E. Jerome McCarthy received his Ph.D. from the University of Minnesota in 1958. Since then he has taught at the Universities of Oregon, Notre Dame, and Michigan State. He has been deeply involved in teaching and developing new teaching materials. Besides writing various articles and monographs, he is the author of textbooks on data processing and social issues in marketing.

Now 59 years old, Dr. McCarthy is active in making presentations to academic conferences and business meetings. He has worked with groups of teachers throughout the country and has addressed international conferences in South America, Africa, and India.

Dr. McCarthy received the American Marketing Association's Trailblazer Award in 1987. And he was voted one of the "top five" leaders in Marketing Thought in 1975 by marketing educators. He was also a Ford Foundation Fellow in 1963–64, studying the role of marketing in economic development. In 1959–60 he was a Ford Foundation Fellow at the Harvard Business School working on mathematical methods in marketing.

Besides his academic interests, Dr. McCarthy is involved in consulting for, and guiding the growth of, several businesses. He has worked with top managers from Dow Chemical, Dow-Corning, 3M, Lear-Siegler, Bemis, Grupo Industrial Alfa, and many smaller companies. He is director of several organizations. His primary interests, however, are in (1) "converting" students to marketing and marketing strategy planning and (2) preparing teaching materials to help others do the same. This is why he has continued to spend a large part of his time revising and improving marketing texts. This is a continuing process, and this edition incorporates the latest thinking in the field.

William D. Perreault, Jr., received his Ph.D. from the University of North Carolina at Chapel Hill in 1973. He has taught at the University of Georgia and Stanford University, and he is currently Hanes Professor at the University of North Carolina School of Business. He has been teaching the introductory marketing course—and many other courses in the marketing curriculum—for over 15 years. In 1978 he was the first recipient of the School's Rendleman Award for teaching excellence. *Ad Week* magazine recently profiled him as one of the "10 best young marketing professors in America."

Dr. Perreault is a well-known author—and his ideas about marketing management, marketing research, and marketing education have been published in many journals. He is a past editor of the *Journal of Marketing Research* and has served on the review board of the *Journal of Marketing* and other publications. In 1985, the American Marketing Association recognized his long-run contributions to marketing research with the prestigious William Odell Award.

Dr. Perreault is a Vice President and serves on the Board of Directors of the AMA, serves on an advisory board to the Marketing Science Institute, and has just completed a term as chairman of an Advisory Committee to the U.S. Bureau of the Census. He has worked as a marketing consultant to many organizations, including Libby-Owens-Ford, Whirlpool, Owens Corning Fiberglas, General Electric, and the Federal Trade Commission, as well as a variety of wholesale and retail firms. He has served as an advisor evaluating educational programs for the U.S. Department of Education, the Venezuelan Ministry of Education, and the American Assembly of Collegiate Schools of Business.

The Irwin Series in Marketing

Consulting Editor
Gilbert A. Churchill, Jr.
University of Wisconsin, Madison

Essentials of Marketing

E. Jerome McCarthy, Ph.D.

Michigan State University

William D. Perreault, Jr., Ph.D.

University of North Carolina

Fourth Edition   1988

Homewood, Illinois 60430

COMPUTER-AIDED PROBLEMS

A free booklet valued at $9.95—*Computer-Aided Problems to Accompany Basic Marketing, Ninth Edition,* by E. Jerome McCarthy and William D. Perreault, Jr.—is shrink-wrapped with the text. Copy your instructor's master disk to work these marketing management problems on a microcomputer.

Computer-Aided Problems for End of Each Chapter
(See separate booklet)

1. Revenue, Cost, and Profit Relationships
2. Target Marketing
3. Segmenting Customers
4. a. Company Resources
   b. Demographic Trend Analysis
5. Marketing Research
6. Consumers' Selective Processes
7. Vendor Analysis
8. Branding Decision
9. Growth Stage Competition
10. a. Intensive vs. Selective Distribution
    b. Physical Distribution Systems
11. Mass-merchandising
12. Merchant vs. Agent Wholesaler
13. Sales Promotion
14. Sales Compensation
15. Advertising Media
16. Cash Discounts
17. Price Setting
18. Export Opportunities

Acquisitions editor: Jeanne M. Teutsch
Production editor: Ethel Shiell
Copyediting coordinator: Merrily D. Mazza
Production manager: Irene H. Sotiroff
Designer: Paula L. Meyers
Cover designer: Bob Mummert
Artists: John Thoeming and Mary Jo Szymanski
Photo researcher: Charlotte Goldman
Compositor: York Graphic Services, Inc.
Typeface: 9/12 Helvetica
Printer: R. R. Donnelley & Sons Company

ISBN 0-256-06009-6

Library of Congress Catalog Card No. 87–82171

Printed in the United States of America

2 3 4 5 6 7 8 9 0 DO 5 4 3 2 1 0 9 8

Preface

This book presents the "essentials" of marketing. A basic objective was to make it easy for students to grasp these very important "essentials"— "accessibility" was a key goal.

Essentials of Marketing is a shortened version of *Basic Marketing*—a book that has been widely used in the first marketing course. While cutting the material down to the *Essentials.* much time and effort was spent on carefully defining terms and finding the "right" word to speed understanding. Similarly, exhibits and pictures were selected to help today's more visual student "see" the material better.

Twenty-eight years ago, the first edition of *Basic Marketing* pioneered an innovative structure—using the "4 Ps" with a managerial approach—for the introductory marketing course. Since then, the book has been continually improved and refined. The response of both teachers and students has been gratifying. *Basic Marketing* and *Essentials of Marketing*—and the supporting materials—have been more widely used than any other teaching materials for introductory marketing. The 4 Ps has proved to be an organizing structure that has worked for millions of students and teachers.

Now, about 50 introductory marketing texts are available—and almost all of them have, in varying degrees, tried to copy the content, structure, and managerial emphasis of *Basic Marketing* and *Essentials of Marketing.* Imitation, they say, is the sincerest form of flattery. But we have responded to this form of "flattery" with an effort and commitment to excellence that should set a new target for the imitators.

We are trying to offer the highest quality teaching resource ever available for the introductory course. We have worked together closely to enhance the best and proven elements of the earlier editions—while blending in new perspectives from our teaching, research, and business experiences.

The whole text has been thoroughly revised, updated, and rewritten. As in past editions, clear and interesting communication has been a priority. Careful explanations—coupled with hundreds of new examples based on well-known companies—bring the concepts alive to heighten interest and motivate learning. We have devoted special attention to changes taking place in today's highly competitive markets. Throughout the text, we have expanded our treatment of services marketing—reflecting the increasing importance of this area in our economy. The Fourth edition is shorter—to provide crisper focus on the important "essentials." The text has been reorganized, too. This edition provides students with a more complete understanding of market segmentation and positioning earlier in their learning process. We have made it even clearer to students how they can find and screen strategic marketing opportunities by studying and understanding the external environments that affect marketing. The revisions also mean that students move more rapidly into the chapters that focus on the 4 Ps. And we have taken major steps to expand and enhance the whole set of teaching and learning materials that are available with *Essentials of Marketing.*

Our society has become more visually oriented. In the previous edition, we saw this trend as both an opportunity and a challenge. We took advantage of new technologies to introduce computer-generated graphs, figures, and full-color photographs to reinforce key points and facilitate learning. With this edition, while other texts are still scrambling to copy what we did before, we continue to refine and improve these learning elements—as part of an overall design that makes exhibits and the concepts they illustrate even clearer.

This edition of *Essentials of Marketing* involves ambitious revisions. But the aim of all our revising is straightforward and has been steadfast from the start. We want to be certain that each student really does get an understanding of our market-directed system and how he or she can help it—and some company—run better. We believe marketing is important and interesting—and we want every student who studies *Essentials of Marketing* to share our enthusiasm.

The emphasis of *Essentials of Marketing* is on marketing strategy planning. Nineteen chapters introduce the important concepts in marketing management—and the student sees marketing through the eyes of the marketing manager. The organization of the chapters and topics was carefully planned. But we took special care in writing so that it's possible to rearrange and use the chapters in many ways—to fit various needs.

The first two chapters introduce the nature of marketing—focusing on its macro role in society and its micro role in both non-profit and for-profit organizations. Chapter 3 provides a strategic planning view of how managers can find target market opportunities with market segmentation. This strategic view alerts students to the importance of evaluating opportunities in the external environments affecting marketing. These topics are then discussed in Chapter 4. Chapter 5 concerns getting information for marketing management planning—and it provides a contemporary view of both marketing information systems and marketing research. Chapters 6 and 7 explore the demographic and behavioral aspects of markets and describe similarities—and differences—between final consumers and intermediate customers—like manufacturers, channel members, and government purchasers.

Chapters 8 through 17 are concerned with developing a marketing mix with the four Ps: Product, Place (involving channels of distribution and customer service levels), Promotion, and Price—emphasizing the important strategy decisions in each of these areas. These chapters provide the frameworks students need to be able to develop the "right" Product and make it available at the "right" Place with the "right" Promotion and the "right" Price—to satisfy target customers and still meet the objectives of the business. These chapters are presented in an integrated, analytical way, so there is a logical development of a student's thinking about planning marketing strategies.

Chapter 18 applies the principles of the text to international marketing.

While there is a multinational emphasis throughout the text, this separate chapter is provided for those wanting special emphasis on international marketing.

The final chapter considers how efficient the marketing process is. Here we discuss many criticisms of marketing and evaluate the effectiveness of both micro and macro marketing.

There are also three special appendices—a concise review of economic fundamentals, a clear explanation of "marketing arithmetic," and ideas about career opportunities in marketing.

Some textbooks treat "special" topics—like services marketing, marketing for non-profit organizations, industrial marketing, and social marketing—in separate chapters. We have not done this because we are convinced that treating such materials as separate topics leads to an unfortunate "compartmentalization" of ideas. We think they are too important to be isolated in that way. Instead, these topics are interwoven and illustrated throughout the text—to emphasize that marketing thinking is crucial in all aspects of our society and economy. Similarly, our examples and case histories are fully integrated with the text discussion—so that they both stimulate interest and deepen understanding of the important concepts they illustrate.

Really understanding marketing and how to plan marketing strategies can build self-confidence—and make a student more ready to take an active part in the business world. To move students in this direction, we deliberately include a variety of frameworks, models, classification systems, and "how-to-do-it" techniques that should speed the development of "marketing sense"—and equip the student to analyze marketing situations in a confident and meaningful way. Taken seriously, they are practical—and they work. By making these materials more interesting and understandable, we hope to help students see marketing as the challenging and rewarding area it is.

So students will see what's coming in each *Essentials of Marketing* chapter, behavioral objectives are included on the first page of each chapter. And to speed student understanding, important new concepts are shown in red and defined immediately. Further, a glossary of these terms is provided at the end of the book. Within chapters, major section headings and second-level headings (placed in the margin for clarity) immediately show how the material is organized *and* summarize key points in the discussion. Further, we have placed pictures in the margin directly beside the paragraph they illustrate—to provide a visual reminder of the ideas. All of these aids help the student understand important concepts—and speed review before exams.

Understanding of the "text material" can be deepened by discussion of the cases suggested at the end of each chapter. In addition, end-of-chapter questions and problems encourage students to investigate the marketing process and develop their own ways of thinking about it.

With this edition of *Essentials of Marketing,* we are introducing a new element—computer-aided problems. We have developed an innovative computer program specifically for use by students who study *Essentials of Marketing.* The program is easy to use—and includes a wide variety of problems that are tied directly to the problem-solving frameworks and concepts developed in

Essentials of Marketing. These exercises complement *Essentials of Marketing*'s approach to marketing strategy planning—and give students "hands-on" microcomputer experience to show how analysis of alternative strategies can help improve decision making. Suggested computer-aided problems are indicated at the end of chapters.

Because of the variety of elements—text, cases, exhibits, questions and problems—*Essentials of Marketing* can be studied and used in many ways. But the *Essentials of Marketing* textbook itself is just the beginning. It is the central component of a complete set of possible *Professional Learning Units Systems* (our *P.L.U.S.*) for students and teachers. Teachers can select from these units to develop their own personalized systems. Many combinations of units are possible—depending on course objectives.

For example, the separate *Student Aid for use with Essentials of Marketing* offers opportunities to get a deeper understanding of the material. The *Student Aid* can be used by the student alone or with teacher direction. If the *Student Aid* is not available at your college bookstore, it can be ordered directly from the publisher.

The *Student Aid* has several objectives. Some elements seek to help students review what they have studied. Other elements are designed to stimulate a deeper understanding of important topics. Specifically, the *Student Aid* provides a brief introduction to each chapter and a list of the important new terms (with text page numbers for easy reference). The *Student Aid* also features true-false questions (with answers and text page numbers) covering *all* the important terms and concepts, as well as multiple-choice questions (with answers) that illustrate the kinds of questions that may appear on exams. In addition, the *Student Aid* offers exercises—cases and problems—with clear instructions and assignments for the student to complete. Some of these exercises are computer-aided. The *Student Aid* exercises can be used as classwork or homework. In fact, reading *Essentials of Marketing* and working with the *Student Aid* can be the basic activity of the course.

Another separate unit, *Readings and Cases in Basic Marketing,* provides carefully selected complementary materials. The readings blend classic and current articles. They are thought-provoking—and illustrate concepts from the text. End-of-reading questions can spark discussion. The longer cases in this separate unit can be used for detailed student analysis—or for instructor presentation.

Another new *P.L.U.S.* element is *The Marketing Game!*—a microcomputer-based competitive simulation. It reinforces the target marketing and marketing strategy planning ideas in *Essentials of Marketing*. Students make marketing management decisions to compete for the business in several target markets. The innovative design of *The Marketing Game!* allows the instructor to increase the number of decision areas—as students learn more about marketing. Some instructors may want to use the advanced level of the game—perhaps in combination with *Readings and Cases in Basic Marketing*—as the basis for a second course.

Essentials of Marketing—and all of our accompanying materials—seek to promote student learning—and get students involved in the excitement and challenges of marketing management. Additional units of *P.L.U.S.* seek to help an instructor offer a truly professional course that meets the objectives he sets for his students. Complete Instructor's Manuals are available. And a separate *Lecture Guide to accompany Essentials of Marketing* is new with this edition—and offers a rich selection of lecture material and ideas. A high-quality selection of Color Transparencies—and the new *Essentials of Marketing Videotapes*—are also available. In addition, thousands of true-false and multiple choice questions—written by the authors to work reliably with the text—are available in a separate *Manual of Objective Tests*. The newly revised COMPUTEST II program for microcomputers allows the instructor to select questions directly from the *Manual of Objective Tests*, change them as desired, or add new questions—and quickly print out a finished test customized to a particular course.

Basic Marketing and *Essentials* have been the leading marketing textbooks for nearly three decades. We take the responsibilities of that leadership seriously. We know you want—and deserve—the very best teaching and learning materials possible. We are committed to providing those materials for you. We will continue to improve them to keep pace with your needs in our ever-changing economy. We encourage your comments. Thoughtful criticisms and suggestions from students and teachers help keep *Basic Marketing* and *Essentials of Marketing* in the forefront of marketing texts.

ACKNOWLEDGMENTS

Planning and preparing this revision of *Essentials of Marketing* has been a consuming, four-year effort. The resulting text—and all of the teaching and learning materials that accompany it—represent a blending of our career-long experiences—and have been influenced and improved by the inputs of more people than it is possible to list.

Faculty and students at our current and past academic institutions—Michigan State University, University of North Carolina, Notre Dame, University of Georgia, Northwestern University, University of Oregon, and University of Minnesota—have significantly shaped the book. Faculty at Notre Dame had a profound effect when the first editions of *Basic Marketing* were developed. Professor Yusaku Furuhashi has had a continuing impact on the multinational emphasis. Similarly, Professor Andrew A. Brogowicz of Western Michigan University and Professor John F. Grashof of Kennesaw College have contributed many fine ideas. We are especially grateful to our many students who have criticized and made comments about teaching materials. Indeed, in many ways, our students have been our best teachers.

Many improvements in the current edition were stimulated by feedback from a number of colleagues around the country. Especially significant were the thought-provoking reviews provided by William R. George of Villanova University, Gilbert A. Churchill, Jr., of the University of Wisconsin, and Barbara A. McCuen of the University of Nebraska at Omaha. In addition, Charlotte H. Mason and Nicholas M. Didow, both at the University of North Carolina, provided a constant flow of valuable suggestions and ideas. In addition, we received helpful recommendations from:

J. Craig Andrews, Marquette University
Jonathan D. Barksy, University of San Francisco
Thomas Bertsch, James Madison University
James P. Boespflug, Arapahoe Community College
Casimir F. Bozek, Purdue University—Calumet
George W. Boulware, David Lipscomb College
James L. Brock, Montana State University
Gul Butaney, Bentley College
William Danko, State University of New York—Albany
Gary A. Ernst, North Central College
William R. George, Villanova University
Kyung-Il (Ed) Ghymn, University of Nevada
Larry A. Haase, Central Missouri State University
Bert Heckel, Sinclair Community College
Charles L. Hilton, Eastern Kentucky University
Earl Honeycutt, University of North Carolina—Wilmington
James C. Johnson, St. Cloud State University
Frederick Langrehr, Brigham Young University
Cyril M. Logar, West Virginia University
Leslie E. Martin, Jr., University of Wisconsin—Whitewater
Lee Meadow, University of Lowell
Michael J. Messina, Gannon University
James Molinari, State University of New York—Oswego
James R. Ogden, Adams State College
Robert W. Ruekert, University of Minnesota
John Schleede, Central Michigan University
Richard Skinner, Kent State University
Gary L. Sullivan, University of Texas—El Paso
Thomas W. Thompson, Virginia Commonwealth University
James P. Tushaus, University of Missouri—St. Louis
Ronald Vogel, Florida International University.

Helpful criticisms and comments on earlier editions were made by Bixby Cooper, David Rink, Homer M. Dalbey, J. H. Faricy, David Lambert, Walter Gross. And Guy R. Banville, Barbara Bart, Robert C. Stephens III, Harry Summers, Gerald Waddell, Donna Rich, Carmen C. Reagan, Dean Almon, Antonio Chriscolo, Chauncy Elkins, Rosann Spiro, John Langly and Dave Sparks participated in focus group discussions at Southern Marketing Association meetings. Many improvements have been incorporated in response to suggestions from these people.

The designers, artists, editors, and production people at Richard D. Irwin, Inc., who worked with us on this edition warrant special recognition. Each has shared our commitment to excellence and brought their own individual creativity to the project.

We owe a special debt of gratitude to Linda G. Davis. She typed thousands of manuscript pages—through countless revisions of the text and all the accompanying materials. Her hard work and dedication to quality throughout the whole process were exemplary. We could not have asked for better support.

Our families have been patient and consistent supporters. The support has been direct and substantive. Joanne McCarthy and Pam Perreault provided invaluable editorial assistance—and many fresh ideas—through each draft and revision. The quality of their inputs is matched only by their energy and enthusiasm about the book. Carol McCarthy helped research and reorient the "Career Planning in Marketing" appendix—reflecting her needs and experiences as a college student looking for a career in advertising. Similarly, Mary Ellen McCarthy Zang provided creative inputs on visual aspects of the project.

We are indebted to all the firms that allowed us to reproduce their proprietary materials here. Similarly, we are grateful to associates from our business experiences who have shared their perspectives and feedback, and heightened our sensitivity to the challenges of marketing management.

A textbook must capsulize existing knowledge—while bringing new perspectives and organization to enhance it. Our thinking has been shaped by the writings of literally thousands of marketing scholars and practitioners. In some cases it is impossible to give unique credit for a particular idea or concept—because so many people have played important roles in anticipating, suggesting, shaping, and developing an area. We gratefully acknowledge these contributors—from the early thought-leaders to contemporary authors—who have shared their creative ideas. We respect their impact on the development of marketing and more specifically this book.

To all of these people—and to the many publishers who graciously granted permission to use their materials—we are deeply grateful. Responsibility for any errors or omissions is certainly ours, but the book would not have been possible without the assistance of many others. Our sincere appreciation goes to everyone who helped in their own special way.

E. Jerome McCarthy
William D. Perreault, Jr.

Contents

Essentials of Marketing

Chapter 1

Marketing's Role in Society

When You Finish This Chapter, You Should

1. Know what marketing is and why you should learn about it.

2. Know why and how macro-marketing systems develop.

3. Know why marketing specialists—including middlemen and facilitators—develop.

4. Know the marketing functions and who performs them.

5. Recognize the important new terms (shown in red).

Marketing affects almost every aspect of your daily life.

When it's time to roll out of bed in the morning, does your General Electric alarm wake you with a buzzer—or playing your favorite radio station? Is the station playing rock, classical, or country music? Will you slip into your Levi's, your shirt from L. L. Bean, and your Nikes—or does the day call for your Brooks Brothers suit? Will breakfast be Kellogg's Corn Flakes—made with corn from America's heartland—or some extra large eggs and Hormel bacon cooked in a Panasonic microwave oven imported from Japan? Will it be Maxwell House coffee—grown in Columbia—or some Minute Maid orange juice? Maybe you're late—and plan to get an Egg McMuffin at McDonald's drive-thru. When you leave home, will it be in a Toyota, or on a Huffy bike, or on the bus the city bought from General Motors?

When you think about it, you can't get very far into a day without bumping into marketing—and what the whole marketing system does for you. It affects every aspect of our lives—often in ways we don't even consider.

In this chapter, you'll see what marketing is all about—and why it's important to you. We will also explore how marketing fits into our whole economic system.

MARKETING—WHAT'S IT ALL ABOUT?

Marketing is more than selling or advertising

If forced to define marketing, most people say that marketing means "selling" or "advertising." It's true that these are parts of marketing. But *marketing is much more than selling and advertising.*

How did all those tennis rackets get here?

Let's think about all the tennis rackets being swung with varying degrees of accuracy by tennis players around the world. Most of us weren't born with a tennis racket in our hand. Nor do most of us make our own tennis rackets. Instead, they are made by firms such as Wilson, Spaulding, Davis, Head, and Prince.

Most tennis rackets look pretty much alike. All are intended to do the same thing—hit the ball over the net. But a tennis player can choose from a wide assortment of rackets. There are different shapes, materials, weights, handle sizes, and types of strings. You can buy a prestrung racket for less than $15. Or you can spend more than $250 just for a frame!

This variety in sizes and materials complicates the production and sale of tennis rackets. The following list shows some of the many things a firm should do *before* and *after* it decides to produce tennis rackets.

1. Analyze the *needs* of people who play tennis and decide if consumers want more or different tennis rackets.
2. Predict what types of rackets—handle sizes, shapes, weights, and materials—different players will want and decide which of these people the firm will try to satisfy.

All tennis rackets can hit the ball over the net—but there are many variations to meet the needs of different people.

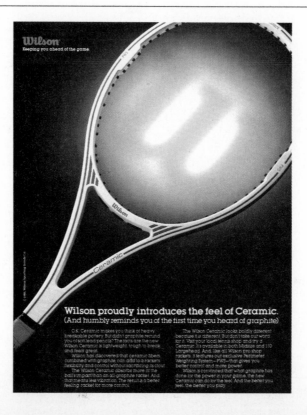

Wilson proudly introduces the feel of Ceramic.
(And humbly reminds you of the first time you heard of graphite)

3. Estimate how many of these people will be playing tennis over the next several years and how many rackets they'll buy.
4. Predict exactly when these players will want to buy tennis rackets.
5. Determine where these tennis players will be—and how to get the firm's rackets to them.
6. Estimate what price they are willing to pay for their rackets—and if the firm can make a profit selling at that price.
7. Decide which kinds of promotion should be used to tell potential customers about the firm's tennis rackets.
8. Estimate how many other companies will be making tennis rackets, how many rackets they'll produce, what kind, and at what prices.

These activities are *not* part of **production**—actually making goods or *performing* services. Rather, they are part of a larger process—called marketing—that provides needed direction for production—and helps make sure that the right products are produced and find their way to consumers.

Our tennis racket example shows that marketing includes much more than selling or advertising. We'll describe these activities in the next chapter—and you'll learn much more about them before you finish this book. For now, you should see that marketing plays a necessary role in providing customers with goods and services that satisfy their needs.

HOW MARKETING RELATES TO PRODUCTION

Production is a very important economic activity. Whether for lack of skill and resources—or just lack of time—most people don't make the products they use. Picture yourself, for example, building a 10-speed bicycle or a stereo system—starting from scratch! And we expect others to produce services—like health care or air transportation. Clearly, the high standard of living that most Americans enjoy is made possible by specialized production.

Tennis rackets, like mousetraps, don't sell themselves

Although production is a necessary economic activity, some people overrate its importance in relation to marketing. Their attitude is reflected in the old saying: "Make a better mousetrap and the world will beat a path to your door." They think that if you just make a good product, customers will line up at your factory door.

The "better mousetrap" idea probably wasn't true in Grandpa's time—and it certainly isn't true today. In modern economies, the grass grows high on the path to the Better Mousetrap Factory—if the new mousetrap is *not* properly marketed. We have already seen, for example, that there's a lot more to selling tennis rackets than just making them. This is true for most goods and services.

The point is that production and marketing are both important parts of a total business system—aimed at providing consumers with need-satisfying goods and services. Together, production and marketing provide the four basic economic utilities—form, time, place, and possession utilities—that are needed to provide consumer satisfaction. Here, **utility** means the power to satisfy human needs.

Tennis rackets do not automatically provide utility

Form utility is provided when someone produces something tangible—say, a tennis racket. But just producing tennis rackets doesn't result in consumer satisfaction. Time, place, and possession utility must also be provided. **Time utility** means having the product available *when* the customer wants it. And **place utility** means having the product available *where* the customer wants it. For example, how much satisfaction does a tennis player in California get from a tennis racket in a producer's warehouse in Pennsylvania. That tennis racket won't win any games unless it's available *when* (time utility) and *where* (place utility) the tennis player wants it. Further, to have the legal right to use the racket, the tennis player has to pay for it before enjoying possession utility. **Possession utility** means obtaining a product and having the right to use or consume it.

Stated simply, marketing provides time, place, and possession utility. It also should guide decisions about what goods and services should be produced to provide form utility. We'll look at how marketing does this later in this chapter. First, we want to tell you why you should study marketing—and then we'll define marketing.

MARKETING AND YOU

Why you should study marketing

One reason for studying marketing is that you—as a consumer—pay for marketing. Marketing costs about 50 cents of each consumer's dollar. For some goods and services, the percentage is much higher.

Another important reason for learning about marketing is that marketing affects your daily life. All the goods and services you buy. The stores where you shop. All that advertising you see and hear. They're all part of marketing. Even your job resumé is part of a marketing campaign to sell yourself to some employer! Some courses are interesting when you take them—but never relevant again once they're over. Not so with marketing—you'll be a consumer dealing with marketing for the rest of your life.

Still another reason for studying marketing is the many exciting and rewarding career opportunities available in marketing. Marketing is often the route to the top. In this book, you'll find information about opportunities in different areas of marketing. (Also see Appendix C on career planning.)

Even if you're aiming at a non-marketing job, you'll be working with marketing people. Knowing something about marketing will help you understand them better. It will also help you do your own job better. Remember, a company that can't sell its products won't need accountants, computer programmers, financial managers, personnel managers, production managers, traffic managers, or credit managers. It's often said: "Nothing happens unless the cash register rings."

Even if you're not planning a business career, marketing concepts and techniques apply to non-profit organizations, too. The same approaches used to

Marketing stimulates product improvement and gives customers a choice.

sell soap are used to "sell" ideas, politicians, mass transportation, health care services, and museums.

An even more basic reason for studying marketing is that marketing plays a big part in economic growth and development. Marketing stimulates research and new ideas—resulting in new goods and services. Marketing gives customers a choice among products. If these products satisfy customers—this can lead to fuller employment, higher incomes, and a higher standard of living. An effective marketing system is important, therefore, to the future of our nation—and all nations.[1]

HOW SHOULD WE DEFINE MARKETING?

As we said earlier, some people define marketing too narrowly as "selling and advertising." On the other hand, one marketing expert defined marketing as "the creation and delivery of a standard of living."[2]

Micro- or macro-marketing?

There is a big difference between these two definitions. The first definition focuses on micro-marketing—the activities of an individual organization. The second focuses on macro-marketing—the economic welfare of a whole society.

Which view is correct? Is marketing a set of activities done by individual firms or organizations? Or is it a social process?

To answer this question, let's go back to our tennis racket example. We saw that a producer of tennis rackets has to perform several customer-related activities besides just making rackets. The same is true for an art museum or a family service agency. This supports the idea of marketing as a set of activities done by individual organizations.

On the other hand, people can't live on tennis rackets and art museums alone! In an advanced economy like ours, it takes thousands of goods and

services to satisfy the many needs of society. A typical K mart stocks 15,000 different items. A society needs some sort of marketing system to organize producers and middlemen to satisfy the needs of all its citizens. So marketing is also an important social process.

The answer to our question is that *marketing is both a set of activities performed by organizations* and *a social process.* In other words, marketing exists at both the micro and macro levels. Therefore, we will use two definitions of marketing—one for *micro*-marketing and another for *macro*-marketing. The first looks at customers and the organizations that serve them. The second takes a broad view of our production-distribution systems.

MICRO-MARKETING DEFINED

Micro-marketing is the performance of activities that seek to accomplish an organization's objectives by anticipating customer or client needs and directing a flow of need-satisfying goods and services from producer to customer or client.[3]

Let's look at this definition.

Applies to profit and non-profit organizations

To begin with, this definition applies to both profit and non-profit organizations. Their customers or clients may be individual consumers, business firms, non-profit organizations, government agencies, or even foreign nations. While most customers and clients pay for the goods and services they receive, others may receive them free of charge or at a reduced cost—through private or government subsidies.

Begins with customer needs

Marketing should begin with potential customer needs—not with the production process. Marketing should try to *anticipate* needs. And then marketing, rather than production, should determine what goods and services are to be developed—including decisions about product design and packaging; prices or fees; credit and collection policies; transporting and storing policies; when and how the products are to be advertised and sold; and after the sale—warranty, service, and perhaps even disposal policies.

Marketing does not do it alone

This does *not* mean that marketing should try to take over production, accounting, and financial activities. Rather, it means that marketing—by interpreting customers' needs—should provide direction for these activities and try to coordinate them. After all, the purpose of a business or non-profit organization is to satisfy customer or client needs. It is *not* to supply goods or service that are *convenient* to produce—and that *may* sell—or be accepted free.

THE FOCUS OF THIS TEXT—MANAGEMENT–ORIENTED MICRO–MARKETING

Since most of you are preparing for a career in business, the main focus of this text will be on micro-marketing. We will see marketing through the eyes of the marketing manager. But most of this material will also be useful for those who plan to work for non-profit organizations.

Marketing managers must never forget that their organizations are just small parts of a larger macro-marketing system. Therefore, the rest of this chapter will look at the macro—or "big picture"—view of marketing. Let's begin by defining macro-marketing—and then review some basic ideas.

MACRO—MARKETING DEFINED

Macro-marketing is a social process that directs an economy's flow of goods and services from producers to consumers in a way which effectively matches supply and demand and accomplishes the objectives of society.

Emphasis is on whole system

Like micro-marketing, macro-marketing is concerned with the flow of need-satisfying goods and services from producer to consumer. However, when we talk about macro-marketing the emphasis is not on the activities of *individual* organizations. Instead, the focus is on *how the whole system works.*[4]

Every society needs an economic system

All societies must provide for the needs of their members. Therefore, every society needs some sort of **economic system**—the way an economy organizes to use scarce resources to produce goods and services and distribute them for consumption among various people and groups in the society.

How an economic system operates depends on a society's objectives and its political system.[5] But all economic systems must decide *what and how much* is to be produced and distributed *by whom, when, and to whom. How* these decisions are made varies from nation to nation—but the macro-level objectives are basically the same: to create goods and services and make them available when and where they are needed—to maintain or improve each nation's standard of living.

HOW ECONOMIC DECISIONS ARE MADE

There are two basic kinds of economic systems: planned systems and market-directed systems. Actually, no economy is *entirely* planned or market-directed. Most are a mixture of the two extremes.

Government planners may make the decisions

In a **planned economic system** government planners decide what and how much is to be produced and distributed by whom, when, and to whom. Producers generally have little choice about what goods and services to produce. Their main task is to meet their assigned production quotas. Prices are set by government planners and tend to be very rigid—not changing according to supply and demand. Consumers usually have *some* freedom of choice. But the assortment of goods and services may be quite limited. Activities such as market research, branding, and advertising usually are neglected—or not done at all.

Government planning may work fairly well as long as an economy is simple—and the variety of goods and services is small. It may even be necessary under certain conditions—during wartime, for example. However, as economies become more complex, government planning becomes more difficult. It may even break down. Planners may face too many complex decisions. And consumers may lose patience if the planners don't meet their needs. To try to reduce consumer dissatisfaction, planners in the Soviet Union and other socialist countries have put more emphasis on marketing (branding, advertising, and market research) in recent years.[6]

A market-directed economy adjusts itself

In a **market-directed economic system**, the individual decisions of the many producers and consumers make the macro-level decisions for the whole economy.

Price is a measure of value

In a pure market-directed economy, consumers make a society's production decisions when they make their choices in the marketplace. They decide what is to be produced and by whom—through their dollar "votes." Prices in the marketplace are a rough measure of how society values particular goods and services. If consumers are willing to pay the market prices, then apparently they feel they are getting at least their money's worth.

The aim of marketing is to identify customers' needs—and to meet those needs so well that the product almost "sells itself."

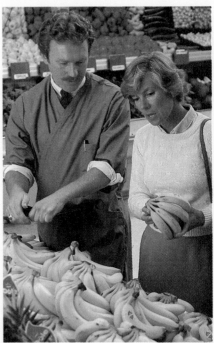

New consumer needs that can be served profitably create opportunities for profit-minded firms. Any consumer needs that can be served profitably will encourage producers to try to meet those needs. Ideally, the control of the economy is completely democratic. Power is spread throughout the economy.

Greatest freedom of choice

Consumers in a market-directed economy enjoy maximum freedom of choice. They aren't forced to buy any goods or services, except those that must be provided for the good of society—like national defense, schools, police and fire protection, mass transportation, and public health services. These are provided by the community—and citizens are taxed to pay for them.

Similarly, producers are free to do whatever they wish—provided that they stay within the rules of the game set by government and receive enough dollar "votes" from consumers. If they do their job well—they earn a profit and stay in business. But profit, survival, and growth are not guaranteed.

The role of government

The American economy is mainly—but not completely—market-directed. For example, besides setting and enforcing the "rules of the game," the federal government controls interest rates and the supply of money. It also sets import and export rules, regulates radio and TV broadcasting, sometimes controls wages and prices, and so on. Government also tries to be sure that prop-

---

In the past decade, there has been less government regulation in markets for services such as banking, transportation, and communications.

erty is protected, contracts are enforced, individuals are not exploited, no group unfairly monopolizes markets, and that producers deliver the kinds and quality of goods and services they claim to be offering.

You can see that some of these government activities are needed to make sure the economy runs smoothly. However, some people worry that increasing government interference is a growing threat to the survival of our market-directed system—and the economic and political freedom that goes with it.[7]

ALL ECONOMIES NEED MACRO–MARKETING SYSTEMS

At this point, you may be saying to yourself: All this sounds like economics—where does *marketing* fit in? Studying a *macro-marketing system* is a lot like studying an economic system except we give more detailed attention to the "marketing" components of the system—including consumers and other customers, middlemen, and marketing specialists. The focus is on the activities they perform—and how the interaction of the components affects the effectiveness and fairness of a particular system.

In general, we can say that no economic system—whether centrally planned or market-directed—can achieve its objectives without an effective macro-marketing system. To see why this is true, we will look at the role of marketing in primitive economies. Then we will see how macro-marketing tends to become more complex in advanced economic systems.

Marketing involves exchange

In a **pure subsistence economy**—each family unit produces everything it consumes. There is no need to exchange goods and services. Each producer-consumer unit is totally self-sufficient. No marketing takes place—because *marketing doesn't take place unless there are two or more parties who want to exchange something for something else.*

What is a market?

The term "marketing" comes from the word **market**—which is a group of sellers and buyers willing to exchange goods and/or services for something of value. This can be done face-to-face at some physical location (for example, a farmers' market). Or it can be done indirectly—through a complex network of middlemen who link buyers and sellers that are far apart.

In primitive economies, exchanges tend to occur in central markets. **Central markets** are convenient places where buyers and sellers can meet face-to-face to exchange goods and services. We can understand macro-marketing better by seeing how and why central markets develop.

Central markets help exchange

Imagine a small village of five families—each with some special skill for producing some need-satisfying product. After meeting basic needs, each family decides to specialize. It's easier for one family to make two pots and another to make two baskets than for each one to make one pot and one basket. Specialization makes labor more efficient and more productive. It can increase the total amount of form utility created.

If these five families specialize in one product each, they will have to trade

Exhibit 1–1   Ten Exchanges Required When a Central Market Is Not Used

Pots

Hats

Baskets

Hoes

Knives

with each other. As Exhibit 1–1 shows, it will take the five families 10 separate exchanges to obtain some of each of the products. If the families live near each other, the exchange process is relatively simple. But if they are far apart, travel back and forth will take time. And who will do the traveling—and when?

Faced with this problem, the families may agree to come to a central market and trade on a certain day. Each family then needs to make only one trip to the market to trade with all the others. This would reduce the total number of trips to five. This makes exchange easier, leaves more time for production and consumption, and also provides for social gatherings. In total, much more time, place, possession, and even form utility is enjoyed by each of the five families.

Money system speeds trading

While a central meeting place simplifies exchange, the individual bartering transactions still take a lot of time. Bartering only works when someone else wants what you have—and vice versa. Each trader must find others who have products of about equal value. After trading with one group, a family may find itself with extra baskets, knives, and pots. Then it has to find others willing to trade for these products.

A money system changes all of this. A seller only has to find a buyer who wants his products and agrees on the price. Then he is free to spend his money to buy whatever he wants.

Middlemen help exchange even more

The development of a central market and a money system simplifies the exchange process among the five families in our imaginary village. But a total of 10 separate transactions are still needed. It still takes much time and effort to carry out exchange among the five families.

This clumsy exchange process is made much simpler by the appearance of a **middleman**—someone who specializes in trade rather than production. A middleman is willing to buy each family's goods—and then sell each family

Exhibit 1–2   Only Five Exchanges Are Required When a Middleman in a Central Market Is Used

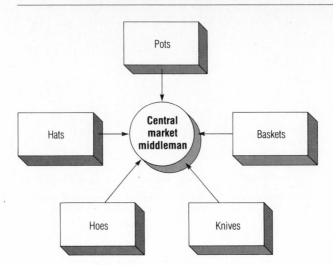

whatever it needs. He charges for the service, of course. But this charge may be more than offset by savings in time and effort.

In our simple example, using the services of a middleman at a central market reduces the necessary number of exchanges for all five families from 10 to 5. See Exhibit 1–2. Each family has more time for production, consumption, and visits with other families. Also, each family can specialize in production—creating more form utility. Meanwhile, by specializing in trade, the middleman provides additional time, place, and possession utility. In total, all the villagers may enjoy greater economic utility—and greater consumer satisfaction—by using a middleman in the central market.

Note that the reduction in transactions resulting from using a middleman in a central market becomes more important as the number of families increases. For example, if the population of our imaginary village increases from 5 to 10 families, 45 transactions are needed without a middleman. Using the middleman reduces the necessary number of transactions to 10—1 for each family.

Today such middlemen—offering permanent trading facilities—are known as *wholesalers* and *retailers*. The advantages of working with them increase as the number of producers and consumers, their distance from each other, and the number and variety of competing products increase. That's why there are so many wholesalers and retailers in modern economies.

THE ROLE OF MARKETING IN ECONOMIC DEVELOPMENT

Modern economies have advanced well beyond the five-family village—but the same ideas still apply. The main purpose of markets and middlemen is to make exchange easier and allow greater time for production, consumption, and other activities—including recreation.

Without an effective macro-marketing system, people can't leave their subsistence way of life.

Effective marketing system is necessary

Although it is tempting to decide that more effective macro-marketing systems are the result of greater economic development, just the opposite is true. *An effective macro-marketing system is necessary for economic development.* Improved marketing may be the *key* to growth in less-developed nations.

Breaking the vicious circle of poverty

Without an effective macro-marketing system, the less-developed nations may not be able to escape the "vicious circle of poverty." They can't leave their subsistence way of life to produce for the market because there are no buyers for what they produce. And there are no buyers because everyone else is producing for their own needs. As a result, distribution systems and middlemen do not develop.

Breaking this vicious circle of poverty may require a major change in the micro- and macro-marketing systems typical in less-developed nations.[8]

CAN MASS PRODUCTION SATISFY A SOCIETY'S CONSUMPTION NEEDS?

Most people must depend on others to produce most of the goods and services they need to satisfy their basic needs. And in advanced economies many consumers have higher incomes. They can afford to satisfy higher-level needs as well. A modern economy faces a real challenge to satisfy all these needs.

Economies of scale mean lower cost

Fortunately, advanced economies can take advantage of mass production with its **economies of scale**—which means that as a company produces larger numbers of a particular product, the cost for each of these products goes down. You can see that a one-of-a-kind, custom-built car would cost *much* more than a mass-produced standard model.

Of course, even in our advanced society not all goods and services can be produced by mass-production—or with economies of scale. For example, it's

difficult to get productivity gains in some labor-intensive medical services. But from a macro-marketing perspective, it's clear that we are able to devote resources to meeting these "quality of life" needs because we are achieving efficiency in other areas.

Modern production skills can help provide great quantities of goods and services to satisfy large numbers of consumers. But mass production alone can't solve the problem of satisfying consumers' needs. Effective marketing is also needed.

Effective marketing is needed to link producers and consumers

Effective marketing means delivering the goods and services that consumers want and need. It means getting products to them at the right time, in the right place, and at a price they're willing to pay. That's not an easy job, especially if you think about the big variety of goods and services a highly developed economy can produce—and the many kinds of goods and services consumers want and can afford.

Effective marketing in an advanced economy is more difficult because producers and consumers are separated in several ways—as Exhibit 1–3 shows. It is also complicated by "discrepancies of quantity" and "discrepancies of assortment" between producers and consumers. This means individual producers specialize in producing and selling large amounts of a narrow assortment of goods and services, but each consumer wants only small quantities of a wide variety of goods and services.[9]

Marketing functions help narrow the gap

The purpose of a macro-marketing system is to overcome these separations and discrepancies. The "universal functions of marketing" do this.

The **universal functions of marketing** are: buying, selling, transporting, storing, standardization and grading, financing, risk taking, and market information. They are *universal* in the sense that they must be performed in *all* macro-marketing systems. *How* these functions are performed—and by *whom*—may differ among nations and economic systems. But they are needed in any macro-marketing system. Let's take a closer look at them now.

The **buying function** means looking for and evaluating goods and services. The **selling function** involves promoting the product. It includes the use of personal selling, advertising, and other mass selling methods. This is probably the best-known function of marketing.

The **transporting function** means moving goods from one place to another. The **storing function** involves holding goods until customers need them.

Standardization and grading involve sorting products according to size and quality. This makes buying and selling easier—because it reduces the need for inspection and sampling. **Financing** provides the necessary cash and credit to produce, transport, store, promote, sell, and buy products. **Risk taking** involves bearing the uncertainties that are part of the marketing process. A firm can never be sure that customers will want to buy its products. Products can also be damaged, stolen, or outdated. The **market information function** involves collecting, analyzing, and distributing the information needed to plan, carry out, and control marketing activities.

Exhibit 1–3   Marketing Facilitates Production and Consumption

PRODUCTION SECTOR	Specialization and division of labor result in heterogeneous supply capabilities

SPATIAL SEPARATION	Producers and consumers are separated geographically. Producers tend to cluster together by industry in a few concentrated locations, while consumers are located in many scattered locations.
SEPARATION IN TIME	Consumers may not want to consume goods at the time they are produced, and time may be required to transport goods from producer to consumer.
SEPARATION OF INFORMATION	Producers do not know who needs what, where, when, and at what price. Consumers do not know what is available from whom, where, when, and at what price.
SEPARATION IN VALUES	Producers value goods and services in terms of costs and competitive prices. Consumers value goods and services in terms of economic utility and ability to pay.
SEPARATION OF OWNERSHIP	Producers hold title to goods and services which they themselves do not want to consume. Consumers want to consume goods and services which they do not own.
DISCREPANCIES OF QUANTITY	Producers prefer to produce and sell in large quantities. Consumers prefer to buy and consume in small quantities.
DISCREPANCIES OF ASSORTMENT	Producers specialize in producing a narrow assortment of goods and services. Consumers need a broad assortment.

Marketing needed to overcome separations & discrepancies

CONSUMPTION SECTOR	Heterogeneous demand for form, time, place, and possession utility to satisfy needs and wants.

WHO DOES MARKETING FUNCTIONS?

Producers, consumers, and marketing specialists

From a macro-level viewpoint, these marketing functions are all part of the marketing process—and must be done by someone. None of them can be eliminated. In a planned economy, some of the functions may be done by government agencies. Others may be left to individual producers and consumers. In a market-directed economy, marketing functions are done by producers, consumers, and a variety of marketing specialists. See Exhibit 1–4.

Earlier in this chapter, you saw how producers and consumers benefited when marketing specialists (middlemen) took over some buying and selling. Producers and consumers also benefit when marketing specialists do the other

Exhibit 1–4   Model of U.S. Macro-Marketing System*

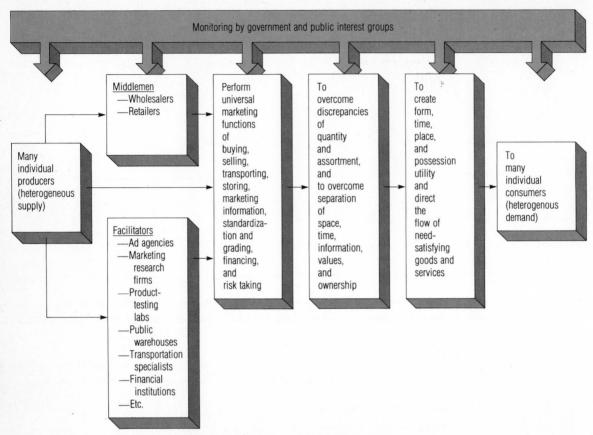

Monitoring by government and public interest groups

Many
individual
producers
(heterogeneous
supply)

Middlemen
—Wholesalers
—Retailers

Facilitators
—Ad agencies
—Marketing
research
firms
—Product-
testing
labs
—Public
warehouses
—Transportation
specialists
—Financial
institutions
—Etc.

Perform
universal
marketing
functions
of
buying,
selling,
transporting,
storing,
marketing
information,
standardiza-
tion and
grading,
financing,
and
risk taking

To
overcome
discrepancies
of
quantity
and
assortment,
and
to overcome
separation
of
space,
time,
information,
values,
and
ownership

To
create
form,
time,
place,
and
possession
utility
and
direct
the
flow of
need-
satisfying
goods and
services

To
many
individual
consumers
(heterogenous
demand)

*Our nation's macro-marketing system must interact with the macro-marketing systems of many other nations.

Source: This model was suggested by Professor A. A. Brogowicz of Western Michigan University.

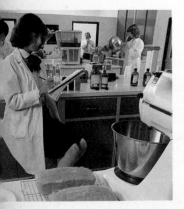

marketing functions. So we find marketing functions being done not only by marketing middlemen—but also by a variety of other **facilitators**—firms that provide one or more of the marketing functions other than buying or selling. These include advertising agencies, marketing research firms, independent product-testing laboratories, public warehouses, transporting firms, and finan-cial institutions (including banks). Through specialization or economies of scale, marketing middlemen and facilitators are often able to do the marketing func-tions better—and at a lower cost—than producers or consumers can. This al-lows producers and consumers to spend more time on production and con-sumption.

Functions can be shifted and shared

From a macro viewpoint, all of the marketing functions must be done by someone. But, *from a micro viewpoint, not every firm must do all of the functions.* Some marketing specialists do all the functions. Others specialize in only one or two. Marketing research firms, for example, specialize only in the market information function. The important idea to remember is this: *Responsibility for doing the marketing functions can be shifted and shared in a variety of ways,* but *no function can be completely eliminated!*

HOW WELL DOES OUR MACRO–MARKETING SYSTEM WORK?

It connects remote producers and consumers

A macro-marketing system does more than just deliver goods and services to consumers—it allows mass production with its economies of scale. Also, mass communication and mass transportation allow products to be shipped where they're needed. Oranges from California are found in Minnesota stores—even in December—and electronic parts made in New York State are used in making products all over the country.[10]

It encourages growth and new ideas

In addition to making mass production possible, our market-directed, macro-marketing system encourages **innovation**—the development and spread of new ideas and products. Competition for consumers' dollars forces firms to think of new and better ways of satisfying consumer needs.

It has its critics

In explaining marketing's role in society, we described some of the benefits of our macro-marketing system. We feel this approach is right because our macro-marketing system has provided us with one of the highest standards of living in the world. It seems to be "effective" and "fair" in many ways. We must admit, however, that marketing—as we know it in the United States—has many critics! Marketing activity is especially open to criticism because it is the part of business most visible to the public. There is nothing like a pocketbook issue for getting consumers excited!

Typical complaints about marketing include:

Advertising is too often annoying, deceptive, and wasteful.

Marketing makes people too materialistic—it motivates them toward "things" instead of social needs.

Easy consumer credit makes people buy things they don't need—and really can't afford.

Packaging and labeling are often confusing and deceptive.

Middlemen add to the cost of distribution—and raise prices without providing anything in return.

Marketing creates interest in products that pollute the environment.

Too many unnecessary products are offered.

Marketing serves the rich—and exploits the poor.

Note that some of these complaints deal with the whole macro-marketing system. Others apply to practices of specific firms—and are micro-marketing oriented.

Consumer complaints should be taken seriously

Such complaints should not be taken lightly.[11] They show that many Americans aren't happy with some parts of our marketing system. Certainly, the strong public support for consumer protection laws proves that not all consumers feel they are being treated like kings and queens. But some of the complaints occur because people don't understand what marketing is all about. As you go through this book, we will try to answer some of these criticisms—to help you understand marketing better.

CONCLUSION

In this chapter, we defined two levels of marketing: micro-marketing and macro-marketing. Macro-marketing is concerned with the way the whole economy works. Micro-marketing focuses on the activities of individual firms. We discussed the role of marketing in economic development—and talked about the functions of marketing and who does them. We ended by raising some of the criticisms of marketing—both of the whole macro system and of the way individual firms work.

We emphasized macro-marketing in this chapter, but the major thrust of this book is on *micro-marketing*. We believe that most criticism of mar-

keting results from ineffective decision making at the micro level. Therefore, the best way to answer some of this criticism is to educate future business people. This will help improve the way individual organizations work. Eventually, it will help our macro-marketing system work better.

The effect of micro-level decisions on society will be discussed throughout the text. Then—in Chapter 19—after you have begun to understand how and why producers and consumers think and behave the way they do—we will look at macro-marketing again. We will evaluate how well both micro-marketing and macro-marketing perform in our market-directed economic system.

Questions and Problems

1. It is fairly easy to see why people do not beat a path to a mousetrap producer's door, but would they be similarly indifferent if some food processor developed a revolutionary new food product that would provide all necessary nutrients in small pills for about $100 per year per person?

2. List your activities for the first two hours after you woke up this morning. Briefly indicate how marketing affected your activities.

3. Distinguish between macro- and micro-marketing. Then explain how they are interrelated, if they are.

4. Distinguish between how economic decisions are made in a planned economic system and how they are made in a market-directed economy.

5. Explain (*a*) how a central market facilitates exchange and (*b*) how the addition of a middleman facilitates exchange even more.

6. Identify a "central market" in your city and explain how it facilitates exchange.

7. Discuss the nature of marketing in a socialist economy. Would the functions that must be

provided and the development of wholesaling and retailing systems be any different than in a market-directed economy?

8. Describe a recent purchase you made and indicate why that particular product was available at a store and, in particular, at that store.

9. Refer to Exhibit 1–3, and give an example of a purchase you recently made that involved spatial separation and separation in time between you and the producer. Briefly explain how these separations were overcome.

10. Define the functions of marketing in your own words. Using an example, explain how they can be shifted and shared.

11. Explain, in your own words, why the emphasis in this text is on micro-marketing.

12. Why is satisfying customers or clients considered equally as important as satisfying an organization's objectives—in the text's definition of micro-marketing?

Suggested Computer-Aided Problem

1. Revenue, Cost, and Profit Relationships

Suggested Cases

1. McDonald's

4. Block Services, Inc.

Chapter 2

Marketing's Role within the Firm

When You Finish This Chapter, You Should

1. Know what the marketing concept is—and how it should affect a firm's strategy planning.

2. Understand what a marketing manager does.

3. Know what marketing strategy planning is—and why it will be the focus of this book.

4. Understand target marketing.

5. Be familiar with the four Ps in a marketing mix.

6. Know the difference between a marketing strategy, a marketing plan; and a marketing program.

7. Recognize the important new terms (shown in red).

"A master plan to hit the target" is not a Rambo *story line—but the goal of a good marketing manager.*

Marketing and marketing management are important in our society—and in business firms. As you saw in Chapter 1, marketing is concerned with anticipating needs and directing the flow of goods and services from producers to consumers. This is done to satisfy the needs of consumers—and achieve the objectives of the firm (the micro view) and of society as a whole (the macro view).

To get a better understanding of marketing, we're going to look at things through the eyes of the marketing manager—the one who makes a company's important marketing decisions. Let's look at just a few decisions recently made by marketing managers—to get you thinking about the ideas we'll be talking about in this chapter—and in the rest of the book.

In 1983, Pillsbury bought Häagen–Dazs ice cream company to gain faster entry into the fast-growing "super premium" ice cream market. This had been a "mom and pop" industry—with many small firms. But with projected growth rates of 20 percent annually, Pillsbury decided to bring modern marketing methods to the "high end" of the ice cream market. This required many decisions.

The company had to develop and test new flavors to be sure customers liked the new tastes. Pillsbury had to decide whether to rely on the familiar Häagen–Dazs name and label—or design a whole new look. Marketing managers also had to decide who would be the main target—and the best way to reach them. This included picking a theme for the advertising campaign, deciding how much to spend on advertising—and where to spend it. Managers also had to decide how to promote the products to their wholesalers and retailers—the middlemen who actually distribute the products to places where customers can buy them.

The marketing managers had other decisions to make. Should the price be the same "high" $2 a pint? Should a special low price be set during Pillsbury's introductory period? Should they pick some introductory regions of the country—or distribute the ice cream in as many places as possible all at once? Pillsbury's efforts paid off. Within a few years, sales more than doubled and were growing—in an increasingly competitive market.[1]

We've mentioned only a few of many decisions Pillsbury's marketing managers had to make—and you can see that each of these decisions affects the others. Making marketing decisions is never easy—but knowing what basic decision areas have to be considered helps to plan a more successful strategy. This chapter will get you started by giving you a framework for thinking about all the marketing management decision areas—which is what the rest of this book is all about.

MARKETING'S ROLE HAS CHANGED A LOT OVER THE YEARS

In our Häagen–Dazs example, it's clear that marketing management is very important. But this hasn't always been true. In fact, only in the last 25 years or so have producers, wholesalers, and retailers adopted modern marketing thinking. These companies used to think mainly of just making a *product.* Now they focus on *customers*—and try to aim the company's total effort toward satisfying them.

We'll discuss five stages in this marketing evolution: (1) the simple trade era, (2) the production era, (3) the sales era, (4) the marketing department era, and (5) the marketing company era. We'll talk about these eras as if all firms are now marketing-oriented—but keep in mind that *some managers haven't made it to the final stages.* They're still stuck in the past.

Specialization permitted trade—and middlemen met the need

When societies first moved toward specialization of production, traders began to play an important role. Early producers made products they—or their neighbors—needed. As local bartering became harder, they moved into the **simple trade era**—a time when families traded or sold their "surplus" output to local middlemen, who then sold these goods to other consumers or distant middlemen. This early role of marketing didn't change much until the Industrial Revolution a little over a hundred years ago.

From the production to the sales era

From the Industrial Revolution until the 1920s, most companies were in the production era. The **production era** is a time when a company focuses on production of a few specific products—perhaps because few of these products are available in the market.

By 1930, new machines made it possible to produce more than ever before. Now the problem wasn't just to produce—but to beat competition and win customers. This led many firms to enter the sales era. The **sales era** is a time when a company emphasizes selling—because of increased competition.

In 1905, a firm could easily sell the washing machines it could produce—because there were few available in the market.

Washing Machines *For the* RESIDENCE

Modern and complete with ample capacity to do all the family linen and do it just right. An absolute necessity in the household.

Saves Time Trouble and Money

Easy to operate. Write for Circular "C."

The Steel Roll Machine Co., *Manufacturers of Household Laundry Equipment.* 8 S. Canal St., Chicago, Ill.

To the marketing department era

For most firms, the sales era continued until at least 1950. By then, sales were growing rapidly. Someone had to tie together the efforts of research, purchasing, production, and sales. The marketing department era replaced the sales era. The **marketing department era** is a time when all marketing activities are brought under the control of one department—to improve short-run policy planning and tie together the firm's activities.

To the marketing company era

Since 1960, many firms have developed at least some staff with a marketing management outlook. Some have moved all the way to the marketing company era. The **marketing company era** is a time when—in addition to short-run marketing planning—marketing people develop long-range plans—and the marketing concept guides the whole company effort.

WHAT DOES THE MARKETING CONCEPT MEAN?

The **marketing concept** means that a firm aims *all* its efforts at satisfying its *customers*—at a *profit*.

It isn't really a new idea in business—it's been around a long time. But some managers act as if they're stuck at the beginning of the production era. They still have a **production orientation**—making products that are easy to produce and *then* trying to sell them.

In well-managed firms, this production orientation has been replaced with a marketing orientation. A **marketing orientation** means trying to carry out the marketing concept. Instead of just trying to get customers to buy what the firm has produced, a marketing-oriented firm tries to produce what customers need.

Three basic ideas are included in the definition of the marketing concept:

1. A customer orientation.
2. A total company effort.
3. Profit—not just sales—as an objective.

These three ideas deserve more discussion.

A customer orientation guides the whole system

"Give the customers what they need" seems so obvious that it may be hard for you to see why the marketing concept deserves special attention. However, people don't always do what's logical and obvious. Twenty years ago—in a typical company—production managers thought mainly about getting out the product. Accountants were interested only in balancing the books. Financial people looked after the company's cash position. And salespeople were mainly concerned with getting orders. Each department thought of its own activity as the center of the business—with others working around it. No one was concerned with the whole system. As long as the company made a profit, each department went merrily on "doing its own thing." Unfortunately, many companies *still* operate this way.

Work together . . . do a better job

Ideally, all managers should work together—because the output from one department may be the input to another. But managers tend to build "fences" around their own departments—as seen in Exhibit 2–1A. There may be meet-

As part of its customer orientation, Ford set up a special group to try to solve consumers' problems.

Exhibit 2–1

A.   A business as a box
     (most departments have high fences)

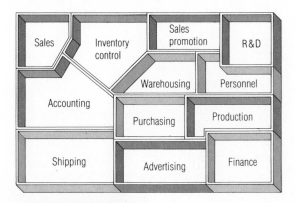

B.   Total system view of a
     business (implementing marketing concept;
     still have departments but all guided by
     what customers want)

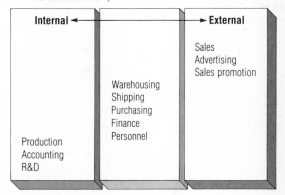

ings to try to get them to work together—but usually department heads come to such meetings worried only about protecting their own "turf."

We use the term "production orientation" to describe this lack of a central focus in a business firm. But keep in mind that this problem is also seen in sales-oriented sales reps, advertising-oriented agency people, finance-oriented finance people, and so on.

In a firm that accepts the marketing concept, however, the fences come down. Departments still exist, of course, because specialization makes sense. But the total system's effort is guided by what customers want—instead of what each department wants to do.

In such a firm, it's more realistic to view the business as a box with both internal and external activities. See Exhibit 2–1B. Some internal departments—production, accounting, and research and development (R&D)—deal mainly with affairs inside the firm. And the external departments deal with outside matters—sales, advertising, and sales promotion. Finally, some departments work with both inside and outside problems—warehousing, shipping, purchasing, finance, and personnel.

The important point is to have a guiding focus that *all* departments adopt. It helps the organization work as a total system—rather than a lot of separate parts. The marketing concept provides this focus. Further, it is more complete than many systems-oriented ideas. It actually specifies a "high-level" objective—customer satisfaction—that makes sense for all parts of the system. It also specifies a profit objective—which is necessary for the system's survival.

A non-profit organization doesn't measure "profit" in the same way as a for-profit firm. But, like any business firm, a non-profit organization needs support to survive and achieve its objectives. If the supporters don't see the benefits produced as worth what it costs to provide them, they will—and should—put their time and money elsewhere. So the marketing concept makes sense for non-profit organizations, too.

Marketing is being more widely accepted by non-profit organizations.

FRY NOW... PAY LATER.

There is a proven connection between sun exposure and skin cancer, as well as premature wrinkling. If you must be in the sun, use sunscreen and common sense.

AMERICAN CANCER SOCIETY

It's easy to slip into a production orientation

It's very easy to slip into a production-oriented way of thinking. For example, a retailer might prefer only weekday hours—avoiding nights, Saturdays, and Sundays, when many customers would like to shop. Or a company might rush to produce a new product developed in its lab—rather than first finding out if it fills a need. A community theater group might choose a play that the actors and the director like—without considering what the audience might want to see.

Take a look at Exhibit 2–2. It shows some differences in outlook between adopters of the marketing concept and typical production-oriented managers. As this suggests, the marketing concept is really powerful—if taken seriously. It forces the company to think through what it does—and why. And it also forces the company to develop plans for reaching its objectives.

ADOPTION OF THE MARKETING CONCEPT HAS NOT BEEN EASY OR UNIVERSAL

The marketing concept seems so logical that you might think most firms would quickly adopt it. In fact, they haven't. Many firms are either production-oriented—or regularly slip back that way—and must consciously bring the customers' interests into their planning.

Consumer products companies—such as General Electric and Procter & Gamble—were first to accept the marketing concept. Competition was intense in some of their markets—and trying to better satisfy customers' needs was a way to win in this competition.[2]

Producers of industrial commodities—steel, coal, paper, glass, chemicals—have accepted the marketing concept more slowly—if at all. Similarly, many

Exhibit 2–2   Some Differences in Outlook between Adopters of the Marketing Concept and the Typical Production-Oriented Managers

Topic	Marketing orientation	Production orientation
Attitudes toward customers	Customer needs determine company plans	They should be glad we exist, trying to cut costs and bring out better products
Product offering	Company makes what it can sell	Company sells what it can make
Role of marketing research	To determine customer needs and how well company is satisfying them	To determine customer reaction, if used at all
Interest in innovation	Focus on locating new opportunities	Focus is on technology and cost cutting
Importance of profit	A critical objective	A residual, what's left after all costs are covered
Role of customer credit	Seen as a customer service	Seen as a necessary evil
Role of packaging	Designed for customer convenience and as a selling tool	Seen merely as protection for the product
Inventory levels	Set with customer requirements and costs in mind	Set with production requirements in mind
Transportation arrangements	Seen as a customer service	Seen as an extension of production and storage activities, with emphasis on cost minimization
Focus of advertising	Need-satisfying benefits of products and services	Product features and quality, maybe how products are made
Role of sales force	Help the customer to buy if the product fits his needs, while coordinating with rest of firm—including production, inventory control, advertising, etc.	Sell the customer, don't worry about coordination with other promotion efforts or rest of firm

retailers have been slow to accept the marketing concept—in part because they are so close to final consumers that they're sure they really know their customers.

Service industries are catching on fast

In the last few years many service industries—including airlines, banks, lawyers, physicians, accountants, and insurance companies—have begun to apply the marketing concept. This is due in part to changes in government regulations that allow these businesses to be more competitive. And some have been forced into it by aggressive competitors who are advertising and using price to attract new customers—contrary to long-accepted professional practice.[3]

Marketing concept applies directly to non-profit organizations

The same ideas apply to non-profit organizations. The objectives are different—but the marketing concept works here, too. The YMCA, the Girl Scouts, colleges, symphony orchestras, and the Post Office are all trying to satisfy some consumer groups and at least survive—even though they aren't seeking profits.[4]

Many service industries have begun to apply the marketing concept.

Throughout this book, we'll be talking about applying the marketing concept.[5] Usually we'll just say "in a firm" or "in a business"—but keep in mind that most of the ideas can be applied in *any* type of organization.

THE MANAGEMENT JOB IN MARKETING

We've talked about the marketing concept as a guide for the whole firm. Now let's look more closely at how a marketing manager helps a firm reach its objectives—using the marketing management process.

The **marketing management process** is the process of (1) *planning* marketing activities, (2) directing the *implementation* of the plans, and (3) *controlling* these plans. See Exhibit 2–3.

In Exhibit 2–3, all the steps are connected to show that the marketing management process is continuous. The planning job sets guidelines for implementing the plans—and specifies expected results. These expected results are compared in the control job—to see if everything has worked out as planned. This feedback is especially important because it can lead to changing the plans.

Exhibit 2–3 also shows that a marketing manager isn't concerned only with present plans. He must also look for attractive new opportunities—and make plans for new strategies.

Strategic management planning concerns the whole firm

The job of planning strategies to guide a *whole company* is called **strategic (management) planning**—the managerial process of developing and maintaining a match between an organization's resources and its market opportunities. This top management job includes planning not only marketing activities but also for production, research and development, and other functional areas.

We won't get into whole company planning in this text—but it is important to see that the marketing department's plans are not whole company plans. On

Exhibit 2–3   The Marketing Management Process

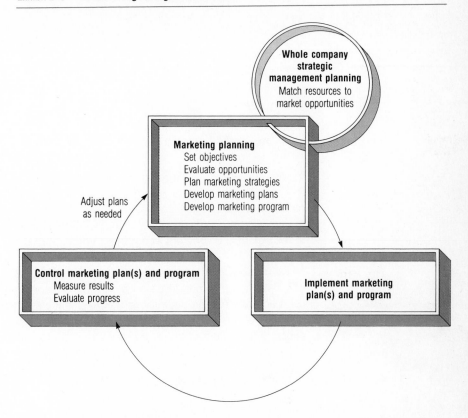

the other hand, company plans should be market-oriented—and the marketing department's plans can help set the tone and direction for the whole company. So we'll use "strategy planning" and "marketing strategy planning" to mean the same thing.[6]

WHAT IS MARKETING STRATEGY PLANNING?

Marketing strategy planning means finding attractive opportunities—and developing profitable marketing strategies and plans. But what is a "marketing strategy" and a "marketing plan?" We have used these words rather casually so far. Now let's see what they really mean.

What is a marketing strategy?

A **marketing strategy** specifies a target market and a related marketing mix. It is a "big picture" of what a firm will do in some market. It has two inter-related parts:

1. A **target market**—a fairly homogeneous (similar) group of customers to whom a company wishes to appeal.
2. A **marketing mix**—the controllable variables the company puts together to satisfy this target group.

Exhibit 2–4   A Marketing Strategy

The importance of target customers in this process can be seen in Exhibit 2–4, where the customer—the "C" at the center of the diagram—is surrounded by the controllable variables we call the "marketing mix." A typical marketing mix includes some product, offered at a price, with some promotion to tell potential customers about the product, and a way to reach the customer's place.

Hanes Corporation's strategy for L'eggs hosiery aims at convenience-oriented young women in urban areas with a dependable product in a distinctive package. The product is made conveniently available at as many grocery and drug stores as possible. Its pricing is more or less competitive. And Hanes supports the whole effort with a great deal of promotion.

SELECTING A MARKET–ORIENTED STRATEGY IS TARGET MARKETING

Target marketing is not mass marketing

Note that a marketing strategy specifies some *particular* target customers. This approach is called "target marketing" to show it's different from "mass marketing." **Target marketing** aims a marketing mix at some specific target customers. **Mass marketing**—the typical production-oriented approach—aims at "everyone" with the same marketing mix. Mass marketing assumes that everyone is the same—and that everyone is a potential customer. See Exhibit 2–5.

"Mass marketers" may do target marketing

Commonly used terms can be confusing here. The terms "mass market*ing*" and "mass market*ers*" do not mean the same thing. Far from it! "Mass marketing" means trying to sell to "everyone," as we explained above—while "mass marketers" like General Foods and Sears, are not aiming at "everyone." They do aim at clearly defined target markets. The confusion with "mass marketing" occurs because their target markets usually are large and spread out.

Target marketing— can mean big markets and profits

Remember that target marketing is not limited to small market segments—only to fairly homogeneous ones. A very large market—even what is sometimes called the "mass market"—may be fairly homogeneous in some cases—and a target marketer will deliberately aim at it. For example, there is a very large group of "young urban professionals" (sometimes called

Exhibit 2–5 Production-Oriented and Marketing-Oriented Managers Have Different Views of the Market

Production-oriented manager sees everyone as basically similar and practices "mass marketing"

Marketing-oriented manager sees everyone as different and practices "target marketing"

"yuppies") who are homogeneous on many dimensions—including a high income level. This group now accounts for about 70 percent of all stereo equipment purchases—so it is a major target market for companies like Sony and Technics.

The reason a marketing manager aims at specific target customers is to gain a competitive advantage—by developing a more satisfying marketing mix that should be more profitable for the firm.

DEVELOPING MARKETING MIXES FOR TARGET MARKETS

There are many marketing mix variables

There are many possible ways to satisfy the needs of target customers. A product can be of various sizes, colors, or materials. The brand names and trademarks can be changed. Various advertising media—newspapers, magazines, radio, television, billboards—may be used. A company's own sales force or other sales specialists can be used. Different prices can be charged—and so on. With so many variables, the question is: Is there any way of simplifying the selection of marketing mixes? The answer is yes.

The four "Ps" make up a marketing mix

It is useful to reduce all the variables in the marketing mix to four basic ones:

Product.   Promotion.

Place.   Price.

Exhibit 2–6
A Marketing Strategy—
Showing the 4 Ps of a
Marketing Mix

It helps to think of the four major parts of a marketing mix as the "four Ps." Exhibit 2–6 emphasizes their relationship and their focus on the customer—"C."

Customer is not part of the marketing mix

The customer is shown surrounded by the four Ps in Exhibit 2–6. Some students assume that the customer is part of the marketing mix—but this isn't so. The customer should be the *target* of all marketing efforts. The customer is placed in the center to show this—the C stands for some specific customers—the target market.

Exhibit 2–7 shows some of the variables in the four Ps that will be discussed in later chapters. For now, let's just describe each P briefly.

Product—the right one for the target

The Product area is concerned with developing the right "product" for the target market. This product may involve a physical good and/or service. The product of H & R Block, for example, is a completed tax form. The important thing to remember in the Product area is that your good—and/or service—should satisfy some customers' needs.

Along with other Product decisions, we'll talk about developing new products and whole product lines. We will also discuss the characteristics of various kinds of products—so you'll be able to make generalizations about product classes. This will help you to develop whole marketing mixes more quickly.

Place—reaching the target

Place is concerned with getting the "right" product to the target market's place. A product isn't much good to a customer if it isn't available when and where it's wanted.

A product reaches customers through channels of distribution. A **channel of**

Exhibit 2–7   Strategy Decision Areas

Product	Place	Promotion	Price
Physical good	Objectives	Objectives	Objectives
Service	Channel type	Promotion blend	Flexibility
Features	Market exposure	Sales people	Level over
Accessories	Kinds of	Kind	product life
Installation	middlemen	Number	cycle
Instructions	Kinds and	Selection	Geographic terms
Warranty	locations of	Training	Discounts
Product lines	stores	Motivation	Allowances
Packaging	Who handles	Advertising	
Branding	transporting	Targets	
	and storing	Kinds of ads	
	Service levels	Media type	
	Recruiting	Copy thrust	
	middlemen	Prepared by	
	Managing	whom	
	channels	Sales promotion	
		Publicity	

Exhibit 2–8   Four Examples of Basic Channels of Distribution for Consumer Products

```
┌─────────────────────────────────────────────────────────────┐
│                   Manufacturer or Producer                    │
└─────────────────────────────────────────────────────────────┘
  ┌──────────┐   ┌──────────┐   ┌──────────┐   ┌──────────┐
  │ Citibank │   │  Apple   │   │   Del    │   │ Procter &│
  │          │   │ Computer │   │  Monte   │   │ Gamble   │
  └──────────┘   └──────────┘   └──────────┘   └──────────┘
                                  ┌──────────┐   ┌──────────┐
                                  │Wholesaler│   │Wholesaler│
                                  └──────────┘   └──────────┘
                                                 ┌──────────┐
                                                 │Wholesaler│
                                                 └──────────┘
                 ┌──────────┐   ┌──────────┐   ┌──────────┐
                 │ Retailer │   │ Retailer │   │ Retailer │
                 └──────────┘   └──────────┘   └──────────┘
┌─────────────────────────────────────────────────────────────┐
│                          Consumer                             │
└─────────────────────────────────────────────────────────────┘
```

distribution is any series of firms (or individuals) from producer to final user or consumer.

Sometimes a channel system is quite short. It may run directly from a producer to a final user or consumer. Usually it is more complex—involving many different kinds of middlemen and specialists. And if a marketing manager has several different target markets, he may need several different channels of distribution. See Exhibit 2–8.

Promotion—telling and selling the customer

The third P—Promotion—is concerned with telling the target market about the "right" product. Promotion includes personal selling, mass selling, and sales promotion. The marketing manager's job is to blend these methods.

Personal selling involves direct face-to-face communication between sellers and potential customers. Personal selling lets the salesperson adapt the firm's marketing mix to each potential customer. But this individual attention comes at a price. Personal selling can be very expensive. Often this personal effort has to be blended with mass selling and sales promotion.

Mass selling is communicating with large numbers of customers at the same time. **Advertising** is any paid form of non-personal presentation of ideas, goods, or services by an identified sponsor. It is the main form of mass selling. **Publicity** is any *unpaid* form of non-personal presentation of ideas, goods, or services.

Sales promotion refers to those promotion activities—other than advertising, publicity, and personal selling—that stimulate interest, trial, or purchase by final customers or others in the channel. Sales promotion people try to help the personal selling and mass selling specialists.

Price—making it right

Besides developing the right Product, Place, and Promotion, marketing managers must also decide the right Price. In setting a price, they must consider the kind of competition in the target market. They must also estimate customer reaction to possible prices.

Price is an important area for the marketing manager. If customers won't accept the Price, all the planning effort will be wasted.

Each of the four Ps contributes to the whole

A good marketing mix needs all four Ps. In fact, they should all be tied together. But is any one more important than the others? Generally speaking, the answer is *no*. When a manager develops a marketing mix, all decisions about the Ps should be made at the same time. That's why the four Ps are arranged around the customer (C) in a circle—to show that they are all equally important.

Strategy guides implementing

Let's sum up our discussion of marketing mix planning so far. We develop a *Product* to satisfy the target customers. We find a way to get our product to our target customer's *Place*. We use *Promotion* to tell the target customers about the availability of the product that has been designed for them. Then we set a *Price*—after estimating expected customer reaction to the total offering and the costs of getting it to them.

Both jobs must be done together

It is important to stress—*it cannot be over-emphasized*—that selecting a target market and developing a marketing mix are interrelated. Both parts must be decided together. Whole *strategies* are evaluated—not alternative target markets or alternative marketing mixes.

These ideas can be seen more clearly with an example in the home decorating market.

Strategy planning in the British home decorating market

The experience of a paint producer in England shows the strategy planning process—and how strategy decisions help decide how the plan is carried out.

First, this paint producer's marketing manager interviewed many potential customers and studied their needs for the products he could offer. By combining several kinds of customer needs and some available demographic data, he came up with the view of the market shown in Exhibit 2–9. In the following description of these markets, note that useful marketing mixes come to mind immediately.

There turned out to be a large market for "general-purpose paint" products. The producer didn't consider this market because he didn't want to compete "head-on" with the many companies already in this market. The other four markets—placed in the four corners of a market diagram to show they are different markets—he called "Helpless Homemaker, Handy Helper, Crafty Craftsman, and Cost-Conscious Couple.

Exhibit 2–9 The Home Decorating Market (Paint Area) in England

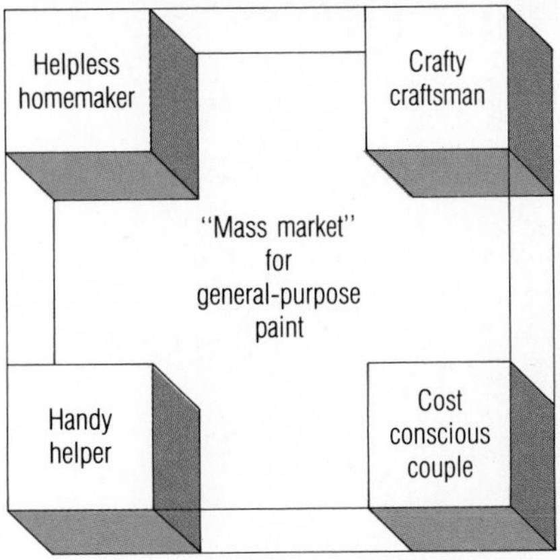

The *Helpless Homemaker*—the producer found—really didn't know much about home painting or specific products. This customer needed a helpful paint retailer who could supply not only paint and other supplies—but also much advice. And the retailer who sold the paint would want it to be of fairly good quality—so that the homemaker would be satisfied with the results.

The *Handy Helper* was a jack-of-all-trades who knew a lot about paint and painting. He wanted a good-quality product and liked to buy from an old-fashioned hardware store or lumber yard—which usually sells mainly to men. The *Crafty Craftsman* had similar needs. But these older men didn't want to buy paint at all. They wanted pigments, oils, and other things to mix their own paint.

Finally, the *Cost-Conscious Couple* was young, had low income, and lived in an apartment. In England, an apartment renter must paint the apartment during the course of the lease. This important factor affects the way some tenants choose their paint. If you were a young apartment renter with limited income, what sort of paint would you want? Some couples in England—the producer found—didn't want very good paint! In fact, something not much better than whitewash would do fine.

The paint producer decided to cater to Cost-Conscious Couples with a marketing mix flowing from the description of that market. That is, knowing what he did about them, he offered a low-quality paint (Product), made it conveniently available in lower-income apartment neighborhoods (Place), aimed his price-oriented ads at these areas (Promotion), and, of course, offered an attractive low price (Price). The producer has been extremely successful with this strategy—giving his customers what they really want—even though the product is of low quality.

Good promotion is important in marketing strategy planning—but a complete marketing mix must include all four Ps.

A MARKETING PLAN IS A GUIDE TO IMPLEMENTATION AND CONTROL

We've been talking about marketing strategy planning. Now let's return to our discussion of the marketing management process. You'll see how a marketing strategy leads to a marketing plan and—finally—to implementation and control (see Exhibit 2–3).

Marketing plan fills out marketing strategy

A marketing strategy is a "big picture" of what a firm will do in some market. A marketing plan goes farther. A **marketing plan** is a written statement of a marketing strategy *and* the time-related details for carrying out the strategy. It should spell out the following—in detail: (1) what marketing mix is to be offered to whom (that is, the target market) and for how long; (2) what company resources (shown as costs) will be needed at what rate (month by month perhaps); and (3) what results are expected (sales and profits—perhaps monthly or quarterly). The plan should also include some control procedures—so that whoever carries out the plan will know when things start to go wrong. This might be something as simple as comparing actual sales against expected sales—with a "warning flag" to be raised whenever total sales fall below a certain level. See Exhibit 2–10.

Exhibit 2–10   Forms to Plan and Control Each of a Firm's Marketing Plans—with Illustrative Comments and Numbers for First Two Pages
(one set of forms for each plan, number of time periods depending on length of plan)

Time period July

	Forecast	Actual	Difference	Cumulative difference
Sales	$ 0	$ 0	$ 0	$ 0
Costs (direct)	700	500	-200	-200
Overhead	$ 3,000	$ 3,000	0	0
Profit (loss)	$ (3,700)	$ (3,500)	$ (200)	$ (200)

Tasks to be done

PRODUCT Be sure that all elements of package are meeting production schedule _____

PLACE _____

PROMOTION Prepare copy for direct mail pieces.
Prepare journal ad copy.
Prepare sales training materials.

PRICE Set tentative price for text and other package elements.

Product Identification McCarthy and Perreault, ESSENTIALS of MARKETING, 4th ed. (and related materials)
Target Market Instructors of first marketing course who want to use a "short" book

PRODUCT-MARKET DEFINITION:
Product type "Short" textbook (and related materials)
Functional needs To aid teaching and learning
Customer types College-level instructors interested in an integrated, analytical, management-oriented
approach to marketing—i.e., logical, organized, pragmatic instructors
Geographic area English language instructors world-wide, except Canada
Competition Other "short book" publishers (actual names used in real situations)
Nature of competition Monopolistic competition
Product life cycle Market maturity

MARKETING MIX

PRODUCT
Type New (revised) component part for instructor (and specialty product to students)
Total product Package of teaching materials and aids
Brand familiarity Recognition to insistence

PLACE
Type of channel Direct to retail bookstores
Degree of market exposure Exclusive OK
Pulling or pushing Push to instructors, contact retailers
Physical distribution service level Immediate delivery to bookstores

PROMOTION
Blend type Heavy on personal selling, with some ads and exhibits at teachers' meetings
Type of salespeople Order getting and taking
Message emphasis "Short" book with integrated, analytical, etc., package
Media emphasis Direct mail and professional journals

PRICE
Flexibility One price
Level Meet competition
Geographic F.O.B. shipping point
Discounts and allowances 20 percent off retail selling price, restricted returns

Exhibit 2–11   Elements of a Firm's Marketing Program

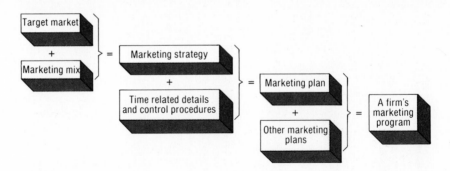

Implementation puts strategies and marketing plans to work

After a marketing plan is developed, a marketing manager focuses on **implementation**—putting a marketing plan into operation. For the marketing manager, this may involve selecting personnel and middlemen, salary administration, selecting promotion materials, getting needed support from others in the firm, and so on.[7]

Several plans make a whole marketing program

Most companies have more than one marketing strategy—and related plan—at the same time. They may have several products—some of them quite different—aimed at different target markets. The other elements of the marketing mix may vary, too. A Bic pen, a Bic windsurfer, and a Bic razor all have different strategies. Yet Bic must implement these strategies at the same time. A **marketing program** blends all of a firm's marketing plans into one "big" plan. See Exhibit 2–11. This program, then, is the responsibility of the whole company. Typically, the whole *marketing program* will be part of the whole-company strategic plans we discussed earlier.

Some people think that only top-level executives of large companies are concerned with planning and control. This isn't true. All organizations—even the smallest farmer, retailer, or wholesaler—should have plans and some kind of control procedures.

This means that marketing strategy planning will be very important to you soon—perhaps in your present job or college activities. In Appendix C on marketing careers, we present some strategy planning ideas for getting a marketing job.

THE IMPORTANCE OF MARKETING STRATEGY PLANNING

Most of our emphasis in this book will be on the planning part of the marketing manager's job—for a good reason. Success or failure for a firm can depend on "one-time" strategy decisions—decisions about what business the company is in and the strategies it will follow. An extremely good plan—carried out badly—might still be profitable. A poor plan—even if well-implemented—can lose money. The examples that follow show the importance of planning—and why we emphasize marketing strategy planning in this text.

Henry Ford's strategy worked—until General Motors caught up

Henry Ford is remembered for developing the mass production techniques that produced a car for the masses. His own view, however, was that mass production developed *because* of his basic decision to build a car for the masses. Cars then were almost custom-built for wealthy buyers. Ford decided on a different strategy. He wanted to make a car that could appeal to most potential buyers.

Certainly, new production ideas were needed to carry out Ford's strategy. But the really important decision was the initial market-oriented decision that there was a market for millions of cars in the $500 price range. Much of what followed was just carrying out his decision. Ford's strategy to offer a low-priced car was an outstanding success—and millions of Model Ts were sold during the 1910s and 1920s. But there was a defect in his strategy. To keep the price down, Ford offered a very basic car—in "any color you want as long as it's black."

In the 1920s, General Motors saw a chance for a new strategy. It hit on the idea of looking at the market as having several segments (based on price and quality). GM decided to offer a full line of cars with different styles and colors in each price range. The GM strategy was not an immediate success. But the company stuck with it and slowly caught up with Ford. In 1927, Ford finally closed down his assembly line for 18 months—switched his strategy—and introduced the more market-oriented Model A to meet the new competition. But GM was already well on its way to the strong market position it still holds.[8]

Airlines seek new strategies

The growth of air travel from 1960 to 1975 left the railroads and bus companies wondering where their customers had gone. The speed and convenience the airlines provided met the needs of many travelers.

The government watched over the airlines carefully—setting safety rules and controlling when and where flights could be offered and at what price. But the Airline Deregulation Act of 1978 gave airlines much more flexibility to make their own marketing decisions. Some airlines developed profitable new strategies for this changed environment—while others went out of business.

Delta Airlines, for example, developed better routes that reduced waiting time in terminals—and made it easier to arrange connecting flights. American Airlines focused on *frequent* business travelers. It avoided price competition—because business travelers were less price sensitive. But now most airlines offer "frequent flyer" programs to try to get a bigger share of this profitable business. Alert marketers will probably continue to offer new airline "Products."[9]

Creative strategy planning needed for survival

Dramatic shifts in strategy may surprise conventional, production-oriented managers. But such changes are becoming much more common—especially in industries where some firms have accepted the marketing concept.

Creative strategy planning is becoming even more important—because companies can no longer win profits just by spending more money on plant and equipment. Also, domestic and foreign competition threatens those who can't create more satisfying goods and services. New markets, new customers, and new ways of doing things must be found if companies are to operate profitably in the future—and contribute to our macro-marketing system.

MARKET–ORIENTED STRATEGY PLANNING HELPS NON–MARKETING PEOPLE, TOO

While market-oriented strategy planning is helpful to marketers, it's also needed by accountants, production, and personnel people—and all other specialists. A market-oriented plan lets everybody in the firm know what "ballpark" they are playing in. It gives direction to the whole business effort. An accountant can't set budgets without a plan. And a financial manager can't estimate cash needs without some idea of expected sales to some customers—and the costs of satisfying them.

We will use the term "marketing manager" for convenience. But when we talk about marketing strategy planning, we're talking about the planning that a market-oriented manager should do when developing a firm's strategic plans. This kind of thinking should be understood by everyone responsible for planning—and this means even the lowest-level sales rep, production supervisor, retail buyer, or personnel counselor.

CONCLUSION

Marketing's role within a marketing-oriented firm is to tie the company effort together. The marketing concept provides direction. It stresses that the firm's efforts should be focused on satisfying some target customers—at a profit. Production-oriented firms forget this. Often various departments in such a firm let their natural conflicts of interest lead them to build "fences" around their areas.

The job of marketing management is one of continuous planning, implementing, and control. The marketing manager must constantly study the environment—seeking attractive opportunities. And new strategies must be planned continually. Potential target markets must be matched with marketing mixes that the firm can offer. Then,

attractive strategies—really, whole marketing plans—are chosen for implementation. Controls make sure that the plans are carried out successfully. If anything goes wrong along the way, this continual feedback should cause the process to be started over again—with the marketing manager planning more attractive marketing strategies.

A marketing mix has four variables—the four Ps—Product, Place, Promotion, and Price. Most of this text is concerned with developing profitable marketing mixes for clearly defined target markets. So after several chapters on selecting target markets, we will discuss the four Ps in greater detail.

Questions and Problems

1. Define the marketing concept in your own words. Explain why the notion of profit is usually included in this definition.

2. Define the marketing concept in your own words. How would acceptance of this concept affect the organization and operation of your college?

3. Distinguish between "production orientation" and "marketing orientation" illustrating with local examples.

4. Explain why a firm should view its internal activities as part of a "total system." Illustrate your answer for (a) a large grocery products producer, (b) a plumbing wholesaler, and (c) a department store chain.

5. Does the acceptance of the marketing concept almost require that a firm view itself as a "total system?"

6. Distinguish clearly between a marketing strategy and a marketing mix. Use an example.

7. Distinguish clearly between mass marketing and target marketing. Use an example.

8. Why is the customer placed in the center of the four Ps in the text diagram of a marketing strategy? Explain, using a specific example from your own experience.

9. Explain, in your own words, what each of the four Ps involves.

10. Distinguish between a strategy, a marketing plan, and a marketing program, illustrating for a local retailer.

11. Outline a marketing strategy for each of the following new products: (a) a radically new design for a hair comb, (b) a new fishing reel, (c) a new "wonder drug," (d) a new industrial stapling machine.

12. Provide a specific illustration of why marketing strategy planning is important for all business people, not just for those in the marketing department.

Suggested Computer-Aided Problem

2. Target Marketing

Suggested Cases

2. West Foods, Inc.

3. Sears' Discover Card

5. TOW Chemical Company

31. Precision Castings, Inc.

Appendix A

Economics Fundamentals

When You Finish This Appendix, You Should

1. Understand the "law of diminishing demand."

2. Know what a market is.

3. Understand demand and supply curves—and how they set the size of a market and its price level.

4. Know about elasticity of demand and supply.

5. Know why demand elasticity can be affected by availability of substitutes.

6. Recognize the important new terms (shown in red).

A good marketing manager should be an expert on markets—and the nature of competition in markets. The economist's traditional demand and supply analyses are useful tools for analyzing markets. In particular, you should master the concepts of a demand curve and demand elasticity. A firm's demand curve shows how the target customers view the firm's Product—really its whole marketing mix. And the interaction of demand and supply curves helps set the size of a market—and the market price. These ideas are discussed more fully in the following sections.

PRODUCTS AND MARKETS AS SEEN BY CUSTOMERS AND POTENTIAL CUSTOMERS

Economists provide useful insights

How potential customers (not the firm) see a firm's product (marketing mix) affects how much they are willing to pay for it, where it should be made available, and how eager they are to obtain it—if at all. In other words, their view has a direct bearing on marketing strategy planning.

Economists have been concerned with market behavior for years. Their analytical tools can be quite helpful in summarizing how customers view products and how markets behave.

Economists see individual customers choosing among alternatives

Economics is sometimes called the "dismal" science—because it says that customers simply cannot buy everything they want. Since most customers have a limited income over any period of time, they must balance their needs and the prices of various products.

Economists usually assume that customers have a fairly definite set of preferences—and that they evaluate alternatives in terms of whether the alternatives will make them feel better (or worse)—or in some way improve (or change) their situation.

But what exactly is the nature of a customer's desire for a particular product?

Usually economists answer this question in terms of the extra utility the customer can obtain by buying more of a particular product—or how much utility would be lost if the customer had less of the product. (Students who wish further discussion of this approach should refer to indifference curve analysis in any standard economics text.)

It may be easier to understand the idea of utility if we look at what happens when the price of one of the customer's usual purchases changes.

The law of diminishing demand

Suppose that a consumer buys potatoes in 10-pound bags at the same time he buys other foods—such as bread and rice. If the consumer is mainly interested in buying a certain amount of food—and the price of the potatoes drops—it seems reasonable to expect that he will switch some of his food money to potatoes and away from some other foods. But if the price of potatoes rises, you expect our consumer to buy fewer potatoes and more of other foods.

The general interaction of price and quantity demanded illustrated by this food example is called the **law of diminishing demand**—which says that if the price of a product is raised, a smaller quantity will be demanded—and if the price of a product is lowered, a greater quantity will be demanded.

A group of customers makes a market

When our hypothetical consumers are considered as a group, we have a "market." It's reasonable to assume that many consumers in a market will behave in a similar way. That is, if price declines, the total quantity demanded will increase—and if price rises, the quantity demanded will decrease. Experience supports this reasoning, especially for broad product categories or commodities such as potatoes.

The relationship between price and quantity demanded in a market is what economists call a "demand schedule." An example is shown in Exhibit A–1. The third column shows that the total revenue (sales) in the potato market—at possible prices—is equal to the quantity demanded times the price at those possible prices. Note that as prices go lower, the total *unit* quantity increases,

Exhibit A–1   Demand Schedule for Potatoes

Point	(1) Price of potatoes per bag (P)	(2) Quantity demanded (bags per month) (Q)	(3) Total revenue per month (P × Q = TR)
A	$0.80	8,000,000	$6,400,000
B	0.65	9,000,000	_____
C	0.50	11,000,000	5,500,000
D	0.35	14,000,000	_____
E	0.20	19,000,000	_____

yet the total *revenue* decreases. Fill in the blank lines in the third column and observe the behavior of total revenue—an important number for the marketing manager. We will explain what you should have noticed—and why—a little later.

The demand curve— usually down-sloping

If your only interest is seeing at which price customers will be willing to pay the greatest total revenue, the demand schedule may be adequate. But a demand curve "shows" more. A **demand curve** is a "picture" of the relationship between price and quantity demanded in a market—assuming that all other things stay the same. It is a graph of the demand schedule. Exhibit A–2 shows the demand curve for potatoes—really just a plotting of the demand schedule. It shows how many potatoes potential customers will demand at various possible prices. This is a "down-sloping demand curve."

Most demand curves are down-sloping. This just means that if prices are decreased, the quantity customers demand will increase.

Note that the demand curve only shows how customers will react to various prices. In a market, we see only one price at a time—not all of these prices. The curve, however, shows what quantities will be demanded—depending on what price is set.

Exhibit A–2   Demand Curve for Potatoes (10-pound bags)

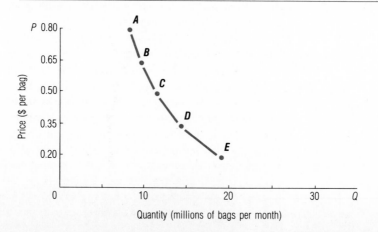

Exhibit A–3   Demand Schedule for 10-Cubic-Foot Refrigerators

Point	(1) Price per refrigerator (P)	(2) Quantity demanded per year (Q)	(3) Total revenue per year (P × Q = TR)
A	$300	20,000	$ 6,000,000
B	250	70,000	17,500,000
C	200	130,000	26,000,000
D	150	210,000	31,500,000
E	100	310,000	31,000,000

You probably think that most business people would like to set a price that would result in a large sales revenue. Before discussing this, however, we should consider the demand schedule and curve for another product to get a more complete picture of demand-curve analysis.

Refrigerator demand curve looks different

A different demand schedule is the one for standard 10-cubic-foot refrigerators shown in Exhibit A–3. Column (3) shows the total revenue that will be obtained at various possible prices and quantities. Again, as the price goes down, the quantity demanded goes up. But here, unlike the potato example, total revenue increases as prices go down—at least until the price drops to $150.

Every market has a demand curve—for some time period

These general demand relationships are typical for all products. But each product has its own demand schedule and curve in each potential market—no matter how small the market. In other words, a particular demand curve has meaning only for a particular market. We can think of demand curves for individuals, regions, and even countries. And the time period covered really should be specified—although this is often neglected, because we usually think of monthly or yearly periods.

The difference between elastic and inelastic

The demand curve for refrigerators (see Exhibit A–4) is down-sloping—but note that it is flatter than the curve for potatoes. It is important that we understand what this flatness means.

We will consider the flatness in terms of total revenue—since this is what interests business managers.*

When you filled in the total revenue column for potatoes, you should have noticed that total revenue drops continually if the price is reduced. This looks undesirable for sellers—and illustrates inelastic demand. **Inelastic demand** means that although the quantity demanded increases if the price is decreased, the quantity demanded will not "stretch" enough—that is, it is not elastic enough—to avoid a decrease in total revenue.

---

*Strictly speaking, two curves should not be compared for flatness if the graph scales are different, but for our purposes now, we will do so to illustrate the idea of "elasticity of demand." Actually, it would be more correct to compare two curves for one product—on the same graph. Then both the shape of the demand curve and its position on the graph would be important.

Exhibit A–4   Demand Curve for 10-Cubic-Foot Refrigerators

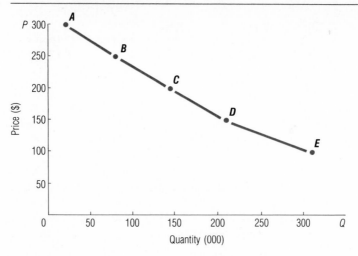

In contrast, **elastic demand** means that if prices are dropped, the quantity demanded will stretch (increase) enough to increase total revenue. The upper part of the refrigerator demand curve is an example of elastic demand.

But note that if the refrigerator price is dropped from $150 to $100, total revenue will decrease. We can say, therefore, that between $150 and $100, demand is inelastic—that is, total revenue will decrease if price is lowered from $150 to $100.

Thus, elasticity can be defined in terms of changes in total revenue. *If total revenue will increase if price is lowered, then demand is elastic. If total revenue will decrease if price is lowered, then demand is inelastic.* (Note: A special case known as "unitary elasticity of demand" occurs if total revenue stays the same when prices change.)

Total revenue may increase if price is raised

A point that is often missed in discussions of demand is what happens when prices are raised instead of lowered. With elastic demand, total revenue will *decrease* if the price is *raised*. With inelastic demand, however, total revenue will *increase* if the price is *raised*.

The possibility of raising price and increasing sales (total revenue) at the same time is attractive to managers. This only occurs if the demand curve is inelastic. Here, total revenue will increase if price is raised, but total costs probably will not increase—and may actually go down—with smaller quantities. So profits will increase as price is increased!

The ways total revenue changes as prices are raised are shown in Exhibit A–5. Here, total revenue is the rectangular area formed by a price and its related quantity.

P_1 is the original price here—and the total potential revenue with this original price is shown by the area with blue shading. The area with red shading

Exhibit A–5   Changes in Total Revenue as Prices Increase

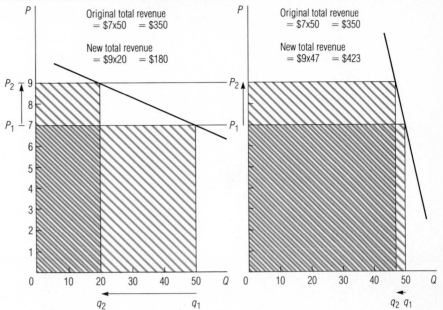

shows the total revenue with the new price, P_2. There is some overlap in the total revenue areas—so the important areas are those with only one color. Note that in the left-hand figure—where demand is elastic—the revenue added (the red-only area) when the price is increased is less than the revenue lost (the blue-only area). When demand is inelastic, however, only a small blue revenue area is given up for a much larger (red) one when price is raised.

An entire curve is not elastic or inelastic

It is important to see that it is *wrong to refer to a whole demand curve as elastic or inelastic*. Rather, elasticity for a particular curve refers to the change in total revenue between two points on a curve—not along the whole curve. You saw the change from elastic to inelastic in the refrigerator example. Generally, however, nearby points are either elastic or inelastic—so it is common to refer to a whole curve by the degree of elasticity in the price range that normally is of interest—the *relevant range.*

Demand elasticities affected by availability of substitutes and urgency of need

At first, it may be difficult to see why one product has an elastic demand and another an inelastic demand. Many factors affect elasticity—such as the availability of substitutes, the importance of the item in the customer's budget, and the urgency of the customer's need and its relation to other needs. By looking at one of these factors—the availability of substitutes—we should better understand why demand elasticities vary.

Substitutes are products that offer the buyer a choice. For example, many consumers see grapefruit as a substitute for oranges and hot dogs as a substitute for hamburgers. The greater the number of "good" substitutes available,

Exhibit A–6   Demand Curve for Hamburger (a product with many substitutes)

the greater will be the elasticity of demand—"good" here referring to the degree of similarity—or homogeneity—that customers see. If they see products
as extremely different—or heterogeneous—then a particular need cannot easily be satisfied by substitutes. And the demand for the most satisfactory product may be quite inelastic.

As an example, if the price of hamburger is lowered (and other prices stay
the same), the quantity demanded will increase a lot—as will total revenue.
The reason is that not only will regular hamburger users buy more hamburger,
but some consumers who formerly bought hot dogs or steaks probably will buy
hamburger, too. But if the price of hamburger is raised, the quantity demanded
will decrease—perhaps sharply. Still, consumers will buy some hamburger—
depending on how much the price has risen, their individual tastes, and what
their guests expect (see Exhibit A–6).

In contrast to a product with many "substitutes"—such as hamburger—
consider a product with few or no substitutes. Its demand curve will tend to be
inelastic. Salt is a good example. Salt is needed to flavor food. Yet no one
person or family uses great quantities of salt. So it is not likely that the quantity of salt purchased will change much as long as price changes are *within a*

Exhibit A–7   Demand Curve for Salt (a product with few substitutes)

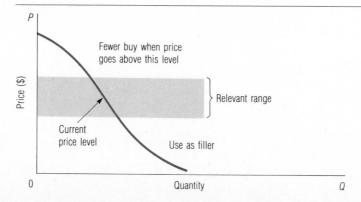

reasonable range. Of course, if the price drops to an extremely low level, producers may buy more—say, for low-cost filler instead of clay or sand (Exhibit A–7). Or, if the price is raised to a staggering figure, many people will have to do without. But these extremes are outside the relevant range.

MARKETS AS SEEN BY SUPPLIERS

Demand curves are introduced here because the degree of elasticity of demand shows how potential customers feel about a product—and especially whether they see substitutes for the product. But to get a better understanding of markets, we must extend this economic analysis.

Customers may want some product—but if suppliers are not willing to supply it, then there is no market. So we'll study the economist's analysis of supply. And then we'll bring supply and demand together for a more complete understanding of markets.

Economists often use the kind of analysis we are discussing here to explain pricing in the marketplace. This is not our intention. Here we are interested in how and why markets work—and the interaction of customers and potential suppliers. The discussion in this appendix does not explain how individual firms set prices—or should set prices. That will come in Chapters 16 and 17.

Supply curves reflect supplier thinking

Generally speaking, suppliers' costs affect the quantity of products they are willing to offer in a market during any period. In other words, their costs affect their supply schedules and supply curves. While a demand curve shows the quantity of products customers will be willing to buy at various prices, a **supply curve** shows the quantity of products that will be supplied at various possible prices. Eventually, only one quantity will be offered and purchased. So a supply curve is really a hypothetical (what-if) description of what will be offered at various prices. It is, however, a very important curve. Together with a demand curve, it summarizes the attitudes and probable behavior of buyers and sellers about a particular product in a particular market—i.e., in a product-market.

Some supply curves are vertical

We usually assume that supply curves tend to slope upward—that is, suppliers will be willing to offer greater quantities at higher prices. If a product's market price is very high, it seems only reasonable that producers will be anxious to produce more of the product—and even put workers on overtime or perhaps hire more workers to increase the quantity they can offer. Going further, it seems likely that producers of other products will switch their resources (farms, factories, labor, or retail facilities) to the product that is in great demand.

On the other hand, if a very low price is being offered for a particular product, it's reasonable to expect that producers will switch to other products—thus reducing supply. A supply schedule (Exhibit A–8) and a supply curve (Exhibit A–9) for potatoes illustrate these ideas. This supply curve shows how many potatoes would be produced and offered for sale at each possible market price in a given month.

Exhibit A–8   Supply Schedule for Potatoes (10-pound bags)

Point	Possible market price per 10-lb. bag	Number of bags sellers will supply per month at each possible market price
A	$0.80	17,000,000
B	0.65	14,000,000
C	0.50	11,000,000
D	0.35	8,000,000
E	0.20	3,000,000

Note: This supply curve is for a month to emphasize that farmers might have some control over when they deliver their potatoes. There would be a different curve for each month.

In the very short run (say, over a few hours, a day, or a week), a supplier may not be able to increase the supply at all. In this situation, we would see a vertical supply curve. This situation is often relevant in the market for fresh produce. Fresh strawberries, for example, continue to ripen, and a supplier wants to sell them quickly—preferably at a higher price—but in any case, he wants to sell them.

If the product is a service, it may not be easy to expand the supply in the short run. Additional barbers or medical doctors are not quickly trained and licensed, and they only have so much time to give each day. Further, the prospect of much higher prices in the near future cannot easily expand the supply of many services. For example, a "hit" play or an "in" restaurant or nightclub is limited in the amount of "product" it can offer at a particular time.

Elasticity of supply

The term *elasticity* also is used to describe supply curves. An extremely steep or almost vertical supply curve—often found in the short run—is called **inelastic supply** because the quantity supplied does not stretch much (if at all) if the price is raised. A flatter curve is called **elastic supply** because the

Exhibit A–9   Supply Curve for Potatoes (10-pound bags)

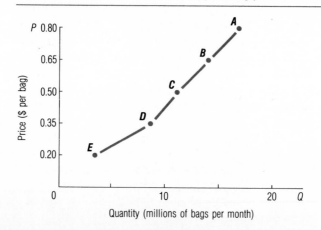

quantity supplied does stretch more if the price is raised. A slightly up-sloping supply curve is typical in longer-run market situations. Given more time, suppliers have a chance to adjust their offerings. And competitors may enter or leave the market.

DEMAND AND SUPPLY INTERACT TO DETERMINE THE SIZE OF THE MARKET AND PRICE LEVEL

We have treated market demand and supply forces separately. Now we must bring them together to show their interaction. The *intersection* of these two forces determines the size of the market and the market price—at which point (price and quantity) the market is said to be in *equilibrium.*

The intersection of demand and supply is shown for the potato data discussed above. The demand curve for potatoes is now graphed against the supply curve in Exhibit A–9. See Exhibit A–10.

In this potato market, demand is inelastic—the total revenue of all the potato producers would be greater at higher prices. But the market price is at the **equilibrium point**—where the quantity and the price sellers are willing to offer are equal to the quantity and price that buyers are willing to accept. The $0.50 equilibrium price for potatoes yields a smaller *total revenue* to potato producers than a higher price would. This lower equilibrium price comes about because the many producers are willing to supply enough potatoes at the lower price. *Demand is not the only determiner of price level. Cost also must be considered—via the supply cuve.*

Some consumers get a surplus

It is important to note that not everyone gets *only* his money's worth in a sales transaction. Presumably, a sale takes place only if both buyer and seller feel they will be better off after the sale. But sometimes the price is better than "right."

Exhibit A–10   Equilibrium of Supply and Demand for Potatoes

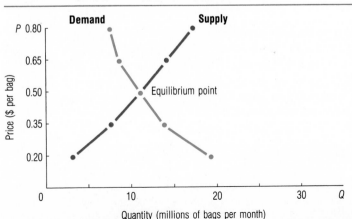

The price we are talking about is the market price set by demand and supply forces. Typically, demand curves are down-sloping, and some of the demand curve is above the equilibrium price. This is simply a graphic way of showing that some customers are willing to pay more than the equilibrium price if they have to. In effect, some of them are getting a "bargain" by being able to buy at the equilibrium price. Economists have traditionally called these bargains the **consumer surplus**—that is, the difference to consumers between the value of a purchase and the price they pay.

It is important to see that there is such a surplus—because some business critics assume that consumers do badly in any business transaction. In fact, a sale takes place only if the consumer feels he is at least "getting his money's worth." As we can see here, some are willing to pay much more than the market price.

DEMAND AND SUPPLY HELP US UNDERSTAND THE NATURE OF COMPETITION

The elasticity of demand and supply curves—and their interaction—help predict the nature of competition a marketing manager is likely to face. For example, an extremely inelastic demand curve means that the manager will have much choice in strategy planning—and especially price setting. Apparently customers like the product and see few substitutes. They are willing to pay higher prices before cutting back much on their purchases.

Clearly, the elasticity of a firm's demand curves makes a big difference in strategy planning—but there are other factors that affect the nature of competition. Among these are the number and size of competitors and the uniqueness of each firm's marketing mix. These ideas are discussed more fully in Chapters 3 and 4. Those discussions presume a real understanding of the contents of this appendix—so now you should be ready to handle them and later material involving demand and supply analysis (especially Chapters 16 and 17).

CONCLUSION

The economist's traditional demand and supply analysis provides useful tools for analyzing the nature of demand and competition. It is especially important that you master the concepts of a demand curve and demand elasticity. How demand and supply interact helps determine the size of a market—and its price level. It also helps explain the nature of competition in different market situations. These ideas are discussed in Chapters 3 and 4 and then built on throughout the text. So careful study of this appendix will build a good foundation for later work.

Questions and Problems

1. Explain in your own words how economists look at markets and arrive at the "law of diminishing demand."

2. Explain what a demand curve is and why it is usually down-sloping.

3.   What is the length of life of the typical demand curve? Illustrate your answer.

4.   If the general market demand for men's shoes is fairly elastic, how does the demand for men's dress shoes compare to it? How does the demand curve for women's shoes compare to the demand curve for men's shoes?

5.   If the demand for razor blades is inelastic above and below the present price, should the price be raised? Why or why not?

6.   If the demand for steak is highly elastic below the present price, should the price be lowered?

7.   Discuss what factors lead to inelastic demand and supply curves. Are they likely to be found together in the same situation?

8.   Why would a marketing manager prefer to sell a product that has no close substitutes? Are "high profits" almost guaranteed?

Chapter 3

Finding Target Market Opportunities with Market Segmentation

When You Finish This Chapter, You Should

1. Understand how to find marketing opportunities.

2. Know about the different kinds of marketing opportunities.

3. Know about defining generic markets and product-markets.

4. Know what market segmentation is.

5. Know three approaches to market-oriented strategy planning.

6. Know how to segment product-markets into sub-markets.

7. Know dimensions that may be useful for segmenting markets.

8. Know a seven-step approach to market segmentation that you can do yourself.

9. Recognize the important new terms (shown in red).

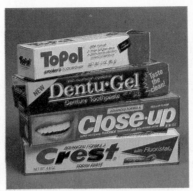

Finding attractive target markets is part of marketing strategy planning.

Frederick Smith likes to tell about the "C" he got on his economics term paper. His professor claimed Smith's ideas for a nationwide, overnight small package delivery service ignored "market demand." After all, most people were happy with the U.S. Postal Service and United Parcel Service. They could deliver most packages within a few days—and for a lot less than Smith's proposal would cost.

You guessed it! Smith is the creator of Federal Express. He showed his economics professor that you don't have to serve *everybody's* needs to be successful. He realized that some customers—a segment of the overall market—really needed pickup and "next-day" delivery. And they were willing to pay extra to get it. Today, a decade later, the Postal Service and several private firms are chasing after Federal Express.[1]

WHAT ARE ATTRACTIVE OPPORTUNITIES?

The main focus of this book is on marketing strategy planning—an important part of which is finding attractive target markets. But what are "attractive target markets"? Should a company that is just delivering letters and packages seek customers who need telecommunications? Should it seek customers who want to buy a transmitting machine—and eliminate its delivery trucks altogether? What is a good target market—and how do you identify it?

Attractive opportunities for a particular firm are those that the firm has some chance of doing something about—given its resources and objectives.

Exhibit 3–1   Finding and Evaluating Market Opportunities

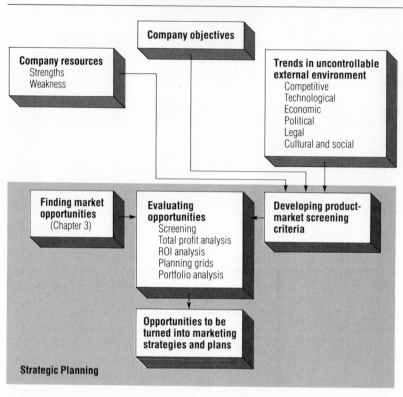

Usually, attractive opportunities are fairly close to markets the firm already knows. It makes sense to build on a firm's strengths and avoid its weaknesses. This may allow the firm to capitalize on changes in its present markets—or more basic changes in the uncontrollable environments.

How many opportunities a firm "sees" depends on the thinking of top management—and the objectives of the firm. Some want to be innovators—and eagerly search out new opportunities. Others are willing to be creative imitators of the leaders. And others are risk-avoiding "me-too" marketers.

Exhibit 3–1 shows the process we'll be talking about in this chapter and the next chapter—finding possible opportunities and screening them to choose the ones to be turned into strategies and plans. As Exhibit 3–1 shows, we'll look first at possible opportunities—and then evaluate them against screening criteria. These criteria grow out of analysis of the firm's resources, the long-run trends facing the firm, as well as the objectives of top management.

Breakthrough opportunities are wanted

Throughout this book, we'll emphasize finding **breakthrough opportunities**—opportunities that help innovators develop hard-to-copy marketing strategies that will be very profitable for a long time. Finding breakthrough opportunities is important because imitators are always waiting to "share" the profits—if they can.

Competitive advantage is needed—at least

Even if a breakthrough opportunity isn't possible, a firm should try to obtain a competitive advantage to increase its chances for profit or survival. **Competitive advantage** means that a firm has a marketing mix that the target market sees as better than a competitor's mix.

The search for breakthrough opportunities and competitive advantage sometimes involves only "fine tuning" a firm's marketing mix(es). But it's vital to have some competitive advantage—so the promotion people have something unique to sell and success doesn't hinge on offering lower and lower prices.[2]

TYPES OF OPPORTUNITIES TO PURSUE

Most people have unsatisfied needs—and alert marketers can find opportunities all around them. Starting with the firm's present product-markets is useful. By carefully defining its markets, the firm may see new opportunities. Or it may see opportunities beyond its present activities.

It helps to see the kinds of opportunities firms may find. Exhibit 3–2 shows the four broad possibilities: market penetration, market development, product development, and diversification.

Market penetration

Market penetration tries to increase sales of a firm's present products in its present markets—probably through a more aggressive marketing mix. The firm may try to increase the customers' rate of use, or attract competitors' customers or current nonusers. New promotion appeals may be effective. The firm may add more stores in present areas—for greater convenience. Short-term price cuts or coupon offers can help. AT&T increased advertising and offered special discounts to encourage customers to choose AT&T over other long-distance telephone services.

Obviously, effective planning is aided by a real understanding of why some people are buying now and what will motivate them to buy more—or motivate others to shift brands—or begin or resume buying.

Exhibit 3–2   Four Basic Types of Opportunities

	Present products	**New products**
Present markets	Market penetration	Product development
New markets	Market development	Diversification

Bic saw an opportunity to develop a new product for its current market.

Market development

  Market development tries to increase sales by selling present products in new markets. This may involve advertising in different media to reach new target customers. Or it may mean adding channels of distribution or new stores in new areas. For example, McDonald's might locate in schools, hospitals, downtown areas, or in foreign countries—as it did when it opened a new store in Rome, Italy.

  Market development may also involve a search for new uses for a product, as when Lipton provides recipes showing how to use its dry soup mixes to make party dip.

Product development

  Product development is offering new or improved products for present markets. Here, the firm should know the market's needs—and may see ways of adding or modifying product features, or creating several quality levels, or adding more types or sizes—to better satisfy the present market. Some McDonald's, for example, now offer salad and soup as well as hamburgers.

Diversification

  Diversification is moving into totally different lines of business—which may include entirely unfamiliar products, markets, or even levels in the production-marketing system. An example is Coca-Cola's move into the entertainment business when it bought Columbia Pictures.[3]

SEARCH FOR OPPORTUNITIES CAN BEGIN BY UNDERSTANDING MARKETS

Breakthrough opportunities from understanding target markets

When marketing managers really understand their target markets, they may see breakthrough opportunities. Eastman Kodak—maker of cameras and photographic supplies—also produces an industrial product, X-ray film. At first, Kodak felt all the target market wanted was faster X-ray pictures at cheaper prices. But closer study showed that the real need in hospitals and health-care units was saving the radiologist's time. Time was precious—but just giving the radiologist a faster picture wasn't enough. Something more was needed to help do the whole job faster—and better.

Kodak came to see that its business was not just supplying X-ray pictures but really helping to improve health care. As a result, Kodak came up with new time-savers for radiologists: a handy cassette film pack and a special identification camera that records all vital patient data directly on the X-ray picture at the time it is made. Before, such tagging had to be done during developing, which took more time and created the risk of error. This new marketing mix aimed at satisfying a different need. And it worked very well.

What is a company's market?

What is a company's market is an important—but sticky—question. A **market** is a group of potential customers with similar needs and sellers offering various products—that is, ways of satisfying those needs.

Market-oriented managers develop marketing mixes for *specific* target markets. Unlike production-oriented managers—who just see a mass market of customers who are pretty much the same—target marketers aim at specific "somebodies."

Getting the firm to focus on specific target markets is vital. Target marketing requires a "narrowing down" process—to get beyond mass market thinking. Exhibit 3–3 shows the narrowing down process we'll be talking about.

Don't just focus on the product

Some production-oriented managers ignore the tough part of defining markets. To make the narrowing down process easier, they just describe their markets in terms of *products* they sell. For example, producers and retailers of greeting cards might define their market as the "greeting-card" market. But this production-oriented approach ignores customers—and customers make a market! This also leads to missed opportunities. Hallmark isn't making that mistake. Instead, Hallmark aims at the "personal-expression" market. It offers all kinds of products that can be sent as "memory makers"—to express one person's feelings toward another. Hallmark has expanded far beyond Christmas and birthday cards—the major greeting card days—to jewelry, gift wrap, plaques, candies, and puzzles as well as all-occasion and humorous cards.

From generic markets to product-markets

It's useful to think of two basic types of market. A **generic market** is a market with *broadly* similar needs—and sellers offering various—*often diverse*—ways of satisfying those needs. In contrast, a **product-market** is a market with *very* similar needs and sellers offering various *close substitute* ways of satisfying those needs.[4]

Exhibit 3–3   Narrowing Down to Target Markets

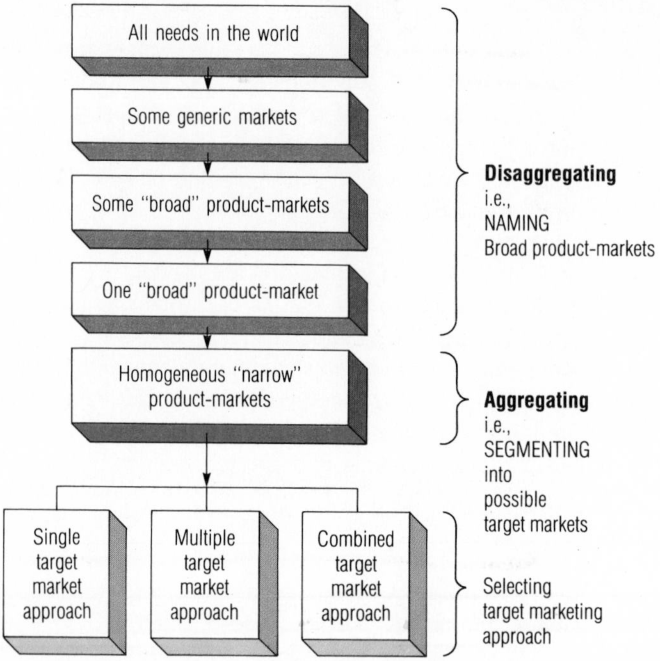

```
┌─────────────────────────────┐
│   All needs in the world    │ ┐
└─────────────────────────────┘ │
              ↓                  │
┌─────────────────────────────┐ │
│    Some generic markets     │ │
└─────────────────────────────┘ │
              ↓                  ├─ Disaggregating
┌─────────────────────────────┐ │   i.e.,
│ Some "broad" product-markets│ │   NAMING
└─────────────────────────────┘ │   Broad product-markets
              ↓                  │
┌─────────────────────────────┐ │
│  One "broad" product-market │ │
└─────────────────────────────┘ ┘
              ↓
┌─────────────────────────────┐ ┐
│  Homogeneous "narrow"       │ │   Aggregating
│     product-markets         │ │   i.e.,
└─────────────────────────────┘ │   SEGMENTING
              ↓                  │   into
                                 │   possible
                                 ┘   target markets
┌─────────┬─────────┬─────────┐
│ Single  │Multiple │Combined │    ┐
│ target  │ target  │ target  │    │  Selecting
│ market  │ market  │ market  │    ├  target marketing
│approach │approach │approach │    │  approach
└─────────┴─────────┴─────────┘    ┘
```

A generic market description looks at markets broadly and from a customer's viewpoint. Status-seekers, for example, have several very different ways to satisfy status needs. A status-seeker might buy a new Mercedes, a Lindblad tour, or designer fashions from Neiman–Marcus. See Exhibit 3–4. Any one of these *very different* products may satisfy this status need. Sellers in this generic status-seeker market have to focus on the need(s) the customers want satisfied—not on how one seller's product (car, vacation, or designer label) is better than another producer's. By really understanding people's needs and attitudes, it may be possible for producers of "status symbols" to encourage shifts to their particular product.

It's sometimes hard to understand and define generic markets because *quite different product types may compete with each other.* But if customers see all these products as substitutes—as competitors in the same generic market—then marketers must deal with this complication.

Suppose, however, that one of our status seekers decides to satisfy this status need with a new, expensive car. Then—in this product-market— Mercedes, Cadillac, and BMW may compete with each other for the status-seeker's dollars. In this *product*-market concerned with cars *and* status (not just transportation!), consumers compare similar products to satisfy their status need.

Most companies quickly narrow their focus to product-markets—because of the firm's past experience, resources, or management preferences. And we will

Exhibit 3–4   The Position of Some Products in a "Status-Seeker" Market

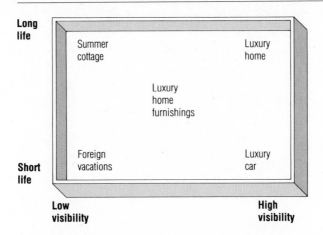

usually be thinking of product-markets when we refer to markets. But, when looking for opportunities, you should consider the broader generic market view, too.

Broaden market definitions to find opportunities

Broader market definitions—including generic market definitions and broader product-market definitions—can help firms find opportunities. But deciding *how* broad to go isn't easy. Too narrow a definition limits a firm's opportunities—but too broad a definition makes the company's efforts and resources seem insignificant.

Our strategy planning process helps in defining relevant markets. Here we are trying to match opportunities to a firm's resources and objectives. So the *relevant market for finding opportunities* should be bigger than the firm's present product-market—but not so big that the firm couldn't expand and be an important competitor. A small manufacturer of screwdrivers, for example, shouldn't define its market as broadly as "the worldwide tool users market" or as narrowly as "our present screwdriver customers." But it may have the production and/or marketing potential to consider "the U.S. handyman's hand tool market." Careful naming of your product-market can help you see possible opportunities.

NAMING PRODUCT–MARKETS AND GENERIC MARKETS

Product-related terms do not—by themselves—give an adequate description of a market. A complete product-market definition includes a four-part description.

What:	1. Product Type
To Meet What:	2. Customer (User) Needs
For Whom:	3. Customer Types
Where:	4. Geographic Area

Video tapes for children compete in a generic market that includes story books and toys.

In other words, a product-market description must include customer-related terms—not just product-related terms. We will refer to these four-part descriptions as product-market "names" because most managers label their markets when they think, write, or talk about them. Such a four-part definition can be clumsy, however, so it's often practical to use a "nickname"—as long as everyone understands the underlying four-part terms. And it's desirable to have the nickname refer to people—not products—because, as we've emphasized, people make markets!

Product type should meet customer needs

Product type describes the goods and/or services the customers want. (Note: a particular product type may include no physical good. Many products are pure services.)

Customer (user) needs refer to the needs the product type will satisfy for the customer. At a very basic level, product types usually provide functional benefits such as nourishing, protecting, warming, cooling, transporting, cleaning, holding, drilling, assembling, etc. We should identify such "basic" needs first. But usually it's necessary to go beyond these basic needs to emotional needs—such as needs for fun, excitement, or status. Correctly defining the need(s) relevant to a market is crucial and requires a good understanding of people's needs and attitudes. These topics are discussed more fully in Chapters 6 and 7.

Both "product type" and "customer need(s)" should be defined together. Sometimes naming the product type reveals the needs at the same time. For example, caulking products are for caulking. In other cases, naming the needs requires much thought—because the same product type may satisfy several needs—or even several sets of needs. Cars, for example, can be for transporting *and* socializing *and* status *and* fun. When a single product can satisfy different needs, marketers have a basis for identifying two or more product-markets.

Customer type refers to the final consumer or user of a product type. Here, we want to choose a name that describes all present (possible) types of customers.

The emphasis in defining customer type should be on identifying the final consumer or user of the product type, rather than the buyer—if they are different. If the product type flows through middlemen on the way to final customers, marketers should avoid treating middlemen as a customer type—unless these middlemen actually use the product in their own business.

The *geographic area* is where a firm is competing—or thinking of competing—for customers. While naming the geographic area may seem trivial, it's not. Just understanding geographic boundaries of a market can suggest new opportunities. A supermarket in Los Angeles is not catering to all consumers in the Los Angeles area—and so there may be opportunities for expansion to unsatisfied customers in that market. Similarly, if a firm is only aiming at the U.S. market, this may suggest world market opportunities.

No product type in generic market names

A generic market description *doesn't include any product-type terms.* It consists of the last three parts of a product-market definition—omitting the product type. This emphasizes that any product type that satisfies the needs of the customer type can compete in this generic market. Recall that in our "status-seeker" market example, very different product types were competitors. Exhibit 3–5 shows the relationship between generic market and product-market definitions.

Creativity is needed in naming markets

Creative analysis of the needs and attitudes of present and potential target markets—in relation to the benefits being offered by the firm and competitors—can reveal new opportunities. Later, we'll study the many possible dimensions of markets. But for now you should see that defining markets only in

Exhibit 3–5   Relationship between Generic and Product-Market Definitions

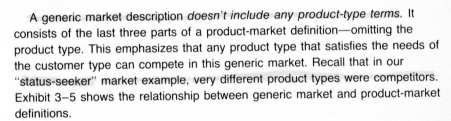

terms of current products is not the best way to find new opportunities—or plan marketing strategies.

MARKET SEGMENTATION DEFINES POSSIBLE TARGET MARKETS

Market segmentation is a two-step process

Market segmentation is a two-step process of: (1) *naming* broad product-markets, and (2) *segmenting* these broad product-markets in order to select target markets and develop suitable marketing mixes.

This two-step process isn't well understood. First-time market segmentation efforts often fail because beginners start with the whole "mass market" and try to find one or two demographic characteristics to segment this market. But customer behavior can't be explained in terms of just one or two demographic characteristics. For example, not all old men—or all young women—buy the same products or brands. Other dimensions usually must be considered—starting with customer needs.

Sometimes many different dimensions are needed to describe the sub-markets within a broad product-market. We saw this in the home-decorating market example in Chapter 2. Recall that the British paint producer finally settled on the "Cost-Conscious Couple" as its target market. This is the kind of market segmentation and target marketing we want to do.

Naming broad product-markets is disaggregating

The first step in effective market segmentation is naming a broad product-market of interest to the firm. This involves "breaking apart"—disaggregating—all possible needs into some generic markets and broad product-markets in which the firm may be able to operate profitably. See Exhibit 3–3. No one firm can satisfy everyone's needs. So, the naming—disaggregating—step involves "brainstorming" about very different solutions to various generic needs and selecting some broad areas—broad product-markets—where the firm has some resources and experience. This means that a car manufacturer would probably ignore all the possible opportunities in food and clothing markets and focus on the generic market, "transporting people in the world," and probably on the broad product-market, "cars and trucks for transporting people in the world."

Disaggregating is a practical "rough and ready" approach. It tries to "narrow down" to product-market areas where the firm will more likely have a competitive advantage—or even find breakthrough opportunities. It looks easy but actually requires a lot of thought and judgment about what the firm can do for some consumers—better than some or all competitors—so it will have a competitive advantage.

Market grid is a visual aid to market segmentation

Assuming that any market may consist of sub-markets, it helps to picture a market as a rectangle with boxes representing smaller, more homogeneous product-markets. See Exhibit 3–6.

Think of the whole rectangle as representing a generic market—or broad

Exhibit 3–6   Market Grid Diagram with Sub-Markets Numbered

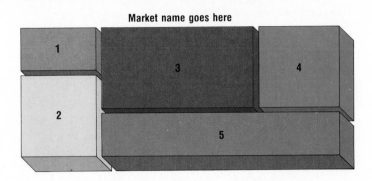

product-market. Now, think of the boxes as sub-markets—product-markets. In the generic "transporting market" discussed above, for example, we might see sub-markets for bicycles, mopeds, motorcycles, airplanes, ships, buses, and "others."

Segmenting is an aggregating process

Marketing-oriented managers think of **segmenting** as an aggregating process—clustering people with similar needs into a "market segment." A **market segment** is a (relatively) homogeneous group of customers who will respond to a marketing mix in a similar way.

This part of the market segmentation process (see Exhibit 3–3) takes a different approach than the naming part. Here, we are looking for similarities rather than basic differences in needs. Segmenters start with the idea that each person is "one of a kind" but that it may be possible to aggregate some more or less "homogeneous" people into a product-market.

Segmenters see each of these "one-of-a-kind" people having a unique set of dimensions. This is shown in Exhibit 3–7A. Here the many dots show each person's position in a product-market with two dimensions—need for status and need for dependability. While each person's position is unique, you can see that many of them are similar in terms of how much status and dependability they want. So a segmenter may aggregate these people into three (an arbitrary number) relatively homogeneous sub-markets—A, B, and C. Group A might be called "Status Oriented" and Group C "Dependability Oriented." Members of Group B want both and might be called the "Demanders."

How far should the aggregating go?

The segmenter wants to aggregate individual customers into some workable number of relatively homogeneous target markets—and then treat each target market differently.

Look again at Exhibit 3–7A. Remember we talked about three segments. But this was an arbitrary number. As Exhibit 3–7B shows, there may really be six segments. What do you think—does this broad product-market consist of three segments or six segments?

Another difficulty with segmenting is that some potential customers don't "fit" neatly into market segments. For example, not everyone in Exhibit 3–7B

Exhibit 3–7A
Every Individual Has His Own Unique Position in the Market—
Those with Similar Positions Can Be Aggregated into Potential
Target Markets

Exhibit 3–7B
How Many Segments Are There?

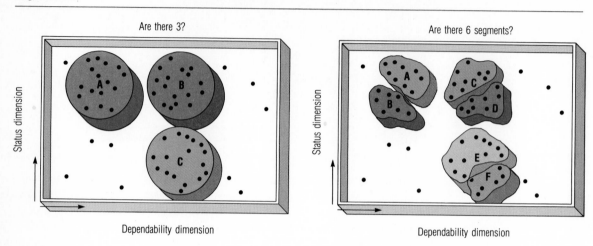

was put into one of the groups. Forcing them into one of the groups would have made these segments more heterogeneous—and harder to please. Further, forming additional segments for them probably wouldn't be profitable. These people are simply too few and too "unique" to cater to and may have to be ignored—unless they are willing to pay a high price for special treatment.

The number of segments that should be formed depends more on judgment than on some scientific rule. But the following guidelines can help.

Criteria for segmenting a broad product-market

Ideally, "good" market segments meet the following criteria:

1. *Homogeneous (similar) within*—the customers in a market segment should be as similar as possible with respect to their likely responses to marketing mix variables *and* their segmenting dimensions.
2. *Heterogeneous (different) between*—the customers in different segments should be as different as possible with respect to their likely responses to marketing mix variables *and* their segmenting dimensions.
3. *Substantial*—the segment should be big enough to be profitable.
4. *Operational*—the segmenting dimensions should be useful for identifying customers and deciding on marketing mix variables.

It is especially important that segments be *operational*. This means you should avoid dimensions that have no practical use. A personality trait such as moodiness, for example, might be found among the traits of a product's heavy buyers, but how could you use this fact? Personal salespeople would have to give a personality test to each buyer—an impossible task. Advertising media buyers or copywriters couldn't make much use of this information either. So although moodiness might be related in some way to previous purchases, it would not be a useful dimension for segmenting.

The need for segments to be operational may lead marketers to include demographic dimensions such as age, income, location, and family size to help in planning marketing mixes. Information on these dimensions is readily available and useful—at least for Place and Promotion planning. In fact, it is difficult to make some Place and Promotion decisions without such information.

Target marketers aim at specific targets

Once you accept the idea that broad product-markets may have sub-markets, you can see that target marketers usually have a choice among many possible target markets.

There are three basic ways of developing market-oriented strategies in a broad product-market.

1. The **single target market approach**—segmenting the market and picking one of the homogeneous segments as the firm's target market.
2. The **multiple target market approach**—segmenting the market, choosing two or more segments, and treating each as a separate target market needing a different marketing mix.
3. The **combined target market approach**—combining two or more sub-markets into one larger target market as a basis for one strategy.

Note that all three approaches involve target marketing—they all aim at specific—and clearly defined—target markets. See Exhibit 3–8. For convenience, we'll call people who follow the first two approaches the "segmenters" and the people who use the third approach "combiners."

Exhibit 3–8 Target Marketers Have Specific Aims

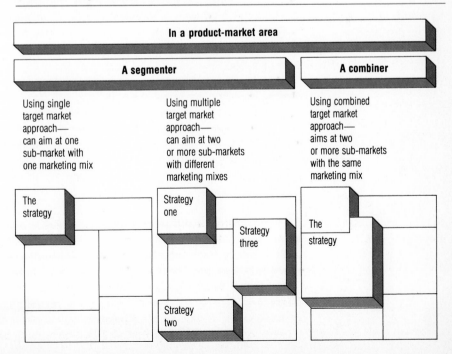

Chicago Tribune advertisers use a combined target market approach.

Combiners try to satisfy pretty well

Combiners try to increase the size of their target markets by combining two or more segments—perhaps to gain some economies of scale, to reduce risk, or just because they don't have enough resources to develop more than one marketing mix.

Combiners look at various sub-markets for similarities rather than differences. Then they try to extend or modify their basic offering to appeal to these "combined" customers with just one marketing mix. See Exhibit 3–8. For example, combiners may try a new package, more service, a new brand, or new flavors. But even if they make product or other marketing mix changes, they don't try to uniquely satisfy smaller sub-markets. Instead, combiners try to improve the general appeal of their marketing mix to appeal to a bigger "combined" target market.

Segmenters try to satisfy very well

Segmenters, on the other hand, aim at one or more homogeneous segments and try to develop a different marketing mix for each segment. They want to satisfy each one very well. Segmenters may make more basic changes in marketing mixes—perhaps in the product itself.

Instead of assuming that the whole market consists of a fairly similar set of customers (like the mass marketer does) or merging various sub-markets together (like the combiner), a segmenter sees sub-markets with their own demand curves—as shown in Exhibit 3–9. Segmenters believe that aiming at

Exhibit 3–9 There May Be Different Demand Curves in Different Market Segments

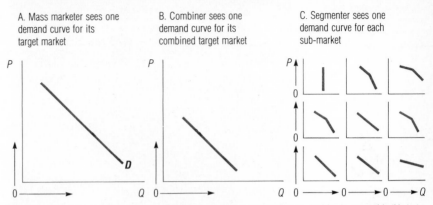

Note: A familiarity with economic analysis, and especially demand curves and demand elasticity, is assumed in this text. Those desiring a review of these materials should see Appendix A at the end of Chapter 2.

one—or some—of these smaller markets produces greater satisfaction to the target customers and greater profit potential for the firm.

Segmenting may produce bigger sales

Note that a segmenter is not settling for a smaller sales potential. Instead, by aiming at only a part of a larger product-market, the segmenter hopes to get a much larger share of his target market(s). In the process, total sales may increase. The segmenter may even get a "monopoly" in "his" market(s).

Should you segment or combine?

Which approach should a firm use? This depends on the firm's resources, the nature of competition, and—most important—the similarity of customer needs, attitudes, and buying behavior.

It's tempting to aim at larger combined markets instead of smaller segmented markets. If successful, such a strategy can result in economies of scale. Also, offering one marketing mix to two or more sub-markets usually requires less investment—and may seem less risky—than offering different marketing mixes to different sub-markets.

Too much aggregating is risky

Combiners must be careful not to aggregate too far in search of profit. As they enlarge the target market, it becomes less homogeneous—and individual differences within each sub-market may begin to outweigh the similarities. This makes it harder to develop marketing mixes that can do an effective job of reaching and satisfying potential customers within each of the sub-markets.

A combiner faces the continual risk of innovative segmenters "chipping away" at the various segments of the combined target market—by offering more attractive marketing mixes to more homogeneous sub-markets.[5]

In the extreme, a combiner may create a fairly attractive marketing mix, but then watch segmenters capture one after another of its sub-markets with more targeted marketing mixes—until finally the combiner is left with no customers at all!

McDonnell Douglas identified a breakthrough opportunity—one that will help it to satisfy some customers very well instead of many just fairly well.

In general, it's usually safer to be a segmenter—that is, to try to satisfy some customers *very* well—instead of many just *fairly* well. That's why many firms use the single or multiple target market approach instead of the combined target market approach. Procter & Gamble, for example, offers many products that seem to compete directly with each other (e.g., Tide versus Cheer or Crest versus Gleem). However, P&G offers "tailor-made" marketing mixes to each sub-market that is large enough—and profitable enough—to deserve a separate marketing mix. This approach can be extremely effective but may not be possible for a smaller firm with more limited resources. A smaller firm may have to use the single target market approach—aiming at the one sub-market that looks "best" for it.

Profit is the balancing point

Target marketers develop and implement whole strategies—they don't just segment markets. In practice, this means that cost considerations probably encourage more aggregating—to obtain economies of scale—while demand considerations suggest less aggregating—to satisfy needs more exactly.

Profit is the balancing point. It determines how unique a marketing mix the firm can afford to offer to a particular group.

WHAT DIMENSIONS ARE USED TO SEGMENT MARKETS?

Market segmentation forces a marketing manager to decide which product-market dimensions will be useful for planning marketing mixes. Exhibit 3–10 shows the kinds of dimensions we'll be talking about in Chapters 4 through 7—and their probable effect on the four Ps. Ideally, we would like to describe any potential product-market in terms of all three types of customer-related dimensions—plus a product type description—because these dimensions will help us develop better marketing mixes.

Consumers have many dimensions. And several may be useful for segmenting a broad product-market. Exhibit 3–11 shows some possible consumer market segmenting dimensions and their typical breakdowns. Note that there are customer-related dimensions and situation-related dimensions—either of which may be more important in some cases.[6]

Exhibit 3–12 shows some possible dimensions for segmenting industrial markets and typical breakdowns.

With so many possible dimensions—and knowing that several dimensions may be needed to show what is really important in specific product-markets—how should we proceed?

Basically, we start with the assumption that potential customers are reasonably sensible problem solvers who have needs they want to satisfy. They may not always solve their problems in a strictly economic way—or the way the marketer might solve them. But research seems to suggest that most customers have only a few really important determining dimensions—so the task is to try to understand the "few" *determining* dimensions of groups of customers.

What are the qualifying and determining dimensions

To select the important segmenting dimensions, it is useful to think about two different types of dimensions. **Qualifying dimensions** are the dimensions relevant to a product-market. **Determining dimensions** actually affect the purchase of a specific product or brand in a product-market. These are the segmenting dimensions we are seeking.

Exhibit 3–10   Relation of Potential Target Market Dimensions to Marketing Mix Decision Areas

Potential target market dimensions	Effects on decision areas
1. Geographic location and other demographic characteristics of potential customers	Affects size of *Target Markets* (economic potential) and *Place* (where products should be made available) and *Promotion* (where and to whom to advertise)
2. Behavioral needs, attitudes, and how present and potential goods or services fit into customers' consumption patterns	Affects *Product* (design, packaging, length or width of product line) and *Promotion* (what potential customers need and want to know about the product offering, and what appeals should be used)
3. Urgency to get need satisfied and desire and willingness to compare and shop	Affects *Place* (how directly products are distributed from producer to consumer, how extensively they are made available, and the level of service needed) and *Price* (how much potential customers are willing to pay)

Exhibit 3–11 Possible Segmenting Dimensions and Typical Breakdowns for Consumer Markets

Dimensions	Typical breakdowns
Customer related	
Geographic	
Region.	Pacific, Mountain, West North Central, West South Central, East North Central, East South Central, South Atlantic, Middle Atlantic, New England
City, county, MSA size. . . .	Under 5,000; 5,000–19,999; 20,000–49,999; 50,000–99,999; 100,000–249,999; 250,000–499,999; 500,000–999,999; 1,000,000–3,999,999; 4,000,000 or over
Demographic	
Age.	Infant, under 6; 6–11; 12–17; 18–24; 25–34; 35–49; 50–64; 65 and over
Sex	Male, female
Family size.	1–2, 3–4, 5 +
Family life cycle	Young, single; young, married, no children; young, married, youngest child under 6; young, married, youngest child 6 or over; older, married, with children; older, married, no children under 18; older, single; other
Income	Under $5,000; $5,000–$7,999; $8,000–$9,999; $10,000–$14,999; $15,000–$24,999; $25,000–$39,999; $40,000 or over
Occupation.	Professional and technical; managers, officials, and proprietors; clerical, sales; craftsmen, foremen; operatives; farmers; retired; students; housewives; unemployed
Education.	Grade school or less, some high school, graduated high school, some college, college graduate, post-graduate
Religion	Catholic, Protestant, Jewish, other
Race	White, Black, Oriental, other
Nationality	American, British, French, German, etc.
Social class	Lower-lower, upper-lower, lower-middle, upper-middle, lower-upper, upper-upper
Situation related	
Benefits offered	
Need satisfiers	PSSP, economic, and more detailed needs
Product features	Situation specific, but to satisfy specific or general needs
Consumption or use patterns	
Rate of use.	Heavy, medium, light, non-users
Use with other products	Situation specific, e.g., gas with a traveling vacation
Brand familiarity	Insistence, preference, recognition, non-recognition, rejection
Buying situation	
Kind of store.	Convenience, shopping, specialty
Kind of shopping.	Serious versus browsing, rushed versus leisurely
Depth of assortment	Out of stock, shallow, deep
Type of product.	Convenience, shopping, specialty, unsought

A prospective car buyer, for example, has to have enough money—or credit—to buy a car. He also must have—or be able to get—a driver's license. This still doesn't guarantee that he'll buy a car. He may just rent one—or continue borrowing his parents' or friends' cars—or take a bus. He may not get around to actually buying a car until his status with his buddies falls because he doesn't have "wheels." This need may lead him to buy *some* car. But this dimension is not determining with respect to a specific brand or a specific model.

Exhibit 3–12   Possible Segmenting Dimensions for Industrial Markets

Type of organization	Manufacturing, institutional, government, public utility, military, farm, etc.
Demographics	Size 　　Employees 　　Sales volume SIC code Number of plants Geographic location: 　　East, Southeast, South, Midwest, Mountains, Southwest, West 　　Large city ⟶ rural
Type of product	Installations, accessories, components, raw materials, supplies, services
Type of buying situation	Decentralized ⟶ centralized Buyer ⟶ multiple buying influence Straight rebuy ⟶ modified rebuy ⟶ new buy
Source loyalty	Weak ⟶ strong loyalty Last resort ⟶ second source ⟶ first source
Kinds of commitments	Contracts, agreements, financial aids
Reciprocity	None ⟶ complete

Determining dimensions may be very specific

How specific the determining dimensions are depends on whether you are concerned with a general product type or a specific brand. See Exhibit 3–13. The more specific you want to be, the more particular the determining dimensions may be. In a particular case, the determining dimensions may seem minor. But they are important because they *are* the determining dimensions. In the car-status-seekers market, for example, paint colors or brand name (e.g., BMW) may determine which cars people buy.

Exhibit 3–13   Finding the Relevant Segmenting Dimensions

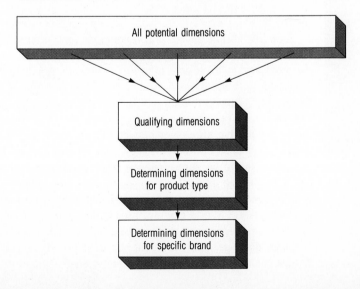

Qualifying dimensions are important, too

The qualifying dimensions help identify the "core features" that must be offered to everyone in a product-market. Qualifying and determining dimensions work together in marketing strategy planning.

Different dimensions needed for different sub-markets

Note that each different sub-market within a broad product-market may be motivated by a different set of dimensions. In the "snack food" market, for example, health food enthusiasts are interested in nutrition, dieters may care only about calories, and economical shoppers with lots of kids may want volume to "fill them up." The related sub-markets might be called: "health-conscious snack food market," "dieters' snack food market," and "kids snack food market." They would be in different boxes in a market grid diagram for the "snack food" market.

A SEVEN–STEP APPROACH TO SEGMENTING CONSUMER PRODUCT–MARKETS

Now let's go on to a logical, seven-step approach to market segmentation that can be used without expensive marketing research or computer analysis. More sophisticated techniques are discussed later—but this one works and has led to successful strategies.

To be sure you understand the approach, we will review each step separately, explain its importance, and use an ongoing example to show how each step works. The example is rental housing—in particular, the apartment market in a big urban area.

1. Name the broad product-market.

First, decide what broad product-market the firm wants to be in. This may be stated in the firm's objectives. Or, if the firm is already in some product-market, this might be a good starting point. If it is just starting out, however, then many more choices are open—although the available resources, both human and financial, will limit the possibilities. It is better to build on the firm's strengths while avoiding its weaknesses—and competitors' strengths.

Example: A firm builds and rents small apartments for low-income families. A narrow view—considering only the products now being produced—might lead the firm to think only of more low-income housing. A bigger view might see such apartments as only a small part of the total apartment market—or total rental housing market—or even the total housing market in the firm's geographic area. Taking an even bigger view, the firm could consider expanding to other geographic areas—or moving into other kinds of products (like office buildings or shopping centers).

There has to be some balance between naming the product-market too narrowly (same old product, same old market) and naming it too broadly (the whole world and all its needs). Here, the firm decided on the whole apartment renter's market in one city—where the firm had some experience.

2. List potential customers' needs.

Write down as many relevant needs as you can—considering all of the potential customers in the broad product-market. This is a "brainstorming" step.

The list doesn't have to be complete yet. But it should provide enough input to really stimulate thinking in the next steps. Possible needs can be seen by thinking about *why* some people buy the present offerings in this broad product-market.

Example: In the apartment renter's market, it is fairly easy to list some possible needs: basic shelter, parking, play space, safety and security, distinctiveness, economy, privacy, convenience (to something), enough living area, attractive interiors, and good supervision and maintenance to assure trouble-free and comfortable living.

3. Form "homogeneous" sub-markets—i.e., "narrow" product-markets.

Assuming that some people have different needs than others, form one sub-market around yourself (or some "typical" customer) and then aggregate similar people into this segment if the same marketing mix would satisfy them. Write the important need dimensions of these people in a column to help decide whether each new person should be included in the first segment. Also, note the people-related characteristics (including demographics) of the product-markets you are forming—so you can name them later.

For example, if the people in one market (column) are college students looking for a "party environment," this will help you understand what they want and why—and will help you name the market (perhaps as "the partyers").

People who are not "homogeneous"—who don't fit in the first segment—should be used to form a new sub-market. List their different need dimensions in another column. Continue this classifying until three or more sub-markets emerge.

Obviously, some judgment is needed here. But you should have some ideas about how you behave—and you can see that others have different needs and attitudes. We all are different, but experienced observers do tend to agree, at least roughly, on how and why people behave.

Example: A college student living off campus probably wants an apartment to provide basic shelter, parking, economy, convenience to school and work, and enough room somewhere to have parties. An older married couple, on the other hand, has quite different needs—perhaps for basic shelter and parking, but *also* for privacy and good supervision so that they don't have to put up with the music that might appeal to the partyers.

4. Identify the determining dimensions.

Review the list of need dimensions for each possible segment (column) and identify the determining dimensions (perhaps putting parentheses around them). Although the qualifying dimensions are important—perhaps reflecting "core needs" that should be satisfied—they are not the *determining* dimensions we are seeking now.

Careful thinking about the needs and attitudes of the people in each possible segment will help to identify the determining dimensions. They may not seem very different from market to market, but if they are determining to those people, then they *are* determining!

Example: With our apartment renters, the need for basic shelter, parking, and safety and security are probably not determining. Everyone has these qualifying needs. Ignoring these common needs helps you see the determining dimensions—such as the needs for privacy, club facilities, strong management, and so on. See Exhibit 3–14.

5. Name (nickname) the possible product-markets.

Review the determining dimensions—market by market—and name (nickname) each one based on the relative importance of the determining dimensions (and aided by your description of the customer-types). A market grid helps to visualize this broad product-market and its "narrow" product-markets.

Draw the market grid as a rectangle with boxes inside representing smaller, more homogeneous segments. See Exhibit 3–14. Think of the whole rectangle as representing the broad product-market with its name on top. Now think of each of the boxes as "narrow" product-markets. Since the markets within a broad product-market usually require very different dimensions, don't try to use the same two dimensions to name the markets—or to label the sides of the market grid boxes. Rather, just think of the grid as showing the relative sizes of product-market segments. Then, label each segment with its nickname.

Example: We can identify the following apartment renter sub-markets: swingers, sophisticates, family-oriented, job-centered, and urban-centered. See Exhibit 3–14. Note that each segment has a different set of determining dimensions (benefits sought), following directly from customer type and needs.

6. Think about why product-market segments behave as they do.

After naming the markets as we did in Step 5, think about what else you know about each segment—and why these markets behave the way they do. Different segments may have similar—but slightly different—needs. This may explain why some competitive offerings succeed better than others. It also can lead to splitting and renaming some segments.

Example: Newly married couples might have been treated as "swingers" in Step 5 because the "married" characteristic did not seem important. But with more thought, we see that while some newly married couples are still swingers at heart, others have begun to shift their focus to buying a home. For these "newly marrieds," the apartment is a temporary place. Further, they are not like the sophisticates and probably should be treated as a separate market. The point here is that these market differences might only be discovered in Step 6. It is at this step that the "newly married" market would be named—and a related column created to describe the new segment.

7. Make a rough estimate of the size of each product-market segment.

Remember, we are looking for *profitable* opportunities. So now we try to tie our product-markets to demographic data—or other customer-related characteristics—to make it easier to estimate the size of these markets. We aren't trying to estimate our likely sales yet. Now we only want to provide a basis for later forecasting and marketing mix planning. The more we know about possible target markets, the easier those jobs will be.

Fortunately, much demographic data is available. And bringing in demographics adds a note of economic reality. Some possible product-markets may have almost no market potential. Without some hard facts, the risks of aiming at such markets are great.

To refine the market grid, redraw the inside boxes so that they give a better

Exhibit 3–14 Segmenting the Broad Apartment Renters Market in a Metropolitan Area

	Need dimensions (benefits sought)	Customer-related characteristics	Nickname of product-market
1	Shelter Parking Security (Common facilities) (Close-in location) (Economy) Friendly management	Young, unmarried, active, fun-loving, party-going	**Swingers**
2	Shelter Parking Security (Distinctive design) (Privacy) (Interior variety) (Strong management) Club facilities	Older and more mature than swingers. Also, more income and education. More desire for comfort and individuality	**Sophisticates**
3	Shelter Parking Security (Room size) (Play space) (Economy)	Young families with children and not enough income to afford own home	**Family**
4	Shelter Parking Security (Close-in location) (Strong management) (Economy)	Single adults, widows, or divorcees. Not much discretionary income and want to be near job	**Job-centered**
5	Shelter Parking Security (Distinctive design) (Close-in location) (Strong management)	Former suburban home owners who now want to be close to city attractions	**Urban-centered**
6	Shelter Parking Security (Privacy) (Strong management) Club facilities	Younger, but no longer swingers. Want a home but don't have enough money yet. Both work so economy not necessary	**Newly married**

Apartment Renters in a Metro Area

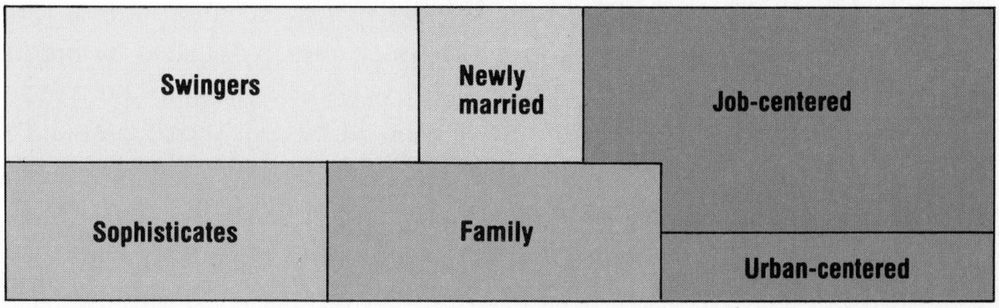

Swingers	Newly married	Job-centered
Sophisticates	**Family**	**Urban-centered**

idea of the size of the various segments. This will help highlight the larger—and perhaps more attractive—opportunities.

Example: It's possible to tie the swingers to demographic data. Most of them are between 21 and 35. The U.S. Census Bureau publishes detailed age data by city. Given age data and an estimate of what percentage are swingers, it's easy to estimate the number of swingers in a metropolitan area.

Once we have followed all seven steps, we should at least see the outlines of the kinds of marketing mixes that would appeal to the various markets. Let's take a look.

We know that "swingers" are active, young, unmarried, fun-loving, and party-going. The determining dimensions (benefits sought) in Exhibit 3–14 show what the swingers want in an apartment. (It's interesting to note what they do *not* want—strong management. Most college students will probably understand why!)

A Dallas-area apartment complex made a very successful appeal to local swingers by offering a swimming pool, a putting green, a night club with bands and other entertainment, poolside parties, receptions for new tenants, and so on. And to maintain the image, management insists that tenants who get married move out shortly—so that new swingers can move in.

As a result, apartment occupancy rates have been extremely high. At the same time, other builders often have difficulty filling their apartments—mostly because their units are just "little boxes" with few unique and appealing features.

Market dimensions suggest a good mix

SEVEN–STEP APPROACH APPLIES IN INDUSTRIAL MARKETS, TOO

A similar seven-step approach can be used for industrial markets, too. The major change is in the first step—selecting the broad product-market. The needs are often different.

Industrial customers' needs derive from final consumer needs—so industrial markets are concerned with purchases that help produce other products. The functions industrial buyers are concerned about include, but are not limited to: forming, bending, grading, digging, cutting, heating, cooling, conducting, transmitting, containing, filling, cleaning, analyzing, sorting, training, and insuring.

Defining the relevant broad product-market using both geographic dimensions and basic functional needs usually ensures a broad focus—that is, one not focused only on the product now being supplied to present customers. But it also keeps the focus from expanding to "all the industrial needs in the world."

It is better to focus on needs satisfied by products *not* product characteristics themselves. New ways of satisfying the need may be found—and completely surprise and upset current producers—if the product-market is defined too narrowly. For example, desktop computers and printers now compete in what some producers thought was the "typewriter market." And telephone calls are replacing letters—further reducing the need for typing. Perhaps this broad product-market is concerned with "thought processing and transmitting." Cer-

tainly, the "typewriter" view is too narrow. Market-oriented strategy planners try to avoid surprises that result from such tunnel vision.

After the first step, the other steps are similar to segmenting consumer markets. Only the segmenting dimensions shown in Exhibit 3–12 and discussed in Chapter 7 are used here.[7]

MORE SOPHISTICATED TECHNIQUES MAY HELP IN SEGMENTING

Clustering techniques try to find similar patterns within sets of data. "Clustering" groups customers with similar segmenting dimensions into homogeneous segments. Clustering approaches use computers to do what previously was done with much intuition and judgment.

The data to be clustered might include such dimensions as demographic characteristics, the importance of different needs, attitudes toward the product, and past buying behavior. The computer searches all the data for homogeneous groups of people. When it finds them, marketers study the dimensions of the people in the groups to see why the computer clustered them together. If the results make some sense, they may suggest new, or at least better, marketing strategies.[8]

A cluster analysis of the toothpaste market, for example, might show that some people buy toothpaste because it tastes good (the sensory segment), while others are concerned with the effect of clean teeth on their social image (the sociables). Others worry about decay (the worriers), and some just look for the best value (the economic men). See Exhibit 3–15. Each of these market segments calls for a different marketing mix—although some of the four Ps may be similar.

Different toothpastes may be targeted at different segments with different needs.

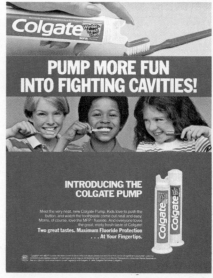

Exhibit 3–15   Toothpaste Market Segment Description

	Segment name			
	The sensory segment	**The sociables segment**	**The worriers segment**	**The independent segment**
Principal benefit sought	Flavor, product appearance	Brightness of teeth	Decay prevention	Price
Demographic strengths	Children	Teens, young people	Large families	Men
Special behavioral characteristics	Users of spearmint flavored toothpaste	Smokers	Heavy users	Heavy users
Brands disproportionately favored	Colgate, Stripe	Macleans, Plus White, Ultra Brite	Crest	Brands on sale
Personality characteristics	High self-involvement	High sociability	High hypochon-driasis	High autonomy
Life-style characteristics	Hedonistic	Active	Conservative	Value-oriented

Finally, a marketing manager has to decide which one (or more) of these segments will be the firm's target market(s).

You can see that these techniques only *aid* the manager. Managers still need judgment to develop an original list of possible dimensions—and then to name the resulting clusters.

Positioning segments by product features

Another approach to segmenting—**positioning**—shows where proposed and/or present brands are located in a market—as seen by customers. It requires some formal marketing research—but may be helpful when competitive offerings are quite similar. The results are usually plotted on graphs to help show the product's "position" in relation to competitors. Usually, the products' positions are related to two product features important to the target customers.

Assuming a reasonably accurate picture, managers then decide whether they want to leave their product (and marketing mix) alone or reposition it. This may mean *physical changes* in the product or simply *image changes based on promotion.* For example, most beer drinkers can't pick out their favorite brand in a blind test—so physical changes might not be necessary (and might not even work) to reposition a beer brand.

The graphs for positioning decisions are obtained by asking product users to make judgments about different brands—including their "ideal" brand—and then computer programs summarize the ratings and plot the results. The details of positioning techniques—sometimes called "perceptual mapping"—are beyond the scope of this text.[9] But Exhibit 3–16 shows the possibilities.

Exhibit 3–16 shows the "product space" for different brands of bar soap using two dimensions—the extent to which consumers think the soaps moisturize and deodorize their skin. For example, consumers see Dial as quite low on moisturizing but high on deodorizing. Lifebuoy and Dial are close to-

Exhibit 3–16   "Product Space" Representing Consumers' Perceptions for Different Brands of Soap

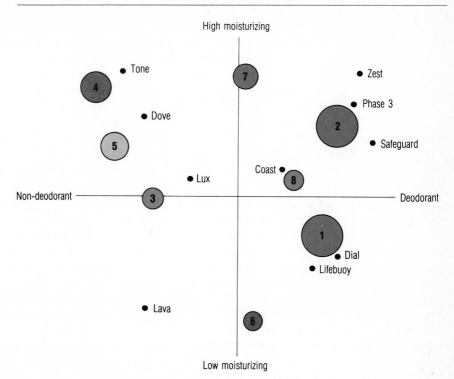

gether—implying that consumers think of them as similar on these characteristics. Dove is viewed as different and is further away on the graph. Remember that positioning maps are based on *customers' perceptions*—the actual characteristics of the products (as determined by a chemical test) might be different!

The circles on Exhibit 3–16 show sets of consumers clustered near their "ideal" soap preferences. Groups of respondents with a similar "ideal" product are circled to show apparent customer concentrations. In this graph, the size of the circles suggests the size of the different "ideal" segments.

Ideal clusters 1 and 2 are the largest and are close to two popular brands—Dial and Safeguard. It appears that customers in cluster 1 want more moisturizing than they see in Dial and Lifebuoy. However, exactly what these brands should do about this isn't clear. Perhaps both of these brands should leave their physical products alone—but emphasize moisturizing more in their promotion to make a stronger appeal to those who want moisturizers.

Note that ideal cluster 7 is not near any of the present brands. This may suggest an opportunity for introducing a new product—a strong moisturizer with some deodorizers. You can see that product positioning can help show how customers see markets—in relation to product features the marketing manager thinks are important to potential customers.

CONCLUSION

Creative strategy planning is needed for survival in our increasingly competitive markets. In this chapter, we discussed how to find attractive target market opportunities. We saw that carefully defining generic markets and product-markets can help find new opportunities. And we emphasized the shortcomings of a too narrow product-oriented view of markets.

We also discussed market segmentation—the process of naming and then segmenting broad product-markets—to find potentially attractive target markets. Some people try to segment markets by starting with the "mass market" and then dividing it into smaller sub-markets based on a few dimensions. But this can lead to poor results. Instead, market segmentation should first focus on a broad product-market and then group similar customers into homogeneous sub-markets. The more similar the potential customers are, the larger the sub-markets can be. Four criteria for evaluating possible product-market segments were presented.

Once a broad product-market has been seg-mented, marketing managers can use one of three approaches to market-oriented strategy planning: (1) the single target market approach, (2) the multiple target market approach, or (3) the combined target market approach. In general, we encourage marketers to be segmenters rather than combiners.

We discussed a practical—"rough and ready"—seven-step approach to market segmentation that works for both consumer and industrial markets. We also discussed some computer-aided segmenting approaches—clustering techniques and positioning.

In summary, good marketers should be experts on markets and likely segmenting dimensions. By creatively segmenting markets, they may spot opportunities—even breakthrough opportunities—and help their firms to succeed against aggressive competitors offering similar products. Segmenting is basic to target marketing. And the more you practice segmenting, the more meaningful market segments you will see.

Questions and Problems

1. Distinguish between an attractive opportunity and a breakthrough opportunity.

2. Explain how new opportunities may be seen by defining a firm's markets more precisely. Illustrate for a situation where you feel there is an opportunity—i.e., an unsatisfied market segment—even if it is not very large.

3. Distinguish between a generic market and a product-market. Illustrate your answer.

4. Explain the major differences among the four basic types of opportunities discussed in the text and cite examples for two of these types of opportunities.

5. Explain why a firm may want to pursue a market penetration opportunity before pursuing one involving product development or diversification.

6. Explain what market segmentation is.

7. List the types of potential segmenting dimensions and explain which you would try to apply first, second, and third in a particular situation. If the nature of the situation would affect your answer, explain how.

8. Explain why segmentation efforts based on attempts to divide the mass market on a few demographic dimensions may be very disappointing.

9. Illustrate the concept that segmenting is an aggregating process by referring to the admis-

sions policies of your own college and a nearby college or university.

10. (a) Evaluate how "good" the seven markets identified in the market for apartments are (Exhibit 3–14) with respect to the four criteria for selecting good market segments. (b) Same as (a) but evaluate the four corner markets in the British home decorating market (Exhibit 2–9).

11. Review the types of segmenting dimensions listed in Exhibits 3–11 and 3–12, and select the ones you think should be combined to fully explain the market segment you personally would be in if you were planning to buy a new car today. List several dimensions and try to develop a short-hand name, like "swinger," to describe your own personal market segment. Then try to estimate what proportion of the total car market would be accounted for by your market segment. Next, explain if there are any offerings that come close to meeting the needs of your market. If not, what sort of a marketing mix is needed? Would it be economically attractive for anyone to try to satisfy your market segment? Why or why not?

12. Identify the determining dimension or dimensions that explain why you bought the specific brand you did in your most recent purchase of a (a) soft drink, (b) pen, (c) shirt or blouse, and a (d) larger, more expensive item, such as a bicycle, camera, boat, and so on. Try to express the determining dimension(s) in terms of your own personal characteristics rather than the product's characteristics. Estimate what share of the market would probably be motivated by the same determining dimension(s).

13. Apply the seven-step approach to segmenting consumer markets to the college-age market for off-campus recreation, which can include eating and drinking. Then evaluate how well the needs in these market segments are being met in your geographic area. Is there an obvious breakthrough opportunity waiting for someone?

14. Explain how the first step in the seven-step approach to segmenting markets would have to be changed to apply it in industrial markets. Illustrate your answer.

15. Explain how positioning can help a marketing manager identify target market opportunities.

Suggested Computer-Aided Problem

3. Segmenting Customers

Suggested Cases

6. Applegate Chevrolet

8. Tony's Place

14. McQueen Ski Shop

31. Precision Castings, Inc.

Chapter 4

Evaluating Opportunities in Uncontrollable Environments

When You Finish This Chapter, You Should

1. Know the uncontrollable variables the marketing manager must work with.

2. Understand why company objectives are important in guiding marketing strategy planning.

3. See how the resources of the firm may limit its search for opportunities.

4. Know the effect of the different kinds of market situations on strategy planning.

5. Understand how the economic and technological environment can affect strategy planning.

6. Know why you can go to prison by ignoring the political and legal environment.

7. Know about population and income trends.

8. Understand how to screen and evaluate marketing strategy opportunities.

9. Recognize the important new terms (shown in red).

Marketing managers do not plan strategies in a vacuum.

Marketing managers don't plan strategies in a vacuum. They must work with several uncontrollable variables when choosing target markets and developing the four Ps.

Tupperware had a successful marketing strategy: using in-home "parties" to sell housewives quality plastic containers for storing food. The parties were organized by Tupperware sales reps—mostly women who worked part-time. Even with little advertising, the company captured a 60 percent share of its market, and sales grew to $800 million! But, by 1984 Tupperware found that it wasn't much fun to have a party if no one came.

The whole environment had changed. Drawn by better job opportunities, a record number of women were working outside the home. Fewer women were interested in coming to the parties—and it was harder to hire good sales reps away from full-time jobs offering more money and prestige.

Microwave cooking was more popular, too—it was a real time-saver for working women. But Tupperware didn't work well in microwaves. Consumers still bought some plastic containers, but the Rubbermaid brand was "stealing share" by selling through retail stores. To cap things off, some states passed laws that made in-home selling tougher.

Tupperware had to change its marketing strategy. It shifted its target market to all homemakers, introduced new products for storing *and* cooking, moved away from in-home parties, and turned to advertising to tell its new story. And sales improved.[1]

THE UNCONTROLLABLE ENVIRONMENT

The Tupperware case shows why marketing managers should understand the uncontrollable environments. You saw in the last chapter that finding target market opportunities takes real understanding of what makes customers tick. But now we'll show you how uncontrollable environments affect the attractiveness of possible opportunities—and marketing strategy planning. The uncontrollable environments—see Exhibit 4–1—fall into five basic areas:

1. Objectives and resources of the firm.
2. Competitive environment.
3. Economic and technological environment.
4. Political and legal environment.
5. Cultural and social environment.

Exhibit 3–1 shows how Chapters 3 and 4 fit together. In Chapter 3 we talked about finding attractive opportunities. Now we'll see how to evaluate them—given the uncontrollable variables facing a marketing manager.

OBJECTIVES SHOULD SET FIRM'S COURSE

A company should know where it's going—or it can fall into this trap: "Having lost sight of our objective, we redoubled our efforts." In spite of their impor-

Exhibit 4–1   Marketing Manager's Framework

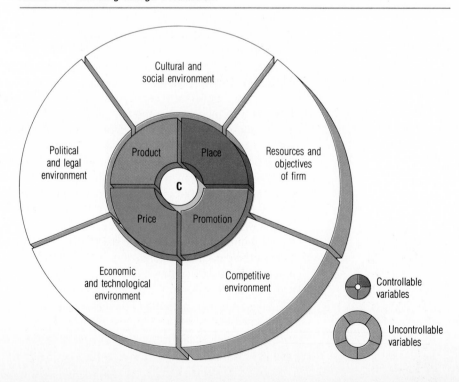

tance, objectives are seldom stated clearly. They may not even be stated at all until *after the strategies are carried out!*

Setting objectives that really guide the present and future of the company isn't easy. It forces top management to look at the whole business—relate its present objectives and resources to the external environment—and then decide what it wants to do in the future.

Three basic objectives provide guidelines

The following three objectives provide a useful starting point for setting a firm's objectives. They should be pursued *together* because—in the long run—a failure in even one of the three areas could lead to total failure of the business.

1. Engage in specific activities that will perform a socially and economically useful function.
2. Develop an organization to carry on the business and implement its strategies.
3. Earn enough profit to survive.[2]

Short-sighted top management may straitjacket marketing

Setting objectives must be taken seriously—or the objectives may limit marketing strategies—perhaps damaging the whole business. A few examples show how the marketing manager may be forced to choose undesirable strategies.

Top management sometimes seeks a quick return on investment. This can force the marketing manager to choose marketing strategies that aim at quick returns in the short run—but that kill brand loyalty in the long run.

Some top managements want a large sales volume or a large market share—because they feel this means higher profits. However, more companies are now shifting their objectives toward *profitable* sales growth rather than just larger market share—as they realize that sales growth doesn't necessarily mean profit growth.[3]

Objectives should lead to marketing objectives

Ideally, the marketing manager should help set a company's objectives— and these objectives should guide the search for and evaluation of opportunities—as well as later planning of marketing strategies. As shown in Exhibit 4–2, there should be a hierarchy of objectives—moving from company objectives to marketing objectives. For each marketing strategy, there should also be objectives for each of the four Ps—as well as sub-objectives. For example, in the Promotion area, we may need advertising objectives, sales promotion objectives, and personal selling objectives.

Both company objectives and marketing objectives should be realistic—and achievable. Objectives that are too ambitious are useless if the firm lacks the resources to achieve them.

COMPANY RESOURCES MAY LIMIT SEARCH FOR OPPORTUNITIES

Every firm has some resources—hopefully some unique resources—that set it apart from other firms. Breakthrough opportunities—or at least some

Exhibit 4–2   A Hierarchy of Objectives

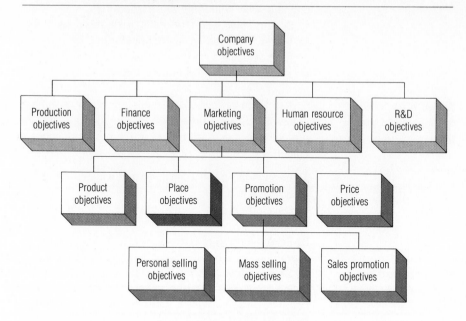

"competitive advantage"—come from using these strengths—while avoiding direct competition with firms having similar strengths.

To find its strengths, the firm must evaluate functional areas (production, research and engineering, marketing, general management, and finance) as well as present products and markets. By analyzing outstanding successes and failures—in relation to the firm's resources—it's possible to discover why it was successful—or why it failed—in the past.

Resources that should be considered—as part of a strengths and weaknesses analysis—are discussed in the following sections.

Financial strength

Some opportunities require large amounts of capital—just to get started. Money may be required for R&D, production facilities, marketing research, or advertising—before the firm makes its first sale. And even a really good opportunity may not be *profitable* for years. So, lack of financial strength is often a "barrier to entry."

Producing capability and flexibility

In many businesses, the cost of production per unit decreases as the quantity produced increases. Therefore, smaller producers can be at a great cost disadvantage if they try to compete against larger competitors having these economies of scale.

On the other hand, new—or smaller—firms sometimes have the advantage of flexibility. They aren't handicapped with large, special-purpose facilities that are obsolete or poorly located. U.S. Steel, Bethlehem, and other large steel producers once enjoyed economies of scale. But today they have trouble competing with producers using smaller, more flexible plants. Similarly, poorly located or obsolete retail or wholesale facilities can severely limit marketing strategy planning.

Firms that own or have assured sources of supply have an important advantage—especially in times of short supply. Big firms often control their own sources of supply. Companies that don't have guaranteed supply sources may have difficulty even staying in business.

Marketing strengths

Our marketing strategy framework helps in analyzing current marketing resources. In the product area, for example, a familiar brand can be a big strength, or a new idea or process may be protected by a *patent*. A patent owner has a 17-year "monopoly" to develop and use a new product, process, or material as he chooses.

Good relations with established middlemen—or control of good locations—can be important resources in reaching some target markets. Similarly, a strong sales force may be able to handle new products and customers. And low-cost facilities may enable a firm to undercut competitors' prices.

Finally, a good understanding of a target market can give a company an edge. Many companies fail in new product-markets because they don't really understand the needs of the new customer—or the new competitive environment.

THE COMPETITIVE ENVIRONMENT

(Note: The following materials assume some familiarity with economic analysis—and especially the nature of demand curves and demand elasticity. For those needing a review of these materials, see Appendix A, which follows Chapter 2.)

A manager may be able to avoid head-on competition

The **competitive environment** affects the number and types of competitors the marketing manager must face—and how they may behave. Although these factors can't be controlled by the marketing manager, he *can* choose strategies that will avoid head-on competition.

A marketing manager operates in one of four kinds of market situations. We'll talk about three kinds: pure competition, oligopoly, and monopolistic competition. The fourth kind, monopoly, isn't found very often and is like monopolistic competition.

Understanding these market situations is important because the freedom of a marketing manager—especially his control over price—is greatly reduced in some situations. The important dimensions of these situations are shown in Exhibit 4–3.

When competition is pure

Many competitors offer about the same thing

Pure competition is a market situation that develops when a market has:

1. Homogeneous (similar) products.
2. Many buyers and sellers, who have full knowledge of the market.

Exhibit 4–3   Some Important Dimensions Regarding Market Situations

Important dimensions \ Types of situations	Pure competition	Oligopoly	Monopolistic competition	Monopoly
Uniqueness of each firm's product	None	None	Some	Unique
Number of competitors	Many	Few	Few to many	None
Size of competitors (compared to size of market)	Small	Large	Large to small	None
Elasticity of demand facing firm	Completely elastic	Kinked demand curve (elastic and inelastic)	Either	Either
Elasticity of industry demand	Either	Inelastic	Either	Either
Control of price by firm	None	Some (with care)	Some	Complete

3. Ease of entry for buyers and sellers; that is, new firms have little difficulty starting in business—and new customers can easily come into the market.

More or less pure competition is found in many agricultural markets. In the potato industry, for example, there are tens of thousands of producers—and they are in pure competition. Let's look more closely at these producers.

In pure competition, each of these many small producers sees an almost perfectly flat demand curve. Exhibit 4–4 shows the relation between the industry demand curve and the demand curve facing the individual farmer in pure competition. Although the potato industry as a whole has a down-sloping demand curve, each individual potato producer has a demand curve that is perfectly flat at the **equilibrium price**—the going market price.

To explain this more clearly, let's look at the demand curve for the individual potato producer. Assume that the equilibrium price for the industry is 50 cents. This means the producer can sell as many potatoes as he chooses at 50 cents. The quantity that all producers choose to sell makes up the supply curve. But acting alone, a small producer can do almost anything he wants to.

If this individual farmer raises 1/10,000th of the quantity offered in the market, for example, you can see that there will be little effect on the market if he goes out of business—or doubles his production.

The reason an individual's demand curve is flat in this example is that he can sell all he can produce *at the market price*. The farmer can't sell any pota-

Exhibit 4–4   Interaction of Demand and Supply in the Potato Industry and the Resulting Demand Curve Facing Individual Potato Producers

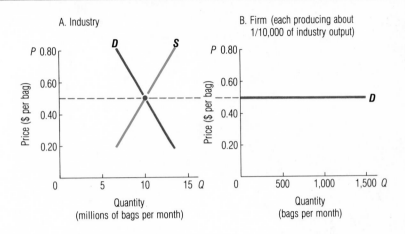

toes above the market price. And there is no need to sell below the market price of 50 cents. So this producer has no control over price.

Markets tend to become more competitive

Not many markets are *purely* competitive. But many are close enough to allow us to talk about "almost" pure competition situations—those in which the marketing manager has to accept the going price.

Such highly competitive situations aren't limited to agriculture. Wherever many competitors sell homogeneous products—such as chemicals, plastics, lumber, coal, printing, and laundry services—the demand curve seen by *each producer* tends to be flat.

Markets tend to become more competitive. In pure competition, prices and profits are pushed down until some competitors are forced out of business. Eventually the price level is only high enough to keep the survivors in business. No one makes much profit—they just cover costs. It's tough to be a marketing manager in this situation!

When competition is oligopolistic

A few competitors offering similar things

Not all markets move toward pure competition. Some become oligopolies.

Oligopoly situations are special market situations that develop when a market has:

1. Essentially homogeneous products—such as basic industrial chemicals or gasoline.
2. Relatively few sellers—or a few large firms and many smaller ones who follow the lead of the larger ones.
3. Fairly inelastic industry demand curves.

The demand curve facing each firm is unusual in an oligopoly situation. Although the industry demand curve can be inelastic throughout the relevant

Exhibit 4–5   Oligopoly—Kinked Demand Curve—Situation

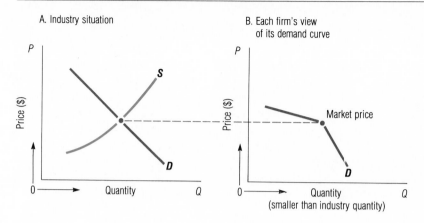

range, the demand curve facing each competitor looks "kinked." See Exhibit 4–5. The current market price is at the kink.

There is a "market price" because the competing firms watch each other carefully—and know it's wise to be at the kink. Each marketing manager must expect that raising his own price above the market would cause a big loss in sales. Few, if any, competitors would follow his price increase. So his demand curve would be relatively flat above the market price. If he lowers his price, he must expect competitors to follow to try to hold their share of the market. Given inelastic industry demand, his own demand curve (his share of the industry demand) would be inelastic at lower prices. Since lowering prices along such a curve would drop total revenue, he should leave his price at the kink—the market price.

Actually, however, there *are* price fluctuations in oligopoly markets. Sometimes this is caused by firms that don't understand the market situation—and cut their prices to get business. In other cases, big increases in demand or supply change the basic nature of the situation—and lead to price cutting. Sometimes the price cuts are drastic—such as Du Pont's Dacron price cut of 25 percent. This happened when Du Pont decided that industry production capacity already exceeded demand—and more plants were due to start into production.

As in pure competition, oligopolists face a long-run trend toward an equilibrium level—with profits driven toward zero. Along the way, a marketing manager may try to avoid price competition—relying more on other elements in the marketing mix. But he has a difficult job because potential customers see the products as homogeneous and tend to focus on price.

When competition is monopolistic

A price must be set

You can see why marketing managers want to avoid pure competition or oligopoly situations. They prefer a market in which they have more control.

Monopolistic competition is a market situation that develops when a market has:

1. Different (heterogeneous) products—in the eyes of some customers.
2. Sellers who feel they do have some competition in this market.

The word *monopolistic* means that each firm is trying to get control of its own little market. But the word *competition* means that there are still substitutes. The vigorous competition of a purely competitive market is reduced. Each firm has its own down-sloping demand curve. But the shape of the curve depends on the similarity of competitors' products and marketing mixes. Each monopolistic competitor has freedom—but not complete freedom—in its own market.

Judging elasticity will help set the price

Since a firm in monopolistic competition has its own down-sloping demand curve, it must make a price level decision as part of its marketing strategy planning. Here, estimating the elasticity of the firm's own demand curve is helpful. If it is highly inelastic, the firm may raise prices—to increase total revenue. But if demand is highly elastic, this may mean many competitors with acceptable substitutes. Then the price may have to be set near "competition." And the marketing manager probably should try to develop a better marketing mix.

Why compete in pure competition?

Why would anyone compete in profitless pure competition? One reason is that the firm is already in the industry. Or the firm enters without knowing what's happening—and must stick it out until it runs out of money.

Production-oriented firms are more likely to make such a mistake. Avoiding pure competition is sensible—and certainly fits with our emphasis on target marketing.

ECONOMIC ENVIRONMENT

The **economic and technological environment** affects the way firms—and the whole economy—use resources. We will treat the economic and technological environments separately—to emphasize that the technological environment provides a *base* for the economic environment. Technical skills and equipment affect the way resources of an economy are converted into output. The economic environment, on the other hand, is affected by the way all of the parts of our macro-economic system interact. This, then, affects such things as national income, economic growth, and inflation.

Economic conditions change rapidly

The economic environment can—and does—change quite rapidly. The effects can be far reaching—and require changes in marketing strategy.

Even a well-planned marketing strategy may fail if the country goes through a rapid business decline. As consumers' incomes drop, they must shift their spending patterns. They may simply have to do without some products. Many companies aren't strong enough to survive such bad times.

Inflation and interest rates affect buying

Inflation is a fact of life in many economies. Some Latin American countries have had from 25 to 100 percent inflation per year for many years. In contrast, the 6 to 20 percent levels reached in recent years in the United States sound low. Still, inflation must be considered in strategy planning. It can lead to government policies that reduce income, employment, *and* consumer spending.

The interest rate—the charge for borrowing money—affects the total price borrowers must pay for products. So the interest rate affects when—and if—they will buy. This is an especially important factor in some industrial markets. But it also affects consumer purchases, especially for homes, cars, and other "high ticket" items usually bought on credit.

World economies are connected

International trade is affected by changes in and between economies. One such factor is the *exchange rate*—how much our dollar is worth in another country's money. When the "dollar is weak," it's worth less in foreign countries. This sounds bad—but it makes U.S. products less expensive overseas and foreign products more expensive in the U.S. In fact, a country's whole economic system can change as the balance of imports and exports shifts—affecting jobs, consumer income, and national productivity.

You can see that the marketing manager must watch the economic environment carefully. In contrast to the cultural and social environment, economic conditions change all the time. And they can move rapidly—up or down—requiring strategy changes.

TECHNOLOGICAL ENVIRONMENT

The technological base affects opportunities

Underlying any economic environment is the **technological base**—the technical skills and equipment that affect the way an economy's resources are converted to output. Technological developments certainly affect marketing. Many argue, for example, that we are moving from an industrial society to an information society. Telecommunications make possible mass promotion via radio, TV, and telephone—reducing the relative importance of other media. Computers allow more sophisticated planning and control of business. And we're in the middle of an explosion of hi-tech products—from robots in factories to home refrigerators that "talk."

As we move through the text, you'll see that some big business successes have come from early recognition of new ways to do things. Marketers should help their firms see such opportunities by trying to understand the "why" of present markets—and what is keeping their firms from being more successful. Then, as new developments come along, the managers will see possible uses—and how opportunities can be turned into profits.

Marketers must also help their firms decide what technical developments will be acceptable to society. With the growing concern about environmental pollution and the quality of life, society may reject some potentially attractive technological developments because of their long-run effects on the environment. Perhaps what's good for the firm and the economy's *economic* growth may not be good for the cultural and social environment—or be acceptable in the political and legal environment. A marketer's closeness to the market should give him a better feel for current trends—and help his firm avoid serious mistakes.[4]

POLITICAL ENVIRONMENT

The attitudes and reactions of people, social critics, and governments all affect the political environment.

Consumerism is here—and basic

Consumerism is a social movement that seeks to increase the rights and powers of consumers. In the last 25 years, consumerism has emerged as a major political force. The basic goals of modern consumerism have not changed much since 1962 when President Kennedy's "Consumer Bill of Rights" affirmed consumers' rights to safety, to be informed, to choose, and to be heard.

Twenty years ago, consumerism was much more visible—with frequent consumer boycotts, protest marches, and much media attention. Today, consumer groups provide information and work on special projects, like product safety standards. Publications like *Consumer Reports* provide product comparisons and information on other consumer concerns.[5]

Business is responding to public expectations

Many companies have responded to the spirit of consumerism. For example, Ford has set up a "consumer board" to help resolve consumer complaints. Many firms have a consumer affairs person—to directly represent consumer interests within the company.

Clearly, top management—and marketing managers—must continue to pay attention to consumer concerns. The old, production-oriented ways of doing things are no longer acceptable.

Nationalism can be limiting in international markets

Strong sentiments of **nationalism**—an emphasis on a country's interests before everything else—may also affect the work of some marketing managers. These feelings can reduce sales—or even block all marketing activity—in some international markets. Oil producers and copper mining firms have felt such pressures in recent years in Latin America, Africa, and the Middle East.

National interests often dictate who a firm can sell to—and how much. Japan has made it difficult for American firms to do business there. But the "Buy American" policy in many government contracts reflects this same attitude in the United States. And there is support for protecting U.S. producers from foreign competition—especially producers of color TVs, footwear, textiles, and cars.

Nationalistic feelings can determine whether a firm can enter markets—because often businesses must get permission to operate. In some political environments, this is only a routine formality. In others, a lot of red tape is in-

volved—and personal influence and/or "bribes" are common. This raises ethical issues for marketing managers—and legal issues, too—since it's illegal for U.S. firms to offer bribes.

Political environment may offer new opportunities

The political environment is not always anti-business. Some governments decide that encouraging business is good for their people. The People's Republic of China is encouraging foreign investors.

Within the United States, special programs and financial incentives have tried to encourage urban redevelopment and minority business. Government loan guarantees made it possible for troubled firms—Lockheed and Chrysler—to develop profitable new marketing strategies. State and local governments also try to attract and hold businesses—sometimes with tax incentives.

Some business managers have become very successful by studying the political environment—and developing strategies that use these political opportunities.

LEGAL ENVIRONMENT

Changes in the political environment often lead to changes in the legal environment—and the way existing laws are enforced.

Trying to encourage competition

American economic and legislative thinking is based on the idea that competition among many small firms helps the economy. Therefore, attempts by business to limit competition are thought to be against the public interest.

As industries grew larger after the Civil War, some became monopolies controlled by wealthy businessmen—the "robber barons." This made it hard for smaller producers to survive. A movement grew—especially among Midwestern farmers—to control monopolists.

Beginning in 1890, Congress passed a series of laws that were basically *antimonopoly* or *procompetition*. The names and dates of these laws are shown in Exhibit 4–6.

Exhibit 4–6   *Outline of Federal Legislation Now Affecting Competition in Marketing*

Year	Antimonopoly (procompetition)	Anticompetition	Antispecific practices
1890	Sherman Act		
1914	Clayton Act Federal Trade Commission Act		Clayton Act
1936	Robinson-Patman Act	Robinson-Patman Act	Robinson-Patman Act
1938			Wheeler-Lea Amendment
1950	Antimerger Act		Antimerger Act
1975	Magnuson-Moss Act		Magnuson-Moss Act

Exhibit 4–7   Focus (mostly prohibitions) of Federal Antimonopoly Laws on the Four Ps

Law	Product	Place	Promotion	Price
Sherman Act (1890) Monopoly or conspiracy in restraint of trade	Monopoly or conspiracy to control a product	Monopoly or conspiracy to control distribution channels		Monopoly or conspiracy to fix or control prices
Clayton Act (1914) Substantially lessen competition	Forcing sale of some products with others— tying contracts	Exclusive dealing contracts (limiting buyers' sources of supply)		Price discrimination by manufacturers
Federal Trade Commission Act (1914) Unfair methods of competition		Unfair policies	Deceptive ads or selling practices	Deceptive pricing
Robinson-Patman Act (1936) Tends to injure competition		Prohibits paying allowances to "direct" buyers in lieu of middlemen costs (brokerage charges)	Prohibits "fake" advertising allowances or discrimination in help offered	Prohibits price discrimination on goods of "like grade and quality" without cost justification, and quantity discounts limited
Wheeler-Lea Amendment (1938) Unfair or deceptive practices	Deceptive packaging or branding		Deceptive ads or selling claims	Deceptive pricing
Antimerger Act (1950) Lessen competition	Buying competitors	Buying producers or distributors		
Magnuson-Moss Act (1975) Unreasonable practices	Product warranties			

Antimonopoly law and marketing mix planning

Specific application of antimonopoly law to the four Ps will be presented in later chapters. For our discussion here, you should know what kind of proof the government must have to get a conviction under each of the major laws. You should also know which of the four Ps are most affected by each law. Exhibit 4–7 provides such a summary—with a phrase following each law to show what the government must prove to get a conviction. Note how the wording of the laws is moving toward protecting *consumers*.

Prosecution is serious—you can go to jail

Businesses and *business managers* are subject to both criminal and civil laws. Penalties for breaking civil laws are limited to blocking or forcing certain actions—along with fines. Where criminal law applies, jail sentences can be imposed. For example, the Sherman Act now provides for fines up to $1 million for corporations—and fines of up to $100,000 and/or up to three years in prison for individuals.[6]

Consumer protection laws are not new

There is more to the legal environment than just the antimonopoly laws. Some consumer protections are built into the English and U.S. common law system. A seller has to tell the truth (if asked a direct question), meet contracts, and stand behind the firm's product (to some reasonable extent). Beyond this, it is expected that vigorous competition in the marketplace will protect consumers—*as long as they are careful.*

Focusing only on competition didn't protect consumers very well in some areas, however. So the government found it necessary to pass other laws—usually involving specific types of products.

Foods and drugs are controlled

Consumer protection laws go back to 1906—when Congress passed the Pure Food and Drug Act. Unsanitary meat-packing practices in the Chicago stockyards stirred consumer support for this act. After much debate, Congress passed a general law to control the quality and labeling of food and drugs in interstate commerce. This was a major victory for consumer protection. Before this, it was assumed that common law and the old warning "let the buyer beware" would take care of consumers.

Later acts corrected some loopholes in the law. The law now bans the shipment of unsanitary and poisonous products—and requires much testing of drugs. The Food and Drug Administration (FDA) attempts to control manufacturers of these products. It can *seize* products that violate its rules—including regulations on branding and labeling.

In general, the FDA has done a good job. But complaints over a proposal to ban the use of saccharin—commonly used to sweeten diet soft drinks—forced the government to rethink how much protection consumers really want. In this case, many users felt that the government should first ban the use of

The government regulates the marketing of many items.

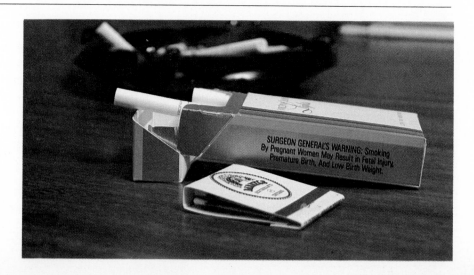

other products whose bad effects had been more thoroughly proven—such as alcohol and cigarettes.

Product safety is controlled

The Consumer Product Safety Act (of 1972) is another important consumer protection law. The act set up the Consumer Product Safety Commission to protect consumers by controlling product safety. This group has broad power to set safety standards—and can impose penalties for failure to meet these standards. Again, there is some question as to how much safety consumers want—the commission found the bicycle the most hazardous product under its control!

But given that the commission has the power to *force* a product off the market, it is obvious that safety must be considered in product design. This is an uncontrollable variable marketing managers must treat seriously.[7]

State and local laws vary, too

Besides federal legislation—which affects interstate commerce—marketers must be aware of state and local laws. There are state and city laws regulating minimum prices and the setting of prices; regulations for starting up a business (licenses, examinations, and even tax payments); and in some communities, regulations prohibiting certain activities—such as door-to-door selling or selling on Sundays or during evenings.

Consumerists and the law say, "let the seller beware"

The old rule about buyer-seller relations—*let the buyer beware*—has shifted to *let the seller beware*. The number of consumer protection laws is increasing. These "pro-consumer" laws and court decisions suggest that there is more interest now in protecting *consumers* instead of protecting *competition*. This may upset production-oriented managers. But times have changed—and they will have to adapt to this new political and legal environment.[8]

CULTURAL AND SOCIAL ENVIRONMENT

The **cultural and social environment** affects how and why people live and behave as they do. This variable is very important—because it has a direct effect on consumer buying behavior in our competitive markets.

Markets consist of real people with money to spend. But the number and location of these people is pretty much set. And many of their attitudes and behavior patterns are fixed—or changing only slowly. In other words, we already know a great deal about our cultural and social environment.

Many people are already born

Over 240 million people live in the United States. Population experts can estimate how long people in various age groups will live and—at least roughly—where they'll live.

Exhibit 4–8 shows that Americans are not spread out equally across the country. The "high areas" emphasize the concentration of population in different areas. Note that California has the largest population—with New York a

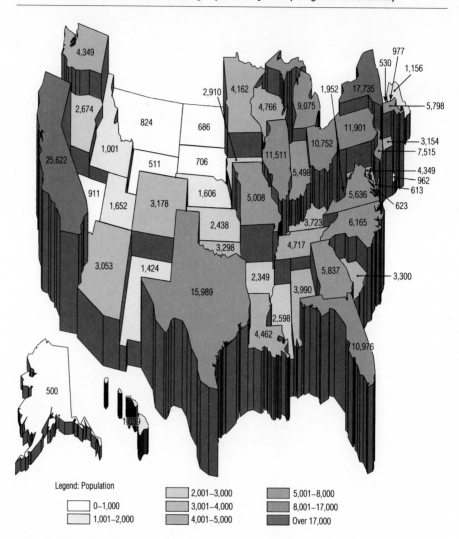

Exhibit 4–8   Map of United States Showing Population by State (all figures in thousands)

Legend: Population

☐ 0–1,000	
☐ 1,001–2,000	
☐ 2,001–3,000	☐ 5,001–8,000
☐ 3,001–4,000	☐ 8,001–17,000
☐ 4,001–5,000	☐ Over 17,000

distant second. But the heavy concentration in the Northeast makes this market much bigger than the whole West Coast. Also notice the importance of the midwestern and southern states. Marketers who want to avoid the tough competition in the East and West Coast markets often see these states as very good target markets. Note, too, the small populations in the plains and mountain states. You can see why some "national" marketers pay less attention to these areas. But these states can be an attractive opportunity for an alert marketer looking for less competitive markets.[9]

Population will keep growing, but...

It seems certain that the U.S. population will continue to grow—at least for another 60 years or so. The big questions are: How much and how fast? The "baby boom" of the 1950s and 1960s turned into the "baby bust" of the

1970s. The **birth rate**—number of babies born per 1,000 people—fell from a post-war high of 25.0 in 1957 to 14.6 in 1976. It's now rising again—but only slightly. And it's expected to drop again in the next decade. This means there will be less need for baby food, toys, teachers, and child-oriented recreation—and more demand for small apartments, travel, and out-of-home entertainment.[10]

Age distribution is changing

Although our population will continue to grow, there will be a major change in our society because the average age is rising. Exhibit 4–9 shows the percentage change—growth or decline—in different age groups for 1980 to 1990 and 1990 to 2000.

The major reason for the changing age distribution is the post-World War II "baby boom"—which produced about one-fourth of our present population. This large group crowded into the schools in the 1950s and 60s. Then they moved into the job market in the 1970s. In the 1980s they are swelling the middle-aged group. And early in the 21st century, they will reach retirement—

Exhibit 4–9   Population Distribution by Age Groups for the Years 1980, 1990, and 2000

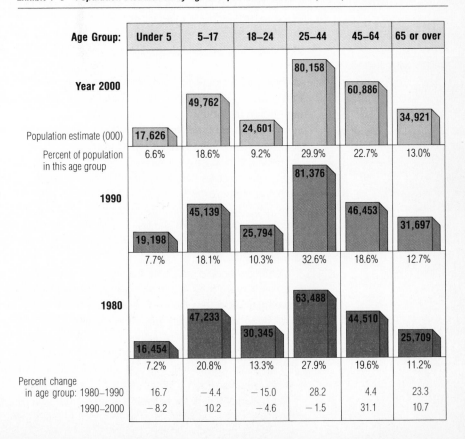

Age Group:	Under 5	5–17	18–24	25–44	45–64	65 or over
Year 2000				80,158	60,886	
		49,762				34,921
Population estimate (000)	17,626		24,601			
Percent of population in this age group	6.6%	18.6%	9.2%	29.9%	22.7%	13.0%
1990				81,376		
		45,139			46,453	31,697
	19,198		25,794			
	7.7%	18.1%	10.3%	32.6%	18.6%	12.7%
1980				63,488		
		47,233	30,345		44,510	
	16,454					25,709
	7.2%	20.8%	13.3%	27.9%	19.6%	11.2%
Percent change in age group: 1980–1990	16.7	−4.4	−15.0	28.2	4.4	23.3
1990–2000	−8.2	10.2	−4.6	−1.5	31.1	10.7

still a large group in the total population. According to one population expert, "It's like a goat passing through a boa constrictor."

Medical advances—that help people live longer—are also adding to the proportion of the population in the senior citizen group. Note from Exhibit 4–9 that the over-65 age group is growing and will continue to grow. This offers opportunities for many industries—like tourism, health care, and financial services.[11]

Household composition is changing

We often think of the "typical" American household as a married couple with two children—living in the suburbs. This never was true—and it's even less true now. Although almost all Americans marry, they are marrying later, delaying child bearing, and having fewer children. Couples with no children under 18 now account for almost half of all families.

And couples don't stay together as long as they used to. The United States has the highest divorce rate in the world—about 38 percent of marriages end in divorce. Almost 80 percent of divorced people remarry—so we see a growing number of "his and hers" families. Still—even with all this shifting around—more than two-thirds of all adults are married.

Non-family households are increasing

Once we get rid of the "couple-with-two-children" image of family life, we should also recognize that many households are not families in the usual sense. *Single-adult households* account for 20 percent of all households— more than 19 million people! These include young adults who leave home when they finish school—as well as divorced and widowed people who live alone.

Such people need smaller apartments, smaller cars, smaller food packages—and in some cases, less expensive household furnishings because they don't have very much money. Other singles have ample discretionary income—and are attractive markets for top-of-the-line stereos, clothing, status cars, travel, and nice restaurants and bars.

There are also several million unmarried people living together—some in groups but most as couples. Some of these arrangements are temporary—as in college towns or in large cities where recent graduates go for their first "real" job. They're setting up households—without much money—and need to buy or rent cheaper furnishings. But some also have more money than they ever thought they would have—and can be good markets for clothing, recreation, and restaurants.

Marketers should probably pay special attention to these non-family households—because they are growing at a much faster rate than traditional family households. And they have different needs and attitudes than the "conventional" American family in the TV comedies.[12]

The shift to urban and suburban areas

Migration from rural to urban areas has continued in the United States since 1800. In 1920, about half the population lived in rural areas. By 1980, the number was less than 4 percent.

After World War II, there was a race to the suburbs. By 1970, more people were living in the suburbs than in the central cities. Retailers moved, too—

following their customers. Lower-income consumers—often with different ethnic backgrounds—moved in, changing the nature of markets in the center of the city.

Some families, however, have become discouraged with the suburban dream. They're tired of commuting, yard and house work, rising local taxes, and gossiping neighbors. These people are reversing the trend to suburbia. The movement back to the city is more common among older—and some-times wealthier—families. These older families are creating a market for luxury condos and apartments close to downtown or other areas with shopping, rec-reation, and office facilities.

Local political bound-aries don't define market areas

Such population shifts mean that the usual way of recording population by cities and counties may not be helpful to marketers. They are more interested in the size of homogeneous (similar) *market* areas—than in the number of people within political boundaries. To meet this need, the U.S. Census Bureau publishes much data for metropolitan statistical areas.

A **Metropolitan Statistical Area (MSA)** is an integrated economic and so-cial unit with a large population nucleus. Usually, a MSA contains one city or urbanized area of at least 50,000 people and bordering "urban" areas.

The largest MSAs—with more than a million people—are called Consoli-dated Metropolitan Statistical Areas. More detailed data is available for these giant urban areas.[13]

The mobile ones are an attractive market

Nearly 20 percent of Americans move each year—about half of them move to a new city. These "mobiles" are an important market. They tend to be younger, better educated people—on the way up in their careers. They have money to spend. They have to make many decisions fairly quickly after they move. They must find new sources of food, clothing, medical and dental care, and household products. Alert marketers should try to locate these mobile people—and tell them about their products.[14]

More people are in middle- and upper-income levels

Unless people have money to spend, they aren't very attractive customers. The amount they can spend also affects what they are likely to buy. For this reason, most marketers study income levels, too.

Income comes from producing and selling goods and services. Family in-comes in the U.S. have increased steadily for about 100 years. Even more important to marketers is the change in income distribution. Many more fami-lies are now in the middle- and upper-income levels.

Fifty years ago, the U.S. income distribution looked something like a pyra-mid. Most families were bunched together at lower-income levels. There were fewer families in the middle range—and a relative handful formed an "elite" market at the top. By the 1970s, real income (buying power) had risen so much that most families—even those near the bottom of the income distribu-tion—could afford a comfortable standard of living. And many more had middle

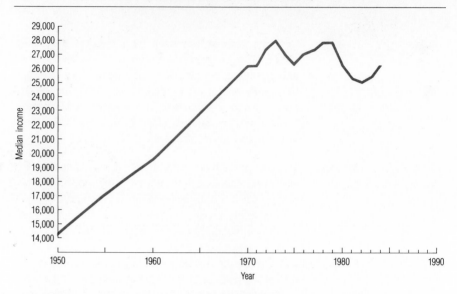

Exhibit 4–10   Median Household Income, 1950–1984 (in 1984 dollars)

and upper incomes. This was a real revolution. It has created an attractive mass market—and drastically changed our marketing system.

Real income growth has dropped—but for how long?

Of course, we hope that family incomes will keep rising—but this may not happen. See Exhibit 4–10. Real income stopped rising during the inflation of the 70s—and actually dropped some. Maybe the peak of real family income in the United States has already passed.

Higher-income groups still receive a big share

Although more people are above the subsistence level, higher-income groups still receive a very large share of the total income and are attractive markets—especially for luxury items. Exhibit 4–11 shows that although the median income of U.S. households in 1984 was about $26,000, the top 20 percent of the households—those with incomes over $45,300—received more than 42 percent of the total income. This gave them extra buying power—especially for luxury items.

At the lower end, more than 12 million families had less than $12,500 income. These account for 20 percent of the families, but receive less than 5 percent of the total income. Even so, they are good markets for some basic commodities—especially food and clothing.

Income is not equally distributed geographically

Population is concentrated in some geographic areas—and consumers in urban areas tend to have higher incomes than their country cousins. Exhibit 4–12 compares median incomes by state. The high spots on the map are areas with high median incomes. Companies often map the income of different areas when picking markets. A market area—a city, county, MSA, or state—with more income is often more attractive. For example, a chain of retail children's wear stores moved into the Washington, D.C., suburbs because a lot of young families with high incomes live there.[15]

Exhibit 4–11   Percent of Total Income Going to Different Income Groups in 1984

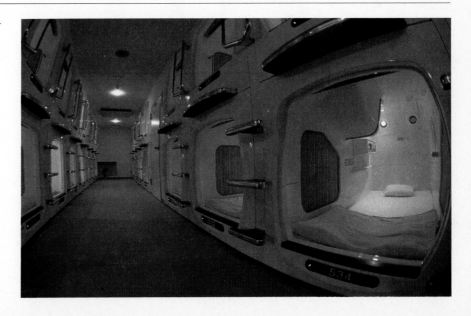

50 —

40 —

30 —

20 —

10 —

4.7%   11.0%   17.0%   24.4%   42.9%

$0 $12,489 $21,709 $31,500 $45,300

Lowest 20%
income group

Middle 20%
income group

Top 20%
income group

Changes come slowly   Changes in the cultural and social environment come slowly. An individual firm can't hope to encourage big changes in the short run. Instead, it should understand the current situation and trends and work within these limits—as it seeks new and better opportunities.

Capsule hotels for traveling busi-nessmen are successful in Japan—but may not catch on here because of cultural and so-cial differences.

Exhibit 4–12   Median per Capita Income by State (1984)

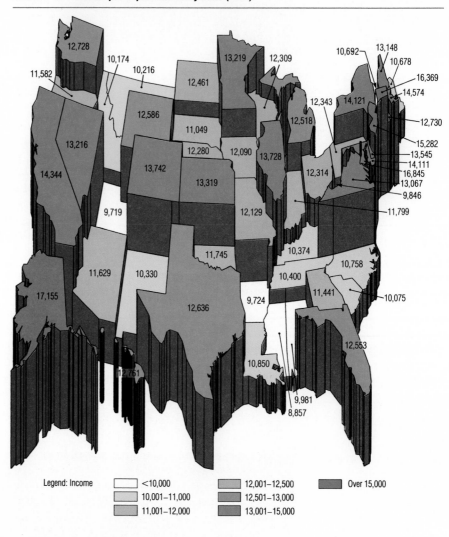

HOW TO EVALUATE OPPORTUNITIES

Once a firm identifies some opportunities, they must be screened and evaluated. A firm can't possibly pursue all of its opportunities. Instead, it must try to match its opportunities to its resources and objectives. The first step is to quickly screen out the obvious mismatches. Then, it can analyze the others more cafefully. Let's look at some methods for screening and evaluating opportunities.

Developing and applying screening criteria

First we have to analyze the firm's resources (for strengths and weaknesses), the environmental trends the firm faces (Chapter 4), and the objectives of top management. Then we can combine them into a set of realistic

Exhibit 4–13   An Example of Product-Market Screening Criteria for a Sales Company (retail and wholesale—$3 million annual sales)

1.   Quantitative criteria

    a. Increase sales by $500,000 per year for the next five years.

    b. Earn ROI of *at least* 25 percent before taxes on new ventures.

    c. Break even within one year on new ventures.

    d. Opportunity must be large enough to justify interest (to help meet objectives) but small enough so company can handle with the resources available.

    e. Several opportunities should be needed to reach the objectives—to spread the risks.

2.   Qualitative criteria

    a. Nature of business preferred.

        1 Goods and services sold to present customers.

        2 "Quality" products that can be sold at "high prices" with full margins.

        3 Competition should be weak and opportunity should be hard to copy for several years.

        4 Should build on our strong sales skills.

        5 There should be strongly felt (even unsatisfied) needs—to reduce promotion costs and permit "high" prices.

    b. Constraints

        1 Nature of businesses to exclude.

            (a) Manufacturing.

            (b) Any requiring large fixed capital investments.

            (c) Any requiring many people who must be "good" all the time and would require much supervision (e.g., "quality" restaurant).

        2 Geographic

            (a) United States and Canada only.

        3 General

            (a) Make use of current strengths.

            (b) Attractiveness of market should be reinforced by *more than one* of the following basic trends: technological, demographic, social, economic, political.

            (c) Market should not be bucking *any* basic trends.

product-market screening criteria. These criteria should include both quantitative and qualitative components. The quantitative components outline the objectives of the firm—sales, profit, and return on investment (ROI) targets.* The qualitative components explain what kinds of businesses the firm wants to be in, what businesses it wants to exclude, what weaknesses it should avoid, and what strengths and trends it should build on.[16] Opportunities that pass the screen ought to be able to be turned into strategies the firm can carry out— with the resources it has.

Exhibit 4–13 shows the product-market screening criteria for a small sales company (retailer and wholesaler). This whole set would help the firm's managers eliminate unsuitable opportunities—and find attractive ones to turn into strategies and plans.

Whole plans should be evaluated

We need forecasts of the probable results of implementing whole strategic plans to apply the quantitative part of the screening criteria. And the forecasts should be for a logical planning period. (Note: Sales forecasting is discussed in

---

*See Appendix B—following Chapter 16—for definitions of these terms.

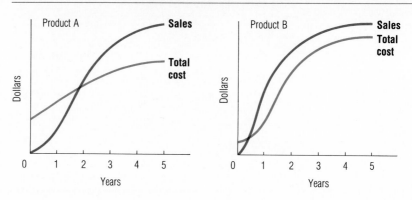

Exhibit 4–14   Expected Sales and Cost Curves of Two Strategies over Five-Year Planning Periods

Appendix B—following Chapter 16.) If a product's life is likely to be five years, for example, then a good strategy may not produce profitable results during the first six months to a year. But if we evaluate the plan over the projected five-year life, it might look like a winner. When evaluating the potential of possible opportunities—strategic plans—it's important to evaluate similar things—that is, *whole* plans.

Note that—as shown in Exhibit 4–14—quite different plans can be evaluated at the same time. In this case, a much improved product (Product A) is being compared with a "me-too" product for the same target market. In the short run, the me-too product will make a profit sooner and might look like the better choice—if we consider only one year's results. The improved product, on the other hand, will take a good deal of pioneering but—over its five-year life—will be much more profitable.

PLANNING GRIDS HELP EVALUATE DIFFERENT KINDS OF OPPORTUNITIES

When a firm has many possibilities to evaluate, it usually has to compare quite different ones. This problem is easier to handle with graphical approaches—such as the nine-box strategic planning grid developed by General Electric.

General Electric looks for green positions

General Electric's strategic planning grid—Exhibit 4–15—forces company managers to make three-part judgments (high, medium, and low) about the business strengths and industry attractiveness of all proposed or existing products or businesses.

GE feels that opportunities that fall into the green boxes in the upper left-hand corner of the grid are its growth opportunities—the ones that will lead the company to invest and grow. The red boxes in the lower right-hand corner of the grid, on the other hand, suggest a no-growth policy. Existing red businesses may continue to generate earnings—but GE figures they no longer

Exhibit 4–15   General Electric's Strategic Planning Grid

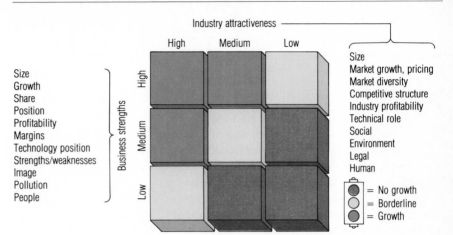

deserve much investment. The yellow businesses are the borderline cases—they can go either way. An existing yellow business may be continued and supported—but top management would probably reject a proposed new yellow business.

GE's "stop light" evaluation method is very subjective because GE feels there is too much chance of error if it tries to use over-simplified criteria—like ROI and market share—for judging "attractiveness" or "strength." Instead, top managers review written summaries of about a dozen factors (see Exhibit 4–15) that help them make summary judgments. Then they make a collective judgment. The approach generally leads to agreement and, further, a good understanding about why some businesses or new opportunities are supported—while others are not. In addition, it appears that high-high green businesses are uniformly good on almost all quantitative and qualitative measures. This interaction among the relevant variables makes it practical to boil them all down into a "stop light" framework.[17]

MULTI–PRODUCT FIRMS HAVE A DIFFICULT STRATEGY PLANNING JOB

Firms with many product lines—like General Electric—obviously have a tougher strategic planning job than a firm with only a few products (or product lines) aimed at the same or similar target markets. Firms like GE have to develop strategic plans for very different businesses. And the corporate level must try to balance the plans and needed resources for this portfolio of businesses so that the whole corporation reaches its objectives. This requires analysis of the various alternatives—using approaches similar to the GE strategic planning grid—and approving strategic plans that make sense for the *whole* corporation.

Details on how to manage such a complicated firm are beyond our scope. But it is important to know (1) that there are such firms and (2) that the principles in this text work—they just have to be applied in a portfolio of strategic plans.

CONCLUSION

Firms need innovative strategy planning to survive in our increasingly competitive markets. In this chapter, we discussed the uncontrollable environments and how they affect marketing strategy planning. We saw how the firm's own resources and objectives may help guide or limit the search for opportunities. Then, we went on to look at the rest of the uncontrollable variables. They are important because changes in these environments present new opportunities—as well as problems—that a marketing manager must deal with in marketing strategy planning.

A manager must study the competitive environment. How well established are competitors? What action might they take? What is the nature of competition: pure competition, oligopoly, or monopolistic competition?

The economic environment—including chances of recession or inflation—also affects the choice of strategies. And the marketer must try to anticipate, understand, and deal with such changes—as well as changes in the technologi-

cal base underlying the economic environment.

The marketing manager must also be aware of legal restrictions—and be sensitive to changing political climates. The growing acceptance of consumerism may force many changes.

The social and cultural environment affects how people behave—and what marketing strategies will be successful.

Developing good marketing strategies within all these uncontrollable environments isn't easy. You can see that marketing management is a challenging job that requires much integration of information from many disciplines.

Eventually, firms need procedures for screening and evaluating opportunities. We explained an approach using screening criteria. We also considered ways for evaluating quite different opportunities—using the GE strategic planning grid.

Now we can go on—in the rest of the book—to discussing how to turn opportunities into profitable marketing plans and programs.

Questions and Problems _____

1. Explain how a firm's objectives may affect its search for opportunities.

2. Specifically, how would various company objectives affect the development of a marketing mix for a new type of baby shoe? If this company were just being formed by a former shoemaker with limited financial resources, list the objectives he might have. Then discuss how they would affect the development of his marketing strategy.

3. Explain how a firm's resources may limit its search for opportunities. Cite a specific example for a specific resource.

4. Discuss how a company's financial strength may have a bearing on the kinds of products it produces. Will it have an impact on the other three Ps as well? If so, how? Use an example in your answer.

5. If a manufacturer's well-known product is sold at the same price by many retailers in the same community, is this an example of pure competition? When a community has many small grocery stores, are they in pure competition? What characteristics are needed to have a purely competitive market?

6.   List three products that are sold in purely competitive markets and three that are sold in monopolistically competitive markets. Do any of these products have anything in common? Can any generalizations be made about competitive situations and marketing mix planning?

7.   Cite a local example of an oligopoly—explaining why it is an oligopoly.

8.   Discuss the probable impact on your home-town of a major technological breakthrough in air transportation that would permit foreign producers to ship into any U.S. market for about the same transportation cost that domestic producers incur.

9.   Which way does the U.S. political and legal environment seem to be moving (with respect to business-related affairs)?

10.   Why is it necessary to have so many laws regulating business? Why hasn't Congress just passed one set of laws to take care of business problems?

11.   What and who is the government attempting to protect in its effort to preserve and regulate competition?

12.   For each of the *major* laws discussed in the text, indicate whether in the long run this law will promote or restrict competition (see Exhibit 4–7). As a consumer without any financial interest in business, what is your reaction to each of these laws?

13.   Are consumer protection laws really new? Discuss the evolution of consumer protection. Is more such legislation likely?

14.   Explain the components of product-market screening criteria—which can be used to evaluate opportunities.

15.   Explain General Electric's strategic planning grid approach to evaluating opportunities.

Suggested Computer-Aided Problems

4a.   Company Resources

4b.   Demographic Trend Analysis

Suggested Cases

2.   West Foods, Inc.

7.   Inland Steel Company

8.   Tony's Place

Chapter 5

Getting Information for Marketing Decisions

When You Finish This Chapter, You Should

1. Know about marketing information systems.

2. Understand a scientific approach to marketing research.

3. Know how to define and solve marketing problems.

4. Know about getting secondary and primary data.

5. Understand the use of observing, questioning, and experimental methods in marketing research.

6. Recognize the important new terms (shown in red).

Marketing research isn't just to prove that you're right. It helps you find out.

In recent years, candy bars seemed to be getting smaller and costing more. Then, suddenly, the wrappers on Snickers and other candies from Mars looked bigger. And the candy bar inside the wrapper was a lot bigger, too. Why did marketing managers at Mars make that decision?

Mars knew that other candy and snack foods were taking customers. But why? Surveys showed that many consumers thought the shrinking candy bar was too small. But they also didn't want to pay more for a larger bar. Mars managers wanted to know if making their candy bar bigger would increase sales enough to offset the higher cost. To decide, they needed more information.

The company carefully varied the size of candy bars sold in *different* markets. Otherwise, the marketing mix stayed the same. Then researchers tracked sales in each market to see the effect of the different sizes. They saw a difference—a big difference—immediately. It was clear that the added sales would more than offset the cost of increasing the size of the candy bar. So marketing managers at Mars made a decision that took them in the opposite direction from other candy companies. And, yes, it proved to be a sweet success.[1]

Marketing managers at Kraft, Inc., faced a different problem. Like many food producers, Kraft's marketing mix relies heavily on promotion. But managers were never certain what level of promotion spending was right. And the "right" level seemed to vary not only for different products, but also in different markets—depending on how Kraft stacked up against competition.

To help its marketing managers plan better strategies, Kraft responded with a computerized information system. A manager can now use a special computer program to help him pick two markets that are very similar for a specific product—in terms of market share, sales volume, competition, promotion spending, and other factors. The manager can then vary the promotion level in one of the two matched markets. After data is collected for a month or two, the system can produce graphs that compare the sales and share in the two markets before and after the test. The system is effective and easy to use. Now over 200 users from brand managers to sales reps—and even Kraft's ad agency people—use the system. And Kraft is making better decisions—faster.[2]

MARKETING MANAGERS NEED INFORMATION

These examples show that successful planning of marketing strategies requires information—information about potential target markets and their likely responses to marketing mixes—and about competition and other uncontrollable variables. Information is also needed for implementation and control. Without good marketing information, managers have to use intuition or guesses—and in our fast-changing and competitive economy, this invites failure.

MARKETING INFORMATION SYSTEMS CAN HELP

MIS makes available data accessible

There is a difference between information that is *available* and information that is *accessible*. Some information is just not available—for example, details of competitors' plans. In other cases, information is available, but not without time-consuming collection. Such information is not really accessible. For example, a company may have records of customer purchases, what sales reps sold last month, or what is in the warehouse. But if a manager can't get to this information when he needs it, it isn't useful.

Some firms, like Kraft, have realized that it doesn't pay to wait until they have important questions they can't answer. They are working to develop a *continual flow of information*—and to make it more accessible to their managers.

A **marketing information system (MIS)** is an organized way of continually gathering and analyzing data to provide marketing managers with information they need to make decisions. In some companies, an MIS is set up by marketing specialists. In other companies, it is set up by a group that provides *all* departments with information.

The technical details of setting up and running an MIS are beyond the scope of this course. But you should understand what an MIS is so you know some of the possibilities. Exhibit 5–1 shows the elements of a complete MIS.

Decision support systems put managers "on-line"

An MIS system organizes incoming data in a database so that it is available when it's needed. Most firms with an MIS have data processing specialists who help managers get standard reports and output from the database.

To get better decisions, some MIS systems provide marketing managers with a **decision support system (DSS)**—a computer program that makes it

Exhibit 5–1   Elements of a Complete Marketing Information System

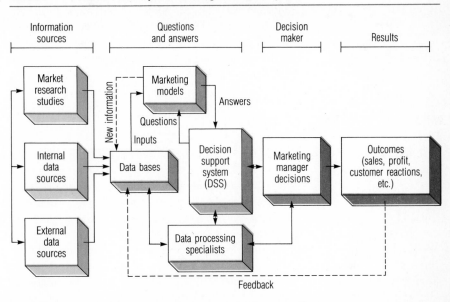

easy for a marketing manager to get and use information *as he is making decisions.* Typically the DSS helps change raw data—like product sales for the previous day—into more *useful information.* For example, it may draw graphs to show relationships in data—perhaps comparing yesterday's sales to sales on the same day for the last four weeks.

Some decision support systems go even further. They allow the manager to see how answers to questions might change in various situations. For example, a manager may want to estimate how much sales will increase if the firm expands into a new market. The DSS asks the manager for *his* judgment about how much business could be won from each competitor in that market. Then, using this input and drawing on data in the database, the system makes an estimate using a **marketing model**—a statement of relationships among marketing variables.

In short, the decision support system puts the individual manager "on-line" so he can study available data and make better marketing decisions—faster.[3]

Information makes managers greedy

Once marketing managers see how a functioning MIS—and perhaps a DSS—can help their decision making, they are eager for more information. They realize that they can improve all aspects of their planning. Further, they can control the implementation of current plans, comparing results against plans and making necessary changes more quickly.

Marketing information systems will become more widespread as managers become more sensitive to the possibilities and computer costs continue to drop.

MIS use is growing—even in small firms. So marketing still has room for able students willing to apply quantitative techniques to solving real marketing problems.[4]

New questions re-
quire new answers

Routinely analyzing incoming data can be valuable to a marketing manager. But it can't be the only source of information for decision making. MIS efforts tend to focus on meeting recurring information needs. But marketing managers must try to satisfy ever-changing needs in dynamic markets. So marketing research must be used—to supplement the data already available in the MIS system.

WHAT IS MARKETING RESEARCH?

Research provides a
bridge to customers

The marketing concept says that marketing managers should meet the needs of customers. But today, many marketing managers are isolated in company offices—far from their potential customers.

This means marketing managers have to rely on help from **marketing research**—procedures to gather and analyze new information to help marketing managers make decisions. One of the important jobs of a marketing researcher is to get the "facts" that are not currently in the MIS.

Who does the work?

Most larger companies have a separate marketing research department to plan and carry out research projects. These departments often use outside specialists—including interviewing and tabulating services—to handle technical assignments.

Small companies—those with less than $4 or $5 million in sales—usually don't have separate marketing research departments. They depend on salespeople or top managers for what research they do.[5]

Effective research
usually requires
cooperation

Good marketing research requires much more than just technical tools. It requires cooperation between researchers and marketing managers. Good marketing researchers must keep both marketing research *and* marketing management in mind—to be sure their research focuses on real problems.

Marketing managers must be involved in marketing research, too. Company or outside experts can handle many marketing research details. But marketing managers must be able to explain their problems—and what kinds of information they need. They should be able to communicate with specialists in *their* language. Marketing managers may only be "consumers" of research. But they should be informed consumers—and able to explain exactly what they want from the research. They should also know about some of the basic decisions made during the research process—so they know the limitation of the findings.

For this reason, our discussion of marketing research won't emphasize mechanics—but rather how to plan and evaluate the work of marketing researchers.[6]

THE SCIENTIFIC METHOD AND MARKETING RESEARCH

The scientific method—combined with the strategy planning framework we discussed in Chapter 2—can help marketing managers make better decisions.

The **scientific method** is a decision-making approach that focuses on being objective and orderly in *testing* ideas before accepting them. With the scientific method, managers don't just *assume* that their intuition is correct. Instead, they use their intuition and observations to develop **hypotheses**—educated guesses about the relationships between things or what will happen in the future. Then they test their hypotheses before making final decisions.

A manager who uses the scientific method might say "I think (hypothesize) that consumers currently using the most popular brand will prefer our new product. Let's run some consumer tests. If at least 60 percent of the consumers prefer our product, we can introduce it in a regional test market. If it doesn't pass the consumer test there, we can make some changes and try again."

The scientific method forces an orderly process. Some managers don't think carefully about what information they need—and blindly move ahead hoping that research will give them "the answer." Other managers may have a clearly defined problem or question but lose their way in the next steps. These hit-or-miss approaches waste both time and money. A scientific approach to solving marketing problems avoids this waste. We'll talk about this approach next.

FIVE–STEP APPROACH TO MARKETING RESEARCH

The **marketing research process** is a five-step application of the scientific method that includes:

1. Defining the problem.
2. Analyzing the situation.
3. Getting problem-specific data.
4. Interpreting the data.
5. Solving the problem.

Exhibit 5–2 shows the five steps in the process. Note that the process may lead to a solution before all of the steps are completed. Or, as the feedback

Exhibit 5–2 Five-Step Scientific Approach to Marketing Research Process

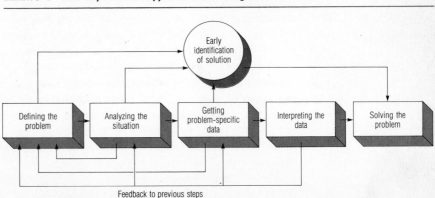

arrows show, the process may return to an earlier step if needed. For example, the interpreting step may point to a new question—or reveal the need for additional information—before making a final decision.

DEFINING THE PROBLEM—STEP 1

Defining the problem is the most important—and often the most difficult—step in the marketing research process. Sometimes it takes over half the time spent on a research project. But it's time well spent if the objectives of the research are clearly defined. The best research job on the wrong problem is wasted effort.

Finding the right problem level almost solves the problem

The strategy planning framework introduced in Chapter 2 can help the researcher identify the real problem area—and what information he needs. Do we really know enough about our target markets to work out all of the four Ps? Do we know enough to decide what celebrity to use in an ad—or how to handle a price war in New York City or Tokyo? If not, we may want to do research—rather than rely on intuition.

The importance of understanding the nature of the problem—and then trying to solve it—can be seen by looking at a Dr Pepper campaign that missed the target. Coke and Pepsi had heated up the competition—and sales of Dr Pepper began to slide. So Dr Pepper's managers decided to go after the "big cola" market—and developed a new promotion effort. Most of us remember an actor dancing his way through Dr Pepper commercials—inviting everyone to join the parade and "be a Pepper too." These snappy ads seemed to be a hit. Consumer surveys rated them among the most remembered on TV.

When sales were still disappointing, Dr Pepper put more personal selling emphasis on food stores—because research showed that the "big cola" customers relied on that channel. But that didn't help either.

At this point, another survey revealed some surprising results. Dr Pepper's customers were very different than the target market selected. An ad agency executive explained: "the Dr Pepper drinker believes he should live life in accordance with his own personal values and not try to meet other people's expectations." In contrast, the cola drinker "tends to follow the latest trends and seek peer approval." "Be a Pepper" turned off customers who might tend to choose Dr Pepper—that is, people like the present Dr Pepper customers.

Having finally identified its most likely consumers, Dr Pepper switched its emphasis to channels these buyers used—like vending machines and fast-food restaurants. And its advertising showed individualists who would stop at nothing to get a Dr Pepper. With these changes, sales began to rise.

In this case, the original strategy planning was sloppy. The choice of target market was based on guesswork. This led to a poor strategy—and wasted promotion money. Preliminary research with consumers—about their needs and attitudes—might have avoided this costly error. Both marketing research and management fumbled the ball—by not studying possible target markets. Then, when sales were poor, the company fumbled again by assuming that the problem was the channel—instead of checking consumers' real attitudes about the product. Fortunately, research finally uncovered the real problem.[7]

The moral of this story is that our strategy planning framework can be useful for guiding the problem definition step—as well as the whole marketing research process. First, marketing managers should understand their target markets—and know that they have unsatisfied needs. Then managers can focus on lower-level problems—i.e., sensitivity to change of one or more of the marketing mix ingredients. Without such a framework, marketing researchers can waste time—and money—working on the wrong problem.

Don't confuse problems with symptoms

Problem definition sounds simple—and that's the danger. It's easy to confuse symptoms with the problem. Suppose a firm's MIS shows that the company's sales are decreasing in certain territories—while expenses remain the same—with a resulting decline in profits. Will it help to define the problem as: How can we stop the sales decline? Probably not.

It's easy to fall into the trap of mistaking symptoms for the definition of the problem. Then, the research objectives are confused. Relevant questions may be ignored—while unimportant questions are analyzed in expensive detail.

Setting research objectives may require more understanding

Sometimes the research objectives are very clear—as when a manager only wants to know if the target households have tried a new product. But often it's not so simple. The manager might also want to know why some didn't buy. Companies rarely have enough time and money to study everything. The manager must narrow his research objectives. One good way is to develop a "research question" list that includes all the possible problem areas. Then, the items on the list can be considered more completely—in the situation analysis step—before setting final research objectives.

ANALYZING THE SITUATION—STEP 2

What information do we already have?

When the marketing manager feels the real problem has begun to surface, a situation analysis is useful. A **situation analysis** is an informal study of information already available in the problem area. It can help define the problem and specify what additional information—if any—is needed.

Pick the brains around you

The situation analysis usually involves informal talks with informed people. Informed people can be others in the firm, a few good middlemen who have close contact with customers, or others knowledgeable about the industry. In industrial markets—where relationships with customers are close—researchers may talk to the customers themselves.

Situation analysis helps educate a researcher

The situation analysis is especially important if the research specialist doesn't know much about the problem—or if the marketing manager is dealing with unfamiliar areas. They both must be sure they understand the nature of the target market, the marketing mix, competition, and other external factors.

Otherwise, the researcher may rush ahead and make costly mistakes—or simply discover "facts" management already knows.

Secondary data may provide the answers—or some background

The situation analysis should also find relevant **secondary data**—information that has been collected or published already. Step 3 will cover **primary data**—information specifically collected to solve a current problem. For now, keep in mind that researchers too often rush out to gather primary data when much relevant secondary information is already available immediately—and at little or no cost! See Exhibit 5–3.

Much secondary data is available

Ideally, the firm's MIS will already have much relevant secondary data. But even if data has not been organized in an MIS, much good secondary data may be available from the company's files and reports. Libraries, trade associations, and government agencies also have secondary data.

One of the first places a researcher should look for secondary data—after looking within the firm—is in a good library. The *Index of Business Periodicals* helps identify all published references to a topic. And some computerized index services are available through libraries and private firms.

Government data is inexpensive

Federal and state governments publish data on almost every subject. Government data is often useful in estimating the size of markets. Almost all gov-

Exhibit 5–3   Sources of Secondary and Primary Data

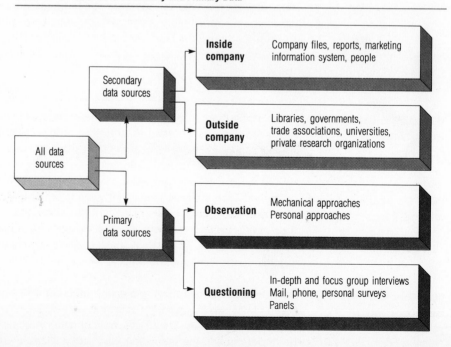

National Data Book and
Guide to Sources

**STATISTICAL
ABSTRACT
OF THE
UNITED
STATES
1986**

106th Edition

US Department
of Commerce
BUREAU OF
THE CENSUS

ernment data is available in inexpensive publications. And some of it is on computer tapes—ready for further analysis if that is needed.

Sometimes it's more practical to use summary publications—to get leads to more detailed documents. The most useful of these summaries—*Statistical Abstract of the United States*—is like an almanac. Issued each year, it lists more than 1,000 summary tables from published sources. It includes references to world markets. Detailed footnotes work as guides to more specific information on a topic.

Private sources are useful, too

Many private research groups—as well as advertising agencies, newspapers, magazines, and trade associations—publish useful data. And a good business library is valuable—for sources such as *Sales & Marketing Management, Industrial Marketing, Advertising Age,* and the publications of the National Industrial Conference Board.[8]

Situation analysis yields a lot—for very little

A good situation analysis can deliver a lot of information—and takes little time. It's inexpensive compared with more formal research efforts—such as a large-scale survey. A clear-cut problem will often be solved at this point—with no added expense. The fact that further research *may* not be necessary is important. The situation analyst is really trying to find the exact nature of the situation—*and* the problem. Too-hasty researchers may try to skip this step—perhaps rushing to get out questionnaires. These researchers may see the real problem only when the questionnaires come back—and they have to start all over. One marketing expert puts it this way: "Some people don't have time to do research right the first time, but they seem to have time to do it over again."

Determine what else is needed

At the end of the situation analysis, you can see which research questions—from the list developed during the problem definition step—remain unanswered. Then you have to decide exactly what information you need to answer those questions—and how to get it.

This often requires discussion between technical experts and the marketing manager. Often a written **research proposal**—a plan that specifies what information will be obtained and how—is used to be sure that no one is surprised later by some misunderstanding. The research proposal may include information about costs, what data will be collected, how it will be collected, who will analyze it and how, and how long it will all take. Then the marketing manager must decide if it makes sense to go ahead—if the time and costs involved seem worthwhile. It's foolish to pay $100,000 for information to solve a $50,000 problem! Often the decision is not so clear-cut—so marketing managers should know more about the next steps in the marketing research process.

GETTING PROBLEM—SPECIFIC DATA—STEP 3

Gathering primary data

The next step is to plan a formal research project to gather data. There are different methods for collecting primary data—and which approach to use depends on how precisely the problem has been defined, the nature of the problem, and how much time and money are available.

Most primary data collection tries to learn what customers think about some topic—or how they behave under some conditions. There are two basic methods for obtaining information about people: *questioning* and *observing.* Questioning can range from qualitative to quantitative research. And many kinds of observing are possible.

Qualitative questioning—open-ended with a hidden purpose

Qualitative research seeks in-depth, open-ended responses—not yes or no answers. The researcher tries to get people to share their thoughts on a topic—without giving them many directions about what to say.

For example, a researcher may ask consumers, "What do you think about when you decide where to shop for food?" One person may talk about convenient location, another about service in the store, and others about the quality of the fresh produce.

The real advantage of this approach is *depth.* Each person can be asked follow-up questions so that the researcher can really learn what *that* respondent thinks.

Focus groups focus the discussion

The most widely used form of qualitative questioning in marketing research is the **focus group interview**—which involves interviewing 6 to 10 people in an informal group setting. It uses the open-ended questions we've been discussing, but here the interviewer wants to get group interaction—to stimulate thinking and get immediate reactions.

A trained focus group leader learns a lot from this approach. A typical session may last an hour—so the group can cover a lot of ground. But conclusions reached from watching a focus group session often vary depending on who watches it! This is a serious criticism of focus groups—really all qualitative research—because the results seem to depend so much on the researcher's point of view.[9]

Some researchers use qualitative research to prepare for quantitative research. The qualitative research can provide good ideas—hypotheses. But the hypotheses have to be tested in some other way.

Structured questioning gives more objective results

With formal questionnaires, many people can be asked questions in the same way. See Exhibit 5–4. Because the same questions and response choices are used for each respondent, information can be summarized quantitatively. Most survey research is **quantitative research**—which seeks structured responses that can be summarized in numbers—like percentages, averages, or other statistics.

Exhibit 5–4   Sample Questioning Methods to Measure Attitudes and Opinions

---

A. Please check your level of agreement with each of the following statements.

	Strongly agree	Agree	Uncertain	Dis-agree	Strongly disagree
1. In general I prefer frozen pizza to a frozen chicken pot pie	____	____	____	____	____
2. A frozen pizza dinner is more expensive than eating at a fast food restaurant	____	____	____	____	____

B. Please rate how important each of the following is to you in selecting a brand of frozen pizza:

	Not at all important					Very important
1. Price per serving	____	____	____	____	____	____
2. Toppings available	____	____	____	____	____	____
3. Amount of cheese	____	____	____	____	____	____
4. Cooking time	____	____	____	____	____	____

C. Please check the rating which best describes your feelings about the last frozen pizza which you prepared.

	Poor	Fair	Good	Excellent
1. Price per serving	____	____	____	____
2. Toppings available	____	____	____	____
3. Amount of cheese	____	____	____	____
4. Cooking time	____	____	____	____

Surveys by mail, phone, or in person

What questions to ask and how to ask them usually depends on how the respondents will be interviewed—by mail, on the phone, or in person.

Mail surveys are the most common and convenient

The mail questionnaire is useful when much questioning is needed. With a mail questionnaire, respondents can answer the questions at their convenience. But the questions must be simple and easy to follow—since there is no interviewer to help.

A big problem with mail questionnaires is that many people don't complete or return them. The **response rate**—the percent of people contacted who complete the questionnaire—is usually around 25 percent in consumer surveys—and it can be even lower.[10]

Mail surveys are economical per questionnaire—if a large number of people respond. But they can be quite expensive if the response rate is poor. In spite of these limits, the convenience and economy of mail surveys makes them a popular approach to collecting primary data.

Telephone surveys—fast and effective

Telephone interviews are growing in popularity. They are effective for getting quick answers to simple questions. Telephone interviews let the interviewer ask several questions to try to understand what the respondent really thinks. On the other hand, the telephone isn't a good way to get confidential personal information—such as details of family income. Respondents are not certain who is calling—or how this personal information might be used.[11]

Personal interview surveys—can be in-depth

A personal interview survey is usually much more expensive per interview than a mail or telephone survey. But it's easier to get and keep the respondent's attention when the interviewer is right there. The interviewer can also help explain confusing directions—and perhaps get better responses. For these reasons, personal interviews are commonly used for interviewing industrial customers.

Researchers have to be careful that having an interviewer involved doesn't affect answers. Sometimes people won't give an answer they consider embarrassing. Or they may try to impress or please the interviewer. For example, when asked what magazines they read, respondents may report a "respectable" magazine like *National Geographic*—even if they never read it—but fail to report magazines like *Playboy* or *Playgirl*.

Sometimes questioning has limitations. Then, observing may be more accurate or economical.

Observing—what you see is what you get

Observing—as a method of collecting data—focuses on a well-defined problem. Here we are not talking about the "casual" observations that may stimulate ideas in the early steps of a research project.

With the observation method, the researcher tries to see or record what the subjects do naturally. You don't want the observing to *influence* what they do.

In some situations, consumers are recorded on videotape. Later, the tape can be studied by running the films at very slow speeds—or actually analyzing each frame. This is used, for example, in studying the routes consumers follow through a grocery store—or how they select products in a department store.

Observation methods are common in advertising research. For example, a device called an audimeter permits adaptation of the observation method to television audience research. The machine is attached to the TV set in the homes of selected families. It records when the set is on—and what station is tuned in.

Check-out scanners see a lot

Computerized "scanners" at retail check-out counters are a major breakthrough in observing—helping researchers to collect very specific information. Often this type of data feeds directly into a firm's MIS. Managers of a big department store can see exactly what products sold *that day*—and how much money each department earns.

The use of scanners to "observe" what customers are actually doing is

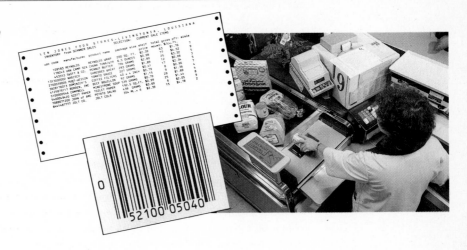

Data from electronic scanning at the supermarket helps retailers to decide what brands they will sell.

changing research methods for many firms. They are no longer limited to surveys that ask consumers about their attitudes. The possibilities are limited more by imagination—and money—than by technology.[12]

Experimental method controls conditions

A marketing manager can get a different kind of information—with either the questioning or observing approaches—using the experimental method. With the **experimental method**, the researcher compares the responses of groups that are similar—except on the characteristic being tested. The researcher wants to learn if the specific characteristic—which varies among groups—causes differences in some response among the groups. The "response" might be an observed behavior—like the purchase of a product—or the answer to a specific question—like "How much do you like the taste of our new product?" Our Mars candy bar example at the beginning of the chapter is an example of a marketing experiment.

The experimental method isn't used as frequently as surveys and focus groups. This is because it's hard to set up controlled situations where only one marketing variable is different. But there are probably other reasons, too. Many managers don't understand the valuable information they can get from this method. Further, they don't like the idea of some researcher "experimenting" with their business.[13]

INTERPRETING THE DATA—STEP 4

What does it really mean?

When data has been collected it has to be analyzed to decide "what it all means." With quantitative research, this step usually involves statistics. **Statistical packages**—easy-to-use computer programs that analyze data—have opened up many new possibilities. Technical specialists often are involved at this step—and the details are beyond the scope of this book. But a good manager should know enough to understand what a research project can—or can't—do.[14]

Is your sample really representative?

For most marketing research, it's impossible to collect all the information you might want about everyone in a population. Here, **population** means the total group you are interested in. In a marketing research study, only a **sample**—a part of the relevant population—may be surveyed. How well a sample represents the total population affects the results. Results from a sample that is not representative may not give a true picture of the whole population.

For example, the manager of a retail store might order a phone survey to learn how consumers feel about the store hours. If interviewers make all of the calls during the day, the sample will not be representative. Consumers who work outside the home during the day won't have an equal chance of being included in the survey. People interviewed might say the limited store hours are "satisfactory." Yet to assume from this that *all* consumers are satisfied would be wrong.

Research results are not exact

Remember that an estimate from a sample—even a representative one—usually varies somewhat from the "true value" for a total population. Many managers forget this. They assume that survey results are exact. Instead, when interpreting sample estimates, it's better to think of them as *suggesting* an approximate result.

The nature of the sample—and how it is selected—makes a big difference in how the results of a study can be interpreted. This should be considered as part of planning data collection—to make sure the marketing manager can use the results with confidence.

Even if the sampling is carefully planned, it's also important to evaluate the quality of research data itself.

Validity problems can destroy research

Marketers often assume that research data really measures what it intends to measure. Managers and researchers should be careful about this—because many of the variables of interest to marketing managers are hard to measure accurately. We can create a questionnaire that lets us assign numbers to consumer responses, but that doesn't mean that the result is precise. For example, an interviewer might ask you, "How much did you spend on soft drinks last week?" You might be perfectly willing to cooperate—and be part of a representative sample—but still not remember the right amount. This problem may increase when trying to assign numbers to consumer attitudes or opinions.

Validity concerns the extent to which data measures what it is intended to measure. Validity problems are important in marketing research because most people want to help and will give an answer—even when they don't know what they're talking about. Sometimes a poorly worded question means different things to different people. Although respondents may not care—a manager should see that he only pays for research results that are representative—and valid.

Poor interpretation can destroy research

Besides sampling and validity problems, a marketing manager must consider whether the analysis of the data supports the conclusions drawn in the interpreting step. Sometimes the technical people pick the right statistical procedure—their calculations are exact—but they misinterpret the data because they don't understand the management problem. In one survey, car buyers were asked to rank five cars in order from "most preferred" to "least preferred." One car was ranked first by slightly more respondents than any other car—so the research reported it as the "most liked car." That interpretation, however, ignored the fact that 70 percent of the respondents ranked the car last!

Interpretation problems like this can make a big difference. Some people draw misleading conclusions—on purpose—to get the results they want. There's even a book called *How to Lie With Statistics*. A marketing manager must decide whether all of the results support the interpretation—and are relevant to his problem.

Marketing manager and researcher should work together

Marketing research involves some technical details. But you can see that the marketing researcher and the marketing manager must work together—to be sure that they really do solve the problems the firm faces. If the whole research process has been a joint effort, then the interpreting step can move quickly to decision making—and solving the problem.

SOLVING THE PROBLEM—STEP 5

The last step is solving the problem

In the problem-solving step, the results of the research are used in making marketing decisions.

Some researchers—and inexperienced managers—are fascinated by the interesting tidbits of information that come from the research process. They're excited if the research reveals something they didn't know before. But if research doesn't have action applications, it has little value—and suggests poor planning by the researcher and the manager.

When the research process is finished, the marketing manager should be able to apply the findings to marketing strategy planning—the choice of a target market or the mix of the four Ps. If the research doesn't provide information to help guide these decisions, the research time and money was wasted.

We are emphasizing this step because it is the logical conclusion to the whole research process. This final step must be anticipated at each of the earlier steps.

HOW MUCH INFORMATION DO YOU NEED

Information is costly—but reduces risk

We've been talking about the benefits of good marketing information. But dependable information can be expensive. A big company may spend millions developing an information system. A large-scale survey can cost from $20,000 to $100,000—or even more. The continuing research available from companies such as A. C. Nielsen can cost a company from $25,000 to well over $100,000 a year. And a market test for 6 to 12 months may cost $100,000 to $300,000 per test market!

Companies willing to pay the cost often find that the marketing information more than pays for itself. They are more likely to select the right target market and marketing mix—or see a potential problem before it becomes a costly crisis.

What is the value of information?

The high cost of good information must be balanced against its probable value to management. You never get all the information you would like to have. Very detailed surveys or experiments may be "too good" or "too expensive" or "too late"—if all that's needed is a rough sampling of retailer attitudes toward a new pricing plan—*by tomorrow*.

Marketing managers must take risks because of incomplete information. That's part of their job—and always will be. They might like more data. But they must weigh the cost of getting it against its likely value. If the risk is not too great, the cost of getting more information may be greater than the potential loss from a poor decision. A decision to expand into a new territory with the present marketing mix, for example, might be made with more confidence after a $25,000 survey. But just sending a sales rep into the territory for a few weeks to try to sell the potential customers would be a lot cheaper—and, if successful, the answer is in *and* so are some sales.[15]

CONCLUSION

Marketing managers face difficult decisions in planning marketing strategies. Rarely does a manager have all the information he would like to have. But, in this chapter we have seen that marketing managers don't have to rely only on intuition. Good information usually *can* be obtained to improve the quality of their decisions.

Computers are helping marketing managers become full-fledged members of the information age. Both large and small firms now set up marketing information systems (MIS)—making routinely needed data available and accessible—quickly.

Marketing managers deal with rapidly changing environments. Available data does not always answer the detailed questions that arise. Then a marketing research project may be needed—to gather new information.

Marketing research should be guided by the scientific method. The scientific approach to solving marketing problems involves five steps: defining the problem, analyzing the situation, obtaining data, interpreting data, and solving the problem. This objective and organized approach helps to keep research on target—reducing the risk of doing costly and unnecessary research that doesn't solve the problem.

Our strategy planning framework can be helpful in finding the real problem. By finding and focusing on the real problem, the researcher and marketing manager may be able to move quickly to a useful solution—without the cost and risks of gathering primary data in a formal research project. With imagination, they may even be able to find the "answers" in their MIS or in other readily available secondary data.

Questions and Problems

1. Discuss the concept of a marketing information system and why it is important for marketing managers to be involved in planning the system.

2. In your own words, explain why a decision support system (DSS) can add to the value of a marketing information system. Give an example of how a decision support system might help.

3. Discuss how output from a MIS might differ from the output of a typical marketing research department.

4. Discuss some of the likely problems facing the marketer in a small firm that has just purchased an inexpensive "personal computer" to help develop a marketing information system.

5. Explain the key characteristics of the scientific method and show why these are important to managers concerned with research.

6. How is the situation analysis different from the data collection step. Can both these steps be done at the same time to obtain answers sooner? Is this wise?

7. Distinguish between primary data and secondary data and illustrate your answer.

8. If a firm were interested in estimating the distribution of income in the state of Florida, how could it proceed? Be specific.

9. If a firm were interested in estimating sand and clay production in Georgia, how could it proceed? Be specific.

10. Go to the library and find (in some government publication) three marketing-oriented "facts" that you did not know existed or were available. Record on one page and show sources.

11. Explain why a company might want to do focus group interviews rather than doing individual interviews with the same people.

12. Distinguish between qualitative and quantitative approaches to research—and give some of the key advantages and limitations of each approach.

13. Define what is meant by response rate and discuss why a marketing manager might be concerned about the response rate achieved in a particular survey. Give an example.

14. Explain how you might use different types of research (focus groups, observation, survey, and experiment) to forecast market reaction to a new kind of margarine that is to receive no promotion other than what the retailer will give it. Further, assume that the new margarine's name will not be associated with other known products. The product will be offered at competitive prices.

15. Marketing research involves expense—sometimes considerable expense. Why does the text recommend the use of marketing research even though a highly experienced marketing executive is available?

16. Discuss the concept that some information may be too expensive to obtain in relation to its value. Illustrate.

Suggested Computer-Aided Problem

5. Marketing Research

Suggested Cases

8. Tony's Place

9. Days Inns vs. Best Western

Chapter 6

Final Consumers and Their Buying Behavior

When You Finish This Chapter, You Should

1. Know how final consumer spending is related to population, income, family life cycle, and other variables.

2. Know how to estimate likely consumer purchases for broad classes of products.

3. Understand how the psychological and social variables affect an individual's and household's buying behavior.

4. Know how consumers use problem-solving processes.

5. Have some feel for how all the behavioral variables and incoming stimuli are handled by a consumer.

6. Recognize the important new terms (shown in red).

Which car will the customer buy—a BMW or a Cadillac Seville?

For years, Cadillac's marketing mix was targeted toward older consumers who wanted a big luxury car with a "living room" quiet drive. Cadillac consistently promoted its image and built a strong customer following. Most people still think about Cadillac—and its market—that way.

But marketing managers at Cadillac are now aiming at the growing number of well-paid professionals in their early 40s who are currently buying BMWs, Mercedes, Turbo Saabs, or Volvos. Cadillac introduced sporty Seville and Eldorado models with sleek new designs, snappy performance, and better handling. Promotion focused on these changes—aiming at the new target market. In spite of this effort, results have been disappointing. In contrast, the "traditional" models continue to sell well to older buyers.

Cadillac is finding that it's hard to change consumer attitudes. The new target market doesn't pay much attention to Cadillac's advertising—even in "their" magazines. These buyers may get a lot of information and compare many cars before buying—but Cadillac isn't in the running. If they want a "status" car, these customers want one that has status with their "group." They think a Cadillac is for somebody else—like their parents![1]

CONSUMER BEHAVIOR—WHY DO THEY BUY WHAT THEY BUY?

How can marketing managers predict which specific products consumers will buy—and in what quantities? Why does a consumer choose a particular product?

This chapter shows that basic data on consumer spending patterns can help forecast trends in consumer buying. But when many firms sell similar products, this data isn't much help in predicting which *products* and *brands* consumers will buy. To find better answers, we need to understand people better. For this reason, many marketers have turned to the behavioral sciences for help. So in this chapter, we'll also explore some of the approaches and thinking in psychology, sociology, and the other behavioral disciplines.

Our discussion will focus on *final consumers,* but keep in mind that many of these behavioral influences apply to industrial and other intermediate buyers, too.

CONSUMER SPENDING PATTERNS RELATED TO POPULATION AND INCOME

Markets are made up of people with money to spend. So consumer spending patterns are related to population *and* income.

Consumer budget studies show that most consumers spend their incomes as part of a family or household unit. The family members usually pool their incomes when planning family purchases. So it makes sense for us to talk about how households or families spend their incomes.

Spending data tells how target markets spend

We have much detailed information on consumer spending patterns. The patterns are more important than the specific dollar figures—because these patterns stay pretty much the same over time. So even as this data gets older, the relationships will help us see how families spend their incomes.

Exhibit 6–1 shows the annual spending by "urban" families at several income levels. This data should keep you from making wild guesses based only on your own experience. The amount families spend on food, housing, clothing, transportation, and so on does vary by income level. The relationships make sense when you realize that many of the purchases are for "necessities."

Data such as that in Exhibit 6–1 can help you understand how potential target customers spend their money. Let's suppose you are a marketing manager for a swimming pool producer. You're thinking of mailing an ad to consumers in an urban neighborhood where average income per family is $25,000 a year. Looking at Exhibit 6–1, you can see how families in this income level spend their money. The exhibit suggests that such families spend about $1,007 a year for "entertainment." If a particular pool costs at least $2,000 a year—including depreciation and maintenance—the average family in this income category would have to make a big change in life style if it bought a pool—i.e., pool expenses would cut into other spending.

Data like this won't tell you whether a specific family will buy the pool. But it does help you make decisions. If you need more information—perhaps about the target market's attitudes toward recreation products—then you may need some marketing research. You might want to see a budget study on con-

Exhibit 6–1   Family Spending (in dollars and percent of spending) for Several Family Income Levels (in 1982 dollars)

Spending category	$15,000–$19,999 $	%	$20,000–$29,999 $	%	$30,000–$39,999 $	%
Food	$ 2,789	17.4%	$ 3,381	16.4%	$ 3,961	15.4%
Housing	4,803	30.0	5,977	29.0	7,423	28.8
Clothing	848	5.3	1,042	5.1	1,384	5.4
Transportation	3,286	20.5	4,342	21.1	5,298	20.6
Health care	795	5.0	893	4.3	902	3.5
Personal care	146	.9	182	.9	222	.9
Education	137	.9	166	.8	272	1.0
Reading	115	.7	142	.7	165	.6
Entertainment	656	4.1	1,007	4.9	1,292	5.0
Alcohol	268	1.7	339	1.6	377	1.5
Tobacco	207	1.3	254	1.2	260	1.0
Insurance and pensions	1,207	7.6	1,982	9.6	2,974	11.5
Contributions	514	3.2	608	2.9	856	3.3
Miscellaneous	224	1.4	308	1.5	394	1.5
Total spending	$15,995	100.0%	$20,623	100.0%	$25,780	100.0%

sumers who already have swimming pools—to see how they adjusted their spending patterns—and how they felt before and after the purchase.[2]

Stage of family life cycle affects spending

Two other demographic dimensions—age and number of children—affect spending patterns. Put together, these dimensions tell us about the life-cycle stage of a family. See Exhibit 6–2 for a summary of family life cycle and buying behavior.[3]

Young people and families accept new ideas

Singles and young couples seem to be more open to new products and brands. And they are careful, price-conscious shoppers. The income of these younger people is often lower than the older groups. But they spend a greater proportion of their income on "discretionary" items—because they don't have big expenses for housing, education, and raising a family. Although many are waiting longer to marry—most young people do "tie the knot" eventually. These younger families—especially those with no children—are still buying durable goods, such as automobiles and home furnishings. They spend less on food. Only as children begin to arrive and grow does family spending shift to soft goods and services—such as education, medical, and personal care. This usually happens when the household head reaches the 35–44 age group.

Teenagers mean shifts in spending

Once children become teenagers, further shifts in spending occur. Teenagers eat more. Their clothing costs more. Their recreation and education

Exhibit 6–2   Stages in the Family Life Cycle

Stage	Characteristics and buying behavior
1. Singles: unmarried people living away from parents	Feel "affluent" and "free." Buy basic household goods. More interested in recreation, cars, vacations, clothes, cosmetics and personal care items.
2. Divorced or separated	May be financially squeezed to pay for alimony or maintaining two households. Buying may be limited to "necessities"—especially for women who have no job skills.
3. Newly married couples: no children	Both may work and so they feel financially well-off. Buy durables: cars, refrigerators, stoves, basic furniture—and recreation equipment and vacations.
4. Full nest I: youngest child under six	Feel squeezed financially because they are buying homes and household durables—furniture, washers, dryers, and TV. Also buying child-related products—food, medicines, clothes, and toys. Really interested in new products.
5. Full nest II: youngest child over five	Financially are better off as husband earns more and/or wife goes to work as last child goes to school. More spent on food, clothing, education, and recreation for growing children.
6. Full nest III: older couples with dependent children	Financially even better off as husband earns more and more wives work. May replace durables and furniture, and buy cars, boats, dental services, and more expensive recreation and travel. May buy bigger houses.
7. Empty nest: older couples, no children living with them, head still working	Feel financially "well-off." Home ownership at peak, and house may be paid for. May make home improvements or move into apartments. And may travel, entertain, go to school, and make gifts and contributions. Not interested in new products.
8. Sole survivor, still working	Income still good. Likely to sell home and continue with previous life style.
9. Senior citizen I: older married couple, no children living with them, head retired	Big drop in income. May keep home but cut back on most buying as purchases of medical care, drugs, and other health-related items go up.
10. Senior citizen II: sole survivor, not working	Same as senior citizen I, except likely to sell home, and has special need for attention, affection, and security.

needs are hard on the family budget. Parents may be forced to change their spending to cover these expenses—by spending less on durable goods, such as appliances, cars, household goods, and houses.

Many teenagers do earn much or all of their own spending money—so they are an attractive market. But marketers who aim at teenagers are beginning to notice the decline in birth rate. Motorcycle manufacturers, for example, have already been hurt—as teenagers are their heaviest buyers.

Selling to the empty nesters

An important group is the **empty nesters**—people whose children are grown and who are now able to spend their money in other ways. Usually these people are in the 50–64 age group. It is the empty nesters who move back into the smaller, more luxurious apartments in the city. They may also be more interested in travel, small sports cars, and other things they couldn't afford before. Much depends on their income, of course. But this is a high-income period for many workers—especially white-collar workers.

Senior citizens are a big new market

Finally, the **senior citizens**—people over 65—should not be neglected. People over 65 now make up over 13 percent of the population—and their number is growing.

Although older people generally have reduced incomes, many do have money—and very different needs. Many firms, in fact, are already catering to the senior citizen market. Travel agents are finding that seniors are an eager market for expensive tours and cruises. And some firms offer special diet supplements and drug products. Others design housing and "life care" centers to appeal to older people.

Do ethnic groups buy differently?

America may be called the "melting pot"—but ethnic groups deserve special attention from marketers. For example, more than 1 out of 10 families speaks a language other than English at home. Some areas have a much higher rate. In Miami and San Antonio, for example, about one out of three households speaks Spanish.

This is an area where stereotype thinking is common—and where a company may need to do some original marketing research—to reach this varied—and growing—market.[4]

The median age of U.S. blacks and Spanish-speaking people is much lower than that of whites. This means that many more are in earlier stages of the life cycle and, therefore, are a better market for certain products—especially durable goods.

Some minority groups seem to be striving for what they believe to be white middle-income standards. Current products may be quite acceptable. Others disregard these objectives in favor of their own traditional values. Clearly, separate strategies may be needed for these ethnically or racially defined markets.[5]

When the wife earns, the family spends

Another factor that deserves attention is the growing number of married women with paying jobs. In 1950, only 24 percent of wives worked outside the home. This figure is more than 55 percent in the 80s.

In families where the wife works for pay, she contributes about 40 percent of all the family spending power. This is why family income is as high as it is.

When a wife works outside the home, it seems to have little effect on the nutritional value of her family's food. But working wives do *spend more* for food—and choose more expensive types of food.

Families with working wives also spend more on clothing, child care, alcohol and tobacco, home furnishings and equipment, and cars. In short, when a wife works, it affects the spending habits of the family. This fact must be considered when planning marketing strategies.[6]

THE BEHAVIORAL SCIENCES HELP UNDERSTAND BUYING PROCESS

Buying in a black box

Exhibit 6–3 shows a simplified—"black box"—view of customer buying behavior. Potential customers are exposed to various stimuli—including the marketing mixes of competitors. Somehow, a person takes in some or all of these stimuli and then, for some reason, responds.

Exhibit 6–3   Simplified Buyer Behavior Model

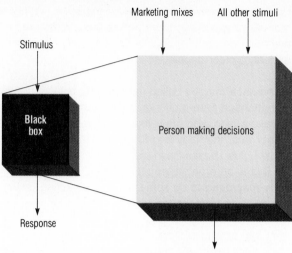

This simple version of the classic **stimulus-response model** says that people respond in some predictable way to a stimulus. The model doesn't explain *why* they behave the way they do.

Although we can't directly observe a consumer's decision-making process, there is much research—and many different opinions—about how it works.

Exhibit 6–4   More Complete Buyer Behavior Model, Showing that Psychological Variables, Social Influences, and the Purchase Situation All Affect the Problem-Solving Process

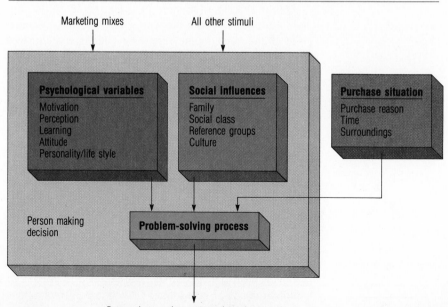

These different theories lead to different forecasts about how consumers will behave.

Most economists assume that consumers are **economic men**—people who logically compare choices in terms of cost and value received—to get the greatest satisfaction from spending their time, energy, and money. A logical extension of the economic-man theory led us to look at consumer spending patterns earlier in the chapter. There is value in this approach. Consumers must at least have income to be in a market. But other behavioral scientists suggest that buyer behavior is not as simple as the economic-man model suggests.

How we will view consumer behavior

Consumers have many dimensions. Let's try to combine these dimensions into a better model of how consumers make decisions. Exhibit 6–4 presents a more detailed view "inside" the black box. Here, we see that *psychological variables, social influences,* and the *purchase situation* all affect the consumer.

These topics will be discussed in the next few pages. Then we'll look at the consumer's problem-solving process.

PSYCHOLOGICAL INFLUENCES WITHIN AN INDIVIDUAL

Motivation determines what consumers want

Everybody is motivated by needs and wants. **Needs** are the basic forces that motivate an individual to do something. Some needs concern a person's physical well-being. Other needs concern the individual's self-view and relationship with others. Needs are more basic than wants. **Wants** are "needs" that are learned during an individual's life. For example, everyone needs water, or some kind of liquid, but some people also have learned to want "Perrier with a twist."

A need that is not satisfied may lead to a drive. The need for liquid, for example, leads to a thirst drive. A **drive** is a strong stimulus that encourages action—to reduce a need. Drives are the reasons behind certain behavior patterns. A product purchase is the result of a drive to satisfy some need.

A marketing mix can't create a drive

Marketing managers can't create drives in consumers. Some critics imply that marketers can somehow make consumers buy products against their will. Most marketing managers realize that trying to get consumers to act against their will just doesn't work. Instead, a good marketing manager studies what consumer drives and needs already exist—and how they can be satisfied better.

We all are a bundle of needs and wants. Exhibit 6–5 lists some important consumer needs. They can also be thought of as *benefits* consumers might seek from a marketing mix.

When a marketing manager defines a product-market, the needs may be quite specific. For example, the food need might be as specific as wanting a thick-crust pepperoni pizza.

Exhibit 6–5   Possible Needs Motivating a Person to Some Action

Physiological needs			
Food	Sleep	Body elimination	Rest
Drink	Warmth	Activity	Self-preservation
Sex—tension release	Coolness		

Psychological needs			
Abasement	Companionship	Exhibition	Playing—relaxing
Acquisition	Conserving	Family preservation	Power
Affiliation	Curiosity	Imitation	Pride
Aggression	Discovery	Independence	Security
Beauty	Deference	Individualism	Self-expression
Belonging	Distinctive	Love	Self-identification
Being constructive	Discriminating	Nurturing	Symmetry
Being part of a group	Discriminatory	Order	Tenderness
Being responsible	Dominance	Personal fulfillment	Striving
Being well thought of	Emulation	Playing—competitive	Understanding (knowledge)

Desire for		
Acceptance	Distinctiveness	Satisfaction with self
Achievement	Fame	Security
Affection	Happiness	Self-confidence
Affiliation	Identification	Sensuous experiences
Appreciation	Prestige	Sexual satisfaction
Comfort	Recognition	Sociability
Contrariness	Respect	Status
Dependence	Retaliation	Sympathy
Distance—"space"		

Freedom from		
Anxiety	Harm—Psychological	Pain
Depression	Harm—Physical	Pressure
Discomfort	Imitation	Ridicule
Fear	Loss of prestige	Sadness

**Several needs at the
same time**

Some psychologists argue that a person may have several reasons for buying—at the same time. Maslow is well known for his five-level hierarchy. But we will discuss a more recent four-level hierarchy that is easier to apply to consumer behavior.[7] The four levels are illustrated in Exhibit 6–6, along with an advertising slogan that illustrates how a company has tried to appeal to each need. The lowest-level needs are physiological. Then come safety, social, and personal needs. As a study aid, think of the "PSSP needs."

The **physiological needs** concern biological needs—food, drink, rest, and sex. The **safety needs** concern protection and physical well-being (perhaps involving health food, medicine, and exercise). The **social needs** concern love, friendship, status, and esteem—things that involve a person's interaction with others. The **personal needs**, on the other hand, concern an individual's need for personal satisfaction—unrelated to what others think or do. Examples here include self-esteem, accomplishment, fun, freedom, and relaxation.

Motivation theory suggests that we never reach a state of complete satisfaction. As soon as lower-level needs are reasonably satisfied, those at higher levels become more dominant. It is important to see, however, that a particular product may satisfy more than one need at the same time. A hamburger in a friendly environment, for example, might satisfy not only the physiological need to satisfy hunger—but also some social need. In fact, marketing managers should realize that most consumers try to fill a *set* of needs—rather than just one need or another in sequence. Also, the set of needs to be satisfied can vary from one group to another.

Exhibit 6–6   The PSSP Hierarchy of Needs

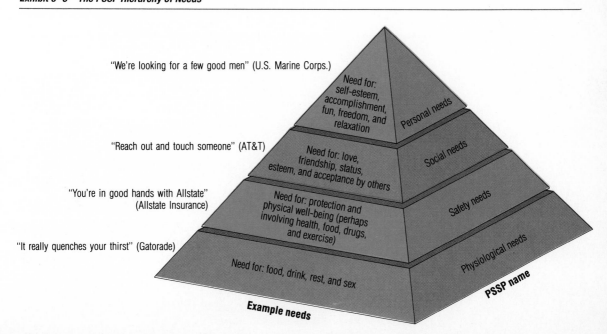

Economic needs affect how we satisfy basic needs

The need hierarchy idea can help explain *what* consumers will buy—but the economic needs help explain *why* they select specific product features.

Economic needs are concerned with making the best use of a consumer's limited resources—as the consumer sees it. Some people look for the best price. Others want the best quality—almost regardless of price. And others settle for the best value. Some economic needs are:

1. Economy of purchase or use.
2. Convenience.
3. Efficiency in operation or use.
4. Dependability in use.
5. Improvement of earnings.

Economic needs often can be explained in terms of factors we can measure—including specific dollar savings, the length of the guarantee, and the time or money saved in using the product.

Perception determines what is seen and felt

We are constantly bombarded by stimuli—ads, products, stores. Yet we may not hear or see anything—because we apply the following selective processes.

1. **Selective exposure**—our eyes and minds seek out and notice only information that interests us.
2. **Selective perception**—we screen out or modify ideas, messages, and information that conflict with previously learned attitudes and beliefs.
3. **Selective retention**—we remember only what we want to remember.

Different products meet different needs.

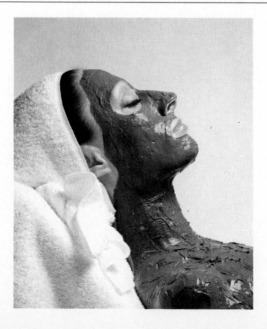

These selective processes help explain why some people are not affected by some advertising—even offensive advertising. They just don't see or remember it!

Our needs affect these selective processes. Decisions of current concern will receive more attention. For example, Goodyear tire retailers advertise a "sale" in the newspaper almost weekly. Most of the time we don't even notice these ads—until we need new tires. Only then do we tune in to Goodyear's ads.

Marketers are interested in these selective processes because they affect how target consumers get and retain information. This is also why marketers are interested in how consumers *learn*.

Learning determines what response is likely

Learning is a change in a person's thought processes caused by prior experience. A little girl tastes her first Häagen Dazs ice cream cone—and learning occurs! In fact, almost *all* consumer behavior is learned.[8]

There are several steps in the learning process. We've already discussed the idea of a *drive* as a strong stimulus that encourages action. Depending on the **cues**—products, signs, ads, and other stimuli in the environment—an individual chooses some specific response. A **response** is an effort to satisfy a drive. The specific response chosen depends on the cues—and the person's past experience.

Reinforcement—of the learning process—occurs when the response is followed by satisfaction—thus reducing the drive. Reinforcement strengthens the relationship between the cue and the response. And it may lead to a similar response the next time the drive occurs. Repeated reinforcement leads to the development of a habit—making the decision process routine for the individual. Exhibit 6–7 shows the relationships of the important variables in the learning process.

Exhibit 6–7   The Learning Process

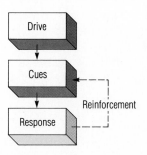

The learning process can be illustrated by a thirsty person. The thirst *drive* could be satisfied in a variety of ways. But if the person happened to walk past a vending machine and a 7UP sign—a *cue*—then he might satisfy the drive with a *response*—buying a 7UP. If the experience is satisfactory, positive *reinforcement* will occur—and our friend may be quicker to satisfy this drive in the same way next time. This emphasizes the importance of developing good products that live up to the promises of the firm's advertising. People can learn to like or dislike 7UP—reinforcement and learning work both ways!

Good experiences can lead to positive attitudes about a firm's product. Bad experiences can lead to negative attitudes—which even good promotion won't be able to change.

Some needs may be learned

Some needs may be culturally (or socially) learned. The need for food, for instance, may lead to many specific food wants. Many Japanese enjoy raw fish—and it's common in their culture. Few Americans, however, have learned to like raw fish.

Some critics argue that marketing efforts encourage people to spend money on learned wants that relate to no "basic need' at all. Europeans, for example, are less concerned about body odor—and few buy or use a deodorant. In the

United States people spend millions of dollars on such products. Advertising says that using Ban deodorant "takes the worry out of being close." But is advertising the cause of the differences in the two cultures? Most research says that advertising can't convince buyers of something that is contrary to their basic *attitudes.*

Attitudes relate to buying

An **attitude** is a person's point of view toward something. The "something" may be a product, an ad, a salesperson, a firm, or an idea. Attitudes are an important topic for marketers—because attitudes affect the selective processes, learning, and eventually buying decisions.

Attitudes involve liking or disliking—so people are willing to take some action. *Beliefs* are not so action-oriented. A **belief** is a person's opinion about something. Beliefs may help shape a consumer's attitudes—but don't necessarily involve any liking or disliking. It is possible to have a belief—say that Listerine has a medicinal taste—without really caring what it tastes like.

Some marketers have stretched the attitude concept to include consumer "preferences" or "intention to buy"—in an attempt to relate attitude more closely to purchase behavior.

The "intention to buy" is of most interest to managers who must forecast how much of their brand customers will buy. This would be easier if attitudes were good predictors of intentions to buy. Unfortunately, the relationships usually aren't that simple. A person might have positive attitudes toward a Jacuzzi hot tub, without having *any* intention of buying one.

Marketers generally try to understand the attitudes of their potential customers—and work with them. This is much easier—and more economical—than trying to *change* them. Attitudes tend to last. Changing present attitudes—especially negative ones—is probably the most difficult job that marketers face.[9]

Personality affects how people see things

Much research has been done on how personality affects people's behavior—but the results have generally been disappointing to marketers. A trait like neatness can be associated with users of certain types of products—like cleaning materials. But personality traits haven't been much help in predicting which specific products or brands people will choose.[10] As a result, marketers have stopped focusing on personality measures borrowed from psychologists and instead developed *life-style analysis.*

Psychographics and life-style analysis focuses on activities, interests, and opinions

Psychographics or **life-style analysis** is the analysis of a person's day-to-day pattern of living—as shown by his *A*ctivities, *I*nterests, and *O*pinions—sometimes referred to as "AIOs." Exhibit 6–8 shows a number of variables for each of the AIO dimensions—along with some demographics that may add useful detail to the life-style profile of a target market.

Life-style analysis assumes that you can plan better strategies to reach your target customers if you know more about them. Understanding the life-style of target customers has helped provide ideas for advertising themes. Let's see how it adds to a typical demographic description. It may not help Mercury marketing managers much to know that an average member of the target market

Exhibit 6–8   Life-Style Dimensions

Activities	Interests	Opinions	Demographics
Work	Family	Themselves	Age
Hobbies	Home	Social issues	Education
Social events	Job	Politics	Income
Vacation	Community	Business	Occupation
Entertainment	Recreation	Economics	Family size
Club membership	Fashion	Education	Dwelling
Community	Food	Products	Geography
Shopping	Media	Future	City size
Sports	Achievements	Culture	Stage in life cycle

for a Sable station wagon is 34.8 years old, married, lives in a three-bedroom home, and has 2.3 children. Life styles help marketers to paint a more human portrait of the target market. Life-style analysis might show that the 34.8-year-old is also a community-oriented consumer with traditional values who especially enjoys spectator sports and spends much time in other activities with the whole family. An ad might show the Sable being used by a happy family at a ball game—so the target market could really identify with the ad.[11]

SOCIAL INFLUENCES AFFECT CONSUMER BEHAVIOR

We have been discussing some of the ways that needs, attitudes, and other psychological variables influence the buying process. Now we'll look at how the individual interacts with family, social class, and other groups who may have influence.

The original Betty, 1936   **1972**   **1980**   **1955**   **1965**   **1986**

General Mills has changed "Betty Crocker's" appearance as consumer attitudes and life styles have changed.

Who is the real decision maker in family purchases?

Although one person in a household usually makes the purchase, in planning strategy it's important to know who the real decision maker is.

Not so long ago, the wife was "the" family purchasing agent. She had the time to shop—and run errands. So most promotion was aimed at women. But now, as more women work outside the home—and as night and weekend shopping become more popular—men are doing more shopping and decision making.

Although one member of the family may go to the store and make a specific purchase, it's important in planning marketing strategy to know who else may be involved. Other family members may have influenced the decision—or really decided what to buy. Still others may use the product.

You don't have to watch much Saturday morning TV to see that Kellogg and General Mills know this. Cartoon characters like "Cap'n Crunch" and "Tony the Tiger" tell kids abouts the goodies found in certain cereal packages—and urge them to remind Dad or Mom to pick up that brand next trip to the store. Older sons and daughters may even influence big purchases—like cars and television sets.

Family considerations may overwhelm personal ones

A husband or wife may do a lot of thinking about which products they prefer. Their choices may be modified if the other spouse has different priorities. One might want to spend more on a family vacation to Disneyland—and the

---

Buying responsibilities and influence vary greatly, depending on the product and the family.

other might want a new RCA video recorder and Sony large-screen TV. The actual outcome in such a situation is hard to predict. The final decision might be determined by social processes—such as power, influence, and affection.[12]

Social class affects attitudes, values, and buying

Up to now, we have been concerned with the individual and his relation to his family. Now let's consider how society looks at an individual and perhaps the family—in terms of social class. A **social class** is a group of people who have approximately equal social position—as viewed by others in the society.

Almost every society has some social class structure. The U.S. class system is far less rigid than in most countries. Children start out in the same social class as their parents—but can move to a different social class depending on their education levels and the jobs they hold.

Marketers want to know what buyers in various social classes are like. Simple approaches for measuring social class groupings are based on a person's *occupation, education,* and *type and location of housing.* These can be studied in marketing research surveys—or in available census data—to get a feel for the social class of a target market.

Note that income level is not included in this list. There is *some* general relationship between income level and social class. But the income level of people within the same social class can vary greatly—and people with the same income level may be in different social classes.

Note, also, that we are using the traditional technical terms "upper," "middle," and "lower." See Exhibit 6–9. These terms are used here because they are in general use—but a word of warning is in order. The terms may seem to imply "superior" and "inferior." But in sociology and marketing usage, no value judgment is intended. We can't say that any one class is "better" or "happier" than another.

Exhibit 6–9   Relative Sizes of Different Social Class Groups

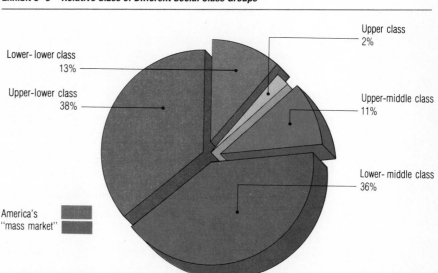

Characteristics of social classes in the United States

The **upper class** (2 percent of the population) consists of people from old, wealthy families (upper-upper)—as well as the socially prominent new rich (lower-upper). They often live in large homes with luxury features.

The **upper-middle class** (11 percent of the population) consists of successful professionals, owners of small businesses, or managers for large corporations. These people are concerned about their quality of life. They view their purchases as symbols of success—so they want quality products.

The **lower-middle class** (36 percent of the population) consists of small business people, office workers, teachers, and technicians—the white-collar workers. The American moral code and the emphasis on hard work have come from this class. This has been the most "conforming" segment of society. They are home- and family-oriented. We speak of America as a middle-class society, but the middle-class value system stops here. More than half of our society is *not* middle class.

The **upper-lower class** (38 percent of the population) consists of factory production line workers, skilled workers, and service people—the blue-collar workers. Most earn good incomes—but are still very concerned about security.

The **lower-lower class** (13 percent of the population) consists of unskilled laborers and people in non-respectable occupations. They usually don't have much income. But they are good markets for "necessities" and products that help them enjoy the present.[13]

What do these classes mean?

Social class studies suggest that an old saying—"A rich man is simply a poor man with more money"—is not true. It appears that a person belonging to the lower classes—given the same income as a middle-class person—handles himself and his money very differently. The various classes shop at different stores. They prefer different treatment from salespeople. They buy different brands of products—even though their prices are about the same—and they have different spending-saving attitudes. Exhibit 6–10 shows some of these differences.

Reference groups are relevant, too

A **reference group** is the people an individual looks to when forming attitudes about a particular topic. We normally have several reference groups—for different topics. Some we meet face-to-face. Others we may just wish to imi-

Exhibit 6–10   Characteristics and Attitudes of Middle and Lower Classes

Middle classes	Lower classes
Plan and save for the future	Live for the present
Analyze alternatives	"Feel" what is "best"
Understand how the world works	Have simplistic ideas about how things work
Feel they have opportunities	Feel controlled by the world
Willing to take risks	"Play it safe"
Confident about decision making	Want help with decision making
Want long-run quality or value	Want short-run satisfaction

tate. In either case, we may take values from these reference groups—and make buying decisions based on what the group might accept.

The importance of reference groups depends on the product—and on whether anyone else will be able to "see" which product and which brand are being used. Exhibit 6–11 shows products with different amounts of reference group influences.[14]

Reaching the opinion leaders who are buyers

An **opinion leader** is a person who influences others. Opinion leaders aren't necessarily wealthier or better educated. And opinion leaders on one subject are not necessarily opinion leaders on another subject. Capable homemakers with large families may be consulted for advice on family budgeting. Young women may be opinion leaders for new clothing styles and cosmetics. Each social class tends to have its own opinion leaders. Some marketing mixes are aimed especially at these people—since their opinions affect others.[15]

Culture surrounds the whole decision-making process

Culture is the whole set of beliefs, attitudes, and ways of doing things of a reasonably homogeneous set of people. We can think of the American culture, the French culture, or the Latin American culture. People within these cultural groups are more similar in outlook and behavior. And sometimes it's useful to think of sub-cultures within such groupings. For example, within the American culture, there are various religious and ethnic sub-cultures. If a marketing manager is aiming at people in two cultures, two different marketing plans may be needed.[16]

The attitudes and beliefs within a culture tend to change slowly. So once you develop a good understanding of the culture you are planning for, it probably will be practical to concentrate on the more dynamic variables discussed above.

Exhibit 6–11   *Examples of Different Levels of Group Influence for Different Types and Brands of Products*

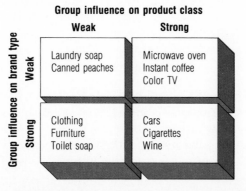

INDIVIDUALS ARE AFFECTED BY THE PURCHASE SITUATION

Purchase reason can vary

The purchase situation can affect buying behavior. For example, a student buying a pen for his own use might pick up an inexpensive Bic. But if the same student wanted a pen as a gift for a friend, he might choose a Cross pen.

Time affects what happens

Time is also a purchase situation influence: *when* a purchase is made—as well as how much time we have to shop—can influence behavior. A leisurely dinner induces different behavior than grabbing a quick cup of 7–11 coffee on the way to work.

Surroundings affect buying, too

Surroundings can affect buying behavior. The excitement of an auction may *stimulate* impulse buying.

Needs, benefits sought, attitudes, motivation, and even how a consumer selects certain products vary—depending on the purchase situation. So different purchase situations may require different marketing mixes—even for the same target market.[17]

CONSUMERS USE PROBLEM–SOLVING PROCESSES

Buyers seem to use a problem-solving process to select particular products. This problem-solving process consists of five steps:

1. Becoming aware of—or interested in—the problem.
2. Recalling and gathering information about possible solutions.
3. Evaluating alternative solutions—perhaps trying some out.
4. Deciding on the appropriate solution.
5. Evaluating the decision.[18]

Exhibit 6–12 presents an expanded version of this basic process. Note that this exhibit integrates the problem-solving process with the whole set of variables we've been reviewing.

Three levels of problem solving are useful

The basic problem-solving process shows the steps a consumer may go through while trying to find a way to satisfy his needs. But it doesn't show how long this will take—or how much thought he will give to each step.

So it's helpful to recognize three levels of problem solving: extensive problem solving, limited problem solving, and routinized response behavior. See Exhibit 6–13. These problem-solving approaches are used for any kind of product.

Extensive problem solving is involved when a need is completely new or important to a consumer—and much effort is taken to decide how to satisfy the need. A new transfer student at a college, for example, may want a place to live that meets his needs for comfort, companionship, and convenience to campus. It may take him some time to figure out what he wants to do—and how to do it.

Exhibit 6–12   Consumer's Problem-Solving Process

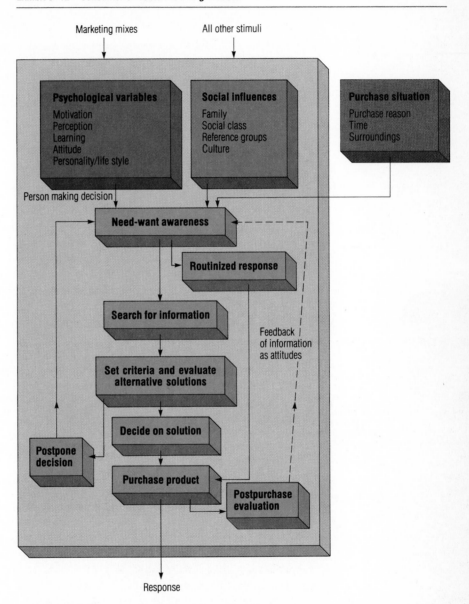

Limited problem solving

Marketing mixes

All other stimuli

Psychological variables
Motivation
Perception
Learning
Attitude
Personality/life style

Social influences
Family
Social class
Reference groups
Culture

Purchase situation
Purchase reason
Time
Surroundings

Person making decision

Need-want awareness

Routinized response

Search for information

Feedback
of information
as attitudes

**Set criteria and evaluate
alternative solutions**

Decide on solution

**Postpone
decision**

Purchase product

**Postpurchase
evaluation**

Response

Limited problem solving is involved when a consumer is willing to put *some* effort into deciding the best way to satisfy a need. Our transfer student has tried different ways of solving his housing needs. He may have lived in a dorm or shared a house with friends. So he would use limited problem solving to decide which choice is best at this time.

Routinized response behavior involves mechanically selecting a particular way of satisfying a need when it occurs. For example, when our college stu-

Exhibit 6–13   Problem-Solving Continuum

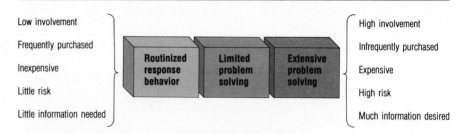

dent finds an apartment that meets his needs, he might routinely renew his lease each year.

Routinized response behavior is typical when a consumer has much experience in how to meet a need. He doesn't need more information.

Routine response behavior is also typical for **low involvement purchases**—purchases that don't have high personal importance or relevance for the customer. Let's face it—buying a box of salt is probably not one of the burning issues in your life. Most marketing managers would like their target consumers to always buy their products in a routinized way.[19]

New concepts require an adoption process

Really new concepts present a problem solver with a harder job—the adoption process. The **adoption process** is the steps individuals go through on the way to accepting or rejecting a new idea. It is similar to the problem-solving process. But the adoption process makes the role of learning clearer—and the potential contribution of promotion in a marketing mix.

The adoption process for an individual moves through some fairly definite steps, as follows:

1. Awareness—the potential customer comes to know about the product but lacks detail. He may not even know how it works or what it will do.
2. Interest—*if* he becomes interested, he gathers general information and facts about the product.
3. Evaluation—he begins to give the product a "mental trial," applying it to his personal situation.
4. Trial—the customer may buy the product so that he can experiment with it in use. A product that is either too expensive to try—or isn't available for trial—may never be adopted.
5. Decision—he decides on either adoption or rejection. A satisfactory evaluation and trial may lead to adoption of the product and regular use. According to psychological learning theory, reinforcement leads to adoption.
6. Confirmation—the adopter continues to rethink the decision and searches for support for the decision—that is, further reinforcement.[20]

Dissonance may set in after the decision

After a buyer makes a decision, he may have second thoughts. He may have had to choose from among several attractive alternatives—weighing the pros and cons and finally making a decision. Later doubts, however, may lead to **dissonance**—tension caused by uncertainty about the rightness of a deci-

Marketing managers offer trial sizes of products free—to speed the adoption process.

sion. Dissonance may lead a buyer to search for additional information—to confirm the wisdom of the decision and so reduce tension.[21]

SEVERAL PROCESSES ARE RELATED AND RELEVANT TO STRATEGY PLANNING

Exhibit 6–14 shows the relation of the problem-solving process, the adoption process, and learning. It is important to see that they can be changed, modified, or accelerated by promotion. Also note that the way buyers solve problems affects the physical distribution system needed. If customers aren't willing to travel far to shop, then more outlets may be needed to get their busi-

Exhibit 6–14   Relation of Problem-Solving Process, Adoption Process, and Learning (given a problem)

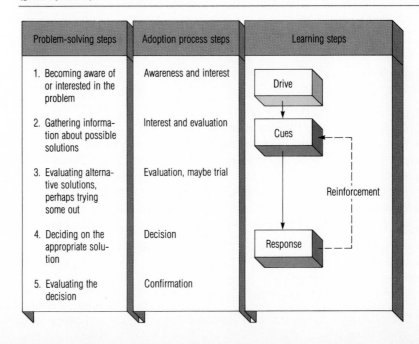

ness. Also, customer attitudes help determine what price to charge. Clearly, knowing how a target market handles these processes will aid marketing strategy planning.

CONCLUSION

In this chapter, we analyzed the individual consumer as a problem solver who is influenced by psychological variables, social influences, and the purchase situation. All of these variables are related. And our model of buyer behavior helps integrate them into one process. A good grasp of this material is needed in marketing strategy planning—because assuming that everyone behaves the way you do—or even like your family or friends do—can lead to expensive marketing errors.

Consumer buying behavior results from the consumer's efforts to satisfy needs and wants. We discussed some reasons why consumers buy—and saw that consumer behavior can't be fully explained by only a list of needs.

We also saw that our society is divided into social classes—which helps explain some consumer behavior. The impact of reference groups and opinion leaders was discussed, too.

A buyer behavior model was presented to help you interpret and integrate the present findings—and any new data you might obtain from marketing research. As of now, the behavioral sciences can only offer insights and theories that the marketing manager must blend with intuition and judgment in developing marketing strategies.

Marketing research may be needed to answer specific questions. But if marketing managers lack either the money or the time for research, they will have to rely on their understanding of present behavior—and "guesstimates" about future behavior.

We have more data and understanding of consumer behavior than business managers generally use. Applying this information may help you find your breakthrough opportunity.

Questions and Problems _____

1. Discuss the impact of our "aging culture" on marketing strategy planning.

2. Some demographic characteristics are likely to be more important than others in determining market potential. For each of the following characteristics, identify two products for which this characteristic is *most* important: (*a*) size of geographic area, (*b*) population, (*c*) income, (*d*) stage of life cycle.

3. Does the growing homogeneity of the consumer market mean there will be fewer opportunities to segment markets? Do you think all consumers of about equal income will spend their incomes similarly—and demand similar products?

4. What behavioral science concept underlies

the "black box" model of consumer behavior? Does this concept have operational relevance to marketing managers; i.e., if it is a valid concept, can they make use of it?

5. Explain what is meant by a hierarchy of needs and provide examples of one or more products that enable you to satisfy each of the four levels of need.

6. Cut out two recent advertisements: one full-page color ad from a magazine and one large display from a newspaper. Indicate which needs each ad is appealing to.

7. Explain how an understanding of consumers' learning processes might affect marketing strategy planning. Give an example.

8.   Briefly describe your own *beliefs* about the potential value of wearing seat belts when driving a car, your *attitude* toward seat belts, and your *intention* about wearing seat belts the next time you drive.

9.   Explain psychographics and life-style analysis. Explain how they might be useful for planning marketing strategies to reach college students as compared to the "average" consumer.

10.   How do cultural values affect purchasing behavior? Give two specific examples.

11.   How should the social class structure affect the planning of a new restaurant in a large city? How might the four Ps be adjusted?

12.   What social class would you associate with each of the following phrases or items?
a.   Sports cars.
b.   The *National Enquirer.*
c.   *The New Yorker* magazine.
d.   *Playboy* magazine.
e.   People watching soap operas.
f.   TV bowling shows.
g.   Men who drink beer after dinner.
h.   Families who dress formally for dinner regularly.
i.   Families who are distrustful of banks (keep money in socks or mattresses).
j.   Owners of French poodles.
  In each case, choose one class if you can. If you can't choose one class, but rather feel that several classes are equally likely, then so indicate. In those cases where you feel that all classes are equally interested or characterized by a particular item, choose all five classes.

13.   Illustrate how the reference group concept may apply in practice by explaining how you personally are influenced by some reference group for some product. What are the implications of such behavior for marketing managers?

14.   Give two examples of recent purchases where your purchase decision was influenced by the specific purchase situation. Briefly explain how your decision was affected.

15.   Illustrate the three levels of problem solving with an example from your personal experience.

16.   On the basis of the data and analysis presented in Chapters 4 and 6, what kind of buying behavior would you expect to find for the following products: (a) canned peas, (b) toothpaste, (c) ballpoint pens, (d) baseball gloves, (e) sport coats, (f) microwave ovens, (g) life insurance, (h) automobiles, and (j) a new checking account? Set up a chart for your answer with products along the left-hand margin as the row headings and the following factors as headings for the columns: (a) how consumers would shop for these products, (b) how far they would go, (c) whether they would buy by brand, (d) whether they would wish to compare with other products, and (e) any other factors they should consider. Insert short answers—words or phrases are satisfactory—in the various boxes. Be prepared to discuss how the answers you put in the chart would affect each product's marketing mix.

Suggested Computer-Aided Problem

6.   Consumers' Selective Processes

Suggested Cases

1.   McDonald's

3.   Sears' Discover Card

9.   Days Inns vs. Best Western

10.   Metro Ice Arena

12.   Nike and the Joggers House

Chapter 7

Industrial and Intermediate Customers and Their Buying Behavior

When You Finish This Chapter, You Should

1. Know who intermediate customers are.

2. Know about the number and distribution of manufacturers.

3. Understand the problem-solving behavior of industrial buyers.

4. Know the basic methods used in industrial buying.

5. Know how buying by service firms, retailers, wholesalers, and governments is similar to—and different from—industrial buying.

6. Recognize the important new terms (shown in red).

Intermediate customers buy more than final consumers!

Duall/Wind, a plastics producer, was a major supplier of small parts for Polaroid instant cameras. But when Duall/Wind decided to raise its prices, Polaroid balked. Polaroid's purchasing manager demanded that Duall/Wind show a breakdown of all its costs, from materials to labor to profit. As Duall/Wind's president said, "I had a tough time getting through my head that Polaroid wanted to come right in here and have us divulge all that." But Polaroid is a big account—and it got the information it wanted.

You can see that Polaroid takes buying seriously. It works at limiting supplier price increases by knowing suppliers' businesses as well as—or better—than they do themselves. Instead of just accepting price hikes, a Polaroid buyer looks for ways to help the supplier operate at lower cost. Then Polaroid refuses to pay a higher price until the supplier streamlines its operation.[1]

Most buyers look at more than price. General Motors needed to cut the weight of its cars—to improve gas mileage and be able to compete with the imports. Dow Chemical assigned a sales rep to the account—because some of its plastics were a possible solution. Meetings were arranged with those involved in the decision. GM engineers, production managers, quality-control, and safety experts all had different concerns. The sales rep listened to each one and offered advice about which parts could be made of tougher plastics—and what technical problems had to be considered.

After more than a year, GM wrote detailed specifications for the parts it wanted—and invited a few suppliers to submit bids. The Dow sales rep was pleased to see that many of his suggestions—favorable to his products—appeared in the GM specifications. He was finally called by a GM buyer—who told him that top GM executives had selected several suppliers—to ensure supply and keep suppliers on their toes—but Dow would get a nice share of the new business.

INTERMEDIATE CUSTOMERS—A BIG OPPORTUNITY

Most of us think *customers* means only final consumers. In fact, more purchases are made by intermediate customers. **Intermediate customers** are any buyers who buy for resale or to produce other goods and services. Some examples include:

Manufacturers, farmers, and other producers of goods and services.

Hospitals, universities, and other non-profit organizations.

Wholesalers and retailers.

Government units—including federal agencies in the United States or other countries, as well as all state and local-level governments.

This chapter will discuss these intermediate consumers: who they are, where they are, and how they buy. We will emphasize the buying behavior of manufacturers. But other intermediate customers seem to buy in much the same way. In fact, often buyers for all kinds of organizations are loosely referred to as "industrial buyers." To keep the discussion specific, we'll focus on the United States—but most of the ideas apply to international markets.

There are great marketing opportunities in serving intermediate customers—and a student heading toward a business career has a good chance of working in this area.

INTERMEDIATE CUSTOMERS ARE DIFFERENT

There are about 15 million intermediate customers in the United States. See Exhibit 7–1. These customers do many different jobs—and we need many different market dimensions to describe all these different markets.

Exhibit 7–1   Kind and Number of Intermediate Customers in 1982–1983

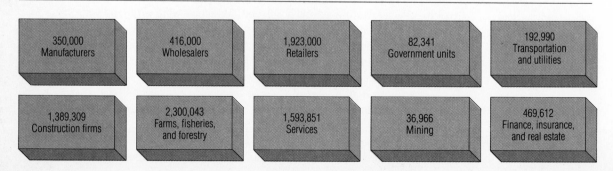

350,000 Manufacturers	416,000 Wholesalers	1,923,000 Retailers	82,341 Government units	192,990 Transportation and utilities
1,389,309 Construction firms	2,300,043 Farms, fisheries, and forestry	1,593,851 Services	36,966 Mining	469,612 Finance, insurance, and real estate

Even small differences are important

Understanding how and why intermediate customers buy is important. Competition is often rough in intermediate markets. Even small differences can affect the success of a marketing mix.

Since sellers usually approach each intermediate customer directly—through a sales rep—there is more chance to adjust the marketing mix for each individual customer. Sellers may even have a special marketing strategy for each individual customer. This is carrying target marketing to its extreme! But when a customer's purchases are large, it may be worth it.

In such situations, the individual sales rep carries more responsibility for strategy planning. This is important to your career planning, since these jobs are very challenging—and pay well.

MANUFACTURERS ARE IMPORTANT CUSTOMERS

There are not many big ones

There are very few manufacturers compared to final consumers. In the industrial market, there are about 350,000 factories. Exhibit 7–2 shows that the majority of these are quite small—half of the plants have less than 10 workers. The owners are often the buyers in small plants. And they buy less formally than buyers in the relatively few large manufacturing plants. Larger plants, however, employ most of the workers and produce a large share of the "value added" by manufacturing. For example, plants with 250 or more employees make up about 4 percent of the total—yet they employ nearly 60 percent of the production employees and produce about two thirds of the "value added" by manufacturers. You can see that these large plants are important markets.

Customers cluster in geographic areas

In addition to concentration by size, industrial markets are concentrated in big metropolitan areas—especially in the Midwest, Middle Atlantic states, and California.

Exhibit 7–2   Size Distribution of Manufacturing Establishments, 1982

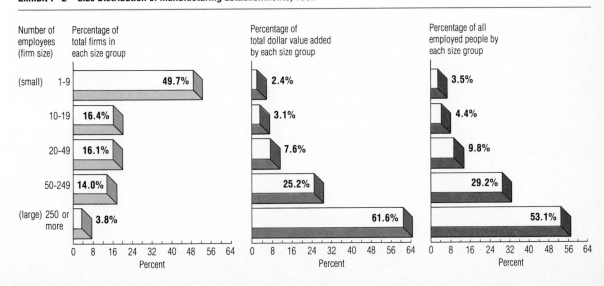

Number of employees (firm size)	Percentage of total firms in each size group	Percentage of total dollar value added by each size group	Percentage of all employed people by each size group
(small) 1-9	49.7%	2.4%	3.5%
10-19	16.4%	3.1%	4.4%
20-49	16.1%	7.6%	9.8%
50-249	14.0%	25.2%	29.2%
(large) 250 or more	3.8%	61.6%	53.1%

The buyers for some of these larger manufacturers are even further concentrated in home offices—often in big cities. U.S. Gypsum, a large building materials manufacturer, does most of its buying for more than 50 plants from its Chicago office. In such a case, a sales rep may be able to sell to plants all over the country without leaving his home city. This makes selling easier for competitors, too—and the market may be very competitive. The importance of these big buyers has led some companies to set up "national account" sales forces—specially trained to cater to these needs. A geographically bound salesperson can be at a real disadvantage against such competitors.

Concentration by industry

Manufacturers also concentrate by industry. Manufacturers of advanced electronics systems are concentrated in California's "Silicon Valley" near San Francisco and along Boston's "Route 128." The steel industry is concentrated in the Pittsburgh, Birmingham (Alabama), and Chicago areas.

Much data is available on industrial markets by SIC Codes

In industrial markets, marketing managers can focus their attention on a relatively few clearly defined markets and reach most of the business. Their efforts can be aided by very detailed census information reported by **Standard Industrial Classification (SIC) Codes**—codes used to identify groups of firms in similar lines of business. The data shows the number of firms, their sales volumes, and number of employees—broken down by industry, county, and MSA. These codes are a real help in marketing research—for those who can relate their own sales to their customers type of business. SIC Code breakdowns start with broad industry categories—such as food and related products (code 20), tobacco products (code 21), textile mill products (code 22), apparel (code 23), and so on.

Within each two-digit industry breakdown, much more detailed data may be available for three-digit and four-digit industries (that is, sub-industries of the two- or three-digit industries). Exhibit 7–3 shows the apparel industry breakdown.[2]

BUYERS ARE PROBLEM SOLVERS

Some people think of industrial buying as entirely different from consumer buying. But there are many similarities. In fact, the problem-solving framework introduced in Chapter 6 can be used here.[3]

Three buying processes are useful

In Chapter 6, we discussed three kinds of buying by consumers: extensive, limited, and routine buying. In industrial markets, it is useful to adapt these ideas a little—and talk about new task buying, a modified rebuy, or a straight rebuy. See Exhibit 7–4.

New-task buying occurs when a firm has a new need and the buyer wants a great deal of information. New-task buying can include setting product specifications and sources of supply.

A **modified rebuy** is the in-between process where some review of the buying situation is done—though not as much as in new-task buying.

Exhibit 7–3   Illustrative SIC Breakdown for Apparel Industries

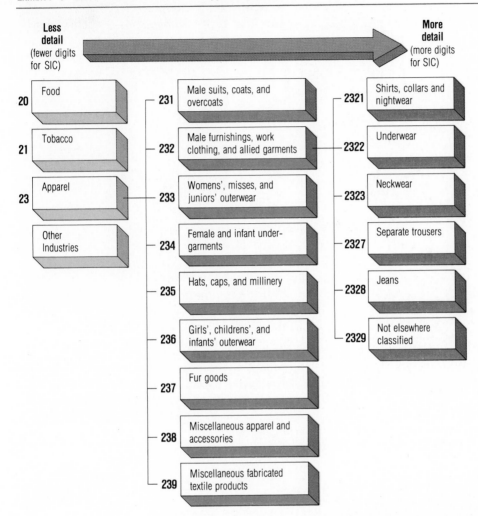

A **straight rebuy** is a routine repurchase that may have been made many times before. Buyers probably would not bother looking for new information—or new sources of supply. Most of a company's small purchases are of this type—but they take only a small part of a good buyer's time.

Note that a particular product might be bought in any of the three ways. Careful market analysis is needed to learn how the firm's products are bought—and by whom. A new-task buy takes much longer than a straight rebuy—and gives much more chance for promotion impact by the seller. Exhibit 7–5 shows the time—and many influences—involved in buying a special drill.[4]

Purchasing agents are buying specialists

The large size of some producers has led to a need for buying specialists. **Purchasing agents** are buying specialists for their employers.

Purchase of major equipment often involves new-task buying. A purchase of a repair item may be a straight rebuy from a reliable supplier.

The purchasing agent usually must be seen first—before contacting any other employee. Purchasing agents have a lot of power—and take a dim view of sales reps who try to go around them. In large companies, purchasing agents usually specialize by product area—and are real experts.

Rather than being "sold," these buyers expect accurate information that will help them buy wisely. They need information on new goods and services—as well as tips on possible price changes, strikes, and other changes in business conditions. Most industrial buyers are serious and well educated. A sales rep should treat them accordingly.

Exhibit 7–4 Industrial Buying Processes

Type of process Characteristics	New-task buying	Modified rebuy	Straight rebuy
Time required	Much	Medium	Little
Multiple influence	Much	Some	Little
Review of suppliers	Much	Some	None
Information needed	Much	Some	Little

Exhibit 7–5   Decision Network Diagram of the Buying Situations: Special Drill

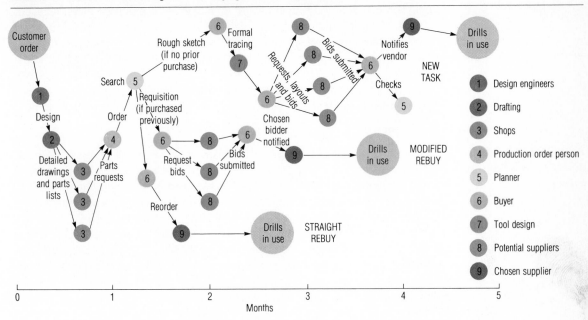

Basic purchasing needs are economic

Industrial buyers are usually less emotional in their buying than final consumers. Buyers look for certain product characteristics—including economy, productivity, uniformity, purity, and ability to make the buyer's final product better.

In addition to product characteristics, buyers consider the seller's reliability, general cooperativeness, ability to provide speedy maintenance and repair—as well as dependable and fast delivery.

Many buyers use **vendor analysis**—formal rating of suppliers on all areas of performance. Evaluating suppliers—and how they are working out—results in better buying decisions.[5]

Emotional needs are relevant, too

Vendor analysis emphasizes economic factors—but industrial purchasing does have an emotional side. Buyers are human—and want friendly relationships with suppliers. Some buyers eagerly imitate progressive competitors—or are the first to try new products. Such "early adopters" might deserve special attention when new products are being introduced.

Buyers also want to protect their own position in the company. "Looking good" isn't easy for purchasing agents. They have to buy a wide variety of products from many sources—and make decisions involving many factors beyond their control. If a new source delivers low-quality materials—you can guess who will be blamed. Poor service—or late delivery—also reflects on the buyer's ability. Therefore, anyone or anything that helps the buyer look good has a definite appeal. In fact, this one factor may make the difference between a successful and an unsuccessful marketing mix.

Supply sources must be dependable

Dependability is very important. Nothing bothers a purchasing agent and a production manager more than having to shut down a production line because sellers haven't delivered the goods. Product quality is important, too. The cost of a small item may have little to do with its importance. If it causes the breakdown of a larger unit, it may result in a large loss—much greater than its own value.

A seller's marketing mix should satisfy both the needs of the buyer's company as well as the buyer's individual needs. Therefore, it helps to find some common area where both can be satisfied. See Exhibit 7–6.

Multiple buying influences in a buying center

Much of the work of the typical purchasing agent consists of straight rebuys. But in some cases—especially in new-task buying—a multiple buying influence may be important. **Multiple buying influence** means the buyer shares the purchasing decision with several people—perhaps even top management. Each of these "influences" may have very different interests.

It is helpful to think of a **buying center** that consists of all the people who participate in or influence a purchase. A salesperson must study each case carefully. Just finding out who to talk with may be hard—but thinking about the various roles in the buying center can help.

A sales rep might have to talk to every member of the buying center—stressing different topics for each. This not only complicates the promotion job—but also lengthens it. Approval of a routine order may take anywhere from a week to several months. On very important purchases—a new computer system, a new plant, or major equipment—the selling period may stretch out to a year or more.[6]

BASIC METHODS AND PRACTICES IN INDUSTRIAL BUYING

Should you inspect, sample, describe, or negotiate

Industrial buyers—really, buyers of all types, including final consumers—use four basic approaches to evaluating and buying products: (1) inspection, (2) sampling, (3) description, and (4) negotiated contracts. Understanding the differences in these buying methods is important in strategy planning—so let's look at each approach now.

Inspection looks at everything

Inspection buying means looking at every item. It's used for products that are not standardized—for example: livestock or used equipment. Such products are often sold in open markets—or at auctions. Buyers inspect the goods and either bargain with the seller—or bid against competitors.

Sampling looks at some

Sampling buying means looking at only part of a potential purchase. As products become more standardized—perhaps because of more careful grading or quality control—buying by sample becomes possible. For example, a power company might buy miles of heavy electric cable. A sample section might be heated to the melting point—to be sure it's safe.

Prices may be based on a sample. Demand and supply forces may set the general price level—but the *actual* price level may vary depending on the

Exhibit 7–6   A Model of Individual Industrial Buyer Behavior—Showing Overlapping Needs

Career
growth

Innovation

Friendships

Survival

**Individual
buyer's
needs**

**Overlap
in
needs**

**Company's
needs**

Money

Job
security

Profit

Growth

Other needs

Other needs

Possible overlaps

Friendships	Survival
Job security	Innovation
Money	Growth
Career growth	Profit

quality of a specific sample. This kind of buying is used in grain markets—for example, where the actual price is based on an analysis of a sample taken from a carload of corn or wheat.

**Description just de-
scribes accurately**

Description (specification) buying means buying from a written (or verbal) description of the product. The products are not inspected. This method is used when quality can be controlled and described—as with many branded products.

Today, most buyers of fruits and vegetables accept government grading

Sampling buying is often used with grain, and the quality of the sample may affect the price for the whole order.

standards for these products. They are packed in the fields and sold without further inspection or sampling. This, of course, reduces the cost of buying and is used by buyers whenever practical.

Services are usually purchased by description. Since a service is usually not performed until it is purchased, there is nothing to inspect ahead of time.

Negotiated contracts explain how to handle relationships

Negotiated contract buying means agreeing to a contract that allows for changes in the purchase arrangements.

Sometimes the buyer knows roughly what's needed—but can't fix all the details in advance. The specifications—or total requirements—may change as the job progresses. This is found, for example, in research and development work—and in the building of special-purpose machinery or buildings. In such cases, the general project is described. Then a basic price may be agreed on—with guidelines for changes and price adjustments up or down. The whole contract may even be subject to bargaining as the work proceeds.

Buyers may favor loyal, helpful suppliers

To be sure of dependable quality, a buyer may develop loyalty to certain suppliers. This is especially important when buying non-standardized products. When a friendly relationship develops over the years, the supplier almost becomes a part of the buyer's organization.

Most buyers have a sense of fair play. When a seller suggests a new idea that saves the buyer's company money, the buyer usually rewards the seller with orders. This also encourages future suggestions.

In contrast, buyers who use a bid system exclusively may not be offered much beyond the basic goods and services. They are interested mainly in price. Marketing managers who have developed better marketing mixes may not seek such business—at least with their better marketing mixes.

Industrial buyers favor helpful suppliers who offer solutions to their problems.

Until recently, Ford, Chrysler, and GM relied heavily on bids—convinced this would result in lower prices from competing suppliers. But Japanese competition made them rethink this approach. Japanese producers and their suppliers often work together very closely. They view the effort as a partnership. Suppliers are consulted before design changes are made—to make sure that a planned change won't create problems. Now, the Detroit automakers also use this approach—often giving a single supplier a long-term contract to supply a needed part. In return, they expect and get more help from the supplier. In fact, Ford credits suggestions from its suppliers for the improved quality of its new cars.[7]

But most buyers seek several sources to spread their risk

Even if a firm has developed the best marketing mix possible, it probably won't get all the business of its industrial customers. Buyers usually look for several dependable sources of supply. They must protect themselves from unpredictable events—such as strikes, fires, or other problems in one of their suppliers' plants. Still, a good marketing mix is likely to win a larger share of the total business.[8]

Most buyers try to routinize buying

Most firms use a buying procedure that tries to routinize the process. When an item is needed, a **requisition**—a request to buy something—is filled out. After approval by a supervisor, the requisition goes to the buyer—for placement with the "best" seller. Now the buyer is responsible for placing a purchase order—and getting delivery by the date requested.

Ordering may be routine after requisitioning

Requisitions are converted to purchase orders as quickly as possible. Straight rebuys are usually made the day the requisition is received. New-task and modified rebuys take longer. If time is important, the buyer may phone in the order—and then send out a confirming purchase order.

It pays to know the buyer

Notice the importance of being one of the regular sources of supply. The buyers don't even call potential suppliers for straight rebuys.

Having a good image is an advantage for a sales rep. It's likely that he'll get a larger share of the orders. Moving from a 20 percent to a 30 percent share may not seem like much from a buyer's point of view, but for the seller it is a 50 percent increase in sales!

Some buy by computer

Some buyers have turned over a large part of their routine order-placing to computers. They program decision rules that tell the computer how to order—and leave the details of following through to the machine. When economic conditions change, the buyers modify the computer instructions. When nothing unusual happens, however, the computer system continues to routinely rebuy as needs develop—printing out new purchase orders to the regular suppliers.

Obviously, it's a big "sale" to be selected as a supplier—and routinely called up by the computer. It's also obvious that such a buyer will be more impressed by an attractive marketing mix for a whole *line* of products—not just a lower price for a particular order. It's too expensive—and too much trouble—to change a whole buying system just because somebody offers a low price on a particular day.[9]

Inventory policy may determine purchases

Industrial firms generally try to maintain an adequate inventory—at least enough to keep production lines moving. There is nothing worse than having a production line close down.

No buyer wants to run out of needed products—but keeping too much inventory is expensive. Firms now pay more attention to these costs—and look for suppliers' help in controlling them. This often means that a supplier must be able to provide **"just-in-time" delivery**—reliably getting products there *just* before the customer needs them.

Adequate inventory is often stated in terms of number of days' supply—for example, 60- or 90-days' supply. But what a 60- or 90-days' supply is depends on the level of demand for the company's products. If the demand rises sharply—say by 10 percent—then total purchases will expand by more than 10 percent to maintain inventory levels *and* meet the new needs. On the other hand, if sales drop 10 percent, actual needs and inventory requirements drop, too. Buying may even stop while inventory is "worked off." During such a cutback, a seller probably can't stimulate sales—even by reducing price. The buyer is just "not in the market."

Reciprocity helps sales, but. . .

Reciprocity means trading sales for sales—that is, "If you buy from me, I'll buy from you." If a company's customers can also supply products that the firm buys, then the sales departments of both buyer and seller may try to "trade" sales for sales. Purchasing agents generally resist reciprocity. But often their sales departments force it on them.

When both prices and quality are competitive, it's hard to ignore pressure from the sales departments. An outside supplier can only hope to become an alternate source of supply—and wait for the "insiders" to let their quality slip or prices rise.

The U.S. Justice Department frowns on reciprocity. It tries to block reciprocal buying on the grounds that it injures competition. This has forced some firms that have depended on reciprocity to rethink their marketing strategies.[10]

PRODUCERS OF SERVICES—SMALLER AND MORE SPREAD OUT

Some marketing managers know that the service side of our economy is large and growing. In fact, the number of service firms increased 40 percent between 1977 and 1982. There may be good opportunities in providing these companies with the products they need to support their operations. But there are also challenges.

As Exhibit 7–1 shows, there are about 10 times as many service firms as there are manufacturers. Some of these—like a large hotel chain or a telephone company—are big companies. But, as you might guess given the large number of firms, most of them are small. They are also more spread out around the country than manufacturing concerns.

Buying is usually not as formal

Purchases by small service firms are often handled by whoever is in charge. This may be a doctor, lawyer, owner of a local insurance agency, or manager of a hotel. Suppliers who usually deal with manufacturers may have trouble adjusting to this market. Personal selling is still an important part of Promotion, but reaching these customers in the first place often requires more advertising. And service firms may need much more help in buying than a large manufacturer.

RETAILERS AND WHOLESALERS BUY FOR THEIR CUSTOMERS

Most retail and wholesale buyers see themselves as purchasing agents for their target customers. They believe the old saying: "Goods well bought are half sold." They do *not* see themselves as sales agents for manufacturers. They buy what they think they can sell. They don't try to make value judgments about the desirability of what they sell. Instead, they focus on the needs and attitudes of *their* target customers. For example, Super Valu—a $5 billion a year food wholesaler—calls itself "the retail support company." And, as a top manager at Super Valu put it, "Our mandate is to try to satisfy our retailer customers with *whatever it takes.*"[11]

They must buy too many items

Most retailers carry a large number of items—drug stores up to 12,000 items, hardware stores from 3,000 to 25,000, and grocery stores up to 20,000 items. They just don't have the time to pay close attention to every item.

Wholesalers, too, handle so many items that they can't give constant attention to each one. Drug wholesalers may stock up to 125,000 items—and wholesalers of textiles and sewing supplies up to 250,000 items.[12]

You can see why retailers and wholesalers buy most of their products as straight rebuys. Many buyers are annoyed by the number of sales reps who call on them with little to say about one or a few items. Sellers to these markets must understand the size of the buyer's job—and have something useful to say and do when they call. For example, besides just improving relations, they might take inventory, set up displays, or arrange shelves—while looking for a chance to talk about specific products and maintain the relationship.

In larger firms, buyers spend more time on individual items. They may specialize in certain lines. Some large chains—like Sears—expect buyers to seek out additional and lower-cost sources of supply.[13]

They must watch inventories and computer output

The large number of items bought and stocked by wholesalers and retailers means that inventories must be watched carefully. Smart retailers and wholesalers try to carry *enough* inventory but not too much—and then depend on a continual flow through the channel.

Most large firms now use computer-controlled inventory control systems. Scanners at retail check-out counters keep track of what's sold—and computers use this data to update the records. Even small firms are using automated control systems that can print daily reports—showing sales of every product on the manager's shelves. This is important to marketing managers selling to them—because buyers with this kind of information know more about how goods move—and where promotion assistance might be helpful.

Automatic computer ordering is a natural outgrowth of such systems. McKesson Corp.—a large wholesaler of drug products—gave computers to drugstores to keep track of inventory and place orders directly to McKesson's computer. Once a retailer started using the service, McKesson's share of that store's business usually doubled or tripled. Many competing wholesalers went out of business—and the survivors now use such computerized systems.[14]

Some are not always "open to buy"

Just as manufacturers sometimes try to reduce their inventory—and are "not in the market"—retailers and wholesalers may stop buying for similar reasons. No special promotions or price cuts will make them buy.

In retailing, another factor affects buying. A buyer may be controlled by a miniature profit and loss statement for each department or merchandise line. In an effort to make a profit, the buyer tries to forecast sales, merchandise costs, and expenses. The figure for "cost of merchandise" is the amount the buyer has to spend during the budget period. If the money hasn't been spent, the buyer is **open to buy**—that is, the buyer has budgeted funds that he can spend during the current time period.[15]

Owners or professional buyers may buy

The buyers in small stores—and for many wholesalers—are the owners or managers. There is a very close relationship between buying and selling. In larger operations, buyers may specialize in certain lines—and supervise the salespeople who sell what they buy. These buyers stay in close contact with their customers—*and* with their salespeople. The salespeople are sensitive to the effectiveness of the buyer's efforts—especially when they are on commission. A buyer may even buy some items to satisfy the preferences of his sales force. A successful promotion effort can't ignore these salespeople. The multiple buying influence may make the difference.

As sales volumes rise, a buyer may specialize in buying only—and have no responsibility for sales. Sears is an extreme case. It has a buying department of more than 3,000—supported by a staff department of over 1,400. These are professional buyers—who often know more about prices, quality, and trends in the market than their suppliers. Obviously, they are big potential customers—and should be approached differently than the typical small retailer.

Resident buyers may help a firm's buyers

Resident buyers are independent buying agents who work—in central markets—for several retailer or wholesaler customers in outlying areas. They work in cities like New York, Chicago, Los Angeles, and San Francisco. They buy new styles and fashions—and fill-in items—as their customers run out of stock during the year. Some resident buyers have hundreds of employees—and buy more than $1 billion worth of goods a year.

Resident buying organizations fill a need—helping small channel members (producers and middlemen) who can't afford large sales forces. Resident buyers usually are paid an annual fee—based on the amount they buy.

Committee buying happens, too

In some large companies—especially chains selling foods and drugs—the major buying decisions may be made by a *buying committee*. The seller still calls and gives a "pitch" to a buyer—but the buyer doesn't have final responsibility. The buyer prepares a form summarizing the proposal for a new product. The seller may help complete this form—but probably won't get to present his story to the buying committee in person.

This rational, almost cold-blooded approach reduces the impact of the persuasive salesperson. It has become necessary because of the flood of new products. Consider the problem facing grocery chains. In an average week, up to 250 new items are offered to the buying offices of a large food chain like Safeway. If all were accepted, 10,000 new items would be added during a single year! Obviously, buyers must be hard-headed and impersonal. Food stores reject about 90 percent of the new items presented to them.

Marketing managers for wholesalers and manufacturers must develop good marketing mixes when buying becomes this organized and competitive.

THE GOVERNMENT MARKET

Size and variety

Some marketers avoid the government market because they think that government "red tape" is "more trouble than it's worth." This is a mistake because government is the largest customer group in the United States. About 21 percent of the U.S. gross national product is spent by various government units. Government buyers spend more than $750 *billion* a year—to buy almost every kind of product. They run schools, police departments, and military organizations. They also run supermarkets, public utilities, research laboratories, offices, hospitals, and even liquor stores. Aggressive marketing managers shouldn't ignore government buyers.

Bid buying is common

Many government buyers buy by description—using a required bidding method that is open to public review. Often the government buyers must accept the lowest bid. You can see how important it is for the buyer to accurately describe his need—so he can write a precise and complete specification. Otherwise, sellers may submit a bid that fits the "specs" but doesn't really match what is needed. By law, the buyer might have to accept the low bid—for an unwanted product. Writing specifications is not easy—and buyers usually appreciate the help of well-informed salespeople.

Specification and bidding difficulties aren't problems in all government orders. Some frequently bought items—or items with widely accepted standards—are purchased routinely by simply placing an order at a previously approved price. To share in this business, a supplier must be on the list of "approved suppliers."

Negotiated contracts are common, too

Negotiation (bargaining) is often necessary when products are not standardized. Unfortunately, this is exactly where "favoritism" and "influence" can slip in. Nevertheless, negotiation is an important buying method in government business. Here, a marketing mix must emphasize more than just low price.

Learning what government wants

There are more than 80,000 local government units—school districts, cities, counties, and states—as well as many federal agencies that make purchases. Since most government contracts are advertised, potential suppliers should focus on the government units they want to sell to—and learn their bidding methods.

A marketer can learn a lot about potential government target markets from various government publications. The Federal Government's *Commerce Business Daily* lists most current purchase bid requests. Similarly, the Small Business Administration's *U.S. Purchasing, Specifications, and Sales Directory* explains government procedures—since it wants to encourage competition for its business. State and local governments also offer help. Trade magazines and trade associations provide information on how to reach schools, hospitals, highway departments, park departments, and so on. These are unique target markets—and must be treated as such when developing marketing strategies.[16]

CONCLUSION

In this chapter, we considered the number, size, location, and buying habits of various intermediate customers—to try to identify logical dimensions for segmenting markets. We saw that the nature of the buyer and the buying situation are important. We also saw that the problem-solving models of buyer behavior introduced in Chapter 6 apply here—with modifications.

The chapter emphasized buying in the industrial market—because more is known about manufacturers' buying behavior. We discussed some differences in buying by retailers and wholesalers. The government market was described as an extremely large, complex set of markets that offer opportunities for target marketers.

A clear understanding of intermediate customer buying behavior can aid marketing strategy planning. And since there are fewer intermediate customers than final consumers, it may even be possible to develop a unique strategy for each potential customer.

Questions and Problems

1. Discuss the importance of thinking "target marketing" when analyzing intermediate customer markets. How easy is it to isolate homogeneous market segments in these markets?

2. Explain how SIC Codes might be helpful in evaluating and understanding industrial markets.

3. Compare and contrast the problem-solving approaches used by final consumers and by industrial buyers.

4. Describe the situations that would lead to the use of the three different buying processes for a particular product—such as computer tapes.

5. Compare and contrast the buying processes of final consumers and industrial buyers.

6. Briefly discuss why a marketing manager should think about who is likely to be involved in the "buying center" for a particular industrial purchase. Is there anything like the buying center in consumer buying? Explain your answer.

7. Distinguish among the four methods of eval-

uating and buying (inspection, sampling, etc.) and indicate which would probably be most suitable for furniture, baseball gloves, coal, and pencils—assuming that some intermediate customer is the buyer.

8.   Discuss the advantages and disadvantages of reciprocity from the industrial buyer's point of view. Are the advantages and disadvantages merely reversed from the seller's point of view?

9.   Is it always advisable to buy the highest quality product?

10.   Discuss how much latitude an industrial buyer has in selecting the specific brand and the specific source of supply for that product, once a product has been requisitioned by some production department. Consider this question with specific reference to pencils, paint for the offices, plastic materials for the production line, a new factory, and a large printing press. How should the buyer's attitudes affect the seller's marketing mix?

11.   How does the kind of industrial product affect manufacturers' buying habits and practices? Consider lumber for furniture, a lathe, nails for a box factory, and a floor cleaner.

12.   Considering the nature of retail buying, outline the basic ingredients of promotion to retail buyers. Does it make any difference what kinds of products are involved? Are any other factors relevant?

13.   The government market is obviously an extremely large one, yet it is often slighted or even ignored by many firms. "Red tape" is certainly one reason, but there are others. Discuss the situation and be sure to include the possibility of segmenting in your analysis.

14.   Based on your understanding of buying by manufacturers and governments, outline the basic ingredients of promotion to each type of customer. Use two products as examples for each type. Is the promotion job the same for each pair?

Suggested Computer-Aided Problem

7.   Vendor Analysis

Suggested Cases

5.   TOW Chemical Company

7.   Inland Steel Company

Chapter 8

Elements of Product Planning

When You Finish This Chapter, You Should

1. Understand what "Product" really means.

2. Know the key differences between goods and services.

3. Know the differences among the various consumer and industrial product classes.

4. Understand how the product classes can help a marketing manager plan marketing strategies.

5. Understand what branding is and how it can be used in strategy planning.

6. Understand the importance of packaging in strategy planning.

7. Understand the importance of warranties in strategy planning.

8. Recognize the important new terms (shown in red).

The product must satisfy customers—what they want is what they'll get.

Developing the "right" product isn't easy—because customer needs and attitudes keep changing. Further, *most customers want some combination of goods and services in their product.*

A sales rep has just bought a new Ford car—and now has a new need. She wants to listen to her compact disk recordings while traveling. A car CD player is a big purchase for her, so she compares units for the best sound. She doesn't have much spare time, so she plans to buy her CD player from a retailer who provides installation service. She wants a well-known brand—like Pioneer—with proven quality. And she wants to avoid costly repairs—so a good warranty on parts and labor must come with the product.

This buying situation includes many of the topics we'll discuss in this chapter. First, we'll look at how customers see a firm's product. Then, we'll talk about product classes—to help you understand marketing strategy planning better.

We'll also talk about branding, packaging, and warranties. Most products need some packaging. And both goods and services should be branded. A successful marketer wants satisfied customers to know what to ask for the next time they buy.

In summary, we'll talk about the strategy decisions of producers—or middlemen—who make these Product decisions. These decisions are shown in Exhibit 8–1.

Exhibit 8–1   Strategy Planning for Product

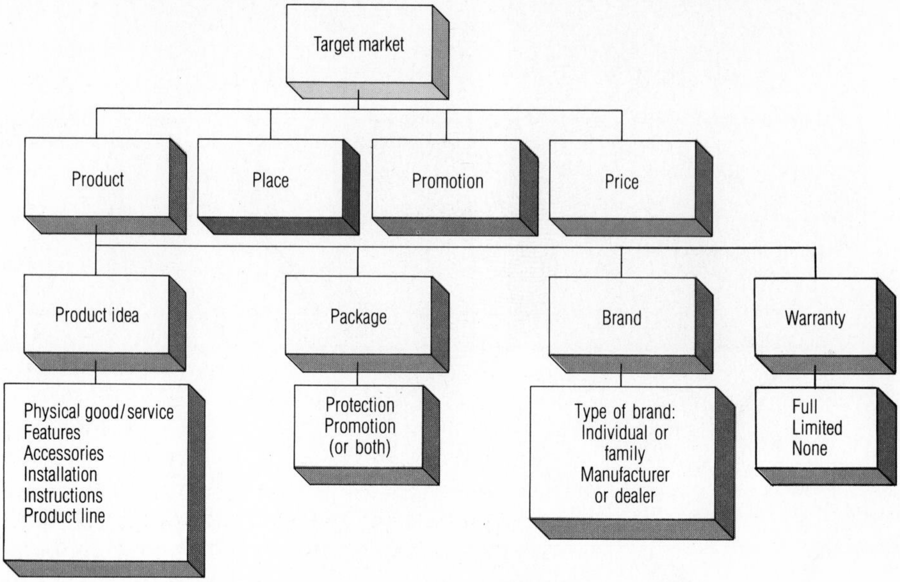

WHAT IS A PRODUCT?

**Customers buy satis-
faction, not parts**

First, we have to define what we mean by a "product." When Chrysler sells a minivan, is it selling a certain number of nuts and bolts, some sheet metal, an engine, and four wheels?

When Procter & Gamble sells a box of Tide laundry detergent is it just selling a box of chemicals?

When Federal Express sells overnight delivery service, is it just selling so much wear and tear on a plane—and so much pilot fatigue?

The answer to all these questions is *no.* Instead, what we are really selling is the satisfaction, use, or profit the customer wants.

All customers care about is that their minivan looks good—and keeps running. They want to clean with their detergent—not analyze it. And when they send something by Federal Express, they really don't care how it gets there. They just want their package to arrive on time.

In the same way, when producers or middlemen buy products, they are interested in the profit they can make from their purchase—through its use or resale—not how the products were made.

Product means the need-satisfying offering of a firm. The idea of "product" as potential customer satisfaction or benefits is very important. Many business managers—trained in the production side of business—get wrapped up in the technical details. They think of Product in terms of physical components—like transitors and screws. These are important to *them,* but they have little effect on the way most customers view the product. What matters to customers is how *they* see the product.

Goods and/or services are the product

Most products are a blend of physical goods *and* services. Exhibit 8–2 emphasizes this by showing that a "product" can range from 100 percent physical good—such as commodities like common nails—to 100 percent service, like a taxi ride.

This bigger view of a product must be understood completely—it's easy to slip into a *physical product* point of view. We want to think of a product in terms of the *needs it satisfies.* If the objective of a firm is to satisfy customer needs, managers must see that service may be part of the product.

Given this view, we won't make a distinction between goods and services—but will call them all *Products.* Sometimes, however, understanding the differences in goods and services can help fine-tune marketing strategy planning. So let's look at some of these differences next.

DIFFERENCES IN GOODS AND SERVICES

How tangible is the product?

Because a good is a physical thing, it can be seen and touched. You can try on a Gant shirt or thumb through the latest *National Geographic* magazine. A good is a *tangible* item. When you buy it, you own it. And it's usually pretty easy to see exactly what you'll get.

Service, on the other hand, is a deed performed by one party for another. When you provide a customer with a service, the customer can't "keep" it. Rather, it's experienced, used, or consumed. You see a Broadway musical, but afterwards all you have is a memory. You ride in a Checker taxi, but you don't own the taxi. Services are *intangible.* You can't "hold" a service. And it may be hard to know exactly what you'll get when you buy it.

Most products are a combination of goods and services. Texaco gas and

Exhibit 8–2   Examples of Possible Blends of Physical Goods and Services in a Product

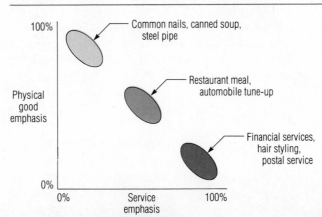

the credit card to buy it are tangible—the credit the card grants is not. A McDonald's hamburger is tangible—but the fast service isn't.

Is the product produced before its sold?

Goods are usually produced in a factory—and then sold. By contrast, services are often sold first, then produced. And they're produced and consumed in the same time frame. Further, goods producers may be far away from the customer, but the service provider often works in the customer's presence.

Services can't be stored or transported

Services can't be stored, and this makes it harder to balance supply and demand. An example explains the problem.

MCI is a major supplier of long-distance telephone services. Even when demand is high—during peak business hours or on Mother's Day—customers expect service. They don't want to hear "Sorry, all lines are busy." So MCI must have enough equipment and employees to deal with peak demand times. But when customers aren't making many calls, MCI's facilities are idle. MCI might be able to save money with less capacity (equipment and people), but then there will be times when they have dissatisfied customers.

It's also hard to have economies of scale when the product is mainly service. Services can't be produced in large, economical quantities and then transported to customers. Also, *services often have to be produced in the customer's presence.* So services often require a duplication of equipment and people—at places where the service is actually provided. E. F. Hutton sells investment advice along with financial "products." That advice could, perhaps, be "produced" more economically in a single building in New York. But E. F. Hutton uses small facilities all over the country—to be conveniently available. Customers want the "personal touch" from the stockbroker who tells them how to invest their money.[1]

WHOLE PRODUCT LINES MUST BE DEVELOPED, TOO

We've been talking about a single product. But most businesses have to offer complete lines of products to satisfy their customers. This makes the job of product planning harder. But if this is what customers want, then complete lines must be offered.

To keep our discussion simple, we'll focus mainly on developing one marketing strategy at a time. But remember that *several* strategies for goods and/or services might have to be planned—to develop an effective marketing program for a whole company.

PRODUCT CLASSES HELP PLAN MARKETING STRATEGIES

It isn't necessary to treat *every* product as unique when planning strategies. Some classes of products require similar marketing mixes. These product classes will be a useful starting point for developing marketing mixes for new products—and evaluating present mixes. Exhibit 8–3 summarizes the product classes.

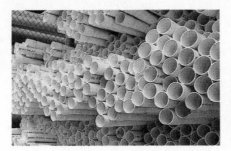 

A good is a physical thing; a service is a deed performed by one party for another.

Product classes start with type of customer

All products fit into one of two broad groups—based on the type of customer that will use them. **Consumer products** are products meant for the final consumer. **Industrial products** are products meant for use in producing other products.

There are product classes within each of these two groups. Consumer product classes are based on *how consumers think about* and shop for products. Industrial product classes are based on *how buyers think about products—and how they'll be used.*

We'll talk about consumer product classes first.

Exhibit 8–3   Product Classes

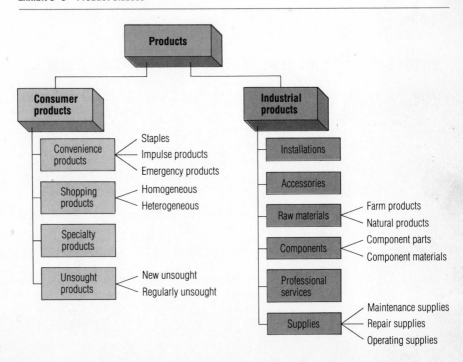

CONSUMER PRODUCTS CLASSES

Consumer products classes are based on the way people buy products. Consumer products divide into four groups: (1) convenience, (2) shopping, (3) specialty, and (4) unsought. See Exhibit 8–4 for a summary of how these product classes relate to marketing mixes.[2]

CONVENIENCE PRODUCTS—PURCHASED QUICKLY WITH LITTLE EFFORT

Convenience products are products a consumer needs but isn't willing to spend much time or effort shopping for. These products are bought often, require little service or selling, don't cost much, and may even be bought by habit.

Convenience products are of three types—staples, impulse products, and emergency products—again based on *how customers think about products*— not the features of the products themselves.

Staples—purchased regularly, by habit

Staples are convenience products that are bought often and routinely— without much thought. Examples include most packaged foods used frequently in every household. Staples are usually sold in convenient places like food stores, discount stores, or vending machines. Branding is important with staples. It helps customers cut shopping effort and encourages repeat buying of satisfying brands.

Impulse products— bought immediately on sight

Impulse products are convenience products that are bought quickly—as *unplanned* purchases—because of a strongly felt need. True impulse products are items that the customer had not planned to buy, decides to buy on sight, may have bought the same way many times before, and wants "right now." An ice cream seller at a beach sells impulse products. If sun bathers don't buy an ice cream bar, the need goes away, and the purchase won't be made later.

Exhibit 8–4   *Consumer Products Classes and Marketing Mix Planning*

---

1. Convenience products.
   a. Staples—need maximum exposure—need widespread distribution at low cost.
   b. Impulse products—need maximum exposure—need widespread distribution but with assurance of preferred display or counter position.
   c. Emergency products—need widespread distribution near probable point of use.
2. Shopping products.
   a. Homogeneous—need enough exposure to facilitate price comparison.
   b. Heterogeneous—need adequate representation in major shopping districts or large shopping centers near other, similar shopping products.
3. Specialty products—can have limited availability, but in general should be treated as a convenience or shopping product (in whichever category product would normally be included), to reach persons not yet sold on its specialty products status.
4. Unsought products—need attention directed to product and aggressive promotion in outlets, or must be available in places where similar products would be sought.

This is important because it affects Place—and the whole marketing mix—for impulse products. If the buyer doesn't see an impulse item at the "right" time, the sale may be lost. As a result, impulse products are put where they will be seen—near check-out counters or in other heavy traffic areas of a store. Gum, candy bars, and magazines are often sold this way in grocery stores. And life insurance is sold at convenient booths—or vending machines—in airports.[3]

Emergency products—purchased only when urgently needed

Emergency products are convenience products that are purchased immediately when the need is great. The consumer doesn't have time to shop around. Price isn't important. Examples are ambulance services, umbrellas or raincoats during a rainstorm, or a bag of ice just before a party.

Meeting customers' emergency needs may require a different marketing mix—especially regarding Place. Some small neighborhood stores carry "emergency" products to meet these needs—staying open "7 till 11" and stocking "fill-in" items like milk and bread. A wrecker service for cars is available 24 hours a day. Customers don't mind the higher prices charged for these products because they think of these products as "emergencies."

SHOPPING PRODUCTS—ARE COMPARED

Shopping products are products that a customer feels are worth the time and effort to compare with competing products.

Shopping products divide into two types—depending on what customers are comparing: (1) homogeneous and (2) heterogeneous shopping products.

Homogeneous shopping products—the price must be right

Homogeneous shopping products are shopping products the customer sees as basically the same—and wants at the lowest price. Some customers feel that certain sizes and types of refrigerators, television sets, washing machines, and even cars are very similar. They're shopping for the best price.

Firms may try to emphasize their product differences. However, if the customers don't believe these differences are real, they'll just look at price.

Even some inexpensive items like butter and coffee may be thought of as homogeneous shopping products. *Some* customers carefully read food store ads for the lowest prices—and then go from store to store getting the items. They don't do this for staples.

Heterogeneous shopping products—must be right

Heterogeneous shopping products are shopping products the customer sees as different—and wants to inspect for quality and suitability. Examples are furniture, clothing, dishes, and some cameras. Quality and style are more important than price.

For non-standardized products, it's harder to compare prices. Once the customer has found the right product, price may not matter—as long as it's "reasonable."

Branding may be less important for heterogeneous shopping products. The more consumers want to make their own comparisons of price and quality, the less they rely on brand names and labels. Some retailers carry competing brands so consumers don't have to go to a competitor to compare items.

Often the buyer of heterogeneous shopping products not only wants—but expects—some kind of help in buying. And if the product is expensive, the buyer may want extra service—such as alteration of clothing or installation of appliances.

SPECIALTY PRODUCTS—NO SUBSTITUTES PLEASE!

Specialty products are consumer products that the customer really wants—and makes a special effort to find. Shopping for a specialty product doesn't mean comparing—the buyer wants that special product and is willing to search for it. It is not the extent of searching, but the customer's *willingness* to search—that makes it a specialty product.

Don't want substitutes!

Specialty products don't have to be expensive, once-in-a-lifetime purchases. Most of us have waited for a specific barber or hairdresser—who provides a "just right" haircut. *Any* branded item that consumers insist on by name is a specialty product. Consumers have been observed asking for a drug product by its brand name and—when offered a chemically identical substitute—actually leaving the store in anger.

UNSOUGHT PRODUCTS—NEED PROMOTION

Unsought products are consumer products that potential customers do not yet want or know they can buy. Therefore, they don't search for them at all. In fact, consumers probably won't buy these products if they see them—unless Promotion can show their value.

There are two types of unsought products. **New unsought products** are products offering really new ideas that potential customers don't know about yet. Informative promotion can help convince customers to accept or even seek out the products—ending their unsought status. When Litton first introduced microwave ovens, customers didn't know what the oven could do. Promotion showed the benefits offered by the new product—and now many consumers buy them.

Regularly unsought products are products—like gravestones, life insurance, and encyclopedias—that stay unsought but not unbought forever. There may be a need—but the potential customers are not motivated to satisfy it. And there probably is little hope that these products will move out of the unsought class for most consumers. For this kind of product, personal selling is *very* important.

ONE PRODUCT MAY BE SEEN AS SEVERAL CONSUMER PRODUCTS

We have been looking at product classes *one at a time*. But the same product might be seen in different ways by different target markets—at the same time. Each of these markets might need a different marketing mix.

A tale of four motels

Motels are a good example of a service that can be seen as *four different* kinds of consumer products. Some tired motorists are satisfied with the first motel they come to—a convenience product. Others shop for just basic facilities at the lowest price—a homogeneous shopping product. Some shop for the kind of place they want at a fair price—a heterogeneous shopping product. And others study tourist guides, talk with traveling friends, and phone ahead to reserve a place in a recommended motel—a specialty product.

Perhaps one motel could satisfy *all* potential customers. But it would be hard to produce a marketing mix attractive to everyone—easy access for convenience, good facilities at the right price for shopping product buyers, and qualities special enough to attract the specialty product travelers. As a result, different kinds of motels at first seem to be competing with each other. But they're really aiming at different markets.

Of course, marketing strategy planners would like to know more about potential customers than how they buy specific products. But these classes are a good place to start strategy planning.

INDUSTRIAL PRODUCTS ARE DIFFERENT

Industrial product classes help in developing marketing mixes, too—since industrial firms use a logical system of buying related to these product classes.

Before looking at industrial product *differences,* however, we will note some important *similarities* that affect marketing strategy planning.

One demand derived from another

The big difference in industrial products markets is **derived demand**—the demand for industrial products is derived from the demand for final consumer products. For example, auto manufacturers buy about one-fifth of all steel products. Even a steel company with a good marketing mix will lose sales to the auto manufacturers if demand for cars is down.[4]

Price increases might not reduce quantity purchased

The fact that demand for most industrial products is derived means that total *industry* demand for many industrial products will be fairly inelastic. To satisfy their customers' needs, industrial firms buy what they need to produce their own products—almost regardless of price, assuming they can still make a profit. Even if the cost of buttons doubles, for example, the shirt producer needs them. And the increased cost of the buttons won't have much effect on the price of the shirt—or on the number of shirts final consumers demand.

But suppliers may face almost pure competition

Although the total industry demand for industrial products may be inelastic, the demand facing *individual sellers* may be extremely elastic. Further, industrial buyers make the market as competitive as they can. Their job is to buy as economically as possible—so they are quick to tell suppliers when competitors offer lower prices.

Tax treatment affects buying, too

How a firm's accountants—and the tax laws—treat a purchase is also important to industrial customers. A **capital item** is a long-lasting product that can be used and depreciated for many years. Often it's very expensive. The customer pays for the capital item when he buys it, but for tax purposes the cost is spread over a number of years. This may increase current profits—and taxes—as well as reducing the cash available for other purchases.

An **expense item** is a product whose total cost is treated as a business expense in the year it's purchased. This reduces current profits and taxes, but it doesn't affect long-run profits. Business managers think about how their decisions affect taxes and profits—and this affects the way they look at the products they buy.

INDUSTRIAL PRODUCTS CLASSES—HOW THEY ARE DEFINED

Industrial products classes are based on how buyers see products—and how the products are used. Capital items are treated differently than expense items. Products that become a part of a firm's own product are seen differently from those that only aid production. Finally, the size of a particular purchase can make a difference. A band-saw might be a very big purchase (installation) for a small cabinet shop but a small item (accessory) for a large furniture maker like Drexel.

The classes of industrial products are: (1) installations, (2) accessories, (3) raw materials, (4) component parts and materials, (5) supplies, and (6) professional services. See Exhibit 8–5 for a summary of how these product classes are related to marketing mix planning.

Exhibit 8–5   Industrial Products and Marketing Mix Planning

1. Installations.
   a. *Buildings (used) and land rights*—need widespread and/or knowledgeable contacts, depending on specialized nature of product.
   b. *Buildings (new)*—need technical and experienced personal contact, probably at top-management level (multiple buying influence).
   c. *Major equipment.*
      i. Custom-made—need technical (design) contacts by person able to visualize and design applications, and present to high-level and technical management.
      ii. Standard—need experienced (not necessarily highly technical) contacts by person able to visualize applications and present to high-level and technical management.
2. Accessory equipment—need fairly widespread and numerous contacts by experienced and sometimes technically trained personnel.
3. Raw materials.
   a. *Farm products*—need contacts with many small farmer producers and fairly widespread contact with users.
   b. *Natural products*—need fairly widespread contacts with users.
4. Component parts and materials—need technical contacts to determine specifications required—widespread contacts usually not necessary.
5. Supplies.
   a. *Maintenance*—need very widespread distribution for prompt delivery.
   b. *Repairs*—need widespread distribution for some, and prompt service from factory for others (depends on customers' preferences).
   c. *Operating supplies*—need fair to widespread distribution for prompt delivery.
6. Professional services—most need very widespread availability.

INSTALLATIONS—MAJOR CAPITAL ITEMS

Installations are important long-lived capital items—buildings, land rights, and major equipment. One-of-a-kind installations—like buildings and custom-made equipment—generally require special negotiations for each sale. Standard major equipment is more homogeneous—and is treated more routinely. All installations, however, are important enough to require high-level—and even top-management—consideration.

Small number of customers at any one time

Installations are long-lasting products—so they aren't bought very often. The number of potential buyers *at any particular time* is usually small. For custom-made machines, there may be only five potential customers—compared to a thousand or more potential buyers for similar standard machines.

Potential customers are generally in the same industry. Their plants are likely to be near each other—which makes personal selling easier. The textile industry, for example, is heavily concentrated in and around North Carolina. The aircraft industry—from a world view—is in the United States.

Buying needs basically economic

Buying needs are basically economic—and concerned with the performance of the installation over its expected life. After comparing expected performance to present costs and figuring interest, the expected return on capital can be determined. Yet emotional needs—such as a desire for industry leadership and status—also may be involved.

Installations may have to be leased or rented

Since installations are relatively expensive, some target markets prefer to lease or rent the product. Leasing makes it easier for a firm to make changes, if necessary. For example, many firms lease computers so they can expand to bigger systems as the firm grows. Leasing also shifts a capital item to an expense.[5]

Specialized services are needed as part of the product

Since the expected return on an installation is based on efficient operation, the supplier may provide special services to assure this efficiency. Firms selling equipment to dentists, for example, may assign a service representative to stay with the dentist until he can use the equipment easily. They will even provide plans for an office building to hold the dental equipment. The cost is included in the price.

ACCESSORIES—IMPORTANT BUT SHORT–LIVED CAPITAL ITEMS

Accessories are short-lived capital items—the tools and equipment used in production or office activities. Examples include Canon's small copy machines, Rockwell's portable drills, Clark's electric lift trucks, IBM's electric typewriters, and Steelcase filing cabinets.

Since these products cost less—and last a shorter time—than installations, multiple buying influence is less important. Operating people and purchasing agents—rather than top managers—may do the buying.

More target markets requiring different marketing mixes

Accessories are more standardized than installations. And they are usually needed by more customers! Prime Computer Company's special-purpose computer-aided design system, for example, might cost $500,000 and be sold as a custom installation for NASA or a state highway department. But its small "desk-top" systems are accessories for many types of businesses—architects, engineering firms, and others. And these different types of customers are likely to be spread out geographically. The larger number of different kinds of customers—and increasing competition—mean that accessories need different marketing mixes than installations.

Might want to lease or rent

Some target markets prefer to lease or rent accessories because the cost can be treated as an expense. A producer of electric lift trucks, for example, expanded sales by selling the basic trucks—and then charging for the expensive battery system by the amount of time it was used. This increased sales because, as one manager said: "Nobody worries about costs that are buried as operating expenses."

RAW MATERIALS—FARM PRODUCTS AND NATURAL PRODUCTS ARE EXPENSE ITEMS

Become part of a physical good

Raw materials are unprocessed expense items—such as logs, iron ore, wheat, and cotton—that are handled as little as needed to move them to the next production process. Unlike installations and accessories, *raw materials become part of a physical good*—and are expense items.

We can divide raw materials into two types: (1) farm products and (2) natural products. **Farm products** are grown by farmers—examples are oranges, wheat, strawberries, sugar cane, cattle, hogs, poultry, eggs, and milk. **Natural products** are products that occur in nature—such as fish and game, lumber, copper, zinc, iron ore, oil, and coal.

Farm products involve grading, storing, and transporting

The need for grading is one of the important differences between farm products and other industrial products. Nature produces what it will—and someone must sort and grade the raw materials to satisfy various market segments. Some of the top grades of fruits and vegetables find their way into consumer products markets. The lower grades are treated as industrial products—and used in juices, sauces, and soup.

Most farm products are produced seasonally—yet the demand is fairly constant. As a result, storing and transporting are important.

Buyers of industrial products usually don't seek suppliers. This complicates the marketing of farm products. The many small farms usually are widely scattered—sometimes far from potential buyers. Selling direct to final users would be difficult. So Place and Promotion are important in marketing mixes for these products.

NATURAL PRODUCTS—QUANTITIES ARE ADJUSTABLE

While farm products have many producers, natural products are usually produced by fewer and larger companies. There are some exceptions—such as the coal and lumber industries, which face almost pure competition—but oligopoly conditions are common for natural products.

The supply of natural products harvested or mined in any one year can be adjusted up or down—at least within limits. And storage is less of a problem—since few are perishable.

As with farm products, buyers of natural products usually need specific grades and dependable supply sources—to keep production rolling in their own plants. Large buyers, therefore, often try to control—or even buy—their supply sources. Some control can be gained through contracts—perhaps negotiated by top-level managers.

COMPONENT PARTS AND MATERIALS—IMPORTANT EXPENSE ITEMS

The whole is no better than . . .

Components are processed expense items that become part of a finished product. They need more processing than raw materials. They require different marketing mixes than raw materials—even though they both become part of a finished product.

Component *parts* include items that are (1) finished and ready for assembly or (2) nearly finished—requiring only minor processing (such as grinding or polishing) before being assembled into the final product. Disk drives included in personal computers, car batteries, and motors for appliances are examples.

Component *materials* are items such as wire, paper, textiles, or cement. They have already been processed—but must be processed further before becoming part of the final product.

Components must meet specifications

Some components are custom-made. Much negotiation may be needed between the engineering staffs of both buyer and seller to arrive at the right specifications. If the price of the item is high—or if it is extremely important in the final product—top managers may be involved.[6]

Other components are produced to commonly accepted standards or specifications—and produced in quantity. Production people in the buying firm may specify quality—but the purchasing agent does the buying. And he will want several dependable sources of supply.

Since components become part of the firm's own product, quality is extremely important. The buyer's own name and whole marketing mix are at stake. Because of this, a buyer tries to buy from sources that help assure a good product.

SUPPLIES—SUPPORT MAINTENANCE, REPAIR, AND OPERATIONS

Supplies are expense items that do not become a part of a finished product. Buyers may treat such items less seriously.

They are called MRO supplies

Supplies can be divided into three types: (1) maintenance, (2) repair, and (3) operating supplies—giving them their common name "MRO supplies."[7]

Maintenance supplies include such things as paint, nails, light bulbs, and sweeping compounds. Repair supplies are parts—like filters, bearings, and gears—needed to fix worn or broken equipment. Operating supplies include lubricating oils and greases, grinding compounds, typing paper, ink, pencils, and paper clips.

Important operating supplies

Some operating supplies are needed regularly—and in large amounts. They receive special treatment from buyers. Some companies buy coal and fuel oil in carload or tank car quantities. Usually there are several sources for such homogeneous products—and large volumes may be purchased in highly competitive markets. Or contracts may be negotiated—perhaps by high-level managers.

Maintenance and small operating supplies

These items are like convenience products. They're so numerous that a buyer can't possibly be an expert in buying all of them.

Each requisition for maintenance and small operating supplies may be for relatively few items. A purchase order may amount to only $1 or $2. Although the cost of handling a purchase order may be from $5 to $10, the item will be ordered—because it's needed—but not much time will be spent on it.

Branding may become important for such products. It makes product identification and buying easier for such "nuisance" items. Width of assortment and

Alcoa's aluminum wheels are sold as components to auto and truck makers. Burroughs sells a complete line of operating supplies for computers.

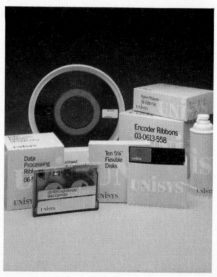

the seller's dependability are important when buying supplies. Middlemen usually handle the many supply items.

Repair supplies

The original supplier of installations or accessories may be the only source of supply for repairs or parts. The cost of repairs in relation to the cost of a production breakdown may be so small that buyers willingly pay the price charged—whatever it is.

PROFESSIONAL SERVICES—PAY TO GET IT DONE

Professional services are specialized services that support a firm's operations. They are usually expense items. Engineering or management consulting services can improve the plant layout—or the company's operation. Design services can supply designs for a physical plant, products, and promotion materials. Maintenance services can handle window-cleaning, painting, or general housekeeping.

Here the emphasis is completely on the *service* part of the product. Goods may be supplied, as with food services, but the customer is primarily interested in the service.

Managers compare the cost of buying services outside the firm with the cost of having company people do them. For special skills needed only occasionally, an outsider can be the best source. And service specialists are growing in number in our complex economy.

BRANDING NEEDS A STRATEGY DECISION, TOO

There are so many brands—and we're so used to seeing them—that we take them for granted. In the grocery products area alone, there are more than 40,000 brands. Brands are of great importance to their owners—because they help identify the company's marketing mix—and help consumers recognize the firm's products and advertising. Branding is an important decision area that many business people ignore. So we'll treat it in some detail.

What is branding, brand name, and trademark

Branding means the use of a name, term, symbol, or design—or a combination of these—to identify a product. It includes the use of brand names, trademarks, and practically all other means of product identification.

Brand name has a narrower meaning. A **brand name** is a word, letter, or a group of words or letters.

Trademark is a legal term. A **trademark** includes only those words, symbols, or marks that are legally registered for use by a single company.

The word *Buick* can be used to explain these differences. The Buick car is branded under the brand name "Buick" (whether it is spoken or printed in any manner). When "Buick" is printed in a certain kind of script, however, it becomes a trademark. A trademark need not be attached to the product. It can be a word—or symbol. Exhibit 8–6 shows some common trademarks.

Exhibit 8–6   Recognized Trademarks and Symbols Help in Promotion

These differences may seem technical. But they are very important to business firms that spend a lot of money to protect and promote their brands.

BRANDING—WHY IT DEVELOPED

Brands meet needs

Branding started during the Middle Ages—when craft guilds (similar to labor unions) and merchant guilds formed to control the quantity and quality of production. Each producer had to mark his goods—so output could be cut back when necessary. This also meant that poor quality—which might reflect unfavorably on other guild products and discourage future trade—could be traced back to the guilty producer. Early trademarks also protected the buyer—who could now know the source of the product.

More recently, firms use brands mainly for identification. The earliest and most aggressive brand promoters in America were the patent medicine companies. They were joined by the food manufacturers—who grew in size after the Civil War. Some of the brands started in the 1860s and 1870s (and still going strong) are Borden's Condensed Milk, Quaker Oats, Pillsbury's Best Flour, and Ivory Soap.

Well-recognized brands make shopping easier. Think of trying to buy groceries, for example, if you had to evaluate the advantages and disadvantages of each of 10,000 items every time you went to a supermarket.

Many customers are willing to buy new things—but having gambled and won, they like to buy a "sure thing" the next time.

CONDITIONS FAVORABLE TO BRANDING

Most marketing managers accept branding—and are concerned with seeing that their brands succeed.

The following conditions are favorable to successful branding:

1. The product is easy to identify by brand or trademark.
2. The product quality is the best "value" for the price. And the quality is easy to maintain.
3. Dependable and widespread availability is possible. When customers start using a brand, they want to be able to continue using it.
4. The demand for the general product class is large.
5. The demand is strong enough so that the market price can be high enough to make the branding effort profitable.
6. There are economies of scale. If the branding is really successful, costs should drop and profits should increase.
7. Favorable shelf locations or display space in stores will help. Retailers can control this when they brand their own products. Producers must use aggressive salespeople to get favorable positions.

ACHIEVING BRAND FAMILIARITY IS NOT EASY

Brand acceptance must be earned with a good product and regular promotion. **Brand familiarity** means how well customers recognize and accept a company's brand. The degree of brand familiarity affects the planning for the rest of the marketing mix—especially where the product should be offered and what promotion is needed.

Five levels of brand familiarity

Five levels of brand familiarity are useful for strategy planning: (1) rejection, (2) non-recognition, (3) recognition, (4) preference, and (5) insistence.

Some brands have been tried and found wanting. **Brand rejection** means potential customers won't buy a brand—unless its image is changed. Rejection may suggest a change in the product—or perhaps only a shift to target customers who have a better image of the brand. Overcoming negative images is difficult—and can be very expensive.

 Brand non-recognition means that final customers don't recognize a brand at all—even though middlemen may use the brand name for identification and inventory control. Examples here are school supplies, novelties, and inexpensive dinnerware.

Brand recognition means that customers remember the brand. This can be a big advantage if there are many "nothing" brands on the market.

Most branders would like to win **brand preference**—which means target customers will usually choose the brand over other brands—perhaps because of habit or past experience.

Brand insistence means customers insist on a firm's branded product and are willing to search for it. This is an objective of many target marketers.

The right brand name can help

A good brand name can help build brand familiarity. It can help tell something important about the company or its product. Exhibit 8–7 lists some characteristics of a good brand name. Some successful brand names seem to break all these rules. Many of these names, however, got started when there was less competition.

Exhibit 8–7   Characteristics of a Good Brand Name

Short and simple.

Easy to spell and read.

Easy to recognize and remember.

Pleasing when read or heard—and easy to pronounce.

Pronounceable in only one way.

Pronounceable in all languages (for goods to be exported).

Always timely (does not get out of date).

Adaptable to packaging or labeling needs.

Legally available for use (not in use by another firm).

Not offensive, obscene, or negative.

Suggestive of product benefits.

Adaptable to any advertising medium (especially billboards and television).

PROTECTING BRAND NAMES AND TRADEMARKS

Common law protects the rights of the owners of trademarks and brand names. And the Lanham Act of 1946 spells out the exact method of protecting trademarks—and what kinds of marks (including brand names) can be protected. The law applies to products shipped in interstate or foreign commerce.

The Lanham Act does not force registration. But a good reason to register under the Lanham Act is to protect a trademark to be used in international markets. Before a trademark can be protected in a foreign country, some nations require that it be registered in its home country.

You must protect your own

A brand can be a real asset to a company. Each firm should try to see that its brand doesn't become a common descriptive term for its kind of product. When this happens, the brand name or trademark becomes public property. The owner loses all rights to it. This happened with the names cellophane, aspirin, shredded wheat, and kerosene. There was concern that "Teflon" and "Scotch Tape" might become public property. And Miller Brewing Company tried—unsuccessfully—to protect its Lite beer by suing other brewers who wanted to use the word "light."[8]

WHAT KIND OF BRAND TO USE?

Keep it in the family

Branders of more than one product must decide whether they are going to use a **family brand**—the same brand name for several products—or individual brands for each product. Examples of family brands are the Kraft food products, the three A&P brands (Ann Page, Sultana, and Iona), and Sears Craftsman tools and Kenmore appliances.

The use of the same brand for many products makes sense if all are similar in type and quality. The goodwill attached to one or two products may help the others, thus cutting promotion costs. It also tends to build loyalty to the family brand—and makes it easier to introduce new products.

A *special* kind of family brand is a **licensed brand**—a well-known brand that sellers pay a fee to use. For example, the creators of "Sesame Street" allow different sellers to brand their products with the Sesame Street name and trademark—for a fee. In this case, many different companies are in the "family."[9]

Individual brands for outside and inside competition

A company uses **individual brands**—separate brand names for each product—when its products vary in quality or type. If the products are really different—such as Elmer's glue and Borden's ice cream—individual brands are better.

Sometimes firms use individual brands to encourage competition within the company. Each brand is managed by a different group within the firm. Management feels that internal competition keeps everyone alert. The theory is that if anyone is going to take business away, it ought to be one of the company's own brands. This kind of competition is found among General Motors' brands. Chevrolet, Pontiac, Oldsmobile, Buick, and even Cadillac compete with each other in some markets.

Generic brands for "commodities"

Products seen by consumers as "commodities" may be difficult to brand. Some manufacturers and middlemen meet this problem with **generic products**—products with no brand at all other than identification of their contents and the manufacturer or middleman. Generic products are most common for staples—especially food products and drug items. Typically, these are offered in plain packages at lower prices.

Some generic products—like paper towels—have been well accepted by some target markets. These consumers don't see big differences among these products—except in price. When generic products were first introduced, many critics predicted that they wouldn't last. It now appears that some products will continue to be offered this way.[10]

WHO SHOULD DO THE BRANDING

Manufacturer brands versus dealer brands

Manufacturer brands are brands created by manufacturers. These are sometimes called "national brands"—because the brand is promoted all across the country or in large regions. Such brands include Kellogg's, Stokely, Whirlpool, Ford, and IBM. And creators of service-oriented firms—like McDonald's, Orkin Pest Control, and Midas Muffler—spend a lot of money promoting their brands in the same way that other producers do.

Dealer brands are brands created by middlemen. These are sometimes called "private brands." Examples of dealer brands include the brands of Kroger, Ace Hardware, Sears, and Radio Shack. Some of these are advertised and distributed more widely than many "national brands."

Who's winning the battle of the brands?

The **battle of the brands** is the competition between dealer brands and manufacturer brands. The "battle" is just a question of popularity—and who will control the market.

At one time, manufacturer brands were much more popular than dealer brands. But they may be losing the battle. Sales of dealer brands have continued to grow. Now sales are about equal—and rising. Middlemen have some advantages in this battle. They can control shelf space. And they often price their own brands lower. Customers benefit from the "battle." Price differences between manufacturer brands and well-known dealer brands have already narrowed due to the competition.[11]

PACKAGING NEEDS A STRATEGY DECISION, TOO

Packaging involves protecting and promoting the product. Packaging can be important to both sellers and customers. It can make a product more convenient to use or store—and prevent spoiling or damage. Good packaging makes products easier to identify—and promotes the brand.

Packaging can make the difference

A new package can make the important difference in a new marketing strategy—by meeting customers' needs better. A better box, wrapper, can, or bottle may help create a "new" product—or a new market. Valvoline put automobile oil in screw-top plastic containers—to appeal to consumers in self-service gas stations. Frozen vegetables in one-pound packages served larger families better. The little 10-ounce packages were too small—but two packages held too much.

Packaging can make the important difference in a marketing strategy—by meeting customer needs better.

Multiple packs were the basis of a new marketing strategy, too. Surveys showed that some customers were buying several units at a time of products like soft drinks, beer, and frozen orange juice. Producers tried packaging in four-, six-, and eight-packs—and have been very successful.

Sometimes a new package improves a product by making it easier to use. Kodak increased sales of its light-sensitive X-ray films by packing each sheet in a separate foil pack—making it easier to handle. Lean Cuisine frozen dinners are now packaged in containers that can be used in microwave ovens.

Packaging can improve product safety: shampoo comes in plastic bottles that won't break if dropped in the shower.

Packaging sends a message—even for services

Packaging can tie the product to the rest of the marketing strategy. Expensive perfume can come in a crystal bottle—adding to the prestige image. L'eggs pantyhose—in plastic eggs—makes the product stand out in store displays and reminds customers of the name.

The appearance of service providers or the area where a service is provided can be a form of "packaging." Disneyland sends the message that it is a good place for family vacations by keeping all its parks spotless. Lawyers put their awards and diplomas on the wall—to show that they provide a high-quality product.

May lower total distribution costs

Better protective packaging is very important to producers and wholesalers. They often have to pay the cost of goods damaged in shipment—and costs for settling such claims. Goods damaged in shipment also may delay production—or cause lost sales.

Retailers need good packaging, too. Packaging that provides better protection can reduce storing costs—by cutting breakage, preventing discoloration, and stopping theft. Packages that are easier to handle can cut costs by speeding price marking, improving handling and display, and saving space.

A good package sometimes gives a firm more promotion effect than it could possibly afford with advertising. The package is seen regularly in retail stores—where customers are actually doing the buying. The package may be seen by many more potential customers than the company's advertising. An attractive package may speed turnover so much that total costs will drop as a percentage of sales.

Or . . . may raise total costs

In other cases, total distribution costs may rise because of packaging. But customers may be more satisfied because the packaging improves the product—by offering much greater convenience or reducing waste.

Packaging costs as a percentage of a producer's selling price vary widely—ranging from 1 to 70 percent. Let's look at sugar as an example. When sugar producers—like Domino—sell sugar in 100-pound bags, the cost of packaging sugar is only 1 percent of the selling price. In two- and five-pound cartons, it's 25 to 30 percent. And for individual serving packages, it's 50 percent. But consumers don't want to haul a 100-pound bag home. They're quite willing to pay for more convenient packages. Restaurants use one-serving envelopes of sugar—finding that they reduce the cost of filling and washing sugar bowls—and that customers prefer the more sanitary little packages. In both cases, packaging adds value to the product. Actually, it creates new products—and new marketing strategies.[12]

WHAT IS SOCIALLY RESPONSIBLE PACKAGING?

Some consumers say that some package designs are misleading—perhaps on purpose. Who hasn't been surprised by a candy bar half the size of the package! Others feel that the great variety of packages makes it hard to compare values. And some are concerned about whether the packages are biodegradable—or can be recycled.

Laws reduce confusion—and clutter

Consumer criticism finally led to passage of the **Federal Fair Packaging and Labeling Act** (of 1966)—which requires that consumer products be clearly labeled in easy-to-understand terms—to give consumers more information. The law also calls on government agencies and industry to try to reduce the number of package sizes—and to make labels more useful.[13]

Food products must now list nutrition information—as well as weight or volume. But there is some question whether many consumers understand this information—or what to do with it—or even if they want this information. At the same time, it is difficult or impossible to provide the kind of information they *do* want—for example, regarding taste and texture.

Unit-pricing is a possible help

Some retailers—especially large supermarket chains—make it easier for consumers to compare packages with different weights or volumes. They use **unit-pricing**—which means placing the price per ounce (or some other standard measure) on or near the product. This makes price comparison easier—and some consumers do appreciate this service.[14]

Universal product codes allow more information

To speed the handling of fast-selling products, government and industry representatives have developed a **universal product code (UPC)**—which identifies each product with marks that can be "read" by electronic scanners. Through a computer, each code is related to the type of product—and its price. Supermarkets and other high-volume retailers have been eager to use these codes. They speed the check-out process—and get rid of the need for marking the price on every item. They also reduce errors by cashiers—and make it easy to control inventory and track sales of specific products. Exhibit 8–8 shows a universal product code mark.

Exhibit 8–8   An Illustration of a Universal Product Code

Some consumers don't like the codes because they can't compare prices—either in the store or at home. To solve this problem, most new systems now include a printed receipt showing the prices of products bought. In the future, the codes probably will become even more widely used—because they do lower operating costs.[15]

GIVING A WARRANTY IS A STRATEGY DECISION, TOO

Warranty should mean something

Common law says that producers must stand behind their products. And now the federal **Magnuson-Moss Act** of 1975 says that warranties offered by producers must be clearly written. A **warranty** explains what the seller promises about its product. The warranty does not have to be strong. But Federal Trade Commission (FTC) guidelines do try to make sure that warranties are clear and definite—and not "deceptive" or "unfair." Some firms used to say their products were "fully warranted" or "absolutely guaranteed." The time period wasn't stated. And the meaning of the warranty was not clear.

Now a company has to make clear whether it offers a "full" or "limited" warranty—if it offers a warranty. And the law defines what "full" means. Also, the warranty must be available for inspection before the purchase. Most firms offer a limited warranty—if they offer one at all.

Some firms use warranties to help create different strategies. They design more quality into their products and offer stronger warranties or replacement—not just repair—if problems occur. In other cases, the basic price for a product may include a warranty for a short time period—or cover parts but not labor. Consumers who want more or better protection pay extra for an extended warranty—or a service contract.

Customers might like a strong warranty, but it can be very expensive—even economically impossible for small firms. Backing up warranties can present problems, too. Some customers abuse products—and demand a lot of service on warranties. Although manufacturers may be responsible, they may have to depend on reluctant or poorly trained middlemen to do the job. For example, when energy prices began to rise, many consumers bought chain saws to cut their own firewood. To reach this target market, Homelite began to distribute its saws through chain stores like K mart. But Homelite had to set up its own service centers because the retail chains had no repair facilities. In situations like this, it's hard for a small firm to compete with larger firms with many service centers.

Deciding on the warranty is a strategic matter. Specific decisions should be made about what the warranty will cover—and then it should be communicated clearly to the target customers. A warranty can make the difference between success and failure for a whole marketing strategy.[16]

CONCLUSION

In this chapter, we looked at Product very broadly. A Product may not be a physical good at all. It may be a service. Or it may be some combination of goods and services—like a meal at a restaurant. We saw that a firm's Product is what satisfies the needs of its target market. This *may* be a physical good—but also could include a package, brand, installation, repair service, or warranty.

Consumer product and industrial product classes were introduced to simplify your study of marketing—and help in planning marketing mixes. The consumer product classes are based on consumers' buying behavior. Industrial product classes are based on how buyers see and use the products. Knowing these product classes—and learning how marketers handle specific products within these classes—will speed the development of your "marketing sense."

The fact that different people may see the same product in different product classes helps explain why seeming competitors may use very different marketing mixes—and succeed.

Packaging and branding can create new and more satisfying products. Variations in packaging can make a product salable in various target markets. A specific package may have to be developed for each strategy. Packaging offers another way to promote the product—and inform customers.

To customers, the main value of brands is as a guarantee of quality. This leads to repeat purchasing. For marketers, such "routine" buying means lower promotion costs and higher sales.

Should brands be stressed? The decision depends on whether the costs of brand promotion and honoring the brand guarantee can be more

than covered by a higher price or more rapid turnover—or both. The cost of branding may reduce other costs—by reducing pressure on the other three Ps.

Branding gives marketing managers choice. They can add brands—and use individual or family brands. In the end, however, customers express their approval or disapproval of the whole Product (including the brand). The degree of brand familiarity is a measure of the marketing manager's ability to carve out a separate market—and affects Place, Price, and Promotion decisions.

Warranties are also important in strategy planning. A warranty need not be strong—it just has to be clearly stated. But some customers find strong warranties attractive.

So it should be clear that Product is concerned with much more than a physical good or service. The marketing manager must also make good strategy decisions about packaging, branding, and warranties—to succeed in our increasingly competitive marketplaces.

Questions and Problems _____

1. Define, in your own words, what a Product is.

2. Discuss several ways in which physical goods are different from pure services. Give an example of a good and then an example of a service that illustrates each of the differences.

3. What "products" are being offered by an exclusive men's shop? By an airline? By a supermarket? By a new car dealer?

4. What kinds of consumer products are the following: (a) fountain pens, (b) men's shirts, (c) cosmetics? Explain your reasoning and draw a picture of the market in each case to help illustrate your thinking.

5. Consumer services tend to be intangible, and goods tend to be tangible. Use an example to explain how the lack of a physical good in a "pure service" might affect efforts to promote the service.

6. How would the marketing mix for a staple convenience product differ from the one for a homogeneous shopping product? How would the mix for a specialty product differ from the mix for a heterogeneous shopping product? Use examples.

7. Give an example of a health care service that would be an unsought product for most people. Briefly explain why it is an unsought product.

8. In what types of stores would you expect to find: (a) convenience products, (b) shopping products, (c) specialty products, and (d) unsought products?

9. Cite two examples of industrial products that require a substantial amount of service in order to be useful "products."

10. Explain why a new furniture store might want to lease a delivery truck rather than buy it.

11. Would you expect to find any wholesalers selling the various types of industrial products? Are retail stores required (or something like retail stores)?

12. What kinds of industrial products are the following: (*a*) paint, (*b*) dust-collecting and ventilating systems, (*c*) a service that provides hot lunches for an employee cafeteria? Explain your reasoning.

13. How do raw materials differ from other industrial products? Do the differences have any impact on their marketing mixes? If so, what specifically?

14. For the kinds of industrial products described in this chapter, complete the following table (use one or a few well-chosen words).

Products	1	2	3
Installations			
Buildings and			
land rights			
Major equipment			
· Standard			
Custom made			
Accessories			
Raw materials			
Farm products			
Natural products			
Components			
Supplies			
Maintenance and			
small operating			
supplies			
Operating supplies			
Professional services			

1—Kind of distribution facility(ies) needed and functions they will provide.
2—Caliber of salespeople required.
3—Kind of advertising required.

15. Is there any difference between a brand name and a trademark? If so, why is this difference important?

16. Is a well-known brand valuable only to the owner of the brand?

17. Suggest an example of a product and a competitive situation where it would *not* be profitable for a firm to spend large sums of money to establish a brand.

18. Evaluate the suitability of the following brand names: (*a*) Star (sausage), (*b*) Rugged (shoes), (*c*) Shiny (shoe polish), (*d*) Lord Jim (ties).

19. Explain family brands. Sears and A&P use family brands, but they have several different family brands. If the idea is a good one, why don't they have just one brand?

20. What major advantages does a large retail chain get from using its own dealer brand?

21. What does the degree of brand familiarity imply about previous and future promotion efforts? How does the degree of brand familiarity affect the Place and Price variables?

22. You operate a small supermarket with emphasis on manufacturers' brands and have barely been breaking even. Evaluate the proposal of a large wholesaler who offers a full line of dealer-branded groceries at substantially lower prices? Specify any assumptions necessary to obtain a definite answer.

23. Give an example where packaging costs probably: (*a*) lower total distribution costs and (*b*) raise total distribution costs.

Suggested Computer-Aided Problem

8. Branding Decision

Suggested Cases

1. McDonald's

3. Sears' Discover Card

6. Applegate Chevrolet

11. Up With People

Chapter 9

Product Management and New-Product Development

When You Finish This Chapter, You Should

1. Understand how product life cycles affect strategy planning.

2. Know what is involved in designing new products and what "new products" really are.

3. Know about the new-product development process.

4. Know about product liability.

5. Understand the need for product or brand managers.

6. Recognize the important new terms (shown in red).

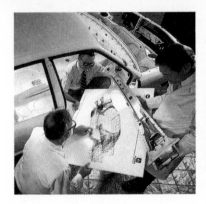

Product management is a dynamic, full-time job for product managers.

The standard-size vacuum cleaner, with its tangle of hoses and cords, has been a symbol of the drudgery of housework for a long time. But in 1979 Black & Decker introduced the Dustbuster—a rechargeable mini-vacuum cleaner. It changed the way consumers attack little messes—like scattered kitty litter and crumbs on the kitchen floor. Black & Decker spent over $3 million on advertising to introduce its new product. By 1985, it had sold more than 10 million Dustbusters. But the Dustbuster success attracted many competitors—with similar products. In fact, some of these products were *too similar*. Black & Decker filed patent-infringement suits against more than a dozen of its competitors.[1]

More music lovers are now buying compact audiodisk players. Experts agree that the disks will soon replace traditional records—just as cassette tapes replaced reel-to-reel tapes a decade ago.

Innovations like these show that products, markets, and competition change over time. This makes marketing management difficult—but exciting. Developing new products and managing existing products in changing conditions is necessary for the success of every firm. In this chapter, we'll look at some important ideas in these areas.

MANAGING PRODUCTS OVER THEIR LIFE CYCLES

Products—like consumers—have life cycles. So product and marketing mix planning are important. Competitors are always developing and copying ideas and products—making existing products out-of-date more quickly than ever.

Product life cycle has four major stages

The **product life cycle** describes the stages a product idea goes through from beginning to end. It is divided into four major stages: (1) market introduction, (2) market growth, (3) market maturity, and (4) sales decline.

A particular firm's marketing mix for a product should change during these stages—for several reasons. Customers' attitudes and needs may change through the course of the product's life cycle. The firm may appeal to entirely different target markets at different stages of the product's life cycle. And the nature of competition moves toward pure competition or oligopoly.

Further, total sales of the product—by all competitors in the industry—vary in each of its four stages. More importantly, the profit picture changes, too. You can see these relationships in Exhibit 9–1. Note that sales and products do not move together over time. *Industry profits start to decline while industry sales are still rising.*[2]

Market introduction— investing in the future

In the **market introduction** stage, sales are low as a new idea is first introduced to a market. Customers aren't looking for the product. They don't even know about it. Informative promotion is needed to tell potential customers about the advantages and uses of the new product.

Even though a firm promotes its new product, it takes time for customers to learn about it. Losses are typical in market introduction—with much money spent for Promotion, Product, and Place development. Money is being invested in the hope of future profits.

Market growth— profits go up and down

In the **market growth** stage, industry sales are growing fast—but industry profits rise and then start falling. The innovator begins to make big profits. But competitors enter the market—each trying to improve on the product design. This results in much product variety. But some competitors just copy the most successful products.

This is the time of biggest profits—*for the industry. But it is also when industry profits begin to decline*—as competition increases. See Exhibit 9–1.

Some firms make big strategy planning mistakes at this stage—by not un-

Exhibit 9–1 Life Cycle of a Typical Product

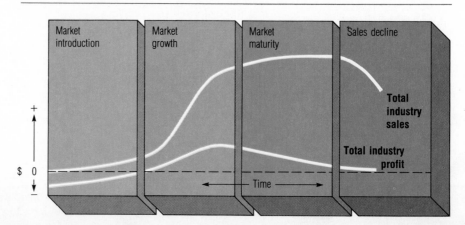

derstanding the product life cycle. They see the big sales and profit opportunities of the early market growth stage—but ignore the competition that will soon follow. When they realize their mistake, it may be too late.

Market maturity— sales level off, profits continue down

The **market maturity** stage is when industry sales level off—and competition gets tougher. Many competitors have entered the race for profits—except in oligopoly. Industry profits continue down during the market maturity stage—because promotion costs rise and some competitors cut prices to attract business. Less efficient firms can't compete with this pressure—and they drop out of the market. Even in oligopoly situations, there's a long-run downward pressure on prices.

New firms may still enter the market at this stage—increasing competition even more. Note that late entries skip the early life-cycle stages—including the profitable market growth stage.

Promotion becomes more important during the market maturity stage. Products may differ only slightly—if at all. Most competitors have discovered the most effective appeals—or copied the leaders. Although each firm may still have its own demand curve, the curves become more elastic—because potential consumers see the various products as almost the same.

In the United States, the markets for most automobiles, TV sets, boats, and many household appliances are in market maturity.[3] This stage may continue for many years—until a basically new product idea comes along. This is true even though individual brands or models may come and go.

Sales decline—a time of replacement

During the **sales decline** stage, new products replace the old. Price competition from dying products increases—but firms with strong brands may make profits almost until the end. These firms have down-sloping demand curves—because they have been able to differentiate their products.

As the new products go through their introduction stage, the old ones may keep some sales—by appealing to the most loyal target customers or those who are slow to try new ideas. These conservative buyers might switch later—smoothing the sales decline.

Product life cycles are getting shorter

The length of a product life cycle may vary from 90 days—in the case of a toy like Rubic's Cube—to possibly 100 years for gas-powered cars.

Although the life of different products varies, in general product life cycles are getting shorter. This is partly due to rapidly changing technology. A top Du Pont manager said: "Lead time is gone . . . there's no company so outstanding technically today that it can expect a long lead time in a new discovery." Du Pont had nylon to itself for 15 years. But in just two years, a major competitor—Celanese Corporation—came out with something very competitive to Delrin—another synthetic fiber discovery that Du Pont hoped would be as important as nylon. Similarly, six months after U.S. Steel came out with a new "thin tin" plate, competitors were out with even better products.[4]

The early bird makes the profits

The increasing speed of product life cycles means that a successful firm must be developing new products all the time. And it must try to have marketing mixes that will make the most of the market growth stage—when profits are highest.

Profits don't necessarily go to the innovator. Sometimes fast copiers of the basic idea will share in the market growth stage. Duncan Hines' new chocolate chip cookies were an instant success. Nabisco, Keebler, Frito-Lay, and other cookie makers followed fast—with product improvements, lower prices—and even more varieties. Within a year, Nabisco's Almost Home brand led the market. At that time, the Duncan Hines brand had lost an estimated $100 million. You can see that copiers can be even faster than the innovator in adapting to the market's needs. Marketers must be flexible but also must fully understand the needs and attitudes of their target markets.[5]

PRODUCT LIFE CYCLES SHOULD BE RELATED TO SPECIFIC MARKETS

Each market should be carefully defined

The way we define a market makes a difference in the way we see product life cycles—and who the competitors are. If a market is defined too broadly, there may be many competitors—and the market may appear to be in market maturity. On the other hand, if we look at a narrow area—and a particular way of satisfying specific needs—then we may see much shorter product life cycles as improved product ideas come along to replace the old. For example, the broad market for power lawnmowers appears to be in the market maturity stage—where only minor product changes are expected. If we think of lawnmowers satisfying more specific needs and using different technical principles, however, we get a different view. "Air-cushion" mowers for very uneven lawns were introduced recently and may take some of the "wheeled" mower business. Power lawnmower producers who defined their market too broadly may miss this opportunity.

Each market segment has its own product life cycle

Too narrow a view of a market segment can lead to misreading the nature of competition—and the speed of the relevant product life cycle. A firm producing exercise machines, for example, may aim at only the "exercise machine" market. But this narrow view can lead it to compete only with other exercise machine producers—when it might make more sense to compete in the "fitness" market. Of course, it can't ignore competitors' machines, but even tougher competition may come from health clubs—and suppliers of jogging suits, athletic shoes, and other fitness-related products. In other words, there may be two markets—and two life cycles—to work with: the exercise machine market and the fitness market. Each may require a different strategy.

Individual products don't have product life cycles

Notice that product life cycles describe industry sales and profits within a particular product-market—*not* the sales and profits of an individual product or brand. Individual products or brands may be introduced—or withdrawn—during any stage of the product life cycle. Further, their sales and profits may vary up and down throughout the life cycle—sometimes moving in the opposite direction of industry sales and profits.

A me-too product introduced during the market growth stage, for example, may reach its peak and start to decline even before market maturity. Or it may never get any sales at all—and suffer a quick death. Market leaders may enjoy high profits during the market maturity stage—even though industry profits are declining. Weaker products, on the other hand, may not earn a profit during any stage of the product life cycle.

This means that sales of *individual* products or brands often don't follow the product life cycle curve shown in Exhibit 9–1—and studying a specific product's past sales patterns can be dangerous for strategy planners. It's the life cycle for the product idea—in the whole product-market—that marketing managers must study when planning their strategies. In fact, it might be better to think in terms of "market life cycles" or "product-market life cycles" rather than product life cycles—but we will use the term *product life cycle* because it is commonly accepted and widely used.

PLANNING FOR DIFFERENT STAGES OF THE PRODUCT LIFE CYCLE

Length of cycle affects strategy planning

The probable length of the cycle affects strategy planning—realistic plans must be made for the later stages. In fact, where a product is in its life cycle—and how fast it's moving to the next stage—should affect strategy planning. Exhibit 9–2 shows the relation of the product life cycle to the marketing mix variables. The new technical terms in this exhibit are discussed later in the book.

Exhibit 9–2 shows that a marketing manager has a tough job introducing a really new product. Even if the product is unique, this doesn't mean that everyone will immediately line up to buy it. The firm will have to build channels of distribution—perhaps offering special incentives to win cooperation. Promotion is needed to build demand *for the whole idea*—not just to sell a specific brand. All of this costs money—so losses can be expected in the market introduction stage of the product life cycle. The marketing manager may try to "skim" the market—charging a relatively high price to help pay for these costs.

The best strategy, however, depends on how fast the product life cycle is likely to move—that is, how quickly the idea will be accepted by customers—and how quickly competitors will follow with their own versions of the product.

Also relevant is how quickly the firm can change its strategy as the life cycle moves on. Some firms are very flexible—and are able to compete effectively with larger, less adaptable competitors.

Managing maturing products

Having some competitive advantage is important as your product moves into market maturity. Even a small advantage can make a big difference—and some firms do very well by careful management of maturing products. They are able to take advantage of a slightly better product—or perhaps lower production and/or marketing costs. Or they are better at promotion—allowing them to differentiate their more-or-less homogeneous product from competitors.

An important point to remember here, however, is that industry profits are

Exhibit 9–2   Typical Changes in Marketing Variables over the Product Life Cycle

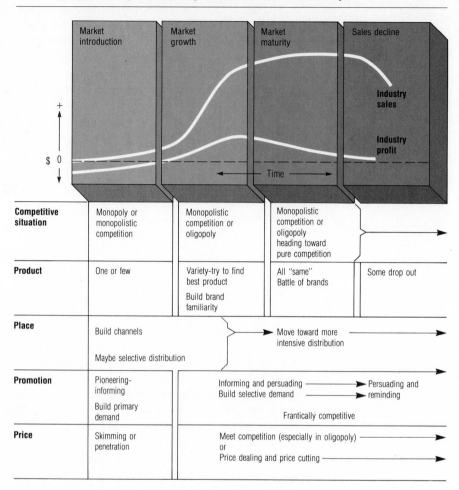

	Market introduction	Market growth	Market maturity	Sales decline
Competitive situation	Monopoly or monopolistic competition	Monopolistic competition or oligopoly	Monopolistic competition or oligopoly heading toward pure competition →	
Product	One or few	Variety-try to find best product Build brand familiarity	All "same" Battle of brands	Some drop out
Place	Build channels Maybe selective distribution		Move toward more intensive distribution →	
Promotion	Pioneering-informing Build primary demand	Informing and persuading → Build selective demand → Frantically competitive	Persuading and reminding	
Price	Skimming or penetration	Meet competition (especially in oligopoly) → or Price dealing and price cutting →		

declining in market maturity. Financially oriented top management must see this—or they will continue to expect the attractive profits of the market growth stage—profits that are no longer possible. If top managers don't understand this, they may place impossible burdens on the marketing department—causing marketing managers to think about collusion with competitors, deceptive advertising, or some other desperate way to try to reach impossible objectives.

Top management must see that there is an upper limit in any product-market. The product life cycle concept has been very useful in communicating this unhappy message. It is one of the powerful tools of marketing that is turning up in finance and top management literature—because it is useful for overall corporate planning and objective setting.

Product life cycles keep moving. But if a company has no competitive advantage, it doesn't have to sit by and watch its products go through a complete product life cycle. It has choices. It can improve the product—to try to win a larger share of the market. Or it can withdraw the product before it completes the cycle. These two choices are shown in Exhibit 9–3.

Product life cycles can be extended

When a firm's product wins the position of "*the* product that meets my needs," its life will last as long as it continues to meet these needs. If the needs change, the product may have to change—but the target consumers will continue to buy it if it still meets their needs. An outstanding example is Procter & Gamble's Tide. Introduced in 1947, this powdered detergent gave consumers a much cleaner wash than they were able to get before—because it did away with soap film. Tide led to a whole new generation of laundry products—because it produced better cleaning with fewer suds. Since 1947 consumers' needs have changed, washing machines have changed, and fabrics have changed—so the Tide sold today is much different than the one sold in 1947. In fact, Tide has had at least 55 (sometimes subtle) modifications. But it continues to sell well—because it continues to meet consumers' needs for a dependable powdered detergent that "does the job."[6]

Do the product changes made with Tide create a new product that should have its own product life cycle—or are they just technical changes in the original product idea? We'll take the second view—focusing on the product *idea* rather than technical changes. Note that for strategy planning purposes, new ~~detergents~~ must be seen as immediately entering the market ~~maturity~~ stion.

Phasing ~~out~~ produc~~ts~~

~~some gro~~wth strategies. If prospects are poor in ~~a "pha~~se-out" strategy may be needed. The need ~~ob~~vious as the sales decline stage arrives. But ~~be~~ clear that a particular product isn't going to ~~meet the~~ company's objectives. The wisest move is to

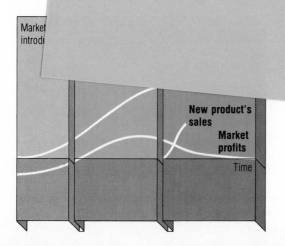

New product's sales

Market profits

Time

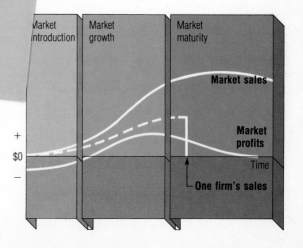

Market introduction

Market growth

Market maturity

Market sales

Market profits

+

$0

–

Time

One firm's sales

develop a strategy that helps the firm phase out of the product-market—perhaps over several years.

Firms carry out marketing plans as "ongoing" strategies—with salespeople making calls, inventory moving in the channel, advertising planned for several months ahead, and so on. So usually it isn't possible for them to avoid losses if they end a plan too quickly. Because of this, it's usually better to "phase out" the product gradually. Managers order materials more selectively—so production can end with a minimum of unused inventory. Salespeople are shifted to other jobs, and advertising and other promotion efforts are cancelled or phased out quickly—since there's no point in promoting for the long run anymore. These various actions obviously affect morale within the company—and may cause channel members to pull back also. So the company may have to offer price inducements in the channels.

Obviously, there are some difficult problems here, but it should be clear that a "phase-out" is also a strategy—and it must be market-oriented to cut losses. In fact, it's even possible to "milk" a dying product for some time if competitors move out more quickly. There is still ongoing demand—although it is declining—and some customers are willing to pay attractive prices to get their "old favorite." For example, in the 1960s Ipana and Pepsodent were the best selling brands of toothpaste—both supported by much promotion. But since then, Pepsodent's market share has fallen by 50 percent, and its producer, Lever Brothers, doesn't think a new ad campaign can bring it back. So the company keeps Pepsodent alive for loyal customers—but puts its promotion money behind its more successful brands—Close-up and Aim. Similarly, Ipana isn't advertised and gets only spotty distribution in less competitive markets.

NEW-PRODUCT PLANNING

Competition is so fierce in most markets that a firm has to keep developing new products—as well as modifying its current products—to meet changing customer needs and competitors' actions. Not having an active new product development process means that consciously—or subconsciously—the firm has decided to "milk" its current products and go out of business. New-product planning *must* be done—just to survive in our dynamic marketplaces.

What is a new product?

A **new product** is one that is new *in any way* for the company concerned. A product can become "new" in many ways. A fresh idea can be turned into a new good or service. For example, Alza Corporation developed time-release "skin patches" that are replacing pills and injections for some medications. Variations on an existing product idea can also make a product "new." 3M—producer of Scotch Tape—recently introduced "Magic Plus" tape—which sticks to paper but can be easily removed without damaging the surface. Even small changes in an existing product can make it "new."

FTC says product is "new" only six months

A product can be called "new" for only six months according to the **Federal Trade Commission (FTC)**—the federal government agency that polices antimonopoly laws. To be called new—says the FTC—a product must be entirely new or changed in a "functionally significant or substantial respect." While six months may seem a very short time for production-oriented managers, it may be reasonable, given the short life cycles of many products.[7]

AN ORGANIZED NEW–PRODUCT DEVELOPMENT PROCESS IS CRITICAL

Identifying and developing new product ideas—and effective strategies to go with them—is often the key to a firm's success and survival. But this isn't easy. New-product development demands effort, time, and talent—and still the risks and costs of failure are high. The failure rate on new products actually placed in the market may be as high as 50 percent.[8]

To improve this effort, it helps to follow an organized new-product development process. Exhibit 9–4 shows such a process—moving logically through five steps: (1) idea generation, (2) screening, (3) idea evaluation, (4) development (of product and marketing mix), and (5) commercialization.[9]

Process tries to kill new ideas— economically

An important element in this new-product development process is continued evaluation of new ideas—and their likely profitability and return on investment. In fact, it's desirable to apply the hypothesis-testing approach discussed in Chapter 5 to new-product development. The hypothesis tested is that the new idea will *not* be profitable. This puts the burden on the new idea to prove it-self—or be rejected. Such a process may seem harsh, but experience shows that most new ideas have some flaw that can lead to problems—and even big losses. Marketers try to discover those flaws early—and either find a remedy or reject the idea completely. Applying this process requires much analysis of the idea—both within and outside the firm—*before* research and development (R&D) or engineering spend any money to develop a physical item. This is a major difference from the usual production-oriented approach—which develops a product first and then asks sales to "get rid of it."

Exhibit 9–4   New-Product Development Process

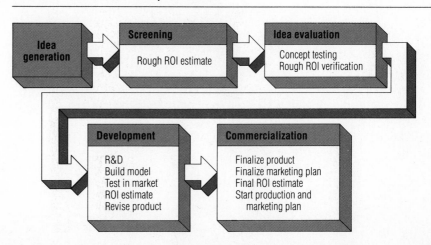

Booz, Allen, & Hamilton—a consulting firm—has studied new product introductions for some time. Its research shows how important it is to have an organized new product development process. In a 1968 study, the firm found that about 58 ideas were evaluated for each successful new product. Of course, as shown in Exhibit 9–5, some ideas were rejected at each stage of the process. When the study was repeated in 1981, only about 7 ideas were required for each successful new product.[10] The firm feels that this dramatic change is because many companies are doing a better job of generating good new product ideas. As a result, they can concentrate their resources—in the later stages of the new-product development process—on those with the highest potential.

Of course, the actual new-product "success rate" varies among industries and companies. But many companies *are* improving the way they develop new products. It's important to see that if a firm doesn't use an organized process like this, it may bring many bad or weak ideas to market—at a big loss.

Remember customers—and middlemen

When looking for new ideas, the consumer's viewpoint is very important. It helps to consider the image that potential customers have of the firm. The Maryland Cup Corporation—the world's largest manufacturer of paper drinking straws and a leading manufacturer of paper drinking cups—was able to move into producing plastic food containers of all types because customers identified the company with the "disposable container" business—rather than just the straw and cup business.

New product planners must consider not only the consumers, however—but the middlemen who will handle or sell the product. There may be special handling or packaging needs. The shelf height in supermarkets, for example, may limit package size. Shipping or handling problems in the warehouse—or on carriers—might call for different types of packaging to keep damage down or make handling easier.

Exhibit 9–5 *Surviving New-Product Ideas during an Organized New-Product Development Process*

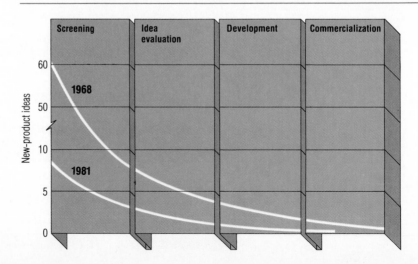

Social responsibility important, too

Exhibit 9–6   Types of New-Product Opportunities

The firm's final choice in product design should fit with the company's overall objectives—and make good use of the firm's resources. But it's also desirable to create a need-satisfying product that will appeal to consumers—in the long run as well as the short run. Different kinds of new-product opportunities are shown in Exhibit 9–6. Obviously, a socially responsible firm tries to find "desirable" opportunities rather than "deficient" ones. This may not be as easy as it sounds, however. Some consumers want "pleasing products" instead of "desirable products." And some competitors are quite willing to offer what consumers want. Creating "socially responsible" new-product ideas is a challenge for new-product planners.

Safety must be considered, too

Real acceptance of the marketing concept should lead to the design of safe products.

The **Consumer Product Safety Act** (of 1972) set up the Consumer Products Safety Commission to encourage more awareness of safety in product design—and better quality control. The commission can set safety standards for products—and it can order costly repairs or return of "unsafe products." And it can back up its orders with fines and jail sentences. The Food and Drug Administration has similar powers for foods and drugs.

Product safety makes strategy planning harder because not all customers—including some who want better safety features—are willing to pay more for safer products. And some features cost a lot to add—increasing prices considerably.

Products can turn to liabilities

Product liability means the legal obligation of sellers to pay damages to individuals who are injured by defective or unsafe products. Product liability is a serious matter. Liability settlements may exceed not only the company's insurance coverage—but its total assets.

The courts have been very strict with product liability cases. Producers may be held responsible for injuries related to their products, no matter how they are used or how well they are designed. Riddell—whose football helmets protect the pros—recently was hit with a $12 million judgment for a high school football player who broke his neck. The jury concluded that Riddell should have put a sticker on the helmet to warn players of the danger of butting into opponents! Cases—and settlements—like this are common.

The question of liability is a serious concern—and changes in state and federal laws are underway. But, until product liability questions are resolved, marketing managers must be very sensitive when screening new product ideas.[11]

Top-level support is vital

New-product development must have the enthusiastic support of top management. New products tend to upset old routines. So someone—or a department or group—has to be in charge of new-product development.[12]

Some organization helps

What specific organization is used may not be too important—as long as there is top-management support. A new-product development department—or committee—can help make sure that new ideas are studied carefully.

A well-organized development process even makes it possible for a firm to copy others' successful ideas—quickly and profitably. This possibility should not be overlooked. Ford Motor Company has new product specialists who buy cars made by other firms as soon as they are available. Then the cars are taken apart, and a search begins for new ideas or improvements made by the other firms. Many other companies use similar approaches. A company should organize to innovate—but no firm can always be first with the best new ideas.[13]

NEED FOR PRODUCT MANAGERS

Product variety leads to product managers

When a firm has only one or a few related products, everyone is interested in them. But when many new products are being developed, someone must be in charge of new-product planning—to be sure it is not neglected. Also, when a firm has several different kinds of products, management may decide to put someone in charge of each kind—or even each brand—to be sure they aren't lost in the rush of everyday business. **Product managers** or **brand managers** manage specific products—often taking over the jobs once handled by an advertising manager. That gives a clue to what is often their major responsibility—Promotion—since the products have already been developed by the "new-product" people.

Product managers are especially common in large companies that produce many kinds of products. Several product managers may work under a marketing manager. Sometimes these product managers are responsible for the profitable operation of the whole marketing effort for a particular product. They must coordinate their efforts with others—including the sales manager, advertising agencies, and production and research people.

In some companies, the product manager has a lot of power—and profit responsibility. In other firms, the product manager may be a "product champion"—concerned with planning and getting the promotion done.

The activities of product managers vary a lot—depending on their experience and aggressiveness and the company's organizational philosophy. Today, companies are emphasizing marketing *experience*—as it becomes clear that this important job takes more than academic training and enthusiasm.[14]

CONCLUSION

Product planning is an increasingly important activity in a modern economy—because it is no longer very profitable to sell just "commodities."

The product life-cycle concept is especially important to marketing strategy planning. It shows that different marketing mixes—and even strategies—are needed as a product moves through its cycle. This is an important point, because profits change during the product life cycle—with most of the profits going to the innovators or fast copiers.

We pointed out that a new product is not limited to physical newness. We will call a product "new" if it is new in any way—to any target market.

New products are so important to business survival that firms need some organized process for developing them. Such a process was discussed—and we stressed that it must be a total company effort to be successful.

The failure rate of new products is high—but it is lower for larger and better-managed firms that recognize product development and management as vital processes. Some firms appoint product or brand managers to manage individual products—and new-product committees to ensure that the process is carried out successfully.

Questions and Problems

1. Explain how industry sales and industry profits behave over the product life cycle.

2. Cite two examples of products that you feel are currently in each of the product life-cycle stages.

3. Explain how different conclusions might be reached with respect to the correct product life-cycle stage(s) in the automobile market—especially if different views of the market are held.

4. Can product life cycles be extended? Illustrate your answer for a specific product.

5. Discuss the life cycle of a product in terms of its probable impact on a manufacturer's marketing mix. Illustrate using compact disc players for stereo music.

6. What are some of the characteristics of a new product that will help it to move through the early stages of the product life cycle more quickly? Briefly discuss each characteristic—illustrating with a product of your choice.

7. What is a new product? Illustrate your answer.

8. Explain the importance of an organized new-product development process and illustrate how it might be used for (*a*) an improved popcorn popper (*b*) new frozen-food items, (*c*) a new children's toy.

9. Explain the role of product or brand managers. Are they usually put in charge of new-product development?

10. Discuss the social value of new-product development activities that seem to encourage people to discard products that are not "all worn out." Is this an economic waste? How worn out is "all worn out?" Must a shirt have holes in it? How big?

Suggested Computer-Aided Problem

9. Growth Stage Competition

Suggested Cases

13. Union Carbide Corporation

20. A–1 Sports, Inc.

Chapter 10

Place and Physical Distribution

When You Finish This Chapter, You Should

1. Understand how and why marketing specialists adjust discrepancies of quantity and assortment.

2. Know why physical distribution is such an important part of Place *and* marketing strategy planning.

3. Know about the transporting and storing possibilities a marketing manager can use.

4. Know about the different kinds of channel systems.

5. Understand how much market exposure would be "ideal."

6. Recognize the important new terms (shown in red).

You may build a "better mousetrap," but if it's not in the right place at the right time, it won't do anyone any good.

In 1981, IBM came out with its first Personal Computer (PC). In the past, IBM sold its large computers directly to industrial customers—without help from middlemen. This allowed IBM to control prices, service quality, and product availability. But IBM realized that many target customers—including most small businesses—were already buying PCs from independent computer stores.

IBM worried that its image might suffer if some of these computer stores did a poor job. Moreover, IBM's objectives were in conflict with those of some of the more aggressive stores. They were already selling competitors' PCs to big firms that bought hundreds at a time. IBM wanted to reserve these accounts for its own sales force.

IBM decided to be very selective and work only with proven stores—like those in the Computerland chain—willing to cooperate with IBM's strategy *and* guarantee attention to IBM products. In addition, IBM also opened some stores of its own—to learn more about this new part of its business.

This approach to distribution proved vital to IBM's early success. As the market continued to grow, IBM added other channels—and dropped its own stores. But IBM PCs continue to hold their edge with computer stores.[1]

As IBM learned, offering customers a good product at a reasonable price is important for a successful marketing strategy—but it isn't enough. Managers must also think about **Place**—making products available in the right quantities and locations—when customers want them. Place requires marketing specialists—middlemen, transporting and storing companies, and facilitators—to provide target customers with time, place, and possession utilities.

There are many ways to provide Place. Magnavox televisions are sold by a select group of stores, while Zenith televisions are sold by many more retailers. Producers sell many industrial products directly to the customer. But most consumer products are sold to middlemen—who later sell to the final consumer.

Place decisions are important strategy decisions. See Exhibit 10–1 for a picture of the strategy decision areas we will discuss in the next three chapters.

"IDEAL" PLACE OBJECTIVES SUGGESTED BY PRODUCT CLASSES

Obviously, firms must consider the needs and attitudes of potential target markets when developing Place. People in a particular target market should have similar needs and attitudes—and therefore should be satisfied with a similar Place system. Their urgency to have needs satisfied—and their willingness to shop—have already been summarized in the product classes. Now we should be able to use these product classes to suggest how to handle Place.

The relationship between product classes and *ideal place objectives* was shown in Exhibit 8–4 for consumer products and Exhibit 8–5 for industrial products. These exhibits deserve careful study—since they set the framework for making Place decisions.

Place system is not automatic

Just as product classes are not automatic, we can't automatically decide on the best Place arrangement. If two or more market segments have different views of a product, different Place arrangements may be needed too. Further, Place depends on both (1) what customers would like best and (2) what channel members can provide profitably.

DIRECT CHANNEL SYSTEMS MAY BE BEST, SOMETIMES

Many producers like to handle the whole distribution job themselves. The advantage in selling directly to the final user or consumer is that marketing research is easier—because the producer's sales reps have direct contact with the target customers. If any special selling effort or technical services are needed, the marketing manager can be sure that the sales force will receive the necessary training and motivation.

Some products typically have short channels of distribution—and a direct-to-user channel is not uncommon. It's not always necessary to use middlemen. On the other hand, it isn't always best to "go direct" either.

SPECIALISTS AND CHANNEL SYSTEMS DEVELOP TO ADJUST DISCREPANCIES

Discrepancies require channel specialists

All producers want to be sure that their products reach the target customers. But the assortment and quantity of products customers want may differ

Exhibit 10–1   Strategy Decision Areas in Place

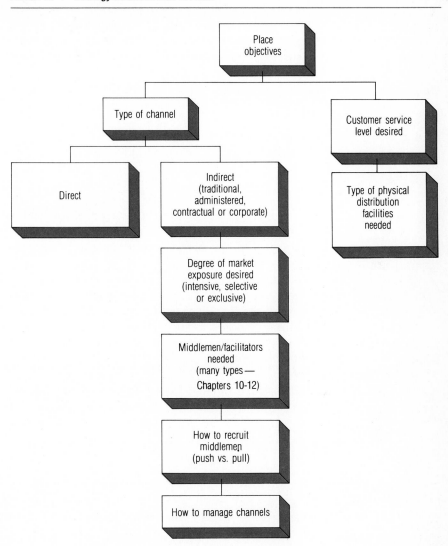

from the assortment and quantity of products normally produced. Specialists develop to adjust these discrepancies.[2]

Discrepancy of quantity means the difference between the quantity of products it's economical for a producer to make and the quantity final users or consumers normally want. For example, most manufacturers of golf balls produce large quantities—perhaps 200,000 to 500,000 in a given time period. The average golfer, however, wants only a few balls at a time. Adjusting for this discrepancy usually requires middlemen—wholesalers and retailers.

Producers typically specialize by product—and therefore another discrepancy develops. **Discrepancy of assortment** means the difference between the

lines the typical producer makes and the assortment final consumers or users want. Most golfers, for example, need more than golf balls. They want golf shoes, gloves, clubs, a bag, and so forth. And probably they would prefer not to shop around for each item. So, again, middlemen are needed to adjust these discrepancies.

Channel specialists adjust discrepancies with regrouping activities

Regrouping activities adjust the quantities and/or assortments of products handled at each level in a channel of distribution.

There are four regrouping activities: accumulating, bulk-breaking, sorting, and assorting. When one or more of these activities is required, a marketing specialist might develop to fill this need.

Adjusting quantity discrepancies by accumulating and bulk-breaking

Accumulating involves collecting products from many small producers. This is common for agricultural products. It is a way of getting the lowest transporting rate—by combining small quantities that can then be shipped in truckload or carload quantities.

Bulk-breaking involves dividing larger quantities into smaller quantities as products get closer to the final market. This may involve several middlemen. Wholesalers may sell smaller quantities to other wholesalers—or directly to retailers. Retailers continue the bulk-breaking as they sell to their customers.

Adjusting assortment discrepancies by sorting and assorting

Different types of specialists are needed to adjust assortment discrepancies. Two types of regrouping activities may be needed: sorting and assorting.

Sorting means separating products into grades and qualities desired by different target markets. This is a common process for agricultural products. Na-

Wholesalers often accumulate products from many producers and then break bulk to provide the smaller quantities needed by retailers.

ture produces what it will—and then these products must be sorted to meet the needs of different target markets.

Assorting means putting together a variety of products to give a target market what it wants. Marketing specialists put together an assortment to satisfy some target market. This usually is done by those close to the final consumer or user—retailers or wholesalers who try to supply a wide assortment of products for the convenience of their customers. A grocery store is a good example. But some assortments involve very different products—a wholesaler selling Yazoo tractors and mowers to golf courses might also carry Pennington grass seed, Scott fertilizer, and even golf ball washers or irrigation systems—for its customers' convenience.

Channel systems can be complex

Adjusting discrepancies can lead to complex channels of distribution. Exhibit 10–2 shows the possibility for competition among different channels. It also shows the many channels used by producers of roofing shingles. Shingles can be both consumer products and industrial products, which helps explain why

Exhibit 10–2   Sales of Roofing Shingles Are Made through Many Kinds of Wholesalers and Retailers

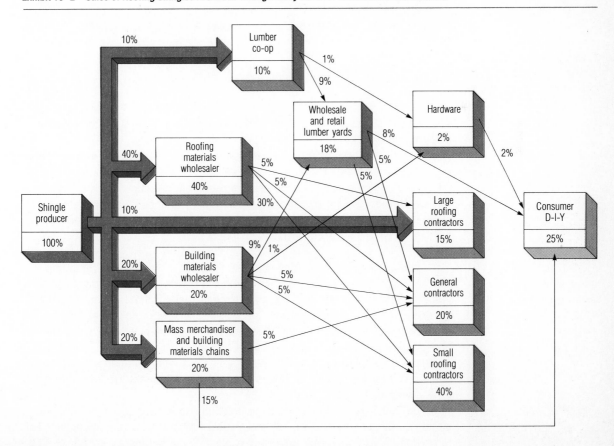

some channels develop. But note that the shingles go through different wholesalers and retailers. This can cause problems—because different wholesalers and retailers are used to different markups. And the different markups may lead to open price wars—especially on well-known and branded products.

Dual distribution occurs when a producer uses several competing channels to reach the same target market—perhaps using several middlemen and selling directly itself. Some established middlemen resent this practice because they don't like *any* competition—especially competition set up by their own suppliers. But producers often are forced to use dual distribution—because their present channels are doing a poor job—or aren't reaching some potential customers.

Sometimes there's not much choice

The roofing shingle example seems to suggest that there are plenty of middlemen around to form almost any kind of channel system. But this isn't true. Sometimes there is only one good middleman serving a market. To reach this market, producers may have no choice but to use this one middleman.

In other cases, there are no middlemen at all! Then a producer may try to go directly to target customers. If this isn't possible, the product may die—because it can't be distributed economically. Some products aren't wanted in big enough volume and/or at high enough prices to justify any middlemen providing the regrouping activities needed to reach potential customers.

PHYSICAL DISTRIBUTION IS AN IMPORTANT PART OF PLACE PLANNING

Physical distribution (PD) is the transporting and storing of goods within individual firms and along a channel of distribution to match target customers' needs with a firm's marketing mix. Physical distribution accounts for nearly half the cost of marketing. These PD activities are very important to a firm—and the macro-marketing system. Goods that remain in a factory or on a farm really have no "use" at all. And possession utility is impossible until time and place utility have been provided. This requires the transporting and storing functions that are a part of physical distribution.

Deciding who will haul and store is strategic

As a marketing manager develops the Place part of a strategy, it is important to decide who will store and transport the goods—and who will pay for these services. A wholesaler may use its own trucks to haul goods from a producer to its warehouse—and from there to retailers—but only because the producer gives a transporting allowance. Another wholesaler may want the goods delivered.

When developing a marketing strategy, the marketing manager must decide how these functions are to be shared—since this will affect the other three Ps—especially Price.

These are important strategy decisions—because they can make or break a strategy. The case of Channel Master, a small producer of "rabbit ear" TV antennas, is an example. The growth of cable TV was hurting sales. So the firm developed a new product—a dish-like antenna used by motels to receive HBO and other satellite TV signals. The product looked like it could be a big success. Because Channel Master couldn't finance a lot of inventory, the firm decided to work only with wholesalers who were willing to buy and stock several units—to be used for demonstrations and to make sure that buyers got immediate delivery. In a few months, the firm had $2 million in sales to its wholesalers—and recovered its development costs just providing inventory for the channel. Here, the wholesalers helped share the risk of the new venture—but it was a good decision for them, too. They won many sales from a competing channel that couldn't offer such fast delivery—because it didn't do any storing and used higher cost transporting. So they easily got back the interest cost of their inventory investment—and more.

THE TRANSPORTING FUNCTION—ADDS VALUE

Transporting is the marketing function of moving goods. It provides time and place utilities. But the value added to products by moving them must be greater than the cost of the transporting—or there is little reason to ship in the first place.

Modern transporting facilities—including railroads, pipe lines, trucks, barges and ships, and airplanes—have changed marketing. Without these transporting facilities, there could be no mass distribution—with its regrouping activities—or any urban life as we know it today.

Seventy-five percent of all U.S. freight moves by trucks—at least part of the way. Railroads carry goods for long distances, but trucks have the bulk of the short-haul business. The trucking industry slogan, "If you have it, it came by truck," is true for consumer products. However, many industrial products are delivered by railroads—or by other transporting methods. See Exhibit 10–3.

Can you afford to hit the target?

Transporting costs may limit the target markets that a marketing manager can consider. Shipping costs increase delivered cost—and that's what really interests customers.

Transporting bulky and low-value products like sand and gravel, for example, costs about 55 percent of their value. At the other extreme, lighter or more valuable items like office machines are transported for 3 percent of their selling price.[3] See Exhibit 10–4.

There used to be many regulations

Until the 1980s, there was much government control over transporting. Routes had to be approved by the government—as did rates and services. Because of these rates, carriers typically did not compete on Price. And some carriers were approved to carry some products but not others.

All of this caused higher prices and much waste. For example, the rules required a carrier that took Cummins diesel engines from the Midwest to California to use an extra long route going out—and make the return trip empty. *Other* carriers took California vegetables to the Midwest—and they too went home empty.[4]

Exhibit 10–3   Intercity Freight Movement in the United States, 1960 and 1984

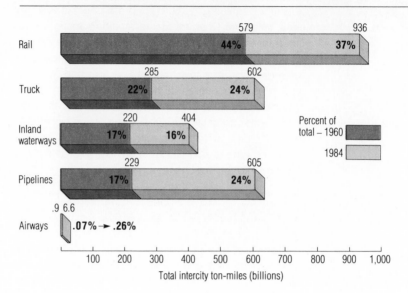

Total intercity ton-miles (billions)

Exhibit 10–4   Transporting Costs as a Percent of Selling Price for Different Products

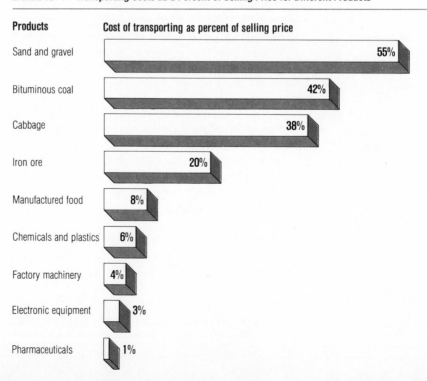

Marketing manager can affect rates

Creative marketing managers—by bargaining for better transporting rates—can help their channel system members with the transporting function. In fact, some manufacturers and middlemen maintain *traffic departments* to deal with carriers. These departments can be a great help—not only to their own firms but also to their suppliers and customers—by finding the best carriers and bargaining for the lowest rates.

Which transporting alternative is best?

The best transporting choice should fit into the whole marketing strategy. What is "best" depends on the product, other physical distribution decisions, and what service level the company wants to offer. See Exhibit 10–5. It is important to see that low transporting cost is *not* the only criterion for selecting the best mode.[5]

Railroads—large loads moved at low cost

The railroads are important mainly for carrying heavy and bulky products—such as chemicals, cars, and canned goods—over long distances at low cost. Railroad freight moves more slowly than truck shipments. And railroads are more efficient at handling full carloads of products. Less-than-carload (LCL) shipments take a lot of handling and rehandling—which slows movement and raises cost.

Railroads had low profits for many years—in part because trucks took a large share of the most profitable business. Now railroads are cutting costs to improve profits. Relaxed government regulations have helped. Many railroads have merged to reduce overlap in equipment—and routes. And they are also catering to the needs of new target customers with a variety of specially designed railcars.[6] Some railroads encourage **pool car service**—which allows groups of shippers to pool their shipments of like goods into a full car. When

Exhibit 10–5   Relative Benefits of Different Transport Modes

Transporting features / Mode	Cost per ton mile	Door-to-door delivery speed	Number of locations served	Ability to handle variety of goods	Frequency of scheduled shipments	Dependability in meeting schedules
Rail	○	○	◒	◒	◒	○
Water	●	◒	◒	●	●	◒
Truck	◒	◒	●	○	◒	●
Pipeline	◒	●	●	●	●	●
Air	●	●	○	◒	○	●

Worst ● ◒ ○ ◒ ● Best

different commodities are shipped in the same car, it is called a *mixed car* rather than a pool car.

Another example of a special railroad service is **diversion in transit**—which allows redirection of carloads already in transit. A Florida grower can ship a carload of oranges toward the northeast, and, while they head north, he can find a buyer or identify the market with the best price. Then—for a small fee—the railroad will reroute the car to this destination.

Trucks are more expensive, but flexible and essential

The flexibility of trucks makes them better at moving small quantities of goods for shorter distances. They go where the rails can't go. And using the interstate highway system, trucks can give extremely fast service.

Critics complain that trucks congest traffic and damage highways. But trucks are essential to our present macro-marketing system.[7]

Ships and barges—slow and seasonal, but inexpensive

Water transporting is the lowest-cost method—but it is also the slowest. When speed is not as important, however, barges or ships are important methods of transporting. Barges on internal waterways are used for bulky, nonperishable products—such as iron ore, grain, steel, oil, cement, gravel, sand, and coal. By a combination of rivers, canals, and locks, it is possible to ship goods from industrial and agricultural regions of inland United States all over the world. Foreign ships regularly move on the Great Lakes. Ocean-going barges can reach as far north as Minneapolis-St. Paul—and deep into Arkansas.

Pipelines move oil and gas

In the United States, pipelines are used primarily by the petroleum industry—to move oil and natural gas. Only a few cities in the United States are more than 200 miles from a major pipeline system. Of course, the majority of the pipelines are in the Southwest—connecting the oil fields and refineries. From there, the more flexible railroads, trucks, and ships usually take over—bringing refined products to customers.

Airplanes may cut the total cost of distribution

The most expensive means of cargo transporting is air freight—but it also is fast! Air freight rates normally are at least twice as high as trucking rates—but the greater speed may be worth the added cost. High-value, light-weight products—like high-fashion clothing or industrial parts for the electronics and metal-working industries—are often shipped by air. Air freight also carries perishable products that just could not be shipped before. Tropical flowers from Hawaii are now jet-flown to points all over the United States. A big advantage of air transport is that the cost of packing, unpacking, and preparing products for sale may be reduced—or eliminated—when products are shipped by air. Air freight can help a producer reduce inventory costs by eliminating outlying warehouses. The greater speed may also reduce spoilage, theft, and damage. So, although the transporting cost may be higher, the total cost of distribution may be lower.[8]

Put it in a container—and move between modes easily

We have described the modes separately. But products are often moved by several different modes and carriers during their journey. This is especially common for international shipments. Japanese firms—like Panasonic—ship stereos to the United States and Canada by boat. When they arrive on the

Containerization makes it easier and more economical to combine different transporting modes.

West Coast, they are loaded on trains and sent across the country. Then, the units are delivered to a wholesaler by truck or rail. Loading and unloading the goods several times raises costs and slows delivery. Sometimes parts of a shipment become separated, damaged, or even stolen.

Many of these problems are reduced with **containerization**—grouping individual items into an economical shipping quantity and sealing them in large protective containers for transit to the final destination.

STORING MAY BE NEEDED IN SOME CHANNELS

Storing is the marketing function of holding goods. It provides time utility. **Inventory** is the amount of goods being stored. Storing is necessary because production doesn't always match consumption. Some products—such as farm produce—are produced seasonally but are in demand year-round. And some items—such as suntan products—are in big demand for short periods.

Storing can be done by both producers and middlemen. It can balance supply and demand—keeping inventory at convenient locations—ready to meet customers' needs. Storing is one of the major activities of some middlemen.[9]

Specialized storing facilities can be very helpful

Private warehouses are storing facilities owned or leased by companies for their own use. Most producers, wholesalers, and retailers have some storing facilities in their own main buildings—or in a warehouse district.

Private warehouses are used when a large volume of goods must be stored regularly. Owning warehouse space can be expensive, however. If the need changes, the extra space may be hard—or impossible—to rent to others.

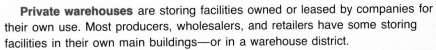

Public warehouses are independent storing facilities. They can provide all the services that a company's own warehouse can provide. A company might choose to use a public warehouse if it doesn't have a regular need for warehouse space. With a public warehouse, the customer pays only for space used—and may buy a variety of other services. Public warehouses are useful to producers who must carry inventory in many locations—including foreign countries. Public warehouses are found in all major urban areas—and many smaller cities. Rural towns also have public warehouses for locally produced agricultural products.[10]

Warehousing facilities have modernized

The cost of physical handling is a major storing cost. The goods must be handled once when put into storage—and again when they come out. Further—in the typical old "downtown" warehouse districts—traffic congestion, crowded storage areas, and slow freight elevators slow the process. This increases the cost.

Today, modern one-story buildings are replacing the old multi-story buildings. They are located away from downtown traffic. They eliminate the need for elevators—and permit the use of power-operated lift trucks, battery-operated motor scooters, roller-skating order pickers, electric hoists for heavy items, and hydraulic ramps to aid loading and unloading. Some even have computer controlled order-picking systems.[11]

Distribution center is a different kind of warehouse

A **distribution center** is a special kind of warehouse designed to speed the flow of goods—and avoid unnecessary storing costs. Basically, it is a bulk-breaking operation. A distribution center increases inventory turnover—and thus reduces the cost of carrying inventory—which leads to bigger profits. This is important—these costs may run as high as 35 percent of the value of the average inventory each year.

Some large food producers and supermarket operators run their own distribution centers. For example, the Pillsbury Company—a large producer of baking mixes and flour—ships products in rail carloads from its many manufacturing plants (which each specialize in a few product lines) directly to distribution centers. Almost no goods are stored at the factories. These distribution centers are able to quickly ship any combination of goods by the most economical transporting route. This lets Pillsbury offer faster service—at lower cost.

PHYSICAL DISTRIBUTION CONCEPT FOCUSES ON WHOLE DISTRIBUTION SYSTEM

We have talked about the transporting and storing functions as separate activities—partly because it's the usual approach. Recently, however, attention has turned to the *whole* physical distribution function—not just storing or transporting.

This 315,000-square-foot distribution center helps to speed the flow of goods from producers to consumers.

Physical distribution concept—an idea for now

The **physical distribution (PD) concept** says that all transporting and storing activities of a business and a channel system should be coordinated as one system—which aims to minimize the cost of distribution for a given customer service level.[12]

Focusing on individual functions may actually increase total distribution costs for the firm—and even the whole channel. It may also lead to the wrong customer service level.

Total cost approach helps

The **total cost approach**—to selecting a PD system—evaluates *all* the costs of possible PD systems. This means that all costs—including those sometimes ignored—should be considered. Inventory costs, for example, are often ignored in marketing decisions—because these costs are buried in "overhead costs." But inventory costs can be very high. In fact, including them may lead to a different decision.

The tools of cost accounting and economics are used with this approach. Sometimes, total cost analyses show that unconventional PD methods will provide service as good as or better than usual methods—and at lower cost, as the following example shows.

Evaluating rail/warehouse versus air freight

The Good Earth Vegetable Company had been shipping produce to distant markets by train. The cost of shipping a ton of vegetables by train averaged less than half the cost of air freight. But when a competitor began using air freight, the Good Earth managers were forced to rethink their PD system. To their surprise, they found the air freight system was not only faster—but cheaper. See Exhibit 10–6.

Exhibit 10–6 compares the costs for the two distribution systems—airplane and railroad. Because shipping by train was slow, Good Earth had to store a large inventory in a warehouse—to fill orders on time. And the company was also surprised at the extra cost of carrying the inventory "in transit." Good Earth's managers also found that the cost of spoiled vegetables—during shipping and in the warehouse—was much, much higher when the firm used rail shipment. By using air freight, Good Earth could offer better service—at lower total cost.

Decide what service level to offer

Early physical distribution efforts emphasized lowering costs—to increase profits. Now there is more emphasis on making physical distribution planning a part of the company's strategy planning. Sometimes, by increasing physical distribution cost a little, the customer service level can be increased so much that, in effect, the company creates a new and better marketing mix.

What aspects of customer service are most important will depend on target market needs. Xerox might focus on how long it takes to deliver copy machine repair parts. When a copier breaks down, customers want the repair "yesterday." The service level might be stated as "we will deliver emergency repair parts within 24 hours." Obviously, supplying this service level will affect the total cost of the PD system. But it may also beat competitors who don't provide this service level.[13]

Customer service level is a measure of how rapidly and dependably a firm

Exhibit 10–6   Comparative Costs of Airplane versus Rail and Warehouse

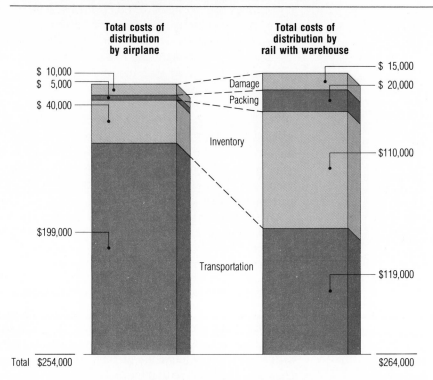

can deliver what customers want. Exhibit 10–7 shows the typical relation between physical distribution costs and customer service level. When a firm decides to lower total cost, it may also be settling for a lower customer service level. Minimizing cost is not always the right answer.

It may be hard to see the PD concept as a startling development. But until just a few years ago, even the most progressive companies treated PD functions as separate—and quite unrelated—activities. Companies spread responsibility for different distribution activities among various departments—production, shipping, sales, warehousing, and others. No individual was responsible for coordinating storing and transporting decisions—or relating them to customer service levels. Unfortunately, this is still true in many firms.

INDIRECT CHANNELS MAY BE BEST, SOMETIMES

Although a producer might prefer to handle the whole distribution job itself, this is just not economical for many kinds of products. When Apple Computer introduced its Macintosh personal computer, it hoped to use its own sales force to sell to corporate customers. But a year after the Macintosh came out, profits from this market were poor—only about 30 percent of Apple's sales came from its sales force. Apple concluded that it had to develop better chan-

Exhibit 10–7   Trade-Offs among Physical Distribution Costs, Customer Service Level, and Sales

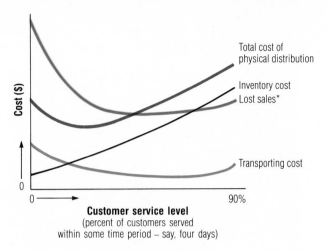

Note: Sales may be lost because of poor customer service or because of the high price charged to pay for too high a customer service level.

nel relationships with computer middlemen to compete profitably.[14] Typically, producers have to use middlemen—like it or not. They join—or develop—one of the indirect channel systems described below—and summarized in Exhibit 10–8.

Traditional channel systems are common

In a **traditional channel system**—the various channel members make little or no effort to cooperate with each other. They buy and sell from each other—and that's all. For example, General Electric wants a wholesaler of electrical building supplies to sell GE products. But if the wholesaler carries products from different producers, he may not care whose products are sold—as long as he has happy customers and a good profit margin.

In some very independent channels, buyers may even wait until sellers desperately need to sell—hoping to force the price down. This leads to erratic production, inventory, and employment patterns—that can only increase total costs. As we will see, such channels are declining in importance—with good reason. But they are still typical in some industries.

Vertical marketing systems focus on final customers

Unlike traditional channel systems, **vertical marketing systems** are channel systems in which the whole channel shares a common focus on the same target market at the end of the channel. Such systems make sense—and are growing in importance—because if the final customer doesn't buy the product, the whole channel suffers. We'll talk about the three types of vertical marketing systems next.

Corporate channel systems—shorten channels

Some firms develop their own vertical marketing systems by internal expansion and/or by buying other firms. With **corporate channel systems**—corporate ownership all along the channel—we might say the firm is going "di-

Exhibit 10–8   Types of Indirect Channel Systems

Type of channel Characteristic	Traditional	Vertical marketing systems		
		Administered	Contractual	Corporate
Amount of cooperation	Little or none	Some to good	Fairly good to good	Complete
Control maintained by	None	Economic power and leadership	Contracts	Ownership by one company
Examples	Typical channel of "independents"	General Electric, Miller's Beer, O.M. Scott & Sons (lawn products)	McDonald's, Holiday Inn, IGA, Ace Hardware, Super Valu, Coca-Cola, Chevrolet	Florsheim Shoes, Firestone Tire

rect." But actually it may be handling manufacturing, wholesaling, *and* retailing—and it is more accurate to think of it as running a vertical marketing system.

Vertical integration is at different levels

Corporate channel systems are often developed by **vertical integration**—acquiring firms at different levels of channel activity. Firestone, for example, has rubber plantations in Liberia, tire plants in Ohio, and Firestone wholesale and retail outlets all over the United States.

Corporate channel systems are not always started by manufacturers. A retailer might integrate into wholesaling—and perhaps even manufacturing. A&P has fish canning plants. Genesco and Florsheim make their own shoes. J. C. Penney controls textile plants.

There are many advantages to vertical integration—stability of operations, assurance of materials and supplies, better control of distribution, better quality control, larger research facilities, greater buying power, and lower executive overhead. The economies of vertical integration benefit the consumer, too, through lower prices and better products.

Provided that discrepancies of quantity and assortment aren't too great at each level in a channel—that is, the firms fit together well—vertical integration can be very efficient and profitable.

Administered and contractual systems may work well

Although a company's managers might prefer to handle the whole distribution job, this just isn't economically practical for many products. So instead of integrating corporately, they may develop an administered or contractual channel system. In **administered channel systems,** the various channel members informally agree to cooperate with each other. This can include agreements to

Southland Corporation has vertically integrated its 7-Eleven stores from its own dairies, food, and ice plants, and even a gasoline refiner.

routinize ordering, standardize accounting, and coordinate promotion efforts. In **contractual channel systems,** the various channel members agree by contract to cooperate with each other. With both of these systems, the members get some of the advantages of corporate integration—but have some of the flexibility of a traditional channel system.

Such systems are run by middlemen in the grocery, hardware, and drug industries. Electronic cash registers keep track of sales. This information is sent to the wholesaler's computer, and an order is entered—automatically. This reduces buying and selling costs, inventory investment, and customer frustration with "out-of-stock" items.

Vertical marketing systems—new wave in the marketplace

Besides their other advantages, smoothly operating channel systems can compete better.

For consumer products, corporate chains that are at least partially vertically integrated account for about 25 percent of total retail sales. Firms linked with other vertical systems account for an additional 37.5 percent. This gives vertical systems in the consumer products area much more than half of retail sales. Such systems will probably continue to increase their share in the future. Vertical marketing systems are becoming the major competitive units in the U.S. distribution system.[15]

THE BEST CHANNEL SYSTEM SHOULD ACHIEVE IDEAL MARKET EXPOSURE

Although it might seem that all marketing managers would want their products to have maximum exposure to potential customers, this isn't true. Some product classes require much less market exposure than others.

Ideal market exposure makes a product widely enough available to satisfy target customers' needs—but not exceed them. Too much exposure only increases the total marketing cost.

Three degrees of market exposure may be ideal

Intensive distribution is selling a product through all responsible and suitable wholesalers or retailers who will stock and/or sell the product. **Selective distribution** is selling through only those middlemen who will give the product special attention. **Exclusive distribution** is selling through only one middleman in each geographic area.

In practice, this means that cigarettes are handled—through intensive distribution—by at least a million U.S. outlets, while Rolls Royces or expensive chinaware are handled—through exclusive distribution—by only a limited number of middlemen across the country.

Intensive distribution—sell it where they buy it

Intensive distribution is commonly needed for convenience products and for industrial supplies—such as pencils, paper clips, and typing paper—used by all plants and offices. Customers want such products nearby.

The seller's *intent* is important here. Intensive distribution refers to the *desire* to sell through *all* responsible and suitable outlets. What this means depends on customer habits and preferences. If target customers normally buy a certain product at a certain type of outlet, ideally you would specify this type of outlet in your Place policies. If customers prefer to buy your hardware items only at hardware stores, you might try to sell all hardware stores.

Selective distribution—sell it where it sells best

Selective distribution covers the area between intensive and exclusive distribution. It can be suitable for all products. Only the better middlemen are used. Here, a firm hopes to get some of the advantages of exclusive distribution—while still getting fairly widespread coverage.

A selective policy might be used to avoid selling to wholesalers or retailers who (1) have a poor credit rating, (2) have a reputation for making too many returns or wanting too much service, (3) place orders that are too small to justify making calls or providing service, or (4) are not in a position to do a good job.

Selective distribution is growing in popularity—as firms see that it isn't necessary to have 100 percent coverage of a market. Often, most of the sales come from relatively few customers—and the others buy too little compared to the cost of working with them. This is called the "80/20 rule"—because 80 percent of a company's sales often come from only 20 percent of its customers—*until it becomes more selective in choosing customers.*

In 1983, Esprit—a producer of colorful, trendy clothing—sold through about 4,000 department stores and specialty shops nationwide. Esprit found, however, that about half of the stores generated most of the sales. Sales analysis also showed that sales in Esprit's own stores were about 400 percent better than in other outlets. As a result, in 1986, it cut back to about 2,000 outlets, and opened more of its own stores—and profits increased.[16]

Exclusive distribution sometimes makes sense

Exclusive distribution means that only one middleman is selected in each geographic area. Manufacturers might use exclusive distribution to help control prices—and the service offered in a channel.

But is limiting market exposure legal?

Antimonopoly laws do not specifically prohibit exclusive distribution. But the courts' current interpretation of these laws gives the impression that almost any exclusive distribution arrangement could be interpreted as an injury to some competitor—somewhere.

The Supreme Court has consistently ruled illegal horizontal arrangements—among competing retailers, wholesalers, or manufacturers—to limit sales by customer or territory. This is seen as collusion—reducing competition and harming customers!

The legality of vertical arrangements—between producers and middlemen—is not as clear. A 1977 Supreme Court decision reversed its 1967 ruling that vertical relationships limiting territories or customers were always illegal. Now possible good effects can be weighed against possible harm to competition. As long as some good reason can be shown for limiting distribution—such as building stronger retailers who can offer advertising and sales support and better repair services, vertical arrangements may be legal.[17]

Caution is suggested

In spite of the recent Supreme Court ruling, firms should be very careful about entering into *any* exclusive distribution arrangements. The antimonopoly rules still apply. The courts can force a change in expensively developed relationships. And—even worse—triple damages can be imposed if the courts rule that competition has been hurt. Apparently, the law will allow some exclusive arrangements—to permit the introduction of a new product or to help a new company enter a market—but these arrangements probably should be short term.

The same cautions apply to selective distribution. Here, however, less formal arrangements are typical—and hurting competition is less likely. It's now more acceptable to carefully select channel members when building a channel system. Refusing to sell to some middlemen, however, should be part of a logical marketing plan that has long-term benefits to consumers.

HOW TO RECRUIT MIDDLEMEN

A producer has a special challenge—making sure its product reaches the end of the channel. To reach the target market, a producer may have to recruit middlemen.

The two basic methods of recruiting middlemen are pushing and pulling.[18]

Pushing policy—get a hand from the firms in the channel

Pushing (a product through a channel) means using normal promotion effort—personal selling and advertising—to help sell the whole marketing mix to possible channel members. The approach emphasizes the importance of building a channel—and getting the cooperation of channel members. In effect, the producer tries to develop a team that will work well—to "push" the product down the channel to the final user.

Pulling policy—make them reach for it out there

By contrast, **pulling** means getting consumers to ask middlemen for the product. This usually involves very aggressive promotion to final consumers—perhaps using coupons or samples—and the temporary bypassing of middlemen. If the promotion works, the middlemen are forced to carry the product—to satisfy customer requests.

This method may be used if many products are already competing in all desired outlets. But channel members should be told about the planned pulling effort—so they can be ready if the promotion works.

CHANNEL CAPTAIN NEEDED TO GUIDE CHANNEL PLANNING

Until now, we have considered an individual marketing manager as the strategy planner. But now we see that there may be several firms and marketing managers in a single distribution channel. It is logical that each channel have a **channel captain**—a manager who helps guide the activities of the whole channel. The question is: Which marketing manager should be the captain?

The idea of a single channel captain makes sense—but some channels don't have such a captain. The various firms may not be acting as a system—because of lack of leadership. Or the members of a channel system may not understand that they are part of a channel.[19]

But even if they don't know it, firms *are* connected by their policies. It makes sense to try to avoid channel conflicts by planning for channel relationships.

Producer or middlemen?

In the United States, producers frequently are the leaders in channel relations. Middlemen wait and see what the producer intends to do—and what he wants done. Then they decide whether their roles will be profitable—and whether they want to join in the producer's plans.

Some middlemen do take the lead—especially in foreign markets where there are fewer large producers. Such middlemen decide what their customers want and seek out producers—perhaps small ones—who can provide these products at reasonable prices.

Large middlemen are closer to the final user or consumer—and in good position to assume the channel captain role. It is even possible that middlemen—especially retailers—may dominate the channel systems of the future.

The captain guides the channel

The channel captain arranges for the necessary marketing activities in the best way. This might be done as shown in Exhibit 10–9 in a producer-domi-

Exhibit 10–9   How Channel Strategy Might Be Handled in a Producer-Dominated System

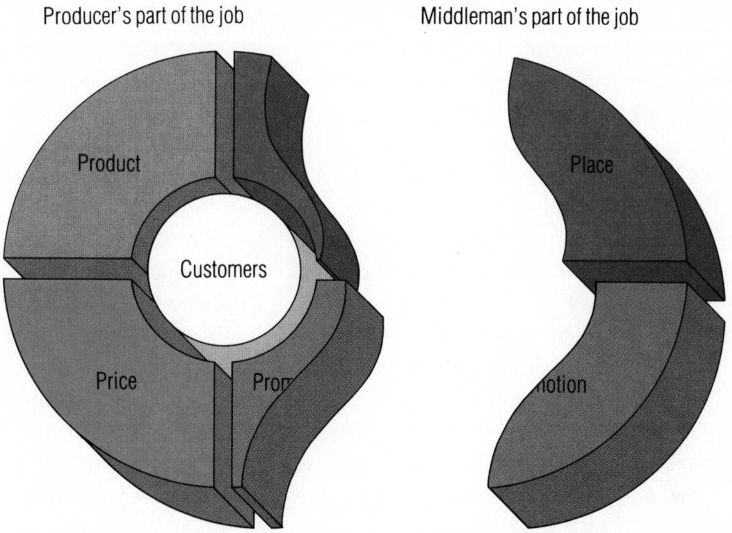

Producer's part of the job

Middleman's part of the job

nated channel system. Here, the producer has picked a target market—and developed a product, set the price structure, done some promotion, and developed the place setup. Middlemen then finish the promotion job—at their own places.

If a middleman is the channel captain, we would see quite a different picture. In the extreme—in a channel like that dominated by Sears—the middleman's part of the job would be larger. Producers would be mainly concerned with making the product to meet Sears' requirements.

A coordinated channel system may help everyone

A channel system in which the members accept leadership of a channel captain can work very well—even though not everyone in the channel system is strongly market-oriented. As long as the channel captain *is* market-oriented, it's possible to win the confidence and support of production-oriented firms—and make the whole channel work well.

Computerland is working with small producers in Korea to develop a Computerland brand of personal computers and accessories. The producers don't know much about the U.S. market. But, if Computerland correctly analyzes market needs and relays them clearly to the producers, the relationship will profit both the producers and Computerland—and the whole channel will compete effectively.

The choice of who will lead a channel system—and who will perform specific marketing functions in a channel—are important strategy decisions. They must be decided not only on the basis of costs but also on how Place (and PD) fits in with the rest of the marketing strategy.[20]

CONCLUSION

This chapter discussed the role of Place and Physical Distribution (PD) in marketing strategy planning. Place decisions are especially important because they may be hard to change.

Marketing specialists and channel systems develop to adjust discrepancies of quantity and assortment. Their regrouping activities are basic in any economic system—and adjusting discrepancies provides opportunities for creative marketers.

Physical distribution functions—transporting and storing—were discussed. These activities are needed to provide time, place, and possession utilities. And, by using the total cost approach, we can find the lowest-cost PD alternative—or the cost of various customer service levels.

The importance of planning channel systems was discussed—along with the role of a channel captain. We stressed that channel systems compete with each other—and that smoothly operating vertical marketing systems seem to be winning out in the marketplace.

Channel planning also requires deciding on the degree of market exposure desired. The legality of limiting market exposure should also be considered—to avoid jail or having to undo an expensively developed channel system.

Finally, we emphasized that producers aren't necessarily channel captains. Often, middlemen control or even dominate channels of distribution. Producers must consider the degree of this control when they decide whether they should try to push or pull products through a channel system.

Questions and Problems

1. Explain "discrepancies of quantity and assortment" using the clothing business as an example. How does the application of these concepts change when selling coal to the steel industry? What impact does this have on the number and kinds of marketing specialists required?

2. Explain the four regrouping activities with an example from the building supply industry (nails, paint, flooring, plumbing fixtures, etc.). Do you think that many specialists develop in this industry, or do producers handle the job themselves? What kinds of marketing channels would you expect to find in this industry, and what functions would various channel members provide?

3. Discuss the relative advantages and disadvantages of railroads, trucks, and airlines as transporting methods.

4. Discuss some of the ways that air transportation can change other aspects of a Place system.

5. Explain which transporting mode would probably be most suitable for shipping the following goods to a large Chicago department store:

a. 300 pounds of Alaskan crab.
b. 15 pounds of screwdrivers from New York.
c. Three dining room tables from High Point, North Carolina.
d. 500 high-fashion dresses from the garment district in New York City.
e. A 10,000-pound shipment of machines from England.
f. 600,000 pounds of various appliances from Evansville, Indiana.

How would your answers change if this department store were the only one in a large factory town in Ohio?

6. Indicate the nearest location where you would expect to find large storing facilities. What kinds of products would be stored there? Why are they stored there instead of some other place?

7. Indicate when a producer or middleman would find it desirable to use a public warehouse rather than a private warehouse. Illustrate, using a specific product or situation.

8. Discuss the distribution center concept. Is this likely to eliminate the storing function of conventional wholesalers? Is it applicable to all products? If not, cite several examples.

9. Clearly differentiate between a warehouse and a distribution center. Explain how a specific product would be handled differently by these marketing institutions.

10. Explain the total cost approach and why it may be controversial in some firms. Give examples of where conflicts might occur between different departments.

11. Explain how adjusting the customer service level could improve a marketing mix. Illustrate.

12. Explain how a "channel captain" could help traditional independent firms compete with a corporate (integrated) channel system.

13. How does the nature of the product relate to the degree of market exposure desired?

14. Why would middlemen want to be exclusive distributors for a product? Why would producers want exclusive distribution? Would middlemen be equally anxious to get exclusive distribution for any type of product? Why or why not? Explain with reference to the following products: chewing gum, razor blades, golf clubs, golf balls, steak knives, stereo equipment, and industrial woodworking machinery.

15. Explain the present legal status of exclusive distribution. Describe a situation where exclusive distribution is almost sure to be legal. Describe the nature and size of competitors and the industry, as well as the nature of the exclusive arrangement. Would this exclusive arrangement be of any value to the producer or middleman?

16. Discuss the promotion a grocery products producer would need in order to develop appropriate channels and move products through those channels. Would the nature of this job change at all for a dress producer? How about for a new small producer of installations?

17. Discuss the advantages and disadvantages of either a pushing or pulling policy for a very small producer just entering the candy business with a line of inexpensive candy bars. Which policy would probably be most appropriate?

Suggested Computer-Aided Problems

10a. Intensive vs. Selective Distribution

10b. Physical Distribution Systems

Suggested Cases

6. Applegate

16. Industrial Sales Company

17. Brogan Lumber Company

27. Orecan, Inc.

Chapter 11

Retailing

When You Finish This Chapter, You Should

1. Understand about retailers planning their own marketing strategies.

2. Know about the many kinds of retailers that might become members of producers' or wholesalers' channel systems.

3. Understand the differences among conventional and non-conventional retailers—including those who accept the mass-merchandising concept.

4. Understand "scrambled merchandising" and the "wheel of retailing."

5. Recognize the important new terms (shown in red).

If the products aren't sold, nobody makes any money.

Sears, the largest U.S. retailer, has decided that the best way to expand is to get smaller. Perhaps that statement needs some explaining. Sears sells a whopping $4 billion a year in home-improvement products—about 15 percent of its total sales. But Sears faces growing competition from firms like Hechingers and Home Depot that sell from warehouse-like stores and offer discounts on up to 25,000 different items. Even local hardware stores are becoming more aggressive—with the help of wholesale groups. This affected Sears' profits, so the company decided to sell hardware at more locations—to compete better. Now Sears is opening new stores—selling only paint and hardware. These smaller stores target consumers living in areas not conveniently served by regular Sears stores.[1]

Retailing covers all of the activities involved in the sale of products to final consumers. Retailing is important to all of us. As consumers, we spend $1.4 *trillion* (that's $1,400,000,000,000!) a year buying goods and services from retailers. If the retailing effort isn't effective, everyone in the channel suffers—and some products aren't sold at all. So retailing is important to marketing managers of consumer products at *all* channel levels.

Retailers must choose their own target markets and marketing mixes very carefully. As our Sears example shows, retailing is very competitive—and always changing.

What are the different kinds of retailers—and why did they develop? How do their strategies vary? What does the future look like for retailers? In this chapter, we'll try to answer these questions. We'll talk about the strategy decision areas shown in Exhibit 11–1.

Exhibit 11–1   Strategy Decision Areas for a Retailer

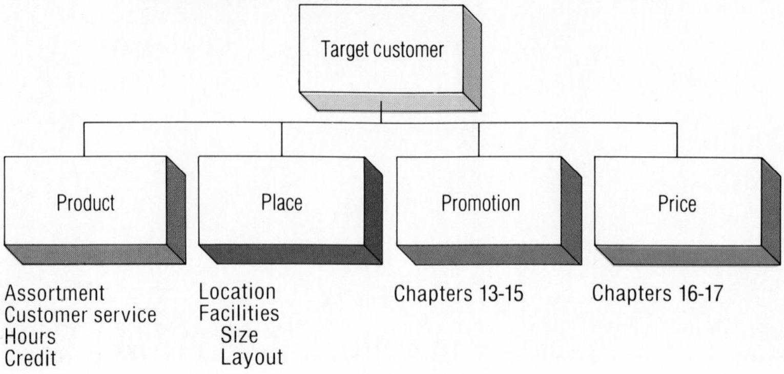

```
                    ┌──────────────────┐
                    │ Target customer  │
                    └──────────────────┘
        ┌──────────────┬──────────────┬──────────────┐
   ┌─────────┐   ┌─────────┐   ┌─────────┐   ┌─────────┐
   │ Product │   │  Place  │   │Promotion│   │  Price  │
   └─────────┘   └─────────┘   └─────────┘   └─────────┘
```

Assortment   Location
Customer service   Facilities   Chapters 13-15   Chapters 16-17
Hours   Size
Credit   Layout

PLANNING A RETAILER'S STRATEGY

Retailers are so directly involved with final consumers that their strategy planning must be done well or they won't survive. This makes *buying* an important activity for retailers. Successful retailers know the truth of the old rule: Goods well bought are half sold.

A retailer usually sells more than just one item. Think of the retailer's whole offering—assortment of goods and services, advice from sales clerks, convenient parking, packing and delivery, etc.—as its Product. Let's look at why customers choose particular retailers.

Consumers have reasons for buying from particular retailers

We know that different consumers prefer different kinds of retailers—but retailers often ignore *why* they do. Many new retailers just rent a store and assume that customers will flock to them. But more than three-fourths of new retailing efforts fail in their first year!

To be successful, retailers should try to adjust to changing conditions by identifying possible target markets and understanding why these people buy where they do.[2]

Economic needs— which store has the best value?

Consumers consider many things when choosing a particular retailer. For example:

1. Convenience.
2. Variety of selection.
3. Quality of products.
4. Help from salespeople.
5. Reputation for integrity and fairness in dealings.
6. Services offered—delivery, credit, return privileges.
7. Value offered.

**Emotional needs—
the importance of
social class**

Customers may prefer particular retailers for emotional reasons. Some may think a certain store has higher social status—and get an ego boost from shopping there.

Different stores do attract customers from different social classes. People like to shop where salespeople and other customers are like themselves. No one wants to feel "out of place."

The emotional needs that a store fills relate to its target market(s). Dollar General Stores—a chain of 1,300 general merchandise stores—has been very successful with a "budget" image that appeals to lower-class shoppers. Saks Fifth Avenue works at its upper-class image. But not all stores have—or want—a particular class image. Some try to avoid creating one because they want to appeal to a wide audience. Macy's, for example, has departments that carry some very expensive items—and others that handle products for the masses.

There is no one "right" answer as to whom a store should appeal. But ignoring emotional dimensions—including social class appeal—could lead to serious errors in marketing strategy planning.[3]

**Product classes help
explain store types**

Retail strategy planning can be simplified by extending our earlier discussion of consumer products classes—convenience products, shopping products, and specialty products—to define three types of stores.

A **convenience store** is a convenient place to shop—either centrally located "downtown" or "in the neighborhood." Such stores attract many customers because they are so handy. **Shopping stores** attract customers from greater distances because of the width and depth of their assortments. **Specialty stores** are those for which customers have developed a strong attraction. For whatever reasons—service, selection, or reputation—some customers will regularly buy at these stores. This is like brand insistence for products.

**Store types based on
how customers see
store**

These store types refer to the way *customers think of the store*—not just the kind of products the store carries. Also, different market segments might see or use a particular store differently. Remember this was true with the products classes, too. So a retailer's strategy planning must consider potential customers' attitudes toward both the product *and* the store. Classifying market segments by how they see both the store and the product—as shown in Exhibit 11–2—helps to make this clear.

A retailer can get a better understanding of a market by estimating the relative size of each of the boxes shown in Exhibit 11–2. By identifying which competitors are satisfying which market segments, the retailer may see that some boxes are already "filled." He may find that he and his competitors are all charging head-on after the same customers—and completely ignoring others.

For example, house plants used to be sold only by florists and greenhouses, satisfying customers who wanted "shopping store" variety. For other people, this was too much trouble—and they just didn't buy plants. When some retailers went after the "convenience store" segment—with small house

Exhibit 11–2   How Customers View Store-Product Combinations

Product class \ Store type	Convenience	Shopping	Specialty
Convenience	Will buy any brand at most accessible store	Shop around to find better service and/or lower prices	Prefer store. Brand may be important
Shopping	Want some selection but will settle for assortment at most accessible store	Want to compare both products and store mixes	Prefer store but insist on adequate assortment
Specialty	Prefer particular product but like place convenience too	Prefer particular product but still seeking best total product and mix	Prefer both store and product

plant departments or stores in neighborhood shopping centers—they found a new, large market segment willing to buy plants—at convenience stores.

While the way consumers see stores can help guide strategy planning, other dimensions of retailers are useful, too. Let's look at the kinds of retailers already competing in the marketplace—and how they developed.

TYPES OF RETAILERS AND THE NATURE OF THEIR OFFERINGS

There are nearly 2 million retailers in the United States—and they are always evolving.

Retailers differ in terms of service, product assortments, and width and depth of product lines. A paint store and a fabric store, for example, both have depth in their different lines. By contrast, a department store might have less depth in any one line—but carry more lines and more variety in each one. Some stores are strictly "self-service"—while others provide helpful sales clerks as well as credit, delivery, trade-ins, gift wrapping, special orders, and returns. Some retailers have "status" locations—downtown or at a mall. Others sell from vending machines or directly to a customer's home—without any store at all.

Each retailer's offering is some mix of these different characteristics. So we can't classify retailers using only a single characteristic. But it is helpful to describe basic types of retailers—and some differences in their strategies.

Let's look first at some of the conventional retailers and then see how others have modified the conventional offering and survived—because they met the needs of *some* customers.

CONVENTIONAL RETAILERS—TRY TO AVOID PRICE COMPETITION

Single-line, limited-line retailers specialized by product

A hundred and fifty years ago, **general stores**—that carried anything they could sell in reasonable volume—were the main retailers. But after the Civil War, the growing number and variety of consumer products made it hard for a general store to offer the depth and width customers wanted. So some stores began to specialize in dry goods, apparel, furniture, or groceries.

Now most conventional retailers are **single-line stores** or **limited-line stores** specializing in certain lines of related products rather than a wide assortment. Some of these stores specialize not only in a single line—such as clothing—but also in a limited-line within the broader line. For example, within the clothing line a store might carry only shoes, or formal wear, or men's casual wear, or even neckties—but offer depth in that limited line. This specialization will probably continue as long as customer demands are varied—and large enough to support such stores.

Single-line, limited-line stores are being squeezed

The main advantage of these stores is that they can satisfy some target markets better. Some even win specialty-store status by changing their marketing mix—including store hours, credit, and product assortment—to suit certain customers. Because these stores are small and must stock some slow-moving items to satisfy their customers, they often have high expenses relative to sales. They have traditionally followed the retailing rule of "buy low and sell high." If there is much competition, they may add more depth—specialize further—trying to keep costs down and prices up by avoiding competition on identical products.

These conventional retailers satisfy some needs and have been around for a long time. But newer retailers with more to offer will continue to squeeze them. See Exhibit 11–3. Let's take a closer look at these newer types of retailers.

EXPAND ASSORTMENT AND SERVICE—TO COMPETE AT A HIGH PRICE

Specialty shops usually sell shopping products

A **specialty shop**—a type of conventional limited-line store—is usually small and has a distinct "personality." Specialty shops aim at a carefully defined market segment by offering a unique product assortment, good service, and salespeople who know their products.[4] For example, specialty shops have developed to satisfy joggers. The clerks are runners themselves and are eager to explain the advantages of different types of running shoes to their customers. These stores also carry books on running—as well as clothes for the jogger.

A specialty shop's major advantage is that it caters to customers the management and salespeople come to know well. Because specialty shops usually offer special types of shopping products, knowing their customers simplifies buying, speeds turnover, and cuts costs. Specialty shops probably will remain

Exhibit 11–3   Types of Retailers and the Nature of Their Offerings

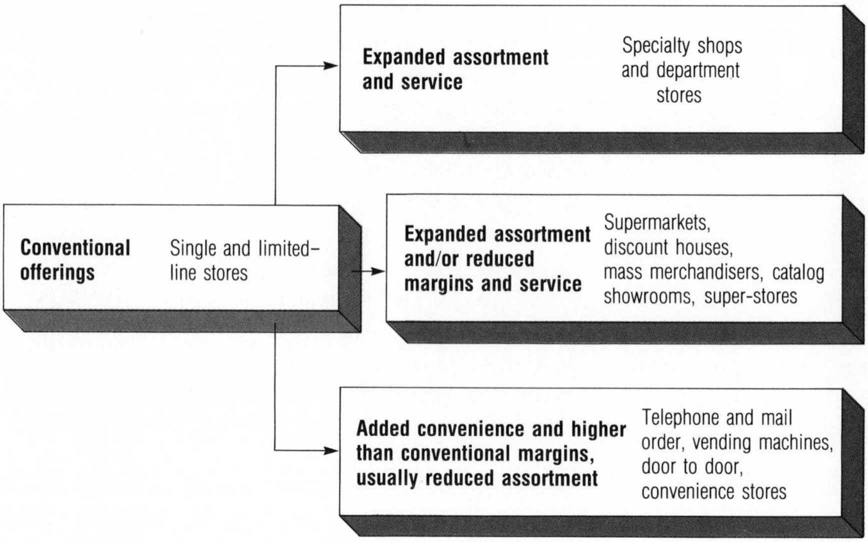

	Expanded assortment and service	Specialty shops and department stores
Conventional offerings Single and limited–line stores	**Expanded assortment and/or reduced margins and service**	Supermarkets, discount houses, mass merchandisers, catalog showrooms, super-stores
	Added convenience and higher than conventional margins, usually reduced assortment	Telephone and mail order, vending machines, door to door, convenience stores

in the retailing scene as long as customers have varied tastes—and the money to satisfy them.

Don't confuse specialty *shops* with specialty *stores*. A specialty store is a store that for some reason (service, quality, etc.) has become *the* store for some customers. For example, some customers see Sears as a specialty store and regularly buy their paint, hardware, and major appliances there—without shopping anywhere else.

Department stores combine many limited-line stores and specialty shops

Department stores are larger stores that are organized into many separate departments and offer many product lines. Each department is like a separate limited-line store or specialty shop. Department stores usually handle a wide variety of products—such as women's ready-to-wear and accessories, men's and boys' wear, textiles, housewares, and home furnishings.

Many see department stores as the retailing leaders in a community. They usually do lead in customer services—including credit, merchandise return, delivery, fashion shows, and Christmas displays. They also are leaders because of their size. The most recent census of retailers showed that U.S. department stores averaged about $10.7 million annual sales—compared to about $550,000 for the average retail store.[5] The biggest—Macy's, May Company, and Dayton-Hudson—each top $500 million in sales annually. Although department stores account for less than 1 percent of the total number of retail stores, they make over 10 percent of total retail sales.

Department stores generally aim at customers seeking shopping products. They are thought of as shopping *stores* by most people. But some department stores have earned specialty store status. They have a strong hold on their market.

Originally, most department stores were located downtown, close to other department stores and potential customers. When many middle- and upper-income people moved to the suburbs after World War II, some department stores opened suburban branches—usually in shopping centers. This helped offset declining sales at the downtown stores. But department stores' share of retail business has been declining since the 1970s. Well-run limited-line stores are competing with good service—and they often carry the same brands. An even bigger threat has come from mass-merchandising retailers who operate with lower costs and sell large volumes.[6] We'll discuss them next.

EVOLUTION OF NEW, MASS–MERCHANDISING RETAILERS

Mass-merchandising is different than conventional retailing

So far we've been describing retailers mainly in terms of product assortment—the traditional way. We could talk about supermarkets and discount houses in these terms, too. But then we would miss an important difference—just as some conventional retailers did when these stores first appeared.

Conventional retailers believe in a fixed demand for a territory—and have a "buy low and sell high" philosophy. Some modern retailers, however, have accepted the **mass-merchandising concept**—which says that retailers should offer low prices to get faster turnover and greater sales volumes—by appealing to larger markets. To understand mass-merchandising better, let's look at its evolution from the development of supermarkets and discounters to the modern mass-merchandisers—like K mart.

Supermarkets started the move to mass-merchandising

A **supermarket** is a large store specializing in groceries—with self-service and wide assortments. As late as 1930, most food stores were relatively small single- or limited-line operations. In the early Depression years, some creative people felt that charging lower prices would increase sales. They introduced self-service, provided a very broad product assortment in large stores, and offered low prices. Their early experiments in vacant warehouses were an immediate success. Profits came from large sales volume—not from traditional "high" markups.[7]

Supermarkets sell convenience products—but in quantity. They typically carry 12,000 product items. Stores are large—around 20,000 square feet—with free parking. According to the Food Marketing Institute, $2 million is the minimum annual sales volume for a store to be called a supermarket. In 1986, there were over 30,500 supermarkets—about 20 percent of all food stores—and they handled more than half of all food store sales. Today, there are almost too many supermarkets, but new ones still do well when they are well located.[8]

Supermarkets are planned so products can be loaded on the shelves easily. The store layout makes it easy for customers to shop. Scanners at check-out counters help analyze the sales and profit of each item—and allow more shelf space for faster moving and higher profit items. This helps sell more products faster, reduces the investment in inventory, makes stocking easier, and reduces the cost of handling products. Such efficiency is very important—

because competition is tough. Net profits (after taxes) in grocery supermarkets usually run a thin 1 percent of sales—*or less!*

Catalog showroom retailers came before discount houses

Catalog showroom retailers sell several lines out of a catalog and display showroom—with backup inventories. Before 1940, these retailers were usually wholesalers who also sold at retail to friends and members of groups—such as labor unions or church groups. In the 1970s, however, these operations expanded rapidly—offering big price savings on jewelry, gifts, luggage, and small appliances. Catalog showrooms—like Service Merchandise, Consumers Distributing, and Best—tend to focus on well-known manufacturers' brands. They offer few services.[9]

The early catalog operations didn't bother the conventional retailers—because they were not well promoted and accounted for only a small part of total retail sales. If these early catalog retailers had moved ahead aggressively—as the current catalog retailers are doing—the retailing scene might be different. But instead, discount houses developed.

Discount houses upset some conventional retailers

Right after World War II, some retailers moved beyond offering discounts to selected customers. These **discount houses** offered "hard goods" (cameras, TVs, appliances)—with big price cuts—to customers who would go to the discounter's low-rent store, pay cash, and take care of any service or repair problems themselves. These retailers sold at 20 to 30 percent below conventional retailers.

In the early 1950s—with war shortages finally over—well-known brands were more available, and discount houses could offer fuller assortments. At this stage, many discounters "turned respectable"—moving to better locations and offering more services and guarantees. They began to act more like regular retailers—but still kept their prices lower than conventional retailers to keep turnover high. And they still do today—frustrating conventional retailers!

Mass-merchandisers are more than discounters

Mass merchandisers are large, self-service stores with many departments—that emphasize "soft goods" (housewares, clothing, and fabrics) but still follow the discount house's emphasis on lower margins to get faster turnover. Mass-merchandisers—like K mart and Zayre—have check-out counters in the front of the store and little or no sales help on the floor. This is different than more conventional retailers—such as Sears and J. C. Penney—who still offer some service and have sales stations and cash registers in most departments. The conventional retailer may try to carry complete stocks and reorder popular sizes or items in the lines it carries. But mass-merchandisers want to move merchandise—fast—and are less concerned with continuity of lines and assortment.

The average mass-merchandiser has nearly 60,000 square feet of floor space—three to four times the size of the average supermarket. Mass-merchandisers grew so rapidly in some areas that they no longer took customers from conventional retailers—but from each other. Lately, profits have dropped, and many stores have failed. Seeing fewer opportunities in big cities, K mart has started moving into smaller towns with a smaller K mart. This has really upset some small-town merchants—who felt safe from this kind of competition.[10]

Super-stores meet all routine needs

Super-stores—are very large stores that try to carry not only foods, but all goods and services that the consumer purchases *routinely.* Although such a store may look like a mass-merchandiser, it tries to meet *all* the customer's routine needs—at a low price.

Super-stores are much bigger than supermarkets or mass-merchandisers. The super-store offers not only foods—but also personal care products, alcoholic beverages, some clothing, some lawn and garden products, gasoline—and services such as laundry, dry cleaning, shoe repair, check cashing, and bill paying. Some mass-merchandisers have moved in this direction—and if super-stores spread, food-oriented supermarkets may suffer because their present buildings and parking lots are not large enough to convert to super-stores.[11]

SOME RETAILERS FOCUS ON ADDED CONVENIENCE

The supermarkets, discounters, and mass-merchandisers sell many different products "under one roof." But they are inconvenient in some ways. They offer fewer customer services, check-out lines may be longer, and stores may be in less convenient, "low-rent" locations. The savings may justify these inconveniences when a consumer has a lot to buy. But sometimes—for some products—convenience is much more important—even if the price is a little higher. Let's look at some retailers who met a need by emphasizing convenience.

Convenience (food) stores must have the right assortment

Convenience (food) stores are a convenience-oriented variation of the conventional limited-line food stores. Instead of carrying a big variety, they limit their stock to "fill-in" items like bread, milk, ice cream, and beer. Stores such as 7-Eleven, Majik Market, and White Hen Pantry fill needs between major shopping trips to a supermarket. They offer convenience—not assortment—and often charge 10 to 20 percent more than nearby supermarkets. They net about 4 percent on sales—rather than the 1 percent supermarkets earn. This helps explain why the number of such stores rose from 2,500 in 1960 to over 30,000 in the 1980s.[12]

Vending machines are convenient

Automatic vending is selling and delivering products through vending machines. Vending machine sales have increased but still are only about 1.5 percent of total U.S. retail sales. In some lines, however, vending machines are very important. Sixteen percent of all cigarettes sold in the United States, 20 percent of the candy bars, and 25 percent of canned and bottled soft drinks are sold through machines.

The major problem with automatic vending is high cost. The machines are expensive to buy, stock, and repair—relative to the volume they sell. Marketers of similar non-vended products can operate profitably on a margin of about 20 percent—while the vending industry needs about 41 percent to break even.

So they must charge higher prices.[13] If costs come down—and consumers continue to want convenience—we may see more growth in this retailing method. The 24-hour bank teller machine—where a customer can use his "money card" to get cash—provides a hint of how technology may change automatic vending.

Shopping at home— with telephone, TV, and direct-mail retailing

Telephone and direct-mail retailing allows consumers to shop at home— placing orders by mail or telephone—and charging the purchase to a credit card. Catalogs and ads on TV let customers "see" the offerings—and purchases are delivered by mail or United Parcel Service (UPS). This "mail-order" method can reach widely scattered markets that conventional retailers can't serve.

"Mail-order" retailing continues to grow—recently at the rapid rate of about 15 percent per year—and now accounts for about 4 percent of retail sales. Mail-order retailing has changed, however. Many companies offer toll-free telephone numbers for ordering and information. They aim at narrower target markets—with more expensive fashion, gift, and luxury items.[14]

The big mail-order houses started it all—but now many department stores and limited-line stores see the profit possibilities and sell by phone and mail, too. Not only can they get additional business this way—but costs may be lower because they can use warehouse-type buildings and limited sales help. After-tax profits for mail-order retailers average 7 percent of sales—more than twice the profit margins for most other types of retailers.

Door-to-door retailers—give personal attention

Door-to-door selling means going directly to the consumer's home. It accounts for less than 1 percent of retail sales—but it meets some consumers' needs for convenience and personal attention. This can be a good way to introduce a new product or sell unsought products. But with more adults working outside the home, it's getting harder to find customers at home—especially during the day.

WHY RETAILERS EVOLVE AND CHANGE

We've talked about different kinds of retailers. Exhibit 11–4 shows the relationship among these different retailers—and their offerings. Now let's look at how retailing is changing.

Scrambled merchandising—mixing product lines for higher profits

Conventional retailers tend to specialize by product line. But most modern retailers have moved toward **scrambled merchandising**—carrying any products they feel they can sell profitably. Supermarkets and "drug stores" are selling anything they can move in volume—while mass-merchandisers sell groceries, cameras, jewelry, and even home computers. Why has scrambled merchandising become so common?

The wheel of retailing keeps rolling

The **wheel of retailing theory** says that new types of retailers enter the market as low-status, low-margin, low-price operators and then—if suc-

Exhibit 11–4   A Three-Dimensional View of the Market for Retail Facilities and the Probable Position of Some Present Offerings

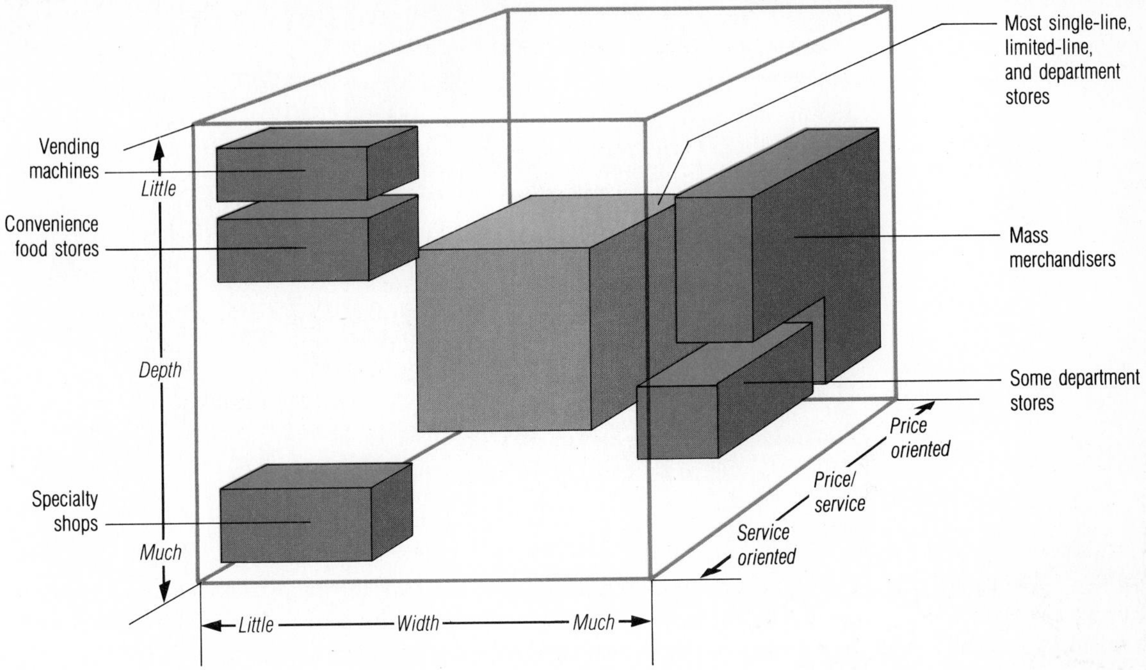

cessful—evolve into more conventional retailers offering more services—with higher operating costs and higher prices. Then they are threatened by new low-status, low-margin, low-price retailers—and the wheel turns again.

Early department stores began this way but slowly raised prices and added "bargain basements" to serve the more price-conscious customers. The supermarket also started with low prices and little service. Mass-merchandisers have gone through the same cycle.

Some innovators start with high margins

The wheel of retailing theory, however, does not explain all major retailing developments. Vending machines entered as high-cost, high-margin operations. Convenience food stores and suburban shopping centers have never had a low-price emphasis either.

Retailing types also explained by consumer needs filled

Consumer needs also affect the type of retailer that develops. Look at Exhibit 11–4. It gives a simplified view of the consumer market. It suggests that three consumer-oriented dimensions affect the kinds of retailers customers choose: (1) width of assortment desired, (2) depth of assortment desired, and (3) price/service combination. Most existing retailers fall within this three-dimensional market. Exhibit 11–4, for example, suggests the "why" of vending machines. Some customers—in the front upper left-hand corner—have a strong need for a specific item—and are *not* interested in the width of assortment, the depth of assortment, *or* the price.

Supermarkets are "scrambling" video movie cassettes because they offer fast turnover and a good profit margin.

Product life-cycle concept applies to retailer types, too

We've seen that people's needs help explain why different kinds of retailers developed. Applying the product life-cycle concept explains this process further. A retailer with a new idea may have big profits—for awhile. But if it's a really good idea, he can count on speedy imitation—and a squeeze on his profits. Other retailers will "scramble" their product mix—to sell products with high profit margins or faster turnover.

Some conventional retailers are far along in their life cycles—and may be declining. Recent innovators are still in the market growth stage. See Exhibit 11–5.

Some retailers are confused by the scrambling going on around them. They don't see this evolutionary process—and don't understand that some of their more successful competitors are aiming at different market segments—instead of just "selling products."

It's not surprising that some modern success stories in retailing include firms that moved into an unsatisfied market and started another "product life cycle"—by aiming at needs along the edges of the broad market shown in Exhibit 11–4. Convenience food stores, for example, don't just sell food. They deliberately sell a particular assortment-service combination to meet a different need. This is also true of specialty shops—and some mass-merchandisers and department store chains.[15]

RETAILER SIZE AND PROFITS

We've talked about different types of retailers—and how they evolved. Now let's look at the size of stores—and how they are owned—because these relate to retailer strategy planning, too.

Exhibit 11–5   Retailer Life Cycles—Timing and Years to Market Maturity

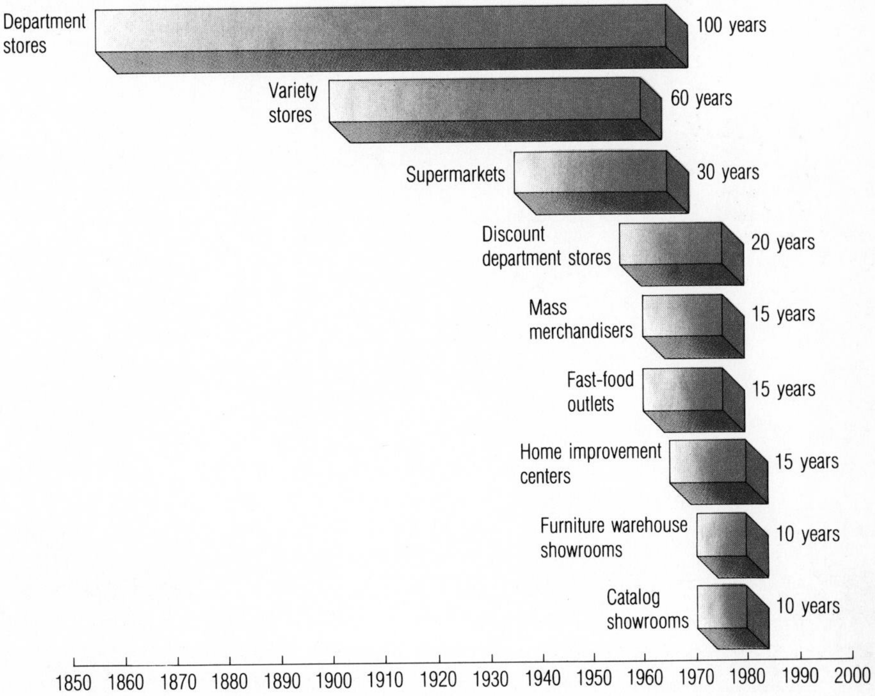

Department stores — 100 years

Variety stores — 60 years

Supermarkets — 30 years

Discount department stores — 20 years

Mass merchandisers — 15 years

Fast-food outlets — 15 years

Home improvement centers — 15 years

Furniture warehouse showrooms — 10 years

Catalog showrooms — 10 years

1850 1860 1870 1880 1890 1900 1910 1920 1930 1940 1950 1960 1970 1980 1990 2000

The number of retailers is very large

There are lots of retailers—in part because it's easy to enter retailing. Kids can open and close a lemonade stand in one day. A more serious retailer can rent an empty store and be in business without putting up much money (capital). When the last census was taken, there were nearly 2 million retailers compared to just over 400,000 wholesalers and 350,000 manufacturers.

But a few big ones do most of the business

The large number of retailers suggests that retailing is a field of small businesses. This is partly true. As shown in Exhibit 11–6, about 60 percent of all retail stores had annual sales of less than $250,000—and such stores had only 8 percent of total sales. The larger retail stores—such as supermarkets and others selling more than $2.5 million annually—do most of the business. Only about 4 percent of the retail stores are this big, yet they account for over 50 percent of all retail sales.

Small retailers reach many consumers—and often are valuable channel members. But they cause problems for producers and wholesalers. Their large number—and relatively small sales volume—make working with them expensive. They often require separate marketing mixes.

Small size may be hard to overcome

A small retailer may satisfy some personal needs—by being his own boss. And his flexibility can be very helpful to some target customers. But a small store may only *seem* profitable because some business costs are ignored. The

Exhibit 11–6 Distribution of Stores by Size and Share of Total Retail Sales (United States, 1982)

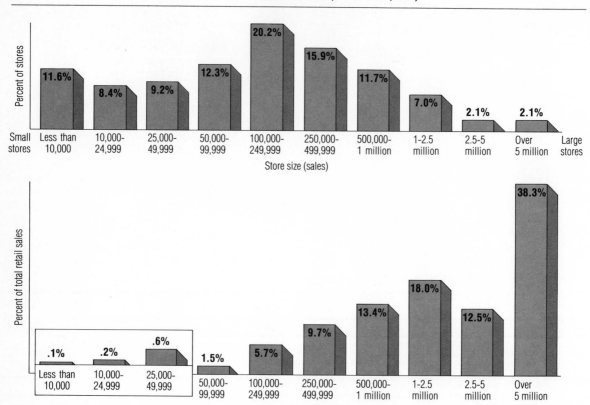

owner may not be allowing for depreciation—or for family members working without pay. About a half million small retailers—one-fourth of the total—sell less than $50,000 per year—which, after expenses, leaves hardly enough to support one person.

Even the average retail store is too small to gain economies of scale. Average annual sales of only $550,000 is not very impressive—especially considering that net profits as a percentage of sales range from 1 to 5 percent.

The disadvantage of small size may even apply to the many departments in a large department store. Its many small departments may not be any larger than independent limited-line stores—so there is little possibility for volume buying.[16]

Being in a chain may help

A corporate chain offers one way for a retailer to gain economies of scale. A **(corporate) chain store** is one of several stores owned and managed by the same firm. Most chains do at least some central buying for different stores—allowing them to take advantage of quantity discounts. They may also have advantages in promotion and management—spreading the costs to many stores.

Chains grew slowly until after World War I—then spurted ahead during the

Chain stores—like Sears—win a very large share of all retail business.

1920s. They now account for about 53 percent of retail sales—and about 22 percent of the retailers.

Chains have done even better in certain lines. They have 99 percent of the department store business. Sears, Montgomery Ward, and J. C. Penney are chains. Safeway, Kroger, A&P, and other supermarket chains have 70 percent of the grocery sales.

Independents form chains, too

The growth of corporate chains has encouraged the development of cooperative chains and voluntary chains.

Cooperative chains are retailer-sponsored groups—formed by independent retailers—to run their own buying organizations and joint promotion efforts. Sales of cooperative chains have risen as they learned how to meet the corporate chain competition. Examples include Associated Grocers, Certified Grocers, and True Value (hardware).

Voluntary chains are wholesaler-sponsored groups that work with "independent" retailers. Some are linked by contracts stating common operating procedures—and the use of common store front designs, store name, and joint promotion efforts. Examples include IGA and Super Valu in groceries, Ace in hardware, and Western Auto in auto supplies.

Franchisers form chains, too

In **franchise operations** the franchiser develops a good marketing strategy—and the franchise holders carry out the strategy in their own units. Each franchise holder benefits from the experience, buying power, and image of the larger company. The parent company also trains its franchise holders, which lowers the failure rate. Government studies show only about 5 percent of new franchise operations fail in the first few years—compared to about 70 percent of other new retailers.[17] Examples of well-known franchise operations are shown in Exhibit 11–7.

LOCATION OF RETAIL FACILITIES

Location can spell success or failure for a retailer. But what's a "good location" can change—as target markets, competitors, costs, and other nearby stores change.

Exhibit 11–7 *Examples of Some Well-Known Franchise Operations*

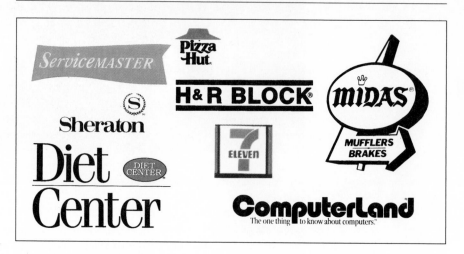

Downtown and shopping strips—evolve without a plan

Most cities have a "central business district" with many retail stores. It may seem that such districts developed according to some plan. Actually, the location of individual stores is more an accident of time—and available space. And, as cities grow, "shopping strips" of convenience stores spring up along major roads. Generally, they emphasize convenience products. But a variety of single-line and limited-line stores may enter, too, adding shopping products to the mix. There may be a lot of turnover—as one goes out of business and another takes its place.

Although some city planners restrict commercial development, most of these retail areas are unplanned—unlike the planned shopping centers developed in the last 30 years.

Planned shopping centers—not just a group of stores

A **planned shopping center** is a set of stores planned as a unit—to satisfy some market needs. Free parking is provided. Many centers are enclosed—to make shopping more pleasant. The stores sometimes act together for promotion purposes.

Neighborhood shopping centers consist of several convenience stores. These centers usually include a supermarket, drug store, hardware store, beauty shop, laundry, dry cleaner, gas station, and perhaps a bakery or appliance shop. They normally serve 7,500 to 40,000 people living within 6 to 10 minutes driving distance.

Community shopping centers are larger and offer some shopping stores as well as the convenience stores found in neighborhood shopping centers. They usually include a small department store that carries shopping products (clothing and home furnishings). But most sales in these centers are convenience products. Such centers serve 40,000 to 150,000 people within a radius of five to six miles.

Regional shopping centers are the largest centers and emphasize shopping stores and shopping products. Most are enclosed malls. They include one or more large department stores—and as many as 200 smaller stores. Stores that feature convenience products are often placed at the edge of the center—so they won't get in the way of customers really interested in shopping.

Regional centers usually serve 150,000 or more people. They are like downtown shopping districts of larger cities and usually are found near suburban areas. They draw customers from a radius of 7 to 10 miles—or even further, from rural areas with limited shopping facilities. Regional shopping centers are often in the 2 million square foot range—as large as 40 football fields!

WHAT DOES THE FUTURE LOOK LIKE?

Retailing continues to change. Scrambled merchandising may become more scrambled. Some people forecast larger stores—while others predict smaller ones.

More customer-oriented retailing may be coming

Forecasting trends is risky—but our three-dimensional picture of the retailing market (Exhibit 11–4) can be helpful. Those who predict bigger stores are looking at the mass market. Those who expect more small stores and specialty shops expect more demanding—but increasingly wealthy—target markets able to afford higher prices for special products.

To serve these markets, convenience stores will continue to spread. And "electronic" retailing is expected to grow. For example, Compusave Corporation now has an "electronic catalog" order system. A videodisk player hooked to a TV-like screen allows a consumer to see pictures and descriptions of thousands of products. The product assortment is similar to that at a catalog store—and the prices are even lower. To make a purchase, the consumer inserts a credit card, and the computer places the order and routes it to the consumer's home. Experts predict that there may be 50,000 of these videodisk vending machines by 1990—with total sales up to $10 billion![18]

American consumers simply don't have as much time to shop as they once did—and a growing number are willing to pay for convenience. Stores probably will continue to make shopping more convenient—by staying open later, carrying assortments that make one-stop shopping possible, and paying greater attention to products that consumers want in stock.

In-home shopping will become more popular

Telephone shopping will become more popular, too. Mail-order houses and department stores already find phone business attractive. Telephone supermarkets now sell only by phone and deliver all orders.

We now have far greater electronic capabilities than we are using. There is no reason why customers can't shop in the home—saving time and gasoline. Such automated retailing could take over a large share of the convenience products and homogeneous shopping products business.

Retailers becoming manufacturers and vice versa

We may also see more horizontal and vertical arrangements in channel systems. This would certainly affect present manufacturers—who already see retailers developing their own brands, using manufacturers as production arms.

Large manufacturers themselves may go into retailing—for self-protection. Rexall Corporation, Sherwin-Williams, B. F. Goodrich, Van Heusen, and others already control their own retail outlets.

Retailing will continue to be needed. But the role of individual retailers—and even the concept of a retail store—may have to change. Customers will always have needs. But retail stores aren't the only way to satisfy them!

Retailers must face the challenge

One thing is certain—retailing will continue to change. For years, conventional retailers' profits have gone down. Even some of the newer discounters and shopping centers have not done well. Department stores and food and drug chains have seen profit declines. Conventional "variety stores" have done even worse. Some shifted into mass-merchandising—but, as we saw, trouble has hit even some mass-merchandisers.

A few firms—especially K mart—avoided this general profit squeeze. But the future doesn't look bright for retailers who can't—or won't—change.

No easy way for more profit

In fact, it seems that there is no easy way to big profit any more. Instead, future success demands careful strategy planning—and great care in carrying out the plans. This means more careful market segmenting to find unsatisfied needs which (1) have a long life expectancy and (2) can be satisfied with low levels of investment. This won't be easy. But the imaginative marketing planner will find more profitable opportunities than the conventional retailer who doesn't know that the product life cycle is moving along—and is just hoping for the best.[19]

CONCLUSION

Modern retailing is scrambled—and we will probably see more changes in the future. A producer's marketing manager must choose very carefully among available retailers. And retailers must plan marketing mixes with target customers' needs in mind.

We described many types of retailers—and saw that each has its advantages and disadvantages. We also saw that some modern retailers have left conventional ways behind. The old "buy low and sell high" idea is no longer a safe rule. Lower margins with faster turnover is the modern idea—as retailers move into mass-merchandising. But even this doesn't guarantee success—as retailers' product life cycles move on.

Scrambled merchandising will probably continue as the "wheel of retailing" continues to roll. But important breakthroughs are still possible—because consumers may continue to move away from conventional retailers. For example, some combination of electronic ordering and home delivery or vending may make convenience products more easily available.

Our society needs a retailing function—but perhaps not all the present retailers. It is safe to say that retailing offers the marketing manager new challenges and opportunities.

Questions and Problems

1. Identify a specialty store selling convenience products in your city. Explain why you think it is that kind of store and why an awareness of this status would be important to a manufacturer. Does it give the retailer any particular advantage? If so, with whom?

2. What sort of a "product" are specialty shops offering? What are the prospects for organizing a chain of specialty shops?

3. Many department stores have a bargain basement. Does the basement represent just another department, like the hat department or the luggage department. Or is some whole new concept involved?

4. Distinguish among discount houses, price cutting by conventional retailers, and mass-merchandising. Forecast the future of low-price selling in food, clothing, and appliances.

5. Discuss a few changes in the uncontrollable environment that you think help to explain why telephone and mail-order retailing has been growing so rapidly.

6. Apply the "wheel of retailing" theory to your local community. What changes seem likely? Will established retailers see the need for change, or will entirely new firms have to develop?

7. Discuss the kinds of markets served by the three types of shopping centers. Are they directly competitive? Do they contain the same kinds of stores? Is the long-run outlook for all of them similar?

8. Explain the growth and decline of various retailers and shopping centers in your own community. Use the text's three-dimensional drawing (Exhibit 11–4) and the product life-cycle concept. Also, treat each retailers' whole offering as a "product."

Suggested Computer-Aided Problem

11. Mass-merchandising

Suggested Cases

12. Nike and the Joggers House

15. Graphic Arts, Inc.

18. Hutton, Inc.

Chapter 12

Wholesaling

When You Finish This Chapter, You Should

1. Understand what wholesalers are and the wholesaling functions they *may* provide for others in channel systems.

2. Know the various kinds of merchant wholesalers and agent middlemen.

3. Understand when and where the various kinds of merchant wholesalers and agent middlemen would be most useful to strategy planners.

4. Understand why wholesalers have lasted.

5. Recognize the important new terms (shown in red).

"I can get it for you wholesale," the man said. But could he? Would it be a good deal?

Baxter Healthcare Corporation provides hospitals with about 70 percent of all the items they need—and does it within 24 hours—no small feat. To help hospitals reduce costs—and to stay the leader in its field—Baxter has developed new strategies. For example, a Baxter sales rep works *full-time* for Nashville's Hospital Corp. of America—which controls purchasing for many hospitals. The Baxter rep helps control inventory and handling costs—which can eat up a large part of a hospital's budget. Baxter also offers a "cash refund" to hospitals that buy in larger quantities. In return, more than 350 hospitals have agreed not to seek competitive bids on products carried by Baxter. Baxter's success has encouraged imitators, so Baxter is seeking new opportunities—by shifting more of its personal selling effort to nursing homes, doctors' offices, and clinics.[1]

You can see from this Baxter example that wholesalers can provide many different functions and be an important link in a channel system—helping both suppliers and customers. Although they are separate business firms that must plan their own strategies, you can understand wholesalers better if you look at them as members of a channel of distribution.

In this chapter, you will learn more about wholesalers. You will see how they have evolved, how they fit into various channels, why they are used, and what functions they perform.

WHAT IS A WHOLESALER?

It's hard to define just what a wholesaler is—because there are so many different wholesalers doing different jobs. Some of their activities may even seem like manufacturing. In fact, some wholesalers call themselves "manufacturer and dealer." Others like to identify themselves with such general terms as merchant, dealer, or distributor. Others just use the name commonly used in their trade—without really thinking about what is means.

To avoid a long technical discussion on the nature of wholesaling, we will use the U.S. Bureau of the Census definition:

Wholesaling is concerned with the activities of those persons or establishments which sell to retailers and other merchants, and/or to industrial, institutional, and commercial users, but who do not sell in large amounts to final consumers.

So **wholesalers** are firms whose main function is providing wholesaling activities.

Note that producers who take over wholesaling activities are not considered wholesalers. However, if separate middlemen firms—such as branch warehouses—are set up by producers, then they are counted as wholesalers by the U.S. Census Bureau. Wholesaling must be seen as a middleman activity.

POSSIBLE WHOLESALING FUNCTIONS

Wholesalers may perform certain functions for both their own customers and their suppliers. These wholesaling functions are just variations of the eight basic marketing functions discussed in Chapter 1. And note that *these functions are provided by some, but not all, wholesalers.*

What a wholesaler might do for customers

1. *Regroup products*—provide the quantity and assortment customers want at the lowest possible cost.
2. *Anticipate needs*—forecast customers' demands and buy for them.
3. *Carry stocks*—carry inventory so customers don't have to store a large inventory.
4. *Deliver products*—provide prompt delivery at low cost.
5. *Grant credit*—give credit to customers, perhaps supplying their working capital. (Note: This financing function may be *very* important to small customers. It is sometimes the main reason why they use wholesalers—rather than buying directly from producers.)
6. *Provide information and advisory service*—supply price and technical information as well as suggestions on how to install and sell products. (Note: The wholesaler's sales force may be experts in the products they sell.)
7. *Provide part of buying function*—offer products to potential customers so they don't have to hunt for supply sources.
8. *Own and transfer title to products*—help by completing a sale without the need for other middlemen—speeding the whole buying and selling process.

A wholesaler often helps its customers by carrying needed products and providing prompt delivery at low cost.

If your store's sales are moving faster than your distributor, make a quick call to us.

For convenience stores, nothing is more inconvenient than running out when customers are running in.

That's why Southland maintains a 99.7% in-stock rate. Why placing an electronic order takes only seconds. Why we deliver on the day we promise, in less than 30 minutes.

Stores with brisk sales need a system that knows how to move.

Call Southland. We're ready to roll.

southland distribution center

What a wholesaler might do for producer-suppliers

1. *Provide part of producer's selling function*—by going to producer-suppliers instead of waiting for their sales reps to call.
2. *Store inventory*—reduce a producer's need to carry large stocks—and so cut his storing expenses.
3. *Supply capital*—reduce a producer's need for working capital by buying his output and carrying it in inventory until it's sold.
4. *Reduce credit risk*—by selling to customers the wholesaler knows—and taking the loss if these customers don't pay.
5. *Provide market information*—as an informed buyer and seller closer to the market, the wholesaler reduces the producer's need for market research.[2]

KINDS AND COSTS OF AVAILABLE WHOLESALERS

Exhibit 12–1 compares the number, sales volume, and operating expenses of some major types of wholesalers. The differences in operating expenses suggest that each of these types does different wholesaling functions. But which ones and why?

Why, for example, do manufacturers use merchant wholesalers—costing 13 percent of sales—when manufacturers' sales branches cost only 6.8 percent? Why use either when agent middlemen cost only 4.5 percent?

To answer these questions, we must understand what these wholesalers do—and don't do. Exhibit 12–2 gives a big-picture view of the wholesalers described in more detail below. Note that a major difference is whether they *own* the products they sell.

Exhibit 12–1   Wholesale Trade by Type of Operation and Cost (as a percent of sales)

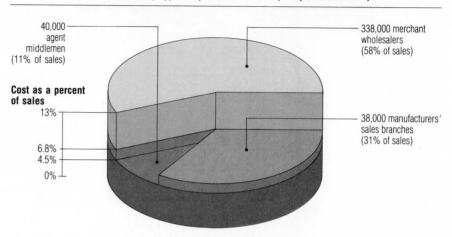

Wholesaler provides access to a target market

One of a wholesaler's main assets is its customers. A certain wholesaler may be the only one who reaches some customers. The producer who wants to reach these customers *may have no choice but to use that wholesaler.* "What customers does this wholesaler serve?" should be one of the first questions you ask when planning a channel of distribution.[3]

Exhibit 12–2   Types of Wholesalers

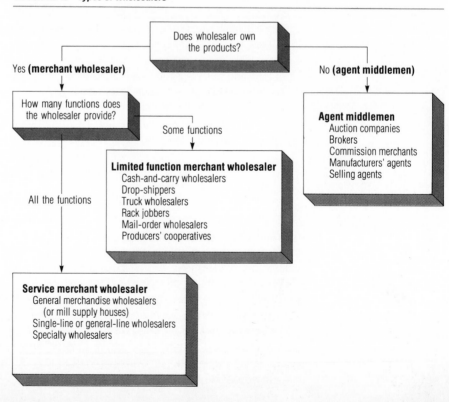

Learn the pure to understand the real

The next important question should be, "What functions does this particular wholesaler provide?" Wholesalers typically specialize by product line. But they do provide different functions. And they probably will keep doing what they're doing—no matter what others might like them to do!

To help you understand wholesaling better, we will describe "pure types" of wholesalers. In practice, it may be hard to find examples of these pure types—because many wholesalers are mixtures. Further, the names commonly used in a particular industry may be misleading. Some so-called "brokers" actually behave as limited-function merchant wholesalers—and some "manufacturers' agents" operate as full-service wholesalers. This casual use of terms make it all the more important for you to understand the pure types before trying to understand the blends—and the names used in the business world.

In the following pages, we'll discuss the major types of wholesalers identified by the U.S. Census Bureau. Remember, detailed data is available by kind of business, by product line, and by geographic territory. Such detailed data can be valuable in strategy planning—to learn whether potential channel members are serving a target market—as well as the sales volumes present middlemen are achieving.

MERCHANT WHOLESALERS ARE THE MOST NUMEROUS

Merchant wholesalers own (take title to) the products they sell. For example, a wholesale lumber yard that buys plywood from a producer is a merchant wholesaler. It actually owns—"takes title to"—the lumber before selling it to its customers.

As you might guess based on the large number of merchant wholesalers, they often specialize by certain types of products or customers. And several wholesalers may be competing for the same customers. For example, restaurants, hotels, and cafeterias purchase about $80 billion worth of food a year—mostly from merchant wholesalers who specialize in food distribution. But over 3,500 wholesalers share this business. Even the very largest—Sysco Corp., Staly, Continental, and Sara Lee's PYA/Monarch—have only about 3 percent share each.[4]

There are two basic kinds of merchant wholesalers: (1) service—sometimes called full-service—wholesalers and (2) limited-function or limited-service wholesalers. Their names explain their difference.

Service wholesalers provide all the functions

Service wholesalers are merchant wholesalers that provide all the wholesaling functions. Within this basic group are three types: (1) general merchandise, (2) single-line, and (3) specialty.

General merchandise wholesalers are service wholesalers who carry a wide variety of non-perishable items such as hardware, electrical supplies, plumbing supplies, furniture, drugs, cosmetics, and automobile equipment. With this broad line of convenience and shopping products, they serve many kinds of retail stores. In the industrial products field, the *mill supply house* operates in a similar way. Somewhat like a retail hardware store, the mill supply house carries a broad variety of accessories and supplies for industrial customers.

Single-line (or general-line) wholesalers are service wholesalers who carry a narrower line than general merchandise wholesalers. For example, they might carry only groceries, or wearing apparel, or certain types of industrial tools or supplies.

Specialty wholesalers are service wholesalers who carry a very narrow line of products—and offer more information and service than other service wholesalers. A consumer products specialty wholesaler might carry only health foods or oriental foods—instead of a full line of groceries.

For industrial products, a specialty wholesaler might limit itself to fields requiring technical knowledge or service. This specialty wholesaler is an expert in selling the product lines it carries. Where there is need for this kind of technical help the specialty wholesaler usually has little difficulty taking business away from less specialized wholesalers.

The Cadillac Plastic and Chemical Company in Detroit, for example, became a specialty wholesaler serving the needs of both plastic makers and users. Neither the large plastics manufacturers nor the merchant wholesalers with wide lines are able to give technical advice to each of the many customers (who often have little knowledge of which product would be best for them). Cadillac carries 10,000 items and sells to 25,000 customers—ranging in size from very small firms to General Motors.

Limited-function wholesalers provide some functions

Limited-function wholesalers are merchant wholesalers that provide only *some* wholesaling functions. Exhibit 12–3 shows the functions typically provided—and not provided. In the following paragraphs, the main features of these wholesalers will be discussed. Some are not very numerous. In fact, they are not counted separately by the U.S. Census Bureau. Nevertheless, these wholesalers are very important for some products.

Cash-and-carry wholesalers want cash

Cash-and-carry wholesalers operate like service wholesalers—except that the customer must pay cash.

Many small retailers—especially small grocers and garages—are too small to be served profitably by a service wholesaler. To handle these markets, service wholesalers often set up cash-and-carry operations—to serve these small retailers for cash on the counter. The cash-and-carry wholesaler can operate at low cost—because the retailers take over many wholesaling functions.

Drop-shipper does not handle the products

Drop-shippers own the products they sell—but do not actually handle, stock, or deliver them. These wholesalers are mainly involved in selling. They get orders—from wholesalers, retailers, or industrial users—and pass these orders to producers. Then the products are shipped directly to the customers. Because drop-shippers do not have to handle the products, their operating costs are lower.

Drop-shippers commonly sell products so bulky that additional handling would be expensive—and possibly damaging. Also, the quantities they usually

Exhibit 12–3   Functions Provided by Limited-Function Merchant Wholesalers

Functions	Cash-and-carry	Drop-shipper	Truck	Mail-order	Coopera-tives	Rack jobbers
For customers						
Anticipates needs	X		X	X	X	X
"Regroups" products (one or more of four steps)	X		X	X	X	X
Carries stocks	X		X	X	X	X
Delivers products			X		X	X
Grants credit		X	Maybe	Maybe	Maybe	Consignment (in some cases)
Provides information and advisory services		X	Some	Some	X	
Provides buying function		X	X	X	Some	X
Owns and transfers title to products	X	X	X	X	X	X
For producers						
Provides producers' selling function	X	X	X	X	X	X
Stores inventory	X		X	X	X	X
Helps finance by owning stocks	X		X	X	X	X
Reduces credit risk	X	X	X	X	X	X
Provides market information	X	X	Some	X	X	Some

sell are so large that there is little need for regrouping—for example, rail carload shipments of coal, lumber, oil, or chemical products.

Truck wholesalers deliver—at a cost

Truck wholesalers specialize in delivering products that they stock in their own trucks. Handling perishable products in general demand—tobacco, candy, and potato chips—truck wholesalers may provide almost the same functions as full-service wholesalers. Their big advantage is that they deliver perishable products that regular wholesalers prefer not to carry. Others call on many small service stations and "back-alley" garages—providing local delivery of the many small items these customers often forget to pick up from a service wholesaler. Truck wholesalers' operating costs are relatively high—because they provide a lot of service for the little they sell.

Mail-order wholesalers reach outlying stores

Mail-order wholesalers sell out of catalogs that are distributed widely to smaller industrial customers or retailers. These wholesalers operate in the hardware, jewelry, sporting goods, and general merchandise lines. Their best markets are often small industrial or retailer customers who are not called on by other middlemen. They often take orders by phone and use United Parcel Service (UPS) for fast delivery.[5]

Producers' cooperatives do sorting

Producers' cooperatives operate almost as full-service wholesalers—with the "profits" going to the cooperative's customer-members. Successful producers' cooperatives have emphasized the sorting process—to improve the quality of farm products offered to the market. Some have also branded their products—and then promoted the brands. Farmers' cooperatives have sometimes had success in limiting output and then increasing prices—by taking advantage of the normally inelastic demand for agricultural commodities.

Examples of producers' cooperatives are the California Fruit Growers Exchange (citrus fruits), Sunmaid Raisin Growers Association, The California Almond Exchange, and Land O'Lakes Creameries, Inc.

Rack jobbers sell hard-to-handle assortments

Rack jobbers specialize in non-food items sold in grocery stores and supermarkets and often displayed on the rack jobbers' own wire racks. Most grocers don't want to bother with non-food items (housewares, hardware items, and books and magazines) because they sell only small quantities of these products. So the rack-jobber specializes in these items. Rack jobbers are almost service wholesalers—except that they usually are paid cash for the amount of stock sold or delivered.

This is a relatively expensive service—operating costs are about 18 percent of sales. The large volume of sales from these racks has encouraged some large food chains to try to handle these items on their own. But they often find that rack jobbers can provide this service as well as—or better than—they can themselves. For example, a rack jobber of paperback books studies which titles are selling in the local area—and applies that knowledge in many stores. The chain may have many stores—but in different areas where preferences vary. It may not be worth trying to study the market in each area.

AGENT MIDDLEMEN ARE STRONG ON SELLING

They don't own the products

Agent middlemen are wholesalers who don't own the products they sell. Their main purpose is to help in buying and selling. They usually provide even fewer functions than the limited-function wholesalers. In some fields, however, they are extremely valuable. They operate at relatively low cost, too—sometimes 2 to 6 percent of their selling price.

In the following paragraphs, we will mention only the most important points about each type. See Exhibit 12–4 for details on the functions provided by each. You can see from the number of empty spaces in Exhibit 12–4 that agent middlemen provide fewer functions than merchant wholesalers.

Exhibit 12–4   Functions Provided by Agent Middlemen

Functions	Manufacturers' agents	Brokers	Com- mission merchants	Selling agents	Auction companies
For customers					
Anticipate needs	Sometimes	Some			
"Regroups" products (one or more of four steps)	Some		X		X
Carries stocks	Sometimes		X		Sometimes
Delivers products	Sometimes		X		
Grants credit			Sometimes	X	Some
Provides information and advisory services	X	X	X	X	
Provides buying function	X	Some	X	X	X
Owns and transfers title to products			Transfers only		Transfers only
For producer					
Provides selling function	X	Some	X	X	X
Stores inventory	Sometimes		X		X
Helps finance by owning stocks					
Reduces credit risk				X	Some
Provides market information	X	X	X	X	

Manufacturers' agents— free-wheeling sales reps

A **manufacturers' agent** sells similar products for several non-competing producers—for a commission on what he actually sells. Such agents work almost as members of each company's sales force—but they are really independent middlemen. Manufacturers' agents account for more than half of all agent middlemen.

Their big "plus" is that they already call on a group of customers and can add another product line at relatively low cost—and no cost to the producer until they sell something! If the sales potential in an area is low, a manufacturers' agent may be used instead of a company's own sales rep because the agent can do the job at lower cost. A small producer often has to use agents—because its sales volume is too small to support its own sales force.

Manufacturers' agents are very useful in fields where there are many small manufacturers who need to call on customers. These agents are often used in the sale of machinery and equipment, electrical products, automobile products, clothing and apparel accessories, and some food products. Each may cover one city or several states—so many may be needed to cover the U.S.

The agent's main job is selling. The agent—or his customer—sends the orders to the producer. The agent, of course, gets credit for the sale. Agents seldom have any part in setting prices—or deciding on the producer's policies. Basically, they are independent, aggressive sales reps.

Agents are especially useful in introducing new products. For this service, they may earn 10 to 15 percent commission. (In contrast, their commission on large-volume established products may be quite low—perhaps only 2 percent.) The higher rates for new products often become the agent's major disadvantage for the producer. The 10 to 15 percent commission rate may have seemed small when the product was new—and sales volume was low. Once the product is selling well, the rate seems high. About this time, the producer often begins using its own sales reps—and the manufacturers' agent must look for other new products to develop. Agents are well aware of this possibility. Most try to work for many producers—so they aren't dependent on only one or a few lines.

Brokers provide information

Brokers bring buyers and sellers together. Their "product" is information about what buyers need—and what supplies are available. They aid in buyer-seller negotiation. When a deal is completed, they earn a commission from whoever hired them.

Brokers are especially useful for selling seasonal products. For example, they could represent a small food canner during the canning season—then go on to other activities.

Brokers also sell used machinery, real estate, and even ships. These products are not similar, but the needed wholesaling functions are. In each case, buyers don't come into the market often. Someone with knowledge of available products is needed to help both buyers and sellers complete the sale quickly—and at a reasonable cost.

Commission merchants handle and sell products in distant markets

Commission merchants handle products shipped to them by sellers, complete the sale, and send the money—minus their commission—to each seller.

Commission merchants are common in farm markets where farmers must ship to big-city central markets. They need someone to handle the products there—as well as to sell them—since the farmer can't go with each shipment. Although commission merchants do not own the products, they generally are allowed to sell them at the market price—or the best price above some stated minimum. Newspapers usually publish prices for these markets, so the producer-seller has a check on the commission merchant. Costs are usually low because commission merchants handle large volumes of products—and buyers usually come to them.

Other fields—such as textiles—sometimes use commission merchants. Here, many small producers wish to reach buyers in a central market—without having to maintain their own sales force.

Selling agents— almost marketing managers

Selling agents take over the whole marketing job of producers—not just the selling function. A selling agent may handle the entire output of one or more producers—even competing producers—with almost complete control of pricing, selling, and advertising. In effect, the agent becomes each producer's marketing manager.

Some kind of broker will develop whenever and wherever market information is inadequate.

Producers often call in a selling agent because of financial trouble. The selling agent may provide working capital—but may also take over the affairs of the business.

Selling agents are common in some highly competitive fields—such as textiles, coal, and lumber. Here, marketing is much more important than production for survival. The selling agent provides the necessary financial assistance and marketing know-how.

Auction companies—display the products

Auction companies provide a place where buyers and sellers can come together and complete a transaction. There aren't many of these middlemen, but they are important in certain lines—such as livestock, fur, tobacco, and used cars. For these products, demand and supply conditions change rapidly. Also, these products must be seen to be evaluated. The auction company allows buyers and sellers to get together—and set the price while the products are being inspected.

Facilities can be simple—keeping overhead low. Often, auction companies are close to transportation so the products can be reshipped quickly. The auction company just charges a set fee or commission for the use of its facilities and services.

International marketing is not so different

We find agent middlemen in international trade, too. Most operate much like those just described. **Export or import agents** are basically manufacturers' agents. **Export or import commission houses** and **export or import brokers** are really brokers. A **combination export manager** is a blend of manufacturers' agent and selling agent—handling the entire export function for several producers of non-competing lines. Agent middlemen are more common in international trade. Financing is usually needed, but many markets have only a few well-financed merchant wholesalers. The best many producers can do is get local representation through agent middlemen—and arrange financing through banks that specialize in international trade.[6]

MANUFACTURERS' SALES BRANCHES PROVIDE WHOLESALING FUNCTIONS, TOO

Manufacturers' sales branches are separate businesses that producers set up away from their factories. For example, computer producers like IBM set up local branches to provide service, display equipment, and handle sales. About 9 percent of wholesale businesses are owned by manufacturers—but they handle 31 percent of total wholesale sales. One reason the sales per branch are so high is that the branches are usually placed in the best market areas. This also helps explain why their operating costs are often lower. But cost comparisons between various channels can be misleading. Sometimes the cost of selling is not charged to the branch. If all the expenses of the manufacturers' sales branches were charged to them, they probably would turn out to be more costly than they seem now.[7]

WHOLESALERS TEND TO CONCENTRATE TOGETHER

Different wholesalers are found in different places

Some wholesalers—such as grain elevator operators—are located close to producers. But most wholesaling is done in or near large cities. About 40 percent of all wholesale sales are made in the 15 largest Metropolitan Statistical Areas.

This heavy concentration of wholesale sales in large cities makes sense because many large wholesalers and industrial buyers are there. Some large producers buy for many plants through one purchasing department located in the general offices in these cities. Also, merchant wholesalers need the trans-

Fully automated warehouse storage and retrieval systems have helped wholesalers to reduce cost and improve service to customers.

porting, storing, and financing facilities found in these big cities. This is true not only in the United States—but also in world markets.

When a number of competing wholesalers are located together, competition can be tough. When Sanyo began exporting consumer products to the United States in 1968, the company had little brand recognition and no established channels of distribution. Small electronics wholesalers—like Pinros and Gar Corp. in New York City—developed retail customers for Sanyo. By 1984, 90 U.S. wholesalers had helped develop a large market share for Sanyo's audio and video equipment lines. But Sanyo was finding it costly to work with so many wholesalers. So the company picked 20 of its largest wholesalers—in different geographic areas—to handle the job. This made sense for Sanyo, but the smaller wholesalers—like Pinros and Gar—lost product lines that had generated millions of dollars in sales each year. Many wholesalers try to protect themselves from such losses by handling competing lines—or demanding long-term arrangements and exclusive territories.[8]

COMEBACK AND FUTURE OF WHOLESALERS

In the 1800s in the United States, wholesalers dominated marketing. The many small producers and small retailers needed their services. As producers became larger, some bypassed the wholesalers. When retail chains began to grow larger, many predicted the end of wholesalers.

Not fat and lazy, but enduring

Some people felt the end of wholesalers might be desirable because many wholesalers had grown "fat and lazy"—contributing little more than bulk-breaking. Their salespeople were often only order takers. And many neglected the selling function. The best managers were not attracted to wholesaling.

We've seen, however, that wholesaling functions *are* necessary—and wholesalers have not disappeared. Their sales volume declined in the 1930s. But by 1954, they had returned to the same importance they had in 1929. And they have continued to hold their own since then.

Producing profits, not chasing orders

Wholesalers have lasted, in part, because of new management and new techniques. Many are still operating in the old ways. But progressive wholesalers are more concerned with their customers—and with channel systems. Some offer more services. Others are developing voluntary chains that bind them more closely to their customers. Some ordering is now done routinely by mail or telephone—or directly by telephone to computer.

Some modern wholesalers no longer make all customers pay for all the services offered—simply because some customers use them. This traditional practice had the effect of encouraging limited-function wholesalers and direct channels. Now some wholesalers make a basic service available at a minimum cost—then charge extra fees for any special services required. In the grocery field, for instance, the basic servicing of a store costs the store 3 to 4 percent of wholesale sales. Promotion assistance and other aids are offered at extra cost.

Modern wholesalers also select customers more carefully—i.e., they choose a selective distribution policy—as cost analysis shows that many of their smaller customers are unprofitable. By cutting out these customers, wholesalers can give more attention to their better customers. In this way, they help promote healthy retailers—who can compete in any market.

Today's progressive wholesalers are no longer just order takers. Some wholesalers have renamed their salespeople "store advisers" or "supervisors" to reflect their new roles. They provide management advisory services—including site selection and store design. They offer legal assistance on new leases or adjustments in old leases. They even provide store-opening services, sales training, and sales promotion and advertising help. Such salespeople—really acting as management consultants—must be more competent than the order takers of the past.

Many wholesalers now use electronic data processing systems to control inventory. And some are modernizing their warehouses and physical handling facilities.

Other wholesalers offer central bookkeeping facilities for their retailers—realizing the link between their own survival and their customers' survival. In this sense, some wholesalers are becoming more channel system minded—no longer trying to overload retailers' shelves. Now they try to clear the merchandise *off* retailers' shelves. They follow the old saying, "Nothing is really sold until it is sold at retail."

Perhaps good-bye to some

Not all wholesalers are progressive, however. Some of the smaller, less efficient ones may fail. While the average operating expense ratio is 13 percent for merchant wholesalers, some small wholesalers have expense ratios of 20 to 30 percent or higher.

Low cost, however, is not all that's needed for success. The higher operating expenses of some wholesalers may be a result of the special services they offer to *some* customers. Truck wholesalers are usually small—and have high operating costs—yet some customers willingly pay the higher cost of this service. Although full-service wholesalers may seem expensive, some will continue operating because they offer the wholesaling functions and sales contacts some small producers need.

To survive, each wholesaler must develop a good marketing strategy. Profit margins are not large in wholesaling—typically ranging from less than 1 percent to 2 percent. And they have been declining in recent years as the competitive squeeze has tightened.

The function of wholesaling will last—but weaker, less progressive wholesalers may not.[9]

CONCLUSION

Wholesalers can provide wholesaling functions for those both above and below them in a channel of distribution. These functions closely relate to the basic marketing functions.

There are many types of wholesalers. Some provide all the wholesaling functions—while others specialize in only a few. Eliminating wholesalers would not eliminate the need for the functions they provide. And we cannot assume that direct channels will be more efficient.

Merchant wholesalers—the most numerous type—account for just over half of wholesale sales. They take title—and often possession—of products. Agent middlemen, on the other hand, act more like sales representatives for sellers or buyers. They *do not* take title.

In spite of various predictions of the end of wholesalers, they're still around. And the more progressive ones have adapted to a changing environment. No such revolutions as we saw in retailing have yet taken place in wholesaling—and none seems likely. But some smaller—and less progressive—wholesalers will probably fail, while larger and more market-oriented wholesalers will continue to provide the necessary wholesaling functions.

Questions and Problems

1. Discuss the difference between wholesaling and retailing.

2. What risks do merchant wholesalers assume by taking title to goods? Is the size of this risk about constant for all merchant wholesalers?

3. Why would a manufacturer set up its own sales branches if established wholesalers were already available?

4. What is an agent middleman's marketing mix? Why don't producers use their own salespeople instead of agent middlemen?

5. Discuss the future growth and nature of wholesaling if low-margin retailing and scrambled merchandising become more important. How will wholesalers have to adjust their mixes if retail establishments become larger and the retail managers more professional? Will wholesalers be eliminated? If not, what wholesaling functions will be most important? Are there any particular lines of trade where wholesalers may have increasing difficulty?

6. Which types of wholesalers would be most appropriate for the following products? If more than one type of wholesaler could be used, describe each situation carefully. For example, if size or financial strength of a company has a bearing, then so indicate. If several wholesalers could be used in this same channel, explain this, too.

a. Fresh tomatoes.
b. Paper-stapling machines.
c. Auto mechanics' tools.
d. Men's shoes.
e. An industrial accessory machine.
f. Ballpoint pens.
g. Shoe laces.

7. Would a drop-shipper be desirable for the following products: coal, lumber, iron ore, sand and gravel, steel, furniture, or tractors? Why or why not? What channels might be used for each of these products if drop-shippers were not used?

8. Discuss some of the ways that use of computer systems affects wholesalers' operations.

9. Which types of wholesalers are likely to become more important in the next 25 years? Why?

Suggested Computer-Aided Problem

12. Merchant vs. Agent Wholesaler

Suggested Cases

16. Industrial Sales Company

17. Brogan Lumber Company

Chapter 13

Promotion—Introduction

When You Finish This Chapter, You Should

1. Know the advantages and disadvantages of the promotion methods a marketing manager can use in strategy planning.

2. Understand the importance of promotion objectives.

3. Know how the communication process should affect promotion planning.

4. Know how the adoption processes can guide promotion planning.

5. Understand how promotion blends should change along the adoption curve.

6. Know how typical promotion budgets are blended.

7. Know who plans and manages promotion blends.

8. Recognize the important new terms (shown in red).

People won't buy your product if they've never heard of it.

Quaker Oats Co. had a problem. Its Cap'n Crunch cereal—a children's favorite for 24 years—was losing sales. In 1985, Quaker launched an $18 million promotion campaign to increase awareness and recapture its share of Cap'n Crunch's major target market—children ages 6 to 12.

Quaker sponsored a contest to encourage children to solve a "Where's the Cap'n?" mystery. The clues were found in boxes of Cap'n Crunch cereal. To tell kids about the contest, Quaker ran ads in children's magazines like *Jack and Jill.* A music video—with its own "Where's the Cap'n" song, and "sky writing" were used to get more attention. TV ads played up Crunch's disappearance. Coupons offering discounts on Cap'n Crunch were aimed at parents. And Quaker sales reps worked with retailers—to make sure they stocked enough of the cereal.

Quaker gave a $100 prize to each of 10,000 children who solved the mystery. And when the Cap'n was "found," Quaker spent another $600,000 for Saturday morning ads on all three networks. In addition, a spoof of the promotion on the "Saturday Night Live" TV program generated a lot of free publicity. The result: awareness increased, and sales of Cap'n Crunch rose 50 percent.[1]

Promotion is communicating information between seller and buyer—to influence attitudes and behavior. The marketing manager's promotion job is to tell target customers that the right Product is available at the right Place at the right Price.

What the marketing manager should communicate is determined when the target customers' needs and attitudes are known. *How* the messages are delivered depends on what promotion methods are chosen.

275

SEVERAL PROMOTION METHODS ARE AVAILABLE

The marketing manager can choose from several promotion methods, as the Cap'n Crunch case showed. These include personal selling, mass selling, and sales promotion. See Exhibit 13–1.

Personal selling—is flexible

Personal selling involves direct face-to-face communication between sellers and potential customers. It lets the salesperson see—immediately—how a customer reacts. This allows salespeople to adapt the company's marketing mix to the needs of each target market. Most marketing mixes include salespeople. However, personal selling is very expensive. It's often necessary to combine personal selling with mass selling and sales promotion.

Mass selling—reaching millions at a price or even free

Mass selling is communicating with large numbers of potential customers at one time. It isn't as flexible as personal selling. But when the target market is large and spread out—mass selling can be less expensive.

Advertising is the main form of mass selling. **Advertising** is any *paid* form of non-personal presentation of ideas, goods, or services by an identified sponsor. It uses media such as magazines, newspapers, radio and TV, signs, and direct mail. While advertising must be paid for, another form of mass selling—publicity—is "free."

Publicity is "free"

Publicity is any *unpaid* form of non-personal presentation of ideas, goods, or services. Although, of course, publicity people get paid, they try to attract

Exhibit 13–1   Basic Promotion Methods and Strategy Planning

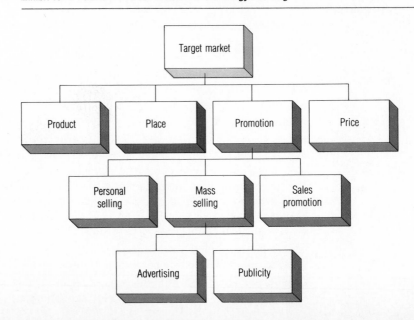

attention to the firm and its offerings without having to pay media costs. For example, Kraft provides food editors with recipes using Kraft products. Book publishers try to get authors on TV "talk shows" because this generates a lot of interest—and book sales—at no cost to the publisher.[2]

If a firm has a really new message, publicity may be more effective than advertising. Trade magazines, for example, may carry articles featuring the newsworthy products of regular advertisers. Often a firm's publicity people write the basic copy—and then try to convince magazine editors to print it. This publicity may even raise more interest than the company's paid advertising. A potential customer might not pay any attention to an ad—but might carefully read a trade magazine story with the same information.

Some companies prepare videotapes for TV news shows that give free publicity to a firm's product. For example, one video—released at Halloween—discussed a government recommendation that parents use makeup rather than masks for young children. The story was effectively tied to a new makeup product for children made by PAAS Products.[3]

Sales promotion tries to spark immediate interest

Sales promotion refers to those promotion activities—other than advertising, publicity, and personal selling—that stimulate interest, trial, or purchase by final customers or others in the channel. Sales promotion can be aimed at consumers, at middlemen, or even at a firm's own sales force. Exhibit 13–2 lists many examples.

Sales promotion for final consumers or users

Sales promotion aimed at final consumers or users usually tries to increase demand—or speed up the time of purchase. This might involve developing displays for retail stores—including banners and streamers, sample

Exhibit 13–2 Examples of Sales Promotion Activities

Aimed at final consumers or users	Aimed at middlemen	Aimed at company's own sales force
Banners	Price deals	Contests
Streamers	Promotion allowances	Bonuses
Samples	Sales contests	Meetings
Calendars	Calendars	Portfolios
Point-of-purchase materials	Gifts	Displays
Aisle displays	Trade shows	Sales aids
Contests	Meetings	Training materials
Coupons	Catalogs	
Trade shows	Merchandising aids	
Trading stamps		

packages, calendars, and various point-of-purchase materials. The sales pro-motion people also might develop the aisle displays for supermarkets. They might be responsible for "jackpot" and "sweepstakes" contests—as well as coupons to persuade customers to try a product. All of these efforts aim at specific promotion objectives.

Sales promotion directed at customers for industrial products might use the same kinds of ideas. In addition, the sales promotion people might set up and staff trade show exhibits, using attractive models to encourage economically oriented buyers to at least look at a firm's product—especially when it is dis-played near other, similar products in a circus-like atmosphere.[4]

Sales promotion for middlemen

Sales promotion aimed at middlemen—sometimes called trade promotion—stresses price—because the objective assigned to sales promotion may be to encourage stocking new items, or buying in larger quantity, or buying early. The tools used here are price and/or merchandise allowances, promotion al-lowances, and perhaps sales contests—to encourage retailers or wholesalers to sell specific items—or the company's whole line. Offering to send contest winners to Hawaii, to example, may increase sales greatly.[5]

Sales promotion for own sales force

Sales promotion aimed at the company's own sales force might try to en-courage getting new customers, selling a new product, or selling the firm's whole line. Depending on the objectives, a firm might use contests, bonuses on sales, and sales meetings at luxury resorts to raise everyone's spirits.[6]

Some large companies try to design ads targeted at customers that also communicate to employees—and boost the employees' image. This is espe-cially important in service-oriented industries—where the quality of the em-ployees' efforts is a big part of the product. General Motors, for example, pro-motes "Mr. Goodwrench"—the well-qualified mechanic who provides friendly, expert service. The ad communicates primarily to customers—but it also reminds service people that what they do is important and appreciated.

 This neglected method is bigger than advertising

Sales promotion—like publicity—is a weak spot in marketing. Sales promo-tion includes a wide variety of activities—each of which may be custom-designed and used only once. Few companies develop their own experts in sales promotion. This lack of experience can cause costly mistakes. One pro-motion sponsored jointly by Polaroid and Trans World Airlines proved to be a disaster. They offered a coupon worth 25 percent off on the purchase of any TWA flight with the purchase of a $20 Polaroid camera. Their aim was to ap-peal to vacationers who take pictures when they travel. Instead, travel agents bought up many of the cameras. For the price of the $20 camera, they made an extra 25 percent on every TWA ticket they sold. And big companies bought thousands of the cameras—to save on overseas travel expenses.[7]

Many companies—even large ones—don't have a separate budget for sales promotion. Few even know what it costs in total. This neglect of sales promotion is a mistake. In total, sales promotion costs almost as much as advertising. This means it deserves more attention—and perhaps separate status—within the marketing organization.

The spending on sales promotion is large and growing—sometimes at the expense of other promotion methods. There are several reasons for this. Sales promotion has proved successful in increasingly competitive markets. Sales promotion can usually be implemented quickly—and get results sooner than advertising.[8] Sales promotion activities can help the product manager win support from an already overworked sales force. Sales people welcome sales promotion—including promotion in the channels—because it makes their job easier.

Creative sales promotion can be very effective, but making it work is a learned skill—not a sideline for amateurs. It can't be delegated to a sales trainee. In fact, sales promotion specialists have developed—both inside firms and as outside consultants. Some are very creative—and might be willing to take over the whole promotion job. But marketing managers must set promotion objectives and policies that fit with the rest of a marketing strategy.[9] So let's look at the whole promotion blend—personal selling, mass selling, and sales promotion combined—to see how promotion fits into the rest of the marketing mix.

WHICH METHODS TO USE DEPENDS ON PROMOTION OBJECTIVES

Overall objective is to affect behavior

The different promotion methods can all be seen as different forms of communication. But good marketers don't want to just "communicate." They want to communicate information that will lead target customers to choose *their* product. They know that if they have a better offering, informed customers are more likely to buy. Therefore, they are interested in (1) reinforcing present attitudes that might lead to favorable behavior or (2) actually changing the attitudes and behavior of the firm's target market.

Informing, persuading, and reminding are basic promotion objectives

For a firm's promotion to work, the firm's promotion objectives must be clearly defined. The right promotion blend depends on what the firm wants to accomplish. It's helpful to think of three basic promotion objectives: to *inform, persuade,* and *remind* target customers about the company and its marketing mix. All aim to affect behavior—by providing more information.

The most useful promotion objectives state exactly who you want to inform, persuade, or remind, and why. But this is unique to each company's strategy—and too detailed to discuss here. Instead, we will limit ourselves to the three basic promotion objectives—and how you might reach them.

Informing is educating

We know that potential customers must know something about a product if they are to buy at all.

A firm with a really new product may not have to do anything but inform consumers about it—and show that it works better than other products. When Compaq introduced its "IBM-compatible" portable computer, the uniqueness of the product simplified the promotion job—and Compaq had the highest ever first year sales for a new company—about $111 million. Excitement about the product also generated much free publicity in computer magazines.

Persuading usually becomes necessary

When competitors offer similar products, the firm must not only inform the customers that its product is available—but also persuade them to buy it. A persuading objective means the firm tries to develop or reinforce a favorable set of attitudes toward the firm's product—hoping to affect buying behavior.

Reminding may be enough, sometimes

If target customers already have positive attitudes about the firm's product, then a *reminding* objective might be used. This objective can be extremely important. Even though customers have been attracted and sold once, they are still targets for competitors' promotion. Reminding them of their past satisfaction may keep them from shifting to a competitor. Campbell realizes that most people already know about its soup—so much of its advertising simply tries to remind.

PROMOTION REQUIRES EFFECTIVE COMMUNICATION

Promotion obviously must get the attention of the target audience—and communicate effectively—or it's wasted. However, this isn't always easy to do. Much promotion doesn't really communicate. You might listen to the radio for several hours—but never really be aware of any of the ads. Communication can break down in many ways.

The same message may be interpreted differently

Different people may see the same message in different ways—or interpret the same words differently. Such differences are common in international marketing—where translation is a problem. General Motors, for example, had trouble in Puerto Rico with its Nova automobile. Then it discovered that—while Nova means "star" in Spanish—when spoken it sounds like "no va," meaning "it doesn't go." The company quickly changed the car's name to Caribe—and it sold well.[10]

Such problems in the same language may not be so obvious—but can cause trouble for marketers. For example, a new children's cough syrup was advertised as "extra strength." The advertising people thought that would assure parents that the product worked well. But worried mothers avoided the product, fearing it might be too strong for their children.

Feedback improves communication

The **communication process** means a source trying to reach a receiver with a message. Exhibit 13–3 shows this process. Here we see that a **source** —the sender of a message—is trying to deliver a message to a **receiver** —a potential customer. Research shows that customers evaluate not only the message—but also the source of the message—in terms of trustworthiness and credibility. For example, information coming from Lee Iacocca—chairman

Exhibit 13–3   The Communication Process

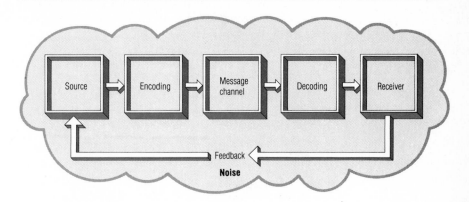

of Chrysler—might be viewed as more impressive than the same message from a junior sales rep.

A source can use many message channels to deliver a message. The personal salesperson does it with voice and action. Advertising must do it with mass media—magazines, newspapers, radio, and TV.

A major advantage of personal selling is that the source—the seller—gets immediate feedback from the receiver. It's easier to judge how the message is being received—and to change it if necessary. Mass sellers must depend on marketing research or total sales figures for feedback—which can take too long.

The **noise**—shown in Exhibit 13–3—is any distraction that reduces the effectiveness of the communication process. Conversations during TV ads are "noise." Advertisers planning messages must recognize that many possible distractions—noise—can interfere with communications.

Encoding and decoding depend on common frame of reference

Exhibit 13–4

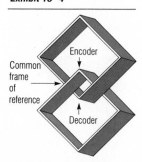

The big difficulty in the communication process occurs during encoding and decoding. **Encoding** is the source deciding what it wants to say and translating it so that it will have the same meaning to the receiver. **Decoding** is the receiver translating the message. This process can be very tricky. The meanings of various words and symbols may differ—depending on the attitudes and experiences of the two groups. People need a common frame of reference to communicate effectively. See Exhibit 13–4.

Maidenform, Inc., encountered this problem with its promotion aimed at working women. The company ran a series of ads depicting women stockbrokers and doctors wearing Maidenform lingerie. The men in the ads were fully dressed. Maidenform was trying to show women in positions of authority, but some women felt the ad presented them as sex objects. In this case, the promotion people who encoded the message didn't understand the attitudes of the target market—and how they would decode the message.[11]

Message channel is important, too

The communication process is complicated even more because the receiver is aware that the message is not only coming from a source but also coming through some **message channel**—the carrier of the message. The receiver may attach more value to a product if the message comes in a well-respected newspaper or magazine, rather than over the radio.

ADOPTION PROCESSES CAN GUIDE PROMOTION PLANNING

The adoption process discussed in Chapter 6 relates to effective communication—and promotion planning. You learned that there are six steps in the adoption process: awareness, interest, evaluation, trial, decision, and confirmation. We saw consumer buying as a problem-solving process in which buyers go through these six steps on the way to adopting (or rejecting) an idea or product.

Now we'll see that the three basic promotion objectives are related to these six steps. See Exhibit 13–5. Informing and persuading may be needed to affect the potential customer's knowledge and attitudes about a product—and then bring about its adoption. Later, promotion can simply remind the customer about that favorable experience—aiming to confirm the adoption decision.

The AIDA model is a practical approach

The basic adoption process fits very neatly with another action-oriented model—called AIDA—which we will use in this and the next two chapters to guide some of our discussion.

The **AIDA model** consists of four promotion jobs—(1) to get *Attention,* (2) to hold *Interest,* (3) to arouse *Desire,* and (4) to obtain *Action.* (As a memory aid, note that the first letters of the four key words spell AIDA—the well-known opera.)

The relation of the adoption process to the AIDA jobs can be seen in Exhibit 13–5. *Getting attention* is necessary to make the potential customer aware of the company's offering. *Holding interest* gives the communication a chance to really build the prospect's interest in the product. *Arousing desire* affects the evaluation process—perhaps building preference. And *obtaining action* includes obtaining trial—which may lead to a purchase decision. Continued promotion is needed to confirm the decision—and encourage continued adoption.

Exhibit 13–5   Relation of Promotion Objectives, Adoption Process, and AIDA Model

Promotion objectives	Adoption process (Chapter 6)	AIDA model
Informing	⎧ Awareness ⎫	Attention
	⎨ Interest	Interest
	⎩ Evaluation ⎫	Desire
Persuading	Trial ⎬	
	Decision ⎫	Action
Reminding	Confirmation ⎭	

Pepsi's "tipping can" shelf display helped to get attention and hold interest.

GOOD COMMUNICATION VARIES PROMOTION BLENDS ALONG ADOPTION CURVE

The AIDA and adoption processes look at individuals. This emphasis on individuals helps us understand how people behave. But it also helps to look at markets as a whole. Different customers within a market behave differently—with some taking the lead in trying new products and, in turn, influencing others.

Adoption curve focuses on market segments, not individuals

Research on how markets accept new ideas has led to the adoption curve model. The **adoption curve** shows when different groups accept ideas. It shows the need to change the promotion effort as time passes. It also shows that some groups act as leaders in accepting new ideas.

Promotion must vary for different adopter groups

Exhibit 13–6 shows the adoption curve for a typical successful product. We'll discuss some of the important characteristics of each of these customer groups below. Which one are you?

Innovators don't mind taking some risk

Innovators are the first to adopt. They eagerly try a new idea—and will take risks. Innovators tend to be young and well educated. They are likely to be mobile—with many contacts outside their local social group and community. Business firms in the innovator group usually are large and rather specialized.

An important characteristic of innovators is that they rely on impersonal and

Exhibit 13–6   The Adoption Curve

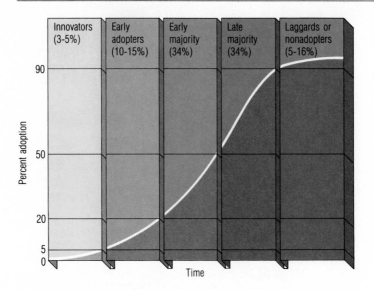

scientific information sources—or other innovators—instead of personal sales-people. They read articles in technical publications—or informative advertise-ments in special-interest magazines or newspapers.

Early adopters are often opinion leaders

Early adopters are well respected by their peers—and often are opinion leaders. They are younger, more mobile, and more creative than later adopt-ers. But, unlike innovators, they have fewer contacts outside their own social group or community. Business firms in this category tend to be specialized.

Of all the groups, this group tends to have the greatest contact with sales-people. Mass media are important information sources, too. Marketers should be very concerned with attracting—and selling—the early adopter group. Their acceptance is really important in reaching the next group—because the early majority look to the early adopters, not the innovators.

Early majority group is deliberate

The **early majority** avoid risk and wait to consider a new idea until many early adopters have tried it—and liked it.

Average-sized business firms with less specialization often fit in this cate-gory. If successful companies in their industry adopt the new idea, they will, too.

The early majority has a great deal of contact with mass media, salespeo-ple, *and* early adopter opinion leaders. They usually are not opinion leaders.

Late majority are cautious

The **late majority** are cautious about new ideas. Often they are older than the early majority group—and more set in their ways. So they are less likely to follow opinion leaders and early adopters. In fact, some social pressure from their own peer group may be needed before they adopt a new product.

Business firms in this group tend to be conservative, smaller-sized firms with little specialization.

The late majority make little use of marketing sources of information—mass media and salespeople. They are influenced more by other late adopters—rather than by outside sources of information.

Laggards or non-adopters hang on to tradition

The **laggards** or **non-adopters** prefer to do things the way they have been done in the past—and are very suspicious of new ideas. They tend to be older and less well educated. They may also be low in social status and income.

The smallest businesses with the least specialization are often in this category. They cling to the status quo—and think it's the safe way.

The main source of information for laggards is other laggards. This certainly is bad news for marketers who want to reach a whole market quickly—or who want to use only one promotion method. In fact, it may not pay to bother with this group.[12]

Opinion leaders help spread the word

Adoption curve research supports our earlier discussion (in Chapter 6) of the importance of opinion leaders. It shows the importance of early adopters. They influence the early majority—and help spread the word to many others.

Marketers know the importance of these personal conversations and recommendations by opinion leaders. If early groups reject the product, it may never get off the ground. For example, some movie goers are usually among the first to see new movies. If they think a movie is dull, they quickly tell their friends not to waste their time and money. As a result—the movie may flop.

Thus "word-of-mouth" may do the real selling job—long before the customer ever walks into a retail store. Some companies try to target promotion to encourage opinion leadership. When Canon—the camera producer—introduced a high-quality new "automatic" 35 mm camera, the firm prepared special ads designed to help opinion leaders explain to others how the camera worked. Other advertisers take a simpler approach—and say "tell your friends."[13]

MAY NEED A DIFFERENT BLEND FOR EACH MARKET SEGMENT

Each market segment may need a separate marketing mix—and a different promotion blend. Some mass selling specialists miss this point. They think in "mass marketing"—rather than "target marketing"—terms. Aiming at large markets may be all right sometimes. But, unfortunately, promotion aimed at everyone can end up hitting no one. In the Promotion area, we should be careful about using a "shotgun" approach when what we really need is a "rifle" approach—with more careful aiming.

SUCCESSFUL PROMOTION MAY BE AN ECONOMICAL BLEND

Once promotion objectives for a strategy are set, a marketing manager may decide to use a blend of promotion methods. Certain jobs can be done more cheaply one way than another. This is seen most clearly in the industrial products market. While personal selling dominates most industrial products promotion budgets, mass selling is necessary, too. Personal salespeople nearly always have to complete the sale. But it is usually too expensive for them to do the whole promotion job. The cost of an industrial sales call is about $240.[14] This relatively high cost is because salespeople have only limited time and must spend much of it on non-selling activities—traveling, paperwork, sales meetings, and service calls. Less than half of their time is available for actual selling.

The constant turnover of buyers and influencers makes the job of reaching all the buying influences more costly and difficult. An industrial salesperson may be responsible for several hundred customers and prospects—with many buying influences per company. He doesn't have enough time to get the company's whole message across to every possible contact. Often, too much is invested in a salesperson to use his time and skill to answer questions that mass selling could handle better. Mass selling "sales calls" cost much less than personal calls. It may cost an industrial advertiser much less than a dollar per reader to advertise in a trade magazine. After mass selling does the ground work, a salesperson can answer specific questions—and close the sale.

HOW TYPICAL PROMOTION BUDGETS ARE BLENDED

There is no one right blend

There is no one *right* promotion blend. Each must be developed as part of a marketing mix. But to round out our discussion of promotion blends, let's look at some typical ways promotion budgets are spread across the three promotion methods.

Exhibit 13–7 shows the percentage of total promotion budgets spent on personal selling, advertising, and sales promotion in various situations. We can see that wholesalers rely on personal selling almost exclusively, while a producer of branded consumer products spends about equally on mass selling to consumers, personal selling (to middlemen), and sales promotion to middlemen and consumers. On the other hand, smaller producers and firms that offer relatively undifferentiated consumer products or industrial products put more emphasis on personal selling, with the rest of the budget going mainly to sales promotion.

Exhibit 13–7   Typical Promotion Blends (percentage of total budget going to personal selling, advertising, and sales promotion)

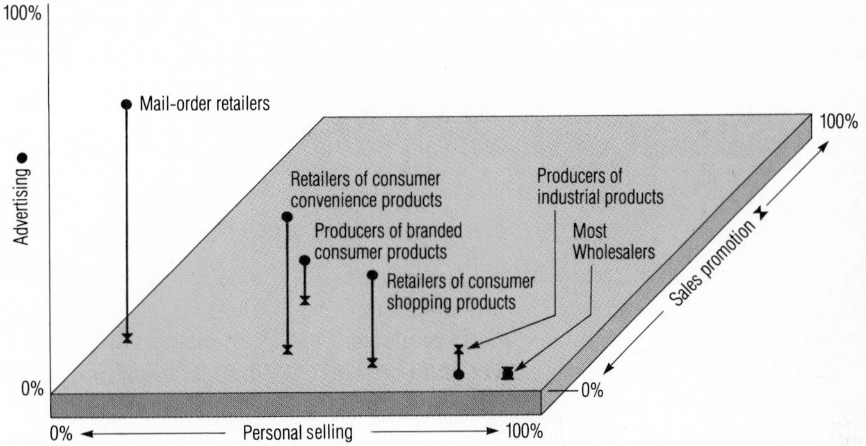

Personal selling usually is dominant

The heavier emphasis on personal selling that you might have assumed from Exhibit 13–7 is correct. The many ads you see in magazines and newspapers—and on television—are impressive and costly. And sales promotions cost about the same amount of money. But sales clerks complete most retail sales. And much personal selling goes on in the channels. In total, personal selling is several times more expensive than mass selling (advertising) or sales promotion.

SOMEONE MUST PLAN AND MANAGE THE PROMOTION BLEND

Choosing a promotion blend is a strategy decision that should fit with the rest of a marketing strategy. This is the job of the marketing manager. Then, specialists—such as sales and advertising managers—must develop and implement more detailed plans.

Sales managers are concerned with managing personal selling. Often the sales manager is responsible for building good distribution channels and implementing Place policies.

Advertising managers manage their company's mass selling effort—in television, newspapers, magazines, and other media. They choose the right media for each purpose—and develop the ads. They may use advertising departments within their own firms—especially if they're in retailing. Or they may use outside advertising agencies. They—or their agencies—may handle publicity, too.

Sales promotion managers manage their company's sales promotion effort. Nearly everything the sales promotion department does *could* be done by the sales or advertising departments. But because sales promotion activities vary so greatly, specialists often develop. In some companies, the sales promotion managers work for the sales managers. In others, they have independent status—and report directly to the marketing manager.

Marketing manager talks to all, blends all
Because of differences in outlook and experience—the advertising, sales, and sales promotion managers may have a hard time working together. It's the marketing manager's job to develop an effective promotion blend—fitting the various departments and personalities into it.

CONCLUSION

Promotion is an important part of any marketing mix. Most consumers and intermediate customers can choose from among many products. A successful producer must do more than offer a good product at a reasonable price. It must also inform potential customers about the product—and where they can buy it. Producers must also tell wholesalers and retailers in the channel about their product—and their marketing mix. These middlemen, in turn, must use promotion to reach *their* customers.

A firm's promotion blend should fit into the strategy that is being developed to satisfy some target market. *What* should be communicated to them—and *how*—should be stated as part of the strategy planning.

The overall promotion objective is to affect buying behavior—but basic promotion objectives include informing, persuading, and reminding.

Various promotion methods can be used to reach these objectives. Behavioral science findings can guide how promotion methods are combined. In particular, we know something about the communication process—and how individuals and groups adopt new products.

An action-oriented model—called AIDA—can help guide planning of promotion blends. But the marketing manager has the final responsibility for blending the promotion methods into one promotion effort—for each marketing mix.

In this chapter, we've studied some basic ideas. In the next two chapters, we'll treat personal and mass selling in more detail. We won't discuss sales promotion again—because it's difficult to generalize about all the possibilities. Further, the fact that most sales promotion activities are short-run efforts—which must be specially tailored—means that sales promotion will probably continue to be a "stepchild"—even though sales promotion costs about as much as advertising. Marketers must find a better way of handling this important decision area.

Questions and Problems

1. Briefly explain the nature of the three basic promotion methods that are available to a marketing manager. Explain why sales promotion is currently a "weak spot" in marketing and suggest what might be done.

2. Relate the three basic promotion objectives to the four jobs (AIDA) of promotion, using a specific example.

3. Discuss the communication process in relation to a producer's promotion of an accessory product, say, a portable air hammer used for breaking up concrete pavement.

4. Explain how an understanding of the way individuals adopt new ideas or products (the adoption process) would be helpful in developing a promotion blend. In particular, explain how it might be desirable to change a promotion blend during the course of the adoption process. To make this more concrete, discuss it in relation to the acceptance of a new men's sportcoat style.

5. Explain how opinion leaders should affect a firm's promotion planning.

6. Discuss how our understanding of the adoption curve should be applied to planning the promotion blend(s) for a new, wireless portable telephone that can be used in cars while traveling.

7. Promotion has been the target of considerable criticism. What specific types of promotion are probably the object of this criticism?

8. Would promotion be successful in expanding the general demand for: (a) pineapples, (b) automobiles, (c) tennis rackets, (d) cashmere sweaters, (e) iron ore, (f) chocolate chip cookies, (g) cement? Explain why or why not in each case.

9. What promotion blend would be most appropriate for producers of the following established products? Assume average- to large-sized firms in each case and support your answer.

a. Candy bars.
b. Men's T-shirts.
c. Castings for car engines.
d. Car tires.
e. Industrial fire insurance.
f. Inexpensive plastic raincoats.
g. A camera that has achieved a specialty-product status.

10. Discuss the potential conflict among the various promotion managers. How could this be reduced?

Suggested Computer-Aided Problem

13. Sales Promotion

Suggested Cases

11. Up With People

19. Mason National Bank

20. A–1 Sports, Inc.

Chapter 14

Personal Selling

When You Finish This Chapter, You Should

1. Understand the importance and nature of personal selling.

2. Know the three basic sales tasks and what the various kinds of salespeople can be expected to do.

3. Know what a sales manager must do to carry out the job assigned to personal selling in a marketing strategy.

4. Understand when and where the three types of sales presentations should be used.

5. Recognize the important new terms (shown in red).

Today, many salespeople are problem-solving professionals.

A producer of allergy tablets wanted to switch to tamper-proof packages for its products. Some of the firm's managers were impressed with Carol Wilson—a sales rep for W. R. Grace, a producer of specialty packaging. So they helped her meet with different departments to learn about their needs and problems. Then Carol made a sales presentation—describing the types of packaging that could be used—as well as the probable cost. The company liked her ideas. But they wanted the packages in a hurry—faster than Carol's company could usually fill an order. To win the sale, she coordinated schedules with her company's design, production, and distribution departments—to get the packages to the customer on time. Then she even held a training session for the customer's sales force—to explain the details of the new package. Now working with this customer is easy. Carol Wilson simply visits occasionally—to write routine orders—and be sure the customer is still happy.

Promotion is communicating with potential customers. Personal selling is often the best way to do it. While face-to-face with prospects, salespeople can get more attention than an ad or a display. Also, they can adjust the presentation as they move along—and adapt to a prospect's feedback. If—and when—the prospect decides "this might be a good idea," the salesperson is there to close the sale—and take the order.

Marketing managers must decide how much—and what kind of—personal selling effort is needed in each marketing mix. As part of their strategy planning, they must decide: (1) how many salespeople are needed, (2) what kind of salespeople are needed, (3) what kind of sales presentation should be used,

Exhibit 14–1   Strategy Planning for Personal Selling

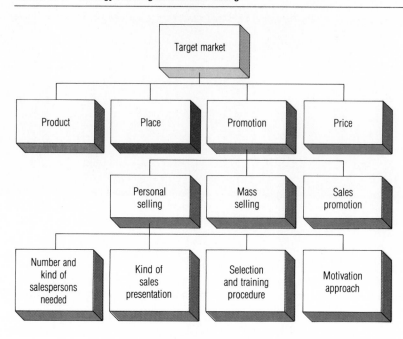

(4) how salespeople should be selected and trained, and (5) how they should be motivated. These strategy decisions can be seen more clearly in Exhibit 14–1.

The sales manager provides inputs into these strategy decisions. And once they're made, it's the sales manager's job to carry out the personal selling part of a marketing strategy.

In this chapter, we'll talk about the importance and nature of personal selling—so you understand the strategy decisions that face sales managers and marketing managers.

THE IMPORTANCE AND ROLE OF PERSONAL SELLING

We have already seen the importance of personal selling to some promotion blends. Some of its supporters feel that personal selling is the dynamic element that keeps our economy going. You would better appreciate the importance of personal selling if you regularly had to meet payrolls, and somehow—almost like magic—your salespeople kept coming in with orders just in time to keep your business from closing.

Our economy does need and use many salespeople. Census Bureau statistics show that about 1 person out of 10 in the labor force is in sales work. That's about 20 times more people than in advertising! Any activity that employs so many people—and is so important to the economy—deserves study.

Good salespeople try to help the customer buy—by understanding the customer's needs.

Helping to buy is good selling

Today, good salespeople don't just try to *sell* the customer. Rather, they try to *help the customer buy*—by showing the advantages and disadvantages of their products and how they satisfy needs and solve problems. This results in satisfied customers—and long-term relationships. "Old-time" salesmen with nothing to offer but funny stories, big expense accounts, and nice smiles are being replaced by real professionals—who solve problems and help bring in sales.

Salespeople represent the whole company—and customers, too

The modern salesperson represents the whole company—by explaining its total effort to target customers—rather than just "getting rid of products." The sales force may be the only link between the firm and its customers—especially for distant customers. Most salespeople provide information about products, explain company policies, and even negotiate prices.

In some cases, the salesperson represents his customers back inside his own firm, too. For example, the sales rep might explain to the production manager why a customer is unhappy with product performance or quality—or show the physical distribution manager why slow shipments cause problems.

As evidence of these changing roles, some companies now give their salespeople such titles as field manager, market specialist, account representative, or sales engineer.

Sales force aids in market information function as well

The sales force can aid in the market information function, too. The sales rep may be the first to hear about a new competitor—or a competitor's new product or strategy. It's important that this information get back to the firm—as the following example shows.

A salesman for Scripto ballpoint pens wondered why sales were dropping off in his California stores—and asked why. He learned that a new Japanese product—a felt-tip writer—was taking sales from ballpoint pens. But months went by before the salesman reported this to management. By then, it was too late. The new felt-tip pens were sweeping the country, and Scripto had none in its product line.

Salespeople can be strategy planners, too

Some salespeople are expected to be marketing managers in their own geographic territories. Or some may have to become "marketing managers"—because top management hasn't provided clear guidelines. Then the salespeople have to develop their own marketing mixes—or even their own strategies. A sales rep may be given a geographic territory—with no specific description of the target customers. He may have to start from scratch with strategy planning—the only limits being the general product line to sell and probably the price structure. The salesperson may have choices about (1) what target customers to aim at, (2) which products in the line to push most aggressively, (3) which middlemen to work with, (4) how to use any promotion money available, and (5) how to adjust prices.

A salesperson who can put together profitable strategies—and carry them out—can rise very rapidly. The opportunity is there—for those who are prepared and willing to work.

Even the starting job may offer many opportunities. Some beginning salespeople—especially those working for manufacturers or wholesalers—are responsible for larger sales volumes than many retail stores achieve. This responsibility must be taken seriously—and should be prepared for.

Further, the sales job is often used as an entry-level position—to find out what a new employee can do. Success in this job can lead to rapid promotion to higher-level sales and marketing jobs—and more money and job security.[1]

WHAT KIND OF PERSONAL SELLING TASKS ARE NEEDED?

If a firm has too few salespeople—or the wrong kind—some important personal selling tasks may not be done. But having too many salespeople—or the wrong kind—wastes money. A sales manager has to find a good balance. He needs the right number of the right kind of salespeople.

One of the difficulties of setting the right number and kind of salespeople is that every sales job is different. While the engineer or accountant can look forward to fairly specific duties, the salesperson's job changes all the time. There are, however, three basic types of sales tasks. This gives us a starting point for understanding what selling tasks have to be done—and how many people will be needed to do them.

Personal selling is divided into three tasks

The **basic sales tasks** are order getting, order taking, and supporting. For convenience, we'll describe salespeople by these terms—referring to their main task—although one person might do all three tasks in some situations.

As the names imply, order getters and order takers are interested in obtaining orders for their company. Every marketing mix must have someone or some way to obtain orders. In contrast, supporting salespeople have no direct interest in orders—they simply help the order-oriented salespeople. With this variety, you can see that personal selling has a place for nearly everyone.

An order-getter may have to deal with multiple buying influences to make a sale.

ORDER GETTERS DEVELOP NEW BUSINESS

Order getters are concerned with getting new business. **Order getting** means seeking possible buyers with a well-organized sales presentation designed to sell a product or idea.

Order-getting salespeople work for producers, wholesalers, and retailers. They normally are well paid. Many earn more than $70,000 a year.

Producers' order getters—find new opportunities

Producers of all kinds of products—but especially industrial products—have a great need for order getters. They are needed to locate new prospects, open new accounts, see new opportunities, and help set up and build channel relationships.

Top-level customers are more interested in ways to save or make more money than in technical details—and good order getters cater to this interest. They sell concepts and ideas—not just physical products. Products are merely the means of achieving the ends the customer desires.

For example, Circadian, Inc., sells "high-tech" medical equipment. Changes in Medicare rules mean that doctors can no longer routinely order expensive tests in hospitals—because the costs can't be recovered easily. But the doctors *can* be paid for tests done in their offices—if they have the right equipment. When a Circadian order getter calls on a doctor, he shows how the firm's testing equipment can improve patient care—and office profits. The rep can often get a $20,000 order "on the spot"—because he can show that the equipment pays for itself in the first year. The doctors don't care about technical details—as long as the machines are accurate and easy to use.[2]

Industrial order getters need the know-how to help solve their customers' problems. Often they have to understand customers' general business concerns—as well as technical details about the product and how it works. To be

Rockwell International gives sales representatives special technical training so they can understand their customers' needs.

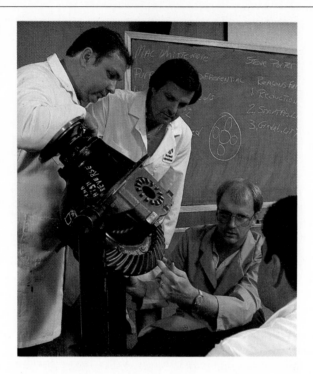

sure of competent order getters, firms often give special technical training to business-trained college graduates. Such salespeople can be a real help to their customers. In fact, they may be more technically able—in their narrow specialty—than anyone in the customer's firm. They provide a unique service.

Wholesalers' order getters—hand it to the customer, almost

Progressive wholesalers are becoming counselors and store advisors—rather than just order takers. Such order getters are almost "partners" of retailers in the job of moving products from the wholesale warehouse through the retail store to consumers. These order getters almost become a part of the retailer's staff—helping to plan stock levels, write orders, conduct demonstrations—as well as planning advertising and special promotions.

Retail order getters—visionaries at the storm window

Order getters are needed for unsought products—and are desirable for some shopping products.

Unsought products need order getters

Convincing customers of the value of products they haven't seriously considered takes a high level of personal selling ability. Order getters must help customers see how a new product can better satisfy needs now being filled by something else. Early order getters for aluminum storm windows—for example—faced a tough job: convincing skeptical customers that this new kind of storm window was not only durable—but would need less maintenance in the long run. Without order getters, many of the products we now accept as part of our standard of living—such as refrigerators and window air-conditioners—might have died in the market introduction stage. The order getter helps bring products out of the market introduction stage—into the market growth stage. Without sales and profits in the early stages, the product may fail—and never be offered again.

They help sell shopping products

Order getters are helpful for selling heterogeneous shopping products. Consumers shop for many of these items on the basis of price *and* quality. They welcome useful information. Cars, furniture and furnishings, cameras, and fashion items can be sold effectively by an order getter. Helpful advice—based on knowledge of the product and its alternatives—may help consumers—and bring profits to the salesperson and retailer.

ORDER TAKERS—KEEP THE BUSINESS COMING

Order takers sell the regular or typical customers. Order takers complete most sales transactions. After a customer becomes interested in the products of a specific firm—from an order getter or a supporting salesperson—or through advertising or sales promotion—an order taker usually is needed to answer any final questions and complete the sales. **Order taking** is the routine completion of sales made regularly to target customers.

Sometimes sales managers or customers use the term "order taker" as a "put down" when referring to some salespeople. While a particular salesperson may perform so poorly that criticism is called for, it's a mistake to downgrade the function of order taking. Order taking is extremely important—whether handled by humans or machines. Many sales are lost because no one asks for the order—and closes the sale.

Producers' order takers—train and explain

After order getters open up industrial, wholesale, or retail accounts, regular follow-up is necessary. Someone has to explain details, make adjustments, handle complaints, and keep customers informed about new developments. Customers' employees may need training to use the product. In sales to middlemen, it may be necessary to train wholesalers' or retailers' salespeople. All these activities are part of the order taker's job.

Usually these salespeople have a regular route with many calls. To handle these calls well, they must have energy, persistence, enthusiasm, and a friendly personality that wears well over time. They sometimes have to "take the heat" when something goes wrong with some other element of the marketing mix.

Sometimes order-taking jobs are used to train potential order getters and managers—since they also offer order-getting possibilities. George Turpin worked for a manufacturer of supplies for automotive body shops—basically an order-taking job. He discovered that one of the biggest body shops in his territory was splitting its orders between several suppliers. George spent more time at this shop—studying the business. He suggested new products that speeded up repairs—and increased the shop's profits. The owners were impressed—and George convinced them that they could save even more if they let him coordinate *all* of their purchases. Since the body shop scheduled all repairs a week ahead, George could study the work list in advance, figure out what supplies and paints were needed, and write up the order. The shop found that this approach meant fewer delays due to supplies that hadn't been ordered or didn't arrive. And it saved them the time of working up orders. George used the same approach with other customers—and increased sales in his territory by 50 percent.

Wholesalers' order takers—not getting orders but keeping them

While producers' order takers handle relatively few items—and sometimes only a single item—wholesalers' order takers may sell 125,000 items or more. Most of these order takers just sell out of their catalogs. They have so many items that they can't possibly give aggressive sales effort to many—except perhaps newer or more profitable items. The strength of this type of order taker is a wide assortment—rather than detailed knowledge of individual products.

The wholesale order taker's main job is to maintain close contact with customers—perhaps once a week—and fill any needs that develop. Some retailers let the sales rep take inventory—and then write the order. Obviously, this position of trust can't be abused. After writing up the order, the order taker normally checks to be sure his company fills the order promptly—and accurately. He also handles any adjustments or complaints—and generally acts as a link between the company and customers.

Such salespeople are usually the low-pressure type—friendly and easy going. Usually these jobs aren't as high paying as the order-getting variety—but are attractive to many because they aren't as demanding. They require relatively little traveling. There is little or no pressure to get new accounts. And some social needs may be satisfied, too. Some order takers become good friends with their customers.

Retail order takers—often they are poor sales clerks

Order taking may be almost mechanical at the retail level—at the supermarket check-out counter, for example. Some retail clerks seem annoyed by having to complete sales. Many are just plain rude. This is too bad—because order taking is important. They may be poor order takers, however, because they aren't paid much—often only the minimum wage. But they may be paid little because they do little. In any case, order taking at the retail level appears to be declining in quality. Probably there will be far fewer such jobs in the future—as more retailers turn to self-service selling.

SUPPORTING SALES FORCE—INFORMS AND PROMOTES IN THE CHANNEL

Supporting salespeople help the order-oriented salespeople—but don't try to get orders themselves. Their activities are aimed at getting sales in the long run. For the short run, however, they are ambassadors of goodwill—who provide specialized services. Almost all supporting salespeople work for producers—or middlemen who do this supporting work for producers. There are two types of supporting salespeople: *missionary salespeople* and *technical specialists.*

Missionary salespeople can increase sales

Missionary salespeople are supporting salespeople who work for producers—calling on their middlemen and their customers. They try to develop goodwill and stimulate demand, help the middlemen train their salespeople, and often take orders for delivery by the middlemen. Missionary salespeople are sometimes called *merchandisers* or *detailers.*

They may be needed if a producer uses the typical merchant wholesaler to obtain widespread distribution—but knows that the retailers will need promotion help that the merchant wholesaler won't provide. These salespeople sometimes give an occasional "shot in the arm" to the producer's regular wholesalers and retailers. Or they may work regularly with these middlemen—setting up displays, arranging special promotions, and, in general, carrying out the sales promotion plans the producer's own specialists develop.

A missionary sales rep can focus on a product that otherwise wouldn't get much attention from the middlemen—because it's just one of many they sell. A missionary salesperson for Vicks' cold remedy products, for example, might visit druggists during the "cold season" and encourage them to use a special end-of-aisle display for Vicks' cough syrup—and even help set it up. The wholesaler that supplies the drug store would benefit from any increased sales, but might not take the time to urge use of the special display.

Such special efforts can double or triple sales. Naturally, this doesn't go unnoticed—and missionary sales jobs often lead to order-oriented jobs. In fact, this position often serves as a training ground for new salespeople.

Missionary salespeople call on middlemen and some focus on retail distribution and display.

Technical specialists are experts who know product applications

    Technical specialists are supporting salespeople who provide technical assistance to order-oriented salespeople. They usually are scientists or engineers with technical know-how—plus the ability to explain the advantages of their firm's product. Since they usually talk with the customer's technical people, there is little need for much sales ability. Before the specialist's call, an order getter probably has stimulated interest. The technical specialist provides the details. Some technical specialists do become fine order getters. But most show more interest in explaining the technical fine points of their product than in actual sales work.

Three tasks may have to be blended

    We've described three sales tasks—order getting, order taking, and supporting. Remember, however, that a particular salesperson might have to do any—or all—of these tasks. Ten percent of a particular job may involve order getting, 80 percent order taking, and the remaining 10 percent supporting. Another company might have three different people handling the different sales tasks. This can lead to **team selling**—when different sales reps work together on a specific account. Team selling is often used by producers of "high ticket" items. AT&T uses team selling to sell office communications systems for a whole business. Different specialists handle different parts of the job—but the efforts of the whole "team" are coordinated to achieve the desired result.

    Strategy planners should set the different types and amounts of selling tasks the sales force must handle. Once these are set, the sales manager can assign responsibility for individual sales jobs.

THE RIGHT STRUCTURE HELPS ASSIGN RESPONSIBILITY

    A sales manager must organize the sales force so that all the necessary tasks are done well. A large organization might have different salespeople who specialize by different selling tasks *and* by the target markets they serve.

Different target markets need different selling tasks

    Sales force responsibilities often are divided based on the type of customer involved. A company that sells upholstery fabrics, for example, might have one sales group that calls on furniture manufacturers and another that calls on wholesalers who sell to small upholstery shops. They may buy the same products—but the marketing mixes are very different.

    Very large customers often require special selling efforts—and different treatment. Moen—a maker of plumbing fixtures—might have a "regular" sales force to call on building material wholesalers and an "elite" **national accounts sales force** that sells direct to large accounts—like Lowe's or other major retail chain stores that carry plumbing fixtures.

Sales tasks are done in sales territories

    Often companies organize selling tasks on the basis of **sales territory**—a geographic area that is the responsibility of one salesperson or several working together. A territory might be a region of the country, a state, or part of a city—depending on the market potential. Companies like Lockheed Aircraft Corporation often consider a whole country as *part* of a sales territory for one salesperson.

Size of sales force depends on workload

Once all the important selling tasks have been set—and the responsibilities divided—the sales manager decides how many salespeople are needed. The first step is estimating how much work can be done by one person in some time period. Then he can make an "educated guess" about the total number of people required—as the following example shows.

For many years the Parker Jewelry Company was very successful—selling its jewelry to department and jewelry stores in the Southwest. But management wanted to expand into the big urban markets of the northeast. They realized that most of the work for the first few years would call for order getters. They felt that a salesperson would have to call on each account at least once a month to get a share of this competitive business. They estimated that a salesperson could make only four calls a day on prospective buyers—and still allow time for travel, waiting, and follow-up on orders that came in. This meant that a sales rep who made calls 20 days a month could handle about 80 stores (4 a day × 20 days).

The managers checked telephone Yellow Pages for target cities—and estimated the total number of jewelry departments and stores. Then they simply divided the total number of stores by 80 to estimate the number of salespeople needed. This helped them set up territories, too—defining areas that included about 80 stores for each salesperson.[3]

When a company is starting a new sales force, managers are concerned about its size. But many ongoing businesses often ignore this strategy decision. Some managers forget that over time the "right" number of salespeople may change—as selling tasks change. Then, when a problem becomes obvious, they try to change everything in a hurry—a big mistake. Finding and training effective salespeople takes time—and is an ongoing job.

SOUND SELECTION AND TRAINING TO BUILD A SALES FORCE

Selecting good salespeople takes judgment, plus

It is important to hire good, well-qualified salespeople. But many companies select on a hit-or-miss basis—without serious thought about exactly what kind of person they need. Friends and relations—or whoever is available—may be hired. This often leads to poor sales—and costly sales force turnover.

Progressive companies try to be more careful. They update lists of possible candidates, and use multiple interviews with various managers as well as psychological tests. Unfortunately, these techniques can't guarantee success—but using some selection method results in a better sales force than using no selection aids at all.

One problem in selecting salespeople is that two different sales jobs with identical titles may involve very different selling tasks—and require different skills. One way to avoid this problem is with a carefully prepared job description.

Job description should be in writing and specific

A **job description** is a written statement of what a salesperson is expected to do. It might list 10 to 20 specific tasks—as well as routine prospecting and sales report writing. Each company must write its own job specifications. They should provide clear guidelines about what specific selling tasks the job requires. This is necessary to decide what kind of salespeople should be selected—and how they should be motivated. A job description also affects the kind of training needed. Later, it can provide a basis for evaluating sales performance.

Good salespeople are trained, not born

The idea that good salespeople are born may have some truth in it—but it isn't the whole story. Studies show that any alert person can be trained to be a good salesperson.

What a salesperson needs to be taught—about the company and its products, about planning and making sales presentations, and about following up after the sale—may seem obvious. But managers often ignore these topics. Many salespeople fail—or do a poor job—because they haven't had good training. New salespeople often are hired and sent out on the road—or retail selling floor—with no sales training and no information about the products or the customer—just a price list and a pat on the back. This isn't enough!

All salespeople need some training

It's up to sales and marketing management to be sure that the salespeople know what they're supposed to do—and how to do it. The kind of sales training should depend on the experience and skills of the group involved. But a company's sales training program should cover at least: (1) company policies and practices, (2) product information, and (3) selling techniques.[4]

COMPENSATING AND MOTIVATING SALESPEOPLE

Public recognition, sales contests, or just personal recognition for a job well done may help stimulate greater sales effort.[5] But most companies emphasize cash incentives to attract and motivate their salespeople.[6]

Many sales are lost because the salesperson doesn't ask for the order.

Two basic decisions must be made in developing a compensation plan: (1) the level of compensation and (2) the method of payment.

Level of compensation depends on needed skills—and job

To attract—and keep—good people, most companies must pay at least the going market wage for different kinds of salespeople. Order getters are paid more than order takers, for example.

The job description explains the salesperson's role in the marketing mix. It should show whether any special skills or responsibilities are needed—requiring higher pay levels. To be sure it can afford a specific type of salesperson, the company should estimate—when the job description is written—how valuable such a salesperson will be. A good order getter may be worth $50,000 to $100,000 to one company, but only $15,000 to $25,000 to another—just because the second firm doesn't have enough to sell! In such a case, the second company must rethink its job specifications—or completely change its promotion plans—because the "going rate" for order getters is much higher than $15,000 a year.

If a job requires extensive traveling, aggressive pioneering, or contacts with difficult customers—the pay may have to be higher. It must be kept in mind, however, that the salesperson's compensation level should compare—at least roughly—with the pay scale of the rest of the firm. Normally, salespeople earn more than the office or production force, but less than top management.

Payment methods vary

Once the general level of compensation has been decided, the method of payment must be set. There are three basic methods of payment: (1) straight salary, (2) straight commission, or (3) a combination plan.

Straight salary gives the salesperson the most security—and straight commission the most incentive. But most companies offer their salespeople some balance between incentive and security. Therefore, the most popular method of payment is a combination plan—which includes some salary and some commission. Bonuses, profit sharing, and fringe benefits may be included, too.

A sales manager's control over a sales rep depends on the compensation plan. A straight salary plan permits the greatest amount of supervision. A person on commission tends to be his own boss.

The marketing manager should try to avoid very complicated compensation plans—or plans that change frequently. Complicated plans are hard for salespeople to understand—and costly for the accounting department to handle. Also, low morale may result if salespeople can't see a direct relationship between their effort and their income.

Simplicity is probably best achieved with straight commission. But, in practice, it is usually better to give up some simplicity to have some control over salespeople—while still providing flexibility and incentive. Exhibit 14–2 shows the general relation between personal selling expenses and sales volume—for the various alternatives.

There are, unfortunately, no easy answers to the compensation problem. It's up to the sales manager—working with the marketing manager—to develop a good compensation plan. The sales manager's efforts have to be part of the

Exhibit 14–2   *Relation between Personal Selling Expenses and Sales Volume—for Basic Personal Selling Compensation Alternatives*

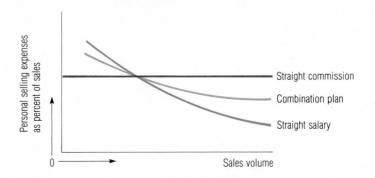

whole marketing program—because he can't accomplish his objectives if enough money isn't allocated for the personal selling job.

PERSONAL SELLING TECHNIQUES—PROSPECTING AND PRESENTING

When we talked about sales training, we mentioned training in selling techniques. Now let's discuss these ideas in more detail—including the basic steps each salesperson should follow—prospecting, planning sales presentations, making sales presentations, and trying to close the sale. Exhibit 14–3 shows the process we'll consider. You can see that the personal salesperson carries out the communication process discussed in the last chapter.[7]

Finding prospects— the big buyer who wasn't there

Finding "live" prospects isn't as easy as it sounds. Although the marketing strategy should specify the target market, we've already seen that some people within a target market may be innovators, while others are late adopters.

Basically, **prospecting** involves following through on all the "leads" in the target market. But which ones are currently "live" and will help make the buying decision? In the industrial products area, for example, about two-thirds of industrial calls are made on the wrong person—because of multiple buying influences and the fact that companies often change their organization structures. This means that constant, detailed customer analysis is needed—requiring many personal calls and telephone calls.

Exhibit 14–3   *Personal Selling Is a Communication Process*

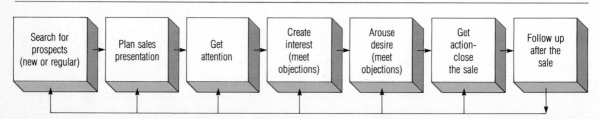

Owens-Illinois uses computer-assisted telephone selling to provide fast service to even the smallest customers.

Telephone selling—using the telephone to find out about a prospect's interest in the company's marketing mix—and even to make a sales presentation or take an order—is becoming more common as an aid in prospecting. A phone call has many of the benefits of a personal visit—including the chance to adjust the message as feedback is received. And it is often more efficient. It cuts the number of costly personal visits—and may even sell "hot" prospects on the phone. At the very least, it provides follow-up information.[8]

How long to spend with whom?

Another part of prospecting involves deciding how much time to spend on prospects. The problem is to "qualify" prospects—to see if they deserve more effort. The rep must weigh the potential sales volume—as well as the likelihood of a sale. This obviously requires judgment—but well-organized salespeople usually develop some system to guide prospecting. They can't afford to "wine and dine" all of their many prospects. Some may deserve only a phone call.

Some firms now provide their reps with personal computers—and specially developed computer programs—to help screen prospects. Using some "grading" system, a sales rep estimates how much each prospect might purchase—and the chances of getting the business, given the competition. The computer combines this information and "grades" each prospect. Attractive accounts—sometimes labeled A—may require weekly calls until the sale is made. B customers might offer somewhat lower potential—and be called on monthly. C accounts might be called on only once a year, and D accounts might be ignored—unless the customer calls the sales rep.[9]

Three kinds of sales presentations may be useful

Once a promising prospect has been found, it's necessary to make a **sales presentation**—a salesperson's effort to make a sale. But someone has to plan the kind of sales presentation. This is a strategy matter—and should be set before the sales rep is sent prospecting. And, in situations where the customer comes to the salesperson—in a retail store, for example—the planners have to make sure that prospects do come to the salespeople. (This may be the job of advertising or sales promotion.) Then the sales presentation must be made.

The marketing manager can choose two basically different approaches to making sales presentations: The prepared approach or the need-satisfaction approach. Another approach—the selling formula approach—combines the two. Each of these has its place.

The prepared sales presentation

The **prepared sales presentation** approach uses a memorized presentation which is not adapted to each individual customer. A prepared ("canned") presentation builds on the black box (stimulus-response) model discussed in Chapter 6. This model says that a customer faced with a particular stimulus will give the desired response—say, a yes answer to the salesperson's request for an order.

The use of prepared sales presentations is shown in Exhibit 14–4. Basically, the salesperson does most of the talking—only occasionally letting the customer talk when the salesperson attempts to close. If one "trial close" doesn't work, the rep tries another prepared presentation—with another attempt at closing. This can go on until the salesperson runs out of material—or the customer either buys or decides to leave.

This approach can be effective—and practical—when the possible sale is low in value—and the rep can spend only a short time on selling. It also makes sense with less skilled salespeople. The company can control what they say—and in what order. For example, a sales rep for *Time* Magazine with little training or ability can call a prospect and basically "read" the prepared presentation.

This approach has the obvious weakness of treating all potential customers alike. It may work for some and not for others—and the salespeople won't know why. This approach is no longer considered good selling for complicated situations.

Need-satisfaction approach—builds on the marketing concept

The **need-satisfaction approach** involves developing a good understanding of the individual customer's needs before trying to close the sale. Here, after making some general "benefit" statements—to get the customer's attention and interest—the salesperson leads the customer to do most of the talking—so he understands the customer's needs. Then the salesperson enters into the conversation more—trying to help the customer understand his own needs better. Once they agree, the seller tries to show how his product fills these spe-

Exhibit 14–4   Prepared Approach to
Sales Presentations

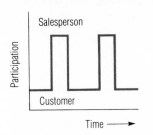

Exhibit 14–5   Need-Satisfaction
Approach to Sales Presentations

Exhibit 14–6   Selling-Formula Approach
to Sales Presentations

cial needs—and close the sale. See Exhibit 14–5. This problem-solving approach requires that the customer and salesperson work together.

The need-satisfaction approach is most useful if there are many differences
among the various customers in a target market. With this approach, the
salesperson is much more on his own. This kind of selling obviously takes
more skill and understanding. The salesperson must be able to analyze what
motivates a particular customer—and show how the company's offering will
help satisfy that customer's needs.

**Selling formula ap-
proach—some of
both**

The **selling formula approach** starts with a prepared presentation outline—much like the prepared approach—and leads the customer through some
logical steps to a final close. The steps are logical because we assume that
we know something about the target customers' needs and attitudes.

The selling formula approach is shown in Exhibit 14–6. The salesperson
does most of the talking at the beginning of the presentation—and communicates basic points early. This part of the presentation may even have been
prepared as part of the marketing strategy. Then the salesperson brings the
customer into the discussion—to see what special needs this customer has.
Next, the salesperson tries to show how his product satisfies this specific customer's needs. Finally, he tries to close the sale.

This approach can be useful for both order-getting and order-taking situations—where potential customers are similar, and relatively untrained salespeople must be used. Some of the office equipment and computer manufacturers use this approach—because they know the kinds of situations their
salespeople meet—and roughly what they want them to say. Using this approach speeds training—and makes the sales force productive sooner.

**AIDA helps plan sales
presentations**

Each sales presentation—except some very simple "canned" types—
follows the AIDA sequence: Attention, Interest, Desire, Action. The "how-to-
do-it" might even be set as part of the marketing strategy. The time spent with
each of the steps varies, depending on the situation—and the selling approach
used. But it is still necessary to begin a presentation by getting the prospect's
attention and, of course, moving him to action through a close.[10]

Each sales manager—and salesperson—must think through this sequence
in deciding what sales approach to use—and in evaluating a possible presen-

tation. Does the presentation do a good job of quickly getting the prospect's attention? Will the presentation hold the prospect's interest? Finally—does the presentation result in action—does the salesperson ask for the order and persuade the customer to buy? It might surprise you to learn that the most common reason for losing a sale is that the seller *never asks for the order!* These ideas may seem very obvious to you. But too often they are overlooked—or ignored—and the sale is lost.

CONCLUSION

In this chapter, we've discussed the importance and nature of personal selling. Selling is much more than just "getting rid of the product." In fact, a salesperson who is not provided with a strategy may have to become his own strategy planner. Ideally, however, the sales manager and marketing manager should work together to set the strategy guidelines: the kind and number of salespersons needed, the kind of sales presentation, and selection, training, and motivation approaches.

Three *basic* sales tasks were discussed: (1) order getting, (2) order taking, and (3) supporting. Most sales jobs combine at least two of these three tasks. Once the important tasks have been set, the structure of the sales organization and the number of salespeople needed to accomplish the tasks can be decided. The nature of the job—and the level and method of compensation—also depends on the blend of these tasks. A job description should be written for each sales job. This, in turn, provides guidelines for selecting, training, and compensating salespeople.

Once the sales manager's basic plan and budget have been set, the job is to implement the plan—including directing and controlling the sales force. This includes assigning sales territories and controlling performance. You can see that a sales manager is deeply involved with the basic management tasks of planning and control—as well as ongoing implementing of the personal selling effort.

Three kinds of sales presentations were discussed. Each has its place—but the need-satisfaction approach seems best for higher-level sales jobs. In jobs like these, personal selling achieves a new, professional status—because of the ability and personal responsibility required of the salesperson. The old-time "glad-hander" is being replaced by the specialist who is creative, hard working, persuasive, and highly trained—and therefore able to help the buyer. This type of salesperson always has been—and probably always will be—in short supply. And the demand for high-level salespeople is growing.

Questions and Problems

1. What strategy decisions are needed in the personal selling area? Why should they be made by the marketing manager?

2. What kind of salesperson (or what blend of the basic sales tasks) is required to sell the following products? If there are several selling jobs in the channel for each product, then indicate the kinds of salespeople required. Specify any assumptions necessary to give definite answers.

a. Soybean oil.
b. Costume jewelry.
c. Personal computers.
d. Handkerchiefs.
e. Mattresses.
f. Corn.
g. Life insurance.

3. Distinguish among the jobs of producers', wholesalers', and retailers' order-getting sales-

people. If one order getter is needed, must all the salespeople in a channel be order getters? Illustrate.

4.   Discuss the role of the manufacturers' agent in a marketing manager's promotion plans. What kind of salesperson is a manufacturers' agent?

5.   Discuss the future of the specialty shop if producers place greater emphasis on mass selling because of the inadequacy of retail order taking.

6.   Compare and contrast missionary salespeople and technical specialists.

7.   How would a straight commission plan provide flexibility in the sale of a line of women's clothing products that continually vary in profitability.

8.   Explain how a compensation plan could be developed to provide incentives for older salespeople and yet make some provision for trainees who have not yet learned their job.

9.   Cite an actual local example of each of the three kinds of sales presentations discussed in the chapter. Explain for each situation whether a different type of presentation would have been better.

10.   Describe a need-satisfaction sales presentation that you experienced recently. How could it have been improved by fuller use of the AIDA framework?

11.   How would our economy operate if personal salespeople were outlawed? Could the economy work? If so, how? If not, what is the minimum personal selling effort necessary? Could this minimum personal selling effort be controlled by law?

Suggested Computer-Aided Problem

14.   Sales Compensation

Suggested Cases

21.   Du Pont

22.   Moore Wire Rope, Inc.

23.   King Furniture Company

29.   Pulte Products, Inc.

Chapter 15

Mass Selling

When You Finish This Chapter, You Should

1. Understand how the various kinds of advertising can be used in marketing strategy planning.

2. Understand how to go about choosing the "best" medium.

3. Understand how to plan the "best" message—that is, the copy thrust.

4. Understand what advertising agencies do—and how they are paid.

5. Understand how to advertise legally.

6. Recognize the important new terms (shown in red).

To reach a lot of people quickly and cheaply—use mass selling.

About 85 million people—one-third of the U.S. population—watched the 1986 Super Bowl. Parts of the game weren't that exciting. But the ads were. Advertisers—who paid a *million dollars a minute* to reach the audience—knew that viewers would head for the refrigerator if an ad didn't get attention within seconds. To hold viewer interest, Timex spent a million dollars for an ad to introduce its $35 Atlantis model sports watch. But the high cost—and the target market—of Super Bowl advertising aren't for everyone. Huggies diapers, Heinz Ketchup, and Windex window cleaner advertise on message boards on shopping carts in grocery stores. Campbell's Soup puts advertising message boards on parking meters in downtown Baltimore. Merrill Lynch advertises on cable channels—like the Arts and Entertainment Network—which targets higher income viewers.[1]

Mass selling makes widespread distribution possible. Although a marketing manager may prefer to use only personal selling, it's often too expensive. Mass selling can be cheaper. It's not as targeted as personal selling, but it can reach large numbers of potential customers at the same time. Today, most promotion blends contain both personal and mass selling.

Marketing managers have many strategy decisions to make about mass selling. Working with advertising managers, they must decide: (1) who the target audience is, (2) what kind of advertising to use, (3) how to reach customers (via which types of media), (4) what to say to customers (the copy thrust), and (5) who will handle the advertising (the firm's own advertising department or an advertising agency). See Exhibit 15–1. We'll talk about these decisions in this chapter.

Exhibit 15–1 Strategy Planning for Advertising

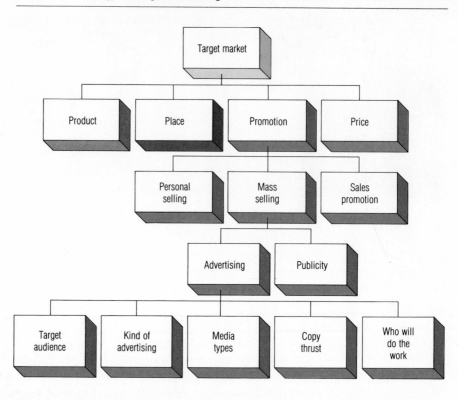

THE IMPORTANCE OF ADVERTISING

$100 billion in ads in 1986

Advertising can get results in a promotion blend. But good advertising results cost money. In the United States, spending for advertising has grown continuously since World War II. And more growth is expected. In 1964, advertising spending was slightly more than $3 billion. By 1982 it was $66 billion—and by 1986 it was about $100 billion.[2]

It's all done by less than half a million people

While total advertising expenditures are large, the advertising industry itself employs relatively few people. The major expense is for media time and space. And, in the United States, the largest share of this—27 percent—goes for newspaper space. Television takes about 22 percent of the total, and direct mail, about 16 percent.[3]

Many students hope for a glamorous job in advertising, but only about 500,000 people work directly in the U.S. advertising industry. This includes all people who help create or sell advertising or advertising media—advertising people in radio and television stations, newspapers, and magazines—as well as those in advertising agencies—and those working for retailers, wholesalers, and producers. U.S. advertising agencies employ only about half of all these people.[4]

Exhibit 15–2   Top 10 U.S. National Advertisers in 1986

Rank	Company name	Total advertising dollars—1986 ($ million)
1	Procter & Gamble Co.	$1,435.5
2	Philip Morris Cos.	1,364.5
3	Sears Roebuck & Co.	1,004.7
4	RJR/Nabisco	935.0
5	General Motors Corp.	839.0
6	Ford Motor Co.	648.5
7	Anheuser-Busch Cos.	643.5
8	McDonald's Corp.	592.0
9	K mart Corp.	590.4
10	PepsiCo Inc.	581.3

Most advertisers aren't really spending that much

U.S. corporations spend only about 1.5 percent of their sales dollar on advertising. This is relatively small compared to the total cost of marketing—which is about 50 percent of the consumer's dollar.

Some industries—and companies—spend a much larger percentage of sales for advertising than the average of 1.5 percent. Soap producers like Procter & Gamble and Unilever spend between 7 and 11 percent of sales on ads. In the food area, General Foods and McDonald's spend about 6 percent of sales on advertising. At the other extreme, some industrial products companies—those who depend on personal selling—may spend less than $\frac{1}{10}$ of 1 percent. And wholesalers and retailers may spend about 1 percent. (See Exhibit 15–2 for the top 10 national advertisers in 1986.)

You can see that advertising is important in certain markets—especially the consumer products markets. Remember, however, that—in total—it costs much less than personal selling.

ADVERTISING OBJECTIVES ARE SET BY MARKETING STRATEGY

Every ad—and every advertising campaign—should have clearly defined objectives. These should grow out of the overall marketing strategy—and the jobs assigned to advertising. It's not enough for the marketing manager just to say, "Promote the product."

A marketing manager should spell out exactly what is wanted. A general objective—"To help in the expansion of market share"—could be stated more specifically—"To increase traffic in our cooperating retail outlets by 25 percent during the next three months."

Such specific objectives obviously affect the kind of promotion used. Adver-

Exhibit 15–3 Advertising Should Vary for Adoption Process Stages

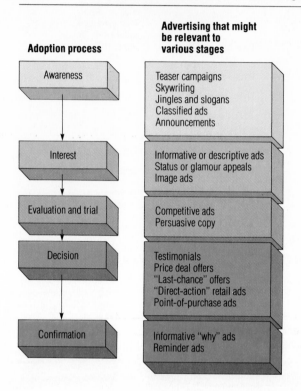

tising that might be right for building a good image among opinion leaders might be all wrong for getting customers into retailers' stores.

Some cases require even more specific objectives. For new products, for example, most of the target market may have to be brought through the early stages of the adoption process. When General Foods developed a sugar-free Kool Aid—sweetened with a new, natural sweetener instead of saccharin—the company mailed samples of the new drink mix to consumers' homes, along with a free coupon offer. For more established products, advertising might have to build brand preference—and help purchasers confirm their decisions. This, too, leads to different kinds of advertising—as shown in Exhibit 15–3.

Advertising objectives should be even more specific than personal selling objectives. One advantage of personal selling is that salespeople can shift their presentations to meet customers' needs. Each ad, however, is a specific communication that has to work, not just for one customer, but for thousands—or millions—of target customers. This means that specific objectives should be set for each ad—as well as a whole advertising campaign. If this isn't done, creative advertising people may set some reasonable objective—like "selling the product"—and then create ads that win artistic awards within the advertising industry—but fail to get the expected results.

OBJECTIVES DETERMINE THE KINDS OF ADVERTISING NEEDED

Advertising objectives determine which of two basic types of advertising to use—product or institutional.

Product advertising tries to sell a product. It may be aimed at final users or channel members.

Institutional advertising tries to develop goodwill for a company or even an industry—instead of a specific product.

Product advertising— know us, like us, remember us

Product advertising falls into three categories: pioneering, competitive, and reminder advertising.

Pioneering advertising—builds primary demand

Pioneering advertising tries to develop **primary demand**—demand for a product category rather than a specific brand. It's needed in the early stages of the adoption process—to inform potential customers about a new product. Pioneering advertising is usually done in the market introduction stage of the product life cycle. In 1985 when Merrell Dow Pharmaceutical introduced a prescription drug to help smokers break their habit, it did pioneering advertising to inform both doctors and smokers about its breakthrough. The ad didn't even mention the name of the drug—but told smokers who wanted to quit that doctors now had a drug to help overcome their dependence on nicotine.

Competitive advertising—emphasizes selective demand

Competitive advertising tries to develop **selective demand**—demand for a specific brand rather than a product category. As the product life cycle moves along, a firm can be forced into competitive advertising to hold its own against competitors. The United Fruit Company gave up a 20-year pioneering effort to promote bananas—in favor of advertising its own Chiquita brand. The reason was simple. While United Fruit was promoting bananas, it slowly lost market share to competitors. The competitive advertising campaign tried to stop further losses.

Competitive advertising may be either direct or indirect. The **direct type** aims for immediate buying action. The **indirect type** points out product advantages—to affect future buying decisions.

Most of Delta Airline's advertising is competitive. Much of it tries for immediate sales—with direct-action ads showing prices, timetables, and phone numbers to call for reservations. The indirect ads focus on the quality of service and number of cities served—and suggest you mention Delta's name the next time you talk to your travel agent.

Comparative advertising is even rougher competitive advertising. **Comparative advertising** means making specific brand comparisons—using actual product names. A recent comparative ad shows a can of Diet Sprite stacked on top of a can of Diet 7UP with the headline "Guess who came out on top in the test? It's official. Diet Sprite Tastes Best."

The Federal Trade Commission encouraged these kinds of ads. But this approach caused legal and ethical problems—and some advertisers and agencies have backed away from it. Research is supposed to support superiority claims, but the rules aren't clear. Some firms just keep testing until they get the results they want. Others talk about minor differences that don't reflect the overall benefits of a product. Some comparative ads leave consumers confused—or even angry—if the product they're using has been criticized. And, in at least one case, comparative ads appear to have helped the competitive product (Tylenol) more than the advertisers' product (Datril, Anacin, and Bayer aspirin).[5]

Many advertisers don't like comparative advertising. But such ads do get attention. So some advertisers will probably continue this approach as long as the government encourages it—and the ad copy is not actually false.[6]

Reminder advertising—reinforces early promotion

Reminder advertising tries to keep the product's name before the public. It may be useful when the product has won brand preference or insistence—perhaps in the market maturity or sales decline stages. Here, the advertiser may use "soft-sell" ads that just mention or show the name—as a reminder.

Comparative advertising makes specific brand comparisons— using actual product names.

Nike uses billboards that show just a Nike shoe and the Nike brand name in bold print.

Institutional advertising—remember our name in Dallas, Seattle, Boston

Institutional advertising focuses on the name and prestige of a company or industry. It tries to inform, persuade, or remind.

Large companies with several divisions sometimes use this kind of promotion. AT&T, for example, advertises the AT&T name—emphasizing the quality and research behind *all* AT&T products.

Sometimes an advertising campaign may have both product and institutional aspects—because the federal government limits tax deductions on some institutional advertising—claiming it has no "business purpose."

COORDINATING ADVERTISING EFFORTS

Vertical cooperation—advertising allowances, cooperative advertising

So far, our discussion suggests that only producers do product or institutional advertising. This isn't true, of course. But producers can affect the advertising done by others. Sometimes a producer knows what he wants advertising to do—but finds that someone further along in the channel can do it better or cheaper. In this case, the producer may offer **advertising allowances**—price reductions to firms further along in the channel to encourage them to promote the firm's products locally.

Cooperative advertising involves middlemen and producers sharing the cost of ads. It helps the producer get more promotion for the advertising dollar—since media usually give local advertisers lower rates than national firms. Also, a retailer is more likely to follow through when he's paying part of the cost.

Cooperative advertising and advertising allowances can be abused. Allowances can be given to retailers without really expecting that they will be used for ads. This may become a hidden price cut—or even price discrimination. The Federal Trade Commission has become more interested in this problem—and some producers have pulled back from cooperative advertising. To avoid legal problems, wise producers insist on proof that the advertising was really done.[7]

CHOOSING THE "BEST" MEDIUM—HOW TO DELIVER THE MESSAGE

For effective promotion, ads have to reach target customers. Unfortunately, not all potential customers read all newspapers and magazines—or listen to all radio and television programs. So not all media are equally effective.

What is the best medium? There is no simple answer. Effectiveness depends on how well it fits with the rest of a marketing strategy—that is, it depends on (1) promotion objectives, (2) target markets, (3) the funds available for advertising, and (4) the nature of the media—including who they *reach,* with what *frequency,* with what *impact,* at what *cost.* Exhibit 15–4 shows some of the pros and cons of major kinds of media—and some typical costs.[8]

Exhibit 15–4 Relative Size and Costs, and Advantages and Disadvantages of Major Kinds of Media

Kinds of media	Sales volume— 1985 ($ billions)	Typical costs— 1986	Advantages	Disadvantages
Newspaper	$25.2	$17,750 for one page weekday, *Milwaukee Journal*	Flexible Timely Local market Credible source	May be expensive Short life No "pass-along"
Television	20.8	$2,000 for a 30-second spot, prime time, Milwaukee	Offers sight, sound, and motion Good attention Wide reach	Expensive in total "Clutter" Short exposure Less selective audience
Direct mail	15.5	$40/1,000 for listing of 593,000 engineers	Selected audience Flexible Can personalize	Relatively expensive per contact "Junk mail"—hard to retain attention
Radio	6.5	$225 for one-minute drive time, Milwaukee	Wide reach Segmented audiences Inexpensive	Offers audio only Weak attention Many different rates Short exposure
Magazine	5.2	$55,300 for one-page, 4-color in *U.S. News & World Report*	Very segmented audiences Credible source Good reproduction Long life Good "pass-along"	Inflexible Long lead times
Outdoor	0.9	$4,200 (painted) for prime billboard, 30–60-day showings, Milwaukee	Flexible Repeat exposure Inexpensive	"Mass market" Very short exposure

Specify promotion objectives

Before choosing the best medium, you must decide on your promotion objectives. If the objective is to inform—telling a long story with a lot of detail and pictures—then magazines and newspapers may be best. Jockey switched its annual budget of more than $1 million to magazines from television when it decided to show the variety of colors, patterns, and styles of men's Jockey briefs. Jockey felt it was too hard to show this in a 30-second TV spot. So it ran ads in men's magazines—such as *Sports Illustrated, Outdoor Life, Field and Stream, Esquire,* and *Playboy.* But aware that women buy over 80 percent of men's ordinary underwear—and 50 percent of fashion styles—Jockey also placed ads in *TV Guide, New Yorker, People, Money, Time,* and *Newsweek.* And a page of scantily clad males appeared in *Cosmopolitan.*[9]

Match your market with the media

To guarantee good media selection, the advertiser first must clearly specify its target market—a step necessary for all marketing strategy planning. Then media can be chosen that will reach those target customers.

Matching target customers and media is the major problem in effective media selection. It's hard to know who sees or hears what. Most of the major media use marketing research to obtain profiles of the people who buy their publications—or live in their broadcasting area. But they can't be as sure about who actually reads each page—or sees or hears each show.[10]

The difficulty of evaluating alternate media has led some media buyers to select media based only on lowest "cost per thousand" figures. But too great concern with numbers of "bodies" may lead to ignoring the target market's dimensions—and slipping into "mass marketing." The media buyer may look only at the relatively low cost (per 1,000 people) of mass media—such as national network radio or TV—when a more specialized medium might be a much better buy. Its audience might have more interest in the product—or more money to spend—or more willingness to buy. Gillette Co. for example, buys advertising time on cable TV—especially MTV—to increase its penetration with the teenager and young adult markets—consumers who are more willing to try new products.

Specialized media help zero in on target markets

Media now try to reach smaller, more defined target markets. Some national media offer regional editions. *Time* magazine, for example, offers not only several regional and metropolitan editions, but also special editions for college students, educators, doctors, and business managers.

Many magazines serve only special-interest groups—such as fishermen, soap opera fans, new parents, and personal computer users. In fact, the most profitable magazines aim at well-defined markets, such as *Car Craft, Skiing, Brides Magazine,* and *Southern Living.*

There are trade magazines in many fields—such as chemical engineering, electrical wholesaling, farming, and the defense market. *Standard Rate and Data* provides a guide to the thousands of magazines now available.

Radio has become a more specialized medium. Some stations aim at nationality, racial, or religious groups—such as Hispanics, Blacks, and Catholics—while others appeal to country, rock, or classical music fans.

Perhaps the most specific medium is **direct-mail advertising**—selling directly to customers via their mailboxes. With this method, a specific message is sent to a carefully selected list of people. Some firms specialize in providing mailing lists—ranging from hundreds to millions of names. The variety of these lists (Exhibit 15–5) shows the importance of knowing your target market.[11]

"Must buys" may use up available money

Selecting which media to use is pretty much an art. The media buyer often starts with a budgeted amount and then tries to buy the best blend to reach the target audience. Some media are obvious "must buys"—such as *the* local newspaper for a retailer in a small or medium-sized town. Such "must buys" may even use up the available promotion money. If not, then the media buyer must compare the relative advantages and disadvantages of alternatives—and select a media *blend* that helps achieve the promotion objectives—given the budget allowed.

Exhibit 15–5   Examples of Available Mailing Lists

Quantity of names	Name of list
425	Small Business Advisors
40,000	Social Register of Canada
5,000	Society of American Bacteriologists
500	South Carolina Engineering Society
2,000	South Dakota State Pharmaceutical Association
250	Southern California Academy of Science
12,000	Texas Manufacturing Executives
720	Trailer Coach Association
1,200	United Community Funds of America
50,000	University of Utah Alumni
19,000	Veterinarians

PLANNING THE "BEST" MESSAGE—WHAT IS TO BE COMMUNICATED

Specifying the copy thrust

Once it has been decided *how* the messages will reach the target audience, then it is necessary to decide on the **copy thrust**—*what* the words and illustrations should communicate. This should flow from the promotion objectives—and the specific jobs assigned to advertising. Advertising specialists usually carry out the copy thrust. But the advertising manager and the marketing manager should understand the process—to be sure that the job is done well.

Let AIDA help guide message planning

There are few set rules in message planning. Basically, the overall marketing strategy should determine *what* should be said in the message. Then management judgment—with the help of marketing research—can decide how to encode this message so it will be decoded as the advertiser intended.

As a guide to message planning, we can make use of the AIDA model: getting *Attention,* holding *Interest,* arousing *Desire,* and obtaining *Action.*

Getting attention

Getting attention is the first job of an ad. If the ad doesn't get attention, it doesn't matter how many people see or hear it. Many readers leaf through magazines and newspapers without paying attention to any of the ads. Many listeners or viewers do chores—or get snacks—during commercials on radio and TV.[12]

There are many ways to catch a customer's attention. A large headline, newsy or shocking statements, pictures of pretty girls, babies, "special effects"—anything that is "different" or eye-catching—may do the trick. But the attention-getting device must not take away from the next step—holding interest.

Holding interest

Holding interest is harder. A pretty girl may get attention. But once you've seen her, then what? A man may pause to admire her. Women may evaluate her. But if there is no relation between the girl and the product, observers of both sexes will move on.

More is known about holding interest than getting attention. The tone and language of the ad must fit with the experience and attitudes of target customers. A Miller Beer ad featuring fox hunters in riding coats, for example, was passed over by most beer drinkers. They just weren't interested in "riding to the hounds."

Besides speaking the target customers' language, the advertising layouts should also look "right" to the customer. Print illustrations and copy should be arranged so that the eye moves smoothly through the ad—i.e., encouraging *gaze motion.*

Arousing desire

Arousing desire for a particular product is one of the most difficult jobs for an ad. The advertiser must communicate with the customer. This means that the advertiser must understand how the target customers think, behave, and make decisions—and then give them a reason to buy. A successful ad must convince customers that the product meets their needs. Although products may satisfy certain emotional needs, many consumers need to justify their purchases on an economic or "rational" basis. Snickers (candy bar) ads, for instance, help ease the guilt for calorie-conscious snackers by assuring them that "Snickers satisfies you when you need an afternoon energy break."

Obtaining action

Getting action is the final requirement—and not an easy one. Communications research shows that potential customers must be led beyond considering how the product *might* fit into their lives—to actually trying it or letting the company's sales rep come in and demonstrate it.

For better communication—the ads might feature strongly felt customer needs. Careful research on attitudes of the target market may help uncover such strongly felt *unsatisfied* needs.

Appealing to these needs can get more action—and also provide the kind of information buyers need to confirm their decisions. Dissonance may set in after the purchase—so providing reassurance may be one important advertising objective. Some customers seem to read more advertising *after* the purchase than before. What the ads communicate to them may be very important if satisfied customers are to start—or keep—the web-of-word-of-mouth going. The ad may reassure them about the correctness of their decision—and also supply the words they use to tell others about the product.

ADVERTISING AGENCIES OFTEN DO THE WORK

An advertising manager manages a company's mass selling effort. Many advertising managers—especially those working for retailers—have their own advertising departments that plan the specific advertising campaigns—and carry out the details. Others use advertising agencies.

Ad agencies are specialists

Advertising agencies are specialists in planning and handling mass selling details for advertisers. Agencies play a useful role—because they are independent of the advertiser—and have an outside viewpoint. They bring experience to an individual client's problems—because they work for many other clients. Further, as specialists they often can do the job more economically than a company's own department.

One of the ad agency's advantages is that the advertiser is free to cancel the arrangement at any time. This provides extreme flexibility for the advertiser. Some companies even use their advertising agency as a scapegoat. Whenever anything goes wrong, it's the agency's fault—and the advertiser shops around for a new one.

Are they paid too much?

The major users of advertising agencies are producers or national middlemen—because of the media rate structure. Normally, media have two prices: one for national advertisers—and another (lower) one for local advertisers, such as retailers. The advertising agency gets a 15 percent commission on national rates *only*. This makes it worthwhile for national advertisers to use agencies. The national advertiser must pay the full media rate anyway. So it makes sense to let the agency experts do the work—and earn their commission. Local retailers—allowed the lower media rate—seldom use agencies.

Resistance to the traditional method of paying agencies is growing. The chief complaints are (1) agencies receive the flat 15 percent commission—regardless of work performed—and (2) this makes it hard for the agencies to be completely objective about lower cost media—or promotion campaigns that use little space or time.

The fixed commission system is most favored by accounts—such as producers of industrial products—that need a lot of service but buy relatively little advertising. Agencies would like to—and sometimes do—charge these firms additional fees.

Large consumer products advertisers who do much of their own advertising research and planning generally oppose the fixed commission system. They need only basic services from their agencies.

Fifteen percent is not required

The Federal Trade Commission worked for many years to change the way advertising agencies are paid. Finally, in 1956, the American Association of Advertising Agencies agreed it would no longer require the 15 percent commission system. This opened the way to fee increases—and decreases.

Du Pont reported recently that it paid agencies an average of 21 percent of billings on industrial accounts and 14 percent on consumer products accounts. Other companies report very different arrangements with their agencies—but most start from the 15 percent base.[13]

MEASURING ADVERTISING EFFECTIVENESS IS NOT EASY

Success depends on the total marketing mix

It would be convenient if we could measure the results of advertising just by looking at sales. Unfortunately, we can't—although the advertising literature is filled with success stories that "prove" advertising has increased sales. The total marketing mix—not just promotion—is responsible for the sales result. The one exception to this rule is direct mail advertising. If it doesn't produce immediate results, it's considered a failure.

Research and testing can improve the odds

Ideally, advertisers should test advertising before it's run—rather than *just* relying on creative people or advertising "experts."

Some progressive advertisers now demand laboratory or market tests to check ads' effectiveness. Sometimes, opinion and attitude research is used before ads are run. American Express, for example, used focus group interviews to get reactions to a series of possible TV ads.[14]

While advertising research techniques aren't foolproof, they are probably far better than just trusting the judgment of advertising "experts." Until better advertising research tools are developed, the present methods seem safest. This means carefully defining specific advertising objectives, choosing media and messages to accomplish these objectives, testing possible ads, and then evaluating the results of actual ads.[15]

HOW TO AVOID UNFAIR ADVERTISING

FTC can control unfair practices

The Federal Trade Commission has the power to control unfair or deceptive business practices—including "deceptive advertising." And it may be getting results—now that advertising agencies as well as advertisers must share equal responsibility for false, misleading, or unfair ads.

This is a serious matter, because if the FTC decides that a particular practice is unfair or deceptive, it can require affirmative disclosures—such as the health warnings on cigarettes—or **corrective advertising**—ads to correct deceptive advertising. Listerine spent millions of dollars on advertising to "correct" earlier ads that claimed the mouthwash helped prevent colds. The FTC concluded that Listerine could not prove its claim. The possibility of large financial penalties and/or the need to pay for corrective ads has caused more agencies and advertisers to stay well within the law.[16]

The FTC has also moved against what it feels are "unfair" practices—since it now finds fewer outright deceptive ads in national campaigns. For example, some in the FTC feel it is unfair for children to be a target for advertising. The FTC is also concerned about effective energy use. An FTC lawyer recently created a stir by criticizing electric hair dryers. He argued that "if you wait 15 minutes, your hair gets dry anyway." There are questions about whether food and drug advertising should be controlled to protect "vulnerable" groups—such as the aged, poor, non-English-speaking, or less educated adults. Some wonder, for example, whether ads for high-calorie foods might cause obesity among low-income women.[17]

What is unfair or deceptive is changing

What is unfair and deceptive is a difficult topic—which marketing managers have to deal with. Clearly, the social and political environment has changed. Practices that were acceptable some years ago are now questioned—or actually considered deceptive. Saying—or even implying—that your product is "best"—even in fun—is now deceptive, unless you have proof.[18]

In the long run, the safest way to avoid "unfair" and "deceptive" criticisms is to stop advertising the typical "me-too" products as "really new" or "better." Already, some advertising agencies refuse such jobs.

CONCLUSION

It may seem simple to develop a mass selling campaign. Just pick the media and develop a message. But it's not that easy. Effectiveness depends on using the "best" medium and the "best" message—considering: (1) promotion objectives, (2) the target markets, and (3) the money available for advertising.

Specific advertising objectives determine what kind of advertising to use—product or institutional. If product advertising is needed, then the particular type must be decided—pioneering, competitive (direct or indirect), or reminder. And advertising allowances and cooperative advertising may be helpful.

Mass selling involves many technical details. Specialists—advertising agencies—handle some of these jobs. But specific objectives must be set for them—or their advertising may have little direction and be almost impossible to evaluate.

Effective advertising should affect sales. But the whole marketing mix affects sales. The results of advertising can't be measured by sales changes alone. Advertising is only a part of promotion. And promotion is only a part of a total marketing mix that the marketing manager must develop to satisfy target customers.

Questions and Problems

1. Identify the strategy decisions a marketing manager must make in the mass selling area.

2. Discuss the relation of advertising objectives to marketing strategy planning and the kinds of advertising actually needed. Illustrate.

3. Give three examples where advertising to middlemen might be necessary. What is the objective(s) of such advertising?

4. What does it mean to say that "money is invested in advertising?" Is all advertising an investment? Illustrate.

5. Find advertisements to final consumers that illustrate the following types of advertising: (a) institutional, (b) pioneering, (c) competitive, (d) reminder. What objective(s) does each of these ads have? List the needs each ad appeals to.

6. Describe the type of media that might be most suitable for promoting: (a) tomato soup, (b) greeting cards, (c) an industrial component

material, (*d*) playground equipment. Specify any assumptions necessary to obtain a definite answer.

7. Discuss the use of testimonials in advertising. Which of the four AIDA steps might testimonials accomplish? Are they suitable for all types of products? If not, for which types are they most suitable?

8. Find an advertisement that seeks to accomplish all four AIDA steps. How does it accomplish each of these steps?

9. Discuss the future of independent advertising agencies now that the 15 percent commission system is not required.

10. Does mass selling cost too much? How can this be measured?

11. How would retailing promotion be affected if all local advertising via mass media such as radio, television, and newspapers were prohibited? Would there be any impact on total sales? If so, would it probably affect all products and stores equally?

12. Is it "unfair" to advertise to children? Is it "unfair" to advertise to less-educated or less-experienced people of any age? Is it "unfair" to advertise "unnecessary" products?

Suggested Computer-Aided Problem

15. Advertising Media

Suggested Cases

11. Up With People

19. Mason National Bank

20. A–1 Sports, Inc.

Chapter 16

Pricing Objectives and Policies

When You Finish This Chapter, You Should

1. Understand how pricing objectives should guide pricing decisions.

2. Understand the marketing strategy choices the marketing manager must make about price flexibility and price levels over the product life cycle.

3. Understand the legality of price level and price flexibility policies.

4, Understand the many possible variations of a price structure, including discounts, allowances, and who pays transporting costs.

5. Recognize the important new terms (shown in red).

Deciding what price to charge can be agonizing.

Recently, Alcoa—one of the largest aluminum producers—found it had too much inventory—and high inventory carrying costs. To solve its problem, Alcoa offered its wholesalers a 30 percent discount off their normal price. Alcoa expected the wholesalers to pass most of the discount along to their customers—to stimulate sales along the channel.

Instead, wholesalers bought *their* aluminum at the lower price, but passed on only a small part of the discount to customers. As a result, the quantity Alcoa sold didn't increase much. Alcoa still had too much inventory—and the wholesalers made more profit on the aluminum they did sell.[1]

Price is one of the four major variables a marketing manager controls. Price decisions affect both sales and profit.

Guided by the company's objectives, marketing managers must develop a set of pricing objectives and policies. These policies should explain: (1) how flexible prices will be, (2) at what level they will be set—over the product life cycle, (3) how transporting costs will be handled, and (4) to whom—and when—discounts and allowances will be given. These strategy decision areas are shown in Exhibit 16–1.

PRICE HAS MANY DIMENSIONS

It's hard to define price in real-life situations—price has many dimensions. If a catalog offered—at $175—a pair of stereo speakers sold by local retailers for $300—this might look like a real bargain. But your view of this "deal" might

Exhibit 16–1 Strategy Planning for Price

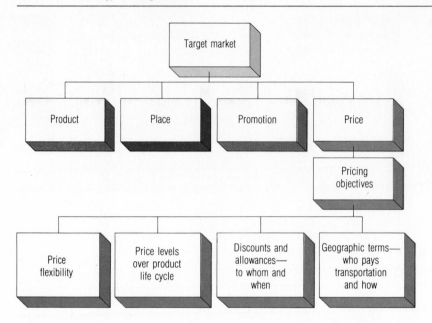

change if you found that the speakers came in a kit for you to assemble—and without a warranty because you were assembling the parts. The price might look even less attractive if you had to pay $35 for insurance and shipping from the factory. Further, how would you feel if you ordered the speakers anyway and then found that delivery takes two months!

The price equation: price equals something

This example shows that price relates to *some* assortment of goods and/or services. So **Price** is what is charged for "something." *Any business transaction can be thought of as an exchange of money—the money being the Price—for Something.*

The something can be a physical product in various stages of completion, with or without the services usually provided, with or without quality guaran-

Exhibit 16–2 Price as Seen by Consumers

Price	equals	Something
List price		*Product:*
Less: *Discounts:*		Physical good
Quantity		Service
Seasonal		Assurance of quality
Cash	equals	Repair facilities
Less: *Allowances:*		Packaging
Trade-ins		Credit
Damaged goods		Trading stamps or coupons
Less: *Rebates*		*Place of delivery or availability*

Exhibit 16-3   *Price as Seen by Channel Members*

Price	equals	Something
List price Less: *Discounts:* Quantity Seasonal Cash Trade or functional Less: *Allowances:* Damaged goods Advertising Push money	equals	*Product:* Branded—well known Guaranteed Warranted Service—repair facilities Convenient packaging for handling *Place:* Availability—when and where *Price:* Price-level guarantee Sufficient margin to allow chance for profit *Promotion:* Promotion aimed at customers

tees, and so on. Or it could be a "pure" service—dry cleaning, a lawyer's advice, or insurance on your car.

The charge for this something depends on what is included. Some customers pay list price. Others get discounts or allowances because something is *not* included. The possible variations are shown in Exhibit 16–2—for consumers or users—and in Exhibit 16–3—for channel members. We'll discuss some of these variations more fully below—but you can see that Price has many dimensions.

PRICING OBJECTIVES SHOULD GUIDE PRICING

Pricing objectives should flow from company-level objectives. Pricing objectives should be *clearly stated*—because they have a direct effect on pricing policies and on the methods used to set prices.

Possible pricing objectives are shown in Exhibit 16–4.

PROFIT—ORIENTED OBJECTIVES

Target returns provide specific guidelines

A **target return objective** sets a specific level of profit as an objective. Often this amount is stated as a percentage of sales—or of capital investment. A large producer like Motorola might aim for a 15 percent return on investment—while the target for Safeway and other grocery chains might be a 1 percent return on sales.

A target return objective has advantages for a large company. Performance can be compared against the target. Some companies cut out divisions—or drop products—that don't earn the target rate of return. General Electric sold its small appliance division to Black & Decker because GE felt it could earn higher returns in other product-markets.

Exhibit 16–4 Possible Pricing Objectives

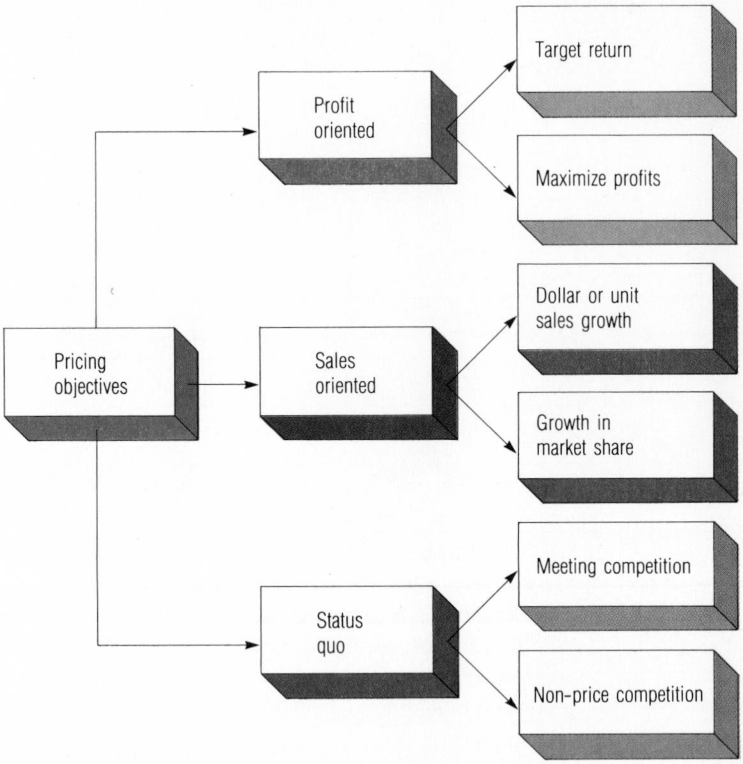

Some just want satisfactory profits

Some managers aim for only "satisfactory" returns. They just want to make enough to stay in business—and convince stockholders that they're "doing a good job." Similarly, some small family-run businesses aim for a profit that provides a "comfortable life style."[2]

Companies that are leaders in their industries—like Alcoa, Du Pont, and General Motors—sometimes pursue only "satisfactory" long-run targets. They know the public—and the government—expect them to follow policies that are "in the public interest" when they play the role of price leader or wage setter. Too large a return might invite government action.[3]

But this kind of situation can lead to decisions that are not in the public interest. For example, before imported cars became popular, many GM managers were afraid of making "too much" profit—so they didn't keep costs and prices low. They thought that lower prices might earn an even larger market share—and antitrust action by the government. Then, when low-cost foreign producers entered the U.S. market, GM was not able to quickly reduce costs—or prices.

Profit maximization can be socially responsible

A **profit maximization objective** seeks to get as much profit as possible. It might be stated as a desire to earn a rapid return on investment. Or—more bluntly—to charge "all the traffic will bear."

Some people believe that anyone seeking a profit maximization objective will charge high prices. Economic theory doesn't support this idea. Profit maximization doesn't always lead to high prices. Demand and supply may bring extremely high prices—if competition can't offer good substitutes. But this happens *if and only if* demand is highly inelastic. But if demand is very elastic, profit maximizers may charge relatively low prices—to increase sales. When prices for electronic calculators were very high, few people bought them. When Texas Instruments and its competitors dropped prices, nearly everyone bought calculators. Contrary to popular belief, a profit maximization objective *can* be socially desirable.

SALES—ORIENTED OBJECTIVES

A **sales-oriented objective** seeks some level of unit sales, dollar sales, or share of market—without referring to profit.

Sales growth doesn't mean big profits

Some managers are more concerned with sales growth than profits. They think sales growth always leads to big profits. This kind of thinking causes problems when a firm's costs grow faster than sales—or when managers don't keep track of costs. Recently, some major corporations have faced declining profits even though their sales were growing. International Harvester kept cutting prices on its tractors—trying to reach its target sales levels in a weak economy—until it had to sell the business. Marketing managers now pay more attention to profits—not just sales.[4]

Market share objectives are popular

Many firms seek a specific share (percent) of a market. One advantage of a market share objective is that it forces a manager to pay attention to what competitors are doing in the market. Also, it's easier to measure a firm's market share than to determine if profits are being maximized. Large consumer products firms—such as Procter & Gamble, Coca-Cola, and General Foods—often use market share objectives.

Aggressive companies often aim to increase market share—or even to control a market. In some businesses, economies of scale encourage a firm to seek increased market share—and probably greater profits.

Sometimes, however, firms blindly follow market growth objectives—setting low prices to get more of the market. This can lead to profitless "success."

Remember: larger sales volume, by itself, doesn't necessarily lead to higher profits.

STATUS QUO PRICING OBJECTIVES

Don't-rock-the-boat objectives

Managers who are satisfied with their current pricing situation and want to reduce risk sometimes adopt **status quo objectives**—"don't-rock-the-*pricing-*

boat'' objectives. They may be stated as ''stabilizing prices,'' ''meeting competition,'' or ''avoiding competition.'' Maintaining stable prices may discourage price competition—and avoid the need for hard decisions.

Or stress non-price competition instead

On the other hand, a status quo pricing objective can be part of an aggressive marketing strategy focusing on **non-price competition**—aggressive action on one or more of the Ps other than Price.[5] Fast-food chains like McDonald's and Hardee's prefer non-price competition.

MOST FIRMS SET SPECIFIC PRICING POLICIES— TO REACH OBJECTIVES

Specific pricing policies are important for any firm. Otherwise, the marketing manager has to rethink his marketing strategy every time a customer asks for a price.

Administered prices help achieve objectives

Price policies usually lead to **administered prices**—consciously set prices. In other words, instead of letting daily market forces decide prices, most firms set their own prices.

Some firms do their pricing without much thought—just ''meeting competition.'' They act as if they have no choice. Managers *do* have many choices. They *should* administer their prices. And they should do it carefully. If customers won't pay the price—the whole marketing mix fails. In the rest of this chapter, we'll talk about price policies a marketing manager must set to do an effective job of administering Price.[6]

PRICE FLEXIBILITY POLICIES

One of the first decisions a marketing manager has to make is about price flexibility. Should he have a one-price—or a flexible-price—policy?

One-price policy— the same price for everyone

A **one-price policy** means offering the same price to all customers who purchase products under the same conditions—and in the same quantities. Most U.S. firms use a one-price policy—for convenience and to maintain goodwill among customers.

A one-price policy makes pricing easier. But a marketing manager must carefully avoid a rigid one-price policy. This can amount to broadcasting a price that competitors can undercut—especially if the price is high. One reason for the growth of discount houses is that conventional retailers used traditional margins—and stuck to them.

Flexible-price policy—different prices for different customers

A **flexible-price policy** means offering the same product and quantities to different customers at different prices.

Flexible pricing is most common in the channels, in direct sales of industrial products, and at retail for more expensive items and homogeneous shopping products. The advantage of flexible pricing is that the sales rep can adjust to market conditions—instead of turning down an order.[7] Most auto dealers use flexible pricing. The producer suggests a list price, but the dealers bargain for what they can get. Their salespeople negotiate prices every day.

Flexible pricing has disadvantages, however. Customers are unhappy if they find that others are getting lower prices. And if customers know that prices are flexible, the cost of selling may rise—as buyers become aware that bargaining can save them money. Also, some sales reps let price cutting become a habit. This can make price useless as a competitive tool—and leads to a lower price level.

PRICE LEVEL POLICIES—OVER THE PRODUCT LIFE CYCLE

When marketing managers administer prices—as most do—they must decide on a price level policy. They must decide if their prices should be above or below or at the same level as the "market price."

Marketing managers should consider the product life cycle when setting the original price level for a new product. Price affects how fast the product moves through the cycle. A high price, for example, may lead to attractive profits—but also to competition and a faster cycle. With this in mind, should the original price be set "high" or "low"?

Skimming pricing— feeling out demand at a high price

A **skimming price policy** tries to sell the top ("skim the cream") of a market—the top of the demand curve—at a high price before aiming at more price-sensitive customers.

When Polaroid first introduced its "instant picture" camera, it set a high price. This high-priced camera sold only in camera stores—mainly to professional photographers and serious amateurs. Soon Polaroid introduced other models with fewer features. These sold at lower prices—to different market

Polaroid initially used a skimming price policy when it introduced "instant" cameras—but over the course of the product life cycle it lowered prices through a series of marketing strategies.

segments. Finally, before its patent ran out, Polaroid introduced a low-price camera—sold through department, drug, and discount stores.

Skimming is useful for getting a better picture of the shape of the demand curve. It's easier to start with a high price and lower it—than to start with a low price and then try to raise it.[8]

Penetration pricing—get volume at a low price

A **penetration pricing policy** tries to sell the whole market at one low price. This approach might be used where there is no "elite" market—where the whole demand curve is fairly elastic.

A penetration policy is more attractive when selling larger quantities results in lower costs—because of economies of scale. And it may be a good idea if the firm expects strong competition very soon after introduction. A low penetration price is a "stay out" price. It discourages competitors from entering the market.

When personal computers became popular, Borland International came out with a complete programming language—including a textbook—for under $50. This was much lower than others' prices. And the low price helped Borland penetrate the market early. IBM, Microsoft, and other big firms have not been able—or willing—to compete directly with Borland.

Introductory price dealing—temporary price cuts

Price cuts do attract customers. So marketers often use **introductory price dealing**—temporary price cuts—to speed new products into a market. These temporary price cuts should not be confused with low penetration prices, however. Prices are raised as soon as the introductory offer ends.

Established competitors often choose not to meet introductory price dealing—as long as the introductory period is not too long or too successful.

"Meeting competition" may be wise sometimes

Regardless of their original pricing policy, most firms face competition sooner or later in the product life cycle. When that happens, how high or low a price seems is relative to the prices charged by competitors.

The nature of competition usually affects whether prices are set below, at, or above competition. The clearest case is in pure competition. The decision is really made by the market. To set a price above or below the market price is foolish.

There also is little choice in oligopoly situations. Pricing "at the market"—that is, meeting competition—may be the only sensible policy. To raise prices might lead to a big loss in sales. And cutting prices would probably cause competitors to cut prices, too. This can only lead to a drop in total revenue for the industry—and probably for each firm. Therefore, a meeting-competition policy makes sense for each firm. And price stability often develops—without any price fixing in the industry.[9]

But above or below what market?

Some firms emphasize "below-the-market" prices in their marketing mixes. Prices offered by discounters and mass-merchandisers—such as K mart—are below the prices charged by conventional retailers. At the other extreme, some firms price "above-the-market"—they may even brag about it. Tiffany's is well known as one of the most expensive jewelry stores in the world. Curtis Mathes advertises that it makes "the most expensive TV you can buy."

The question is: Do these various strategies contain prices that are "above" or "below" the market—or are they really different prices for different market segments? Perhaps some target customers do see important differences in the physical product or the whole marketing mix. Then what we're talking about is different marketing strategies—not just different price levels.

K mart may have lower TV prices than conventional television retailers, but it offers less help in the store and depends on outside repair services. K mart may be appealing to budget-oriented shoppers who are comparing prices among different mass-merchandisers. A specialty TV store—appealing to different customers—may not be a direct competitor! So it may be better to think of K mart's price as part of a different marketing mix for a different target market—not as a "below-the-market" price.

MOST PRICE STRUCTURES ARE BUILT AROUND LIST PRICES

Prices start with a list price

Basic list prices are the prices that final customers or users are normally asked to pay for products. Unless noted otherwise, "list price" refers to "basic list price" in this book.

How these list prices are set is discussed in the next chapter. Now, however, we will consider when—and why—adjustments are made to list price.

DISCOUNT POLICIES—REDUCTIONS FROM LIST PRICES

Discounts are reductions from list price given by a seller to a buyer who either gives up some marketing function or provides the function himself. Discounts can be useful in marketing strategy planning. In the following discussion, think about what functions the buyers are giving up—or providing—when they get each of these discounts.

Quantity discounts encourage volume buying

Quantity discounts are discounts offered to encourage customers to buy in larger amounts. This lets a seller get more of a buyer's business, shifts some of the storing function to the buyer, reduces shipping and selling costs—or all of these. These discounts are of two kinds: cumulative and non-cumulative.

Cumulative quantity discounts apply to purchases over a given period—such as a year—and the discount usually increases as the amount purchased increases. Cumulative discounts are intended to encourage buying from one company—by reducing the price for additional purchases. A Lowes lumber yard might give a cumulative quantity discount to a building contractor who can't afford to buy all of the needed materials at once—because Lowes wants to keep the contractor's business and discourage shopping around.

Non-cumulative quantity discounts apply only to individual orders. Such discounts encourage larger orders but don't tie a buyer to the seller after that one purchase. Our Lowes lumber yard may purchase and resell insulation products made by several competing producers. Owens-Corning might try to encourage Lowes to stock larger quantities of its insulation by offering a non-cumulative quantity discount.

Quantity discounts may be based on the dollar value of the entire order, or on the number of units purchased, or on the size of the package purchased. While quantity discounts are usually given as price cuts, sometimes they are given as "free" or "bonus" products.

Quantity discounts can be a very useful marketing strategy variable for the marketing manager. Some customers are eager to get them. But marketing managers must use quantity discounts carefully—offering them to all customers on equal terms—to avoid price discrimination.

Seasonal discounts— buy sooner and store

Seasonal discounts are discounts offered to encourage buyers to stock earlier than present demand requires. If used by producers, this discount tends to shift the storing function further along in the channel. It also tends to even out sales over the year—permitting year-round operation. If seasonal discounts are large, channel members may pass them along to their customers. For example, the producer of Merry Tiller garden tillers offers its wholesalers a seasonal discount in the fall—when sales are slow. The wholesalers can then offer a discount to retailers—who may then sell the tillers during a special "fall sale."

Payment terms and cash discounts set payment dates

Most sales to channel members and other intermediate customers are made on credit. The seller sends a bill (invoice)—and the buyer sends it through for payment. Some firms depend on their suppliers for temporary working capital (credit). Therefore, it's very important for both sides to clearly

Hertz uses a discounted price during the summer season and on weekends when demand from business travelers is low.

state the terms of payment—including the availability of cash discounts. The following terms of payment are commonly used.

Net means that payment for the face value of the invoice is due immediately. "Net 10" or "net 30" means payment is within 10 or 30 days of the date on the invoice.

Cash discounts are reductions in the price to encourage buyers to pay their bills quickly. The terms for a cash discount usually modify the "net" terms.

2/10, net 30 means that a 2 percent discount off the face value of the invoice is allowed if the invoice is paid within 10 days. Otherwise, the full face is due within 30 days. Usually an interest charge is made after the 30-day free credit period.

Why cash discounts are given and should be taken

Smart buyers take advantage of cash discounts. A discount of 2/10, net 30 may not look like very much at first. But the 2 percent discount is earned just for paying 20 days before the full amount is due anyway. And if it is *not* taken, the company—in effect—is borrowing at an annual interest rate of about 36 percent. The firm would be better off to borrow at a bank—if necessary—to pay such invoices by the earlier date.

While the marketing manager can often use the cash discount as a marketing strategy variable, this isn't always true. Purchasing agents who value cash discounts may insist that the marketing manager offer the same terms offered by competitors. In fact, some buyers automatically deduct the traditional cash discount from their invoices—regardless of the seller's invoice terms!

Trade discounts often are set by tradition

A **trade (functional) discount** is a list price reduction given to channel members for the job they are going to do.

A producer, for example, might allow retailers a 30 percent trade discount from the suggested retail list price—to cover the cost of the retailing function and their profit. Similarly, the producer might allow wholesalers a chain discount of 30 percent and 10 percent off the suggested price. The wholesalers then would be expected to pass the 30 percent discount on to retailers.

Trade discounts might seem to offer a producer's or wholesaler's marketing manager great flexibility in varying a marketing mix. In fact, they may limit him greatly. The customary trade discount can be so well established that he has to accept it when setting prices.

ALLOWANCE POLICIES—OFF LIST PRICES

Allowances—like discounts—are given to final consumers, customers, or channel members for doing "something" or accepting less of "something."

Bring in the old, ring up the new—with trade-ins

A **trade-in allowance** is a price reduction given for used products when similar new products are bought.

Trade-ins give the marketing manager an easy way to lower the price without reducing list price. Proper handling of trade-ins is important when selling durable products. Customers buying machinery or buildings, for example, buy long-term satisfaction—in terms of more producing capacity. If the list price less the trade-in allowance doesn't offer greater satisfaction—as the customer sees it—then no sales will be made.

Many firms replace machinery slowly—perhaps too slowly—because they value their old equipment above market value. This also applies to cars. Customers want higher trade-ins for their old cars than the current market value. This encourages the use of high, perhaps "phony" list prices so that high trade-in allowances can be given.

Advertising allowances—something for something

Advertising allowances are price reductions given to firms in the channel to encourage them to advertise or otherwise promote the supplier's products locally. General Electric gave an allowance (1.5 percent of sales) to its wholesalers of housewares and radios. They, in turn, were expected to provide something—in this case, local advertising.

PMs—push for cash

Push money (or prize money) allowances are given to retailers by producers or wholesalers to pass on to the retailers' sales clerks—for aggressively selling certain items. PM allowances are used for new items, slower-moving items, or higher-margin items. They are especially common in the furniture, clothing, and consumer electronics industries. A sales clerk, for example, might earn an additional $5 for each new model Technics turntable sold.

SOME CUSTOMERS GET EXTRA SOMETHINGS

Trading stamps—something for nothing?

Trading stamps are free stamps (such as "Green Stamps") given by some retailers with each purchase.

Retailers buy trading stamps from trading-stamp companies—or set up their own plans. In either case, customers trade the stamps for merchandise premiums or cash.

Trading stamps were widely used in the 1950s and 60s. The early users of stamps seemed to gain a competitive advantage. But this soon disappeared as competitors started offering stamps. Now their use has declined—especially in grocery retailing.

Clipping coupons brings other extras

Many producers and retailers offer discounts—or free items—through coupons distributed in packages, mailings, newspaper ads—or at the store. By presenting a coupon to a retailer, the consumer is given a discount off list price. This is especially common in the grocery business—but the use of price-off coupons is growing in other lines of business. Coupons are so popular that new firms have been set up to help repay retailers for redeeming them.

Cash rebates when you buy

Some producers offer **rebates**—refunds paid to customers after making a purchase. Rebates ensure that final consumers—not the middlemen—actually get the price reduction. Some rebates are large. Following Chrysler's example, some auto makers offer rebates of $500 to $1,500—to promote sales of less popular models. Rebates are offered on lower-priced items, too—from Duracell batteries to Paul Masson wines.

LIST PRICE MAY DEPEND ON GEOGRAPHIC PRICING POLICIES

Retail list prices often include free delivery—because the cost may be small. But producers and middlemen must take the matter of who pays for transporting seriously. Usually, purchase orders spell out these details—because transporting costs can be as much as half the delivered cost of products! Many possible variations are open to a creative marketing manager. Some special terms are discussed in the following paragraphs.

F.O.B. pricing is easy

A commonly used transporting term is **F.O.B.**—which means "free on board" some vehicle at some place. Typically it is used with the place named—often the location of the seller's factory or warehouse—as in "F.O.B. Detroit" or "F.O.B. mill." This means the seller pays the cost of loading the products onto some vehicle—usually a truck, railroad car, or ship. At the point of loading, title to the products passes to the buyer. Then the buyer pays the freight and takes responsibility for damage in transit—except as covered by the transporting company.

Variations are made easily—by changing the place part of the term. If the marketing manager wants to pay the freight for the convenience of customers—he can use: "F.O.B. delivered" or "F.O.B. buyer's factory." In this case, title does not pass until the products are delivered. If the seller wants title to pass immediately—but is willing to pay the freight (and then include it in the invoice)—"F.O.B. seller's factory—freight prepaid" can be used.

"F.O.B. shipping point" pricing simplifies the seller's pricing—but it may narrow the market. Since the delivered cost of products varies depending on the buyer's location, a customer located farther from the seller must pay more—and might buy from closer suppliers.

Zone pricing smooths delivered prices

Zone pricing means making an average freight charge to all buyers within specific geographic areas. The seller pays the actual freight charges and bills each customer for an average charge. A firm might divide the United States into seven zones, for example. All customers in the same zone pay the same amount for freight, even though shipping costs may vary.

Zone pricing reduces the wide variation in delivered prices that result from an F.O.B. shipping point pricing policy. It also simplifies charging for transporting.

Uniform delivered pricing—one price to all

Uniform delivered pricing means making an average freight charge to all buyers. It is a kind of zone pricing. The whole market is considered as one zone—and the price includes the average cost of delivery. It is most often used when (1) transporting costs are relatively low, and (2) the seller wants to sell in all geographic areas at one price—perhaps a nationally advertised price.

Freight-absorption pricing—competing on equal grounds in another territory

When all firms in an industry use F.O.B. shipping point pricing, a firm usually does well near its shipping point—but not farther away. As sales reps look for business farther away, delivered prices rise. The firm finds itself priced out of the market.

This problem can be reduced with **freight absorption pricing**—which means absorbing freight cost so that a firm's delivered price meets the nearest competitor's. This amounts to cutting list price to appeal to new market segments.

With freight absorption pricing, the only limit on the size of a firm's territory is the amount of freight cost it is willing to absorb. These absorbed costs cut net return on each sale—but the new business may raise total profit.

LEGALITY OF PRICING POLICIES

Generally speaking, companies can charge any price they wish for their products. Governments do put some restrictions on pricing, however.[10]

Unfair trade practice acts control some minimum prices

Unfair trade practice acts put a lower limit on prices, especially at the wholesale and retail levels. They have been passed in more than half the states. Selling below cost in these states is illegal. Wholesalers and retailers are usually required to take a certain minimum percentage markup over their merchandise-plus-transportation costs. The most common markup figures are 6 percent at retail and 2 percent at wholesale.

Most retailers know enough about their costs to set markups larger than these minimums. In practice, these laws protect certain limited-line food retailers—such as dairy stores—from the kind of "ruinous" competition that full-line stores might offer if they sold milk as a "leader"—offering it below cost—for a long time.

Even very high prices are OK—if you don't lie

A firm can charge high prices—even "outrageously high" prices—as long as they aren't fixed with competitors. Also, a firm can't lie about prices.

Phony list prices are prices that suggest to customers that the price they are to pay has been discounted from "list." Some customers seem more interested in the supposed discount than in the actual price. Most businesses, Better Business Bureaus, and government agencies consider the use of phony list prices unethical. And the FTC tries to stop such pricing—using the **Wheeler Lea Amendment**—which bans "unfair or deceptive acts in commerce."[11]

Price fixing is illegal—you can go to jail

Difficulties with pricing—and violations of price legislation—usually occur when competing marketing mixes are quite similar. When the success of an entire marketing strategy depends on price, pressure (and temptation) to make agreements with competitors (conspire) increases. And **price fixing**—competitors getting together to raise, lower, or stabilize prices—is common and relatively easy. *But it is also completely illegal.* It is "conspiracy" under the

Sherman Act and the Federal Trade Commission Act. To discourage price fixing, both companies and individual managers are held responsible. Some managers have already gone to jail! And governments are getting tougher on price fixing.[12]

Antimonopoly legislation bans price discrimination unless. . .

Price level and price flexibility policies can lead to price discrimination. The **Robinson-Patman Act** (of 1936) makes illegal any **price discrimination**— selling the same products to different buyers at different prices—if it injures competition. This law does permit some price differences—but they must be based on (1) cost differences or (2) the need to meet competition. Both buyers and sellers are guilty if they know they are entering into discriminatory agreements. This is a serious matter—and price discrimination suits are common.

What does "like grade and quality" mean?

The Robinson-Patman Act lets a marketing manager charge different prices for *similar* products if they are *not* of "like grade and quality." But how similar can they be? The FTC position is that if the physical characteristics of a product are similar, then they are of like grade and quality. A 1966 U.S. Supreme Court ruling against the Borden Company upheld the FTC position. The court held that a well-known label *alone* does not make a product different from the one with an unknown label. The issue was rather clear-cut in the Borden case. The company agreed that the physical characteristics of the canned milk it sold at different prices under different labels were basically the same.

The FTC's "victory" in the *Borden* case was not complete, however. Although the U.S. Supreme Court agreed with the FTC in the *Borden* case— with respect to like grade and quality—it sent the case back to the U.S. Court of Appeals to determine whether the price difference actually injured competition—which is also required by the law. In 1967, this court found no evidence of injury and further noted that there could be no injury unless Borden's price difference was more than the "recognized consumer appeal of the Borden label." How to measure "consumer appeal" was not spelled out—and may lead to more court cases.

In the end, it's what the consumer thinks about the product that may be the deciding factor. For now, however, it's safer for producers who want to sell several brands at lower prices than their main brand to offer physical differences—and differences that are really useful to the consumer.[13]

Can cost analysis justify price differences?

The Robinson-Patman Act allows price differences if there are cost differences—perhaps for larger quantity shipments.

Justifying cost differences is difficult. Costs usually must be charged to several products—perhaps using logical assumptions. It's easy—then—for the FTC to raise objections to whatever method is used. And the FTC often does raise objections because it is concerned about the impact of price differences on competition—especially on small competitors.[14]

Can you legally meet price cuts?

Meeting competition is permitted as a defense in price discrimination cases—although the FTC normally takes a dim view of this argument.

A major aim of antimonopoly legislation is to protect competition—not competitors—and "meeting competition" in "good faith" still seems to be legal.

Special promotion allowances might not be allowed

Some firms have violated the Robinson-Patman Act by providing PMs (push money), demonstrations, advertising allowances, or other promotion allowances to some customers and not others. The act bans such allowances—*unless they are made available to all customers on "proportionately equal" terms.* No proof of injury to competition is necessary. The FTC has been fairly successful in prosecuting such cases.

The need for such a rule is clear—once price regulation begins. Otherwise allowances for promotion could be granted to retailers or wholesalers without expecting that any promotion would be done. This plainly is price discrimination in disguise.

The law does cause hardships, however. It's hard to provide allowances on "proportionately equal" terms to both large and small customers. The Robinson-Patman Act does not say clearly whether a small store should be allowed the same dollar allowance as a large one or in proportion to sales. But the latter probably would not buy the same promotion impact.

It may also be difficult to decide which customers are competitors. The FTC might define competitors much more broadly than either the seller or the competing buyers. Supermarket operators might only be concerned about other supermarkets and the food discounters. But the FTC might feel small drug stores were also competitors for health and beauty aids.[15]

How to avoid discriminating

Because the price discrimination laws are complicated—and penalties heavy—many business managers play down price as a marketing variable. They think it's safer to offer the same cost-based prices to *all* customers—or just "meet competition."

CONCLUSION

Price offers an alert marketing manager many possibilities while planning marketing strategies. Which pricing policies should be used depends on the pricing objectives. We looked at profit-oriented, sales-oriented, and status quo-oriented objectives.

A marketing manager must set policies about price flexibility, price levels over the product life cycle, who will pay the transporting costs, and who will get discounts and allowances. The manager also should be aware of pricing legislation affecting these policies.

In most cases, a marketing manager must set

prices—that is, administer prices. Starting with a list price, a variety of discounts and allowances may be offered to adjust for the "something" being offered in the marketing mix.

Throughout this chapter, we assumed that a list price has already been set. We talked about what may be included (or excluded) in the "something"—and what objectives a firm might set to guide its pricing policies. Price setting itself was not discussed. It will be covered in the next chapter—showing ways of carrying out the various pricing objectives and policies.

Questions and Problems

1.   Identify the strategy decisions a marketing manager must make in the Price area. Illustrate your answer for a local retailer.

2.   How should the acceptance of a profit-oriented, a sales-oriented, or a status quo-oriented pricing objective affect the development

of a company's marketing strategy? Illustrate for each.

3. Distinguish between one-price and flexible-price policies. Which is most appropriate for a supermarket? Why?

4. Cite two examples of continuously selling above the market price. Describe the situations.

5. Explain the types of competitive situations that might lead to a "meeting competition" pricing policy.

6. What pricing objective(s) is a skimming pricing policy most likely implementing? Is the same true for a penetration pricing policy? Which policy is probably most appropriate for each of the following products: (*a*) a new type of home lawn-sprinkling system, (*b*) a new low-cost meat substitute, (*c*) a new type of children's toy, (*d*) a faster computer?

7. Discuss unfair trade practice acts. Who are they "unfair" to?

8. How would our marketing system change if manufacturers were required to set fixed prices on *all* products sold at retail and *all* retailers were required to use these prices? Would a manufacturer's marketing mix be easier to develop? What kind of an operation would retailing be in this situation? Would consumers receive more or less service?

9. Is price discrimination involved if a large oil company sells gasoline to taxicab associations for resale to individual taxicab operators for 2½ cents a gallon less than the price charged to retail service stations? What happens if the cab associations resell gasoline not only to taxicab operators, but to the general public as well?

10. What does the final consumer really obtain when paying the list price for the following "products": (*a*) a car, (*b*) a portable radio, (*c*) a package of frozen peas, and (*d*) a lipstick in a jeweled case?

11. Are seasonal discounts appropriate in agricultural businesses (which are certainly seasonal)?

12. What are the "effective" annual interest rates for the following cash discount terms: (*a*) 1/10, net 30; (*b*) 1/5, net 10; (*c*) net 30?

13. Why would a manufacturer offer a rebate instead of lowering the suggested list price?

14. How can a marketing manager change his F.O.B. terms to make his otherwise competitive marketing mix more attractive?

15. What type of geographic pricing policy is most appropriate for the following products (specify any assumptions necessary to obtain a definite answer): (*a*) a chemical by-product, (*b*) nationally advertised candy bars, (*c*) rebuilt auto parts, (*d*) tricycles?

16. How would a ban on freight absorption (that is, requiring F.O.B factory pricing) affect a producer with substantial economies of scale in production?

Suggested Computer-Aided Problem ───────────────

16. Cash Discounts

Suggested Cases ──────────────────────────

25. Tale Labs, Inc.

26. Eaton Mfg., Inc.

Marketing Arithmetic

When You Finish This Appendix, You Should

1. Understand the components of an operating statement (profit and loss statement).

2. Know how to compute the stockturn rate.

3. Understand how operating ratios can help analyze a business.

4. Understand how to calculate markups and markdowns.

5. Understand how to calculate return on investment (ROI) and return on assets (ROA).

6. Understand the basic sales forecasting approaches.

7. Recognize the important new terms (shown in red).

Marketing students must become familiar with the essentials of the "language of business." Business people commonly use accounting and other "business" terms when talking about costs, prices, and profit. And analyzing available data is common in solving marketing problems.

THE OPERATING STATEMENT

An **operating statement** is a simple summary of the financial results of a company's operations over a specified period of time. Some beginning students may feel that the operating statement is complex—but as we'll soon see, this really isn't true. *The main purpose of the operating statement is determining the net profit figure—and presenting data to support that figure.* This is why the operating statement is often referred to as the *profit and loss statement.*

An operating statement for a wholesale or retail business is presented in Exhibit B–1. A complete and detailed statement is shown so you will see the framework throughout the discussion—but the amount of detail on an operating statement is *not* standardized. Many companies use financial statements with much less detail than this one. They emphasize clarity and readability—rather than detail. To really understand an operating statement, however, you must know about its components.

Exhibit B–1   *An Operating Statement (profit and loss statement)*

XYZ COMPANY
Operating Statement
For the Year Ended December 31, 198X

Gross sales			$54,000
Less: Returns and allowances			4,000
Net sales			$50,000
Cost of sales:			
Beginning inventory at cost		$ 8,000	
Purchases at billed cost	$31,000		
Less: Purchase discounts	4,000		
Purchases at net cost	27,000		
Plus freight-in	2,000		
Net cost of delivered purchases		29,000	
Cost of products available for sale		37,000	
Less: Ending inventory at cost		7,000	
Cost of sales			30,000
Gross margin (gross profit)			20,000
Expenses:			
Selling expenses:			
Sales salaries	6,000		
Advertising expense	2,000		
Delivery expense	2,000		
Total selling expense		10,000	
Administrative expense			
Office salaries	3,000		
Office supplies	1,000		
Miscellaneous administrative expense	500		
Total administrative expense		4,500	
General expense:			
Rent expense	1,000		
Miscellaneous general expenses	500		
Total general expense		1,500	
Total expenses			16,000
Net profit from operation			$ 4,000

Only three basic components

The basic components of an operating statement are *sales*—which come from the sale of goods and services; *costs*—which come from the making and selling process; and the balance—called *profit* or *loss*—which is just the difference between sales and costs. So there are only three basic components in the statement: sales, costs, and profit (or loss). Other items on an operating statement are there only to provide supporting details.

Time period covered may vary

There is no one time period that an operating statement covers. Rather, statements are prepared to satisfy the needs of a particular business. This may be at the end of each day—or at the end of each week. Usually, however, an operating statement summarizes results for one month, three months, six months, or a full year. Since the time period does vary, this information is included in the heading of the statement as follows:

XYZ COMPANY
Operating Statement
For the (Period) Ended (Date)

Also, see Exhibit B–1.

Management uses of operating statements

Before going on to a more detailed discussion of the components of our operating statement, let's think about some of the uses for such a statement. Exhibit B–1 shows that a lot of information is presented in a clear and concise manner. With this information, a manager can easily find the relation of net sales to the cost of sales, the gross margin, expenses, and net profit. Opening and closing inventory figures are available—as is the amount spent during the period for the purchase of goods for resale. Total expenses are listed to make it easier to compare them with previous statements—and to help control these expenses.

All this information is important to a company's managers. Assume that a particular company prepares monthly operating statements. A series of these statements is a valuable tool for controlling the business. By comparing results from one month to the next, managers can uncover unfavorable trends in the sales, costs, or profit areas of the business—and take any needed action.

A skeleton statement gets down to essential details

Let's refer to Exhibit B–1 and begin to analyze this seemingly detailed statement—to get first-hand knowledge of the components of the operating statement.

As a first step, suppose we take all the items that have dollar amounts extended to the third, or right-hand, column. Using these items only, the operating statement looks like this:

Gross sales	$54,000
Less: Returns and allowances	4,000
Net sales	50,000
Less: Cost of sales	30,000
Gross margin	20,000
Less: Total expenses	16,000
Net profit (loss)	$ 4,000

Is this a complete operating statement? The answer is **yes.** This skeleton statement differs from Exhibit B–1 only in supporting detail. All the basic components are included. In fact, the only items we must list to have a complete operating statement are:

```
Net sales ................................ $50,000
    Less: Costs ..........................   46,000
Net profit (loss).........................  $ 4,000
```

These three items are the essentials of an operating statement. All other subdivisions or details are just useful additions.

Meaning of "sales"

Now let's define the meaning of the terms in the skeleton statement.

The first item is "sales." What do we mean by sales? The term **gross sales** is the total amount charged to all customers during some time period. It is certain, however, that there will be some customer dissatisfaction—or just plain errors in ordering and shipping products. This results in returns and allowances—which reduce gross sales.

A **return** occurs when a customer sends back purchased products. The company either refunds the purchase price or allows the customer dollar credit on other purchases.

An **allowance** occurs when a customer is not satisfied with a purchase for some reason. The company gives a price reduction on the original invoice (bill), but the customer keeps the goods and services.

These refunds and price reductions must be considered when the firm computes its net sales figure for the period. Really, we're only interested in the revenue the company manages to keep. This is **net sales**—the actual sales dollars the company receives. Therefore, all reductions, refunds, cancellations, and so forth—made because of returns and allowances—are deducted from the original total (gross sales) to get net sales. This is shown below:

```
Gross sales ............................. $54,000
    Less: Returns and allowances ........   4,000
Net sales ...............................  $50,000
```

Meaning of "cost of sales"

The next item in the operating statement—**cost of sales**—is the total value (at cost) of the sales during the period. We'll discuss this computation later. Meanwhile, note that after we obtain the cost of sales figure, we subtract it from the net sales figure to get the gross margin.

Meaning of "gross margin" and "expenses"

Gross margin (gross profit) is the money left to cover the expenses of selling the products and operating the business. Firms hope that a profit will be left after subtracting these expenses.

Selling expense is commonly the major expense below the gross margin. Note that in Exhibit B–1, **expenses** are all the remaining costs that are subtracted from the gross margin to get the net profit. The expenses in this case are the selling, administrative, and general expenses. (Note that the cost of purchases and cost of sales are not included in this total expense figure—they were subtracted from net sales earlier to get the gross margin. Note, also, that some accountants refer to "cost of sales" as "cost of goods sold.")

Net profit—at the bottom of the statement—is what the company earned from its operations during a particular period. It is the amount left after the cost of sales and the expenses are subtracted from net sales. *Net sales and net profit are not the same.* Many firms have large sales and no profits—they may even have losses!

DETAILED ANALYSIS OF SECTIONS OF THE OPERATING STATEMENT

Cost of sales for a wholesale or retail company

The cost of sales section includes details that are used to find the "cost of sales" ($30,000 in our example).

In Exhibit B–1, you can see that beginning and ending inventory, purchases, purchase discounts, and freight-in are all necessary in calculating costs of sales. If we pull the cost of sales section from the operating statement, it looks like this:

Cost of sales:			
Beginning inventory at cost			$ 8,000
Purchases at billed cost	$31,000		
Less: Purchase discounts	4,000		
Purchases at net cost	$27,000		
Plus: Freight-in	2,000		
Net cost of delivered purchases		29,000	
Cost of products available for sale		$37,000	
Less: Ending inventory at cost		7,000	
Cost of sales			$30,000

"Cost of sales" is the cost value of what is *sold*—not the cost of products on hand at any given time.

The inventory figures merely show the cost of products on hand at the beginning and end of the period the statement covers. These figures may be obtained by a physical count of the products on hand on these dates—or they may be estimated by "perpetual inventory" records that show the inventory balance at any given time. The methods used in determining the inventory should be as accurate as possible—because these figures affect the cost of sales during the period, and net profit.

The net cost of delivered purchases must include freight charges and purchase discounts received—since these items affect the money actually spent to buy products and bring them to the place of business. A **purchase discount** is a reduction of the original invoice amount for some business reason. For example, a cash discount may be given for prompt payment of the amount due. We subtract the total of such discounts from the original invoice cost of purchases to get the *net* cost of purchases. To this figure we add the freight charges for bringing the products to the place of business. This gives the net cost of *delivered* purchases. When we add the net cost of delivered purchases to the beginning inventory at cost, we have the total cost of products available for sale during the period. If we now subtract the ending inventory at cost from the cost of the products available for sale, we finally get the cost of sales.

One important point should be noted about cost of sales. The way the value of inventory is calculated varies from one company to another—and can cause big differences in the cost of sales and profit. (See any basic accounting textbook for how the various inventory valuation methods work.)

Cost of sales for a manufacturing company

Exhibit B–1 shows the way the manager of a wholesale or retail business arrives at his cost of sales. Such a business *purchases* finished products and resells them. In a manufacturing company, the "purchases" section of this operating statement is replaced by a section called "cost of production." This section includes purchases of raw materials and parts, direct and indirect labor costs, and factory overhead charges (such as heat, light, and power)—which are necessary to produce finished products. The cost of production is added to the beginning finished products inventory to arrive at the cost of products available for sale. Often, a separate cost of production statement is prepared—and only the total cost of production is shown in the operating statement. See Exhibit B–2 for an illustration of the cost of sales section of an operating statement for a manufacturing company.

Expenses

"Expenses" go below the gross margin. They usually include the costs of selling and the costs of administering the business. They do not include the cost of sales—either purchased or produced.

There is no "right" method for classifying the expense accounts or arranging them on the operating statement. They can just as easily be arranged alphabetically—or according to amount, with the largest placed at the top and so on down the line. In a business of any size, though, it is clearer to group the expenses in some way—and to use sub-totals by groups for analysis and control purposes. This was done in Exhibit B–1.

Summary on operating statements

The statement presented in Exhibit B–1 contains all the major components in an operating statement—together with a normal amount of supporting detail. Further detail can be added to the statement under any of the major headings without changing the nature of the statement. The amount of detail normally is determined by how the statement will be used. A stockholder may be given a sketchy operating statement—while the one prepared for internal company use may have a lot of detail.

COMPUTING THE STOCKTURN RATE

A detailed operating statement can provide the data needed to compute the **stockturn rate**—a measure of the number of times the average inventory is sold during a year. Note that the stockturn rate is related to the *turnover during a year*—not the length of time covered by a particular operating statement.

The stockturn rate is a very important measure because it shows how rap-

Exhibit B–2   Cost of Sales Section of an Operating Statement for a Manufacturing Firm

Cost of sales:

Finished products inventory (beginning)	$ 20,000	
Cost of production (Schedule 1)	100,000	
Total cost of finished products available for sale	120,000	
Less: Finished products inventory (ending)	30,000	
Cost of sales		$ 90,000

Schedule 1, Schedule of cost of production

Beginning work in process inventory			$ 15,000
Raw materials			
Beginning raw materials inventory		$ 10,000	
Net cost of delivered purchases		80,000	
Total cost of materials available for use		90,000	
Less: Ending raw materials inventory		15,000	
Cost of materials placed in production		75,000	
Direct labor		20,000	
Manufacturing expenses			
Indirect labor	$4,000		
Maintenance and repairs	3,000		
Factory supplies	1,000		
Heat, light, and power	2,000		
Total manufacturing expenses		10,000	
Total manufacturing costs			105,000
Total work in process during period			120,000
Less: Ending work in process inventory			20,000
Cost of production			$100,000

Note: The last item, cost of production, is used in the operating statement to determine the cost of sales, as in Exhibit B–1.

idly the firm's inventory is moving. Some businesses typically have slower turnover than others. But a drop in turnover in a particular business can be very alarming. It may mean that the firm's assortment of products is no longer as attractive as it was. Also, it may mean that the firm will need more working capital to handle the same volume of sales. Most businesses pay a lot of attention to the stockturn rate—trying to get faster turnover.

Three methods—all basically similar—can be used to compute the stockturn rate. Which method is used depends on the data available. These three methods are shown below—and usually give approximately the same results.*

$$\frac{\text{Cost of sales}}{\text{Average inventory at cost}} \tag{1}$$

$$\frac{\text{Net sales}}{\text{Average inventory at selling price}} \tag{2}$$

$$\frac{\text{Sales in units}}{\text{Average inventory in units}} \tag{3}$$

*Differences occur because of varied markups and non-homogeneous product assortments. In an assortment of tires, for example, those with high markups might have sold much better than those with small markups. But with Formula 3, all tires would be treated equally.

Computing the stockturn rate will be illustrated only for Formula 1—since all are similar. The only difference is that the cost figures used in Formula 1 are changed to a selling price or numerical count basis in Formulas 2 and 3. Note: Regardless of the method used, you must have both the numerator and denominator of the formula in the same terms.

If the inventory level varies a lot during the year, you may need detailed information about the inventory level at different times to compute the average inventory. If it stays at about the same level during the year, however, it's easy to get an estimate. For example, using Formula 1, the average inventory at cost is computed by adding the beginning and ending inventories at cost—and dividing by 2. This average inventory figure is then divided into the cost of sales (in cost terms) to get the stockturn rate.

For example, suppose that the cost of sales for one year was $100,000. Beginning inventory was $25,000 and ending inventory $15,000. Adding the two inventory figures and dividing by 2, we get an average inventory of $20,000. We next divide the cost of sales by the average inventory ($100,000 divided by $20,000) and get a stockturn rate of 5.

The stockturn rate is covered further in Chapter 17.

OPERATING RATIOS HELP ANALYZE THE BUSINESS

Many business people use the operating statement to calculate **operating ratios**—the ratio of items on the operating statement to net sales—and compare these ratios from one time period to another. They can also compare their own operating ratios with those of competitors. Such competitive data is often available through trade associations. Each firm may report its results to the trade association—which then distributes summary results to its members. These ratios help managers control their operations. If some expense ratios are rising, for example, those particular costs are singled out for special attention.

Operating ratios are computed by dividing net sales into the various operating statement items that appear below the net sales level in the operating statement. Net sales is used as the denominator in the operating ratio—because this figure shows the sales the firm actually won.

We can see the relation of operating ratios to the operating statement if we think of there being another column to the right of the dollar figures in an operating statement. This column contains percentage figures—using net sales as 100 percent. This can be seen below:

Gross sales	$540.00	
Less: Returns and allowances	40.00	
Net sales	500.00	100%
Cost of sales	350.00	70
Gross margin	150.00	30
Expenses	100.00	20
Net profit	$ 50.00	10%

The 30 percent ratio of gross margin to net sales in the above example shows that 30 percent of the net sales dollar is available to cover sales expenses and administering the business—and provide a profit. Note that the ratio of expenses to sales added to the ratio of profit to sales equals the 30 percent gross margin ratio. The net profit ratio of 10 percent shows that 10 percent of the net sales dollar is left for profit.

The value of percentage ratios should be obvious. The percentages are easily figured—and much easier to compare than large dollar figures.

Note that because these operating statement categories are interrelated, only a few pieces of information are needed to figure the others. In this case, for example, knowing the gross margin percent and net profit percent makes it possible to figure the expense and cost of sales percentages. Further, knowing just one dollar amount and the percentages lets you figure all the other dollar amounts.

MARKUPS

A **markup** is the dollar amount added to the cost of sales per unit to get the selling price. The markup usually is similar to the firm's gross margin per unit—because the markup amount added onto the unit cost of a product by a retailer or wholesaler is expected to cover the selling and administrative expenses—and to provide a profit.

The markup approach to pricing is discussed in Chapter 17, so it will not be discussed at length here. But a simple example illustrates the idea. If a retailer buys an article that cost $1 when delivered to his store, he must sell it for more than this cost if he hopes to make a profit. So he might add 50 cents onto the cost of the article to cover his selling and other costs and, hopefully, to provide a profit. The 50 cents is the markup.

The 50 cents is also the gross margin or gross profit from that item *if* it is sold. But note that it is *not* the net profit. The selling expenses may amount to 35 cents, 45 cents, or even 55 cents. In other words, there is no guarantee that the markup will cover costs. Further, there is no guarantee that customers will buy at the marked-up price. This may require markdowns, which are discussed later in this appendix.

Markup conversions

Often it is convenient to use markups as percentages—rather than focusing on the actual dollar amounts. But markups can be figured as a percent of cost or selling price. To have some agreement, *markup (percent)* will mean percentage of selling price—unless stated otherwise. So the 50-cent markup on the $1.50 selling price is a markup of $33\frac{1}{3}$ percent. On the other hand, the 50-cent markup is a 50 percent markup on cost.

Some retailers and wholesalers use markup conversion tables. This way they can easily convert from cost to selling price—depending on the markup on selling price they want. To see the interrelation, look at the two formulas below. They can be used to convert either type of markup to the other.

$$\text{Percent markup on selling price} = \frac{\text{Percent markup on cost}}{100\% + \text{Percent markup on cost}} \qquad (4)$$

$$\text{Percent markup on cost} = \frac{\text{Percent markup on selling price}}{100\% - \text{Percent markup on selling price}} \qquad (5)$$

In the previous example, we had a cost of $1, a markup of 50 cents, and a selling price of $1.50. We saw that the markup on selling price was 33⅓ percent—and on cost, it was 50 percent. Let's substitute these percentage figures—in Formulas 4 and 5—to see how to convert from one basis to the other. Assume first of all that we only know the markup on selling price—and want to convert to markup on cost. Using Formula 5, we get:

$$\text{Percent markup on cost} = \frac{33\tfrac{1}{3}\%}{100\% - 33\tfrac{1}{3}\%} = \frac{33\tfrac{1}{3}\%}{66\tfrac{2}{3}\%} = 50\%$$

On the other hand, if we know only the percent markup on cost, we can convert to markup on selling price as follows:

$$\text{Percent markup on selling price} = \frac{50\%}{100\% + 50\%} = \frac{50\%}{150\%} = 33\tfrac{1}{3}\%$$

These results can be proved and summarized as follows:

$$\begin{array}{l} \text{Markup \$0.50} = 50\% \text{ of cost, or } 33\tfrac{1}{3}\% \text{ of selling price} \\ \underline{+ \text{ Cost \$1.00} = 100\% \text{ of cost, or } 66\tfrac{2}{3}\% \text{ of selling price}} \\ \text{Selling price \$1.50} = 150\% \text{ of cost, or } 100\% \text{ of selling price} \end{array}$$

It is important to see that only the percentage figures change—while the money amounts of cost, markup, and selling price stay the same. Note, too, that when selling price is the base for the calculation (100 percent), then the cost percentage plus the markup percentage equal 100 percent. But when the cost of the product is used as the base figure (100 percent), the selling price percentage must be greater than 100 percent—by the markup on cost.

MARKDOWN RATIOS HELP CONTROL RETAIL OPERATIONS

The ratios we discussed above were concerned with figures on the operating statement. Another important ratio, the **markdown ratio**—is a tool used by many retailers to measure the efficiency of various departments and their whole business. But note—it is *not directly related to the operating statement.* It requires special calculations.

A **markdown** is a retail price reduction that is required because customers won't buy some item at the originally marked-up price. This refusal to buy may be due to a variety of reasons—soiling, style changes, fading, damage caused by handling, or an original price that was too high. To get rid of these products, the retailer offers them at a lower price.

Markdowns are generally considered to be due to "business errors"—perhaps because of poor buying, too high original markups, and other reasons. Regardless of the cause, however, markdowns are reductions in the original price—and are important to managers who want to measure the effectiveness of their operations.

Markdowns are similar to allowances because price reductions are made. Thus, in computing a markdown ratio, markdowns and allowances are usually added together and then divided by net sales. The markdown ratio is computed as follows:

$$\text{Markdown \%} = \frac{\text{\$ Markdowns} + \text{\$ Allowances}}{\text{\$ Net sales}} \times 100$$

The 100 is multiplied by the fraction to get rid of decimal points.

Returns are *not* included when figuring the markdown ratio. Returns are treated as "consumer errors"—not business errors—and therefore are not included in this measure of business efficiency.

Retailers who use markdown ratios keep a record of the amount of markdowns and allowances in each department—and then divide the total by the net sales in each department. Over a period of time, these ratios give management one measure of the efficiency of buyers and salespeople in various departments.

It should be stressed again that the markdown ratio is not calculated directly from data on the operating statement—since the markdowns take place before the products are sold. In fact, some products may be marked down and still not sold. Even if the marked-down items are not sold, the markdowns—that is, the reevaluations of their value—are included in the calculations in the time period when they are taken.

The markdown ratio is calculated for a whole department (or profit center)—*not* individual items. What we are seeking is a measure of the effectiveness of a whole department—not how well the department did on individual items.

RETURN ON INVESTMENT (ROI) REFLECTS ASSET USE

Another "off the operating statement" ratio is **return on investment (ROI)**—the ratio of net profit (after taxes) to the investment used to make the net profit—multiplied by 100 to get rid of decimals. "Investment" is not shown on the operating statement. But it is on the **balance sheet** (statement of financial condition)—another accounting statement—that shows a company's assets, liabilities, and net worth. It may take some "digging" or special analysis, however, to find the right investment number.

"Investment" means the dollar resources the firm has "invested" in a project or business. For example, a new product may require $400,000 in new money—for inventory, accounts receivable, promotion, and so on—and its attractiveness may be judged by its likely ROI. If the net profit (after taxes) for this new product is expected to be $100,000 in the first year, then the ROI is 25 percent—that is, ($100,000 ÷ $400,000) × 100.

There are two ways to figure ROI. The *direct* way is:

$$\text{ROI (in \%)} = \frac{\text{Net profit (after taxes)}}{\text{Investment}} \times 100$$

The *indirect* way is:

$$\text{ROI (in \%)} = \frac{\text{Net profit (after taxes)}}{\text{Sales}} \times \frac{\text{Sales}}{\text{Investment}} \times 100$$

This way is concerned with net profit margin and turnover—that is:

$$\text{ROI (in \%)} = \text{Net profit margin} \times \text{Turnover} \times 100$$

This indirect way makes it clearer how to *increase* ROI. There are three ways:

1. Increase profit margin.
2. Increase sales.
3. Decrease investment.

Effective marketing strategy planning and implementation can increase profit margins and/or sales. And careful asset management can decrease investment.

ROI is a revealing measure of how well managers are doing. Most companies have alternative uses for their funds. If the returns in a business aren't at least as high as outside uses, then the money probably should be shifted to the more profitable uses.

Some firms borrow more than others to make "investments." In other words, they invest less of their own money to acquire assets—what we called "investments." If ROI calculations use only the firm's own "investment," this gives higher ROI figures to those who borrow a lot—which is called leveraging. To adjust for different borrowing proportions—to make comparisons among projects, departments, divisions, and companies easier—another ratio (ROA) has come into use. **Return on assets (ROA)** is the ratio of net profit (after taxes) to the assets used to make the net profit—times 100.

Both ROI and ROA measures are trying to get at the same thing—how effectively the company is using resources. These measures became increasingly popular as profit rates dropped and it became more obvious that increasing sales volume doesn't necessarily lead to higher profits—or ROI—or ROA. Inflation and higher costs for borrowed funds also force more concern for ROI and ROA. Marketers must include these measures in their thinking or top managers are likely to ignore their plans—and requests for financial resources.

FORECASTING TARGET MARKET POTENTIAL AND SALES

Estimates of target **market potential**—what a whole market segment might buy—and a **sales forecast**—an estimate of how much an industry or firm hopes to sell to a market segment—are necessary for effective strategy planning. Without such information, it's hard to know if a strategy is potentially profitable.

We must first try to judge market potential before we can estimate what share a particular firm may be able to win with its particular marketing mix.

TWO APPROACHES TO FORECASTING

Many methods are used to forecast market potential and sales—but they can all be grouped into two basic approaches: (1) extending past behavior and (2) predicting future behavior. The large number of methods may seem confusing at first, but this variety is an advantage. Forecasts are so important that management often prefers to develop forecasts in two or three different ways—and then compare the differences before preparing a final forecast.

Extending past behavior

Trend extension can miss important turning points

When we forecast for existing products, we usually have some past data to go on. The basic approach—called **trend extension**—extends past experience into the future. See Exhibit B–3.

Ideally, when extending past sales behavior, we should decide why sales vary. This is the difficult and time-consuming part of sales forecasting. Usually we can gather a lot of data about the product or market—or about the economic environment. But unless we know the *reason* for past sales variations, it's hard to predict in what direction—and by how much—sales will move. Graphing the data and statistical techniques—including correlation and regression analysis—can be useful here. (These techniques, which are beyond our scope, are discussed in beginning statistics courses.)

Once we know why sales vary, we can usually develop a specific forecast. Sales may be moving directly up as population grows, for example. So we can just get an estimate of how population is expected to grow—and project the impact on sales.

The weakness of the trend extension method is that it assumes past conditions will continue unchanged into the future. In fact, the future isn't always like the past. And, unfortunately, trend extension estimates will be wrong whenever big changes occur. For this reason—although they may extend past behavior for one estimate—most managers look for another way to help them forecast sharp economic changes.

Exhibit B–3   Straight-Line Trend Projection—Extends Past Sales into the Future

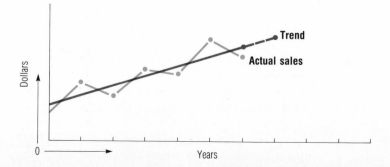

Predicting future behavior takes judgment

When we try to predict what will happen in the future—instead of just extending the past—we have to use other methods and add a bit more judgment. Some of these methods (to be discussed later) include juries of executive opinion, salespeople's estimates, surveys, panels, and market tests.

THREE LEVELS OF FORECAST ARE USEFUL

We are interested in forecasting the potential in specific market segments. To do this, it helps to make three levels of forecasts.

Some economic conditions affect the entire economy. Others may influence only one industry. And some may affect only one company or one product's sales potential. For this reason, a common approach to forecasting is to:

1. Develop a *national income forecast* and use this to:
2. Develop an *industry sales forecast,* which then is used to:
3. Develop *specific company* and *product forecasts.*

Generally, a marketing manager doesn't have to make forecasts for the national economy or his industry. This kind of forecasting—basically trend projecting—is a specialty in itself. Such forecasts are available in business and government publications. Managers can just use one source's forecast or combine several together. Unfortunately, however, the more targeted the marketing manager's segmenting efforts are, the less likely that industry forecasts will match the firm's product-markets. So a manager has to move directly to estimating potential for his own company—and specific products.

FORECASTING COMPANY AND PRODUCT SALES BY EXTENDING PAST BEHAVIOR

Past sales can be extended

At the very least, a marketing manager ought to know what the firm's present markets look like—and what it has sold to them in the past. A detailed sales analysis—for products and geographic areas—helps to project future results.

Just extending past sales into the future may not seem like much of a forecasting method. But it's better than just assuming that next year's total sales will be the same as this year's.

Factor method includes more than time

Simple extension of past sales gives one forecast. But it's usually desirable to tie future sales to something more than the passage of time. The factor method tries to do this.

The **factor method** tries to forecast sales by finding a relation between the company's sales and some other factor (or factors). The basic formula is: something (past sales, industry sales, etc.) *times* some factor *equals* sales forecast. A **factor** is a variable that shows the relation of some other variable to the item being forecast.

A bread producer example

The following example—about a bread producer—shows how firms can make forecasts for many geographic market segments—using the factor method and available data. This general approach can be useful for any firm—producer, wholesaler, or retailer.

Analysis of past sales relationships showed that the bread manufacturer regularly sold one half of 1 percent (0.005) of the total retail food sales in its various target markets. This is a single factor. By using this single factor, a manager could estimate the producer's sales for the coming period by multiplying a forecast of expected retail food sales in each market by 0.005.

Sales & Marketing Management magazine makes retail food sales estimates each year. Exhibit B–4 shows the kind of geographically detailed data available.

Factor method can use several factors

The factor method is not limited to using just one factor. Several factors can be used together. For example, *Sales & Marketing Management* regularly gives a "buying power index" (BPI) as a measure of the potential in different geographic areas. See Exhibit B–4. This index considers (1) the population in a market, (2) the market's income, and (3) retail sales in that market. And this index can be used in the same way that 0.005 was applied in the bread example above.

PREDICTING FUTURE BEHAVIOR CALLS FOR MORE JUDGMENT AND SOME OPINIONS

These past-extending methods use quantitative data—projecting past experience into the future and assuming that the future will be like the past. But this is risky in competitive markets. Usually, it's desirable to add some judgment to get other forecasts—before making the final forecast.

Jury of executive opinion adds judgment

One of the oldest and simplest methods of forecasting—the **jury of executive opinion**—combines the opinions of experienced executives—perhaps from marketing, production, finance, purchasing, and top management. Each executive estimates market potential and sales for the *coming years.* Then they try to work out a consensus.

The main advantage of the jury approach is that it can be done quickly and easily. On the other hand, the results may not be very good. There may be too much extending of the past. Some of the executives may have little contact with outside market influences. But their estimates could point to major shifts in customer demand or competition.

Estimates from salespeople can help, too

Using salespeople's estimates to forecast is like the jury approach. But salespeople are more likely than home office managers to be familiar with customer reactions—and what competitors are doing. Their estimates are especially useful in some industrial markets—where the few customers may be well known to the salespeople. But this approach is useful in any type of market.

Exhibit B–4   Sample of Pages from Sales & Marketing Management's "Survey of Buying Power"

ILL. S&MM ESTIMATES — METRO AREA County City	POPULATION—12/31/85 Total Population (Thousands)	% Of U.S.	Median Age of Pop.	% of Population by Age Group 18-24 Years	25-34 Years	35-49 Years	50 & Over	House-holds (Thousands)	RETAIL SALES BY STORE GROUP 1985 Total Retail Sales ($000)	Food ($000)	Eating & Drinking Places ($000)	General Mdse. ($000)	Furniture/Furnish./Appliance ($000)	Auto-motive ($000)	Drug ($000)
CHAMPAIGN - URBANA - RANTOUL	168.8	.0701	26.4	26.0	19.7	15.3	17.7	61.5	997,214	170,392	110,840	143,096	44,329	191,828	38,264
Champaign	168.8	.0701	26.4	26.0	19.7	15.3	17.7	61.5	997,214	170,392	110,840	143,096	44,329	191,828	38,264
• Champaign	60.0	.0249	25.1	32.7	19.1	13.1	18.1	23.2	524,434	87,094	64,387	90,481	22,709	71,864	25,407
• Rantoul	19.9	.0083	23.5	29.0	19.5	13.6	10.4	5.9	95,706	7,721	8,606	7,658	3,231	41,985	1,089
• Urbana	33.7	.0140	25.0	35.1	20.9	11.6	17.5	11.9	157,056	33,759	23,354	20,326	4,702	16,281	8,542
SUBURBAN TOTAL	55.2	.0229	30.1	12.0	19.9	20.3	19.9	20.5	220,018	41,818	14,493	24,631	13,687	61,698	3,226
CHICAGO	6,127.1	2.5441	32.0	11.5	17.8	19.2	25.6	2,238.0	35,627,510	6,283,706	3,422,880	4,163,874	1,972,348	6,946,431	1,782,885
Cook	5,221.8	2.1682	32.3	11.6	17.5	18.7	26.5	1,916.3	29,317,980	5,356,747	2,963,725	3,411,498	1,706,864	5,493,163	1,536,350
Arlington Heights	68.5	.0284	33.9	9.4	15.8	24.7	23.6	23.6	540,742	93,395	43,014	25,544	34,780	191,417	23,570
Berwyn	45.1	.0187	42.9	9.5	14.4	16.6	42.7	19.3	216,766	26,385	26,365	18,548	12,730	49,782	18,976
• Chicago	2,996.7	1.2443	31.5	12.1	17.8	17.5	26.3	1,122.2	13,053,879	2,591,234	1,549,443	1,449,372	774,748	1,683,807	798,950
• Chicago Heights	35.2	.0146	29.7	12.3	16.0	16.8	24.8	11.7	303,125	38,465	21,901	15,507	5,440	151,063	7,554
Cicero	60.6	.0252	34.3	10.9	16.0	16.8	34.8	24.6	173,354	41,854	28,865	2,463	5,770	35,585	7,976
Des Plaines	56.7	.0235	35.0	10.5	16.2	21.5	28.5	20.5	409,485	56,492	55,610	15,699	7,095	139,556	19,033
• Evanston	71.2	.0296	32.6	16.5	20.3	17.4	27.6	27.8	503,494	76,659	39,190	22,965	34,791	182,561	17,017

ILL. S&MM ESTIMATES — METRO AREA County City	EFFECTIVE BUYING INCOME 1985 Total EBI ($000)	Median Hsld. EBI	% of Hslds. by EBI Group (A) $10,000-$19,999	(B) $20,000-$34,999	(C) $35,000-$49,999	(D) $50,000 & Over	Buying Power Index
CHAMPAIGN - URBANA - RANTOUL	1,908,985	21,541	25.9	26.9	15.3	11.1	.0695
Champaign	1,908,985	21,541	25.9	26.9	15.3	11.1	.0695
• Champaign	679,598	19,320	25.1	24.8	13.6	10.1	.0284
• Rantoul	196,323	19,840	36.5	26.9	15.5	7.0	.0072
• Urbana	351,110	18,886	27.1	23.9	13.0	6.0	.0125
SUBURBAN TOTAL	681,954	26,004	23.3	30.8	18.4	13.7	.0214
CHICAGO	81,641,854	28,217	18.8	25.7	19.2	19.3	2.7327
Cook	66,788,818	26,471	19.8	25.7	18.1	17.5	2.2566
CHICAGO (continued)							
Arlington Heights	1,163,858	41,862	11.6	21.2	25.8	36.1	.0381
Berwyn	623,892	25,096	22.7	27.8	17.9	14.4	.0196
• Chicago	33,100,411	21,115	22.4	25.2	14.7	12.4	1.1206
• Chicago Heights	371,592	25,174	20.2	27.2	19.3	13.3	.0161
Cicero	733,055	23,131	25.1	29.0	16.5	11.0	.0219
Des Plaines	855,424	35,308	15.4	26.6	25.9	24.5	.0288
• Evanston	1,170,408	29,201	20.1	27.2	17.1	23.5	.0376

Good retail clerks have a "feel" for their markets—their opinions shouldn't be ignored.

However, a manager should keep two points in mind when using such estimates. First, salespeople usually don't know about possible changes in the national economic climate—or even about changes in the company's marketing mix. Second, salespeople who change jobs often may have little to offer.

Surveys, panels, and market tests

Special surveys of final buyers, retailers, and/or wholesalers can show what's happening in different market segments. Some firms use panels of stores—or final consumers—to keep track of buying behavior and to decide when just extending past behavior isn't enough.

Surveys are sometimes combined with market tests—when the company wants to estimate customers' reactions to possible changes in its marketing mix. A market test might show that a product increased its share of the market by 10 percent when its price was dropped one cent below competition. But this extra business might be quickly lost if the price were increased one cent above competition. Such market experiments help the marketing manager make good estimates of future sales when one or more of the four Ps are changed.

ACCURACY OF FORECASTS

The accuracy of forecasts varies a lot. The more general the number being forecast, the more accurate the forecast is likely to be. This is because small errors in various parts of the estimate tend to offset each other—and make the whole estimate more accurate. Annual forecasts of national totals—such as GNP—may be accurate within 5 percent. When style and innovation are important in an industry, forecast errors of 10 to 20 percent for *established products* are common. The accuracy of specific *new-product* forecasts is even lower.[1]

Accuracy depends on the marketing mix

Forecasting can help a marketing manager estimate the size of possible market opportunities. But the accuracy of any sales forecast depends on whether the firm selects and implements a marketing mix that turns these opportunities into sales and profits.

Questions and Problems

1. Distinguish between the following pairs of items that appear on operating statements: (*a*) gross sales and net sales and (*b*) purchases at billed cost and purchases at net cost.

2. How does gross margin differ from gross profit? From net profit?

3. Explain the similarity between markups and gross margin. What connection do markdowns have with the operating statement?

4. Compute the net profit for a company with the following data:

Beginning inventory (cost)	$ 15,000
Purchases at billed cost	33,000
Sales returns and allowances	25,000
Rent	5,000
Salaries	40,000
Heat and light	18,000
Ending inventory (cost)	25,000
Freight cost (inbound)	8,000
Gross sales	130,000

5. Construct an operating statement from the following data:

Returns and allowances	$ 15,000
Expenses	20%
Closing inventory at cost	60,000
Markdowns	2%
Inward transportation	3,000
Purchases	100,000
Net profit (5%)	30,000

6. Data given:

Markdowns	$ 20,000
Gross sales	200,000
Returns	16,000
Allowances	24,000

Compute net sales and percent of markdowns.

7. (*a*) What percentage markups on cost are equivalent to the following percentage markups on selling price: 20, 37½, 50, and 66⅔? (*b*) What percentage markups on selling price are equivalent to the following percentage markups on cost: 33⅓, 20, 40, and 50?

8. What net sales volume is required to obtain a stockturn rate of 20 times a year on an average inventory at cost of $100,000, with a gross margin of 30 percent?

9. Explain how the general manager of a department store might use the markdown ratios computed for his various departments? Is this a fair measure? Of what?

10. Compare and contrast return on investment (ROI) and return on assets (ROA) measures. Which would be best for a retailer with no bank borrowing or other outside sources of funds; i.e., the retailer has put up all the money that the business needs?

11.   Explain the difference between a forecast of market potential and a sales forecast.

12.   Suggest a plausible explanation for sales fluctuations for (*a*) bicycles, (*b*) baby food, (*c*) motor boats, (*d*) baseball gloves, (*e*) wheat, (*f*) wood-working tools, and (*g*) latex for rubber-based paint.

13.   Explain the factor method. Illustrate your answer.

14.   Discuss the relative accuracy of the various forecasting methods. Explain why some are more accurate than others.

15.   Given the following annual sales data for a company that is not planning any spectacular marketing strategy changes, forecast sales for the coming year (7) and explain your method and reasoning.

(a)		(b)	
Year	Sales ($000)	Year	Sales ($000)
1	$200	1	$160
2	230	2	155
3	210	3	165
4	220	4	160
5	200	5	170
6	220	6	165

Chapter 17

Price Setting in the Real World

When You Finish This Chapter, You Should

1. Understand how most wholesalers and retailers set their prices—using markups.

2. Understand why turnover is so important in pricing.

3. Understand the advantages and disadvantages of average-cost pricing.

4. Know how to find the most profitable price and quantity for a marketing strategy.

5. Know the many ways that price setters use demand estimates in their pricing.

6. Recognize the important new terms (shown in red).

"How should I price this product?" is a common problem facing marketing managers.

In the last chapter, we talked about variations from list price. Now, let's see how the basic list price might be set in the first place.

How should a Computerland Store price a new item—for example, Hewlett Packard's Laser Jet printer for personal computers? The store could just use the list price suggested by the producer—or Computerland might arrive at a list price by adding the same dollar markup amount it adds to any item costing $2,200. The manager might even price the printer very close to cost—if the customer also buys a computer system that provides a good profit. Or the manager may price the printer based on estimates of demand at different price levels.[1]

There are many ways to set list prices. But—for simplicity—we'll talk about two basic approaches: *cost-oriented* and *demand-oriented* price setting. We'll look at cost-oriented approaches first since they are most common. As we'll see, however, cost-oriented pricing isn't foolproof. Ideally, the marketing manager considers potential demand—as well as his own costs—when setting prices. Let's begin by looking at how most retailers and wholesalers set cost-oriented prices.

PRICING BY WHOLESALERS AND RETAILERS

Markups guide pricing by middlemen

Most retailers and wholesalers set prices by using a **markup**—a dollar amount added to the cost of products to get the selling price. For example, suppose a Dart drug store buys a case of shampoo for $1 a bottle. To make a profit, the store obviously must sell each bottle for more than $1. If Dart adds 50 cents to cover operating costs—and provide a profit—we say that the store is marking up the item 50 cents.

Markups, however, usually are stated as percentages—rather than dollar amounts. And this is where the confusion begins. Is a markup of 50 cents on a cost of $1 a markup of 50 percent? Or should the markup be figured as a percentage of the selling price—$1.50—and therefore be 33⅓ percent? A clear definition is needed.

Markup percent is based on selling price—a convenient rule

Unless otherwise stated, **markup (percent)** means percentage of selling price that is added to the cost to get the selling price. So the 50-cent markup on the $1.50 selling price is a markup of 33⅓ percent. Markups are related to selling price for convenience.

There is nothing wrong, however, with the idea of markup on cost. The important thing is to state clearly which markup percent we're using—to avoid confusion.

Managers often need to change a markup on cost to one based on selling price—or vice versa.[2] The calculations to do this are simple. (See the section on markup conversion in Appendix B.)

Many use a "standard" markup percent

It's very common for a middleman to set prices on all of his products by applying the same markup percent. This makes pricing easier! When you think of the large number of items the average retailer and wholesaler carry—and the small sales volume of any one item—this approach makes sense. Spending the time to find the "best" price to charge on every item in stock (day-to-day or week-to-week) just wouldn't pay.

Markups are related to gross margins

How do managers decide on a standard markup in the first place? It's usually based on information about the firm's *gross margin.* Managers regularly see gross margins on their profit and loss statements. (See Appendix B on Marketing Arithmetic if you are not familiar with these ideas.) Our Computerland manager knows that unless the gross margin is large enough, there won't be any profit. For this reason, he might accept a markup percent on the printer that is close to his usual gross margin.

Smart producers pay attention to the gross margins and standard markups of middlemen in their channel. They usually allow trade (functional) discounts similar to the standard markups expected by these middlemen.

Markup chain may be used in channel pricing

The markup used by different firms in a channel often varies. A **markup chain**—the sequence of markups used by firms at different levels in a channel—sets the price structure in the whole channel. A markup is figured on the *selling price* at each level of the channel. For example, Black & Decker's selling price for an electric drill becomes the cost paid by the Ace Hardware wholesaler—the wholesaler's selling price becomes the hardware retailer's cost—and this cost plus a retail markup becomes the retail selling price. Each markup should cover the costs of running the business—and leave a profit.

Exhibit 17–1   *Example of a Markup Chain and Channel Pricing*

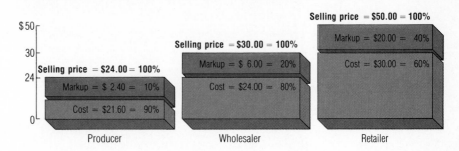

Exhibit 17–1 shows how a markup chain might work for an electric drill. The production (factory) cost of the drill is $21.60. In this case, the producer takes a 10 percent markup and sells the drill for $24. The markup is 10 percent of $24 or $2.40. The producer's selling price now becomes the wholesaler's cost—$24. If the wholesaler is used to taking a 20 percent markup on selling price, the markup is $6—and the wholesaler's selling price becomes $30. $30 now becomes the cost for a hardware retailer. And if the retailer is used to a 40 percent markup, $20 is added, and the retail selling price becomes $50.

High markups don't always mean big profits

Some people—including many retailers—think high markups mean high profits. But often this isn't true. A high markup may result in a price that's too high—and few customers will buy. And you can't earn much if you don't sell much—no matter how high your markup. But many retailers and wholesalers seem more concerned with the size of their markup than with their total profit.

Lower markups can speed turnover—and the stockturn rate

Some retailers and wholesalers, however, try to speed turnover to increase profits—even if this means reducing the markup. They know that the business runs up costs over time. If they can sell much more in the same time period, they may be able to take a lower markup—and still have a higher profit at the end of the period.

An important idea here is the **stockturn rate**—the number of times the average inventory is sold in a year. Various methods of figuring stockturn rates can be used. (See "Computing the Stockturn Rate" in Appendix B.) If the stockturn rate is low, profits may suffer.

At the very least, a low stockturn increases costs by tying up working capital. If a firm with a stockturn of 1 (once per year) sells products that cost it $100,000, that much money is tied up in inventory all the time. But a stockturn of 5 requires only $20,000 worth of inventory ($100,000 cost divided by 5 turnovers a year).

Whether a stockturn rate is high or low depends on the industry. An annual rate of 1 or 2 may be expected by a jewelry store, while an A&P store might expect 10 to 12 stockturns for soap and detergents and 40 to 50 stockturns for fresh fruits and vegetables.

Items with a high stockturn rate may have a lower markup.

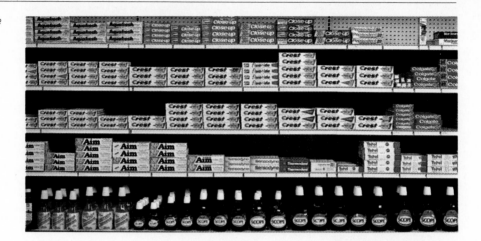

Supermarkets and mass-merchandisers run in fast company

Supermarkets and mass-merchandisers know the importance of fast turnover. They put low markups on fast-selling items—and higher markups on items that sell less frequently. For example, K mart may put a small markup (like 20 percent) on fast-selling health and beauty aids (toothpaste or shampoo) but higher margins on appliances and clothing. Supermarket operators put low markups on fast-selling items like milk, sugar, and detergents. (Sugar, for example, may have a markup of only 9 percent.) Since supermarket expenses are 18 to 22 percent of sales—it looks as if many of these items are carried at a loss. But this may not be true. A small profit per unit is earned more often. Fast-moving products are less expensive to sell. They take up valuable space for shorter periods, are damaged less, and tie up less working capital.

PRICING BY PRODUCERS

It's up to the producer to set the list price

Some markups eventually become customary in a trade. Most of the channel members tend to follow a similar process—adding a certain percentage to the previous price. Who sets price in the first place?

The basic list price usually is decided by the producer and/or brander of the product—a large retailer, a large wholesaler, or, most often, the producer. Now we'll look at the pricing approaches of such firms. For convenience, we will call them "producers."

AVERAGE–COST PRICING IS COMMON AND DANGEROUS

Average-cost pricing is adding a "reasonable" markup to the average cost of a product. The average cost per unit is usually found by studying past records. The total cost for the last year is divided by all the units produced and sold in that period—to get the "expected" average cost per unit for the next

Exhibit 17–2   Results of Average-Cost Pricing

Calculation of planned profit if 10,000 items are sold	**Calculation of actual profit if only 5,000 items are sold**
Calculation of costs:	Calculation of costs:
Fixed overhead expenses . . . . $ 5,000	Fixed overhead expenses $5,000
Labor and materials 5,000	Labor and materials 2,500
Total costs 10,000	Total costs $7,500
"Reasonable" profit 1,000	
Total costs and planned profit $11,000	

Calculation of "reasonable" price for both possibilities:

$$\frac{\text{Total costs and planned profit}}{\text{Planned number of items to be sold}} = \frac{\$11,000}{10,000} = \$1.10 = \text{"Reasonable" price}$$

Calculation of profit or (loss):	Calculation of profit or (loss):
Actual unit sales (10,000) times price	Actual unit sales (5,000) times price
($1.10) = ... $11,000	($1.10) = ... $5,500
Minus: Total costs 10,000	Minus: Total costs 7,500
Profit (loss) . . . . $ 1,000	Profit (loss) . . . . ($2,000)
Therefore: Planned ("reasonable") profit of $1,000 is earned if 10,000 items are sold at $1.10 each.	Therefore: Planned ("reasonable") profit of $1,000 is not earned. Instead, $2,000 loss results if 5,000 items are sold at $1.10 each.

year. If the total cost was $5,000 for labor and materials and $5,000 for fixed overhead costs—such as selling expenses, rent, and manager salaries—then "expected" total cost is $10,000. If the company produced 10,000 items in that time period, the "expected" average cost is $1 per unit. To get the price, the producer decides how much profit per unit seems "reasonable." This is added to the average cost per unit. If 10 cents is considered a reasonable profit for each unit, then the new price is set at $1.10. See Exhibit 17–2.

This approach is simple. But it can also be dangerous. It's easy to lose money with average-cost pricing. To see why, let's follow this example further.

First, remember that the price of $1.10 per unit was based on output of 10,000 units. But if only 5,000 units are produced and sold in the next year, the firm may be in trouble. Five thousand units sold at $1.10 each ($1.00 cost plus $.10 for "profit") yields a total revenue of only $5,500. The overhead is still fixed at $5,000. And the variable material and labor cost drops in half to $2,500—for a total cost of $7,500. This means a loss of $7,000—or 40 cents a unit. The method that was supposed to allow a profit of 10 cents a unit actually causes a loss of 40 cents a unit! See Exhibit 17–2.

It does not make allowances for cost variations as output changes

Exhibit 17–3   Typical Shape of Average Cost Curve

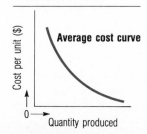

The problem arises because this method doesn't allow for cost variations at different levels of output. In a typical situation, economies of scale set in. But the average costs per unit are high when only a few units are produced. Average costs drop as the quantity produced increases. (See Exhibit 17–3 for the typical shape of the average cost curve.) This is why mass production and mass distribution often make sense. This behavior of costs must be considered when setting prices.

MARKETING MANAGER MUST CONSIDER VARIOUS KINDS OF COSTS

Average-cost pricing may fail because total cost includes a variety of costs. And each of these costs changes in a different way as output changes. Any pricing method that uses cost must consider these changes. To understand why, however, we need to define six types of costs.

There are three kinds of total cost

1. **Total fixed cost** is the sum of those costs that are fixed in total—no matter how much is produced. Among these fixed costs are rent, depreciation, managers' salaries, property taxes, and insurance. Such costs stay the same even if production stops temporarily.

2. **Total variable cost**, on the other hand, is the sum of those changing expenses closely related to output—expenses for parts, wages, packaging materials, outgoing freight, and sales commissions.

At zero output, total variable cost is zero. As output increases, so do variable costs. If Wrangler doubles its output of jeans in a year, the total cost of cloth also (roughly) doubles.

3. **Total cost** is the sum of total fixed and total variable costs. Changes in total cost depend on changes in total variable cost—since total fixed cost stays the same.

There are three kinds of average cost

The marketing manager usually is more interested in cost per unit ("average cost") than total cost—because prices are usually quoted per unit.

1. **Average cost** (per unit) is obtained by dividing total cost by the related quantity (that is, the total quantity that causes the total cost). See Exhibit 17–4.

2. **Average fixed cost** (per unit) is obtained by dividing total fixed cost by the related quantity. See Exhibit 17–4.

3. **Average variable cost** (per unit) is obtained by dividing total variable cost by the related quantity. See Exhibit 17–4.

An example shows cost relations

Exhibit 17–4 shows typical cost data for one firm. Here we assume that average variable cost is the same for each unit. Note how average fixed cost goes down steadily as the quantity increases. Note also how total variable cost increases when quantity increases, although the average variable cost stays the same. Average cost decreases continually, too. This is because average variable cost is the same—but average fixed cost is decreasing. Exhibit 17–5 shows the three "average" curves.

Exhibit 17–4   Cost Structure of a Firm

Quantity (Q)	Total fixed costs (TFC)	Average fixed costs (AFC)	Average variable costs (AVC)	Total variable costs (TVC)	Total cost (TC)	Average cost (AC)
0	$30,000	—	—	—	$ 30,000	—
10,000	30,000	$3.00	$0.80	$ 8,000	38,000	$3.80
20,000	30,000	1.50	0.80	16,000	46,000	2.30
30,000	30,000	1.00	0.80	24,000	54,000	1.80
40,000	30,000	0.75	0.80	32,000	62,000	1.55
50.000	30,000	0.60	0.80	40,000	70,000	1.40
60,000	30,000	0.50	0.80	48,000	78,000	1.30
70,000	30,000	0.43	0.80	56,000	86,000	1.23
80,000	30,000	0.38	0.80	64,000	94,000	1.18
90,000	30,000	0.33	0.80	72,000	102,000	1.13
100,000	30,000	0.30	0.80	80,000	110,000	1.10

$$\begin{bmatrix} 110,000 \ (TC) \\ -\ 80,000 \ (TVC) \\ \hline 30,000 \ (TFC) \end{bmatrix}$$ $$\dfrac{0.30 \ (AFC)}{(Q) \ 100,000)\overline{30,000} \ (TFC)}$$ $$\begin{bmatrix} 100,000 \ (Q) \\ \times 0.80 \ (AVC) \\ \hline 80,000 \ (TVC) \end{bmatrix}$$ $$\begin{bmatrix} 30,000 \ (TFC) \\ +80,000 \ (TVC) \\ \hline 110,000 \ (TC) \end{bmatrix}$$ $$\dfrac{1.10 \ (AC)}{(Q) \ 100,000)\overline{110,000} \ (TC)}$$

Ignoring demand is the major weakness of average-cost pricing

Average-cost pricing works well if the firm actually sells the quantity used in setting the average cost price. Losses may result, however, if actual sales are much lower than expected. On the other hand, profits may be very good if sales are much higher than expected. But this will only happen by luck—that is, because the quantity demanded is much larger than expected.

To use average-cost pricing, a marketing manager must make *some* estimate of the quantity to be sold in the coming period. But unless this quantity is related to price—that is, unless the firm's demand curve is considered—the marketing manager may set a price that doesn't even cover a firm's total cost! This can be seen in a simple example for a firm with the cost curves shown in

Exhibit 17–5   Typical Shape of Cost (per unit) Curves when AVC Is Assumed Constant per Unit

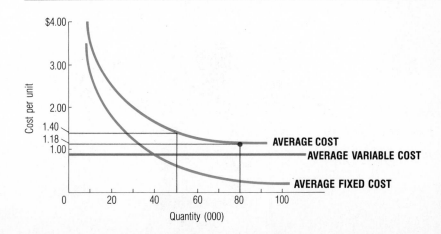

Exhibit 17–6 Evaluation of Various Prices along a Firm's Demand Curve

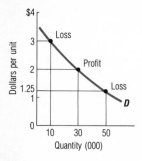

Exhibit 17–5. This firm's demand curve is shown in Exhibit 17–6. You can see that customers' demands (and their demand curve) are important—whether management takes time to analyze the demand curve or not.

In this example, whether management sets the price at a high $3—or a low $1.25—it will have a loss. At $3, only 10,000 units will be sold for a total revenue of $30,000. But total cost will be $38,000—a loss of $8,000. At the $1.25 price, 50,000 units will be sold—for a loss of $7,500. If management tries to estimate the demand curve—however roughly—the price probably will be set in the middle of the range—say at $2—earning a profit of $6,000. See Exhibit 17–6.

In short, average-cost pricing is simple in theory—but often fails in practice. In stable situations, prices set by this method may yield profits—but not necessarily maximum profits. And note that such cost-based prices might be higher than a price that would be more profitable for the firm—as shown in Exhibit 17–6. When demand conditions are changing, average-cost pricing is even more risky.

Exhibit 17–7 shows the relationships we've been discussing. Cost-oriented pricing suggests that the total number of units to be sold determines the *average* fixed cost per unit—and thus the average total cost. Then some amount of profit per unit is added to average total cost to get the cost-oriented selling price. But we're back where we started—when demand is considered— because the number of units sold will depend on the selling price—and the quantity sold (times price) determines total revenue (and total profit or loss). A decision made in one area affects each of the others—directly or indirectly.[3] A manager who forgets this can make bad pricing decisions.

Exhibit 17–7 Summary of Relationships among Quantity, Cost, and Price Using Cost-Oriented Pricing

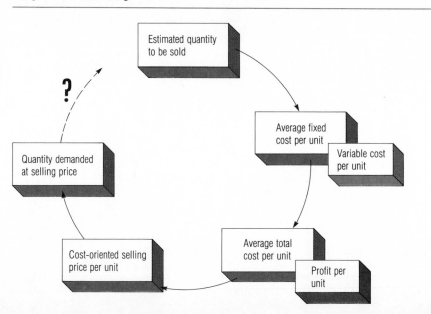

FINDING THE MOST PROFITABLE PRICE AND QUANTITY TO PRODUCE

A marketing manager must choose only *one* price (for a time period). His problem is which price to choose. This price, of course, sets the quantity that will be sold.

To maximize profit, the marketing manager should choose the price that will lead to the greatest difference between total revenue and total cost. Finding this best price and quantity requires an estimate of the firm's demand curve. This should be seen as an "iffy" curve—*if* price A is set, then quantity A will be sold—*if* price B is set, then quantity B will be sold—and so on. By multiplying all these possible prices by their related quantities, you can find the possible total revenues. Then, by estimating the firm's likely costs—at various quantities—it is possible to draw a total cost curve. The difference between these two curves shows possible total profits. You can see that the best price would be the one that has the greatest distance between the total revenue and total cost curves. These ideas are shown in Exhibit 17–8 and Exhibit 17–9, where the data is plotted on a graph. In this example, you can see that the best price is $79—and the best quantity is six units.[4]

A profit range is reassuring

Estimating demand curves isn't easy. But we need some estimate of demand to set prices. This is just one of the tough jobs a marketing manager faces. Ignoring demand curves doesn't make them go away! So some estimates must be made.

Note that demand estimates don't have to be exact. Exhibit 17–10 shows that there is a *range* of profitable prices. This strategy would be profitable all the way from a price of $53 to $117—$79 is just the "best" price.

The marketing manager should try to estimate the price that will "hit" the middle of the profit range. But a slight "miss" doesn't mean failure. At least trying to estimate demand will probably lead to being some place in the profitable

Exhibit 17–8   Revenue, Cost, and Profit for an Individual Firm

(1) Quantity Q	(2) Price P	(3) Total revenue TR	(4) Total cost TC	(5) Profit TR-TC
0	$150	$ 0	$200	$−200
1	140	140	296	−156
2	130	260	316	− 56
3	117	351	331	+ 20
4	105	420	344	+ 76
5	92	460	355	+105
6	79	474	368	+106
7	66	462	383	+ 79
8	53	424	423	+ 1
9	42	378	507	−129
10	31	310	710	−400

Exhibit 17–9   Graphic Determination of the Output Giving the Greatest Total Profit for a Firm

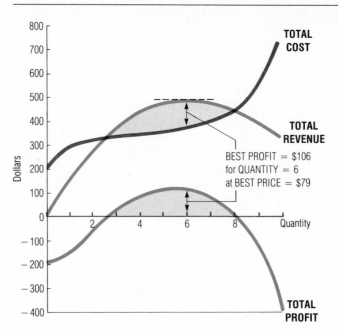

range. In contrast, mechanical use of average-cost pricing could lead to a price that is much too high—or much too low. This is why estimating demand isn't just desirable—it's necessary.

SOME PRICE SETTERS DO ESTIMATE DEMAND

Full use of demand curves isn't very common in business. But we do find marketers setting prices as though they believe demand curves exist. The following sections discuss examples of demand-oriented pricing.

Value-in-use pricing—how much will the customer save?

Industrial buyers are very aware of costs. Some marketers who aim at industrial markets keep this in mind in setting prices. They use **value-in-use pricing**—setting prices that will capture some of what customers will save by substituting the firm's product for the one being used. For example, a producer of computer-controlled machines used to assemble automobiles knows that his product doesn't just replace a standard machine. It will also reduce labor costs, quality control costs, and—after the car is sold—costs of warranty repairs. He can estimate what the auto producer will save by using the new machine—and then set a price that makes it cheaper for the auto producer to buy the computerized machine than to stick with his old methods.[5]

Exhibit 17–10   Range of Profitable Prices for Illustrative Data in Exhibits 17–8 and 17–9

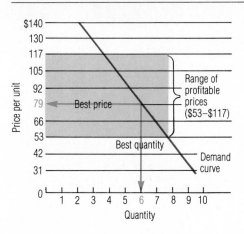

**Leader pricing—
make it low to attract
customers**

Leader pricing is setting some very low prices—real bargains—to get customers into retail stores. The aim isn't to sell large quantities of the leader items—but to get customers into the store to buy other products.[6] Certain products are picked for their promotion value and priced low—but above cost. In food stores, the leader prices are the "specials" that are advertised regularly—to give an image of low prices. Leader items usually are well-known, widely used items that customers don't stock heavily—milk, butter, eggs, or coffee. Customers quickly recognize price cuts on these items.

Leader pricing may appeal to customers who normally shop elsewhere. But it can backfire—if they buy only the low-price leaders. To avoid hurting profits, managers may select leader items that aren't directly competitive with major lines—as when a stereo equipment store offers bargain-priced recording tape.

**Bait pricing—offer a
"steal" but sell under
protest**

Bait pricing is setting some very low prices to attract customers—but trying to sell more expensive models or brands once the customer is in the store. For example, a furniture store may advertise a color TV for $199. But when bargain hunters come to buy it, sales clerks point out the disadvantages of the low-price TV—and try to convince them to "trade up" to a better (and more expensive) set. It's something like leader pricing. But here the seller *doesn't* plan to sell much at the low price. Some stores even make it very difficult to buy the "bait" item.

If bait pricing works—the demand for higher-quality products expands. But extremely aggressive—and sometimes dishonest—bait-pricing advertising has given this method a bad name. The Federal Trade Commission considers bait pricing a deceptive act—and has banned its use in interstate commerce. Even Sears, the nation's largest retail chain, has been criticized for "bait-and-switch" pricing. But some retailers who operate only within one state continue to advertise bait prices.

Value in use pricing considers what a customer will save by buying a product.

Psychological pricing—some prices just seem right

Psychological pricing is setting prices that have special appeal to target customers. Some marketers feel potential consumers see whole ranges of prices as the same. So price cuts in these ranges don't increase the quantity sold. But just below this range, customers may buy more. Then, at even lower prices, the quantity demanded stays the same again, and so on.

Exhibit 17–11 shows the kind of demand curve that leads to psychological pricing. Vertical drops mark the price ranges that customers see as the same. Pricing research shows that there are such demand curves.[7]

Odd-even pricing is setting prices that end in certain numbers. For example, products selling below $50 often end in the number 5 or the number 9—such as $.49 or $24.95.

Some marketers use odd-even pricing because they feel that consumers react better to these prices. They seem to assume that they have a rather jagged demand curve—that slightly higher prices will greatly reduce the quantity demanded. Long ago, some retailers used odd-even prices to force their clerks to make change. Then the clerks had to record the sale and couldn't pocket the money. Today, however, it isn't always clear why these prices are used—or whether they really work. Perhaps it's done just because "everyone else does it."[8]

Prestige pricing: make it high—but not cheap

Prestige pricing is setting a rather high price to suggest high quality or high status. Some target customers want the "best." If prices are dropped a little below this "high" level, they may see a bargain. But if the price seems "cheap," they worry about quality and don't buy.[9]

Prestige pricing is most common for luxury products—such as furs and jewelry. It's also common in service industries—where the customer can't see the product in advance and relies on price to judge the quality. Target customers who respond to prestige pricing give the marketing manager an unusual demand curve. Instead of a normal down-sloping curve, the curve goes down for a while and then bends back to the left again. See Exhibit 17–12.

Price lining—a few prices cover the field

Price lining is setting a few price levels for a product line and then marking all items at these prices. This approach assumes that customers have a certain price in mind that they expect to pay for a product. For example, most neckties are priced between $10 and $25. In price lining, there will only be a few prices within this range. Ties won't be priced at $10, $10.50, $11, and so on. They might be priced at four levels—$10, $12.50, $15, and $25.

The main advantage of price lining is simplicity—for both clerks and customers. It's less confusing than having many prices. Some customers may consider items at only one price level. Their big decision, then, is which item(s) to choose at that price.

Price lining has several advantages for retailers. Sales may increase because (1) they can offer a bigger variety in each price line, and (2) it's easier to get customers to make decisions within one price line. Stock planning is simpler—because demand is larger at the relatively few prices. Price lining also can reduce costs because inventory needs are lower.

Demand-backward pricing— market-minus pricing

Demand-backward pricing is setting an acceptable final consumer price and working backward to what a producer can charge. It's commonly used by producers of final consumer products—especially shopping products like women's and children's clothing. It's also used for toys or gifts for which customers will spend a specific amount—because they need a $5 or a $10 gift. Here, a reverse cost-plus pricing process is used. This method has been called "market-minus" pricing.

The producer starts with the typical retail price for an item and then works

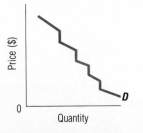

Exhibit 17–11   Demand Curve when Psychological Pricing Is Appropriate

Price ($)

Quantity

0

D

D

Exhibit 17–12   Demand Curve Showing a Prestige Pricing Situation

Price ($)

Quantity

0

D

D'

backward—subtracting the typical margins channel members expect. This gives the approximate price he can charge. Then he subtracts the planned marketing expenses from this price to find how much he can spend producing the item.

Successful demand-backward pricing needs some estimates of demand. The quantity demanded affects production costs—that is, where the firm will be on its average cost curve. Also, since competitors can be expected to make the best product possible, it's important to know customer needs—to set the best amount to spend on production costs. By increasing costs a little, the product may be so improved in consumers' eyes that the firm will sell many more units. But if consumers only want novelty, additional quality may not increase the quantity demanded—and shouldn't be offered.

PRICING A FULL LINE

Our emphasis has been—and will continue to be—on the problem of pricing a single product—mainly because this makes our discussion clearer. But most marketing managers are responsible for more than one product. In fact, their "product" may be the whole company line!

Full-line pricing— market- or firm- oriented?

Full-line pricing is setting prices for a whole line of products. How to do this depends on which of two basic situations a firm is facing.

In one case, all products in the company's line aim at the same general target market—which makes it important for all prices to be related. A producer of TV sets could offer several price and quality levels to give its target customers some choice. But the different prices should appear "reasonable" to the target customers.

In the other case, the different products in the line are aimed at entirely different target markets—and so the various prices need not be related. A chemical manufacturer of a wide variety of products for several target markets, for example, probably should price each product separately.

Cost is not much help in full-line pricing

The marketing manager must try to recover all costs on the whole line— perhaps by pricing quite low on competitive items and much higher on less competitive items. But costs aren't much help in full-line pricing. There is no one "right" way to assign a company's fixed costs to each of the products. And, if any method is carried through without considering demand, it may lead to very unrealistic prices. The marketing manager should judge demand for the whole line—as well as demand for each individual product in each target market—to avoid mistakes.

Complementary product pricing

Complementary product pricing is setting prices on several products as a group. One product may be priced very low—so the profits from another product will increase—and increase the group's total profit. A Gillette razor, for example, may be priced low to sell the blades—which must be replaced regularly.

Complementary product pricing differs from full-line pricing because quite different products and production facilities may be involved. So there's no cost allocation problem. Instead, the problem is really understanding the target market and the demand curves for each of the complementary products.

BID PRICING DEPENDS HEAVILY ON COSTS

A new price for every job

Bid pricing is offering a specific price for each possible job—rather than setting a price that applies for all customers. Building contractors, for example, must bid on possible projects. And many companies selling services (such as cleaning or data processing) must submit bids for jobs they would like to have.

The big problem in bid pricing is estimating all the costs that will apply to each job. This may sound easy, but thousands of cost components may have to go into a complicated bid. Further, management must include an overhead charge and a charge for profit.

Demand must be considered, too

Competition must be considered when adding in overhead and profit. Usually, the customer will get several bids and accept the lowest one. So mechanical rules for adding overhead and profit should be avoided. Some bidders use the same overhead and profit rates on all jobs—regardless of competition—and then are surprised when they don't get some jobs.

Bidding can be expensive. So a marketing manager may want to carefully select which jobs to bid on—and choose those where he feels he has the greatest chance of success. Thousands—or even millions—of dollars have been spent just developing bids for large industrial or government orders.[10]

Sometimes bids are bargained

Some buying situations (including much government buying) require the use of bids—and the purchasing agent must take the lowest bid. In other cases, however, bids may be called for, and then the company submitting the *most attractive* bid—not necessarily the lowest—will be singled out for further bargaining. This may include price adjustments—but it also may concern how additions to the job will be priced, what guarantees will be provided, and the quality of labor and supervisors. Some projects—such as construction projects—are hard to define exactly. So it's important that the buyer be satisfied about the whole marketing mix—not just the price. Obviously, effective personal selling can be important here.

CONCLUSION

In this chapter, we discussed various approaches to price setting. Generally, retailers and wholesalers use the traditional markups. Some use the same markups for all their items. Others have found that varying the markups may increase turnover and profit. In other words, demand is considered!

Cost-oriented pricing seems to make sense for middlemen—because they handle small quantities of many items. Producers must take price setting more seriously—because they set the "list price" to which others apply markups.

Producers commonly use average cost curves to help set their prices. But such an approach sometimes ignores demand completely. A more realistic approach to average-cost pricing requires a sales forecast. This may just mean assuming that sales in the next period will roughly match those in the last period. This will enable the marketing manager to set a price—but the price may or may not cover all costs and earn the desired profit.

We discussed how demand could be brought into pricing. And it appears that some marketers do consider demand in their pricing. We saw this with value-in-use pricing, leader pricing, bait pricing, odd-even pricing, psychological pricing, prestige pricing, price lining, demand-backward pricing, full-line pricing, complementary product pricing, and bid pricing.

We have stressed throughout the book that the customer should be considered before anything is done. This certainly applies to pricing. It means that when marketing managers set a price, they should consider what customers will be willing to pay. This isn't always easy, but it's nice to know that there is a profit range around the "best" price. Therefore, even "guesstimates" about what potential customers will buy at various prices will probably lead to a better price than mechanical use of traditional markups or cost-oriented pricing.[11]

Questions and Problems

1. Why do department stores seek a markup of about 40 percent when some discount houses operate on a 20 percent markup?

2. A producer distributed its lawnmowers through wholesalers and retailers. The retail selling price was $200, and the manufacturing cost

to the company was $100. The retail markup was 35 percent and the wholesale markup 20 percent. (a) What was the cost to the wholesaler? To the retailer? (b) What percentage markup did the producer take?

3. Relate the concept of stock turnover to the growth of mass-merchandising. Use a simple example in your answer.

4. If total fixed costs are $200,000 and total variable costs are $100,000 at the output of 20,500 units, what are the probable total fixed costs and total variable costs at an output of 10,000 units? What are the average fixed costs, average variable costs, and average costs at these two output levels? Determine what price should be charged. Make any assumptions necessary to obtain a definite answer.

5. Construct an example showing that mechanical use of a very large or very small markup might still lead to unprofitable operation while some intermediate price would be profitable.

6. Discuss the idea of drawing separate demand curves for different market segments. It seems logical because each target market should have its own marketing mix. But won't this lead to many demand curves and possible prices? And what will this mean with respect to functional discounts and varying prices in the marketplace? Will it be legal? Will it be practical?

7. How does a prestige pricing policy fit into a marketing mix? Would exclusive distribution be necessary?

8. Cite a local example of odd-even pricing and evaluate whether it makes sense.

9. Cite a local example of psychological pricing and evaluate whether it makes sense.

10. Distinguish between leader pricing and bait pricing. What do they have in common? How can their use affect a marketing mix?

11. Is a full-line pricing policy available only to producers? Cite local examples of full-line pricing. Why is full-line pricing important.?

Suggested Computer-Aided Problem

17. Price Setting

Suggested Cases

24. Meyer, Inc.

28. Plasto, Inc.

30. Dishcom, Inc.

Chapter 18

Marketing Strategy Planning for International Markets

When You Finish This Chapter, You Should

1. Understand the various ways that businesses can get into international marketing.

2. Understand what multinational corporations are.

3. Understand the kinds of opportunities in international markets.

4. Understand the market dimensions that may be useful in segmenting international markets and planning marketing strategies.

5. Recognize the important new terms (shown in red).

  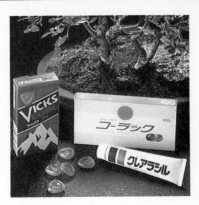

International marketing offers new frontiers.

Goodyear Tire Company must sometimes take products in trade to do business in developing countries. To reduce the currency flows from their economies, these governments often ban imports requiring cash payments. Instead, they encourage Goodyear to trade tires for minerals, textiles, agricultural products, or whatever else is produced locally. Goodyear must then find buyers for these products somewhere else. Companies as varied as Coca-Cola and General Electric are regularly involved in such "counter-trading." In fact, experts at General Electric claim that as much as one-third of the world's trillion dollars in trade involves such trading.[1]

Planning strategies for international markets can be even harder than for domestic markets—because of important cultural differences. Each foreign market must be treated as a separate market—with its own sub-markets. Lumping together all people outside the United States as "foreigners"—or assuming they are just like U.S. customers—almost guarantees failure.

There has been too much narrow thinking about international marketing: "We wouldn't want to risk putting a plant over there and then having it nationalized," or "Fighting all that 'red tape' would be too much trouble," or "It sold here—it'll sell there," or "Just put the ad into Spanish (or French, or German, or—) and run it in all their papers."

This chapter tries to get rid of some of these wrong ideas—and to suggest how strategy planning must change when a firm enters international markets. We'll see that a marketing manager must make several strategy decisions about international marketing: (1) whether the firm even wants to work in international markets at all and, if so, its degree of involvement, (2) in which mar-

Exhibit 18–1   Strategy Decisions about International Marketing

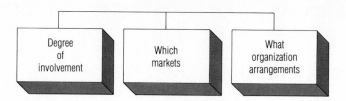

| Degree of involvement | Which markets | What organization arrangements |

kets, and (3) what organization arrangements should be made when it moves beyond its domestic activities. See Exhibit 18–1.

THE IMPORTANCE OF INTERNATIONAL MARKETS TO THE UNITED STATES

As a nation grows, its trade grows

You may be surprised to know that the United States is the largest exporter and importer of products in the world. Our share of the world's foreign trade is about 12 percent. Even the United Kingdom and Japan—which built their growth on exports and imports—rank below the United States. Most of the largest traders are highly developed nations. Trade seems to expand as a country develops and industrializes.

But while the United States is the biggest trading nation in the world, foreign trade does not dominate our economy. This is because of the large size of our national income. Our foreign trade makes up a relatively small part of our income—about 10 percent—but this is still greater in total dollars than in other major trading countries.[2]

DEGREES OF INVOLVEMENT IN INTERNATIONAL MARKETING

Opportunities in foreign countries have led many companies into worldwide operations. The marketing concept is less understood in some foreign markets. So there are exciting opportunities for those who apply it abroad—from just exporting to joint ventures to investment in foreign operations. See Exhibit 18–2.

Many companies are very interested in foreign market opportunities—because they find their foreign operations becoming more profitable than domestic activities. Coca-Cola, for example, sees the day coming when as much as 75 percent of its earnings will be from abroad—because there will be more young people there than in aging America.

Exporting often comes first

Some companies get into international marketing just by **exporting**—selling some of what they already produce to foreign markets. Sometimes this is just a way of "getting rid of" surplus output. For others, it comes from a real effort to look for new opportunities.

Exhibit 18–2   Kinds of Involvement in International Marketing That a Marketing Manager Can Choose

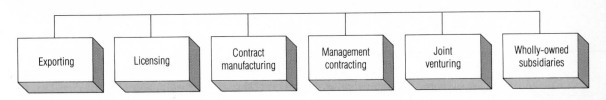

| Exporting | Licensing | Contract manufacturing | Management contracting | Joint venturing | Wholly-owned subsidiaries |

Some firms try exporting without changing the physical product—or even the service or instruction manuals! As a result, some early efforts are not very satisfying—to buyers or sellers. When Toyota first exported cars to the United States, the effort was a failure. Americans were not at all interested in the Toyota model that sold well in Japan. Toyota tried again three years later with a new design—and a new marketing mix. This second effort was a success.[3]

Exporting gets a firm involved in a lot of government "red tape." Beginning exporters build their own staffs—or depend on specialized middlemen to handle these details. Export agents can handle the paperwork as the products are shipped outside the country. Then agents or merchant wholesalers can handle the importing details. Even large producers with many foreign operations use international middlemen for some products or markets. These specialists know how to handle the sometimes confusing formalities and specialized functions. Even a small mistake can tie products up at national borders for days—or months.[4]

Exporting is often the first step into international marketing.

Some relationships get a firm more involved

Exporting doesn't have to involve permanent relationships. Of course, channel relationships take time to build—and shouldn't be treated lightly. Sales reps' contacts in foreign countries are "investments." But it is relatively easy to cut back on these relationships—or even drop them.

Some firms, on the other hand, develop more formal and permanent relationships with nationals in foreign countries—including licensing, contract manufacturing, management contracting, and joint venturing.

Licensing is an easy way

Licensing is a relatively easy way to enter foreign markets. **Licensing** means selling the right to use some process, trademark, patent, or other right—for a fee or royalty. The licensee takes most of the risk—because it must invest some capital to use the right.

This can be an effective way of entering a market if good partners are available. (Gerber entered the Japanese baby food market in this way, but Gerber still exports to other countries.)[5]

Contract manufacturing takes care of the production problems

Contract manufacturing means turning over production to others while retaining the marketing process. Sears used this approach as it opened stores in Latin America and Spain.

This approach can be especially good where labor relations are difficult—or there are problems getting supplies and "buying" government cooperation. Growing nationalistic feelings may make this approach more attractive in the future.

Management contracting sells know-how

Management contracting means the seller provides only management skills—the production facilities are owned by others. Some mines and oil refineries operate this way. And Hilton operates hotels all over the world for local owners. This is a relatively low-risk approach to international marketing. No commitment is made to fixed facilities—which can be taken over or damaged in riots or wars. If conditions get too bad, the key managers can fly off on the next plane—and leave the nationals to manage the operation.

Joint venturing is more involved

Joint venturing means a domestic firm enters into a partnership with a foreign firm. As with any partnership, there can be honest disagreements over objectives—for example, about how much profit is desired—how fast it should be paid out—and operating policies. Where a close working relationship can be developed—perhaps based on a U.S. firm's technical and marketing know-how and the foreign partner's political connections and knowledge of the market—this approach can be very attractive to both parties. At its worst, it can be a nightmare—and cause the U.S. firm to want a wholly-owned operation. But the terms of the joint venture may block this for years.[6]

Wholly-owned subsidiaries give more control

When a firm feels that a foreign market looks really promising, it may want to go the final step. A **wholly-owned subsidiary** is a separate firm—owned by a parent company. This gives complete control—and helps a foreign branch work more easily with the rest of the company.

Some multinational companies have gone this way. It gives them a great deal of freedom to move products from one country to another. If a firm has too much capacity in a country with low production costs, for example, some production may be moved there from other plants—and then exported to countries with higher production costs. This is the same way that large firms in the United States ship products from one area to another—depending on costs and local needs.

MULTINATIONAL CORPORATIONS EVOLVE TO MEET INTERNATIONAL CHALLENGE

Multinational corporations have a direct investment in several countries and run their businesses depending on the choices available anywhere in the world. Well-known U.S.-based multinational firms include Coca-Cola, Eastman Kodak, Warner-Lambert, Pfizer, Anaconda, Goodyear, Ford, IBM, ITT, Corn Products, 3M, National Cash Register, H. J. Heinz, and Gillette. They regularly earn over a third of their total sales or profits abroad.[7]

Many multinational companies are American. But there are also many well-known foreign-based companies—such as Nestle's, Shell (Royal Dutch Shell), Lever Brothers (Unilever), Sony, and Honda. They have well-accepted "foreign" brands—not only in the United States, but around the world.

Multinational operations make sense to more firms

As firms become more involved in international marketing, some reach the point where the firm sees itself as a worldwide business. Said a chief executive of Abbott Laboratories—a pharmaceutical company with plants in 22 countries—"We are no longer just a U.S. company with interests abroad. Abbott is a worldwide enterprise, and many major fundamental decisions must be made on a global basis."

A Texas Instruments manager had a similar view: "When we consider new opportunities and one is abroad and the other domestic, we can't afford to look upon the alternative here as an inherently superior business opportunity simply because it is in the United States. We view an overseas market just as we do our market, say, in Arizona, as one more market in the world."

A General Motors manager sees this trend as "the emergence of the modern industrial corporation as an institution that is transcending national boundaries."[8]

Much of the multinational activity of the 1960s and early 1970s involved U.S.-based firms expanding to other countries. As these opportunities became less attractive in the mid-1970s—due to the energy crisis, inflation, currency devaluations, labor unrest, and unstable governments—foreign multinational companies began moving into the United States. The United States is, after all, one of the richest markets in the world.

Foreign firms are beginning to see the attraction of operating in this large—if competitive—market. The Japanese "invasion" with all kinds of electronic products is well known. Now they are building plants here, too. For example,

Sony has a TV assembly plant and a TV tube plant in southern California. And Honda makes cars in Ohio.[9]

Multinational companies overcome national boundaries

From an international view, multinational firms do—as the GM manager says—"transcend national boundaries." They see world market opportunities—and locate their production and distribution facilities for greatest effectiveness. This has upset some nationalistic business managers and politicians. But these multinational operations may be hard to stop. They no longer just export or import. They hire local residents—and build local plants. They have business relationships with local business managers and politicians. These powerful organizations have learned to deal with nationalistic feelings and typical border barriers—treating them simply as uncontrollable variables.

We do not have "one world" politically as yet—but business is moving in that direction. We may have to develop new kinds of corporations and laws to govern multinational operations. The limitations of national boundaries on business and politics will make less and less sense in the future.

FINDING INTERNATIONAL OPPORTUNITIES

Firms usually start from where they are

A multinational firm that has accepted the marketing concept will look for opportunities in the same way we've been discussing throughout the text. That is, it will look for unsatisfied needs—anywhere—that it might be able to satisfy—given its resources and objectives.

The typical approach starts with the firm's current products—and the needs it knows how to satisfy. Then it tries to find new markets—wherever they may be—with the same or similar unsatisfied needs. Next, the firm might adapt its Product—and perhaps its Promotion. Later, the firm might develop new products and new promotion policies. Some of these possibilities are shown in Exhibit 18–3. Here, we only look at Product and Promotion—because Place and Price would obviously have to be changed in new markets.

The "Same-Same" box in Exhibit 18–3 can be illustrated with McDonald's (fast-food chain) entry into European markets. Its director of international marketing says, "Ronald McDonald speaks eight languages. Our target audience is the same worldwide—young families with children—and our advertising is designed to appeal to them." The basic promotion messages must be translated, of course, but the same strategy decisions that were made in the U.S. market apply. However, McDonald's has adapted its Product in Germany by adding beer to appeal to adults who prefer beer to soft drinks. Its efforts have been extremely successful so far.[10]

McDonald's and other firms expanding into international markets usually move first into markets with good economic potential—such as Western Europe and Japan. But if McDonald's or some other fast-food company wanted to move into much lower-income areas, it might have to develop a whole new Product—perhaps a traveling street vendor with "hamburgers" made from soybean products. This kind of opportunity is shown in the upper right-hand corner of Exhibit 18–3.

Exhibit 18–3   International Marketing Opportunities as Seen by a U.S. Firm from the Viewpoint of Its Usual Product-Market in the United States

	Product		
	Same	**Adaptation**	**New**
Same (Promotion)	Same needs and use conditions (McDonald's usual strategy)	Basically same needs and use conditions (McDonald's strategy with beer in Germany)	Basically same needs, but different incomes and/or applications (street vendor with low-cost hamburgers)
Adaptation (Promotion)	Different needs but same use conditions (bicycles)	Different needs and use conditions (clothing)	Different needs and different incomes and/or applications (hand-powered washing machines)

The lower left-hand box in this exhibit is illustrated by the different kind of Promotion needed for a simple bicycle. In some parts of the world, a bicycle provides basic transportation—while in the United States, it's mainly for recreation. So a different promotion emphasis is needed in these different target markets.

Both Product and Promotion changes are needed as one moves to the right along the bottom row of Exhibit 18–3. Such moves increase the risk—and obviously require more market knowledge.

The risk of opportunities varies by environmental sensitivity

International marketing means going into unfamiliar markets. The farther you go from familiar territory, the greater the chance of making big mistakes. But not all products offer the same risk. It's useful to think of the risks running along a "range of environmental sensitivity." See Exhibit 18–4. Some products are relatively insensitive to the economic or cultural environment. These products may be accepted "as is"—or may need just a little change to make them suitable for local use. Most industrial products are near the insensitive end of this range.

At the other end of the range are highly sensitive products that may be difficult or impossible to adapt to all international situations—for example, "faddy" or high-style consumer products. It is sometimes difficult to understand why a particular product is well accepted in a home market—which makes it even harder to know how it might be received in a different environment.

This range of sensitivity helps explain why many of the early successes in international marketing were basic commodities such as gasoline, soap, transporting vehicles, mining equipment, and agricultural machinery. It also suggests that firms producing and/or selling highly sensitive products should carefully

Exhibit 18–4   Range of Environmental Sensitivity

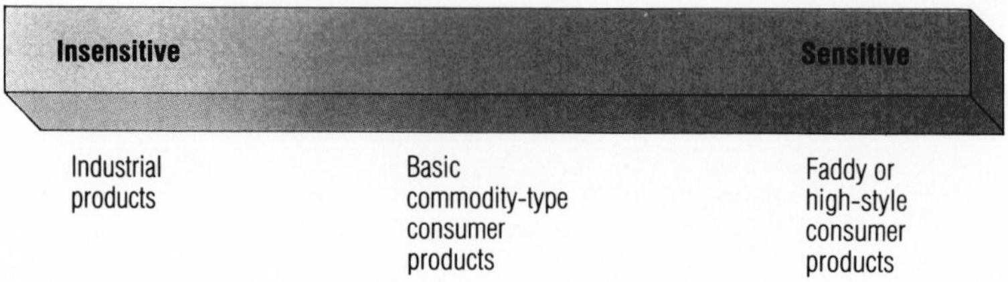

Insensitive		Sensitive
Industrial products	Basic commodity-type consumer products	Faddy or high-style consumer products

study how their products will be seen and used in new environments—and plan their strategies accordingly.[11] American-made blue jeans, for example, have become "status symbols" in Western Europe and Latin America—and producers have been able to sell them at premium prices through the "best" middlemen.

Evaluating opportunities in possible international markets

Judging opportunities in international markets uses the same principles we've been discussing. Basically, each opportunity must be evaluated—within the limits of the uncontrollable variables. But there may be more of these variables—and they may be harder to evaluate—in international markets. Estimating the risk in some opportunities may be very difficult. Some countries are not as politically stable as the United States. Their governments and constitutions come and go. An investment that was safe under one government might become the target for a take-over under another. Further, the possibility of foreign exchange controls—and tax rate changes—can reduce the chance of getting profits and capital back to the home country.[12]

Because the risks are hard to judge, it may be wise to enter international marketing by exporting first—building know-how and confidence over time. Experience and judgment are needed even more in unfamiliar areas. It makes sense to allow time for a firm's top managers—and its international managers—to develop these skills. This puts the firm in a better position to estimate the prospects—and risks—of going further into international marketing.

INTERNATIONAL MARKETING REQUIRES EVEN MORE SEGMENTING

Success in international marketing requires even more attention to segmenting. There are over 140 nations—each with its own unique differences! There can be big differences in language, customs, beliefs, religions, race, and even income distribution from one country to another. This obviously complicates the segmenting process. But what makes it even worse is the lack of good data about international markets. While the number of variables increases, the quantity and quality of data go down. Because of this, some multinational firms insist that local operations be handled by natives. They, at least, have a "feel" for their markets.

There are more dimensions—but there is a way

Segmenting international markets may require more dimensions. But a practical method adds just one step before the seven-step approach discussed in Chapter 3. See Exhibit 18–5. First, segment by country or region—looking at demographic, cultural, and other characteristics—including stage of economic development. This may help the firm find reasonably similar sub-markets. Then—depending on whether the firm is aiming at final consumers or intermediate customers—it can apply the seven-step approach discussed earlier.

In the rest of this chapter we'll emphasize final consumer differences—because they're likely to be greater than intermediate customer differences. Also, we'll consider regional groupings and stages of economic development—which can aid your segmenting.

REGIONAL GROUPINGS MAY MEAN MORE THAN NATIONAL BOUNDARIES

National boundaries are a common and logical dimension for segmenting markets. But sometimes it makes more sense to treat several nearby countries with similar cultures as one region—Central America or Latin America, for example. Or, if several nations have banded together to have common economic boundaries, then these nations may be treated as a unit. The outstanding example is the European Economic Community (EEC)—or "Common Market." Member countries dared to discard old ideas and nationalistic prejudices—in favor of cooperative efforts to reduce tariffs and other controls usually applied at national boundaries.

These cooperative arrangements are very important because the taxes and

Exhibit 18–5   Segmenting in International Markets

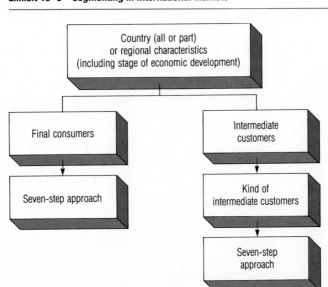

restrictions at national borders can not only be annoying—but also greatly reduce marketing opportunities. **Tariffs**—taxes on imported products—vary depending on whether the country is trying to raise revenue or limit trade. Restrictive tariffs often block all movement. But even revenue-producing tariffs cause red tape and discourage free movement of products. **Quotas** set the specific quantities of products that can move in or out of a country. They act like restrictive tariffs. Great opportunities may exist in a country, but import quotas (or export controls applied against a specific country) may discourage outsiders from entering. The U.S. government, for example, has controlled Japan's export of cars to the United States. (Otherwise, we would have had even more Japanese cars in the U.S. market!)[13]

STAGES OF ECONOMIC DEVELOPMENT HELP DEFINE MARKETS

International markets vary so much that we can't make general rules for all of them. Some markets grow and advance more rapidly than others. And some countries—or parts of a country—are at different stages of economic development. This means their demands—and marketing systems—will vary.

To get some idea of the many possible differences in potential markets—and how they affect strategy planning—let's discuss six stages of economic development. These stages are oversimplified, of course. But they can help you to understand economic development better—and how it affects marketing.

Stage 1—agricultural—self-supporting

In this stage, most people are subsistence farmers. There may be a simple marketing system—perhaps weekly markets—but most of the people are not even in a money economy. Some parts of Africa and New Guinea are in this stage. In a practical sense, these people are not a market—they have no money to buy products.

Stage 2—preindustrial or commercial

Some countries in Sub-Sahara Africa and the Middle East are in this second stage. During this stage, we see more market-oriented activity. Raw materials such as oil, tin, and copper are extracted and exported. Agricultural and forest crops such as sugar, rubber, and timber are grown and exported. Often foreign technical skills and capital help in this process. A commercial economy may develop along with—but not related to—the subsistence economy. These activities may require the beginning of a transporting system—to tie the extracting or growing areas to shipping points. A money economy operates in this stage.

Industrial machinery and equipment are imported. And huge construction projects may import component materials and supplies. Buying for these needs may be handled by purchasing agents in developed countries. Imports—including luxury products—are also required to meet the living standards of technical and supervisory people. These may be handled by company stores—rather than local retailers.

The few large landowners—and those who benefit by this business activity—may develop expensive tastes. The few natives employed by these larger firms—and the small business managers who serve them—may form a small middle-income class. But most of the population is still in the first stage. For practical purposes, they are not in the market. This total market may be so small that local importers can easily handle the demand. There is little reason for local producers to try to supply it.

Stage 3—primary manufacturing

In this third stage, there is some processing of the metal ores or agricultural products that once were shipped out of the country in raw form. Indonesia, for example, produces and processes sugar and rubber. The same is true for oil on the Persian Gulf. Multinational companies may set up factories to take advantage of low-cost labor. They may export most of the output—but they do stimulate local development. More local labor is involved—and a domestic market develops. Small local businesses start to handle some of the raw material processing.

Even though the local market expands in this third stage, a large part of the population stays at the subsistence level—almost entirely outside the money economy. A large foreign population of professionals and technicians may still be needed to run the developing agricultural-industrial complex. The demands of this group—and the growing number of wealthy natives—still differ greatly from the needs of the lower class and the growing middle class. A domestic market among the local people begins to develop—but often without enough demand to keep local producers in business.

Stage 4—non-durable and semi-durable consumer products manufacturing

At this stage, small local manufacturing begins—especially in those lines that need only a small investment to get started. Often these industries grow out of small firms that developed to supply the processors dominating the last stage. For example, plants making sulfuric acid and explosives for extracting mineral resources might expand into soap manufacturing. And recently multinational firms have speeded development of countries in this stage by investing in promising opportunities.

Now paint, drug, food and beverage, and textile industries begin to develop. The textile industry usually develops first. Clothing is a necessity, and economies of scale are possible. This early emphasis on the textile industry in developing nations is one reason the world textile market is so competitive.

Some of the small manufacturers become members of the middle- or even upper-income class. They help to expand the demand for imported products. As this market grows, local businesses begin to see enough volume to operate profitably. So the need for imports to supply non-durable and semi-durable products is less. But consumer durable and capital items are still imported.

Stage 5—capital items and consumer durable products manufacturing

In this stage, the production of capital items and consumer durable products begins. This includes cars, refrigerators, and machinery for local industries. Such manufacturing creates other demands—raw materials for the local factories, and food and fibers for clothing for the rural population entering the industrial labor force.

Industrialization has begun. But the economy still depends on exports of raw materials—either unprocessed or slightly processed.

It may still be necessary to import special heavy machinery and equipment in this stage. Imports of consumer durable products may still compete with local products. The foreign community and the status-conscious wealthy may prefer these imports.

Stage 6—exporting manufactured products

Countries that have not gone beyond the fifth stage mainly export raw materials. They import manufactured products to build their industrial base. In the sixth stage, exporting manufactured products becomes most important. The country specializes in certain types of manufactured products—iron and steel, watches, cameras, electronic equipment, or processed food.

There are many opportunities for importing and exporting at this stage. These countries have grown richer and have needs—and the buying power—for a wide variety of products. In fact, countries in this stage often carry on a great deal of trade with each other. Each trades those products in which it has production advantages. In this stage almost all consumers are in the money economy. There may be a large middle-income class. The United States, most of the Western European countries, and Japan are at this last stage.[14]

Notice that it's not necessary to label a whole country or geographic region as being in one stage. Certainly, different parts of the United States have developed differently—and can be placed in different stages.

HOW THESE STAGES CAN BE USEFUL IN FINDING MARKET OPPORTUNITIES

A good starting point for estimating present and future market potentials in a country—or part of a country—is to estimate its present stage of economic development and how fast it is moving to another stage. Actually, the speed of movement, if any—and the possibility that stages may be skipped—may suggest whether market opportunities are there or are likely to open. But just naming the present stage can be very useful in deciding what to look for—and whether there are prospects for a firm's products.

Fitting the firm to market needs

Producers of cars, expensive cameras, or other consumer durable products, for example, should not plan to set up a mass distribution system in an area that is in Stage 2 (the preindustrial stage) or even Stage 3 (the primary manufacturing stage). To sell these consumer products profitably requires a large base of cash or credit customers—but, as yet, too few are part of the money economy.

On the other hand, a market in the non-durable products manufacturing stage (Stage 4) has more potential—especially for durable products producers. Incomes and the number of potential customers are growing. There is no local competition yet.

Opportunities might still be good for durable products imports in Stage 5—even though domestic producers are trying to get started. But, more likely, the local government will raise some controls to aid local industry. Then the foreign producer has to license local producers—or build a local plant.

Pursuing that tempting mass market

Areas or countries in the final stage often are the biggest and most profitable markets. While there may be more competition, many more customers have higher incomes. We've already seen how income distribution shifted in the United States so there are now more families with middle and upper incomes. This can be expected during the latter stages—when a "mass market" develops.

OTHER MARKET DIMENSIONS MAY SUGGEST OPPORTUNITIES, TOO

Considering country or regional differences—including stages of economic development—can be useful as a first step in segmenting international markets. After finding some possible areas (and eliminating less attractive ones), we must look at more specific market characteristics.

We discussed many potential dimensions in the U.S. market. It's impossible to cover all possible dimensions in all world markets. But some of the ideas discussed for the United States certainly apply in other countries. So here we'll just outline some dimensions of international markets—and give examples to emphasize that depending on half-truths about "foreigners" won't work in increasingly competitive international markets.

The number of people in our world is staggering

Although our cities may seem crowded with people, the U.S. population of over 240 million makes up less than 5 percent of the world's population—which is over 5 billion.

Numbers are important

Instead of a boring breakdown of population statistics, let's look at a map showing area in proportion to population. Exhibit 18–6 makes the United States look unimportant—because of our small population in relation to land area. This is also true of Latin America and Africa. In contrast, Western Europe is much larger—and the Far Eastern countries are even bigger.

But people are not spread out evenly

People everywhere are moving off the farm and into urban areas. Shifts in population—combined with already dense populations—have led to extreme crowding in some parts of the world.

Exhibit 18–6   Map of the World Showing Area in Proportion to Population

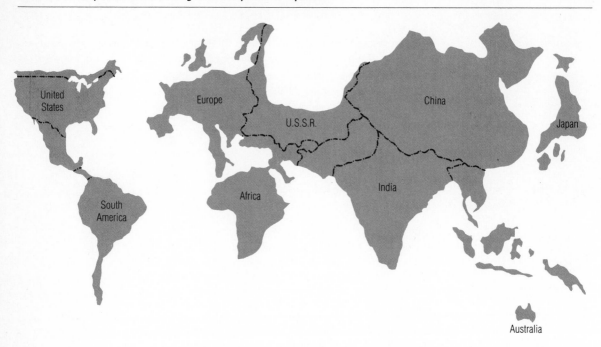

Exhibit 18–7 shows a map of the world emphasizing density of population. The darkest shading shows areas with more than 250 people per square mile.

The urban areas in the United States show up clearly as densely populated areas. Similar areas are found in Western Europe, along the Nile River Valley in Egypt, and in many parts of Asia. In contrast, many parts of the world (like our western plains and mountain states) have few people.

Population densities are likely to increase in the near future. Birth rates in most parts of the world are high—higher in Africa, Latin America, and Asia than in the United States—and death rates are declining as modern medicine is more widely accepted. Generally, population growth is expected in most countries. But the big questions are: How rapidly?—and—Will output increase faster than population? This is important to marketers—because it affects how rapidly these countries move to higher stages of development—and become new markets for different kinds of products.

You must sell where the income is

Profitable markets require income—as well as people. The best available measure of income in most countries is **gross national product (GNP)**—the total market value of goods and services produced in a year. Unfortunately, this may not give a true picture of consumer well-being in many countries—because the method commonly used for figuring GNP may not be accurate for very different cultures and economies. For instance, GNP does not usually include do-it-yourself activities, household services, and the growing of produce

Exhibit 18–7   *Map of the World Emphasizing Density of Population*

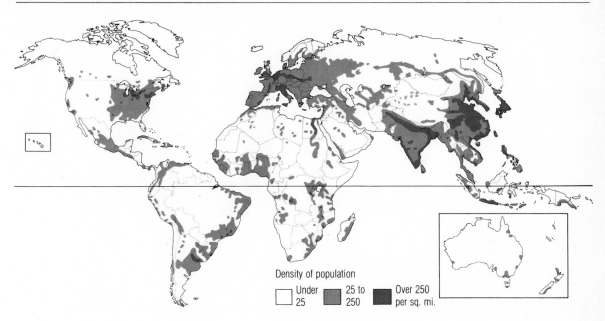

Density of population

☐ Under 25   ▨ 25 to 250   ■ Over 250 per sq. mi.

or meat by family members for their own use. So GNP can give a false picture of economic well-being in less-developed countries.

But gross national product is useful—and in many countries it's the only available measure of market potential. Exhibit 18–8 shows the population and GNP of major regions of the world—except the USSR and mainland China. You can see that the more developed regions have the biggest share of the world's GNP. This is why there is so much trade between these countries— and why many companies see them as the more important markets.

Income per person can be more helpful

GNP per person is a commonly available figure—but it can also be a misleading estimate of market potential. When GNP per person is used for comparison, we assume that the wealth of each country is distributed evenly among all consumers. This is seldom true. In a developing economy, 75 percent of the population may live on farms and receive 25 percent or less of the income. And there may be an unequal distribution along class or racial lines.

To provide some examples, the GNP per person for several countries is shown in Exhibit 18–9. The range is wide, from $132 (in U.S. dollars) per person per year in Ethiopia to $40,587 in the United Arab Emirates.

A business, and a human opportunity

Much of the world's population lives in extreme poverty. Many countries are in the early stages of economic development. Most of their people work on farms—and live barely within the money economy.

These people, however, have needs. And many are eager to improve them-

Exhibit 18–8 Estimated Population (1990) and Gross National Product (1980) of Major Geographic Regions of the World

Population (millions) / GNP (in U.S. $ billions)

- Population
- Gross National Product

Region:	North America	Latin America	Europe	Africa	Asia East and South	Oceania
Population	275	453	500	645	3,057	27
Gross National Product	$2,852.4	$824.1	$3,453.5	$421.3	$1,549.5	$179.5

selves. But they may not be able to raise their living standards without outside help. This presents a challenge—and an opportunity—to the developed nations—and to their business firms.

Some companies—including American firms—try to help the people of developing countries. Corporations such as Pillsbury, Corn Products, Monsanto, and Coca-Cola have developed nutritious foods that can be sold cheaply—but still profitably—in poorer countries. One firm sells a milk-based drink (Samson)—with 10 grams of protein—in the Middle East and Caribbean areas. Such a drink can make an important addition to diets. Poor people in developing nations usually get only 8 to 12 grams of protein per day in their normal diet (60 to 75 grams are considered necessary for an adult).[15]

Reading, writing, and marketing problems

The ability of a country's people to read and write has a direct influence on the development of the economy—and on marketing strategy planning. Certainly, the degree of literacy affects the way information is delivered—which, in marketing, means promotion. Literacy studies show that only about two-thirds of the world's population can read and write.

Low literacy sometimes causes difficulties with product labels and instructions—for which we normally use words. In very illiterate countries, some producers found that placing a baby's picture on food packages is unwise. Natives believed that the product was just that—a ground-up baby! Singer Sewing Machine Company met this lack of literacy with an instruction book that uses pictures instead of words.

Even in Latin America—where literacy is generally higher than in Africa or Asia—large numbers of people cannot read or write. Marketers have to use symbols, colors, and other non-verbal means of communication if they want to reach the masses.

Exhibit 18–9   Gross National Product per Capita for Major Regions of the World and Selected Countries (in 1980 U.S. dollars)

	GNP per capita for countries	GNP per capita for regions
North America		$11,340
United States	$11,416	
Canada	10,585	
Latin America		2,320
Brazil	2,021	
Mexico	2,591	
Venezuela	4,315	
Haiti	283	
Europe		9,860
United Kingdom	9,351	
France	12,137	
West Germany	13,304	
Italy	6,907	
Sweden	14,882	
Portugal (1978)	2,474	
Middle East		3,160
Israel	5,431	
United Arab Emirates	40,587	
Africa		900
Algeria	1,639	
Egypt	435	
Ethiopia	132	
Kenya	426	
South Africa	2,639	
East and South Asia		1,150
India	241	
Pakistan	339	
Japan	8,873	
Indonesia	472	
Oceania		7,850
Australia	10,210	
New Zealand	7,578	

CAREFUL MARKET ANALYSIS IS BASIC

The opportunities in international marketing are exciting. But market differences present a real challenge to target marketers. Careful market analysis is especially important—since subtle but important differences are easy to miss.

What are you drinking?

Tastes do differ across national boundaries. French Burgundy wine going to Belgium must have a higher sugar content than the Burgundy staying in France. Burgundy going to Sweden must have still higher sugar content to sell successfully there.

Milk-drinking habits also differ greatly. Scandinavians consider milk a daily staple—while Latins feel that milk is only for children. A former French premier was able to get his picture on the front page of every Paris newspaper just by drinking a glass of milk in public.

ORGANIZING FOR INTERNATIONAL MARKETING

Until a firm develops a truly worldwide view of its operations, it's usually wise to have someone in charge of international marketing. The basic concern should be to see that the firm transfers its domestic know-how into international operations.

Organization should transfer know-how

As the firm moves beyond just a few international locations, the managers may develop regional groupings of similar kinds of countries. It's important to develop an organization that allows local managers to control matters that require "local feel," while sharing their larger experience with others in the firm.

Top management may delegate a great deal of responsibility for strategy planning to these local managers. These managers may be given a lot of freedom in planning—but still be tightly controlled against their own plans. When the firm reaches this stage, it is being managed like a well-organized domestic corporation—which insists that its managers (of divisions and territories) meet their own plans, so that the whole company's program works out as intended.[16]

CONCLUSION

The international market is large—and keeps growing in population and income. Many American companies now see the opportunities for alert and aggressive marketers.

The great variations in stages of economic development, income, population, literacy, and other factors, however, mean that foreign markets must be treated as many separate target markets—and studied carefully. Lumping foreign nations together under the common and vague heading of "foreigners"—or, at the other extreme, assuming that they are just like U.S. customers—almost guarantees failure.

Involvement in international marketing usually begins with exporting. Then a firm may go into joint ventures or wholly-owned subsidiaries in several countries. Companies that become this involved are called multinational corporations.

Some of these corporations have a global outlook—and are willing to move across national boundaries as easily as our national firms move across state boundaries.

Much of what we have said about marketing strategy planning throughout the text applies directly in international marketing. Sometimes Product adaptions or changes are needed. Promotion messages must be translated into the local languages. And, of course, new Place arrangements and Prices are needed. But blending the four Ps still requires a knowledge of the all-important customer.

The major "roadblock" to success in international marketing is an unwillingness to learn about—and adjust to—different peoples and cultures. To those who are willing to make these adjustments, the returns can be great.

Questions and Problems

1.   Discuss the "typical" evolution of corporate involvement in international marketing. What impact would complete acceptance of the marketing concept have on the evolutionary process?

2.   Distinguish between licensing and contract manufacturing in a foreign country.

3.   Distinguish between joint ventures and wholly-owned subsidiaries.

4.   Discuss the long-run prospects for (a) multinational marketing by U.S. firms producing in the United States only and (b) multinational firms willing to operate anywhere.

5.   How can a producer interested in finding new international marketing opportunities organize its search process? What kinds of opportunities would it look for first, second, and so on?

6.   Discuss how market segmenting (discussed in Chapter 3) might have to be modified when a firm moves into international markets.

7.   Evaluate the growth of the EEC in relation to its members' phases of economic development.

8.   Discuss the prospects for a Latin American entrepreneur who is considering building a factory to produce machines that make cans for the food industry. His country is in Stage 4—the non-durable and semi-durable consumer products manufacturing stage. The country's population is approximately 20 million, and there is some possibility of establishing sales contacts in a few nearby countries.

9.   Discuss the value of gross national product per capita as a measure of market potential. Refer to specific data in your answer.

10.   Discuss the possibility of a multinational marketer using the same promotion campaign in the United States and in many international markets.

11.   What kinds of products may become popular in Europe in the near future? Why? Does the material on U.S. consumption behavior—discussed earlier in the text—have any relevance here?

12.   Describe an effective organization for a multinational firm.

Suggested Computer-Aided Problem

18.   Export Opportunities

Suggested Cases

32.   Lever Limited

34.   Black & Decker Company

Chapter 19

Marketing in a Consumer-Oriented Society: Appraisal and Challenges

---

When You Finish This Chapter, You Should

1. Understand why marketing must be evaluated differently at the micro and macro levels.

2. Understand why the text argues that micro-marketing costs too much.

3. Understand why the text argues that macro-marketing does not cost too much.

4. Know some of the challenges facing marketers in the future.

Does marketing cost too much?

Most of us live fast-paced lives—and we like it that way.

We expect our Domino's Pizza to arrive in less than 30 minutes. We want McDonald's to have our burgers and fries hot and ready whenever we pull up at the "drive-thru." We want supermarkets and drug stores handy—and expect everything from fresh tropical fruits to camera batteries to be available when—and where—we want them. There are few other places in the world where consumers expect—and get—so much. All of this has a price—and we as consumers pay the bill.[1]

Does marketing cost too much? This is a very basic question. Many people feel strongly that marketing does cost too much—that it wastes resources which would be better used elsewhere. Now that you have a better understanding of what the marketing manager does—and how he contributes to the *macro*-marketing process—you should be able to consider whether marketing costs too much. That's what this chapter is about.

Your answer is very important. It will affect your own business career—and the economy you'll live in. Do car producers, for example, produce as high quality cars as they could—or did in the "good old days"? Do producers of food and drug products spend too much advertising their own brands instead of offering more generics—at lower prices? Do we have too many retailers and wholesalers—all taking "too big" markups? Some critics of marketing answer Yes! to *all* these important questions. These critics believe we should change our political and legal environments—and the world in which you'll live and work. Do you agree with these critics? Or are you fairly satisfied with the way our system works? How will you "vote" on your consumer ballot?

MARKETING MUST BE EVALUATED AT TWO LEVELS

As we saw in Chapter 1, we look at marketing at two levels: the *micro* level (how individual firms run) and the *macro* level (how the whole system works). Some complaints against marketing are aimed at only one of these levels. In other cases, the criticism seems to be directed to one level—but actually aims at the other. Some critics of specific ads, for example, probably would not be satisfied with *any* advertising. When evaluating marketing, we must treat each of these levels separately.

HOW SHOULD MARKETING BE EVALUATED?

Different nations have different social and economic objectives. Dictatorships may be concerned mainly with satisfying the needs of the people at the top. In a socialist state, the objective is to satisfy the needs of the people—as defined by government planners.

Consumer satisfaction is the objective in the United States

In the United States, *the aim of our economic system has been to satisfy consumer needs as they—the consumers—see them.* This is no place for a long discussion of whether this objective is right or wrong. Our democratic political process decides such matters.

Therefore, let's try to evaluate the operation of marketing in the American economy—where the objective is to satisfy consumer needs *as consumers see them.* This is the basis of our system. The business firm that ignores this fact is in for trouble.

CAN CONSUMER SATISFACTION BE MEASURED?

Since consumer satisfaction is our objective, marketing's effectiveness must be measured by how well it satisfies consumers. Unfortunately, consumer satisfaction is hard to define—and harder to measure.

Measuring macro-marketing isn't easy

Economists believe that consumer satisfaction comes from economic utility—remember form, time, place, and possession utility. However, we don't have a practical way to measure utility since satisfaction seems to depend on each person's own view of things. Further, products that satisfied one day may not satisfy the next day—or vice versa. Most of us now expect cars to work—almost without maintenance. For car owners in the 1910s and 20s, breakdowns and flat tires were common. A Sunday drive often included fixing several flats—on a dusty road—with no helpful AAA on call! So you can see that consumer satisfaction is a very personal concept that doesn't provide a very good standard for evaluating marketing effectiveness.

The final measure, probably, is whether the macro-marketing system satisfies enough consumer/citizens so that they vote—at the ballot box—to keep it running. So far, we've done so in the United States.

There are ways to measure micro-marketing

Measuring micro-marketing effectiveness is also difficult. But individual business firms can measure how well their products satisfy their customers by using such methods as attitude studies, analysis of consumer complaints, opinions of middlemen and salespeople, market test results—and profits.[2]

Since every company uses slightly different marketing strategies, each customer must decide how well individual firms satisfy his or her needs. Usually, customers are willing to pay higher prices for—or buy more of—products that satisfy them. So profits are a rough measure of a firm's success in satisfying customers.

Evaluating marketing effectiveness is difficult—but not impossible

Because it's hard to measure consumer satisfaction—and therefore marketing's effectiveness—it's easy to see why people view the subject differently. If the objective of the economy is clearly defined, however, the big questions about marketing effectiveness probably *can* be answered.

In this chapter, we'll argue that micro-marketing (how individual firms and channels operate) frequently *does* cost too much but that macro-marketing (how the whole marketing system operates) *does not* cost too much, *given the present objective of the American economy—consumer satisfaction.* In the end, you must make your own decision.[3]

Many companies ask for customer feedback to be sure that their customers are satisfied.

MICRO—MARKETING OFTEN DOES COST TOO MUCH

Throughout the text, we talked about what marketing managers could or should do to help their firms do a better job of satisfying customers—while achieving company objectives. Many firms do carry out very successful marketing programs. But many more firms are still too production-oriented and inefficient. Many consumers are not happy with the marketing efforts of some firms. "Helping consumers get a fair deal when shopping" ranks very high among public concerns. Only inflation, unemployment, government spending, welfare, and taxes rank higher.[4]

The failure rate is high

Further evidence that most firms are too production-oriented—and not nearly as efficient as they could be—is the fact that many new products fail. New and old businesses fail regularly, too.

These failures are caused by one or more of three reasons:

1. Lack of interest in—or understanding of—the sometimes fickle customer.
2. Poor blending of the four Ps—because of a lack of customer orientation.
3. Lack of understanding of—or failure to adjust to—uncontrollable variables.

The company can get in the way of the customer

Serving the customer should be the role of business—but some producers seem to feel that customers eagerly wait for any product they turn out. They don't see a business as a "total system" responsible for satisfying customer needs.

Middlemen, too, often get tied up in their own internal problems. Products may be stocked where it's easy for the retailer to handle them—rather than for consumers to find them. And fast-moving, hard-to-handle products may not be stocked at all—because "they're too much trouble" or "we're always running out."

In the same way, accounting and finance departments try to cut costs by encouraging the production of standardized, "me-too" products—even though they aren't what customers want.

Company objectives may force higher-cost operation

Top-management decisions on company objectives may increase the cost of marketing. Seeking growth for growth's sake, for example, might lead to too much spending for promotion.

For these reasons, the marketing manager should take a big part in shaping the firm's objectives. Recognizing the importance of marketing, progressive firms have given marketing managers more control in setting company objectives. Unfortunately, though, in many more firms marketing is still looked on as the department that "gets rid of" the product.

Micro-marketing does cost too much—but things are changing

Marketing *does* cost too much in many firms. The sales manager is renamed "marketing manager"—and the vice president of sales is called "vice president of marketing"—but nothing else changes. Marketing mixes are still put together by production-oriented managers in the same old ways.

But not all business firms are so old-fashioned. More firms *are* becoming customer-oriented. And some are paying more attention to market-oriented strategy planning—to better carry out the marketing concept.[5]

One hopeful sign is the end of the idea that anybody can run a business successfully. This never was true. Today the growing complexity of business is drawing more and more professionals into the field. This includes not only professional business managers but psychologists, sociologists, statisticians, and economists.

Managers who adopt the marketing concept as a way of business life do a better job. As more of these managers enter business, micro-marketing costs will go down.

MACRO—MARKETING DOES *NOT* COST TOO MUCH

Many critics of marketing take aim at the macro-marketing system. They think that (1) advertising—and promotion in general—are socially undesirable and (2) that the macro-marketing system causes poor use of resources, limits income and employment, and leads to unfair distribution of income. Most of these complaints imply that some micro-marketing activities should not be allowed—and, because of them, our macro-marketing system does a poor job.

Many of these critics have their own version of the ideal way to run an economy. Some of the most severe critics of our marketing system are economists who use pure competition as their ideal. They want consumers and producers to have free choice in the market—but they criticize the way the present market operates. Other critics would scrap our market-directed system and substitute the decisions of central planners for those of individual producers and consumers—reducing freedom of choice in the market place. These different views should be kept in mind when evaluating criticisms of marketing.

Is pure competition the welfare ideal?

One criticism of our macro-marketing system is that it permits—or even encourages—the use of too many resources for marketing activities—and that this may actually reduce consumer "welfare." This argument is concerned with how the economy's resources (land, labor, and capital) are used for producing and distributing products. These critics usually argue that scarce resources should be spent on producing products—not on marketing them. They believe that marketing activities are unnecessary and do not create value. These critics feel that pure competition would result in the greatest consumer benefit.

In pure competition, you remember, we assume that consumers are "economic men"—that they know all about all the homogeneous offerings and will make "wise" choices. Economic analysis can show that pure competition will provide greater consumer welfare than monopolistic competition—*if all the conditions of pure competition are met.* But are they?

Different people want different things

Our present knowledge of consumer behavior and people's desire for different products pretty well destroys the economists' "economic man" idea—and therefore the pure-competition ideal. People, in fact, are different—and they want different products. With this type of demand (down-sloping demand curves), monopoly elements naturally develop. A pioneer in this kind of analysis concluded that "monopoly is necessarily a part of the welfare ideal."[6]

Once we admit that not all consumers know everything—and that they have many different demands—the need for a variety of micro-marketing activities becomes clear.

Micro-efforts help the economy grow

Some critics feel that marketing helps create monopolistic competition—and that this leads to higher prices, limits production, and reduces national income and employment.

It is true that firms in a market-directed economy try to carve out separate monopolistic markets for themselves with new products. But customers don't have to buy a new product unless they feel it's a better value. The old products are still available. The prices may even be lower on the old products to meet the new competition.

The profits of the innovator may rise over several years—but the rising profits also encourage more innovation by competitors. This leads to new investments—which contribute to economic growth and raise the level of national income and employment.

Does marketing make people buy things they don't need?

From our discussion so far, it seems that the individual firm's efforts to satisfy consumer needs will lead to a better division of national income. Giving customers what they want, after all, is the purpose of our market-directed economic system. However, some critics feel that most firms—especially large corporations—don't really try to satisfy consumers. Instead—these critics argue—they use clever ads to persuade consumers to buy whatever the firms want to sell.

Historian Arnold Toynbee, for example, felt that American consumers have been manipulated into buying products that are not necessary to satisfy "the minimum material requirements of life." Toynbee saw American firms as mainly trying to fulfill "unwanted demand"—demand created by advertising—rather than "genuine wants." He defined genuine wants as "wants that we become aware of spontaneously, without having to be told by Madison Avenue that we want something that we should never have thought of wanting if we had been left in peace to find out our wants for ourselves."[7]

What are the minimum requirements of life?

The problem with this kind of thinking is how to decide what "the minimum material requirements of life" *are*. Which products used today are unnecessary—and should be taken off the market? One critic has suggested that Americans could and *should* do without items such as pets, newspaper comic strips, second family cars, motorcycles, snowmobiles, campers, recreational boats and planes, cigarettes, pop and beer cans, and hats.[8] You may agree with some of those. But who should decide "minimum material requirements of life"—consumers or critics?

Consumers are not puppets

The idea that firms can persuade consumers to buy anything the company wants to produce just isn't true. A consumer who buys a can of soda pop that tastes terrible won't buy another can of that brand—regardless of how much it's advertised. In fact, many new products fail the test of the marketplace. Not even large corporations can be sure of success when they offer a new product. Consider, for example, the sad fate of products such as Ford's Edsel, Du Pont's Corfam, Campbell's Red Kettle Soups, and RCA's computers.

Needs and wants change

Consumer needs and wants change constantly. Few of us want to live the way our grandparents lived—let alone like the pioneers who traveled west in covered wagons. Marketing's job is not just to satisfy consumer wants today. Rather, marketing must keep looking for new—and better—ways to serve customers.

Does marketing make people materialistic?

There is no doubt that marketing caters to materialistic values. But there is a lot of disagreement as to whether marketing creates these values—or just appeals to values already there.

Anthropologists tell us that even in the most primitive societies people decorate themselves with trinkets—and accumulate possessions. Surely the desire of ancient pharaohs and kings to surround themselves with wealth and treasures can hardly be blamed on the persuasive powers of advertising agencies!

The idea that marketers create and serve "false tastes" has been answered by a well-known economist who said:

The marketplace responds to the tastes of consumers with the goods and services that are salable, whether the tastes are elevated or depraved. It is

Marketing can help a firm provide better solutions to consumers' needs than consumers might think of themselves.

unfair to criticize the marketplace for fulfilling these desires, when clearly the defects lie in the popular tastes themselves. I consider it a cowardly concession to a false extension of the idea of democracy to make sub rosa attacks on public tastes by denouncing the people who serve them. It is like blaming waiters in restaurants for obesity.[9]

Marketing reflects our own values

Experts who study materialism seem to agree that—in the short run—marketing reflects social values, while—in the long run—it reinforces them. One expert pointed out that consumers vote for what they want in the marketplace *and* in the polling place. To say that what they choose is wrong, he said, is to criticize the basic idea of free choice and democracy![10]

Products do improve the quality of life

More isn't always better. The quality of life can't be measured just in terms of quantities of material goods. But when products are seen as the means to an end—rather than the end itself—we can see that they do make it possible to satisfy higher-level needs. Microwave ovens, for example, have greatly reduced the amount of time and effort spent preparing meals—giving people time for other interests. And more dependable cars have expanded people's geographic horizons—affecting where they live, work, and play. Not having "wheels" would drastically change many people's life styles—and even their self images.

Consumers ask for it, consumers pay for it

The monopolistic competition typical of our economy is the result of customer preferences—not control of markets by business. Monopolistic competition may seem expensive at times—but if the role of the marketing system is to serve consumers, then the cost of whatever they demand cannot be considered too expensive. It's just the cost of serving consumers the way they want to be served.

Does macro-marketing cost enough?

The question, Does marketing cost too much? has been answered by one well-known financial expert with another question, Does distribution cost enough?[11] He meant that marketing is such an important part of our economic system that perhaps even more should be spent on marketing—since "distribution is the delivery of a standard of living"—that is, the satisfaction of consumers' basic needs and wants. In this sense, then, macro-marketing does *not* cost too much. Some of the activities of individual business firms may cost too much—and if these micro-level activities are improved, the performance of the macro system probably will improve. But regardless, our macro-marketing system performs a vital role in our economic system—and *does not cost too much.*

CHALLENGES FACING MARKETERS

We've said that our macro-marketing system does not cost too much—given the present objective of our economy—while admitting that the performance of many business firms is inefficient. This presents a challenge to all of us. What needs to be done—if anything?

We need better performance at the micro level

Some business executives seem to feel that—in a market-directed economy—they should be completely "free." They don't understand that ours is a market-directed system—and that the needs of consumer/citizens must be met. Instead, they focus on their own internal problems—and don't satisfy consumers very well.

We need better market-oriented planning

Most firms are still production-oriented. Some hardly plan at all. Others just extend this year's plans into next year. Progressive firms are beginning to realize that this doesn't work in our fast-changing markets. Many companies now emphasize market-oriented strategy planning. More attention is being given to the product life cycle—because marketing variables should change through the product life cycle.

Exhibit 9–3 showed some of the typical changes in marketing variables that might be needed over the course of a product life cycle. This exhibit should be a good review now—but it also makes clear the need for better planning. As the product life cycle moves on, the marketing manager should expect to find more products entering "his" market—and pushing the market closer to pure competition or oligopoly. As the cycle moves along, he might want to shift from a selective to an intensive distribution policy *and* move from skimming to a penetration pricing policy. The original marketing plan might include these adjustments—and the probable timing.

May need more social responsibility

A good business manager should put himself in the consumer's place. This means developing more satisfying marketing mixes for specific target markets. It may mean building in more quality or more safety. The consumer's long-run satisfaction should be considered, too. How will the product hold up in use? What about service guarantees?

This doesn't always mean producing the "highest quality" that can be produced. Low-quality, short-lived products may be "right" sometimes—as long as the target market understands what it's getting. (Recall our cost-conscious couple in the home-decorating market in Chapter 2.) Low-cost products—such as the paint in that example—might be seen as a "good value" by some market segments. In other markets, an entirely different product and/or marketing mix might be needed.

Production-oriented methods won't work in the future. Tougher competition—and more watchful government agencies—may force the typical production-oriented business managers to change.

May need attention to consumer privacy

While focusing on consumers' needs, marketers also must be aware of other consumer concerns. Advanced marketing research methods and new technologies now make it easier to abuse our rights to privacy.

Most consumers don't realize how much data about their personal lives—some of it incorrect but treated as factual—is collected and available. A simple computer billing error may land a consumer on a computer "bad credit" list—without his knowledge. Marketing managers must use technology responsibly—to improve the quality of life, not disrupt it.

We may need new laws

One of the advantages of a market-directed economic system is its relatively automatic operation. But in our version of this system, consumer/citizens provide certain limits (laws). These laws can be strengthened—or modified—at any time.

Need tougher enforcement of present laws

Before piling on too many new laws, however, we should enforce the ones we have. The antimonopoly laws, for example, have often been used to protect competitors from each other—when they really were intended to protect competition.

Laws should affect top managers

The results of strict enforcement of present laws could be far reaching if more price fixers, dishonest advertisers, and other obvious law breakers were sent to jail or given heavy fines. A quick change in attitudes would occur if top managers—those who plan overall business strategy—were prosecuted, rather than the salespeople or advertisers who are expected to "deliver" on weak strategies.

In other words, if the government made it clear that it was serious about improving the performance of our economic system, much could be achieved within the present system—without adding new laws or trying to "patch up" the present ones.

Need better-informed consumers

We also may need some changes to help potential customers become better informed about the many goods and services on the market. Laws to ensure that consumers have a way of comparing products (for example, life expectancy of light bulbs and appliances) would be useful. Consumer education designed to teach people how to buy more wisely could be helpful, too.

Need socially responsible consumers

We've been stressing the obligation of producers to act responsibly—but consumers have responsibilities, too. This is usually ignored by consumer advocates.[12] Some consumers abuse return policies, change price tags in self-serve stores, and expect attractive surroundings and courteous, well-trained sales and service people—but want discount prices. Others think nothing of "ripping off" businesses.

Americans tend to perform their dual role of consumer/citizens with something of a split personality. We often behave one way as consumers—and then take the opposite stand at the ballot box. For example, while our beaches and parks are covered with garbage and litter, we call for stiff action to curb pollution. We protest sex and violence in the media—and then flock to see the latest R- or X-rated movies.

Let's face it. There's a lot of information already available to aid consumer decision making. We now have nutritional labeling, unit pricing, truth-in-lending, and plain-language contracts and warranties. And government agencies publish many consumer buying guides—as do groups such as Consumers Union. Yet most consumers ignore this information!

We may need to modify our macro-marketing system

Our macro-marketing system is built on the idea of consumer satisfaction. But how far should the marketing concept be allowed to go?

Should marketing managers limit consumers' freedom of choice?

A "better" macro-marketing system is certainly a good idea. But what should marketers do in their roles as producers? Should they, for example, deliberately refuse to produce dangerous products—like skis or motorcycles—even though there is a strong demand? Or should they install safety devices that increase costs—but that customers don't want?

Consumer/citizens should vote on the changes

Marketing managers should be expected to improve and expand the range of goods and services they make available to consumers—always trying to better satisfy their needs and preferences. This is the job we've assigned to business.

If this objective makes "excessive" demands on scarce resources—or causes a "dangerous" level of ecological damage—then consumer/citizens have every right to vote for laws to limit individual firms. These firms can't be expected to fully understand the impact of all their actions. We as consumers have assigned this role to the government—to make sure that the macro-marketing system works effectively.

You should be aware that some critics of marketing are really interested in basic changes in our macro-marketing system.

Consumer/citizens must be careful to see the difference between changes designed just to modify our system and those designed to change it—perhaps completely. Some laws could seriously reduce our "right" to freedom of choice—including "bad" choices. Bicycles, for example, are dangerous consumer products—should they be sold? The consumer/citizen must make such decisions—through elected representatives. These decisions should not be left in the hands of a few well-placed managers—or government planners.[13]

Marketing people may be even more necessary in the future

No matter what changes consumer/citizens might vote for, some kind of a marketing system will be needed in the future. If satisfying more subtle needs—such as for the "good life"—becomes our objective, it could be even more important to have market-oriented firms. It may be necessary, for example, not only to define individuals' needs, but also society's needs—perhaps for a "better neighborhood" or "better quality of life." As we go beyond physical goods—into more sophisticated need-satisfying blends of goods and services—the trial-and-error approach of the typical production-oriented manager becomes even less acceptable.

CONCLUSION

Macro-marketing does *not* cost too much. Business has been assigned the role—by consumers—of satisfying their needs as they (the consumers) see them. Customers find it satisfactory—and even desirable—to permit businesses to cater to them. As long as consumers are satisfied, macro-marketing will not cost too much—and business firms will be permitted to continue as profit-making organizations.

It must always be remembered that business exists at the consumer's approval. It is only by satisfying consumers that a particular business firm—and our economic system—can justify its existence and hope to keep operating.

In carrying out this role granted by consumers, business firms are not always as effective as they might be. Many business managers do not understand the marketing concept—or the role that marketing plays in our way of life. They seem to feel that business has a God-given right to operate as it chooses. And they proceed in their typical production-oriented ways. Further, many managers have had little or no training in business management—and are not as competent as they should be. In this sense, micromarketing *does* cost too much. The situation is improving, however, as training for business expands—and as more competent people are attracted to marketing and business. Clearly, *you* have a role to play in improving marketing in the future.

Marketing faces new challenges in the future. All consumers may have to settle for a lower standard of living. Resource shortages, high energy costs, and slowing population growth all combine to reduce income growth. This will force consumers to shift their consumption patterns—and politicians to change some of the rules governing business. Even our present market-directed system may be threatened.

To keep our system working well, individual business firms should carry out the marketing concept in a more efficient and socially responsible way. At the same time, individual consumers have the responsibility to use goods and services in an intelligent and socially responsible way. Further, they have the responsibility to vote and make sure that they get the kind of macro-marketing system they want. What kind do you want? What can—and should—you do to see that fellow consumer/citizens will vote for your system? Is your system likely to satisfy you, personally, as well as another macro-marketing system? You don't have to answer these questions right now. But your answers will affect the future you'll live in—as well as how satisfied you'll be.

Questions and Problems

1. Explain why marketing must be evaluated at two levels. What criteria should be used to evaluate each level of marketing? Defend your answer. Explain why your criteria are "better" than alternative criteria.

2. Discuss the merits of various economic system objectives. Is the objective of the American economic system sensible? Do you feel more consumer satisfaction might be achieved by permitting some sociologists—or some public offi-

cials—to determine how the needs of the lower-income or less-educated members of the society should be satisfied? If you approve of this latter suggestion, what education or income level should be required before an individual is granted free choice by the social planners?

3. Should the objective of our economy be maximum efficiency? If your answer is yes, efficiency in what? If not, what should the objective be?

4. Cite an example of a critic using his own value system when evaluating marketing.

5. Discuss the conflict of interests among production, finance, accounting, and marketing executives. How does this conflict affect the operation of an individual firm? Of the economic system? Why does this conflict exist?

6. Why does adoption of the marketing concept encourage a firm to operate more efficiently? Be specific about the impact of the marketing concept on the various departments of a firm.

7. In the short run, competition sometimes leads to inefficiency in the operation of the economic system. Many people argue for monopoly in order to eliminate this inefficiency. Discuss this solution to the problem of inefficiency.

8. How would officially granted monopolies affect the operation of our economic system? Consider the effect on allocation of resources, the level of income and employment, and the distribution of income. Is the effect any different if a firm obtains a monopoly by winning out in a competitive market?

9. Could a pure-competition economy evolve naturally? Could legislation force a pure-competition economy?

10. Comment on the following statement: "Ultimately, the high cost of marketing is due only to consumers."

11. How far should the marketing concept go? How should we decide this issue?

12. Should marketing managers, or business managers in general, refrain from producing profitable products that some target customers want but that may not be in their long-run interest? Should firms be expected to produce "good" products that offer a lower rate of profitability than usual? A break-even level? What if the products will be unprofitable, but the company makes other products that are profitable—so on balance it will still make some profit? What criteria are you using for each of your answers?

13. Should a marketing manager or a business refuse to produce an "energy-gobbling" appliance that some consumers are demanding? Should a firm install an expensive safety device that will increase costs but that customers don't want? Are the same principles involved in both these questions? Explain.

14. Discuss how slower economic growth or no economic growth would affect your college community—in particular, its marketing institutions.

Suggested Cases

27. Orecan, Inc.

28. Plasto, Inc.

29. Pulte Products, Inc.

31. Precision Castings, Inc.

34. Black & Decker Company

Appendix C

Career Planning in Marketing

When You Finish This Appendix, You Should

1. Know that there is a job—or a career—for you in marketing.

2. Know that marketing jobs can pay well.

3. Understand the difference between "people-oriented" and "thing-oriented" jobs.

4. Know about the many marketing jobs you can choose from.

One of the hardest jobs facing most college students is the choice of a career. Of course, we can't make this decision for you. You must be the judge of your own objectives, interests, and abilities. Only you can decide what career *you* should pursue. However, you owe it to yourself to at least consider the possibility of a career in marketing.

THERE'S A PLACE IN MARKETING FOR YOU

We're happy to tell you that many opportunities are available in marketing. Regardless of your abilities or training, there's a place in marketing for everyone—from a supermarket bagger to a vice president of marketing in a large consumer products company such as Procter & Gamble or General Foods. The opportunities range widely—so it will help to be more specific. In the following pages, we'll discuss (1) the typical pay for different marketing jobs, (2) setting your own objectives and evaluating your interests and abilities, and (3) the kinds of jobs available in marketing.

MARKETING JOBS CAN PAY WELL

The supermarket bagger may earn only the minimum wage, but there are many more challenging jobs for those with marketing training.

Fortunately, marketing jobs open to college-level students do pay well! At the time this went to press, marketing undergraduates were being offered starting salaries ranging from $13,000 to $30,000 a year. Of course, these figures are extremes. Starting salaries can vary considerably—depending on your background, experience, and location.

As shown in Exhibit C–1, starting salaries in sales-marketing compare favorably with many other fields—although they are lower than those in such fields as engineering where college graduates are currently in very high demand. How far and fast your income rises above the starting level, however, depends on many factors—including your willingness to work, how well you get along with people, and your individual abilities. But most of all, it depends on *getting results*—individually and through other people. And this is where many marketing jobs offer the newcomer great opportunities. It is possible to show initiative, ability, and judgment in marketing jobs. And some young people move up very rapidly in marketing. Some even end up at the top in large companies—or as owners of their own businesses.

Marketing is often the route to the top

Marketing is where the action is! In the final analysis, a firm's success or failure depends on the effectiveness of its marketing program. This doesn't mean the other functional areas aren't important. It merely reflects the fact that a firm won't have much need for accountants, finance people, production managers, and so on if it can't successfully sell its products.

Because marketing is so vital to a firm's survival, many companies look for people with training and experience in marketing when filling key executive positions. A recent survey of the nation's largest corporations showed that the greatest proportion of chief executive officers had backgrounds in marketing and distribution (see Exhibit C–2).

Exhibit C–1   *Average Starting Salaries of 1985 College Graduates (with bachelor's degrees) in Selected Fields*

Field	Average starting salary (per year)
Engineering	$26,880
Chemistry	24,216
Computer Science	24,156
Mathematics or statistics	22,704
Accounting	20,628
Sales—marketing	20,616
Business administration	19,896
Liberal arts	18,828

Exhibit C–2   Main Career Emphasis of Corporate Chief Executive Officers*

Career emphasis	Percent
Marketing, distribution	27.9
Financial	25.3
Production, operations	18.6
Legal	13.6
Engineering, R&D	7.4
General management	5.3
Other	3.8

Percent

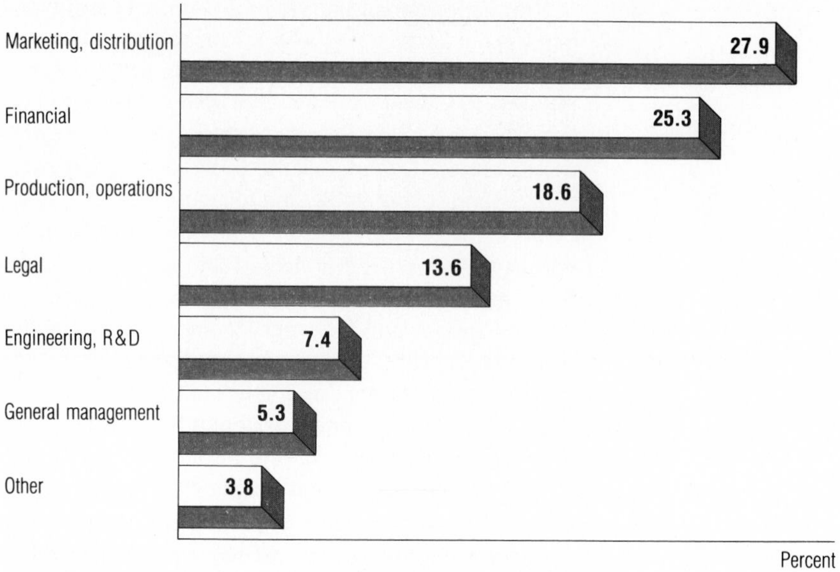

*Based on a survey of the chief executive officers of the nation's 500 largest industrial corporations and 300 non-industrial corporations (including commercial banks, life insurance firms, retailers, transportation companies, utilities, and diversified financial enterprises).

DEVELOP YOUR OWN PERSONAL MARKETING STRATEGY

Now that you know there are many opportunities in marketing, your problem is matching the opportunities to your own personal objectives and strengths. Basically the problem is a marketing problem: developing a marketing strategy to "sell" a product—yourself—to potential employers. Just as in planning strategies for products, developing your own strategy takes careful thought. Exhibit C–3 shows how you can organize your own strategy planning. This exhibit shows that you should evaluate yourself first—a personal analysis—and then analyze the environment for opportunities. This will help you sharpen your own long- and short-run objectives—which will lead to developing a strategy. And, finally, you should start implementing your own personal marketing strategy. These ideas are explained more fully below.

CONDUCT YOUR OWN PERSONAL ANALYSIS

You are the "Product" you are going to include in your own marketing plan. So first you have to decide what your long-run objectives are—what you want to do, how hard you want to work, and how quickly you want to reach your objectives. Be honest with yourself—or you will eventually face frustration. Evaluate your own personal strengths and weaknesses—and decide what factors may become the key to your success. Finally, as part of your personal

Exhibit C–3   Organizing Your Own Personal Marketing Strategy Planning

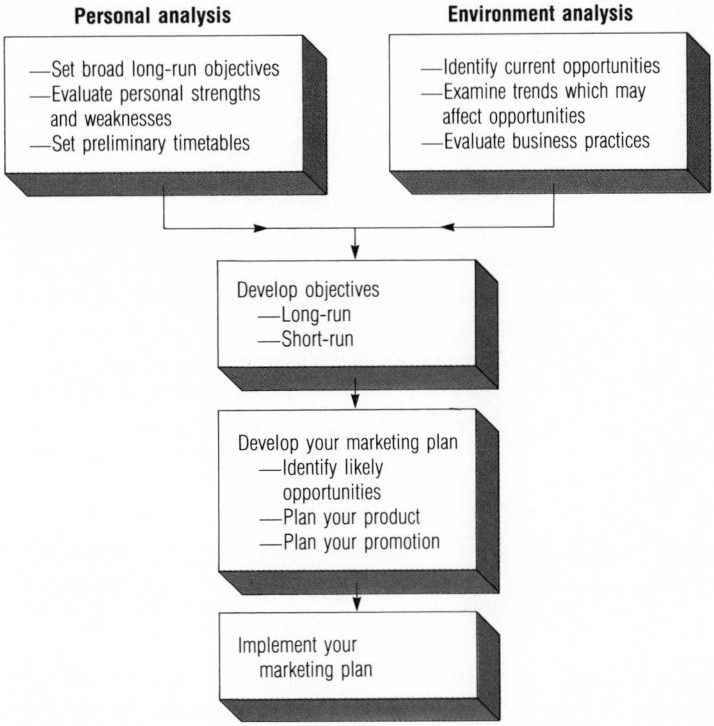

Personal analysis

- —Set broad long-run objectives
- —Evaluate personal strengths and weaknesses
- —Set preliminary timetables

Environment analysis

- —Identify current opportunities
- —Examine trends which may affect opportunities
- —Evaluate business practices

Develop objectives
- —Long-run
- —Short-run

Develop your marketing plan
- —Identify likely opportunities
- —Plan your product
- —Plan your promotion

Implement your marketing plan

analysis, set some preliminary timetables to guide your strategy planning and implementation efforts. Let's spell this out in detail.

Set broad long-run objectives

Strategy planning requires much "trial-and-error" decision making. But at the very beginning, you should make some tentative decisions about your own objectives—what you want out of a job—and out of life. At the very least, you should decide whether you are just looking for a "job"—or whether you want to build a "career." Beyond this, do you want the position to be personally satisfying—or is the financial return enough? And just how much financial return do you need—or are you willing to work for? Some people work only to support themselves and their leisure-time activities. Others work to support themselves and their families. These people seek only financial rewards from a job. They try to find job opportunities that provide adequate financial returns but aren't too demanding of their time or effort. Other people, however, look first for satisfaction in their job—and seek opportunities for career advancement. Financial rewards may be important, too, but these are used only as measures of success. In the extreme, the career-oriented individual may be willing to sacrifice a lot—including leisure and social activities—to achieve success in a career.

Once you've tentatively decided these matters, then you can get more serious about whether you should seek a job—or a career—in marketing. If you decide to pursue a career, you should set your broad long-run objectives to achieve it. For example, one long-run objective might be to pursue a career in marketing management (or marketing research). This might require more academic training than you planned—as well as a different kind of training.

Evaluate personal strengths and weaknesses

What kind of a job is right for you?

Because of the great variety of marketing jobs, it's hard to generalize about what aptitudes you need to pursue a career in marketing. Different jobs attract people with various interests and abilities. We'll give you some guidelines about what kinds of interests and abilities marketers should have. Note: If you're completely "lost" about your own interests and abilities, see your campus career counselor and take some vocational aptitude and interest tests. These tests will help you to compare yourself with people who are now working in various career positions. They will *not* tell you what you should do, but they can help—especially in eliminating possibilities you are less interested in and/or less able to do well.

Are you "people-oriented" or "thing-oriented?"

One of the first things you need to decide is whether you are basically "people-oriented" or "thing-oriented." This is a very important decision. A people-oriented person might be very unhappy in a bookkeeping job, for example, while a thing-oriented person might be miserable in a personal selling job that involves a lot of customer contact.

Marketing has both people-oriented and thing-oriented jobs. People-oriented jobs are primarily in the promotion area—where you must contact potential customers. This may be direct personal selling or customer service activities— for example, in technical service or installation and repair. Thing-oriented jobs focus more on creative activities and analyzing data—as in advertising and marketing research—or on organizing and scheduling work—as in operating warehouses, transportation agencies, or the "back-end" of retailers.

People-oriented jobs tend to pay more, in part because such jobs are more likely to affect sales—the life blood of any business. Thing-oriented jobs, on the other hand, are often seen as "cost-generators" rather than "sales-generators."

Thing-oriented jobs are usually done at a company's facilities. Further, especially in lower-level jobs, the amount of work to be done—and even the nature of the work—may be spelled out quite clearly. The time it takes to design questionnaires and tabulate results, for example, can be estimated with reasonable accuracy. Similarly, running a warehouse, totaling inventories, scheduling outgoing shipments, and so on are more like production operations. It's fairly easy to measure an employee's effectiveness and productivity in a thing-oriented job. At the least, time spent can be used to measure an employee's contribution.

A sales rep, on the other hand, might spend all weekend thinking and planning how to make a half-hour sales presentation on Monday. For what should the sales rep be compensated—the half-hour presentation, all of the planning and thinking that went into it, or the results? Typically, sales reps are rewarded for their sales results—and this helps account for the sometimes extremely high incomes earned by effective order getters. At the same time, some people-oriented jobs can be routinized and are lower paid. For example, sales clerks in some retail stores are paid at or near the minimum wage.

Managers needed for both kinds of jobs

Here we have oversimplified deliberately to emphasize the differences among types of jobs. Actually, of course, there are many variations between the two extremes. Some sales reps must do a great deal of analytical work before they make a presentation. Similarly, some marketing researchers must be extremely people-sensitive to get potential customers to reveal their true feelings. But the division is still useful—because it focuses on the primary emphasis in different kinds of jobs.

Managers are needed for the people in both kinds of jobs. Managing others requires a blend of both people and analytical skills—but people skills may be the more important of the two. Therefore, people-oriented persons are often promoted into managerial positions.

What will differenti-ate your "product"?

After deciding whether you're generally people-oriented or thing-oriented, you're ready for the next step—trying to identify your specific strengths (to be built on) and weaknesses (to be avoided or remedied). It is important to be as specific as possible so you can develop a better marketing plan. For example, if you decide you are more people-oriented, are you more skilled in verbal *or* in written communication? Or if you are more thing-oriented, what specific analytical or technical skills do you have? Are you good at working with numbers, solving complex problems, or coming to the root of a problem? Other possible strengths include past experience (career-related or otherwise), academic performance, an outgoing personality, enthusiasm, drive, motivation, and so on.

It is important to see that your plan should build on your strengths. An employer will be hiring you to do something—so "promote" yourself as someone who is able to do something *well.* In other words, find your "competitive advantage" in your unique strengths—and then "promote" these unique things about *you* and what you can do.

While trying to identify strengths, you also must realize that you may have some important weaknesses—depending on your objectives. If you are seeking a career that requires technical skills, for example, then you need to get these skills. Or if you are seeking a career that requires a lot of self-motivation and drive, then you should try to develop these characteristics in yourself—or change your objectives.

Set some timetables

At this point in your strategy planning, set some timetables—to organize your thinking and the rest of your planning. You need to make some decisions at this point to be sure you see where you're going. You might simply focus on getting your "first job," or you might decide to work on two marketing plans: (1) a short-run plan to get your first job and (2) a longer-run plan—perhaps a five-year plan—to show how you're going to accomplish your long-run objectives. People who are basically job-oriented may "get away with" only a short-run plan—just drifting from one opportunity to another as their own objectives and opportunities change. But those interested in careers need a longer-run plan. Otherwise, they may find themselves pursuing attractive first job opportunities that satisfy short-run objectives—but quickly leave them frustrated when they realize that they can't achieve their long-run objectives without additional training or other experiences.

ENVIRONMENT ANALYSIS

Strategy planning is a matching process. Here this means matching yourself to career opportunities. So let's look at opportunities available in the marketing environment. (The same approach applies, of course, in the whole business area.) Some of the possibilities and salary ranges are shown in Exhibit C–4.

Identifying current opportunities in marketing

Because of the wide range of opportunities in marketing, it's helpful to narrow your possibilities. After deciding on your own objectives, strengths, and weaknesses, think about where in the marketing system you might like to work. Would you like to work for producers, or wholesalers, or retailers? Or doesn't it really matter? Do you want to be involved with consumer products or industrial products? By analyzing your feelings about these possibilities, you can begin to zero in on the kind of job you might like most.

One simple way to get a better idea of the kinds of jobs available in marketing is to review the chapters of this text—this time with an eye for job opportunities rather than new concepts. The following paragraphs contain brief descriptions of job areas that marketing graduates are often interested in—with references to specific chapters in the text. Some, as noted below, offer good starting opportunities, while others do not. While reading these paragraphs, keep your own objectives, interests, and strengths in mind.

Marketing manager (Chapter 2)

This is usually not an entry-level job, although aggressive students may move quickly into this role in smaller companies.

Marketing research opportunities (Chapter 5)

There are entry-level opportunities at all levels in the channel (but especially in large firms where more formal marketing research is done) and in advertising agencies and marketing research firms. Quantitative and behavioral science skills are extremely important in marketing research. So many firms prefer to hire statistics or psychology graduates rather than business graduates. But there still are many opportunities in marketing research for marketing graduates. A recent graduate might begin in a training program—conducting interviews or summarizing open-ended answers from questionnaires—before being promoted to assistant project manager and subsequent management positions.

Exhibit C–4 Some Career Paths and Salary Ranges

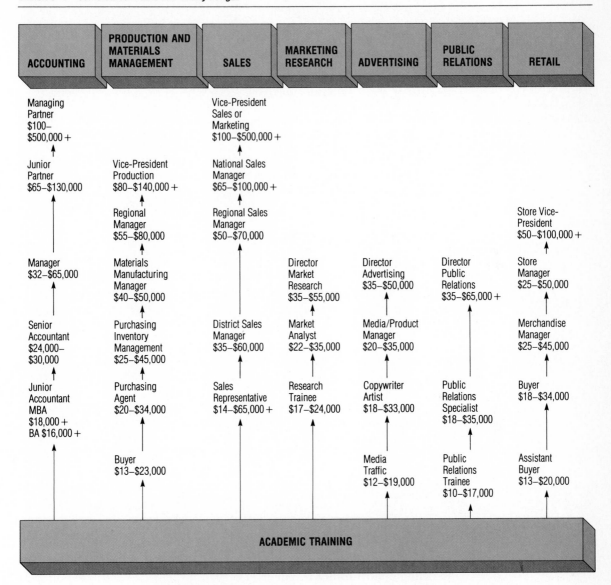

ACCOUNTING	PRODUCTION AND MATERIALS MANAGEMENT	SALES	MARKETING RESEARCH	ADVERTISING	PUBLIC RELATIONS	RETAIL
Managing Partner $100–$500,000 +		Vice-President Sales or Marketing $100–$500,000 +				
Junior Partner $65–$130,000	Vice-President Production $80–$140,000 +	National Sales Manager $65–$100,000 +				
	Regional Manager $55–$80,000	Regional Sales Manager $50–$70,000				Store Vice-President $50–$100,000 +
Manager $32–$65,000	Materials Manufacturing Manager $40–$50,000		Director Market Research $35–$55,000	Director Advertising $35–$50,000	Director Public Relations $35–$65,000 +	Store Manager $25–$50,000
Senior Accountant $24,000–$30,000	Purchasing Inventory Management $25–$45,000	District Sales Manager $35–$60,000	Market Analyst $22–$35,000	Media/Product Manager $20–$35,000		Merchandise Manager $25–$45,000
Junior Accountant MBA $18,000 + BA $16,000 +	Purchasing Agent $20–$34,000	Sales Representative $14–$65,000 +	Research Trainee $17–$24,000	Copywriter Artist $18–$33,000	Public Relations Specialist $18–$35,000	Buyer $18–$34,000
	Buyer $13–$23,000			Media Traffic $12–$19,000	Public Relations Trainee $10–$17,000	Assistant Buyer $13–$20,000

ACADEMIC TRAINING

Consumer researcher or market analyst (Chapters 3 and 5)

Opportunities as consumer analysts and market analysts are commonly found in large companies, marketing research organizations, and advertising agencies. Beginners start in thing-oriented jobs until their judgment and people-oriented skills are tested. Because knowledge of statistics and/or behavioral sciences is very important, marketing graduates often find themselves competing with majors in fields such as psychology, sociology, statistics, and computer science. Graduates who have courses in marketing *and* one or more of these areas may be preferred.

Purchasing agent/buyer (Chapter 7)

Opportunities are commonly found in large companies. Beginners start as trainees or assistant buyers under the supervision of experienced buyers.

Product planner (Chapter 9)

This is usually not an entry-level position. Instead, people with experience on the technical side of the business and/or in sales might be moved into new product development as they demonstrate judgment and analytical skills

Product/brand manager (Chapters 8 and 9)

Many multi-product firms have brand or product managers handling individual products—in effect, managing each product as a separate business. Some firms hire marketing graduates as assistant brand or product managers, although typically only MBAs are considered. Most firms prefer that recent graduates spend some time doing sales work before moving into brand or product management positions.

Packaging specialists (Chapter 8)

Packaging producers tend to hire and train interested people from various backgrounds—because there is little formal academic training in packaging. There are many sales opportunities in this field—and with training, interested people can become specialists fairly quickly in this growing area.

Distribution channel management (Chapter 10)

This work is typically handled or directed by sales managers—and therefore is not an entry-level position.

Retailing opportunities (Chapter 11)

Most entry-level marketing positions in retailing involve some kind of sales work. Retailing positions tend to offer lower-than-average starting salaries—but often provide opportunities for very rapid advancement. Most retailers require new employees to have some selling experience before managing others—or buying. A typical marketing graduate can expect to do some sales work and manage one or several departments before advancing to a store management position—or to a staff position that might involve buying, advertising, marketing research, and so on.

Physical distribution opportunities (Chapter 10)

There are many sales opportunities with physical distribution specialists—but there are also many thing-oriented jobs involving traffic management, warehousing, and materials handling. Here, training in accounting, finance, and quantitative methods could be very useful. These kinds of jobs are available at all levels in the channels of distribution. Remember that about half the cost of marketing comes from physical distribution activities.

Sales promotion opportunities (Chapter 13)

There are not many entry-level positions in this area. Creativity and judgment are required—and it is difficult for an inexperienced person to demonstrate these skills. A beginner would probably move from sales or advertising jobs into sales promotion.

Personal sales opportunities (Chapter 14)

Most of the job opportunities—especially entry-level jobs—are in personal selling. This might be order getting, order taking, or missionary sales. Many students are reluctant to get into personal selling—but this field offers benefits that are hard to match in any other field. These include the opportunity to earn extremely high salaries and commissions—quickly—a chance to develop your self-confidence and resourcefulness, an opportunity to work with minimal supervision—almost to the point of being your own boss—and a chance to acquire product and customer knowledge that many firms consider necessary for a successful career in product/brand management, sales management, and marketing management. Many salespeople spend their entire careers in selling—preferring the freedom and earning potential that go with a sales job over the headaches and sometimes lower salaries of sales management positions.

Advertising opportunities (Chapter 15)

Job opportunities are varied in this area—and highly competitive. And because the ability to communicate and knowledge of the behavioral sciences are important, marketing graduates often find themselves competing with majors from fields such as English, journalism, psychology, and sociology. There are thing-oriented jobs such as copywriting, media buying, art, and so on. And there are people-oriented positions involving sales—which are probably of more interest to marketing graduates. This is a glamorous, but small and extremely competitive industry where young people can rise very rapidly—but can also be as easily displaced by new "bright young people." Entry-level salaries in advertising are typically low.

Pricing opportunities (Chapters 16 and 17)

Pricing is generally handled by experienced managers, so there are no entry-level opportunities here. In fact, in some production-oriented companies pricing is not even handled by the sales or marketing people.

International marketing opportunities (Chapter 18)

Many marketing students are intrigued with the adventure and foreign travel promised by careers in international marketing. However, very few firms hire recent college graduates for positions in international marketing—except some MBA graduates from schools that specialize in international trade. Graduates aiming for a career in international marketing usually must spend time mastering the firm's domestic marketing operations before being sent abroad.

Customer relations/consumer affairs opportunities (Chapters 14 and 19)

Some firms are becoming more concerned about their relations with customers and the general public. Employees in this kind of work, however, usually have held various positions with the firm before doing customer relations.

Study trends that may affect your opportunities

A strategy planner should always be evaluating the future—because it's easier to go along with trends than to buck them. This means you should watch for political, technical, or economic changes that might open—or close—career opportunities.

If you can spot a trend early, you may be able to prepare yourself to take advantage of it as part of your long-run strategy planning. Other trends might mean you should avoid certain career options. For example, rapid technological changes in computers and communications are likely to lead to major changes in retailing and advertising—as well as in personal selling. Cable television, telephone selling, and direct-mail selling may reduce the need for routine order takers—while increasing the need for higher-level order getters. More targeted and imaginative sales presentations—to be delivered by mail and by phone or TV screen may be needed. The retailers who survive will need a better understanding of their target markets. And they will need to be supported by wholesalers and manufacturers who can plan targeted promotions that make economic sense. This will require a better understanding of the production and physical distribution side of business—as well as the financial side. And this means better training in accounting, finance, inventory control, and so on. So plan your personal strategy with such trends in mind.

Evaluate business practices

Finally, you need to know how businesses really operate—and the kind of training required for various jobs. We've already seen that there are many opportunities in marketing—but not all jobs are open to everyone, and not all jobs are entry jobs. Positions such as marketing manager, brand manager, and sales manager are higher rungs on the marketing career ladder. They become available only when you have a few years of experience—and have shown leadership and judgment. Some positions require more education than others. So take a hard look at your long-run objectives—and then see what you need for the kinds of opportunities you might like. Will a two-year degree get you where you want to go? Or will you need a four-year degree or even a graduate degree? Is a degree really necessary, or will it only be "helpful"—perhaps to make up for lack of experience or to speed your progress toward your objective?

DEVELOP OBJECTIVES

Once you've done a personal analysis and environment analysis—identifying your personal interests, strengths and weaknesses, and opportunities in the environment—you must define your objectives more specifically—both long-run and short-run.

Develop long-run objectives

Your long-run objectives should clearly state what you want to do—and what you will do for potential employers. You might be as specific as indicating the exact career area you want to pursue over the next 5 to 10 years. For example, your long-run objective might be to apply marketing research and marketing management tools in the food processing industry—with the objective of becoming director of marketing research in a small food company.

Your long-run objectives should be realistic and attainable. They should be objectives for which you think you have the necessary skills (or the capabilities to develop those skills) as well as the necessary motivation.

Develop short-run objectives

To achieve your long-run objective(s), you should develop one or more short-run objectives. These should spell out what is needed to reach your long-run objective(s). For example, you might need to develop a variety of marketing research skills *and* marketing management skills—because both are needed to reach the longer-run objective. Or you might need an entry-level position in marketing research with a large food processor—to gain experience and background. An even shorter-run objective might be to take the academic courses that are necessary to get that desired entry-level job. In this example, you would probably need a minimum of an undergraduate degree in marketing—with an emphasis on marketing research. (Note that, given the longer-run objective of managerial responsibility, a business degree would probably be better than a degree in statistics or psychology.)

DEVELOPING YOUR MARKETING PLAN

Now that you've developed your objectives, move on to developing your own personal marketing plan. This means zeroing in on likely opportunities and developing a specific marketing strategy for these opportunities. Let's talk about that now.

Identify likely opportunities

An important step in strategy planning is identifying potentially attractive opportunities. Depending on where you are in your academic training, this can vary all the way from preliminary exploration to making detailed lists of companies that offer the kinds of jobs that interest you. If you're just getting started, talk to your school's career counselors and placement officers about the kinds of jobs being offered to your school's graduates. Your marketing instructors can help you be more realistic about ways you can match your training, abilities, and interests to job opportunities. Also, it helps to read business publications such as *Business Week, Fortune, The Wall Street Journal, Sales & Marketing Management,* and *Advertising Age.* Don't overlook the business sections of your local newspapers to keep in touch with marketing developments in your area. And take advantage of any opportunity to talk with marketers directly. Ask them what they're doing—and what satisfactions they find in their jobs. Also, if your college has a marketing club, join it and participate actively in the club's programs. It will help you meet marketers and students with serious interest in the field. Some may have had interesting job experiences and can provide you with leads on part-time jobs or exciting career opportunities.

If you're far along in your present academic training, list companies that you know something about or are willing to investigate—trying to match your skills and interests with possible opportunities. Narrow your list to a few companies you might like to work for.

If you have trouble narrowing down to specific companies, make a list of your personal interest areas—sports, travel, reading, music, or whatever. Think about the companies that compete in markets related to these interests. Often your own knowledge about these areas—and interest in them—can give you a competitive advantage in getting a job. This helps you focus on companies that serve needs you think are important or interesting.

Then do some research on these companies. Find out how they are organized, their product lines, and their strategies. Try to get clear job descriptions for the kinds of positions you're seeking. Match these job descriptions against your understanding of these jobs and your objectives. Jobs with similar titles may offer very different opportunities. By researching job positions and companies in depth, you will begin to have a feel for where you will be comfortable as an employee. This will help you narrow your "target market" of possible employers to perhaps five firms. For example, you may decide that your "target market" for an entry position is large corporations with: (1) in-depth training programs, (2) a wide product line, and (3) a wide variety of marketing jobs that will enable you to get a range of experiences and responsibilities within the same company.

Planning your "Product"

Just like any strategy planner, you must decide what "Product" features are necessary to appeal to your target market. Identify which "credentials" are mandatory—and which are optional. For example, is your present academic program enough, or will you need more training? Also, identify what technical skills are needed—such as computer programming or accounting. Further, are there any business experiences or extra-curricular activities that might help make your "Product" more attractive to employers? This might involve active participation in college organizations—or work experience—either on the job or in internships.

Planning your Promotion

Once you identify target companies and develop a Product you hope will be attractive to them, you have to tell these potential customers about your Product. You can write directly to prospective employers—sending a carefully developed resumé that reflects your strategy planning. Or you can visit them in person (with your resumé). Many colleges run well-organized interviewing services. Seek their advice early in your strategy planning effort.

IMPLEMENTING YOUR MARKETING PLAN

When you complete your personal marketing plan, you have to implement it—starting with working to accomplish your short-run objectives. If, as part of your plan, you decide that you need specific outside experience—then arrange to get it. This may mean taking a "low-paying" job—or even volunteering to work in political organizations or volunteer organizations where you can get that kind of experience. If you decide that you need skills you can learn in academic courses, plan to take these courses. Similarly, if you don't have a good understanding of your opportunities, then learn as much as you can about possible jobs—by talking to professors, taking advanced courses, and talking to business people. And, of course, trends and opportunities can change—so continue to read business publications, talk with professionals in your areas of interest, and be sure that the planning you've done still makes sense.

Strategy planning must adapt to the environment. If the environment changes or your personal objectives change, you have to develop a new plan. This is an ongoing process—and you may never be completely satisfied with your strategy planning. But even trying will make you look much more impressive when you begin your job interviews. Remember, while all employers would like to hire a "Superman" or a "Wonder Woman," they are also impressed with candidates who know what they want to do and are looking for a place where they can fit in—and make a contribution. So planning a personal strategy and implementing it almost guarantee you'll do a better job of career planning, and this will help ensure that you reach your own objectives—whatever they are.

Whether or not you decide to pursue a marketing career, the authors wish you the best of luck in your search for a challenging and rewarding career—wherever your interests and abilities may take you.

Cases

GUIDE TO THE USE OF THESE CASES

Cases can be used in many ways. And the same case can be analyzed several times for different purposes.

"Suggested cases" are listed at the end of most chapters, but these cases can also be used later in the text. The main criterion for the order of the cases is the amount of technical vocabulary—or text principles—that are needed to read the case meaningfully. The first cases are easiest in this regard. This is why an early case can easily be used two or three times—with different emphasis. Some early cases might require some consideration of Product and Price, for example, and might be used twice, perhaps in regard to place planning and later pricing. In contrast, later cases that focus more on Price might be treated more effectively *after* the Price chapters are covered.

1.   McDonald's

Wilma Ming manages a McDonald's restaurant. She has noticed that some senior citizens have become not just regular patrons—but patrons who come for breakfast and stay on until about 3 P.M. Many of these older customers were attracted initially by a monthly breakfast special for people aged 55 and older. The meal costs $.99, and coffee refills are free. Every fourth Monday, between 100 and 150 seniors jam Wilma's McDonald's for the special offer. But now almost as many of them are coming every day—turning the fast-food restaurant into a meeting place. They sit for hours with a cup of coffee, chatting with friends. On most days, as many as 100 will stay from one to five hours.

About a year ago, as a "goodwill" gesture, Wilma brought in a team from the American Red Cross to check her regular customers' blood pressure—free of charge. Wilma's employees have been very friendly to the seniors, calling them by their first names and visiting with them each day. In fact, Wilma's McDonald's is a "happy place"—and her employees have developed close relationships with the seniors. Some employees have even visited customers who have been hospitalized. "You know," Wilma says, "I really get attached to the customers. They're like my family. I really care about these people." They are all "friends," and being friendly with the customers is a part of McDonald's corporate philosophy.

These older customers are an orderly group—and very friendly to anyone who comes in. Further, they are neater than most customers and carefully clean up their tables before they leave. Nevertheless, Wilma is beginning to wonder if anything should be done about her growing "non-fast-food" clientele. There's no crowding problem yet during the time when the seniors like to come. But if the size of the senior citizens group continues to grow, crowding could become a problem. Further, Wilma is concerned that her restaurant might come to be known as an "old people's" restaurant—which might discourage some younger customers. And if customers feel the restaurant is crowded, some might think that they wouldn't get fast service. On the other hand, a place that seems busy might be seen as "a good place to go" and a "friendly place."

Wilma also worries about the image she's projecting. McDonald's is a "fast-food restaurant," and normally customers are expected to "eat and run." Will encouraging—or not discouraging—people to stay and visit change the whole concept? In the extreme, Wilma's McDonald's might become more like a "European style" restaurant where the customers are never rushed—and feel very comfortable lingering over coffee for an hour or two! Wilma Ming knows that the amount her senior customers spend is similar to the average customer's purchase—but the seniors do use the facilities for a much longer time. However, most of the older customers leave McDonald's by 3—before the "after school" crowd comes in.

Evaluate Wilma Ming's current strategy with respect to the senior citizens. Does her current strategy enhance McDonald's image? What should she do about the senior citizen market—i.e., should she encourage, ignore, or discourage her seniors? Explain.

2.   West Foods, Inc.

It is now 1986, and Ken McDonald, newly elected president of West Foods, Inc., faces some serious problems. West Foods is a 115-year-old California-based food processor. Its multi-product lines are widely accepted under the "West" brand. The company and subsidiaries prepare, can, package, and sell canned and frozen foods—including fruits, vegetables, pickles, and condiments. West, which operates more than 27 processing plants in the United States, is one of the largest U.S. food processors—with annual sales (in 1985) of about $600 million.

Until 1983, West Foods was a subsidiary of a major midwestern food processor (Betty, Inc.), and many of the present managers came from the parent company. West's last president recently said: "Betty's influence is still with us. As long as new products show a potential for increasing the company's sales volume, we produce them. Traditionally, there has been little, if any, attention paid to margins. We are well aware that profits will come through good products.''

Bill Watson, a 25-year employee and now production manager, fully agrees with the multi-product-line policy. Mr. Watson says: "Volume comes from satisfying needs. We will can, pack, or freeze any vegetable or fruit we think the consumer might want." He also admits that much of the expansion in product lines was encouraged by economics. The typical plants in the industry are not fully used. By adding new products to use this excess capacity, costs are spread over greater volume. So the production department is always looking for new ways to make more effective use of its present facilities.

The wide expansion of product lines coupled with West's line-forcing policy has resulted in 85 percent of the firm's sales coming from supermarket chain stores—such as Safeway, Kroger, and A&P. Smaller stores are generally not willing to accept the West policy—which requires that any store wanting to carry its brand name must be willing to carry the whole line of 68 varieties of fruits and vegetables. Mr. Watson explains, "We know that only large stores can afford to invest the amount of money in inventory that it would take to adequately stock our products. But the large stores are the volume! We give consumers the choice of any West product they want, and the result is maximum sales." Many small retailers have complained about West's policy, but they have been considered to be too small in potential sales volume per store to be of any significance.

In 1986, a stockholders' revolt over low profits (in 1985, they were only $50,000) resulted in the removal of West's president and two of its five directors. Ken McDonald, a lawyer who had been a staff assistant to the chairman of the board, was elected president. One of the first things he decided to focus on was the variable and low levels of profits earned in the past several years. A comparison of West's results with comparable operations of some large competitors supported

Mr. McDonald's concern. In the past 10 years, West's closest competitors had an average profit return on shareholder's investment of 6 to 12 percent, while West averaged only 3.8 percent. Further, West's sales volume, $600 million in 1985, had not increased much from the 1956 level (after adjusting for inflation)—while operating costs soared upward. Profits for the firm were about $8 million in 1956. The closest they came since then was about $6 million—in 1964.

The outgoing president blamed his failure on an inefficient marketing department. He said, "Our marketing department has deteriorated. I can't exactly put my finger on it, but the overall quality of marketing people has dropped, and morale is bad. The team just didn't perform." When Mr. McDonald confronted Ron Frank—the vice president of marketing—with this charge, his reply was, "It's not our fault. I think the company made a key mistake after World War II. It expanded horizontally—by increasing its number of product offerings—while major competitors were expanding vertically, growing their own raw materials and making all of their packing materials. They can control quality and make profits in manufacturing that can be used in marketing. I lost some of my best people from frustration. We just aren't competitive enough to reach the market the way we should with a comparable product and price."

In further conversation with Ron Frank, Mr. McDonald learned more about the nature of West's market. Although all the firms in the food-processing industry advertise heavily, the size of the market for most processed foods hasn't grown much. Further, consumers aren't very selective. If they can't find the brand of food they are looking for, they'll pick up another brand rather than go without a basic part of their diet. No company in the industry has much effect on the price at which its products are sold. Chain store buyers are used to paying about the same price per case for any competitor's product—and won't exceed it. They will, however, charge any price they wish on a given brand sold at retail. (That is, a 48-can case of sweet peas might be purchased from any supplier for $17.60, no matter whose product it is. Generally, the shelf price for each is no more than a few pennies different, but chain stores occasionally attract customers by placing a well-known brand on "sale.")

At this point, Mr. McDonald is wondering why West Foods isn't as profitable as it once was. Also, he is puzzled as to why the competition is putting products on the market with low potential sales volume. For example, one major competitor recently introduced a line of "gourmet" fruits and vegetables.

Evaluate West Foods' situation. What should Mr. McDonald do to improve West's situation? Explain.

3. Sears' Discover Card

Sears, Roebuck launched its Discover card in 1985. The company sees the Discover as more than "just another credit card" like VISA, Master-Card, and American Express. Sears envisions the new card as a "financial services card," which can serve not only as a credit card—with all of the usual extra services—but also as access to Sears' various financial and insurance subsidiaries. These include savings accounts and automatic teller machines, as well as individual retirement accounts. Longer term, Discover may supply a full range of banking services and stock and bond sales through Sears' Dean Witter brokerage group.

Sears hoped that Discover would break even in about three years, but industry analysts estimate that the venture lost $25 to $35 million in 1985—and probably more than $100 million in 1986. And even more losses are expected before the card is well entrenched in an already competitive market.

Sears seems quite willing to invest in Discover because the possible returns are so big. The total U.S. retail credit charge market is estimated at over $200 billion per year. And cardholders normally pay interest of 18 to 22 percent, while the cost of funds is under 8 percent. Further, Sears is not a newcomer to the charge card business.

There are 60 million Sears charge card owners—making Sears the country's largest single provider of revolving credit.

Initial promotion plans called for Discover to solicit Sears credit cardholders. Early returns indicate that more that 25 percent of those offered a card accept it. In addition to targeting present Sears credit cardholders, Sears used aggressive advertising on television as well as ads in newspapers and major news magazines. The initial promotion in Georgia, for example, was so aggressive that almost all of the state's consumers were exposed to multiple Discover "messages." Sears also promoted the card by telephone—and solicited new holders when they applied for a regular Sears card.

To attract customers in the initial promotion effort, Sears offered Discover cards free of charge—compared with an average fee of about $20 for most bankcards and $45 for American Express. In addition, Discover offered a 1 percent "dividend" on every Discover charge purchase. These dividends could be used for gift certificates for Sears merchandise—deposited in a Discover Saver's account—or even credited to the Discover card account to reduce the balance. As further inducement, Discover offered coupons worth hundreds of dollars in services. $100 in Sears car services were offered for $9.99. And a $30 discount was offered off any Sears catalog purchase. Further, Discover offered 25 percent off a first-year membership in the Allstate Motor Club. In addition, special discounts were offered from various service suppliers—for example, Budget Rent-A-Car offered 15 percent off. And, as an extra service, $100,000 travel accident insurance coverage is offered to any card member traveling on a common carrier—providing tickets are charged to the member's Discover card. This insurance coverage is provided automatically by a Sears subsidiary—Allstate Life Insurance Co.

Some bankers feared the Discover card would try to "buy" market share by offering a "below the market" interest rate. But Sears did not do this, in part because it would undercut the standard Sears credit card—which carries an average 19.35 percent interest rate and is a major profit source for Sears. In fact, Sears charged 19.8 percent nationwide on Discover credit balances.

Sears *is* meeting or undercutting competition when signing up retailers, however. Normally, retail merchants pay 2 percent to 5 percent of a transaction's value for bankcards and up to 7 percent for American Express. By undercutting the normal charges, Discover's sales force was able to sign up many small retailers as well as major chains, such as Days Inns of America, Inc., Holiday Corporation (operator of Holiday Inns), some major airlines, Montgomery Ward, F. W. Woolworth, and some units of Dayton-Hudson. Some major hold-outs were retailers who saw Sears as a direct competitor. Sears promised to keep Discover transactions out of the hands of its merchandise group, but many large retailers were still concerned that Sears might learn too much about their business.

Two years after the introduction of Discover, Sears remains optimistic about its new "financial services card." Sears feels that more and more people will begin to change the way they think about credit cards—and come to regard Sears' Discover card as *the* "one-stop" financial services card. And, although the initial promotion thrust emphasized the usual credit card features, Sears seems to be willing to spend much more than industry experts expected to "buy" market share in the "financial services market."

Evaluate Sears' introductory strategy for its Discover card. Will it succeed? Explain.

4.   *Block Services, Inc.*

Bill Block is frustrated in his new business. He's not sure he can make a go of it—and he really wants to stay in his hometown of Traverse City, Michigan. This is a beautiful summer resort area along the eastern shore of Lake Michigan. The area's permanent population of 25,000 more than triples in the summer months.

Bill spent seven years in the Navy after high school graduation, returning home in June 1981. He decided to go into business for himself be-

cause he couldn't find a good job in the Traverse City area. He set up Block Services, Inc. He thought that his savings would allow him to start the business without borrowing any money. His estimates of required expenditures were: $5,600 for a used panel truck, $525 for a steam-cleaning machine adaptable to carpets and furniture, $375 for a heavy-duty commercial vacuum cleaner, $50 for special brushes and attachments, $75 for the initial supply of cleaning fluids and compounds, and $200 for insurance and other incidental expenses. This total of $6,825 still left Bill with about $2,800 in savings to cover living expenses while getting started.

One of the reasons Bill chose the cleaning business was his previous work experience. From the time he was 16, Bill had worked part-time for Joel Bullard. Mr. Bullard operates the only other successful carpet-cleaning company in Traverse City. There is one other company in Traverse City, but it is rumored to be near bankruptcy.

Mr. Bullard prides himself on quality work and has a loyal clientele. Specializing in residential carpet cleaning, Bullard has built a strong customer franchise. For 35 years, Bullard's major source of new business—besides retailer recommendations—has been satisfied customers who tell friends about the quality service received from Mr. Bullard. He is so highly thought of that the leading carpet and furniture stores in Traverse City always recommend Bullard's for preventive maintenance in quality carpet and furniture care. Often Bullard is trusted with the keys to Traverse City's finest homes for months at a time—when owners are out-of-town and want his services. Bullard's customers are so loyal, in fact, that Vita-Clean—a national household carpet-cleaning franchise—found it impossible to compete with him. Even price cutting was not an effective weapon against Mr. Bullard.

Bill Block thought that he knew the business as well as Mr. Bullard—having worked for him many years. Bill was anxious to reach his $50,000-per-year sales objective because he thought this would provide him with a comfortable living in Traverse City. While aware of opportunities for carpet cleaning in businesses like office buildings and motels, Bill felt that the sales volume available there was only about $20,000 because most businesses had their own cleaning staffs. As Bill saw it, his only opportunity was direct competition with Bullard.

To get started, he allocated $800 to advertise his business in the local newspaper. With this money he bought two large "announcement" ads and 52 weeks of daily three-line ads in the classified section—listed under Miscellaneous Residential Services. All that was left was to paint a sign on his truck and wait for business to "take off."

Bill had a few customers and was able to gross about $100 a week. Of course, he had expected much more. These customers were usually Bullard regulars who, for one reason or another (usually stains, spills, or house guests), weren't able to wait the two weeks until Bullard could work them in. While these people agreed that Bill's work was of the same quality as Mr. Bullard's, they preferred Bullard's "quality-care" image. Sometimes Bill did get more work than he could handle. This happened during April and May—when resort owners were preparing for summer openings and owners of summer homes were ready to "open the cottage." The same rush occurred in September and October—as resorts and homes were being closed for the winter. During these months, Bill was able to gross about $100 to $120 a day—working 10 hours.

Toward the end of his discouraging first year in business, Bill Block is thinking about quitting. While he hates to think about leaving Traverse City, he can't see any way of making a living in the carpet- and furniture-cleaning business in Traverse City. Mr. Bullard has the whole residential market sewed up—except in the rush seasons and for people who need emergency cleaning.

Why wasn't Bill Block able to reach his objective of $50,000? What should Bill do?

5. TOW Chemical Company

Brian Long, a research engineer in TOW Chemical Company's polymer resins laboratory, is trying to decide how hard to fight for the new product he has developed. Brian's job is to find new, more profitable applications for the company's present resin products—and his current efforts are running into unexpected problems.

During the last five years, Brian has been under heavy pressure from top management to come up with an idea that will open up new markets for the company's foamed polystyrene.

Two years ago, Brian developed the "spiral-dome concept"—a method of using the foamed polystyrene to make dome-shaped roofs and other structures. He described the procedure for making domes as follows: The construction of a spiral dome involves the use of a specially designed machine that bends, places, and bonds pieces of plastic foam together into a predetermined dome shape. In forming a dome, the machine head is mounted on a boom, which swings around a pivot like the hands of a clock, laying and bonding layer upon layer of foam board in a rising spherical form.

According to Brian, polystyrene foamed boards have several advantages:

1. Foam board is stiff—but can be formed or bonded to itself by heat alone.
2. Foam board is extremely lightweight and easy to handle. It has good structural rigidity.
3. Foam board has excellent and permanent insulating characteristics. (In fact, the major use for foamed board is as an insulator.)
4. Foam board provides an excellent base on which to apply a variety of surface finishes.

Using his good selling abilities, Brian easily convinced top management that his idea had potential.

According to a preliminary study by the marketing department, the following were areas of construction that could be served by the domes:

1. Bulk storage.
2. Cold storage.
3. Educational construction.
4. Industrial tanks (covers for).
5. Light commercial construction.
6. Planetariums.
7. Recreational construction (such as a golf course starter house).

The study focused on uses for existing dome structures. Most of the existing domes are made of concrete or some cement base material. The study showed that large savings would result from using foam boards—due to the reduction of construction time.

Because of the new technology involved, the company decided to do its own contracting (at least for the first four to five years after starting the sales program). Brian thought this was necessary to make sure that no mistakes were made by inexperienced contractor crews. (For example, if not applied properly, the plastic may burn.)

After building a few domes to demonstrate the concept, Brian contacted some leading architects across the country. Reactions were as follows:

It's very interesting, but we're not sure the fire marshall of Chicago would ever give his OK.

Your tests show that foamed domes can be protected against fires, but there are no *good* tests for unconventional building materials as far as I am concerned.

I like the idea, but foam board does not have the impact resistance of cement.

We design a lot of recreational facilities, and kids will find a way of poking holes in the foam.

Building codes in our area are written for wood and cement structures. Maybe when the codes change.

After this unexpected reaction, management didn't know what to do. Brian still thinks TOW should go ahead. He is convinced that a few reports of well-constructed domes in leading newspapers will go a long way toward selling the idea. But his managers aren't sure they want to OK spending more money on "his" product.

What should Brian do? What should TOW Chemical do? Explain how TOW Chemical got into the present situation.

6. Applegate Chevrolet

Joe Travis, general manager of the Applegate Chevrolet dealership, must decide if he should seek the Yugo franchise for his area. The Yugo car is produced in Yugoslavia and sells in the United States for about $4,000—which is several thousand dollars below most "small" cars. Joe knows that the Yugo is quite small and perhaps not as well-built as some of the Japanese small cars, but he thinks the low price will attract some customers. Further, Joe is greatly concerned about selling only U.S. cars because foreign producers seem to be getting a larger and larger share of the car market. Their costs—and prices—are much lower than U.S. cars.

Joe's dealership is located in Petoskey, Michigan. Petoskey has a metro area population of about 10,000 that swells to over 50,000 in the tourist seasons. This isn't a large market, but most of the major auto producers—both domestic and foreign—are represented. So Joe's choice of a foreign franchise is Yugo or some South Korean lines that are entering the U.S. market. Joe is giving the Yugo brand more serious consideration because of the much lower price—which has received a lot of media attention. Joe feels this publicity may help speed acceptance of the car in the U.S. market

Joe is also considering adding another car line because there is a national movement toward the development of "super-dealers" or "mega-dealers" who sell up to a dozen different brands of cars from different manufacturers—in multiple locations. Some industry analysts are suggesting that the day of the "Ma and Pa" operations are about over. Joe is concerned that he may have to grow internally by adding lines, or buy other dealerships, or be squeezed out as competing dealers add to their lines. Economies of scale will allow these "mega-dealers" to promote more effectively and provide service at lower cost—thereby enabling them to lower prices. Some industry experts are already comparing the "neighborhood dealers"—like Joe—to the corner grocery stores that were driven out by supermarkets after World War II.

The "super-dealers" already sell over 15 percent of all cars in the U.S., and it is expected that this number may go to 30 percent by 1990. This is already shifting some of the power in the industry toward the super-dealers—forcing the Big Three U.S. auto makers to be more cooperative with dealers. The producers aren't blocking dealers like Jim from adding foreign car lines. In fact, it is estimated that about one-third of all U.S. auto dealers now sell both foreign and domestic cars, although Joe's dealership would be the first domestic dealer in Petoskey to take on a foreign line. All of the other foreign lines in the area are handled exclusively by dealers who specialize in one or more foreign lines.

Joe is becoming quite positive about taking on the Yugo line. He has some extra space on his lot (although there would be little or no extra space in his showroom). He also feels that his salespeople could easily handle another line—especially since the primary emphasis would be on the much lower price. Joe's mechanics say they would be able to handle the necessary warranty work and repairs without too much difficulty. Further, Joe would only have to carry a few Yugos to have an adequate display because the company only produces a very basic car with few options.

Joe's major doubts about taking on the Yugo line are: (1) whether it will take too many managerial resources in relation to the likely profit and (2) whether it may affect his image as a "quality" dealer. On the first concern, he is worried that profit as a percentage of sales is usually only 2 to 3 percent in the car business—so there will be a relatively low dollar profit on a $4,000 sale. Further, there is the possibility that some of his "low-end" customers might buy a Yugo instead of a Chevrolet—resulting in a lower profit per car sold.

With respect to his second concern—a quality image—Joe feels that his regular customers are basically rather conservative people who have "bought American" for many years. He knows that many of them won't switch from an American product. But he is aware that some of his formerly "loyal" customers have purchased foreign cars in recent years. By offering the lowest-priced car on the market, Joe might attract some of these people back—as well as some new customers who are shopping for the most economi-

cal car. He sees the possibility of increasing sales by appealing to these price-conscious shoppers who would not otherwise buy from him. And Joe thinks that his salesmen could probably deflect the criticisms of some of his "buy American" customers by simply joking about how "some people always want to buy the *cheapest* product and that's what they are going to get if they buy a Yugo."

Evaluate Joe's present strategy and current line of thinking about adding the Yugo car. What should he do?

7. *Inland Steel Company*

Inland Steel Company is one of the two major producers of wide-flange beams in the Chicago area. The other major producer in the area is the U.S. Steel Corporation (now USX)—which is several times larger than Inland in terms of production capacity on this particular product. Bethlehem Steel Company and U.S. Steel have eastern plants that also produce this product. There are some small competitors, but generally, U.S. Steel and Inland Steel are the major competitors in wide-flange beams in the Chicago area— because typically the mill price charged by all producers is the same and customers must pay freight from the mill. Therefore, the large eastern mills' delivered prices wouldn't be competitive in the Chicago area.

Wide-flange beams are one of the principal steel products used in construction. They are the modern version of what are commonly known as "I-beams." U.S. Steel rolls a full range of wide flanges from 6 to 36 inches. Inland entered the field about 25 years ago—when it converted an existing mill to produce this product. Inland's mill is limited to flanges up to 24 inches, however. At the time of the conversion, Inland felt that customer usage of sizes over 24 inches was likely to be small. In the past few years, however, there has been a definite trend toward the larger and heavier sections.

The beams produced by the various competitors are almost identical— since customers buy according to standard dimensional and physical-property specifications. In the smaller size range, there are a number of competitors. But above 14 inches only U.S. Steel and Inland compete in the Chicago area. Above 24 inches, U.S. Steel has had no competition.

All the steel companies sell these beams through their own sales forces. The customer for these beams is called a "structural fabricator." This fabricator typically buys unshaped beams and other steel products from the mills and shapes them according to the specifications of each customer. The fabricator sells to the contractor or owner of a building or structure being built.

The structural fabricator usually sells on a competitive-bid basis. The bidding is done on the plans and specifications prepared by an architectural or structural engineering firm—and forwarded to him by the contractor who wants the bid. Although several hundred structural fabricators compete in the region, relatively few account for the majority of wide-flange tonnage. Since the price is the same from all producers, they typically buy beams on the basis of availability (i.e., availability to meet production schedules) and performance (i.e., reliability in meeting the promised delivery schedule).

Several years ago, Inland production schedulers saw that they were going to have an excess of hot-rolled plate capacity in the near future. At the same time, a new production technique was developed that would enable a steel company to weld three plates together into a section with the same dimensional and physical properties and almost the same cross-section as a rolled wide-flange beam. This technical development appeared to offer two advantages to Inland. (1) It would enable Inland to use some of the excess plate capacity. (2) Larger sizes of wide-flange beams could be offered. Cost analysts showed that by using a fully depreciated plate mill and the new welding process it would be possible to produce and sell larger wide-flange beams at competitive prices—i.e., at the same price charged by U.S. Steel.

Inland's managers were excited about the possibilities—because customers usually appreciate having a second source of supply. Also, the new approach would allow the production of up to a 60-inch flange. With a little imagination, these larger sizes might offer a significant breakthrough for the construction industry.

Inland decided to go ahead with the new project. As the production capacity was being converted, the salespeople were kept well informed of the progress. They, in turn, promoted this new capability to their customers—emphasizing that soon they would be able to offer a full range of beam products. Several general information letters were sent to a broad mailing list, but no advertising was used. The market development section of the sales department was very busy explaining the new possibilities of the process—particularly to fabricators—at engineering trade associations and shows.

When the new production line was finally ready to go, the market reaction was disappointing. In general, the customers were wary of the new product. The structural fabricators felt they couldn't use it without the approval of their customers—because it would involve deviating from the specified rolled sections. And, as long as they could still get the rolled section, why make the extra effort for something unfamiliar—especially with no price advantage. The salespeople were also bothered with a very common question: How can you take plate that you sell for about $450 per ton and make a product that you can sell for $460? This question came up frequently and tended to divert the whole discussion to the cost of production—rather than to the way the new product might be used.

Evaluate Inland's situation. What should Inland do?

8.   *Tony's Place*

Tony DeLuca, the owner of Tony's Place, is reviewing the slow growth of his restaurant. He's also thinking about the future and wondering if he should change his strategy. Tony's Place is a fairly large restaurant—about 20,000 square feet—located in the center of a small shopping center that was completed early in 1984. In addition to Tony's restaurant, other businesses in the shopping center include a bakery, a beauty shop, a liquor store, and a meat market. Ample parking space is available.

The shopping center is located in a residential section of a growing suburb in the East—along a heavily traveled major traffic artery. The nearby population is middle-income families. Although the ethnic background of the residents is fairly heterogeneous, a large proportion are Italians.

Tony's Place sells mostly full-course dinners (no bar) and is owned and managed by Tony DeLuca. He graduated from a local high school and a nearby university and has lived in this town with his wife and two children for many years. He has been in the restaurant business (self-employed) since his graduation from college in 1956. His most recent venture—before opening Tony's Place—was a large restaurant that he operated successfully with his brother from 1974 to 1980. In 1980, Tony sold out his share because of illness. Following his recovery, Tony was anxious for something to do and opened the present restaurant in April 1984.

Tony feels his plans for the business and his opening were well thought out. When he was ready to start his new restaurant, he looked at several possible locations before finally deciding on the present one. Tony explained: "I looked everywhere, and this is one of the areas I inspected. I particularly noticed the heavy traffic when I first looked at it. This is the crossroads from north to south for practically every main artery statewide. So obviously the potential is here."

Having decided on the location, Tony eagerly attacked the problem of the new building. He tiled the floor, put in walls of surfwood, installed new plumbing and electrical fixtures and an extra washroom, and purchased the necessary restaurant equipment. All this cost $60,000—which came from his own cash savings. He then spent an additional $1,200 for glassware, $2,000 for his initial food stock, and $1,525 to advertise his opening in the local newspaper. The paper served the whole metro area, so the $1,525 bought only three quarter-page ads. These expenditures also came from his own personal savings. Next, he hired five waitresses at $100 a week and one chef at $250 a week. Then, with $15,000 cash reserve for the business, he was ready to open. (His wife—a high school teacher—was willing to support the family until the restaurant caught on.) Reflecting his "sound business sense," Tony knew he would need a substantial cash reserve to fall back on until the business got on its feet. He expected this to take about one year. He had no expectations of "getting rich overnight."

The restaurant opened in April and by August had a weekly gross revenue of only $1,500. Tony was a little discouraged with this, but he was still able to meet all his operating expenses without investing any "new money" in the business. By September business was still slow, and Tony had to invest an additional $1,500 in the business "for survival purposes."

Business had not improved in November, and Tony stepped up his advertising—hoping this would help. In December, he spent $500 of his cash reserve for radio advertising—10 late evening spots on a news program at a station that aims at "middle-income America." Tony also spent $1,000 more during the next several weeks for some metro newspaper ads.

By April 1985, the situation had begun to improve, and by June his weekly gross was up to between $2,000 and $2,100. By March of 1986, the weekly gross had risen to about $2,500. Tony increased the working hours of his staff six to seven hours a week—and added another cook to handle the increasing number of customers. Tony was more optimistic for the future because he was finally doing a little better than "breaking even." His full-time involvement seemed to be paying off. He had not put any new money into the business since the summer of 1985 and expected business to continue to rise. He had not yet taken any salary for himself, even though he had built up a small "surplus" of about $7,000.

Instead, he planned to put in an air-conditioning system at a cost of $5,000—and was also planning to use what salary he might have taken for himself to hire two new waitresses to handle the growing volume of business. And he saw that if business increased much more he would have to add another cook.

Evaluate Tony's past and present marketing strategy. What should he do now?

9. Days Inns vs. Best Western

Jim Salem has a problem. Should he make some minor changes in the way he operates his Sleepy-Time motel, or should he join either the Days Inns or Best Western motel chains? Some decision must be made soon because his present operation is losing money. But joining either of the chains will require fairly substantial changes, including new capital investment if he goes with Best Western.

Jim bought the recently completed 60-room motel two years ago, after leaving a successful career as a production manager for a producer of industrial machinery. He was looking for an interesting opportunity that would be less demanding than the production manager position. The Sleepy-Time is located at the edge of a small town in a rapidly expanding resort area and about one-half mile off an interstate highway. It is 15 miles from a tourist area with several nationally franchised full-service resort motels suitable for "destination" vacations. There is a Holiday Inn, a Ramada Inn, and a Hilton Inn, as well as many "mom and pop" motels in the tourist area. The interstate highway carries a great deal of traffic since the resort area is between several major metropolitan areas.

Initially, Jim was satisfied with his purchase. He had traveled a lot himself and stayed in many different hotels and motels—so he had some definite ideas about what travelers wanted in their accommodations. He felt that a relatively plain but modern room with a comfortable bed, standard bath facilities, and air-conditioning would appeal to most customers. Further, Jim thought a swimming pool or any other non-revenue producing additions were not necessary. And he felt a restaurant would be a greater management problem than benefits it would offer. However, after many customers commented, Jim arranged to serve a free Continental breakfast of coffee and rolls in a room next to the registration desk.

Day-to-day operations went fairly smoothly in the first two years, in part because Jim and his wife handled registration and office duties—as well as general management. During the first year of operation, occupancy began to stabilize around 55 percent of capacity. But according to industry figures, this was far below the average of 68 percent for his classification—motels without restaurants.

After two years of operation, Jim was concerned because his occupancy rates continued to be below average. He decided to evaluate his operation, looking for ways to increase both occupancy rate and profitability—and still maintain his independence.

Jim wanted to avoid direct competition with the resort areas offering much more complete services. He stressed a price appeal in his signs and brochures—and was quite proud of the fact that he had been able to avoid all the "unnecessary expenses" of the resorts. As a result, Jim was able to offer lodging at a very modest price—about 30 percent below that of even the lowest-priced resort area motels. The customers who stayed at the Sleepy-Time said they found it quite acceptable. But he was troubled by what seemed to be a large number of people driving into his parking lot, looking around, and not coming in to register.

Jim was particularly interested in the results of a recent study by the regional tourist bureau. This study revealed the following information about area vacationers:

1. 68 percent of the visitors to the area are young couples and older couples without children.
2. 40 percent of the visitors plan their vacations and reserve rooms more than 60 days in advance.

3. 66 percent of the visitors stay more than three days in the area and at the same location.

4. 78 percent of the visitors indicated that recreational facilities were important in their choice of accommodations.

5. 13 percent of the visitors had family incomes of less than $15,000 per year.

6. 38 percent of the visitors indicated that it was their first visit to the area.

After much thought, Jim began to seriously consider affiliating with a national motel chain. After some investigating, he focused on two: Days Inns and Best Western.

Days Inns of America, Inc., is an Atlanta-based chain of economy lodgings. It has been growing rapidly—and is willing to take on new franchisees. A major advantage of Days Inns is that it would not require a major capital investment by Jim Salem. The firm is targeting people interested in lower-priced motels—in particular senior citizens, the military, school sports teams, educators, and business travelers. In contrast, Best Western would probably require Jim to upgrade some of the Sleepy-Time facilities, including the addition of a swimming pool. The total new capital investment would be between $200,000 and $400,000 depending on how "fancy" he got. But then Jim would be able to charge higher prices—perhaps $50 per day on the average, rather than the $35 per day per room he's charging now.

The major advantages of going with either of these national chains would be their central reservations system—and their national names. Both companies offer toll-free reservation lines—nationwide—and these reservations produce about 40% of all bookings in affiliated motels.

A major difference between the two national chains is their method of promotion. Days Inns uses no TV advertising and less print advertising than Best Western. Instead, Days Inns emphasizes sales promotions. In a recent campaign, for example, Blue Bonnet margarine users could exchange "proof-of-purchase seals" for a free night at a Days Inn. This tie-in led to the Days Inns system *selling* an additional 10,000 rooms.

Further, Days Inns operates a "September Days Club" for over 300,000 senior citizens who receive such benefits as discount rates and a quarterly travel magazine. This club accounts for about 10 percent of the chain's room revenues.

Both firms charge 8 percent of gross room revenues for belonging to their chain—to cover the costs of the reservation service and national promotion. This amount is payable monthly. In addition, franchise members must agree to maintain their facilities—and make repairs and improvements as required. Failure to maintain facilities can result in losing the franchise. Periodic inspections are conducted as part of supervising the whole chain and helping the members operate more effectively.

Evaluate Jim Salem's present strategy. What should he do to improve the occupancy rate and profitability of the motel?

10. Metro Ice Arena

Bob Born, the manager of Metro Ice Arena, is trying to decide what strategies he should use to do better than break even.

Metro is an ice-skating rink with a conventional hockey rink surface (85 feet × 200 feet). It is the only indoor rink in a northern city of about 250,000. Some outdoor rinks are operated by the city in the winter, but they don't offer regular ice skating programs.

Bob has a successful hockey program and is almost breaking even—which is about all he can expect if he emphasizes hockey. To try to improve his financial condition, Bob is trying to develop a public skating program. With such a program, he could have as many as 700 people in a public session at one time, instead of limiting the use of the ice to 12 to 24 people per hour. While the receipts from hockey can be as high as $125 an hour (plus concessions), the receipts from a two-hour public skating session—charging $3 per person—could yield up to $2,100 for a two-hour period (plus much higher concession revenue). The potential revenue from such large public skating sessions could add significantly to total receipts—and make Metro a profitable operation.

Bob has included several public skating sessions in his ice schedule, but so far they haven't attracted as many people as he hoped. In fact, on the average, they don't generate any more revenue than if the times were sold for hockey use. Even worse, more staff people are needed to handle a public skating session—guards, a ticket seller, skate rental, and more concession help.

The Sunday afternoon public skating sessions have been the most successful—with an average of 200 people attending during the winter season. Typically, this is a "kid-sitting" session. More than half of the patrons are young children who have been dropped off by their parents for several hours. There are some family groups.

In general, the kids and the families do seem to have a good time—and a fairly loyal group comes every Sunday during the winter season. In the spring and fall, however, attendance drops about in half, depending on how nice the weather is. (Bob schedules no public sessions in the summer—focusing instead on hockey clinics and figure skating.)

It is the Friday and Saturday evening public sessions that are a big disappointment. The sessions run from 8 until 10—a time when he had hoped to attract couples. At $3 per person, plus 75 cents for skate rental, this would be a more economical date than going to the movies. In fact, Bob has seen quite a few young couples—and some keep coming back. But he also sees a surprising number of 8- to 12-year-olds who have been dropped off by their parents. The younger kids tend to race around the rink, playing tag. This affects the whole atmosphere—making it less appealing for dating couples.

Bob feels that it should be possible to develop a teenage and young-adult market—adapting the format used by roller-skating rinks. Their public skating sessions feature a variety of "couples-only" and "group games" as well as individual skating to dance music. Turning ice skating sessions into social activities is not common, however, although industry "rumors" suggest that a few operators have had success with the roller-skating format.

Bob installed some soft lights to try to change the evening atmosphere. The music was designed to encourage couples to skate together. For a few sessions, Bob even tried to have some "couples-only" skates, but this was strongly resisted by the young boys who felt that they had paid their money and there was no reason why they should be "kicked off the ice." Bob also tried to attract more young couples by bringing in a local disk jockey to broadcast from Metro—playing music and advertising the public sessions. But all this has had little effect on attendance—which varies from 50 to 100 per two-hour session.

Bob seriously considered the possibility of limiting the weekend evening sessions to people over 13—to try to change the environment. But when he counted the customers, he realized this would be risky. More than half of his customers on an average weekend night are 12 or under. This means that he would have to make a serious commitment to building the teenage and young-adult market. And, so far, his efforts haven't been successful. He has already invested over $2,000 in lighting changes, and over $6,000 promoting the sessions over the rock music radio station—with disappointing results.

Some days, Bob feels it's hopeless. Maybe he should accept that a public ice skating session is a "mixed-bag." Or maybe he should just sell the time to hockey groups.

Evaluate Metro Ice Arena's situation. What should Bob do? Why?

11.   Up With People

Barbara McKinley is a newly appointed marketing manager for one of the four traveling casts of "Up With People"—and is trying to set her plans for the next year. Up With People is an international, non-profit educational organization that seeks to encourage understanding among people of all nations. It offers a diverse program

Facts About

Up with People ®

Type of Organization

Up With People was incorporated in 1968 as an independent, nonprofit, educational organization. It is classified by the United States Internal Revenue Service as a 501(c)(3) educational charitable organization exempt from Federal Income Tax. Up With People has no political or religious affiliations.

Mission Statement

The aim of Up With People is
TO ENCOURAGE UNDERSTANDING
AMONG PEOPLE OF ALL NATIONS
through an international educational program
involving young men and women
from many countries
who travel for a year
and learn from the people and places they visit
while staging a musical show.

Student Profile

Up With People maintains five international casts, each composed of approximately 135 students and staff members from throughout the world. These 675 young people are selected from 9,000 applicants annually and this year represent 25 countries and 46 states in the United States. The medium age is 21 in an age range of 18 to 25.

Although musical talent is needed for each cast, individual selection is based upon a personal interview rather than a musical audition. Maturity, personality, motivation, interest in the world around them, ability to communicate and the desire to serve others are among the attributes for which Up With People is looking.

It is the organization's goal that some day young men and women from every nation may have the opportunity to spend a year in this nonsectarian, apolitical program, so that together they may contribute to a more peaceful world.

The Educational Program

Up With People provides its participants with a year-long learning experience that will help them better understand the world, other cultures and themselves and will encourage them to utilize what they have learned when they return to their colleges, jobs and communities.

Students participate in interrelated activities which provide them with an experiential education during their 32,000-mile tour. The educational experiences in Up With People are divided into four components:

- **Cross-Cultural** – The students learn about other people and cultures by living and working with other international students, traveling throughout the U.S. and Europe, South America or Asia, living with different host families, hearing lectures, participating in tours and discussing world issues.
- **Career Development** – Through the program's various work internships, valuable career skills are developed in business management, sales, marketing, advertising, personnel interviewing and recruiting, show production, communications and organizational management.
- **Service-Learning** – Through community performances and involvement in schools, hospitals, prisons, centers for the handicapped and homes for the elderly, the students learn about community needs and develop a desire to serve others.
- **Academic Credit** – Students can receive credit through the University of Arizona in Tucson, Arizona, for their year in Up With People. Many design their own independent study programs and receive credit from their home universities.

The Up With People Show

Up With People began with the belief that music is one of the best means for young people to communicate their enthusiasm for life, as well as their concerns and hopes for the future. Up With People also believes that most young men and women, even the untrained, have enormous reserves of talent that quickly develop when they are given the chance to work and perform for the benefit of others.

The two-hour show performed by the casts is the medium with which Up With People is able to travel throughout the world bringing people together.

The Up With People show is a fresh, contemporary production featuring a talented cast and band. It is one of the few live musical shows in production that provides family-type entertainment to audiences of all ages.

The professionally produced entertainment has been acclaimed around the world and features both popular and original material. From the nostalgic hits of yesterday to today's contemporary sounds, the colorful pageantry of authentic national songs and dances to thoughtful ballads, the Up With People show offers dynamic, high-energy entertainment.

Traveling Around the World

Each cast travels approximately 32,000 miles visiting 80–90 towns and cities. During the past 18 years, Up With People has performed "live" to an estimated twelve million people in 48 countries on six continents.

Performances have taken place in Radio City Music Hall (New York), Tivoli Gardens (Copenhagen), Royal Albert Hall (London), at the Olympic Games (Munich), Ontario Place (Toronto), the Conservatory of Music (Beijing), St. Peter's Square (Rome), at the National Football League Super Bowls X, XIV, XVI, and XX, and the Jerash Festival (Jordan).

In most cites, Up With People is invited by local sponsors who range from businesses and newspapers to service clubs and school groups. For each of them, Up With People is a cost-effective community relations opportunity, drawing people together with high-quality entertainment presented in a spirit of public service.

Host Families

An important part of Up With People's educational and cultural exchange is the hospitality provided to the students in each community by local host families. During the average one-year tour, each student will stay with 80–90 families from every walk of life and many cultures.

Host families provide lodging and some meals and an important opportunity for the students to participate in and learn about their lifestyles and the rich cultural diversity of the world. These contributions are vital to the continuation and existence of Up With People.

Funding

Up With People operates on an annual budget of $17.5 million. Its sources of revenue are:

Performance and related product sales	28%
Student Fees	21%
Gifts, grants and investments	9%
Gifts in kind	42%

Students pay a program fee ($6,300) toward their year of travel. In many cases they spend months before joining the program raising the funds themselves. However, many of the students receive some scholarship assistance for which an endowment fund is being built.

The contribution of food and lodging provided by host families, donated meals, loaned vehicles and other gifts in kind represented $7.1 million in fiscal 1985.

During 1985 over 3,000 individuals, companies, and foundations contributed more than $900,000 to Up With People's annual fund, scholarship fund and endowment.

A gift to Up With People is an investment in young people and helps in the important task of building better understanding among people of the world.

In the United States, contributions, bequests, transfers or gifts to Up With People are deductible for federal income, estate and gift tax purposes as provided by law.

History

Up With People was founded by J. Blanton Belk in the mid-1960's to provide a positive channel for the idealism and energy he saw evidenced in student movements around the world.

"Our aim then, as now, was to help young people gain a new understanding of the world and begin to discover their own potential," Belk said.

Up With People incorporated in 1968 with only 100 students touring eight countries. Since then, Up With People has visited more than 3,000 cities in 48 countries, presenting 9,200 two-hour shows and giving 32,000 informal performances to an estimated 33 million people.

More than 10,000 young men and women from 56 countries have completed their year in Up With People, returning as contributing members of their communities, taking with them their experiences and the global friendships they have made.

Up With People Office

3103 North Campbell Ave.
Tucson, AZ 85719, U.S.A.
Telephone (602) 327-7351
Telex 666 482 uwp tuc
FAX (602) 325-3716

---

in which young people of many different countries travel for a year and learn about the people and places they visit, while staging a two-hour musical show. The casts also participate in various community involvement activities—such as visiting senior citizens' homes, handicapped students, and so on. While the two-hour show is a focal point of the students' activities, they spend much more of their time learning about each community by visiting with local people—including the host families—with whom cast members live while on tour. Up With People is thought of as an "educational experience." The students are expected to pay a program fee (about $6,300) to help cover some of the costs of the program. While touring with a cast, students can also earn college credits through the University of Arizona in Tucson.

The typical cast of about 100 young people visits 80 to 90 cities during the course of a year. A scheduler arranges their itinerary 12 months in advance. The marketing manager for each touring cast is primarily responsible for promoting the group and trying to increase attendance (and revenue) for the two-hour performances, while staying within the fixed promotion budget. The marketing manager is also concerned with obtaining as much publicity as possible, because future students are recruited from people the cast meets during the tour. In fact, at the end of each show, young people have a chance to talk with cast members and—if interested—fill out an application form.

Barbara McKinley will do much of her work through "promotion representatives" who precede the cast by several weeks—setting up and following through on previously arranged publicity. These promotion representatives are also responsible for working with the sponsor in each city to line up host families and community involvement activities that will add to the varied experiences of the students—and also meet the sponsors' objectives.

Barbara is trying to develop a plan for herself and her promotion representatives. As a starting point, she is trying to clarify what "product" she is offering—and to whom. Further, Barbara must decide exactly what she should communicate—and to whom—and what media should be used. As a starting point, she is reviewing the following position statements that have been prepared by "Up With People." She has also studied a carefully prepared PR release called "Facts About Up With People."

POSITIONING STATEMENT
PUBLIC SECTOR—
ENTERTAINMENT MARKET

Up With People is one of the few live musical shows in production today that pro-vides family-type entertainment for audiences of all ages and cultures.

It is a contemporary, high-energy show, performed with sincere enthusiasm by a talented, international cast and band of 100 young men and women.

The Up With People Show has something for everyone . . . full cast production numbers as well as soloists and feature dancers who present music that appeals to everyone's tastes, from the nostalgic hits of yesterday to today's contemporary sounds . . . and the colorful pageantry of authentic nationality songs and dances to whimsical novelty numbers.

The theme behind the 1986–87 shows, The Beat of the Future, is the near future and the changes, challenges, and hopes it brings.

Up With People is acclaimed worldwide for two hours of professionally produced entertainment that makes their audiences become emotionally involved with the exuberance and energy of the outgoing cast. They leave feeling good about themselves and the world around them.

Up With People is an excellent entertainment value.

POSITIONING STATEMENT—
SPONSOR MARKET

Up With People provides a unique and cost-effective vehicle to enable organizations to achieve their community and employee relations goals and objectives.

Through the medium of music, Up With People provides a family oriented communications package that reaches out to all population segments and breaks down barriers and turns negative attitudes into positive ones that last.

In addition to presenting a lively and spirited show performed by an international cast and band of 100 young men and women, these people permeate into the community and become involved in public service events and activities on behalf of the sponsoring firm . . . and this occurs in a non-commercial way that benefits the sponsor favorably.

Up With People can execute a program designed to fulfill a company's needs usually at no greater cost than other more conventional community or employee relations efforts, and achieve a lasting positive impact as well.

Evaluate Up With People's strategy. What is its "product"? What messages should Barbara McKinley try to communicate—and to whom? And what kinds of media should be used?

12.   *Nike and the Joggers House*

Bob and Mike Brown, owners of the Joggers House, are trying to decide in what direction they should go with their retail store and how committed they should be to Nike.

The Brown brothers are runners—and Joggers House grew with the "jogging boom." But that has now flattened out and may actually be declining as many people find that jogging is hard work—and hard on the body, especially the knees. The jogging boom helped make Joggers House a profitable business. Throughout this period, Bob and Mike emphasized Nike shoes, which were well-accepted and seen as "top quality." This positive image made it possible to get $5 to $7 "above the market" for Nike shoes—and some of this was left with the retailers, which led to attractive profits for Bob and Mike Brown.

Committing so heavily to Nike seemed like a good idea when its quality was up and the name was good. But around 1985, Nike quality began to slip. It hurt not only Nike, but retailers such as the Browns, who were heavily committed to them. By 1986, Nike had gotten its house in order again, but the company began to put greater emphasis on other kinds of athletic equipment— and on walking shoes in particular. This forced the Brown brothers to reconsider the emphasis in their store and to question whether they should continue committing so completely to Nike.

Nike's move into the walking market is supported by U.S. Census Bureau estimates that between 50 and 80 million Americans walk for exercise—with between 15 and 20 million of these considering themselves serious "health" walkers. After several years of internal research, Nike is introducing shoes designed specifically for walkers. Nike found that walkers' feet are on the ground more often than a runner's feet—but receive about half the impact. So Nike reduced the size of its mid-sole and grooved it for flexibility. Nike also eliminated inside seams at the toe to avoid irritation and lowered the back tab of the shoe to avoid pressure on the Achilles tendon. The manager of the Nike walking shoe effort is optimistic about the potential for walking shoes. In fact, she's convinced it's a lot larger than the jogging market—especially since no experience or practice is necessary to be "good right away."

Many competitors are entering the walking shoe market, including the popular Avia, but the exact nature and size of the market isn't too clear. For one thing, it's likely that some ex-runners may just stop exercising—especially if they've damaged their knees. Further, the medical and biomechanical evidence about the need for specific walking shoes is not at all clear. One problem is that a shoe made for running can be used for walking, but not vice versa. Only very serious walkers may be interested in "only a walking shoe." Further, fashion has invaded the athletic wear markets, so it may be necessary to have many different colors and quality levels. But Nike has tended to emphasize function. Their initial walking shoes will be offered only in gray— and this could be a problem because about 75 percent of current walkers are women, many of them older. Other colors are planned for future models, however.

The main question that Bob and Mike are debating is whether there really is a market for walking shoes. Further, is there a market for the Nike version of walking shoes—that will emphasize function more than fashion? What the Browns must decide is whether they should shift the emphasis within their store to walking shoes, while continuing to carry jogging shoes for their regular customers—and perhaps carry brands other than Nike.

Just a small shift in emphasis probably won't make much of a difference. But a real switch to a heavy emphasis on walking shoes might require the Browns to change the name of the store—and perhaps even hire salespeople who will be more sympathetic with "non-joggers" and their needs.

Bob and Mike must also decide whether they should continue to commit so firmly to Nike or begin to add other jogging shoes—and perhaps other walking shoes. And should they put much greater emphasis on fashion rather than function? This too would require, at the least, retraining current salespeople, and perhaps bringing in more fashion-oriented salespeople.

One of the reasons they might want to broaden their line beyond Nike, is that many other companies have entered the athletic shoe market, including Avia—with its cantilevered sole—as well as Adidas and many lesser-known and unknown brands. Prices have dropped, and many producers are emphasizing fashion over function. Many customers have purchased "running shoes" with no intention of ever running with them. "Running shoes" are the new "casual shoe."

Still another problem that worries Bob and Mike is whether they really want to help pioneer a "specialty walking shoe" market. Those people who accept the need for "quality" walking shoes seem to be satisfied with running shoes—or hiking boots. Selling a whole new walking shoe concept will require a lot of expensive introductory promotion. And, if it is successful, lower-priced versions will probably enter the market and be sold in most sporting goods stores—as well as large shoe stores. So the larger margins that are available now will erode as the size of the "specialty walking shoe" market becomes clearer. The basic questions bothering Bob and Mike are: Is there really a "specialty walking shoe" market and, if so, how big is it? To get a better idea of how people feel about "specialty walking shoes," they started asking some of their present custom-

ers how they felt about special shoes for walking. The following are "representative" responses:

"What? I can walk in my running shoes!"

"I might be interested if I could really notice the difference, but I think my running shoes will work fine."

"No, my running shoes walk good!"

To get a better feel for how non-customers felt, they talked to some friends and neighbors and a few people in a nearby shopping mall. Typical responses were:

"My regular shoes are fine for walking."

"I really don't do much walking and don't see any need for such things!"

"I might be interested if you could explain to me why they were better than my present running shoes, which I got at K mart."

"My hiking boots work pretty well, but I'd be willing to hear how yours are better."

"I do a lot of walking and might be really interested if they were a lot better than the running shoes I'm using now."

"I'm always interested in looking at new products!"

Evaluate Bob and Mike Brown's present strategy. Evaluate the alternative strategies they are considering and explain which one you would suggest and why.

13. Union Carbide Corporation

Mary Tudor, a new product manager for Union Carbide, must decide what to do with a new antifreeze product that is not doing as well as management had expected. Union Carbide is one of the large chemical companies in the United States—making a wide line of organic and inorganic chemicals, plastics, bio-products, and metals. Technical research has played a vital role in the company's growth.

Recently, one of Carbide's research laboratories developed a new antifreeze product—C-10. Much research was devoted to the technical phase, involving various experiments concerned with the quality of the new product. Then Mary Tudor took over and has been trying to develop a strategy for the product.

The antifreeze commonly used now is ethylene glycol. If it leaks into the crankcase oil, it forms a thick, pasty sludge that can cause bearing damage, cylinder scoring, or a dozen other costly and time-consuming troubles for both the operator and the owner of heavy-duty equipment.

Carbide researchers believed that the new product—C-10—would be very valuable to the owners of heavy-duty diesel and gasoline trucks—as well as other heavy-equipment owners. Chemically, C-10 uses a propanol product—instead of the conventional glycol and alcohol products. It cannot prevent leakage, but if it does get into the crankcase, it won't cause any problems.

The suggested price of C-10 is $16 per gallon—more than twice the price of regular antifreeze. The higher price is due to higher production costs and a "premium" for making a better type of antifreeze.

At first, Mary thought she had two attractive markets for C-10: (1) the manufacturers of heavy-duty equipment and (2) the users of heavy-duty equipment. Carbide sales reps have made numerous calls. So far neither type of customer has been very interested, and the sales manager is discouraging any more calls for C-10. The manufacturers are reluctant to show interest in the product until it has been proven in actual use. The buyers for construction companies and other firms using heavy-duty equipment have also been hesitant. Some said the suggested price was far too high for the advantages offered. Others didn't understand what was wrong with the present antifreeze—and refused to talk any more about paying extra for "just another" antifreeze.

Explain what has happened so far. What should Mary Tudor do?

14.   *McQueen's Ski Shop*

Jim and Joan McQueen are trying to decide what skis to carry in their new store in Aspen. They graduated from a state university in California in 1984 and, with some family help, plan to open a small ski equipment shop in Aspen, Colorado. The McQueens are sure that by offering friendly, personal service they will have something unique—and be able to compete with the many other ski shops in town. They are well aware that they will have many competitors because many "ski bums" choose the Aspen area as a place to live—and then try to find a way to earn a living there. By keeping the shop small, however, the McQueens hope they'll be able to manage most of the activities themselves—keeping costs down and also being sure of good service for their customers.

Their current problem is deciding which line—or lines—of skis they should carry. Almost all the major manufacturers' skis are offered in the competing shops, so Jim and Joan are seriously considering specializing in the King brand—which is not now carried by any local stores. In fact, the King sales rep has assured them that if they are willing to carry the line exclusively, then King will not sell its skis to any other retailers in Colorado. This appeals to Jim and Joan because it would give them something unique—a new kind of "American-made" ski that is just being introduced into the U.S. market with supporting full-page ads in skiing magazines. The skis have an injected foam core that is anchored to boron and fiberglass layers above and below by a patented process that causes the fiberglass to penetrate the foam. The process is the result of several years of experimenting by a retired space capsule designer—Kurt King. Finally, he applied "space technology" to building lighter and more responsive skis. Now his small firm—King Manufacturing Company—is ready to sell the new design as "recreational skis" for the large "beginner" and "intermediate" markets. Eric Zuma, the King sales rep, is excited about the possibilities and compares the King ski development to the

Head ski (first metal ski) and Prince tennis racket (first "outsize" racket) developments, which were big winners. Both of these successes were built on the pioneering work of one man—Mr. Head—who Eric thinks is very much like Mr. King—a "hard-working genius."

The McQueens are interested because they would have a unique story to tell about skis that could satisfy almost every skier's needs. Further, the suggested retail prices and markups were similar to those of other manufacturers, so the McQueen Ski Shop could emphasize the unique features of the King skis—and still keep their prices competitive.

The only thing that worries the McQueens about committing so completely to the King line is that there are many other manufacturers—both domestic and foreign—that claim to offer unique features. In fact, most ski manufacturers regularly come out with new models and features, and the McQueens realize that most consumers are confused about the relative merits of all of the offerings. In the past, Jim himself has been reluctant to buy "off-brand" skis—preferring instead to stay with major names like Hart, Head, K2, and Rossignol. So Jim wonders if a complete commitment to the King line is wise. On the other hand, the McQueens want to offer something unique. They don't want to run just another ski shop carrying lines available "everywhere." The King line isn't their only possibility, of course. There are other "off-brands" that are not yet carried in Aspen. But the McQueens like the idea that King is planning to give national promotion support to the skis during the introductory campaign. They think that this might make a big difference in how rapidly the new skis are accepted. And if they provide friendly sales assistance and quick binding-mounting service, perhaps their chances for success will be even greater. Another reason for committing to the King line is that they like the sales rep, Eric Zuma, and are sure he would be a big help in their initial stocking and set-up efforts. They talked briefly with some other firms' salespeople at the major trade shows, but had not gotten along nearly so well with any of them. In fact, most of the sales reps didn't seem too

interested in helping a newcomer—preferring instead to talk with and entertain buyers from established stores. The major ski shows are over, so any more contacts with manufacturers will mean the McQueens must take the initiative. But from their past experience, this doesn't sound too appealing. Therefore, they seem to be drifting fast toward specializing in the King line.

Evaluate the McQueens' and Eric Zuma's thinking. What should the McQueens do?

15. Graphic Arts, Inc.

Ken Woods, manager of Graphic Arts, Inc., is searching for ways to increase profits. But he's turning cautious after seeing the poor results of his last effort—during the previous Christmas season. Graphic Arts, Inc., is located in a residential area, along a cross-town street, about two miles from the downtown of a metropolitan area of 450,000 and near a large university. It sells high-quality still and movie cameras, accessories, and projection equipment—including 8mm and 16mm movie projectors, 35mm slide projectors, opaque and overhead projectors, and a large assortment of projection screens. Most of the sales of this specialized equipment are made to area school boards for classroom use, to industry for use in research and sales, and to the university for use in research and instruction.

Graphic Arts (GA) also offers a wide selection of film and a specialized film-processing service. Instead of processing film on a mass production basis, GA gives each roll of film individual attention—to bring out the particular features requested by a customer. This service is used extensively by local firms that need high-quality pictures of lab or manufacturing processes for analytical and sales work.

To encourage the school and industrial trade, GA offers a graphics consultation service. If a customer wants to build a display—whether large or small—professional advice is readily available.

Along with this free service, GA carries a full line of graphic arts supplies.

GA employs four full-time store clerks and two outside sales reps. These sales reps make calls on business firms, attend trade shows, make presentations for schools, and help both present and potential customers in their use and choice of visual aids.

The people who make most of the over-the-counter purchases are (1) serious amateur photographers and (2) some professional photographers who buy in small quantities. Price discounts of up to 25 percent of the suggested retail price are given to customers who buy more than $1,200 worth of goods per year. Most regular customers qualify for the discount.

In the last few years, many more "amateurs" have been taking 35mm pictures (slides) using compact automatic and semi-automatic full-frame cameras priced under $150. These cameras are easy to carry and use—and have attracted many people who had never taken 35mm pictures (slides)—or any pictures (slides)—before. Because of this, Ken Woods felt that there ought to be a good opportunity to expand sales during the Christmas "gift-giving" season. Therefore, he planned a special pre-Christmas sale of three of the most popular brands of these compact cameras and discounted the prices to competitive "discount store" levels. To promote the sale, he posted large signs in the store windows and ran ads in a Christmas-gift-suggestion edition of the local newspaper. This edition appeared each Wednesday during the four weeks before Christmas. At these prices and with this promotion, Ken hoped to sell at least 500 cameras. However, when the Christmas returns were in, total sales were 57 cameras. Ken was most disappointed with these results—especially because trade estimates suggested that sales of compact cameras in this price and quality range were up 300 percent over last year.

Evaluate what Graphic Arts is doing and what happened with the special promotion. What should Ken Woods do to increase sales and profits?

16. Industrial Sales Company

Tom Miller, owner of Industrial Sales Company, is trying to decide whether to take on a new line. He is very concerned, however, because although he wants to carry more lines he feels that something is "wrong" with his latest possibility.

Tom Miller graduated from a large midwestern university in 1982 with a B.S. in business. He worked as a car salesman for a year. Then Tom decided to go into business for himself and formed Industrial Sales Company. Looking for opportunities, Tom placed several ads in his local newspaper in Cleveland, Ohio, explaining that he was interested in becoming a sales representative in the local area. He was quite pleased to receive a number of responses. Eventually, he became the sales representative in the Cleveland area for three local manufacturers: Boxer Company, which manufactures portable drills; Silver Company, a manufacturer of portable sanding machines; and Tower Mfg. Company, a producer of small lathes. All of these companies were relatively small—and were represented in other areas by other sales representatives like Tom Miller.

Tom's main job was to call on industrial customers. Once he made a sale, he would send the order to the respective manufacturer, who would in turn ship the goods directly to the customer. The manufacturer would bill the customer, and Miller would receive a commission varying from 5 percent to 10 percent of the dollar value of the sale. Miller was expected to pay his own expenses.

Miller called on anyone in the Cleveland area who might use the products he handled. At first, his job was relatively easy, and sales came quickly because he had little competition. Many national companies make similar products, but at that time, they were not well represented in the Cleveland area.

In 1984, Miller sold $200,000 worth of drills, earning a 10 percent commission; $75,000 worth of sanding machines, also earning a 10 percent commission; and $100,000 worth of small lathes, earning a 5 percent commission. He was encouraged with his progress and looked forward to expanding sales in the future. He was especially optimistic because he had achieved these sales volumes without overtaxing himself. In fact, he felt he was operating at about 70 percent of his capacity.

Early in 1985, however, a local manufacturer with a very good reputation—the Tucker Mfg. Company—started making a line of portable drills. By April 1985, Tucker had captured approximately one half of Boxer's Cleveland drill market by charging a substantially lower price. Tucker used its own sales force locally and probably would continue to do so.

The Boxer Company assured Miller that Tucker couldn't afford to continue to sell at such a low price and that shortly Boxer's price would be competitive with Tucker's price. Tom Miller was not nearly as optimistic about the short-run prospects, however. He began looking for other products he could sell in the Cleveland area. A manufacturer of hand trucks had recently approached him, but Tom wasn't too enthusiastic about this offer because the commission was only 2 percent on potential annual sales of $150,000.

Now Tom Miller is faced with another decision. The Quality Paint Company, also in Cleveland, has made what looks like an attractive offer. They heard what a fine job Tom was doing and felt that he could help them solve their present problem. Quality is having trouble with its whole marketing effort and would like Tom Miller to take over.

The Quality Paint Company sells mainly to industrial customers in the Cleveland area and is faced with many competitors selling essentially the same products and charging the same low prices. Quality Paint is a small manufacturer. Last year's sales were $300,000. They could handle at least four times this sales volume with ease—and are willing to expand to increase sales—their main objective in the short run. They are offering Tom a 12 percent commission on all sales if he will take charge of their pricing, advertising, and sales efforts. Tom is flattered by their offer, but

he is a little worried because the job might require a great deal more traveling than he is doing now. For one thing, he would have to call on new customers in Cleveland, and he might have to travel up to 200 miles around Cleveland to expand the paint business. Further, he realizes that he is being asked to do more than just sell. But he did have marketing courses in college, and thinks the new opportunity might be challenging.

Evaluate what Tom Miller has been doing. What should he do now? Why?

17. Brogan Lumber Company

Andy Brogan, owner of Brogan Company, feels his business is threatened by a tough new competitor. Andy is being pressured to make a decision on an offer that may save his business.

Andy Brogan has been a salesman for over 30 years. He started selling in a clothing store, but gave it up after 10 years to work in a lumber yard because the future looked much better in the building materials industry. After drifting from one job to another, Andy finally settled down and worked his way up to manager of a large wholesale building materials distribution warehouse in Charlotte, North Carolina. In 1965, he formed Brogan Company and went into business for himself, selling carload lots of lumber to large retail yards in the western parts of North and South Carolina.

Andy works with five large lumber mills on the West Coast. They notify him when a carload of lumber is available to be shipped, specifying the grade, condition, and number of each size board in the shipment. Andy isn't the only person selling for these mills—but he is the only one in his area. He isn't required to take any particular number of carloads per month—but once he tells a mill he wants a particular shipment, title passes to him and he has to sell it to someone. Andy's main function is to buy the lumber from the mill as it's being shipped, find a buyer, and have the railroad divert the car to the buyer.

Andy has been in this business for 20 years,

so he knows all of the lumber yard buyers in his area very well—and is on good working terms with them. Most of his business is done over the telephone from his small office, but he tries to see each of the buyers about once a month. He has been marking up the lumber between 4 and 6 percent—the standard markup, depending on the grades and mix in each car—and has been able to make a good living for himself and his family. The "going prices" are widely publicized in trade publications, so the buyers can easily check to be sure Andy's prices are competitive.

In the last few years, however, the building boom slowed down. Andy's profits did too, but he decided to stick it out—figuring that people still needed housing, and that business would pick up again.

Six months ago, an aggressive young salesman set up in the same business, covering about the same area but representing different lumber mills. This new salesman charges about the same prices as Andy, but undersells him once or twice a week in order to get the sale. Many lumber buyers—feeling that they were dealing with a homogeneous product—seem to be willing to buy from the lowest-cost source. This has hurt Andy financially and personally—because even some of his "old friends" are willing to buy from the new man if the price is lower. The near-term outlook seems dark, since Andy doubts that there is enough business to support two firms like his, especially if the markup gets shaved any closer. Now, they seem to be splitting the business about equally—as the newcomer keeps shaving his markup. The main reason Andy is getting some orders is because the lumber mills make up different kinds of carloads (varying the number of different sized products) and specific lumber yards want his cars rather than his competitor's cars.

A week ago, Andy was contacted by Mr. Short, representing Talbord Mfg. Co., a new particleboard manufacturing firm. Mr. Short knew Andy was well acquainted with the local building supply dealers and wanted to know if he would like to be the sole distributor for Talbord Mfg. Co. in his area—selling carload lots, just as he did

lumber. Mr. Short gave Andy a brochure on particleboard, a product introduced about 20 years ago by another company. The brochure explains how particleboard can be used as a cheaper and better subflooring than the standard lumber usually used. Particleboard is also made with a wood veneer so that it can be used as paneling in homes and offices. Mr. Short told Andy that the lumber yards could specify the types and grades of particleboard they needed—unlike lumber where they must choose from carloads that are already made up. Andy knows that a carload of particleboard costs about 30 percent more than a carload of lumber—and that sales will be less frequent. In fact, he knows that this kind of product is not as well accepted in his area as many others because no one has done much promotion there. But the 20 percent average markup is very tempting—and the particleboard market is expanding nationwide. Further, the other particleboard manufacturers don't have anyone calling on lumber yards in his area at this time.

Andy thinks he has three choices:

1. Take Mr. Short's offer and sell both products.
2. Take the offer and drop lumber sales.
3. Stay strictly with lumber and forget the offer.

Mr. Short is expecting an answer within one week, so Andy has to decide soon.

Evaluate what Andy Brogan has been doing. What should he do now? Why?

18. Hutton, Inc.

Mary True, manager of Hutton's cosmetic and drug sundries department, is considering an offer from the Troy Drug Company. She thinks it might be attractive to senior citizens but has doubts about whether it really "fits" with the rest of Hutton's strategies.

Hutton, Inc., is a full-line department store chain operating in and around Los Angeles, California. The company began in the 1920s in the downtown business district of Los Angeles, and has now expanded until it operates not only the downtown store but also branches in eight major shopping centers around Los Angeles.

One of the more successful departments in the Hutton stores is the cosmetic and drug sundries department. This department sells a wide variety of products—ranging from face powder to vitamins. But it has not been in the prescription business—and does not have a registered pharmacist in the department. Its focus in the drug area has been on "proprietary" items—packaged and branded items that are sold without professional advice or supervision—rather than on the "ethical" drugs—which are normally sold only with a doctor's prescription that is filled by a registered pharmacist.

Mary now has a proposal from Troy Drug Company to introduce a wholesale prescription service into Hutton's cosmetic and drug sundries departments. Troy is a well-established drug wholesaler that is trying to expand its business by serving retailers such as Hutton.

Basically, the Troy Drug Company's proposal is as follows:

1. Hutton's customers will leave their prescriptions in the drug sundries department one day and then pick up their medicines the following day.
2. A Troy representative will pick up the prescriptions every evening at closing time and return the filled prescriptions before each store opens the following day. Hutton stores will not have to hire any pharmacists or carry any drug inventories.
3. Hutton could offer savings of from 35 to 40 percent to all customers—and an extra 10 percent discount for senior citizens. These savings will be due to the economies of the operation, including the absence of pharmacists and the elimination of inventories in each store.
4. Hutton will earn a 40 percent commission on the retail selling price of each prescription sale.
5. Hutton's name will be identified with the service and be printed on all bags, bottles, and other materials. In other words, the Troy Drug Company will serve as a wholesaler in the operation, and will not be identified to Hutton's customers.

Troy's sales rep, Anne Butler, pointed out that

retail drug sales are expanding and continued growth is expected as the average age of the population continues to rise—and especially as more people become "senior citizens" (a major market for medicines). Further, she says that prescription drug prices are rising, so Hutton will participate in an expanding business. By offering cost savings to its customers, Hutton will be providing another service—and also building return business and stimulating store traffic. Since Hutton won't need to hire additional personnel or carry inventory, the 40 percent margin will be almost all net profit.

The Troy Drug Company is anxious to begin offering this service to the Los Angeles area and has asked Mary to make a decision very soon. If Hutton accepts Troy's proposal, the Troy executives have agreed not to offer their service to any other Los Angeles stores. Otherwise, Troy plans to approach other Los Angeles retailers.

Evaluate the Troy proposal. What should Mary True do? Why?

19.   *Mason National Bank*

Bob Trane isn't having much luck trying to convince his father that their bank needs a "new look."

Bob Trane was recently appointed director of marketing by his father, Trevor Trane, long-time president of the Mason National Bank. Bob is a recent graduate of the marketing program at the nearby state college. He has worked in the bank during summer vacations—but this is his first full-time job.

The Mason National Bank is a profitable, family-run business located in Mason—the county seat. The town itself has only about 10,000 population, but it serves farmers as far away as 20 miles. About 20 miles north is a metropolitan area of 350,000. Banking competition is quite strong there. But Mason has only one other bank—of about the same size. The Mason National Bank has been quite profitable, last year earning about $325,000—or 1 percent of assets—a profit margin that would look very attractive to big-city bankers.

Mason National Bank has prospered over the years by emphasizing its friendly, small-town atmosphere. The employees are all local residents and are trained to be friendly with all customers—greeting them on a first-name basis. Even Bob's father tries to know all the customers personally and often comes out of his office to talk with them. The bank has followed a conservative policy—for example, insisting on 25 percent down payments on homes and relatively short maturities on loans. The interest rates charged are competitive or slightly higher than in the nearby city, but they are similar to those charged by the other bank in town. In fact, the two local banks seem to be following more or less the same approach—friendly, small-town service. Since they both have fairly convenient downtown locations, Bob feels that the two banks will continue to share the business equally unless some change is made.

Bob has developed an idea that he thinks will attract a greater share of the local business. At a recent luncheon meeting with his father, he presented his plan and was disappointed when it wasn't enthusiastically received. Nevertheless, he has continued to push the idea.

Basically, Bob wants to differentiate the bank by promoting a new image. In particular, his proposal is to try to get all the people in town to think of the bank as "Today's Bank." Bob wants to paint the inside and outside of the bank in current designers' colors (e.g., pastels) and have all the bank's advertising and printed materials refer to the "Today's Bank" campaign. The bank would give away "pastel" shopping bags, offer "pastel" deposit slips, mail out "pastel" interest checks, advertise on "pastel" billboards, and have "pastel" stationery for the bank's correspondence. Bob realizes that his proposal is "different" for a conservative bank. But that's exactly why he thinks it will work. He wants people to notice the Mason National Bank, instead of just assuming that both banks are alike. He thinks that after the initial surprise, the local people will think even more positively about Mason National. Its reputa-

tion is very good now, but he would like it to be recognized as "different." Bob feels that this will help attract a larger share of new residents and businesses. Further, he hopes that his "Today's Bank" campaign will cause people to talk about Mason National Bank—and given that word-of-mouth comments are likely to be positive, the bank might win a bigger share of the present business.

Bob's father, Trevor, is less excited about his son's proposal. He thinks the bank has done very well under his direction—and he is concerned about changing a "good thing." He worries that some of the older farmers who are loyal customers will question the integrity of the bank. His initial request to Bob was to come up with some other way of differentiating the bank without offending present customers. Further, Trevor Trane thinks that Bob is talking about an important change that will be hard to undo once the decision is made. On the plus side, Trevor feels that the proposal will make the bank appear quite different from its competitor. Further, people are continuing to move into Mason, and he wants an increasing share of this business.

Evaluate Mason National Bank's situation and Bob's proposal. What should the bank do to differentiate itself?

20. A-1 Sports, Inc.

Jack Gibson, owner of A-1 Sports, is worried about his business future. He has tried various strategies for two years now, and he's still barely breaking even.

Two years ago, Jack Gibson bought the inventory, supplies, equipment, and business of Washington Sport Sales—located in a suburb of Seattle, Washington. The business is in an older building along a major highway leading out of town—several miles from any body of water. The previous owner had sales of about $300,000 a year—but was just breaking even. For this reason—plus the desire to retire to southern California—the owner sold to Jack for roughly the value of the inventory.

Washington Sport Sales had been selling two well-known brands of small pleasure boats, a leading outboard motor, two brands of snow-mobiles, and a line of trailer and pickup-truck campers. The total inventory was valued at $80,000—and Jack used all of his own savings and borrowed some from two friends to buy the inventory. At the same time, he took over the lease on the building—so he was able to begin operations immediately.

Jack had never operated a business of his own before, but he was sure that he would be able to do well. He had worked in a variety of jobs—as an auto repair man, service man, and generally a jack-of-all-trades in the maintenance departments of several local businesses.

Soon after starting his business, Jack hired his friend, Bud, who had a similar background. To-gether, they handle all selling and set-up work on new sales and do maintenance work as needed. Sometimes the two men are extremely busy—at the peaks of each sport season. Then both sales and maintenance keep them going up to 16 hours a day. At these times it's difficult to have both new and repaired equipment available as soon as customers want it. At other times how-ever, Jack and Bud have almost nothing to do.

Jack usually charges the prices suggested by the various manufacturers—except at the end of a weather season when he is willing to make deals to clear out his inventory. He is annoyed that some of his competitors sell mainly on a price basis—offering 10 to 30 percent off a man-ufacturer's suggested list prices. Jack doesn't want to get into that kind of business, however. He hopes to build a loyal following based on friendship and personal service. Further, he doesn't think he really has to cut price because all of his lines are "exclusive" for his store. No stores within a 10-mile radius carry any of his brands, although many brands of similar products are offered by nearby retailers.

To try to build a favorable image for his com-pany, Jack occasionally places ads in local pa-pers and buys some radio spots. The basic theme of this advertising is that A-1 Sports is a good place to buy the equipment needed for the current season. Sometimes he mentions the brand names he carries, but generally Jack tries to build his own image for friendly service—both in new sales and repairs. He chose this approach because, although he has exclusives on the brands he carries, there generally are 10 to 15 different manufacturers' products being sold in each product category at any one time—and most of the products are quite similar. Jack feels that this similarity among competing products almost forces him to try to differentiate himself on the basis of his own store's services.

The first year's operation wasn't profitable. In fact, after paying minimal salaries to Bud and himself, the business just about broke even. And this was without making any provision for return on his investment.

In hopes of improving profitability, Jack jumped at a chance to add a line of lawn mowers, trac-tors, and trimmers as he was starting into his second year of business. This line was offered by a well-known equipment manufacturer who was expanding into Jack's market. The equipment is similar to that offered by other lawn equipment manufacturers. The manufacturer's willingness to do some local advertising and to provide some point-of-purchase displays appealed to Jack. And he also liked the idea that customers probably would want this equipment sometime earlier than boats and other summer items. So he could han-dle this business without interfering with his other peak selling seasons.

It's two years since Jack started A-1 Sports, Inc.—and he's still only breaking even. Sales have increased a little, but costs have gone up too because he had to hire some part-time help. The lawn equipment helped to expand sales—as he had expected—but unfortunately, it did not increase profits. The part-time helpers were needed to handle this business—in part because the manufacturer's advertising had generated a lot of sales inquiries. Relatively few of these re-sulted in sales, however, because many people seemed to be shopping for "deals." So Jack may have even lost money handling the new line. But he hesitates to give up on it because he has no other attractive choices right now—and he doesn't want to lose that sales volume. Further, the manufacturer's sales rep has been most encouraging—assuring Jack that things will get better and that his company will be glad to continue its promotion support during the coming year.

Evaluate Jack Gibson's overall strategy. What should he do now?

21. Du Pont

Tom Corns is marketing manager of Du Pont's plastic business. Tom is reconsidering Du Pont's promotion effort. He is evaluating what kind of promotion—and how much—should be directed to the "Big Three" U.S. car producers. Currently, Tom has one salesperson who devotes most of his time to the car industry. This man is based in the Detroit area and calls on both the "Big Three"—GM, Ford, Chrysler—and the various molders who supply the car industry. This approach was adequate as long as relatively little plastic was used in each car *and* the auto producers did all of the designing themselves and then sent out specifications for very price-oriented bidding. But now the Big Three's whole product planning and buying system is changing.

The "new system" can be explained in terms of Ford's "program management" approach—developed in 1980 and used on the Taurus-Sable project. Instead of the normal five-year process of creating a new automobile in sequential steps, the new system is a "team approach." Under the old system, product planners would come up with a general concept and then expect the design team to give it "artistic" form. Next Engineering would develop the specifications and pass them on to Manufacturing and suppliers. There was little communication between the groups—and no overall project responsibility. Under the new "program management" approach, representatives from all the various functions—Planning, Design, Engineering, Marketing, and Manufacturing—work together. The whole team takes final responsibility for a car. Because all of the departments are involved from the start, problems are resolved as

the project moves on—before they cause a crisis. Manufacturing, for example, can suggest changes in design that will result in higher productivity—or better quality.

In the Taurus-Sable project, Ford engineers followed the Japanese lead and did some "reverse engineering" of their own. This helped them learn how the parts were assembled—and how they were designed. Ford actually bought several Japanese cars and dismantled them, piece by piece, looking for ideas they could copy or improve. Further, Ford engineers carefully analyzed over 50 similar cars to find the best parts of each. The Audi 5000 had the best accelerator-pedal feel. The Toyota Supra was best for fuel-gauge accuracy. The best tire and jack storage was in the BMW 228e. Eventually, Ford incorporated almost all of the "best" features into their new Taurus-Sable.

In addition to "reverse engineering," Ford researchers conducted the largest series of market studies the company had ever done. This led to the inclusion of additional features, such as oil dipsticks painted a bright yellow for faster identification, and a net in the trunk to hold grocery bags upright.

At the same time, a five-member "ergonomics" group studied ways to make cars more comfortable and easier to operate. They took seats from competing cars and tested them in Ford cars to learn what customers liked—and disliked. Similarly, dashboard instruments and controls were tested. Eventually the best elements in competing models were incorporated into the Taurus-Sable.

Ford also asked assembly-line workers for suggestions before the car was designed—and then incorporated their ideas into the new car. All bolts had the same-size head, for example, so workers didn't have to switch from one wrench to another.

Finally, Ford consulted its suppliers as part of the program management effort. Instead of turning to a supplier after the car's design was completed, the Ford team signed long-term contracts with suppliers—and invited them to participate in product planning. This project is so successful it is likely that not only Ford—but other auto producers—will follow a similar approach in the future.

The suppliers selected for the Taurus project were major suppliers who had already demonstrated a serious commitment to the car industry and who had not only the facilities, but the technical and professional managerial staff who could understand—and become part of—the program management approach. Ford expected that these major suppliers would be able to provide the "just-in-time delivery system" pioneered by the Japanese—and that the suppliers could apply statistical quality-control procedures in their manufacturing processes. These criteria led Ford to ignore suppliers whose primary sales technique is to entertain buyers and then submit bids on standard specifications. Other car makers probably will switch to more service-oriented suppliers, too.

Assuming that the program management approach will spread through the car industry and that plastics will be used more extensively in cars in the 1990s, Tom Corns is trying to determine if Du Pont's present effort is adequate or whether a more aggressive effort will be necessary in the future. Tom's effort has focused primarily on responding to inquiries and bringing in Du Pont technical people as the situation seems to require. Potential customers with technical questions are sometimes referred to other customers already using the materials or to a Du Pont plant—to be sure that all questions are answered. But basically, car producer customers are treated like any other customers. The sales representative makes calls and tries to find good business wherever he can.

Tom now sees that some of his major competitors—including General Electric and Dow Chemical—are becoming more aggressive in the car industry. They are seeking to affect specifications and product design from the start, rather than after the car design is completed. This takes a lot more effort and resources, but Tom thinks that it may get better results. A major problem he sees, however, is that he may have to drastically change the nature of Du Pont's promotion. Instead of focusing primarily on buyers and responding to questions, it may be necessary to try to contact *all* the multiple buying influences, and not only answer their questions, but help them understand what questions should be raised—and then help them answer them. Some competitors are already moving in this direction.

But it is too soon to be sure how effective their efforts are because the car industry is just beginning to think more seriously about plastics as it moves further into "program management."

Contrast Ford Motor Company's previous approach to designing and producing cars to its program management approach. Assuming U.S. car producers will move in this direction, what strategy should Tom Corns develop for Du Pont? Explain.

22. / Moore Wire Rope, Inc.

Phil Moore, sole owner of Moore Wire Rope, Inc., is trying to decide how to organize and train his sales force—and what to do about Mike Brown.

Moore Wire Rope, Inc,. produces wire cable—ranging from one-half inch to four inches in diameter. The plant is in Chicago, Illinois. Moore sells throughout the United States. Principal users of the products are firms using cranes and various other overhead lifts in their own operations. Ski resorts and amusement parks, for example, are good customers because cables are used in the various lifts. The main customers, however, are cement plants, railroad and boat yards, heavy-equipment manufacturers, mining operations, construction companies, and steel manufacturers.

Moore employs its own "sales specialists" to call on the purchasing agents of potential users. All of Moore's sales reps are engineers who go through an extensive training program covering the different applications, product strengths, and other technical details concerning rope and cable. Then they are assigned their own district—the size depending on the number of customers. They are paid a good salary plus generous travel expenses—with small bonuses and prizes to reward special efforts.

Mike Brown went to work for Moore in 1955, immediately after receiving a civil engineering degree from the University of Minnesota. After going through the training program, he took over as the only rep in the Ohio district. His job was to service and give technical help to present customers of wire and cable. He was also expected to call on new customers, especially when inquiries came in. But his main activities were to: (1) call on present customers and supply the technical assistance needed to use cable in the most efficient and safe manner, (2) handle complaints, and (3) provide evaluation reports to customers' management regarding their use of cabling.

Mike Brown soon became Moore's outstanding representative. His exceptional ability to handle customer complaints and provide technical assistance was noted by many of the firm's customers. He also brought in a great deal of new business —mostly from heavy equipment manufacturers in Ohio.

Mike's success established Ohio as Moore's largest-volume district. Although the company's sales in Ohio have not continued to grow in the past few years, the replacement market has been steady and profitable. This fact is mainly due to Mike Brown. As one of the purchasing agents for a large machinery manufacturer mentioned, "When Mike makes a recommendation regarding use of our equipment and cabling, even if it is a competitor's cable we are using, we are sure it's for the best of our company. Last week, for example, a cable of one of his competitors broke, and we were going to give him a contract. He told us it was not a defective cable that caused the break, but rather the way we were using it. He told us how it should be used and what we needed to do to correct our operation. We took his advice and gave him the contract as well!"

Four years ago, Moore introduced a unique and newly patented wire sling device for holding cable groupings together. The sling makes operations around the cable much safer—and its use could reduce hospital and lost-time costs due to accidents. The slings are expensive—and the profit margin is high. Moore urged all its repre-

sentatives to push the sling, but the only sales rep to sell the sling with any success was Mike Brown. Eighty percent of his customers are currently using the wire sling. In other areas, sling sales are disappointing.

As a result of his success, Moore is now considering forming a separate department for sling sales and putting Mike Brown in charge. His duties would include traveling to the various sales districts and training other representatives to sell the sling. The Ohio district would be handled by a new rep.

Evaluate Phil Moore's strategy(ies). What should he do about Mike Brown—and his sales force? Explain.

23. *King Furniture Company*

Carol King is frustrated with her salespeople and is even thinking about hiring some "new blood." Mrs. King has been operating the King Furniture Company for 10 years and has slowly built the sales to $950,000 a year. Her store is located in the downtown shopping area of a growing city of 150,000 population. This is basically a factory city, and she has deliberately selected "blue-collar" workers as her target market. She carries some higher-priced furniture lines but emphasizes budget combinations and easy credit terms.

Mrs. King is concerned that she may have reached the limit of her sales growth—her sales have not been increasing during the last two years even though total furniture sales have been increasing in the city as new people move in. Her newspaper advertising seems to attract her target customers, but many of these people come in, shop around, and leave. Some of them come back—but most do not. She thinks her product selections are very suitable for her target market and is concerned that her salespeople don't close more sales with potential customers. She has discussed this matter several times with her 10 salespeople. Her staff feels they should treat all customers alike—the way they personally want to be treated. They argue that their role is just to answer questions when asked—not to make suggestions or help customers make decisions. They think this would be too "hard sell."

Mrs. King argues that their behavior is interpreted as indifference by the customers attracted to the store by her advertising. She has tried to convince her salespeople that customers must be treated on an individual basis—and that some customers need more encouragement and suggestion than others. Moreover, Mrs. King is convinced that some customers actually appreciate more help and suggestions than the salespeople themselves might. To support her views, she showed her staff the data from a study of furniture store customers (Tables 1 and 2). She tried

Table 1

In shopping for furniture I found (find) that	Demographic groups				Marital Status	
	Group A	Group B	Group C	Group D	Newly-weds	Married 3–10 yrs.
I looked at furniture in many stores before I made a purchase	78%	57%	52%	50%	66%	71%
I went (am going) to only one store and bought (buy) what I found (find) there	2	9	10	11	9	12
To make my purchase I went (am going) back to one of the stores I shopped in previously...........................	48	45	39	34	51	49
I looked (am looking) at furniture in no more than three stores and made (will make) my purchase in one of these	20	25	24	45	37	30
No answer	10	18	27	27	6	4

Table 2   The Sample Design

Demographic status

Upper class (group A); 13% of sample
  This group consisted of managers, proprietors, or executives of large businesses. Professionals, including doctors, lawyers, engineers, college professors and school administrators, research personnel. Sales personnel, including managers, executives, and upper-income sales people above level of clerks.
  Family income over $30,000.

Middle class (group B); 37% of sample
  Group B consists of white-collar workers including clerical, secretarial, sales clerks, bookkeepers, etc.
  It also includes school teachers, social workers, semiprofessionals, proprietors or managers of small businesses; industrial foremen and other supervisory personnel.
  Family income between $20,000 and $40,000.

Lower middle class (group C); 36% of sample
  Skilled workers and semiskilled technicians were in this category along with custodians, elevator operators, telephone linemen, factory operatives, construction workers, and some domestic and personal service employees.
  Family income between $10,000 and $40,000.
  No one in this group had above a high school education.

Lower class (group D); 14% of sample
  Nonskilled employees, day laborers. It also includes some factory operatives, domestic and service people.
  Family income under $15,000.
  None had completed high school; some had only grade school education.

to explain the differences in demographic groups and pointed out that her store was definitely trying to aim at specific people. She argued that they (the salespeople) should cater to the needs and attitudes of their customers—and think less about how they would like to be treated themselves. Further, Mrs. King announced that she is considering changing the sales compensation plan or hiring "new blood" if the present employees can't "do a better job." Currently, the sales reps are paid $20,000 per year plus a 1 percent commission on sales.

Evaluate Mrs. King's strategy planning and thinking about her salespeople. What should she do now? Explain.

24. Meyer, Inc.

Carol Kidd, marketing manager of consumer products for Meyer, Inc., is trying to decide what price to charge for her most promising new product—a kitchen towel holder. Meyer, Inc.—located in Atlanta, Georgia—is a custom producer of industrial wire products. The company has a lot of experience bending wire into many shapes—and also can chrome- or gold-plate finished products. The company was started 10 years ago and has slowly built its sales volume to $1.2 million a year. Just one year ago, Carol Kidd was appointed marketing manager of the consumer products division. It is her responsibility to develop this division as a producer and marketer of the company's own branded products—as distinguished from custom orders, which the industrial division produces for others.

Carol Kidd has been working on a number of different product ideas for almost a year now and has developed several designs for letter holders, message holders, flowerpot holders, key and pencil holders, and other novelties. Her most promising product is a towel holder that can stand over kitchen sink faucets. It is very similar

to one the industrial division produced for a number of years for another company. In fact, it was experience with the sales volume of that product that interested Meyer, Inc., in the market—and led to the development of the consumer products division.

Carol has sold hundreds of units of her products to various local food and general merchandise stores and wholesalers on a trial basis, but each time the price has been negotiated, and no firm policy has been set. Now she must determine what price to set on the kitchen towel holder—which she plans to push aggressively wherever she can. Actually, she hasn't decided on exactly which channels of distribution to use. But trials in the local area have been encouraging, and, as noted above, the experience in the industrial division suggests that there is a large market for this type of product.

The manufacturing cost on this product—when made in reasonable quantities—is approximately 30 cents if it is painted black and 40 cents if it is chromed or gold-plated. Similar products have been selling at retail in the $1.25 to $2.50 range. The sales and administrative overhead to be charged to the division will amount to $60,000 a year. This will include Carol's salary and some office expenses. It is expected that a number of other products will be developed in the near future, but for the coming year, it is hoped that this towel holder will account for about half the consumer products division's sales volume.

Evaluate Carol Kidd's strategy planning so far. What should she do now? What price should she set for the towel holder? Explain.

25. Tale Labs, Inc.

Jack Sutton, marketing manager of Tale Labs, is faced with some price-cutting and wants to fight "fire with fire." But his boss argues that they should promote harder to retailers and/or final consumers.

Tale Labs, Inc., is one of the four major Colorado-based photo-finishers—each with annual sales of about $6 million.

Tale was started in 1950 by three people who had a lot of experience in the photo-finishing industry—working in Kodak's photo-finishing division in Rochester, New York. Tale started in a small rented warehouse in Boulder, Colorado. Today the company has seven company-owned plants in five cities in Colorado and western Kansas. They are located in Boulder, Pueblo, Denver, and Colorado Springs, Colorado, and Hays, Kansas.

Tale does all of its own black-and-white processing. While it has color-processing capability, Tale finds it more economical to have most color film processed by the regional Kodak processing plant. The color film processed by Tale is either "off-brand" film—or special work done for professional photographers. Tale has always given its customers fast, quality service. All pictures—including those processed by Kodak—can be returned within three days of receipt by Tale.

Tale started as a wholesale photo-finisher—and later developed its own processing plants in a drive for greater profit. Tale's major customers are drug stores, camera stores, department stores, photographic studios, and any other retail outlets where photo-finishing is offered to consumers. These retailers insert film rolls, cartridges, negatives, and so on, into separate bags—marking on the outside the kind of work to be done. The customer is handed a receipt, but seldom sees the bag into which the film has been placed. The bag has the retailer's name on it—not Tale's.

Each processing plant has a small retail outlet for drop-in customers who live near the plant. This is a minor part of Tale's business.

The company also does direct-mail photo-finishing within the state of Colorado. Each processing plant in Colorado is capable of receiving direct-mail orders from consumers. All film received is handled in the same way as the other retail business.

A breakdown of the dollar volume by type of business is shown in Table 1.

Table 1

Type of business	Percent of dollar volume
Sales to retail outlets	80
Direct-mail sales	17
Retail walk-in sales	3
	100

All processing is priced at the level established by local competition—and all major competitors charge the same prices. Tale sets a retail list price, and each retailer then is offered a trade discount based on the volume of business generated for Tale. The pricing schedule used by each of the major competitors in the Colorado-Kansas market is shown in Table 2.

All direct-mail processing for final consumers is priced at 33⅓ percent discount off retail price. But this is done under the Colorado Prints name—not the Tale name—to avoid complaints from retailer customers. Retail walk-in accounts are charged the full list price for all services.

Retail stores offering photo-finishing are served by Tale's own sales force. Each processing plant has at least three people servicing accounts. Their duties include daily visits to all present accounts to pick up and deliver all photo-finishing work. These sales reps also make daily trips to the nearby bus terminal to pick up and drop off color film to be processed by Kodak. The reps are not expected to call on possible new accounts.

Since the final consumer does not come in contact with Tale, the firm has not advertised its retail business to final consumers. Similarly, possible retailer accounts are not called on or advertised to —except that Tale is listed under

Table 2

Monthly dollar volume (12-month average)	Discount (2/10, net 30)
$ 0–$ 100	33⅓%
$ 101–$ 500	40
$ 501–$1,000	45
$1,001–above	50

"Photo-finishing: Wholesale"—in the Yellow Pages of all telephone books in cities and towns served by its seven plants. Any phone inquiries are followed up by the nearest sales rep.

The direct-mail business—under the Colorado Prints name—is generated by regular ads in the Sunday pictorial sections of newspapers serving Pueblo, Denver, Colorado Springs, and Boulder. These ads usually stress low price, fast service, and fine quality. Mailers are provided for consumers to send to the plant. Some people in the company feel this part of the business might have great potential if pursued more aggressively.

Tale's president, Mr. Miki, is worried about the loss of several retail accounts in the $500 to $1,000 discount range. He has been with the company since its beginning—and has always stressed quality and rapid delivery of the finished products. Demanding that all plants produce the finest quality, Mr. Miki personally conducts periodic quality tests of each plant through the direct-mail service. Plant managers are advised of any slips in quality.

To find out what is causing the loss in retail accounts, Mr. Miki is reviewing sales reps' reports and talking to employees. In their weekly reports, Tale's sales reps report a major threat to the company—price cutting. Speedy-Film—a competitor of equal size that offers the same services as Tale—is offering an additional 5 percent trade discount in each sales volume category. This really makes a difference at some stores— because these retailers think that all the major processors do an equally good job. Further, they note, consumers apparently feel that the quality is acceptable because no complaints have been heard so far.

Tale has faced price cutting before—but never by an equally well-established company. Mr. Miki can't understand why these retailer customers would leave Tale because Tale is offering higher quality and the price difference is not that large. Mr. Miki thinks the sales reps should sell "quality" a lot harder. He is also considering a direct-mail and newspaper campaign to consumers to persuade them to demand Tale's quality service from their favorite retailer. Mr. Miki is convinced

that consumers demanding quality will force retailers to stay with—or return to—Tale. He says: "If we can't get the business by convincing the retailer of our fine quality, we'll get it by convincing the consumer."

Jack Sutton, the marketing manager, disagrees with Mr. Miki. Jack thinks that they ought to at least meet the price cut or cut prices another 5 percent wherever Speedy-Film has taken a Tale account. This would do two things: (1) get the business back and (2) signal that continued price cutting will be met by still deeper price cuts. Further, he says: "If Speedy-Film doesn't get the message, we ought to go after a few of their big accounts with 10 percent discounts. That ought to shape them up."

Evaluate Tale's present and proposed strategies. What should they do now? Explain.

26. Eaton Mfg., Inc.

Bob Nixon, the marketing manager of Eaton Mfg., Inc., wants to add sales reps rather than "play with price." That's how Bob describes what Jim Tryon, Eaton's president, is suggesting. Jim is not sure what they should do; but he does want to increase sales, and this means that something "new" is needed.

Eaton, Mfg., Inc.—of Los Angeles, California—is a leading manufacturer in the wire machinery industry. It has patents covering over 200 machine variations, but it's rare for Eaton's customers to buy more than 30 different types in a year. The machines are sold to wire and small-tubing manufacturers when they are increasing production capacity or replacing old equipment.

Established in 1895, the company has enjoyed a steady growth to its present position with annual sales of $40 million.

Ten U.S. firms compete in the U.S. wire machinery market—no foreign firms have appeared yet. Each is about the same size and manufactures basically similar machinery. Each of the competitors has tended to specialize in its own geographic area. None has exported much because of high labor costs in the United States. Five of the competitors are in the East, three in the Midwest, and two—including Eaton—on the West Coast. The other West Coast firm operates out of Portland, Oregon. All of the competitors offer similar prices and sell F.O.B. their factories. Demand has been fairly strong in recent years. As a result, all of the competitors have been satisfied to sell in their geographic areas and avoid price cutting. In fact, price cutting is not a popular idea in this industry. About 20 years ago, one firm tried to win more business and found that others immediately met the price cut—but industry sales (in units) did not increase at all. Within a few years, prices returned to their earlier level, and since then competition has tended to focus on promotion.

Eaton's promotion depends mainly on six company sales reps, who cover the West Coast. These reps cost about $200,000 per year when all the costs of salary, bonuses, supervision, travel, and entertaining are added. When the sales reps are close to making a sale, they are supported by two sales engineers—at a cost of about $100,000 per year per engineer. Eaton does some advertising in trade journals—less than $25,000—and occasionally uses direct mailings. But the main promotion emphasis is on personal selling. Personal contact outside the West Coast market, however, is handled by manufacturers' agents who are paid 4 percent on sales.

Jim Tryon, Eaton's president, is not satisfied with the present situation. Industry sales have leveled off and so have Eaton's sales—although the firm continues to hold its share of the market. Jim would like to find a way to compete more effectively in the other regions because he sees great potential outside of the West Coast.

Competitors and buyers agree that Eaton is the top-quality producer in the industry. Its machines have generally been somewhat superior to others in terms of reliability, durability, and productive capacity. The difference, however, usually has not been great enough to justify a higher price—because the others are able to do the necessary job—unless an Eaton sales rep con-

vinces the customer that the extra quality will improve the customer's product and lead to fewer production line breakdowns. The sales rep also tries to "sell" the company's better sales engineers and technical service people—and sometimes is successful. But if a buyer is only interested in comparing delivered prices for basic machines, Eaton's price must be competitive to get the business. In short, if such a buyer has a choice between Eaton's and another machine *at the same price,* Eaton will usually win the business in "its" part of the West Coast market. But it's clear that Eaton's price has to be at least competitive in such cases.

The average wire machine sells for about $150,000, F.O.B. shipping point. Shipping costs within any of the three major regions average about $2,500—but another $2,000 must be added on shipments between the West Coast and the Midwest (either way) and another $2,000 between the Midwest and the East.

Jim Tryon is thinking about expanding sales by absorbing the extra $2,000 to $4,000 in freight cost that occurs if a midwestern or eastern customer buys from his West Coast location. By doing this, he would not be cutting price in those markets but rather reducing his net return. He thinks that his competitors would not see this as price competition—and therefore would not resort to cutting prices themselves.

Bob Nixon, the marketing manager, thinks that the proposed freight absorption plan might actually stimulate price competition in the Midwest and East—and perhaps on the West Coast. He proposes instead that Eaton hire some sales reps to work the Midwest and Eastern regions—selling "quality"—rather than relying on the manufacturers' agents. He argues that two additional sales reps in each of these regions would not increase costs too much—and might greatly increase the sales from these markets over that brought in by the agents. With this plan, there would be no need to absorb the freight and risk disrupting the status quo. This is especially important, he argues, because competition in the Midwest and East is somewhat "hotter" than on the West Coast—due to the number of competitors in those regions. A lot of expensive entertaining, for example, seems to be required just to be considered as a potential supplier. In contrast, the situation has been rather quiet in the West—because only two firms are sharing this market and working harder near their home offices. The "Eastern" competitors don't send any sales reps to the West Coast—and if they have any manufacturers' agents, they haven't gotten any business in recent years.

Jim Tryon agrees that Bob Nixon has a point, but industry sales are leveling off and Jim wants to increase sales. Further, he thinks the competitive situation may change drastically in the near future anyway, and he would rather be a leader in anything that is likely to happen—rather than a follower. He is impressed with Bob Nixon's comments about the greater competitiveness in the other markets, however, and therefore is unsure about what should be done.

Evaluate Eaton's strategies. Given Jim Tryon's objective to increase sales, what should Eaton do? Explain

27. *Orecan, Inc.*

Jerry Turner, President of Orecan, Inc. (formerly Oregon Canning, Inc.) is confused about what he should propose to the board of directors. His recent strategy change isn't working. And Kevin Miller, Orecan's only sales rep (and a board member), is so discouraged that he refuses to continue his frustrating sales efforts. Miller wants Jerry Turner to hire a sales force instead, or do something else.

Orecan, Inc., is a long-time processor in the highly seasonal fruit canning industry. Orecan packs and sells canned raspberries, boysenberries, plums, strawberries, apples, cherries, and "mixed fruit." Sales are made mainly through food brokers to merchant wholesalers, supermarket chains (such as Kroger, Safeway, A&P, and Jewel), cooperatives, and other outlets—mostly in the San Francisco Bay area. Of less

importance, by volume, are sales to local institutions, grocery stores, and supermarkets—and sales of dented canned goods at low prices to walk-in customers.

Orecan is in Oregon's Willamette River Valley. The company has more than $20 million in sales annually (exact sales data is not published by the closely held corporation). Plants are located in strategic places along the valley—with main offices in Eugene. The Orecan brand is used only on canned goods sold in the local market. Most of the goods are sold and shipped under a retailer's label or a broker's/wholesaler's label.

Orecan is well-known for the consistent quality of its product offerings. And it's always willing to offer competitive prices. Strong channel relations were built by Orecan's former chairman of the board and chief executive officer, J. Morgan. Mr. Morgan—who owns controlling interest in the firm—"worked" the Bay area as the company's salesman in its earlier years—before he took over from his father as president in 1940. Morgan was an ambitious and hard-working top manager—the firm prospered under his direction. He became well known within the canned food processing industry for technical/product innovations.

During the off-canning season, Mr. Morgan traveled widely. In the course of his travels, he arranged several important business deals. His 1968 and 1975 trips resulted in the following two events: (1) inexpensive pineapple was imported from Formosa and sold by Orecan—primarily to expand the product line; and (2) a technically advanced continuous process cooker (65 feet high) was imported from England and installed at the Eugene plant in February-March 1980. It was the first of its kind in the United States and cut process time sharply.

Mr. Morgan retired in 1980 and named his son-in-law, 35-year-old Jerry Turner, as his successor. Mr. Turner is intelligent and hard-working. He had been concerned primarily with the company's financial matters and only recently with marketing problems. During his seven-year tenure as financial director, the firm received its highest credit rating ever—and was able to borrow working capital ($4 million to meet seasonal can and wage requirements) at the lowest rate ever received by the company.

The fact that the firm isn't unionized allows some competitive advantage. However, minimum wage law changes have increased costs. And these and other rising costs have squeezed profit margins. This led to the recent closing of two plants—as they became less efficient to operate. The remaining two plants were expanded in capacity (especially warehouse facilities) so that they could operate more profitably due to maximum use of existing processing equipment.

Shortly after Mr. Morgan's retirement, Jerry Turner reviewed the company's situation with his managers. He pointed to narrowing profit margins, debts contracted for new plant and equipment, and an increasingly competitive environment. Even considering the temporary labor-saving competitive advantage of the new cooker system, there seemed to be no way to improve the "status quo" unless the firm could sell direct—as they do in the local market—absorbing the food brokers' 5 percent commission on sales. This was the plan decided on, and Kevin Miller was given the new sales job for six months.

Miller is the only full-time salesman for the firm and lives in Eugene, Oregon. Other top managers do some selling—but not much. Being a nephew of Mr. Morgan, Kevin Miller is also a member of the board of directors. He is well qualified in technical matters and has a college degree in food chemistry. Although Mr. Miller formerly did call on some important customers with the brokers' sales reps, he is not well known in the industry or even by Orecan's usual customers.

It is now five months later. Kevin Miller is not doing very well. He has made several selling trips and hundreds of telephone calls with discouraging results. He is unwilling to continue sales efforts on his own. There seem to be too many potential customers for one person to reach. And more "wining and dining" is needed. Miller insists that a sales staff be formed if the present way of operating is to continue. Sales are down in comparison both to expectations and to the previous year's results. Some regular supermarket chain customers have stopped buying—though basic consumer demand has not changed. Further, some potential new customers have demanded quantity guarantees much larger than the firm can supply. Expanding supply would be difficult in the short run—because the firm typically must contract with growers to assure supplies of the type and quality they normally offer.

Evaluate Orecan's strategy planning. What should Jerry Turner do now?

28.   Plasto, Inc.

Bob McGill is trying to decide whether to leave his present job for what looks like a great chance to buy into a business and be part of "top management."

Bob is now a sales rep for a plastics components manufacturer. He calls mostly on large industrial accounts—such as refrigerator manufacturers—who might need large quantities of custom-made products, like door liners. He is on a straight salary of $25,000 per year, plus expenses and a company car. He expects some salary increases but doesn't see much long-run opportunity with this company. As a result, he is seriously considering changing jobs and investing $30,000 in Plasto, Inc.—an established Long Island (New York) thermoplastic molder (manufacturer). Mr. Larson, the present owner, is nearing retirement and has not developed anyone to take over the business. He has agreed to sell the business to Jim Mayer, a lawyer, who has invited Bob McGill to invest and become the sales manager. Jim Mayer has agreed to match Bob's current salary plus expenses, plus a bonus of 2 percent of profits. However, Bob must invest to become part of the new company. He will get a 5 percent interest in the business for the necessary $30,000 investment.

Plasto, Inc., is well established—and last year had sales of $1.8 million, but zero profits (after paying Mr. Larson a salary of $25,000). In terms of sales, cost of materials was 46 percent; direct labor, 13 percent; indirect factory labor, 15 percent; factory overhead, 13 percent; and sales overhead and general expenses, 13 percent. The company has not been making any profit for several years—but has been continually adding new machines to replace those made obsolete by technological developments. The machinery is well maintained and modern, but most of it is similar to that used by its many competitors. Most of the machines in the industry are standard. Special products are made by using specially made dies with these machines.

Sales have been split about two thirds custom-molded products (that is, made to the specification of other producers or merchandising concerns) and the balance proprietary items (such as housewares and game items, like poker chips and cribbage sets). The housewares are copies of articles developed by others—and indicate neither originality nor style. Mr. Larson is in charge of selling the proprietary items, which are distributed through any available wholesale channels. The custom-molded products are sold through three full-time sales engineers—who receive a 5 percent commission on individual orders up to $10,000 and then 3 percent above that level—and also by three manufacturers' reps who get the same commissions.

The company seems to be in fairly good financial condition—at least as far as book value is concerned. The $30,000 investment will buy approximately $40,000 in assets—and ongoing operations should pay off the seven-year note. See Table 1.

Mr. Mayer thinks that—with new management—the company has a good chance to make big profits. He expects to make some economies in the production process—because he feels most production operations can be improved. He plans to keep custom-molding sales to approximately the present $1.2 million level. The new strategy will try to increase the proprietary sales volume from $600,000 to $2 million a year. Bob McGill is expected to be a big help here because of his sales experience. This will bring the firm up to about capacity level—but it will mean adding additional employees and costs. The major advantage of expanding sales will be spreading overhead.

Some of the products proposed by Jim Mayer for expanding proprietary sales are listed below.

New products for consideration:

Six-bottle soft drink case.

Picnic lunch boxes.

Home storage box for milk cartons.

Short legs for furniture.

Step-on garbage can without liner.

Formed wall coverings.

Outside house shutters.

Bird houses.

Importing and distributing foreign housewares.

Table 1   Custom Manufacturing Company, Statement of Financial Condition, December 31, 198x

Assets			Liabilities and Net Worth		
Cash		$ 13,000	Liabilities:		
Accounts receivable		35,000	Accounts payable		$ 51,000
Building	$ 125,000		Notes payable—		
Less: depreciation	75,000		7 years (machinery)		194,000
		50,000	Net worth:		
			Capital stock		600,000
Machinery	1,200,000		Retained earnings		4,000
Less: depreciation	450,000				
		750,000	Total liabilities and net worth		$848,000
Total assets		$848,000			

Plasto faces heavy competition from many other similar companies. Further, most retailers expect a wide margin—sometimes 50 to 60 percent. Even so, manufacturing costs are low enough so Plasto can spend some money for promotion, while still keeping the price competitive. Apparently, many customers are willing to pay for novel new products—if they see them in stores. And Bob isn't worried too much by tough competition. He sees plenty of that in his present job. And he does like the idea of being an "owner and sales manager."

Evaluate Plasto, Inc.'s situation and Jim Mayer's strategy. What should Bob McGill do? Why?

29. Pulte Products, Inc.

Paul Pulte, president and marketing manager of Pulte Products, Inc., must decide what strategy—or strategies—he should pursue.

Pulte Products, Inc., is a manufacturer of industrial cutting tools. These tools include such items as lathe blades, drill press bits, and various other cutting edges used in the operation of large metal cutting, boring, or stamping machines. Paul Pulte takes great pride in the fact that his company—whose $3,400,000 sales in 1985 is small by industry standards—is recognized as a producer of the highest-quality line of cutting tools.

Competition in the cutting-tool industry is intense. Pulte Products competes not only with the original machine manufacturers, but also with many other larger manufacturers offering cutting tools as one of their many different product lines. This has had the effect, over the years, of standardizing the price, specifications, and, in turn, the quality of the competing products of all manufacturers.

About a year ago, Mr. Pulte was tiring of the financial pressure of competing with larger companies enjoying economies of scale. At the same time, he noted that more and more potential cutting-tool customers were turning to small tool-and-die shops because of specialized needs that could not be met by the mass production firms. Mr. Pulte thought perhaps he should consider

some basic strategy changes. Although he was unwilling to become strictly a custom producer, Mr. Pulte thought that the recent trend toward buying customized cutting edges suggested new markets might be developing—markets too small for the large, multi-product-line companies to serve profitably, but large enough to earn a good profit for a flexible company of Pulte's size.

An outside company, Gramm Associates, was hired to study the feasibility of serving these markets. The initial results were encouraging. It was estimated that Pulte might increase sales by 60 percent and profits by 80 percent by serving the emerging markets.

Next, Mr. Pulte had the sales manager hire two technical specialists (at a total cost of $50,000 each per year) to maintain continuous contact with potential cutting-tool customers. The specialists were supposed to identify any present—or future—needs that might exist in enough cases to make it possible to profitably produce a specialized product. The technical specialists were not to take orders or "sell" Pulte to the potential customers. Mr Pulte felt that only through this policy could these reps talk to the right people.

The initial feedback from the technical specialists was most encouraging. Many firms (large and small) had special needs—although it often was necessary to talk to the shop foreman or individual machine operators to find these needs. Most operators were "making do" with the tools available. Either they didn't know customizing was possible or doubted that their supervisors would do anything about it if they suggested that a more specialized tool would increase productivity. But these operators were encouraging because they said that it would be easier to persuade supervisors to order specialized tools if the tools were already produced and in stock than if they had to be custom-made. So Pulte decided to continually add high-quality products to meet the ever-changing, specialized needs of users of cutting tools and edges.

The potential customers of Pulte's specialized tools are located all over the country. The average sale per customer is likely to be less than

$350, but the sale will be repeated several times within a year. Because of the widespread market and the small order size, Mr. Pulte doesn't think that selling direct—as is done by small custom shops—is practical. At the present time, Pulte Products, Inc., sells 90 percent of its regular output through a large industrial wholesaler—Millco, Inc.—which serves the area east of the Mississippi River. This wholesaler, although very large and well known, is having trouble moving cutting tools. Millco is losing sales of cutting tools in some cities to newer wholesalers specializing in the cutting-tool industry. The new wholesalers are able to give more technical help to potential customers, and therefore better service. Millco's president is convinced that the newer, less-experienced concerns will either realize that a substantial profit margin can't be maintained along with their aggressive strategies, or they will eventually go broke trying to "overspecialize."

From Mr. Pulte's standpoint, the present wholesaler has a good reputation and has served Pulte Products well in the past. Millco has been of great help in holding down Pulte's inventory costs—by increasing the inventory in Millco's 34 branch locations. Although Mr. Pulte has received several complaints about the lack of technical assistance given by the wholesaler's sales reps—as well as their lack of knowledge about the new Pulte products—he feels that the present wholesaler is providing the best service it can. All its sales reps have been told about the new products at a special training session, and a new page has been added to the catalog they carry with them. So, regarding the complaints, Mr. Pulte says: "The usual things you hear when you're in business."

Mr. Pulte thinks that there are more urgent problems than a few complaints. Profits are declining and sales of the new cutting tools are not nearly as high as forecast—even though all reports indicate the company's new products meet the intended markets' needs perfectly. The high costs involved in producing small quantities of special products and in adding the technical specialist team—together with lower-than-expected sales—have significantly reduced Pulte's profits.

Mr. Pulte is wondering whether it is wise to continue to try to cater to the needs of specific target markets when the results are this discouraging. He also is considering increasing advertising expenditures in the hope that customers will "pull" the new products through the channel.

Evaluate Pulte Products' situation and Paul Pulte's strategy. What should he do now?

30.   *Dishcom, Inc.*

Charles Tucker is president of Dishcom, Inc., which sells satellite receiving dishes to final consumers. Business has been very good for the last year, but now some TV channels are being "scrambled" and there is a good deal of uncertainty about the legality of using decoders. As a result, Dishcom's sales are off more that half over several months ago. And uncertainty may continue in the industry because the issue is now being considered by the U.S. Congress—which is not known for settling such matters very quickly.

Dishcom, Inc., has been selling satellite dishes for several years. A satellite receiving dish enables an ordinary TV set to receive over 100 channels of programming—almost every program that's broadcast—directly from orbiting satellite transmitters. Until recently, anyone with a dish was able to receive programming free. There is some controversy about whether dish users should be paying some fee, but it's just not practical to try to collect from all the individual owners. As a result, dish owners were able to tune in "premium programs" such as HBO, Cinemax, Showtime, The Movie Channel, ESPN, Nickelodeon, and Playboy Channel—without charge. Some industry experts estimate that between $500 million and $700 million is lost through "signal theft."

The dish owners don't see it that way, however. They paid from $2,000 to $6,000 for their dishes and feel they should be able to see whatever is being broadcast, just as they tune in—free—to radio or network TV. Further, the majority of dish owners live in suburban or rural areas where they don't have access to cable systems anyway and therefore aren't trying to avoid the cable operators' charges. They have a special situation. Their outlying locations make it easier to install the dishes, which are large (6 to 8 feet in diameter) and unsightly and require enough room so they can be aimed at a satellite. In spite of the cost and installation problems, over 2 million dishes were in use in 1985.

Dishcom, Inc., has been selling and installing these large satellite dishes for three years—growing with the business. But profits have not been very impressive. About a year ago, however, business started to pick up. Dishcom signed an agreement to sell the Beam-Down II—a new, much smaller device for receiving TV broadcasts from satellites.

Beam-Down II was developed by Sukomoko, a Japanese electronics company. Beam-Down II uses an 18-inch diameter receiving dish, so it can easily be mounted out of sight on the roof of a home. Installation and wiring are simple—normally it only takes about one hour to install the unit. The suggested retail price is only $650—much cheaper than the large dishes—and an optional remote control unit to change channels costs another $75. Even at this price, there's a good margin for middlemen. Dishcom pays $300 per unit, plus $50 for the remote control unit. The only disadvantage of Beam-Down II is that it should have some preventive maintenance every two years, at a cost of about $75.

At present, Dishcom is the only dealer for Beam-Down II in North Carolina. So far Sukomoko has moved slowly in setting up distribution in the southeast. The company has indicated that it won't distribute the product through other companies in North Carolina as long as "Dishcom is doing an aggressive job in reaching the target market." The current contract prevents Dishcom from selling competing products.

Charles Tucker started Dishcom with an investment of about $15,000 and hasn't invested much additional capital in the company. Dishcom is located in a leased building. There is a small showroom with a demonstration unit and a few offices with desks and telephones. Sukomoko will send additional units from its New York warehouse by UPS at only $3 shipping each, with delivery in a few days. Thus, Tucker doesn't need to maintain much inventory.

There is little showroom space because most of the selling is done "in the field" by the five full-time sales reps. Each sales rep follows up on leads and demonstrates the units at the prospect's home. The salesperson installs the unit when a sale is made. The sales reps are paid on a commission basis—and pay their own expenses. They receive $120 for each unit sold, unless the sale results from a telephone appointment set up by the office. Then the commission is $100. Last year sales reps sold an average of about 20 units per month.

Appointments set up by the office account for about half of the sales. Some of these result from inquires stimulated by ads in local newspapers. The ads cost about $4,000 a month. To help find prospects, Tucker employs four part-time students who make telephone calls to potential customers—setting up appointments for the sales reps to demonstrate the dish system at the customer's home. The students are paid $5 for each appointment that they set up—and an additional $10 if the appointment results in a sale. About one out of every five appointments scheduled in this way results in a sale. But it is not unusual for a "prospector" to make 15 calls before setting up an appointment.

Sukomoko has been helpful to Dishcom by providing color brochures that describe the product and how it works, sales training materials on videotape, and materials to be used in sales presentations. Sukomoko also provides (at low cost) portable units that can be demonstrated by sales reps without any elaborate setup. Sukomoko even provides print copy for newspaper ads. All Dishcom has to do is buy the space.

Dishcom has operating expenses (beyond advertising and sales-related compensation) of only about $4,000 a month. (That, of course, does not include the cost of the units.)

Sales were going very well—and growing—until about January 1, 1986, when HBO began scrambling its programs. By July 1, 1986, HBO was joined by Cinemax, Showtime, The Movie Channel, Cable News Network (CNN), and CNN Headline News. And other channels—even the three major networks—were considering scrambling. The reduction in the available programming and the likelihood of having to buy a decoder for $395—and perhaps even paying for programming—caused Dishcom's sales to drop off precipitously. Mr. Tucker finds that some of his customers would be willing to buy a decoder, but they aren't happy about the possibility of paying monthly fees for their programming. A spokesman for dish manufacturers says the cable fees are artificially high because they are based on selling the limited number of people who subscribe to cable services. Some people argue that TV programming prices should be much lower. They feel that many more people would willingly pay—at lower prices.

Currently, a number of bills are in Congress to guarantee dish owners access to cable programs—at a reasonable monthly rate. One bill would require the Federal Communications Commission to make sure that the cable programmers' monthly rates for dish owners are no higher than the fees charged to cable customers. This might set an upper rate for Mr. Tucker's customers.

Among the possibilities that Mr. Tucker is considering is to continue selling Beam-Down II along with decoders, which cost $395 (his cost is $200). These decoders unscramble the present signals— and probably will be able to handle any scrambling for the next few years. But depending on the owners' locations, they still may have to pay an "unscrambling fee." In fact, most of Dishcom's customers are close enough to Charlotte, North Carolina, to be within range of any scrambling devices the program owners or local cable companies may use to "force" owners of dishes and decoders to pay some fees.

Evaluate Dishcom, Inc.'s present strategy. What strategy should Mr. Tucker follow for the near future? Be sure to consider the cost and price information provided in the case.

31.   *Precision Castings, Inc.*

Jack Tang, marketing manager for Precision Castings, is trying to figure out how to explain to his boss why a proposed new product line doesn't make sense for them. Jack is sure it's wrong—but can't seem to explain why.

Precision Castings, Inc., is a producer of malleable iron castings for automobile and aircraft manufacturers—and a variety of other users of castings. Last year's sales of castings amounted to over $55 million.

Precision also produces about 60 percent of all the original equipment bumper jacks installed in new automobiles each year. This is a very price-competitive business, but Precision has been able to obtain its large market share with frequent personal contact between the company's executives and its customers—supported by very close cooperation between the company's engineering department and its customers' buyers. This has been extremely important because the wide variety of models and model changes frequently requires alterations in the specifications of the bumper jacks. All of Precision's bumper jacks are sold directly to the automobile manufacturers. No attempt has been made to sell bumper jacks to final consumers through hardware and automotive channels—although they are available through the manufacturers' automobile dealers.

Mr. Sam Selim, Precision's production manager, now wants to begin producing hydraulic jacks for sale through automobile-parts wholesalers to retail auto parts stores. Mr. Selim saw a variety of hydraulic jacks at a recent automotive show—and knew immediately that his plant could produce these products. This especially interested him because of the possibility of using excess capacity—now that auto sales are down. Further, he thinks "jacks are jacks," and that the company would merely be broadening its product line by introducing hydraulic jacks. As he became more enthusiastic about the idea, he found that Precision's engineering department already had a design that appeared to be at least comparable to the products now offered on the market. None of these products have any patent protection.

Further, Mr. Selim says that the company would be able to produce a product that is better made than the competitive products (i.e., smoother castings, etc.)—although he agrees that customers probably wouldn't notice the differences. The production department's costs for making products comparable to those currently offered by competitors would be about one half the current prices at retail auto parts stores.

Jack Tang, the marketing manager, has just received a memo from Bill Miller, the company president, explaining the production department's enthusiasm for broadening Precision's jack line into hydraulic jacks. Miller seems enthusiastic about the idea, too, noting that it may be a way to make fuller use of the company's resources and increase its sales. Recognizing this enthusiasm, Jack Tang is trying to develop a good explanation of why he can't get very excited about the proposal. He knows he's already overworked and couldn't possibly promote this new line himself—and he's the only salesman the company has. So it would be necessary to hire someone to promote the line. And this "sales manager" would probably have to recruit manufacturers' agents (who probably will want a 15 percent commission on sales) to sell to automotive wholesalers who will stock the jacks and sell to the auto parts retailers. These wholesalers will probably expect trade discounts of 20 to 30 percent, trade show exhibits, some national advertising, and sales promotion help (catalog sheets, mailers, and point-of-purchase displays). And the retailers will probably expect trade discounts of 30 to 50 percent. Further, Jack Tang sees that the billing and collection system will have to be expanded because many more customers will be involved. It will also be necessary to keep track of agent commissions and accounts receivable. In summary, Jack feels that the proposed hydraulic-jack line is not very closely related to the company's present emphasis. He has already indicated his lack of enthusiasm to Sam Selim, but this made little difference in Sam's thinking. Now it's clear that Jack will have to convince the president or he will soon be responsible for selling hydraulic jacks.

Evaluate Precision's strategy and the proposed strategy. What should Jack Tang say to Bill Miller?

32. Lever, Limited*

Al Feta, marketing manager of Lever, Ltd., is being urged to okay the development of a separate marketing plan for Quebec.

Al Feta has been the marketing manager of Lever, Ltd., for the last four years—since he arrived from international headquarters in New York. Lever, Ltd.—headquartered in Toronto—is a subsidiary of a large U.S.-based consumer packaged-food company with world-wide sales of more than $2 billion in 1985. Its Canadian sales are just under $300 million—with the Quebec and Ontario markets accounting for 65 percent of the company's Canadian sales.

The company's product line includes such items as cake mixes, puddings, pie fillings, pancakes, and prepared foods. The company has successfully introduced at least six new products every year for the last five years. Its most recent new product was a line of frozen dinners successfully launched last year. Products from Lever are known for their high quality and enjoy much brand preference throughout Canada—including the Province of Quebec.

The company's sales have risen every year since Mr. Feta took over as marketing manager. In fact, the company's market share has increased steadily in each of the product categories in which it competes. The Quebec market has closely followed the national trend except that, in the past two years, total sales growth in that market began to lag.

According to Al Feta, a big advantage of Lever over its competitors is the ability to coordinate all phases of the food business from Toronto. For this reason, Mr. Feta meets at least once a month with his product managers—to discuss developments in local markets that might affect

---

*This case was adapted from one written by Professor Roberta Tamilia, University of Windsor, Canada.

marketing plans. While each manager is free to make suggestions—and even to suggest major departures from current marketing practices—Al Feta has the final say.

One of the product managers, Tom Rhone, expressed great concern at the last monthly meeting about the poor performance of some of the company's products in the Quebec market. While a broad range of possible reasons—ranging from inflation to politics—were reviewed to try to explain the situation, Tom insisted that it was due to a basic lack of understanding of that market because not enough managerial time and money had been spent on the Quebec market.

As a result, Tom Rhone felt the current marketing approach to the Quebec market should be reevaluated. An inappropriate marketing plan may be responsible for the sales slowdown. After all, he said, "80 percent of the market is French-speaking. It's in the best interest of the company to treat that market as being separate and distinct from the rest of Canada."

Tom Rhone supported his position by showing that Quebec's per capita consumption of many product categories (in which the firm competes) is above the national average (Table 1). Research projects conducted by Lever also support the "separate and distinct" argument. Over the years, the firm has found many French-English differences in brand attitudes, life styles, usage rates, and so on.

Tom argued that the company should develop a unique Quebec marketing plan for some or all of its brands. He specifically suggested that the French-language advertising plan for a particular brand be developed independently of the plan for English Canada. Currently, the agency assigned to the brand just translates its English-language

ads for the French market. Al Feta pointed out that the existing advertising approach assured Lever of a uniform brand image across Canada. However, the discussion that followed suggested that a different brand image might be needed in the French market if the company wanted to stop the brand's decline in sales.

The managers also discussed the food distribution system in Quebec. The major supermarket chains have their lowest market share in that province. Independents are strongest there—the "mom-and-pop" food stores fast disappearing outside Quebec remain alive and well in the province. Traditionally, these stores have stocked a higher proportion (than supermarkets) of their shelf space with national brands—an advantage for Lever.

Finally, various issues related to discount policies, pricing structure, sales promotion, and cooperative advertising were discussed. All of this suggested that things were different in Quebec—and that future marketing plans should reflect these differences to a greater extent than they do now.

After the meeting, Al Feta stayed in his office to think about the situation. Although he agreed with the basic idea that the Quebec market was in many ways different, he wasn't sure how far his company should go in recognizing this fact. He knew that regional differences in food tastes and brand purchases existed not only in Quebec, but in other parts of Canada as well. People were people, on the other hand, with far more similarities than differences.

Mr. Feta was afraid that giving special status to one region might conflict with top management's objective of achieving standardization whenever possible. He was also worried about the long-term effect of such a policy change on costs, organizational structure, and brand image. Still, enough product managers had expressed their concern over the years about the Quebec market to make him wonder if he shouldn't modify the current approach. Perhaps he could experiment with a few brands—and just in Quebec. He could cite the "language difference" as the reason for trying Quebec rather than any of the

Table 1   Per Capita Consumption Index, Province of Quebec (Canada = 100)

Cake mixes	103	Soft drinks	122
Pancakes	91	Pie fillings	115
Puddings	111	Frozen dinners	84
Salad dressings	87	Prepared packaged foods	89
Molasses	129	Cookies	119

other provinces. But Al realizes that any change of policy could be seen as the beginning of more change, and what would New York think? Could he explain it successfully there?

Evaluate Lever's present strategy. What should Al Feta do now? Explain.

33. *Visiting Nurses Services (VNS)*

Kay Brand, director of VNS, is attempting to clarify her agency's strategies. She's sure some changes are needed, but she's less sure about how much change is needed and/or can be handled by her people.

The Visiting Nurses Services (VNS) is a non-profit organization that has been operating—with varying degrees of success—for 20 years. Some of its funding comes from the local United Way—to provide emergency nursing services for those who can't afford to pay. The balance of the revenues—about 90 percent of the $1.4 million annual budget—comes from charges made directly to the client or to third-party payers—including insurance companies and the federal government—for Medicare or Medicaid services.

Kay Brand has been executive director of VNS for two years now. She has developed a well-functioning organization that is able to meet most requests for service that come from some local doctors and from the discharge officers at local hospitals. Some business also comes by self-referral—the client finds the VNS name in the Yellow Pages of the local phone directory.

The last two years have been a rebuilding time—because the previous director had personnel problems. This led to a weakening of the agency's image with the local referring agencies. Now the image is more positive. But Kay is not completely satisfied with the situation. By definition, the Visiting Nurses Services is a non-profit organization. But it still must cover all its costs in order to meet the payroll, rent payments, phone expenses, and so on—including Kay's own salary. She can see that while VNS is growing slightly and is now breaking even, it doesn't have

much of a cash "cushion" to fall back on if (1) the demand for VNS nursing services declines, (2) the government changes its rules about paying for the VNS's kind of nursing services—either cutting back on what it will pay for or reducing the amount it will pay for specific services—or (3) new competitors enter the market. In fact, the latter possibility is of great concern to Kay. Some hospitals—squeezed for revenue—are expanding into home health care. And "for-profit" organizations (e.g., Kelly Home Care Services) are expanding around the country—to provide home health care services—including nursing services of the kind offered by VNS. These for-profit organizations appear to be efficiently run—offering good service at competitive and sometimes even lower prices than some non-profit organizations. And they seem to be doing this at a profit—which suggests that it would be possible for these for-profit companies to lower their prices if non-profit organizations try to compete on price.

Kay is considering whether she should ask her board of directors to let her move into the whole "home health care" market—i.e., move beyond just nursing.

Currently, the VNS is primarily concerned with providing professional nursing care in the home. But VNS nurses are much too expensive for routine health care activities—helping fix meals, bathing and dressing patients, and so on. The "full cost" of a nurse to VNS (including benefits and overhead) is about $52 per hour. Besides, a registered nurse is not needed for routine jobs. All that is required is someone who can get along with all kinds of people and is willing to do this kind of work. Generally, any mature person can be trained fairly quickly to do the job—following the instructions and under the general supervision of a physician, a nurse, or family members. The "full cost" of aides is $5 to $10 per hour for short visits—and as low as $50 per 24 hours for a live-in aide who has room and board supplied by the client.

The demand for home health care services seems to be growing as more women join the work force and can't take over home health care when the need arises—due to emergencies or long-term disabilities. And with people living longer, there are more single-survivor family situations where there is no one nearby to take care of the needs of these older people. But often some family members—or third-party payers such as the government or insurers—are willing to pay home care services. Now Kay occasionally assigns nurses to this work—because the VNS has no regular home health care aides. Sometimes Kay recommends other agencies, or suggests one or another of three women who have been doing this work on their own—part-time. But with growing demand, Kay wonders if the VNS should get into this business—hiring aides as needed.

Kay is concerned that a new, full-service home health care organization may come into "her" market and provide both nursing services *and* less-skilled home health care services. This has happened already in two nearby, but somewhat larger cities. Kay fears that this might be more appealing than VNS to the local hospitals and other referrers. In other words, she can see the possibility of losing nursing service business if the VNS does not begin to offer a more complete service. This would cause real problems for the VNS—because overhead costs are more or less fixed. A loss in revenue of as little as 10 percent would require some cutbacks—perhaps laying off some nurses or secretaries, giving up part of the office, and so on.

Another reason for expanding beyond nursing services—using para-professionals and relatively unskilled personnel—is to offer a better service to present customers *and* make more effective use of the organization structure that has been developed over the last two years. Kay estimates that the administrative and office capabilities could handle 50 to 100 percent more clients without straining the system. It would be necessary to add some clerical help—if the expansion were quite large—as well as expanding the hours when the switchboard is open. But these increases in overhead would be minor compared to the present proportion of total revenue that goes to covering overhead. In other words, additional

clients could increase revenue and assure the survival of the VNS, provide a cushion to cover the normal fluctuations in demand, and assure more job security for the administrative personnel.

Further, Kay thinks that if the VNS were successful in expanding its services—and therefore could generate some surplus—it could extend services to those who aren't now able to pay. Kay says one of the worst parts of her job is refusing service to clients whose third-party benefits have run out or for whatever reason can no longer afford to pay. Kay is uncomfortable about having to cut off service, but she must schedule her nurses to provide revenue-producing services if she's going to meet the payroll every two weeks. By expanding to provide more services, she might be able to keep serving more of these non-paying clients. This possibility excites Kay because her nurse's training has instilled a deep desire to serve people—whether they can pay or not. This continual need to cut off service because people can't pay has been at the root of many disagreements—and even arguments—between the nurses serving the clients and Kay, as director and representative of the board of directors.

Kay knows that expanding into home health care services won't be easy. The nurses' union must be convinced that the nurses should be available on a 24-hour schedule—rather than the eight-to-five schedule six days a week that is typical now. Some decisions would be needed about relative pay levels for nurses, para-professionals, and home health care aides. VNS would also set prices for these different services and tell the present customers and referral agencies about the expanded services.

These problems aren't bothering Kay too much, however—she thinks she can handle them. She is sure that home health care services are in demand and could be supplied at competitive prices.

Her primary concern is whether this is the right thing for a nurses' organization to do. The name of her group is the Visiting Nurses Services, and its whole history has been oriented to supplying *nurses' services.* Nurses are dedicated professionals who bring high standards to any job they undertake. The question is whether the VNS should offer "less professional" services. Inevitably, some of the home health care aides will not be as dedicated as the nurses might like them to be. And this could reflect unfavorably on the nurse image. At the same time, however, Kay worries about the future of VNS—and her own future.

Evaluate VNS' present strategy. What should Kay Brand propose to the board of directors? Explain.

34. Black & Decker Company*

In April 1984, the management of Black & Decker (B&D) was poised on the brink of an extremely challenging time. The $300 million (U.S.) acquisition of General Electric's small appliance division had just been completed, representing B&D's attempt to dramatically expand its product line. Black & Decker, Canada, Inc., and Canadian General Electric were included in the deal. According to the agreement, B&D had three years to make the transition from GE's brand name.

B&D faced the question of rebuilding its image to include household products. Laurence Farley, chief executive officer for B&D, told a group of GE retailers at a meeting in February 1984, "Changing the GE brand name will not be easy, nor will it happen overnight. But we're convinced that it can be done successfully."

The Black & Decker Manufacturing Company of Towson, Maryland, was founded in 1910. In 1984, B&D was the world's leader in producing and selling both industrial and consumer power tools. However, the company faced saturation in its core business (consumer power tools) with limited growth potential. B&D also faced competition from the Japanese, who were experts in low-cost production. One Japanese firm, Makita,

was already milking profits from B&D's cash cow, industrial power tools, matching B&D's market share of 20 percent within a three-year period.

One of B&D's divisions had over-expanded during the 1970s. Sales for this division had then plummeted, causing it to be largely responsible for the $77 million loss suffered by B&D in 1982.

Farley began housecleaning to streamline operations worldwide and capitalize on B&D's strengths. Unprofitable divisions were sold, three plants were closed, and a layer of corporate management was eliminated. These moves strengthened the company's financial position by increasing liquidity and reducing leverage. In 1983 the company had a profit of $44 million. The first quarter of 1984 was encouraging. Unit sales were up by 20 percent, and profits increased by 85 percent to a record of $26.7 million.

In 1983 the company had experienced major restructuring and was revamping its entire strategy under the new president, Laurence Farley. In the past, B&D had allowed each subsidiary to have complete control over all operations in the belief that the individual companies knew their own markets best. This autonomy included the design of component parts and decisions regarding which products were offered. Several of B&D's products had been available in some markets and not in others. The DUSTBUSTER (a cordless vacuum), for example, was marketed in only three countries—France, the United Kingdom, and the United States.

The new president believed that the old policy was incompatible with his concept of "globalization"—the marketing of a standard product suitable for sale worldwide rather than a custom product intended for a specific market only. The GE acquisition provided the opportunity to expand sales dramatically since small appliances were thought to lend themselves to standardization. It was also a field where the Japanese were not yet a major factor.

B&D had launched several household items via their expertise in cordless appliance technology. These products bore their own brand name and were designed to capture market niches that

---

*This case was prepared by Ms. Shelagh M. Deely under the direction of Professors Carl Lawrence and Ken Wong, who at the time of its preparation were associated with Queen's University.

were previously unidentified. They accounted for 13 percent of B&D's total sales in 1983. Items such as the DUSTBUSTER, which were marketed under their trade name rather than the B&D logo, were runaway successes and paved the way into the household appliance market.

Prior to the acquisition, GE was number one in the small appliance business, holding a 50 percent market share in items such as toaster ovens, portable mixers, and irons. Sales for 1983 topped $470 million, but after-tax profits were only 3 percent of sales due to GE's high manufacturing costs. B&D could provide lower costs with its more efficient factories. GE top management decided that it could use its own technology and financial resources more effectively in markets for major appliances and high technology. The management and 125-person sales force of the GE small appliance operations were retained and transferred to B&D after the acquisition.

Black & Decker was determined to triple its size and become a $5 billion company by 1989. Farley believed that the small appliance business could be made more profitable by increasing sales volume. He wanted to try to push the brand image harder and thereby command higher prices. He reasoned that when products are similar, price becomes the deciding factor for the consumer and profits suffer as a result. The SPACEMAKER series, developed and introduced by GE, was a perfect test case. The SPACE-MAKER series was designed to hang beneath kitchen cabinets, thereby saving counter space, and consisted of a toaster oven, electric knife, can opener, and coffee maker. The series would be sold as a high-priced, color-coordinated group that could be bought separately, with the intention that when consumers returned for a particular item, they would choose one that matched what they already had.

Several crucial questions faced the top management of B&D after the acquisition. Among these were the following:

1. A powerful brand name has character and helps a high-quality product to be perceived as

such. Establishing an enduring brand name would not be an easy task:

a.   Appliance sales historically followed the rate of growth of the population and, as that rate slowed, increased competition for market share was likely to ensue.
b.   The quality of products from different manufacturers had become increasingly similar since major marketers had access to the same technology. Thus, marketing expenses were growing, as manufacturers responded to the ever-higher cost of reaching the consumer.
c.   The influence of the retailer and retailers' own store brands was growing in many parts of the world.

The "recognition level"* and reputation of GE needed to be transferred to B&D. Management was aware that a well-conceived and smooth transition was vital for success. How was the switch of brand name to be accomplished over the next few years?
2. Contribution towards retailers' profits from housewares products had always been low, and the retailers wanted reassurance that these skimpy margins would be improved under the B&D name. The SPACEMAKER line of products had proved to be successful beyond all expectations, and retailers were continually disappointed that demands were always in excess of deliveries. They had to be reassured that B&D would live up to its promise that five times the number of SPACEMAKER items would be produced in 1984 in order to meet this demand and alleviate the back-order problem. Some retail purchasing agents had already been stocking up on competitors' brands to guard against the possibility of losing sales due to inadequate inventories.
3. Decisions had to be made concerning whether or not B&D should continue GE's "stock balancing policy," under which retailers could return unsold merchandise to GE at year-end in exchange for new models. Retailers were clearly

*"Recognition level" refers to the extent to which the general public is familiar with the brand name in question.

concerned about being left with old stock under the B&D current policy of "you bought it, it's yours."

4. Traditional hardware stores, home centers, catalog showrooms, and discount department stores were the distribution outlets for power tools that were familiar to B&D. These were somewhat different from the retail and discount departments that carried housewares. B&D had to face the frenzy that accompanied the competition with other housewares manufacturers for retail shelf space. This would be a new experience for the B&D marketing staff, and management was concerned with how this task should be handled.

5. Black & Decker made its name through the power tool industry and now faced a completely different target market. Research had shown that women were more familiar with Black & Decker than first thought, mainly because they bought drills, etc., as gifts for their husbands or friends. Retailers were not quite so sure, though, how easy it would be to "sell a lady on a Black & Decker toaster."

Did the GE purchase make sense for Black & Decker? Would you bet on the company doing well in the small appliance business?

Notes

Chapter 1

1. Gregory D. Upah and Richard E. Wokutch, "Assessing Social Impacts of New Products: An Attempt to Operationalize the Macromarketing Concept," *Journal of Public Policy and Marketing* 4 (1985), pp. 166–78; Christopher H. Lovelock and Charles B. Weinberg, *Marketing for Public and Nonprofit Managers* (New York: John Wiley & Sons, 1984); and Ruby Roy Dholakia, "A Macromarketing Perspective on Social Marketing: The Case of Family Planning in India," *Journal of Macromarketing* 4, no. 1 (1984), pp. 53–61.

2. Malcolm P. McNair, "Marketing and the Social Challenge of Our Times," in *A New Measure of Responsibility for Marketing,* ed. Keith Cox and Ben M. Enis (Chicago: American Marketing Association, 1968).

3. An American Marketing Association committee developed a similar—but more complicated—definition of marketing: "Marketing is the process of planning and executing conception, pricing, promotion, and distribution of ideas, goods, and services to create exchanges that satisfy individual and organizational objectives." See *Marketing News,* March 1, 1985, p. 1. See also Ernest F. Cooke, C. L. Abercrombie, and J. Michael Rayburn, "Problems with the AMA's New Definition of Marketing Offer Opportunity to Develop an Even Better Definition," *Marketing Educator,* Spring 1986, p. 1f.

4. George Fisk, "Editor's Working Definiton of Macromarketing," *Journal of Macromarketing* 2, no. 1 (1982), pp. 3–4; Shelby D. Hunt and John J. Burnett, "The Macromarketing/Micromarketing Dichotomy: A Taxonomical Model," *Journal of Marketing,* Summer 1982, pp. 11–26; J. F. Grashof and A. Kelman, *Introduction to Macro-Marketing* (Columbus, Ohio: Grid, 1973); John L. Cromption and Charles W. Lamb, Jr., "The Importance of the Equity Concept in the Allocation of Public Services," *Journal of Macromarketing* 3, no. 1 (1983), pp. 28–39.

5. For a more complete discussion of this topic see Y. H. Furuhashi and E. J. McCarthy, *Social Issues of Marketing in the American Economy* (Columbus, Ohio: Grid, 1971), pp. 4–6.

6. Jacob Naor, "Towards a Socialist Marketing Concept—The Case of Romania," *Journal of Marketing,* January 1986, pp. 28–39; *Advertising Age,* September 16, 1985, pp. 74–79; "Free Enterprise Helps to Keep Russians Fed but Creates Problems," *The Wall Street Journal,* May 2, 1983, p. 1f; Coskun Samli, *Marketing and Distribution Systems in Eastern Europe* (New York: Praeger Publishers, 1978); John F. Gaski, "Current Russian Marketing Practice: A Report of the 1982 AMA Study Tour of the Soviet Union," in *1983 American Marketing Association Educators' Proceedings,* ed. P. Murphy et al. (Chicago: American Marketing Association, 1983), pp. 74–77; "Economic Problems Spur Soviets to Consider Changes in Industrial Organization—Even a 'Profit' Experiment," *The Wall Street Journal,* November 7, 1984, p. 36.

7. J. L. Badaracco, Jr., and D. B. Yoffie, "'Industrial Policy': It Can't Happen Here," *Harvard Business Review,* November-December 1983, pp 96–105; Murray L. Weidenbaum, *Business Government, and the Public* (Englewood Cliffs, N.J.: Prentice-Hall, 1977); John Kenneth Galbraith, *Economics and the Public Purpose* (Boston: Houghton-Mifflin, 1973); Bernard J. Cunningham, S. Prakash Sethi, and Thomas Turicchi, "Public Perception of Government Regulation," *Journal of Macromarketing* 2, no. 2 (1982), pp. 43–51; Robert G. Harris and James M. Carman, "A Typology of Regulatory Failures and Implications for Marketing and Public Policy," *Journal of Macromarketing* 6, no. 1 (1986), pp. 51–64; Venkatakrishna V. Bellur et al., "Strategic Adaptations to Price Controls: The Case of Indian Drug Industry," *Journal of the Academy of Marketing Science,* Winter/Spring 1985, pp. 143–59.

8. Van R. Wood and Scott J. Vitell, "Marketing and Economic Development: Review, Synthesis and Evaluation," *Journal of Macromarketing* 6, no. 1 (1986), pp. 28–48; Robert W. Nason and Phillip D. White, "The Visions of Charles C. Slater: Social Consequences of Marketing," *Journal of Macromarketing* 1, no. 2 (1981), pp. 4–18; D. F. Dixon, "The Role of Marketing in Early Theories of Economic Development," *Journal of Macromarketing* 1, no. 2 (1981), pp. 19–27; Jean C. Darian, "Marketing and Economic Development: A Case Study from Classical India," *Journal of Macromarketing* 5, no. 2 (1985), pp. 14–26.

9. William McInnes, "A Conceptual Approach to Marketing," in *Theory in Marketing,* second series, ed. Reavis Cox, Wroe Alderson, and Stanley J. Shapiro (Homewood, Ill.: Richard D. Irwin, 1964), pp. 51–67.

10. Reed Moyer, *Macro Marketing: A Social Perspective* (New York: John Wiley & Sons, 1972), pp. 3–5.

11. *Forging America's Future: Strategies for National Growth and Development,* Report of the Advisory Committee on National Growth Policy Processes, reprinted in *Challenge,* January/February 1977.

Chapter 2

1. "Pricey Ice Cream Is Scooping the Market," *Business Week,* June 30, 1986, pp. 60–61; "Work Out, Pig Out," *Insight,* May 19, 1986, p. 53; "A Taste for the Cream of the Crop," *Insight,* May 26, 1986, p. 49

2. "Marketing: The New Priority," *Business Week,* November 21, 1983, pp. 96–106; Neal Gilliatt and Pamela Cuming, "The Chief Marketing Officer: A Maverick Whose Time Has Come," *Business Horizons,* January/February 1986, pp. 41–48. For an early example of how the marketing revolution affected one firm, see Robert J. Keith, "The Marketing Revolution," *Journal of Marketing,* January 1960, pp. 35–38. For an overview of some of Procter & Gamble's current marketing effort, see "P&G's Rusty Marketing Machine," *Business Week,* October 21, 1985, pp. 111–12; "Procter & Gamble Co. Starts to Reformulate Tried and True Ways," *The Wall Street Journal,* March 30, 1983, p. 1.

3. Valarie A. Zeithaml, A. Parasuraman, and Leonard L. Berry, "Problems and Strategies in Services Marketing," *Journal of Marketing,* Spring 1985, pp. 33–46; Paul N. Bloom, "Effective Marketing for Professional Services," *Harvard Business Review,* September-October 1984, pp. 102–10; "Doctors Find a Dose of Marketing Can Cure Pain of Sluggish Practice," *The Wall Street Journal,* March 15, 1985, p. 21; "Hospitals Compete for Affluent Patients by Offering Luxury Suites and Hot Tubs," *The Wall Street Journal,* February 3, 1986, p. 19; "A High-Powered Pitch to Cure Hospitals' Ills," *Business Week,* September 2, 1985, pp. 60–61; "Lawyers Learn the Hard Sell—and Companies Shudder," *Business Week,* June 10, 1985, pp. 70–71; "Banks Get Aggressive," *Advertising Age,* March 10, 1986, p. S84; "A New Marketing Blitz in the War of Plastic Cards," *Business Week,* July 23, 1984, pp. 126–28.

4. Alan R. Andreasen, "Nonprofits: Check Your Attention to Customers," *Harvard Business Review,* May-June 1982, pp. 105–10; Jeffrey A. Barach, "Applying Marketing Principles to Social Causes," *Business Horizons,* July/August 1984, pp. 65–69; J. N. Green, "Strategy, Structure, and Survival: The Application of Marketing Principles in Higher Education During the 1980s," *Journal of Business* 10 (1982), pp. 24–28; Philip Kotler, "Strategies for Introducing Marketing into Nonprofit Organizations," *Journal of Marketing,* January 1979, pp. 37–44; C. Scott Greene and Paul Miesing, "Public Policy, Technology, and Ethics: Marketing Decisions for NASA's Space Shuttle," *Journal of Marketing,* Summer 1984, pp. 56–67.

5. Franklin S. Houston, "The Marketing Concept: What It Is and What It Is Not," *Journal of Marketing,* April 1986, pp. 81–87; Roger C. Bennett and Robert G. Cooper, "The Misuses of Marketing: An American Tragedy," *Business Horizons,* November/December 1981, pp. 51–61; Alan R. Andreasen, "Judging Marketing in the 1980s," *Journal of Macromarketing* 2, no. 1 (1982), pp. 7–13; Leslie M. Dawson, "Marketing for Human Needs in a Humane Future," *Business Horizons,* June 1980, pp. 72–82; Peter C. Riesz, "Revenge of the Marketing Concept," *Business Horizons,* June 1980, pp. 49–53; G. R. Laczniak, R. F. Lusch, and P. E. Murphy, "Social Marketing: Its Ethical Dimensions," *Journal of Marketing,* Spring 1979, pp. 29–36.

6. Barton A. Weitz and Robin Wensley, eds., *Strategic Marketing: Planning, Implementation and Control* (Boston: Kent, 1984); Ravi Singh Achrol and David L. Appel, "New Developments in Corporate Strategy Planning," in *1983 American Marketing Association Educators' Proceedings,* ed. P. Murphy et al. (Chicago: American Marketing Association, 1983), pp. 305–10; Derek F. Abell and John S. Hammond, *Strategic Market Planning: Problems and Analytical Approaches* (Englewood Cliffs, N.J.: Prentice Hall, 1979); Robert H. Hayes, "Strategic Planning—Forward In Reverse?" *Harvard Business Review,* November-December 1985, pp. 111–19.

7. Thomas V. Bonoma, "Making Your Marketing Strategy Work," *Harvard Business Review,* March-April 1984, pp. 68–76; Barbara J. Coe, "Key Differentiating Factors and Problems Associated with Implementation of Strategic Market Planning," in *1985 American Marketing Association Educators' Proceedings,* ed. R. F. Lusch et al. (Chicago: American Marketing Association, 1985), pp. 275–81; Robert E. Spekman and Kjell Gron-

haug, "Insights on Implementation: A Conceptual Framework for Better Understanding the Strategic Marketing Planning Process," in *1983 American Marketing Association Educators' Proceedings,* ed. P. Murphy et al. (Chicago: American Marketing Association, 1983), pp. 311–14.

8. Alfred P. Sloan, Jr., *My Years with General Motors* (New York: MacFadden Books, 1965), Introduction, chaps. 4 and 9; "Consumer Signals: Why U.S. Auto Makers Ignored Them," *Advertising Age,* August 4, 1980, pp. 43–48; "U.S. Auto Makers Reshape the World Competition," *Business Week,* June 21, 1982; "Ford's Fragile Recovery," *Fortune,* April 2, 1984, pp. 42–48; "GM Aims Saturn at a Blurred Target," *The Wall Street Journal,* December 16, 1985; "The American Small Car Keeps Getting More Japanese," *Business Week,* June 24, 1985, p. 50; "A Maxirush to Chrysler's Minivans," *Time,* February, 1984, p. 50.

9. Thomas S. Robertson and Scott Ward, "Management Lessons from Airline Deregulation," *Harvard Business Review,* January-February 1983, pp. 40–45; "Major Airlines Step up Battle for Key Markets, Endanger Weak Lines," *The Wall Street Journal,* June 18, 1985, p. 1f; "Decontrol of Airlines Shifts Pricing from a Cost to a Competition Basis," *The Wall Street Journal,* December 4, 1981; "Growing Pains at People Express," *Business Week,* January 28, 1985, pp. 90–91; "Airlines Vie for Share of Pie in Sky," *USA Today,* February 28, 1986, pp. B1–2.

Chapter 3

1. *1985 Annual Report,* Federal Express Corporation; "Federal Express Tries to Put More Zip in ZapMail," *Business Week,* December 17, 1984, pp. 110–11; "The Battle of the Overnights," *Newsweek,* February 7, 1983, pp. 55–56.

2. "Forget Satisfying the Consumer—Just Outfox the Other Guy," *Business Week,* October 7, 1985, p. 55f; Bruce D. Henderson, "The Anatomy of Competition," *Journal of Marketing,* Spring 1983, pp. 7–11; Kevin P. Coyne, "Sustainable Competitive Advantage—What It Is, What It Isn't," *Business Horizons,* January/February 1986, pp. 54–61; William A. Cohen, "War in the Marketplace," *Business Horizons,* March/April 1986, pp. 10–20; Peter Wright, "The Strategic Options of Least-Cost, Differentiation, and Niche," *Business Horizons,* March/April 1986, pp. 21–26; Michael E. Porter, *Competitive Strategy: Techniques for Analyzing Industries and Competitors* (New York: Free Press, 1980).

3. Igor Ansoff, *Corporate Strategy* (New York: McGraw-Hill, 1965); "Coca-Cola to Expand Its Entertainment Line," *The Wall Street Journal,* July 12, 1985, p. 6; "Holiday Inn Scrambles for New Profits," *New York Times,* April 22, 1984.

4. F. R. Bacon, Jr., T. W. Butler, Jr., and E. J. McCarthy, *Planned Innovation Procedures* (printed by authors, 1983). See also George S. Day, A. D. Shocker, and R. K. Srivastava, "Customer-Oriented Approaches to Identifying Product-Markets, *Journal of Marketing,* Fall 1979, pp. 8–19; Rajendra K. Srivastava, Mark I. Alpert, and Allan D. Shocker, "A Customer-Oriented Approach for Determining Market Structures," *Journal of Marketing,* Spring 1984, pp. 32–45. See also the classic article by T. Levitt, "Marketing Myopia," *Harvard Business Review,* September-October 1975, p. 1f.

5. Terry Elrod and Russell S. Winer, "An Empirical Evaluation of Aggregation Approaches for Developing Market Segments,"

Journal of Marketing, Fall 1982, pp. 32–34; Frederick W. Winter, "A Cost-Benefit Approach to Market Segmentation," *Journal of Marketing,* Fall 1979, pp. 103–11.

6. Russell I. Haley, "Benefit Segmentation—20 Years Later," *Journal of Consumer Marketing* 1, no. 2 (1984), pp. 5–14; Peter R. Dickerson, "Person-Situation: Segmentation's Missing Link," *Journal of Marketing,* Fall 1982, pp. 56–64. See also Richard M. Johnson, "Marketing Segmentation: A Strategic Management Tool," *Journal of Marketing Research,* February 1971, pp. 13–18; Roger J. Calantone and Alan G. Sawyer, "The Stability of Benefit Segments," *Journal of Marketing Research,* August 1978, pp. 395–404; Valarie A. Zeithaml, "The New Demographics and Market Fragmentation," *Journal of Marketing,* Summer 1985, pp. 64–75; "The Mass Market Is Splitting Apart," *Fortune,* November 28, 1983, pp. 76–82; "Companies Seek Ways to Put Coupons Where They'll Count," *The Wall Street Journal,* August 8, 1985, p. 25.

7. Peter Doyle and John Saunders, "Market Segmentation and Positioning in Specialized Industrial Markets," *Journal of Marketing,* Spring 1985, pp. 24–32; Richard E. Plank, "A Critical Review of Industrial Market Segmentation," *Industrial Marketing Management,* May 1985, pp. 79–92.

8. Girish Punj and David W. Stewart, "Cluster Analysis in Marketing Research: Review and Suggestions for Application," *Journal of Marketing Research,* May 1983, pp. 134–48; Fernando Robles and Ravi Sarathy, "Segmenting the Computer Aircraft Market with Cluster Analysis," *Industrial Marketing Management,* February 1986, pp. 1–12; Rajendra K. Srivastava, Robert P. Leone, and Allen D. Shocker, "Market Structure Analysis: Hierarchical Clustering of Products Based on Substitution-in-Use," *Journal of Marketing,* Summer 1981, pp. 38–48; Henry Assael, "Segmenting Markets by Response Elasticity," *Journal of Advertising Research,* April 1976, pp. 27–35.

9. David A. Aaker and J. Gary Shansby, "Positioning Your Product," *Business Horizons,* May/June 1982, pp. 56–62; Al Ries and Jack Trout, *Positioning: The Battle for Your Mind* (New York: McGraw-Hill, 1981), p. 53; D. W. Cravens, "Marketing Strategy Positioning," *Business Horizons,* December 1975, pp. 47–54; "Playing for Position," *Inc.,* April 1985, pp. 92–97; Phillip E. Downs and Joel B. Haynes, "Examining Retail Image before and after a Repositioning Strategy," *Academy of Marketing Science,* Fall 1984, pp. 1–24.

Chapter 4

1. "Tupperware: Sales Rebound Underway," *Advertising Age,* March 3, 1986, p. 32; "New Hustle for an Old Product," *Newsweek,* August 26, 1985, p. 48; "How Tupperware Hopes to Liven up the Party," *Business Week,* February 25, 1985, pp. 108–9.

2. See Peter F. Drucker, "Management: Tasks, Responsibilities, Practices, and Plans (New York: Harper & Row, 1973).

3. "Reichhold Chemicals: Now the Emphasis Is on Profits Rather Than Volume," *Business Week,* June 20, 1983, pp. 178–79; Carolyn Y. Woo, "Market-Share Leadership—Not Always So Good," *Harvard Business Review,* January-February 1984, pp. 50–55; Robert Jacobson and David A. Aaker, "Is Market Share All That It's Cracked up to Be?" *Journal of Marketing,* Fall 1985, pp. 11–22.

4. John D. Ela and Manley R. Irwin, "Technology Changes Market Boundaries," *Industrial Marketing Management,* July 1983, pp. 153–56; Geoffrey Kiel, "Technology and Marketing: The Magic Mix?" *Business Horizons,* May/June 1984, pp. 7–14; "Information Power: How Companies Are Using New Technologies to Gain a Competitive Edge," *Business Week,* October 14, 1985, pp. 108–14; Henry R. Norman and Patricia Blair, "The Coming Growth in 'Appropriate' Technology," *Harvard Business Review,* November-December 1982, pp. 62–67; Alan L. Frohman, "Technology as a Competitive Weapon," *Harvard Business Review,* January-February 1982, pp. 97–104.

5. "Consumers Union Tests Products in Ways Manufacturers Don't," *The Wall Street Journal,* January 14, 1985, p. 19; Paul N. Bloom and Stephen A. Greyser, "The Maturing of Consumerism," *Harvard Business Review,* November-December 1981, pp. 130–39; Robert Pitofsky, "Beyond Nader: Consumer Protection and the Regulation of Advertising," *Harvard Law Review,* February 1977, pp. 661–701.

6. Louis W. Stern and Thomas L. Eovaldi, *Legal Aspects of Marketing Strategy: Antitrust and Consumer Protection Issues* (Englewood Cliffs, N.J.: Prentice-Hall, 1984); "Packaging Firm Is Found Guilty of Price Conspiracy," *The Wall Street Journal,* January 21, 1977, p. 3. See also T. McAdams and R. C. Milgus, "Growing Criminal Liability of Executives," *Harvard Business Review,* March-April 1977, pp. 36–40.

7. Joseph C. Miller and Michael D. Hutt, "Assessing Societal Effects of Product Regulations: Toward an Analytic Framework," in *1983 American Marketing Association Educators' Proceedings,* ed. P. E. Murphy et al. (Chicago: American Marketing Association, 1983), pp. 364–68; Rachel Dardis and B. F. Smith, "Cost-Benefit Analysis of Consumer Product Safety Standards," *Journal of Consumer Affairs,* Summer 1977, pp. 34–46; Paul Busch, "A Review and Critical Evaluation of The Consumer Product Safety Commission: Marketing Management Implications," *Journal of Marketing,* October 1976, pp. 41–49.

8. Ray O. Werner, "Marketing and the Supreme Court in Transition, 1982–1984," *Journal of Marketing,* Summer 1985, pp. 97–105; Ray O. Werner, "Marketing and the United States Supreme Court, 1975–1981," *Journal of Marketing,* Spring 1982, pp. 73–81; Ben M. Enis and E. Thomas Sullivan, "The AT&T Settlement: Legal Summary, Economic Analysis, and Marketing Implications," *Journal of Marketing,* Winter 1985, pp. 127–36; Dorothy Cohen, "Trademark Strategy," *Journal of Marketing,* January 1986, pp. 61–74; A. R. Beckenstein, H. L. Gabel, and Karlene Roberts, "An Executive's Guide to Antitrust Compliance," *Harvard Business Review,* September-October 1983, pp. 94–102.

9. "Second Sunbelt Seen Emerging in the 1980s," *The Wall Street Journal,* October 23, 1981, p. 28; "Where You Live Often Affects the Kinds of Goods You Buy," *The Wall Street Journal,* September 14, 1983, p. 33; Gregory A. Jackson and George S. Masnick, "Take Another Look at Regional U.S. Growth," *Harvard Business Review,* March-April 1983, pp. 76–86; "New England's Big Recovery: The 'Most Spectacular' Event," *The Wall Street Journal,* December 18, 1984, p. 37.

10. Based on U.S. Census data and "Growing Pains at 40," *Time,* May 19, 1986, pp. 22–41; "Bringing up Baby: A New Kind of Marketing Boom," *Business Week,* April 22, 1985, p. 58f; Landon Y. Jones, "The Baby-Boom Consumer," *American Demographics,* February 1981, pp. 28–35; "A Portrait of America," *Newsweek,* January 17, 1983, pp. 20–33; "Ten Forces Reshaping America," *U.S. News & World Report,* March 19, 1984, pp. 40–52; "The Last Yuppie Story You Will Ever Have to Read," *Forbes,* February 25, 1985, pp. 134–35.

11. H. Lee Meadow, Stephen C. Cosmas, and Andy Plotkin, "The Elderly Consumer: Past, Present and Future," in *Advances in Consumer Research,* ed. Kent B. Monroe (Ann Arbor, Mich.: Association for Consumer Research, 1980), pp. 742–47; Betsy Gelb, "Discovering the 65+ Consumer," *Business Horizons,* May–June 1982, pp. 42–46; "What's New in Products for the Aged," *New York Times,* December 2, 1984; "'The New Old': Where the Economic Action Is," *Business Week,* November 25, 1985, pp. 137–40; "Last Year It Was Yuppies—This Year It's Their Parents," *Business Week,* March 10, 1986, pp. 68–74; "Yuppies Have Appeal, but Older Americans have Assets," *Business Week,* July 15, 1985, p. 24.

12. For more on the changing nature of families, see "How American Families Are Changing," *American Demographics,* January 1984, pp. 20–27; "Trends/Suprising Singles," *American Demographics,* August 1984, pp. 16–19.

13. "Prospects for Metropolitan Growth," *American Demographics,* April 1984, pp. 32–37; Rogene A. Buchholz, "Business and the Cities: New Directions for the Eighties," *Business Horizons,* January/February 1983, pp. 79–84; "The Suburban Life: Trees, Grass plus Noise, Traffic and Pollution," *The Wall Street Journal,* June 20, 1985, p. 32; "Gentrification of Cities Loses Much of Former Vigor," *The Wall Street Journal,* April 31, 1984, p. 33; Ernest F. Cooke, "Why The Retail Action Is East of the Mississippi," *American Demographics,* November 1984, pp. 21–24.

14. John Gottko, "Marketing Strategy Implications of the Emerging Patterns of Consumer Geographic Mobility," in *1985 American Marketing Association Educators' Proceedings,* ed. R. F. Lusch et al. (Chicago: American Marketing Association, 1985), pp. 290–95; Gerald Albaum and Del I. Hawkins, "Geographic Mobility and Demographic and Socioeconomic Market Segmentation," *Academy of Marketing Science,* Spring 1983, pp. 97–113; "Mobile Americans: A Moving Target with Sales Potential," *Sales & Marketing Management,* April 7, 1980, p. 40.

15. William Lazer, "How Rising Affluence Will Reshape Markets," *American Demographics,* February 1984, pp. 16–21; Thomas J. Stanley and George P. Moschis, "America's Affluent," *American Demographics,* March 1984, pp. 28–33; William Dunn, "In Pursuit of the Downscale," *American Demographics,* May 1986, pp. 26–33; "The Upbeat Outlook for Family Incomes," *Fortune,* February 25, 1980, pp. 122–30.

16. Frank R. Bacon, Jr., and Thomas W. Butler, Jr., *Planned Innovation,* rev. ed. (Ann Arbor: Institute of Science and Technology, University of Michigan, 1980).

17. Paul F. Anderson, "Marketing, Strategic Planning and the Theory of the Firm," *Journal of Marketing,* Spring 1982, pp. 15–26; George S. Day, "Analytical Approaches to Strategic Market Planning," in *Review of Marketing 1981,* ed. Ben M. Enis and Kenneth J. Roering (Chicago: American Marketing Association, 1981), pp. 89–105; Michael E. Porter, "How Competitive Forces Shape Strategy," *Harvard Business Review,* March/April 1979, pp. 137–45.

Chapter 5

1. "Bar Wars: Hershey Bites Mars," *Fortune,* July 8, 1985, pp. 52–57; "Market for Hard Candy Going Soft," *USA Today,* June 1983, pp. B1–2.

2. "Modified Computer System Helps Kraft Make Plans," *Marketing News,* May 23, 1986, p. 31.

3. Bernard C. Reimann, "Decision Support Systems: Strategic Management Tools for the Eighties," *Business Horizons,* September/October 1985, pp. 71–77; "Business Support Systems Cited by AMA," *Marketing News,* May 23, 1986, p. 1f; "So You Found the Needle, Now What?" *Nielsen Researcher,* no. 4 (1982), pp. 2–7; Allen S. King, "Computer Decision Support Systems Must be Credible, Consistent, and Provide Timely Data," *Marketing News,* December 12, 1980, p. 11; Martin D. Goslar and Stephen W. Brown, "Decision Support Systems in Marketing Management Settings," in *1984 American Marketing Association Educators' Proceedings,* ed. R. W. Belk et al. (Chicago: American Marketing Association, 1984), pp. 217–21.

4. F. Warren McFarlan, "Information Technology Changes the Way You Compete," *Harvard Business Review,* May-June 1984, pp. 98–103; M.E. Porter and V.E. Millar, "How Information Gives You Competitive Advantage," *Harvard Business Review,* July-August 1985, pp. 149–61; Donald F. Cox and Robert E. Good, "How to Build a Marketing Information System," *Harvard Business Review,* May–June 1967, pp. 145–56; Martin D. J. Buss, "Managing International Information Systems," *Harvard Business Review,* September-October 1982, pp. 153–62; Lindsay Meredith, "Developing and Using a Customer Profile Data Bank," *Industrial Marketing Management,* November 1985, pp. 255–68.

5. Dik Warren Twedt, *1983 Survey of Marketing Research* (Chicago: American Marketing Association, 1983).

6. For more details on doing marketing research, see Harper W. Boyd, Jr., Ralph Westfall, and Stanley F. Stasch, *Marketing Research: Text and Cases* (Homewood, Ill.: Richard D. Irwin, 1985.) See also Rohit Deshpande and Gerald Zaltman, "A Comparison of Factors Affecting Researcher and Manager Perceptions of Market Research Use," *Journal of Marketing Research,* February 1984, pp. 32–38.

7. "Dr. Pepper Is Bubbling Again after Its 'Be a Pepper' Setback," *The Wall Street Journal,* September 25, 1985, p. B1.

8. An excellent review of commercially available secondary data may be found in Donald R. Lehmann, *Marketing Research and Analysis,* 2nd ed. (Homewood, Ill.: Richard D. Irwin, 1985), pp. 231–72. See also "Everything You Always Wanted to Know May Soon Be On Line," *Fortune,* May 5, 1980, pp. 226–40; Ronald L. Vaughn, "Demographic Data Banks: A New Management Resource," *Business Horizons,* November/December 1984, pp. 38–56.

9. Kathleen M. Wallace, "The Use and Value of Qualitative Research Studies," *Industrial Marketing Management,* August 1984, pp. 181–86; Thomas V. Bonoma, "Case Research in Marketing: Opportunities, Problems, and a Process," *Journal of Marketing Research,* May 1985, pp. 199–208. For more on focus groups, see William Wells, "Group Interviewing," in *Handbook of Marketing Research,* ed. R. Ferber (New York: McGraw-Hill, 1975); Bobby J. Calder, "Focus Groups and the Nature of Qualitative Marketing Research," *Journal of Marketing Research,* August 1977, pp. 353–64; Joe L. Welch, "Researching Marketing Problems and Opportunities with Focus Groups," *Industrial Marketing Management,* November 1985, pp. 245–54.

10. Frederick Wiseman and Maryann Billington, "Comment on a Standard Definition of Response Rates," *Journal of Marketing Research,* August 1984, pp. 336–38.

11. Tyzoon T. Tyebjee, "Telephone Survey Methods: The State of the Art," *Journal of Marketing,* Summer 1979, pp. 68–77.

12. For more detail on observational approachs, see "Buy the Numbers," *Inc.,* March, 1985; "Market Research by Scanner," *Business Week,* May 5, 1980, pp. 113–16; "License Plates Locate Customers," *The Wall Street Journal,* February 5, 1981, p. 23; "Taking Measure of the People Meter," *Marketing and Media Decisions,* August 1985, p. 62f; Eugene Webb et al., *Unobstrusive Measures: Nonreactive Research in the Social Sciences* (Chicago: Rand McNally, 1966).

13. Alan G. Sawyer, Parker M. Worthing, and Paul E. Fendak, "The Role of Laboratory Experiments to Test Marketing Strategies," *Journal of Marketing,* Summer 1979, pp. 60–67; "Test Marketing—The Next Generation," *Nielsen Researcher,* no. 3 (1984), pp. 21–23; "Test Marketing Enters a New Era," *Dun's Business Month,* October 1985, p. 86f.

14. A number of surveys reveal which marketing research areas and techniques are most common. See for example Barnett A. Greenberg, Jac L. Goldstucker, and Danny N. Bellenger, "What Techniques Are Used by Marketing Researchers in Business," *Journal of Marketing,* April 1977, pp. 62–68.

15. Alan R. Andreasen, "Cost-Conscious Marketing Research," *Harvard Business Review,* July-August 1983, pp. 74–81; A. Parasuraman, "Research's Place in the Marketing Budget," *Business Horizons,* March/April 1983, pp. 25–29; R. J. Small and L. J. Rosenberg, "The Marketing Researcher as a Decision Maker: Myth or Reality?" *Journal of Marketing,* January 1975, pp. 2–7; Danny N. Bellenger, "The Marketing Manager's View of Marketing Research," *Business Horizons,* June 1979, pp. 59–65.

Chapter 6

1. "Cadillac Wants to Attract Younger Buyers But Its 'Old Man' Image Gets in the Way," *The Wall Street Journal,* November 18, 1985, p. 33; "Detroit Beware: Japan Is Ready to Sell Luxury," *Business Week,* December 9, 1985, pp. 114–18; "Cadillac Keeps Thinking BIG," *USA Today,* June 19, 1986, p. B1.

2. *Consumer Expenditure Survey: Interview Survey, 1982–83,* Bulletin No. 2246, U.S. Department of Labor, February, 1986; David E. Bloom and Sanders D. Korenman, "Spending Habits of American Consumers," *American Demographics,* March 1986, pp. 22–25.

3. Patrick E. Murphy and William A. Staples, "A Modernized Family Life Cycle," *Journal of Consumer Research,* June 1979, pp. 12–22; William D. Wells and George Gubar, "Life Cycle Concept in Marketing Research," *Journal of Marketing Research,* November 1966, pp. 355–63; Janet Wagner and Sherman Hanna, "The Effectiveness of Family Life Cycle Variables in Consumer Expenditure Research," *Journal of Consumer Research,* December 1983, pp. 281–91; "Companies Target Big-Spending Teens," *Dun's Business Month,* March 1985, pp. 48–49.

4. "Segmenting the Black Market," *Marketing Communications,* July 1985, p. 17f; "Black Market? It's Virtually Untapped," *Advertising Age,* April 16, 1979, p. S14; "Black Middle Class Emerges as Dominant Consumer Force," *Advertising Age,* April 16, 1979, p. S27; A. A. Brogowicz, "Race as a Basis for Market Segmentation: An Exploratory Analysis," Ph.D. thesis, Michigan State University, 1977.

5. "Special Report: Hispanic Marketing," *Advertising Age,* February 27, 1986, pp. 11–12; Robert Wilkes and Humberto Valencia, "Shopping Orientations of Mexican-Americans," *1984 American Marketing Association Educators' Proceedings* (Chicago:
American Marketing Association, 1984), pp. 26–31; Danny N. Bellenger and Humberto Valencia, "Understanding the Hispanic Market," *Business Horizons,* May/June 1982, pp. 47–50; "Hispanics in the United States: Yesterday, Today and Tomorrow," *Futurist,* August 1980, pp. 25–31.

6. "A Special Report: The Corporate Woman," *The Wall Street Journal,* May 24, 1986, pp. D2–32; "Women at Work," *Business Week,* January 28, 1985, pp. 80–85; "The Lasting Changes Brought by Women Workers," *Business Week,* March 15, 1982, pp. 59–67; Michael D. Reilly, "Working Wives and Convenience Consumption," *Journal of Consumer Research,* March 1982, pp. 407–18; "Two-Income Families Will Reshape the Consumer Markets," *Fortune,* March 10, 1980; Myra Strober and Charles B. Weinberg, "Strategies Used by Working and Nonworking Wives to Reduce Time Pressures," *Journal of Consumer Research,* March 1979, pp. 338–47; "More Food Advertisers Woo the Male Shopper as He Shares the Load," *The Wall Street Journal,* August 26, 1980, p. 1; "Wives Are Bringing Home More of the Bacon," *Business Week,* June 23, 1986, pp. 33–34.

7. K. H. Chung, *Motivational Theories and Practices* (Columbus, Ohio: Grid,1977), pp. 40–43; A. H. Maslow, *Motivation and Personality* (New York: Harper & Row, 1970).

8. Frances K. McSweeney and Calvin Bierley, "Recent Developments in Classical Conditioning," *Journal of Consumer Research,* September 1984, pp. 619–31; Walter R. Nord and J. Paul Peter, "A Behavior Modification Perspective on Marketing," *Journal of Marketing,* Spring 1980, pp. 36–47; James R. Bettman, "Memory Factors in Consumer Choice: A Review," *Journal of Marketing,* Spring 1979, pp. 37–53.

9. For just a few references, see Alvin A. Achenbaum, "Advertising Doesn't Manipulate Consumers," *Journal of Advertising Research,* April 1972, pp. 3–14; Steven J. Gross and C. Michael Niman, "Attitude-Behavior Consistency: A Review," *Public Opinion Quarterly,* Fall 1975, pp. 358–68; J. Pavasars and W. D. Wells, "Measures of Brand Attitudes Can Be Used to Predict Buying Behavior," *Marketing News,* April 11, 1975, p. 6; Calvin P. Duncan and Richard W. Olshavsky, "External Search: The Role of Consumer Beliefs," *Journal of Marketing Research,* February 1982, pp. 32–43; M. Joseph Sirgy, "Self-Concept in Consumer Behavior: A Critical Review," *Journal of Consumer Research,* December 1982, pp. 287–300.

10. Harold H. Kassarjian and Mary Jane Sheffet, "Personality and Consumer Behavior: An Update," in *Perspectives in Consumer Behavior,* ed. H. Kassarjian and T. Robertson, (Glenview, Ill.: Scott Foresman, 1981), p. 160; H. H. Kassarjian, "Personality and Consumer Behavior: A Review," *Journal of Marketing Research,* November 1971, pp. 409–18; Raymond L. Horton, *Buyer Behavior: A Decision Making Approach* (Columbus, Ohio: Charles E. Merrill, 1984).

11. "The ABCs of Psychographics," *American Demographics,* November 1983, pp. 25–29; "Psychographic Glitter and Gold," *American Demographics,* November 1985, pp. 22–29; W. D. Wells, "Psychographics: A Critical Review," *Journal of Marketing Research,* May 1975, pp. 196–213; Alvin C. Burns and Mary C. Harrison, "A Test of the Reliability of Psychographics," *Journal of Marketing Research,* February 1979, pp. 32–38; Jack A. Lesser and Marie Adele Hughes, "The Generalizability of Psychographic Market Segments across Geographic Locations," *Journal of Marketing,* January 1986, pp. 18–27.

12. G. M. Munsinger, J. E. Weber, and R. W. Hansen, "Joint Home Purchasing Decisions by Husbands and Wives," *Journal of Consumer Research,* March 1975, pp. 60–66; E. P. Cox III,

"Family Purchase Decision Making and the Process of Adjustment," *Journal of Marketing Research,* May 1975, pp. 189–95; I. C. M. Cunningham and R. R. Green, "Purchasing Roles in the U.S. Family, 1955 & 1973," *Journal of Marketing,* October 1974, pp. 61–64; Harry L. Davis, "Decision Making within the Household," *Journal of Consumer Research,* March 1976, pp. 241–60; George J. Szybillo et al., "Family Member Influence in Household Decision Making," *Journal of Consumer Research,* December 1979, pp. 312–16.

13. Richard P. Coleman, "The Continuing Significance of Social Class to Marketing," *Journal of Consumer Research,* December 1983, pp. 264–80; "What Is Happening to the Middle Class?" *American Demographics,* January 1985, pp. 18–25.

14. James H. Donnelly, Jr., "Social Character and Acceptance of New Products," *Journal of Marketing Research,* February 1970, pp. 111–16; Jeffrey D. Ford and Elwood A. Ellis, "A Reexamination of Group Influence on Member Brand Preference," *Journal of Marketing Research,* February 1980, pp. 125–32; George P. Moschis, "Social Comparison and Informal Group Influence," *Journal of Marketing Research,* August 1976, pp. 237–44.

15. James H. Myers and Thomas S. Robertson, "Dimensions of Opinion Leadership," *Journal of Marketing Research,* February 1972, pp. 41–46; Charles W. King and John O. Summers, "Overlap of Opinion Leadership across Consumer Product Categories," *Journal of Marketing Research,* February 1970, pp. 43–50.

16. Grant McCracken, "Culture and Consumption: A Theoretical Account of the Structure and Movement of the Cultural Meaning of Consumer Goods," *Journal of Consumer Research,* June 1986, pp. 71–84; Walter A. Henry, "Cultural Values Do Correlate with Consumer Behavior," *Journal of Marketing Research,* May 1976, pp. 121–27. See also Lynn R. Kahle, "The Nine Nations of North America and the Value Basis of Geographic Segmentation," *Journal of Marketing,* April 1986, pp. 37–47.

17. Russell W. Belk, "Situational Variables and Consumer Behavior," *Journal of Consumer Research* 2 (1975), pp. 157–64; John F. Sherry, Jr., "Gift Giving in Anthropological Perspective," *Journal of Consumer Research,* September 1983, pp. 157–68.

18. Adapted and updated from James H. Myers and William H. Reynolds, *Consumer Behavior and Marketing Management* (Boston: Houghton-Mifflin, 1967), p. 49. See also Wayne D. Hoyer, "An Examination of Consumer Decision Making for a Common Repeat Purchase Product," *Journal of Consumer Research,* December 1984, pp. 822–29; James R. Bettman, *An Information Processing Theory of Consumer Choice* (Reading, Mass.: Addison-Wesley, 1979); Richard W. Olshavsky and Donald H. Granbois, "Consumer Decision Making—Fact or Fiction?" *Journal of Consumer Research,* September 1979, pp. 93–100; Lawrence X. Tarpey, Sr., and J. Paul Peter, "A Comparative Analysis of Three Consumer Decision Strategies," *Journal of Consumer Research,* June 1975, pp. 29–37; J. H. Myers and M. I. Alpert, "Determinant Buying Attributes: Meaning and Measurement," *Journal of Marketing,* October 1968, pp. 13–20.

19. Raj Arora, "Consumer Involvement—What It Offers to Advertising Strategy," *International Journal of Advertising* 4, no. 2 (1985), pp. 119–30; John A. Howard, *Consumer Behavior: Theory and Action* (New York: McGraw-Hill, 1977), pp. 9–10; Mark E. Slama and Armen Tashchian, "Selected Socioeconomic and Demographic Characteristics Associated with Purchasing Involvement," *Journal of Marketing,* Winter 1985, pp. 72–82.

20. Adapted from E. M. Rogers, *The Diffusion of Innovations* (New York: Free Press, 1962); E. M. Rogers with F. Shoemaker, *Communication of Innovation: A Cross Cultural Approach* (New York: Free Press, 1968).

21. William Cunnings and Mark Venkatesan, "Cognitive Dissonance and Consumer Behavior: A Review of the Evidence," *Journal of Marketing Research,* August 1976, pp. 303–8.

Chapter 7

1. "Polaroid Corp. Is Selling Its Technique for Limiting Supplier Price Increases," *The Wall Street Journal,* February 13, 1985, p. 36.

2. For more detail, see "SIC: The System Explained," *Sales & Marketing Management,* April 22, 1985, pp. 52–113.

3. Edward F. Fern and James R. Brown, "The Industrial/Consumer Marketing Dichotomy: A Case of Insufficient Justification," *Journal of Marketing,* Spring 1984, pp. 68–77; Peter Banting et al., "Similarities in Industrial Procurement across Four Countries," *Industrial Marketing Management,* May 1985, pp. 133–44; John Seminerio, "What Buyers Like From Salesmen," *Industrial Marketing Management,* May 1985, pp. 75–78.

4. Patrick J. Robinson and Charles W. Faris, *Industrial Buying and Creative Marketing* (Boston: Allyn & Bacon, 1967), chap. 2. See also Frederick E. Webster, Jr., and Yoram Wind, "A General Model for Understanding Organizational Buying Behavior," *Journal of Marketing,* April 1972, pp. 12–19; Joseph A. Bellizzi and Phillip McVey, "How Valid Is the Buy-Grid Model?" *Industrial Marketing Management,* February 1983, pp. 57–62; Rowland T. Moriarty, Jr., and Robert E. Spekman, "An Empirical Investigation of the Information Sources Used During the Industrial Buying Process," *Journal of Marketing Research,* May 1984, pp. 137–47.

5. Vincent G. Reuter, "What Good Are Value Analysis Programs?" *Business Horizons,* March/April 1986, pp. 73–79.

6. Donald W. Jackson, Jr., Janet E. Keith, and Richard K. Burdick, "Purchasing Agents' Perceptions of Industrial Buying Center Influence: A Situational Approach," *Journal of Marketing,* Fall 1984, pp. 75–83; Wesley J. Johnston and Thomas V. Bonoma, "The Buying Center: Structure and Interaction Patterns," *Journal of Marketing,* Summer 1981, pp. 143–56; Lowell E. Crow and Jay D. Lindquist, "Impact of Organizational and Buyer Characteristics on the Buying Center," *Industrial Marketing Management,* February 1985, pp. 49–58; Marvin Berkowitz, "New Product Adoption by the Buying Organization: Who Are the Real Influencers?" *Industrial Marketing Management,* February 1986, pp. 33–44; W. E. Patton III, Christopher P. Puto, and Ronald H. King, "Which Buying Decisions Are Made by Individuals and Not by Groups?" *Industrial Marketing Management,* May 1986, pp. 129–38; Michael H. Morris and Stanley M. Freedman, "Coalitions in Organizational Buying," *Industrial Marketing Management,* May 1984, pp. 123–32.

7. "Detroit Raises the Ante for Parts Suppliers," *Business Week,* October 14, 1985, pp. 94–97.

8. Peter Kraljic, "Purchasing Must Become Supply Management," *Harvard Business Review,* September-October 1983, pp. 109–17; Christopher P. Puto, Wesley E. Patton III, and Ronald H. King, "Risk Handling Strategies in Industrial Vendor Selection Decisions," *Journal of Marketing,* Winter 1985, pp. 89–98.

9. Ralph W. Jackson and William M. Pride, "The Use of Approved Vendor Lists," *Industrial Marketing Management,* August 1986, pp. 165–70.

10. "Federal Suit Charges GE with Reciprocity on Purchasing; Vigorous Defense Is Vowed," *The Wall Street Journal,* May 19, 1972, p. 2. See also Robert E. Weigand, "The Problems of Managing Reciprocity," *California Management Review,* Fall 1973, pp. 40–48.

11. *1985 Annual Report,* Super Valu.

12. Dan Hicks, "MEGA Means Superior Service and Super Selection," *Boise Cascade Quarterly,* August 1985, p. 9.

13. For a detailed discussion of supermarket chain buying, see J. F. Grashof, *Information Management for Supermarket Chain Product Mix Decisions,* Ph.D. thesis, Michigan State University, 1968.

14. "For Drug Distributors, Information Is the Rx for Survival," *Business Week,* October 14, 1985, p. 116.

15. "Create Open-to-Buy Plans the Easy Way," *Retail Control,* December 1984, pp. 21–31.

16. Warren H. Suss, "How to Sell to Uncle Sam," *Harvard Business Review,* November-December 1984, pp. 136–44; David E. Gumpert and Jeffry A. Timmons, "Penetrating the Government Procurement Maze," *Harvard Business Review,* September-October 1982, pp. 14–23.

Chapter 8

1. Leonard L. Berry, "Services Marketing Is Different," in Christopher H. Lovelock, *Services Marketing* (Englewood Cliffs, N.J.: Prentice-Hall, 1984), pp. 29–37: G. Lynn Shostack, "Designing Services That Deliver," *Harvard Business Review,* January-February 1984, pp. 133–39; Richard B. Chase, "Where Does the Customer Fit in a Service Operation?" *Harvard Business Review,* November-December 1978, pp. 137–42; Dan R. E. Thomas, "Strategy Is Different in Service Industries," *Harvard Business Review,* July-August 1978, pp. 158–65; Leonard L. Berry, Valarie A. Zeithaml, and A. Parasuraman, "Quality Counts in Services, Too," *Business Horizons,* May/June 1985, pp. 44–52; Phillip D. White and Edward W. Cundiff, "Assessing the Quality of Industrial Products," *Journal of Marketing,* January 1978, pp. 80–86; Gorden E. Greenley, "Tactical Product Decisions," *Industrial Marketing Management,* February 1983, pp. 13–18; Jack Reddy and Abe Berger, "Three Essentials of Product Quality," *Harvard Business Review,* July-August 1983, pp. 153–59.

2. J. B. Mason and M. L. Mayer, "Empirical Observations of Consumer Behavior as Related to Goods Classification and Retail Strategy," *Journal of Retailing,* Fall 1972, pp. 17–31; Arno K. Kleinenhagen, "Shopping, Specialty, or Convenience Goods?" *Journal of Retailing,* Winter 1966–67, p. 32f; Perry Bliss, "Supply Considerations and Shopper Convenience," *Journal of Marketing,* July 1966, pp. 43–45; W. P. Dommermuth and E. W. Cundiff, "Shopping Goods, Shopping Centers, and Selling Strategies," *Journal of Marketing,* October 1967, pp. 28–36; Edward M. Tauber, "Why Do People Shop?" *Journal of Marketing,* October 1972, pp. 46–49; Christopher H. Lovelock, "Classifying Services to Gain Strategic Marketing Insights," *Journal of Marketing,* Summer 1983, pp. 9–20:

3. "Even Star Insurers Are Feeling the Heat," *Business Week,* January 14, 1985, p. 119. See also David T. Kollat and Ronald

P. Willett, "Is Impulse Purchasing Really a Useful Concept for Marketing Decisions?" *Journal of Marketing,* January 1969, pp. 79–83; Danny N. Bellenger, Dan H. Robertson. and Elizabeth C. Hirschman, "Impulse Buying Varies by Product," *Journal of Advertising Research,* December 1978, pp. 15–18.

4. William S. Bishop, John L. Graham, and Michael H. Jones, "Volatility of Derived Demand in Industrial Markets and Its Management Implications," *Journal of Marketing,* Fall 1984, pp. 95–103.

5. Paul F. Anderson and William Lazer, "Industrial Lease Marketing," *Journal of Marketing,* January 1978, pp. 71–79.

6. P. Matthyssens and W. Faes, "OEM Buying Process for New Components: Purchasing and Marketing Implications," *Industrial Marketing Management,* August 1985, pp. 145–57.

7. Ruth H. Krieger and Jack R. Meredith, "Emergency and Routine MRO Part Buying," *Industrial Marketing Management,* November 1985, pp. 277–82; Warren A. French et al., "MRO Parts Service in the Machine Tool Industry," *Industrial Marketing Management,* November 1985, pp. 283–88.

8. "Name-Calling: What the Name of Your Company and Products Says About You and Your Business," *Inc.,* July 1984; "In Marketing, 'Lite' Is a Heavy," *The Chicago Tribune,* November 5, 1985, Sec. 3, p. 6; "Putting Muscle into Trademark Protection," *Advertising Age,* June 9, 1986, p. S13; "Judge Takes a 'Functional' Look at Trademarks," *Advertising Age,* April 21, 1986, p. 52; "Putting Teeth in the Trademark Laws," *Business Week,* November 8, 1984, pp. 75–79; "DuPont's Teflon Trademark Survives Attack," *Advertising Age,* July 14, 1975, p. 93; George Miaoulis and Nancy D'Amato, "Consumer Confusion and Trademark Infringement," *Journal of Marketing,* April 1978, pp. 48–55; Thomas M. S. Hemnes, "How Can You Find a Safe Trademark?" *Harvard Business Review,* March-April 1985, pp. 36–51.

9. "The Marketing of Licensed Characters for Kids, or How the Lovable Care Bears Were Conceived," *The Wall Street Journal,* September 24, 1982, p. 44; "Coca-Cola Finds Murjani Clothes Are It," *Advertising Age,* June 9, 1986, p. S4–S5; "What's in a Name? Millions, if It's Licensed," *Business Week,* April 8, 1985, pp. 97–98; "I'll Wear the Coke Pants Tonight; They Go Well with My Harley-Davidson Ring," *The Wall Street Journal,* July 6, 1985, p. 31.

10. Brian F. Harris and Roger A. Strang, "Marketing Strategies in the Age of Generics," *Journal of Marketing,* Fall 1985, pp. 70–81; "No-Frills Products: 'An Idea Whose Time Has Gone,'" *Business Week,* June 17, 1985, pp. 64–65; Martha R. McEnally and Jon M. Hawes, "The Market for Generic Brand Grocery Products: A Review and Extension," *Journal of Marketing,* Winter 1984, pp. 75–83; K. L. Granzin, "An Investigation of the Market for Generic Products," *Journal of Retailing* 57, 1981, pp. 39–55; "Checklist Tells if Generic Products 'Threaten' Your Brand," *Marketing News,* October 31, 1980; "Co-opting Generics," *Advertising Age,* March 31, 1981.

11. J. A. Bellizzi et al., "Consumer Perceptions of National, Private, and Generic Brands," *Journal of Retailing* 57, 1981, pp. 56–70; I. C. M. Cunningham, A. P. Hardy, and G. Imperia, "Generic Brands versus National Brands and Store Brands," *Journal of Advertising Research,* October/November 1982, pp. 25–32; "Private-Label Firms Aided by Inflation, Expected to Post Healthy Growth in 1980," *The Wall Street Journal,* March 31, 1980, p. 20; "The Drugmaker's Rx for Living with Generics," *Business Week,* November 6, 1978, pp. 205–8.

12. "Package Redesign Helps Soft Cookie Contender Attract National Attention," *Food Processing,* March 1986, pp. 69–70; "Inflatable Campaign Toasts Wine Packaging," *Advertising Age,* May 12, 1986, p. S14; "Containers and Packaging" (chap. 7), *U.S. Industrial Outlook 1980,* p. 75; "Packaging for the Elderly," *Modern Packaging,* October 1979, pp. 38–39; "Is the Bar of Soap Washed up?" *Business Week,* January 12, 1982, pp. 109–16; "Consumers Examine Packages Very Closely Since Tylenol Tragedy," *The Wall Street Journal,* November 5, 1982, p. 1; "Paper Bottles Are Coming on Strong," *Business Week,* January 16, 1984, pp. 56–57; "Wrapping up Sales," *Nation's Business,* October 1985, pp. 41–42; "Quaker State Expects Sales Gains with New Packaging System for Oil," *Marketing News,* February 3, 1984; James H. Barnes, Jr., "Recycling: A Problem in Reverse Logistics," *Journal of Macromarketing,* 2, no. 2 (1982), pp. 31–37.

13. Dennis L. McNeill and William L. Wilkie, "Public Policy and Consumer Information: Impact of the New Energy Labels," *Journal of Consumer Research,* June 1979, pp. 1–11; W. A. French and L. O. Schroeder, "Packge Information Legislation: Trends and Viewpoints," *MSU Business Topics,* Summer 1972, pp. 39–42. See also J. A. Miller, D. G. Topel, and R. E. Rust, "USDA Beef Grading: A Failure in Consumer Information?" *Journal of Marketing,* January 1976, pp. 25–31.

14. J. E. Russo, "The Value of Unit Price Information," *Journal of Marketing Research,* May 1977, pp. 193–201; K. B. Monroe and P. J. LaPlaca, "What Are the Benefits of Unit Pricing?" *Journal of Marketing,* July 1972, pp. 16–22; David A. Aaker and Gary T. Ford, "Unit Pricing Ten Years Later: A Replication," *Journal of Marketing,* Winter 1983, pp. 118–22.

15. "UPC Registers Retailing Impact," *Advertising Age,* April 7, 1986, p. 3f; "Bar Codes: Beyond the Checkout Counter," *Business Week,* April 8, 1985, p. 90; "Bar Codes are Black-and-White Stripes and Soon They Will Be Read All Over," *The Wall Street Journal,* January 8, 1985, p. 39; "Firms Line up to Check out Bar Codes," *USA Today,* December 4, 1985, pp. B1–2.

16. Joshua Lyle Wiener, "Are Warranties Accurate Signals of Product Reliability?" *Journal of Consumer Research,* September 1985, p. 245f; Laurence P. Feldman, "New Legislation and the Prospects for Real Warranty Reform," *Journal of Marketing,* July 1976, pp. 41–47; F. K. Shuptrine and Ellen Moore, "Even after the Magnuson-Moss Act of 1975, Warranties Are Not Easy to Understand," *Journal of Consumer Affairs,* Winter 1980, pp. 394–404; C. L. Kendall and Frederick A. Russ, "Warranty and Complaint Policies: An Opportunity for Marketing Management," *Journal of Marketing,* April 1975, pp. 36–43; David L. Malickson, "Are You Ready for a Product Recall?" *Business Horizons,* January/February 1983, pp. 31–35.

Chapter 9

1. "Marketbuster," *Time,* February 1, 1985, p. 72.

2. George Day, "The Product Life Cycle: Analysis and Applications Issues," *Journal of Marketing,* Fall 1981, pp. 60–67; John E. Swan and David R. Rink, "Fitting Marketing Strategy to Varying Product Life Cycles," *Business Horizons,* January/February 1982, pp. 72–76; Igal Ayal, "International Product Life Cycle: A Reassessment and Product Policy Implications," *Journal of Marketing,* Fall 1981, pp. 91–96; William Qualls, Richard W. Olshavsky, and Ronald E. Michaels, "Shortening of the PLC—An Empirical Test," *Journal of Marketing,* Fall 1981, pp. 76–80; Hans B. Thorelli and Stephen C. Burnett, "The Nature of Product Life Cycles for Industrial Goods Businesses," *Journal of Marketing,* Fall 1981, pp. 97–108; Roger C. Bennett and Robert G. Cooper, "The Product Life Cycle Trap," *Business Horizons,* September/October, 1984, pp. 7–16; Sak Onkvisit and John J. Shaw, "Competition and Product Management: Can the Product Life Cycle Help?" *Business Horizons,* July/August 1986, pp. 51–62; John E. Smallwood, "The Product Life Cycle: A Key to Strategic Marketing Planning," *MSU Business Topics,* Winter 1973, pp. 29–35; Richard F. Savach and Laurence A. Thompson, "Resource Allocation within the Product Life Cycle," *MSU Business Topics,* Autumn 1978, pp. 35–44; Peter F. Kaminski and David R. Rink, "PLC: The Missing Link between Physical Distribution and Marketing Planning," *International Journal of Physical Distribution and Materials Management* 14, no. 6 (1984), pp. 77–92.

3. "RCA to Cut Prices on Eight Color TVs in Promotion Effort," *The Wall Street Journal,* December 31, 1976, p. 16; "Sales of Major Appliances, TV Sets Gain but Profits Fail to Keep up: Gap May Widen," *The Wall Street Journal,* August 21, 1972, p. 22; "What Do You Do when Snowmobiles Go on a Steep Slide?" *The Wall Street Journal,* March 8, 1978, p. 1f; "After Their Slow Year, Fast-Food Chains Use Ploys to Speed up Sales," *The Wall Street Journal,* April 4, 1980, p. 1f; "Home Smoke Detectors Fall on Hard Times as Sales Apparently Peaked," *The Wall Street Journal,* April 3, 1980, p. 1; "As Once Bright Market for CAT Scanners Dims, Smaller Makers of the X-Ray Devices Fade out," *The Wall Street Journal,* May 6, 1980, p. 40.

4. Susan Fraker, "High-Speed Management for the High-Tech Age," *Fortune,* March 5, 1984, pp. 62–68; "How Xerox Speeds up the Birth of New Products," *Business Week,* March 19, 1984, pp. 58–59.

5. "Cookie Marketers Keep Mixing It up," *Advertising Age,* February 24, 1986, p. 12; Steven P. Schnaars, "When Entering Growth Markets, Are Pioneers Better than Poachers?" *Business Horizons,* March/April 1986, pp. 27–36.

6. "Tide Unleashes Flood of New Tide Products," *Advertising Age,* June 16, 1986, p. 3f; "'Good Products Don't Die,' P&G Chairman Declares," *Advertising Age,* November 1, 1976, p. 8; "Ten Ways to Restore Vitality to Old, Worn-Out Products," *The Wall Street Journal,* February 18, 1982, p. 25; William Lazer, Mushtaq Luqmani, and Zahir Quraeshi, "Product Rejuvenation Strategies," *Business Horizons,* November/December 1984, pp. 21–28.

7. "3M's Aggressive New Consumer Drive," *Business Week,* July 16, 1984, pp. 114–22; "Sixteen Years and $100 Million Later, Alza Gets a Dose of Success," *Business Week,* February 4, 1985, pp. 84–86; "Videodisks Make a Comeback as Instructors and Sales Tools," *The Wall Street Journal,* February 15, 1985, p. 25; Patrick M. Dunne, "What Really Are New Products?" *Journal of Business,* December 1974, pp. 20–25.

8. *Marketing News,* February 8, 1980; C. Merle Crawford, "Marketing Research and the New-Product Failure Rate," *Journal of Marketing,* April 1977, pp. 51–61.

9. Adapted from Frank R. Bacon, Jr., and Thomas W. Butler, Jr., *Planned Innovation,* rev. ed. (Ann Arbor: Institute of Science and Technology, University of Michigan, 1980). See also John R. Rockwell and Marc C. Particelli, "New Product Strategy: How the Pros Do It," *Industrial Marketing,* May 1982, p. 49f; G. Urban and J. Hauser, *Design and Marketing of New Products* (Englewood Cliffs, N.J.: Prentice Hall, 1980); David S. Hopkins, "New Emphasis in Product Planning and Strategy Development," *Industrial Marketing Management Journal* 6, 1977, pp. 410–19; Eric von Hippel, "Get New Products from Customers," *Harvard Business Review,* March-April 1982, pp. 117–22;

Shelby H. McIntyre and Meir Statman, "Managing the Risk of New Product Development," *Business Horizons,* May/June 1982, pp. 51–55; "Listening to the Voice of the Marketplace," *Business Week,* February 21, 1983, p. 90f; Hirotaka Takeuchi and Ikujiro Nonaka, "The New New Product Development Game," *Harvard Business Review,* January-February 1986, pp. 137–46.

10. Booz, Allen & Hamilton, *Management of New Products* (1968); "More New Products Die Abourning than in 1968," *Marketing and Media Decisions,* May 1982, p. 48.

11. T. M. Dworkin and M. J. Sheffet, "Product Liability in the 80s," *Journal of Public Policy and Marketing,* 4, 1985, pp. 69–79; Michael Brody, "When Products Turn Liabilities," *Fortune,* March 3, 1986, pp. 20–24; Fred W. Morgan, "Marketing and Product Liability: A Review and Update," *Journal of Marketing,* Summer 1982, pp. 69–78; "The Insurance Crisis: Now Everyone Is in a Risky Business, *Business Week,* March 10, 1986, pp. 88–92; "Marketers Feel Product Liability Pressure," *Advertising Age,* May 12, 1986, p. 3f; "Did Searle Close Its Eye to a Health Hazard," *Business Week,* October 14, 1985, pp. 120–22; George Eads and Peter Reuter, "Designing Safer Products: Corporate Responses of Product Liability Law and Regulation," *Journal of Products Liability* 7, no. 3 (1984), pp. 263–94.

12. Phillip R. McDonald and Joseph O. Eastlack, Jr., "Top Management Involvement with New Products," *Business Horizons,* December 1971, pp. 23–31; Peter F. Drucker, "A Prescription for Entrepreneurial Management," *Industry Week,* April 29, 1985, p. 33f; E. F. McDonough III and F. C. Spital, "Quick-Response New Product Development," *Harvard Business Review,* September-October 1984, pp. 52–61.

13. "How Ford Hit the Bull's Eye with Taurus," *Business Week,* June 30, 1986, pp. 69–70. See also T. Levitt, "Innovation Imitation," *Harvard Business Review,* September-October 1966, pp. 63–70; Shelby H. McIntyre, "Obstacles to Corporate Innovation," *Business Horizons,* January/February 1982, pp. 23–28.

14. Richard T. Hise and J. Patrick Kelly, "Product Management on Trial," *Journal of Marketing,* October 1978, pp. 28–33; Victor P. Buell, "The Changing Role of the Product Manager in Consumer Goods Companies," *Journal of Marketing,* July 1975, pp. 3–11; Robert W. Eckles and Timothy J. Novotny, "Industrial Product Managers: Authority and Responsibility," *Industrial Marketing Management,* May 1984, pp. 71–76; William Theodore Cummings, Donald W. Jackson, Jr., and Lonnie L. Ostrom, "Differences between Industrial and Consumer Product Managers," *Industrial Marketing Management,* August 1984, pp. 171–80; Thomas J. Cosse and John E. Swan, "Strategic Marketing Planning by Product Managers—Room for Improvement?" *Journal of Marketing,* Summer 1983, pp. 92–102.

Chapter 10

1. "Now Big Blue Is Making Waves in Shallower Waters," *Business Week,* September 30, 1985, pp. 102–4.

2. For a classic discussion of the discrepancy concepts, see Wroe Alderson, "Factors Governing the Development of Marketing Channels," in *Marketing Channels for Manufactured Goods,* ed. Richard M. Clewett (Homewood, Ill.: Richard D. Irwin, 1954), pp. 7–9; Louis W. Stern and Adel I. El-Ansary, *Marketing Channels* (Englewood Cliffs, N.J.: Prentice-Hall, 1982). See also R. D. Michman and S. D. Sibley, *Marketing Channels and Strategies* (Columbus, Ohio: Grid, 1980); "Distributors: No Endangered Species," *Industry Week,* January 24, 1983, pp. 47–52.

3. Bernard J. LaLonde and P. H. Zinszer, *Customer Service: Meaning and Measurement* (Chicago: National Council of Distribution Management, 1976).

4. For more detail on deregulation of transportation, see J. J. Coyle, Edward J. Bardi, and Joseph L. Cavinato, *Transportation* (St. Paul, Minn.: West Publishing, 1986); "Deregulating America," *Business Week,* November 28, 1983. See also C. H. White and R. B. Felder, "Turn Your Truck Fleet into a Profit Center," *Harvard Business Review,* May-June 1983, pp. 14–17; "Push for Tighter U.S. Supervision of Railroads Is a Threat to Success of Reagan Deregulators," *The Wall Street Journal,* January 7, 1985, p. 50; "Living without Shackles," *Time,* December 12, 1983, p. 51; "Big Carriers Rely on Commuter Lines," *The Wall Street Journal,* September 13, 1985, p. 6.

5. For a more detailed comparison of mode characteristics, see Donald J. Bowersox, David L. Closs, and Omar K. Helferich, *Logistical Management* (New York: Macmillan Publishing, 1986); Edward R. Bruning and Peter M. Lynagh, "Carrier Evaluation in Physical Distribution Management," *Journal of Business Logistics,* September 1984, pp. 30–47.

6. "Why Santa Fe Wants the Southern Pacific," *Business Week,* June 2, 1980, p. 29; "N&W and Southern Railroads Propose $2 Billion Merger, Response to Big Consolidation Announced This Year," *The Wall Street Journal,* June 3, 1980, p. 3; "Back to Railroading for a New Era," *Business Week,* July 14, 1980, p. 64.

7. George L. Stern, "Surface Transportation: Middle-of-the-Road Solution," *Harvard Business Review,* December 1975, p. 82.

8. Gunna K. Sletmo and Jacques Picard, "International Distribution Policies and the Role of Air Freight," *Journal of Business Logistics* 6, no. 1 (1985), pp. 35–53; "Federal Express Rides the Small-Package Boom," *Business Week,* March 31, 1980, p. 108.

9. Michael D. Hutt and Thomas W. Speh, "Realigning Industrial Marketing Channels," *Industrial Marketing Management,* July 1983, pp. 171–78; "How Just-in-Time Inventories Combat Foreign Competition," *Business Week,* May 14, 1984, pp. 176D–76G; David J. Armstrong, "Sharpening Inventory Management," *Harvard Business Review,* November-December 1985, pp. 42–59; Hall E. Mather, "The Case for Skimpy Inventories," *Harvard Business Review,* January-February 1984, pp. 40–49.

10. Wade Ferguson, "Buying an Industrial Service Warehouse Space," *Industrial Marketing Management,* February 1983, pp. 63–66; "Warehousing: Should You Go Public?" *Sales & Marketing Management,* June 14, 1976, p. 52; G. O. Pattino, "Public Warehousing: Supermarket for Distribution Services," *Handling and Shipping,* March 1977, p. 59; "Public Warehouses Perform Many Marketing Functions," *Marketing News,* February 8, 1980, p. 12.

11. Kenneth B. Ackerman and Bernard J. LaLonde, "Making Warehousing More Efficient," *Harvard Business Review,* April 1980, pp. 94–102.

12. Roy D. Shapiro, "Get Leverage from Logistics," *Harvard Business Review,* May-June 1984, pp.119–26; James E. Morehouse, "Operating in the New Logistics Era," *Harvard Business Review,* September-October 1983, pp. 18–19; Graham Sharman, "The Rediscovery of Logistics," *Harvard Business Review,* September-October 1984, pp. 71–79.

13. Ernest B. Uhr, Ernest C. Houck, and John C. Rogers, "Physical Distribution Service," *Journal of Business Logistics* 2, no. 2 (1981), pp. 158–69; Martin Christopher, "Creating Effective Policies for Customer Service," *International Journal of Physical Distribution and Materials Management* 13, no. 2 (1983), pp. 3–24; William D. Perreault, Jr., and Frederick A. Russ, "Physical Distribution Service in Industrial Purchase Decisions," *Journal of Marketing,* April 1976, pp. 3–10; Harvey N. Shycon and Christopher R. Sprague, "Put a Price Tag on Your Customer Servicing Levels," *Harvard Business Review,* July-August 1979, pp. 71–78; Richard A. Matteis, "The New Back Office Focuses on Customer Service," *Harvard Business Review,* March-April 1979, pp. 146–59; William D. Perreault, Jr., and Frederick R. Russ, "Physical Distribution Service: A Neglected Aspect of Marketing Management," *MSU Business Topics,* Summer 1974, pp. 37–46; Philip B. Schary, "Customer Service as a System Process," *Contemporary Issues in Marketing Channels,* eds. R. Lusch and P. Zinszer (Norman: University of Oklahoma, 1979), pp. 165–75; Frances G. Tucker, "Creative Customer Service Management," *International Journal of Physical Distribution and Materials Management* 13, no. 3 (1983), pp. 34–50.

14. Michael W. Miller, "Apple Promises Big Role for Retailers and Producers of Computer Accessories," *The Wall Street Journal,* June 27, 1985, p 8.

15. Robert D. Buzzell, "Is Vertical Integration Profitable?" *Harvard Busines Review,* January-February 1983, pp. 92–102; Louis W. Stern and Torger Reve, "Distribution Channels as Political Economies: A Framework for Comparative Analysis," *Journal of Marketing,* Summer 1980. pp. 52–64; Michael Etgar and Aharon Valency, "Determinants of the Use of Contracts in Conventional Marketing Channels," *Journal of Retailing,* Winter 1983, pp. 81–92; "Why Manufacturers Are Doubling as Distributors," *Business Week,* January 17, 1983, p. 41; "Beer and Antitrust," *Fortune,* December 9, 1985, pp. 135–36; "Car Megadealers Loosen Detroit's Tight Rein," *The Wall Street Journal,* July 1, 1985, p. 6; Wilke D. English and Donald A. Michie, "The Impact of Electronic Technology upon the Marketing Channel," *Academy of Marketing Science,* Summer 1985, pp. 57–71.

16. "Esprit's Spirited Style Is Hot Seller," *USA Today,* March 25, 1986, p. B5; "Apparel Firm Makes Profits, Takes Risks by Flouting Tradition, *The Wall Street Journal,* June 11, 1985, p. 1f.

17. "Antitrust Issues and Marketing Channel Strategy" and "Case 1—Continental T.V., Inc. et al. v. GTE Sylvania, Inc.," in Louis W. Stern and Thomas L. Eovaldi, *Legal Aspects of Marketing Strategy* (Englewood Cliffs, N.J.: Prentice-Hall, 1984), pp. 300–61. See also James R. Burley, "Territorial Restriction and Distribution Systems: Current Legal Developments," *Journal of Marketing,* October 1975, pp. 52–56; "Justice Takes Aim at Dual Distribution," *Business Week,* July 7, 1980, pp. 24–25; Saul Sands and Robert J. Posch, Jr., "A Checklist of Questions for Firms Considering a Vertical Territorial Distribution Plan," *Journal of Marketing,* Summer 1982, pp. 38–43.

18. See, for example, Michael Levy, John Webster, and Roger Kerin, "Formulating Push Marketing Strategies: A Method and Application," *Journal of Marketing,* Winter 1983, pp. 25–34; "Gillette Puts $8,000,000 Ad Push into Trac II National Introduction," *Advertising Age,* September 6, 1971, p. 4.

19. Bruce J. Walker, Janet E. Keith, and Donald W. Jackson, Jr., "The Channels Manager: Now, Soon or Never?" *Academy of Marketing Science,* Summer 1985, pp. 82–96; Robert W. Little, "The Marketing Channel: Who Should Lead This Extra Corporate Organization?" *Journal of Marketing,* January 1970, pp. 31–39; Patrick L. Schul, William M. Pride, and Taylor L. Little, "The Impact of Channel Leadership Behavior on Intrachannel

Conflict," *Journal of Marketing,* Summer 1983, pp. 21–34; Gary L. Frazier, "On the Measurement of Interfirm Power in Channels of Distribution," *Journal of Marketing Research,* May 1983, pp. 158–66; Bert Rosenbloom and Rolph Anderson, "Channel Management and Sales Management: Some Key Interfaces," *Academy of Marketing Science,* Summer 1985, pp. 97–106.

20. Shelby D. Hunt, Nina M. Ray, and Van R. Wood, "Behavioral Dimensions of Channels of Distribution: Review and Synthesis," *Academy of Marketing Science,* Summer 1985, pp. 1–24; Peter R. Dickson, "Distributor Portfolio Analysis and the Channel Dependence Matrix: New Techniques for Understanding and Managing the Channel," *Journal of Marketing,* Summer 1983, pp. 35–44; Robert F. Lusch, "Sources of Power: Their Impact on Intrachannel Conflict," *Journal of Marketing Research,* November 1976, pp. 382–90; William P. Dommermuth, "Profiting from Distribution Conflicts," *Business Horizons,* December 1976, pp. 4–13; Shelby D. Hunt and John R. Nevin, "Power in a Channel of Distribution: Sources and Consequences," *Journal of Marketing Research,* May 1974, pp. 186–93; Louis P. Bucklin, "A Theory of Channel Control," *Journal of Marketing,* January 1973, pp. 39–47; James R. Brown, "A Cross-Channel Comparison of Supplier-Retailer Relations," *Journal of Retailing,* Winter 1981, pp. 3–18; John E. Robbins, Thomas W. Speh, and Morris L. Mayer, "Retailers' Perceptions of Channel Conflict Issues," *Journal of Retailing,* Winter 1982, pp. 46–67; John F. Gaski, "The Theory of Power and Conflict in Channels of Distribuiion," *Journal of Marketing,* Summer 1984, pp. 9–29.

Chapter 11

1. "Sears, Ward's: Get Small," *Advertising Age,* March 31, 1986, p. 85; "Hechinger's: Nobody Does It Better in Do-It-Yourself," *Business Week,* May 5, 1986, p. 96; "Hardware Wars: The Big Boys Might Lose This One," *Business Week,* October 14, 1985, pp. 84–92; "Hardware Stores Forced to Alter Marketing Tack," *The Wall Street Journal,* August 13, 1985, p. 35.

2. *Client's Monthly Alert,* June 1977, p. 3.

3. For additional examples, see "Zayre's Strategy of Ethnic Merchandising Proves to Be Successful in Inner-City Stores," *The Wall Street Journal,* September 25, 1984, p. 31; "Selling to the Poor: Retailers That Target Low-Income Shoppers Are Growing Rapidly," *The Wall Street Journal,* June 24, 1985, p. 1f.

4. "Bonwit's Turns up the Heat," *Business Week,* October 11, 1976, pp. 120–22.

5. *Census of Retailers 1982* (Washington, D.C.: U.S. Bureau of the Census, 1985).

6. "How Department Stores Plan to Get the Registers Ringing Again," *Business Week,* November 18, 1985, pp. 66–67; "Why Profits Shrink at a Grand Old Name (Marshall Field)," *Business Week,* April 11, 1977, pp. 66–78; Louis H. Grossman, "Merchandising Strategies of a Department Store Facing Change," *MSU Business Topics,* Winter 1970, pp. 31–42; "Suburban Malls Go Downtown," *Business Week,* November 10, 1973, pp. 90–94.

7. David Appel, "The Supermarket: Early Development of an Institutional Innovation," *Journal of Retailing,* Spring 1972, pp. 39–53.

8. "Special Report: Grocery Marketing," *Advertising Age,* April 28, 1986, p. S1f; *Industry Surveys,* January 26, 1984, pp. R1–7; "The Transformation of the Nation's Supermarkets," *The New*

York Times, September 2, 1984, p. 1f: Edward W. McLaughlin and Gene A. German, "Supermarketing Success," *American Demographics,* August 1985, pp. 34–37.

9. "Catalog Showrooms Revamp to Keep Their Identity," *Business Week,* Industrial/Technology Edition, June 10, 1985, pp. 117–20; "Discount Catalogs: A New Way to Sell," *Business Week,* April 29, 1972, pp. 72–74; Pradeep K. Korgaonkar, "Consumer Preferences for Catalog Showrooms and Discount Stores," *Journal of Retailing,* Fall 1982, pp. 76–88; "Best Products: Too Much Too Soon at the No. 1 Catalog Showroom," *Business Week,* July 23, 1984, pp. 136–38.

10. "Mass Merchandisers Move toward Stability," *Nielsen Researcher,* no. 3 (1976), pp. 19–25; "Where K mart Goes Next Now That It's No. 2," *Business Week,* June 2, 1980, p. 109; "Mass Merchandisers: A Maturing Retail Concept," *Nielsen Researcher,* no. 3 (1984), pp. 14–20; "Electronics Superstores Are Devouring Their Rivals," *Business Week,* June 24, 1985, pp. 84–85; "Hechinger's: Nobody Does It Better in Do-It-Yourself," *Business Week,* May 5, 1986, p. 96.

11. "Special Report: Grocery Marketing," *Advertising Age,* April 28, 1986, p. S1f. For a discussion of the early superstore concept, see W. J. Salmon, R. D. Buzzell, and S. G. Cort, "Today the Shopping Center, Tomorrow the Superstore," *Harvard Business Review,* January-February 1974, pp. 89–98.

12. "Convenience Chains Chase Buying Trends," *USA Today,* June 11, 1986, p. B3; "Convenience Stores: A $7.4 Billion Mushroom," *Business Week,* March 21, 1977, pp. 61–64; "Convenience Stores Battle Lagging Sales by Adding Items and Cleaning up Image," *The Wall Street Journal,* March 28, 1980, p. 16; "Arco Takes on Convenience Stores," *Advertising Age,* December 17, 1979, p. 1f.

13. "How Sweet It Is for Granola Bars," *Business Week,* August 12, 1985, pp. 61–62; "Vendors Pull out All Stops," *Business Week,* August 15, 1970, pp. 52–54.

14. "Magalogs in the Mailbox," *Time,* September 2, 1985, p. 73; "Catalog Merchants Try New Strategies as the Field Crowds with Competitors," *The Wall Street Journal,* January 20, 1986, p.17; "Catalogue Cornucopia," *Time,* November 8, 1982, pp. 72–79; "Baby-Goods Firms See Direct Mail as the Perfect Pitch for New Moms," *The Wall Street Journal,* January 29, 1986, p. 31; "Mail Order: Continuing Its Maturation, Competitiveness," *Direct Marketing,* July 1985, pp. 64–86; "Montgomery Ward Is Planning to Shut 300 Catalog Stores," *The Wall Street Journal,* January 14, 1985, p. 6; "Competition Heats up for and with Consumer Mailbox," *Direct Marketing,* February 1985, pp. 46–57.

15. Rom J. Markin and Calvin P. Duncan, "The Transformation of Retailing Institutions: Beyond the Wheel of Retailing and Life Cycle Theories," *Journal of Macromarketing* 1, no. 1 (1981), pp. 58–66; R. C. Curhan, W. J. Salmon, and R. D. Buzzell, "Sales and Profitability of Health and Beauty Aids and General Merchandise in Supermarkets," *Journal of Retailing,* Spring 1983, pp. 77–99; Ronald Savitt, "The 'Wheel of Retailing' and Retail Product Management," *European Journal of Marketing* 18, no. 6/7 (1984), pp. 43–54; "Safeway: Selling Nongrocery Items to Cure the Supermarket Blahs," *Business Week,* March 7, 1977, pp. 52–58; William R. Davidson, Albert D. Bates, and Stephen J. Bass, "Retail Life Cycle," *Harvard Business Review,* November-December 1976, pp. 89–96.

16. Dale D. Achabal, John M. Heineke, and Shelby H. McIntyre, "Issues and Perspectives on Retail Productivity," *Journal of Retailing,* Fall 1984, p. 107f; Charles A. Ingene, "Scale

Economies in American Retailing: A Cross-Industry Comparison," *Journal of Macromarketing,* 4, no. 2 (1984), pp. 49–63; "Mom-and-Pop Videotape Shops Are Fading out," *Business Week,* September 2, 1985, pp. 34–35.

17. "The Stunning Franchise Explosion," *The New York Times,* January 20, 1985; "Franchisee Cuts Risk of Going into Business," *USA Today,* February 10, 1986, p. E6; "Franchising across the USA," *USA Today,* November 1, 1985, pp. B5–7. See also the special issue on franchising in the *Journal of Retailing,* Winter 1968–69.

18. "Electronic Retailing Goes to the Supermarket," *Business Week,* March 25, 1985, pp. 78–79.

19. "Computer Users Shop at Home over the Phone," *The Wall Street Journal,* February 20, 1985, p. 35; Terry R. Hiller, "Going Shopping in the 1990s," *The Futurist,* December 1983, pp. 63–68; Larry J. Rosenberg and Elizabeth C. Hirschman, "Retailing without Stores," *Harvard Business Review,* July-August 1980, pp. 103–12; Albert D. Bates, "The Troubled Future of Retailing," *Business Horizons,* August 1976, pp. 22–28; Ronald D. Michman, "Changing Patterns in Retailing," *Business Horizons,* October 1979, pp. 33–38; "Sears Mulls Test of Catalog Sales via Warner Cable," *Advertising Age,* February 18, 1980, p. 1f; Patrick J. Kelly and William R. George, "Strategic Management Issues for the Retailing of Services," *Journal of Retailing,* Summer 1982, pp. 26–43; "Shoppers Tune in National Cable Network," *Advertising Age,* March 6, 1986, p. 35; "Home Shopping Gets Push from Cable Systems," *Advertising Age,* June 9, 1986, p. 64; Joel E. Urbany and W. Wayne Talarzyk, "Videotex: Implications for Retailing," *Journal of Retailing,* Fall 1983, pp. 76–92; George P. Moschis, Jac L. Goldstucker, and Thomas J. Stanley, "At-Home Shopping: Will Consumers Let Their Computers Do the Walking?" *Business Horizons,* March/April 1985, pp. 22–29; Jack G. Kaikati, "Don't Discount Off-Price Retailers," *Harvard Business Review,* May-June 1985, pp. 85–92.

Chapter 12

1. "American Hospital Supply: Snaring New Business with Freebies and Bonuses," *Business Week,* April 8, 1985, pp. 88–89; "Baxter Eases into Its Big Acquisition," *The Wall Street Journal,* July 19, 1985, p. 6.

2. For interesting case studies of the activities of different types of wholesalers, see M. P. Brown, William Applebaum, and W. J. Salmon, *Strategy Problems of Mass Retailers and Wholesalers* (Homewood, Ill.: Richard D. Irwin, 1970). See also Richard Greene, "Wholesaling," *Forbes,* January 2, 1984, pp. 226–28.

3. James D. Hlavacek and Tommy J. McCuistion, "Industrial Distributors—When, Who, and How?" *Harvard Business Review,* January-February 1983, pp. 96–101; Steven Flax, "Wholesalers," *Forbes,* January 4, 1982; N. Mohan Reddy and Michael P. Marvin, "Developing a Manufacturer-Distributor Information Partnership," *Industrial Marketing Management,* May 1986, pp. 157–64; Michael Levy and Michael Van Breda, "How to Determine Whether to Buy Direct or through a Wholesaler," *Retail Control,* June/July 1985, pp. 35–55.

4. "Food Distribution: The Leaders Are Getting Hungry for More," *Business Week,* March 24, 1986, pp. 106–8.

5. "Business-to-Business Mail Order Sales Reached $31B in '84," *Direct Marketing,* September 1985, pp. 72–82.

6. "Brazil Captures a Big Share of the U.S. Shoe Market," *The Wall Street Journal,* August 27, 1985, p. 35; Jim Gibbons, "Selling Abroad with Manufacturers' Agents," *Sales & Marketing Management,* September 9, 1985, pp. 67–69; Evelyn A. Thomchick and Lisa Rosenbaum, "The Role of U.S. Export Trading Companies in International Logistics," *Journal of Business Logistics,* September 1984, pp. 85–105.

7. "Why Manufacturers Are Doubling as Distributors," *Business Week,* January 17, 1983, p. 41.

8. "Sanyo Sales Strategy Illustrates Problems of Little Distributors," *The Wall Street Journal,* September 10, 1984, p. 33.

9. J. A. Narus, N. M. Reddy, and G. L. Pinchak, "Key Problems Facing Industrial Distributors," *Industrial Marketing Management,* August 1984, pp. 139–48; J. A. Narus and J. C. Anderson, "Turn Your Industrial Distributors into Partners," *Harvard Business Review,* March-April 1986, pp. 66–71; J. R. Moore and K. A. Adams, "Functional Wholesaler Sales: Trends and Analysis," in *Combined Proceedings of the American Marketing Association,* ed. E. M. Mazze (Chicago: American Marketing Association, 1976), pp. 403–5; R. S. Lopata, "Faster Pace in Wholesaling," *Harvard Business Review,* July-August 1969, pp. 130–43; J. J. Withey, "Realities of Channel Dynamics: A Wholesaling Example," *Academy of Marketing Science,* Summer 1985, pp. 72–81; "Napco: Seeking a National Network as a Nonfood Supermarket Supplier," *Business Week,* November 8, 1982, p.70.

Chapter 13

1. "Quaker Oats Finds Cap'n Crunch Loot with Hide-And-Seek," *Advertising Age,* May 26, 1986, pp. 52–56.

2. "Attention to Public Opinion Helps Firms Avoid Blunders," *The Wall Street Journal,* June 15, 1981, p. 21; Robert S. Mason, "What's a PR Director for, Anyway?" *Harvard Business Review,* September-October 1974, pp. 120–26; Raymond Simon, *Public Relations: Concepts and Practices* (Columbus Ohio: Grid, 1980); "Success of Flashy 'Miami Vice' TV Show May Be Rubbing off on Troubled Miami," *The Wall Street Journal,* August 5, 1985, p. 23.

3. Jeanne Saddler, "Public Relations Firms Offer 'News' to TV," *The Wall Street Journal,* April 2, 1985, p. 6.

4. Christopher H. Lovelock and John A. Quelch, "Consumer Promotions in Service Marketing," *Business Horizons,* May/June 1983, pp. 66–75; Thomas V. Bonoma, "Get More out of Your Trade Shows," *Harvard Business Review,* January-February 1983, pp. 75–83; Kenneth G. Hardy, "Key Success Factors for Manufacturers' Sales Promotions in Package Goods," *Journal of Marketing,* July 1986, pp. 13–23; "Airlines Try New Efforts to Lure Overseas Fliers," *Advertising Age,* May 26, 1986, p. 89; "The Selling of the Biggest Game on Earth," *Business Week,* June 9, 1986, pp. 102–3; "How Coors Picks Its Winners in Sports," *Business Week,* August 26, 1985, pp. 56–61; "Promotions Hit Creative High Tide," *Advertising Age,* February 27, 1986, p. 54; "Product Sampling Getting off the Ground," *Advertising Age,* May 5, 1986, p. S30; "Retailers Turn to Glitzy 'Special Events,' to Create Excitement and Lure Shoppers," *The Wall Street Journal,* September 10, 1985, p. 33.

5. John A. Quelch, "It's Time to Make Trade Promotion More Productive," *Harvard Business Review,* May-June 1983, pp. 130–36; "Retailing May Have Overdosed on Coupons," *Business Week,* June 13, 1983, p. 147.

6. Joanne Y. Cleaver, "Employee Incentives Rising to Top of Industry," *Advertising Age,* May 5, 1986, p. S1f; Curt Schleier, "Travel Business Gets Mileage Out of Incentives," *Advertising Age,* May 5, 1986, p. S14.

7. "What's New in Joint Promotions," *The New York Times,* March 10, 1985; Roger A. Strang, "Sales Promotion—Fast Growth, Faulty Management," *Harvard Business Review,* July-August 1976, pp. 115–24; Henry H. Beam, "Preparing for Promotion Pays Off," *Business Horizons,* January/February 1984, pp. 6–13.

8. "Sales-Promo Surge Has Shops Scrambling," *Advertising Age,* April 14, 1986, p. 114; "New Tactics Attempt to Speed Coupon Clip," *USA Today,* May 13, 1986.

9. J. F. Engel, M. R. Warshaw, and T. C. Kinnear, *Promotional Strategy,* 5th ed. (Homewood, Ill.: Richard D. Irwin, 1983).

10. "More Firms Turn to Translation Experts to Avoid Costly Embarrassing Mistakes," *The Wall Street Journal,* January 13, 1977, p. 32.

11. "Prisoners of the Past: When It Comes to Understanding Women, Most Marketers Are Caught in a Time Warp," *The Wall Street Journal,* March 24, 1986, pp. D17–18. For interesting perspectives on this issue, see Jacob Jacoby and Wayne D. Hoyer, "Viewer Miscomprehension of Televised Communication: Selected Findings," *Journal of Marketing,* Fall 1982, pp. 12–26; Gary T. Ford and Richard Yalch, "Viewer Miscomprehension of Televised Communication—A Comment," *Journal of Marketing,* Fall 1982, pp. 27–31. See also Reed Sanderlin, "Information Is Not Communication," *Business Horizons,* March/April 1982, pp. 40–42.

12. Everett M. Rogers and F. Floyd Shoemaker, *Communication of Innovations: A Cross-Cultural Approach* (New York: Free Press, 1971), pp. 203–9; Kenneth Uhl, Roman Andrus, and Lance Poulsen, "How Are Laggards Different? An Empirical Inquiry," *Journal of Marketing Research,* February 1970, pp. 43–50; Thomas S. Robertson, "The Process of Innovation and the Diffusion of Innovation," *Journal of Marketing,* January 1967, pp. 14–19; Joseph Cherian and Rohit Deshpande, "The Impact of Organizational Culture on the Adoption of Industrial Innovations," in *1985 American Marketing Association Educators' Proceedings,* ed. R. F. Lusch et al. (Chicago: American Marketing Association, 1985), pp. 30–34; Mary Dee Dickerson and James W. Gentry, "Characteristics of Adopters and Non-Adopters of Home Computers," *Journal of Consumer Research,* September 1983, pp. 225–35; Robin N. Shaw and Anna Bodi, "Diffusion of Product Code Scanning Systems," *Industrial Marketing Management,* August 1986, pp. 225–36.

13. Marsha L. Richins, "Negative Word-of-Mouth by Dissatisfied Consumers: A Pilot Study," *Journal of Marketing,* Winter 1983, pp. 68–78; Joseph R. Mancuso, "Why Not Create Opinion Leaders for New Product Introductions?" *Journal of Marketing,* July 1969, pp. 20–25; Leon G. Schiffman and Vincent Gaccione, "Opinion Leaders in Institutional Markets," *Journal of Marketing,* April 1974, pp. 49–53; John A. Czepiel, "Word-of-Mouth Processes in the Diffusion of a Major Technological Innovation," *Journal of Marketing Research,* May 1974, pp. 172–80; Diane Lynn Kastiel, "Converse Takes a Test Run," *Advertising Age,* February 6, 1986, p. 34; John A. Martilla, "Word-of-Mouth Communication in the Industrial Adoption Process," *Journal of Marketing Research,* May 1971, pp. 173–78.

14. "Survey: Business Sales Calls Costing $229.70," *Marketing News,* August 1, 1986, p. 1.

Chapter 14

1. Kenneth R. Evans and John L. Schlacter, "The Role of Sales Managers and Salespeople in a Marketing Information System," *Journal of Personal Selling & Sales Management,* November 1985, pp. 49–58; P. Ronald Stephenson, William L. Cron, and Gary L. Frazier, "Delegating Pricing Authority to the Sales Force: The Effects on Sales and Profit Performance," *Journal of Marketing,* Spring 1979, pp. 21–24; "Reach out and Sell Something," *Fortune,* November 26, 1984, p. 127f; James H. Fouss and Elaine Solomon, "Salespeople as Researchers: Help or Hazard?" *Journal of Marketing,* Summer 1980, pp. 36–39; Douglas N. Behrman and William D. Perreault, Jr., "Measuring the Performance of Industrial Salespersons," *Journal of Business Research,* September 1982, pp. 350–70; Gilbert A. Churchill, Jr., Neil M. Ford, and Orville C. Walker, Jr., *Sales Force Management: Planning, Implementation and Control* (Homewood, Ill.: Richard D. Irwin, 1985).

2. "Pushing Doctors to Buy High Tech for the Office," *Business Week,* September 2, 1985, pp. 84–85.

3. David W. Cravens and Raymond W. LaForge, "Salesforce Deployment Analysis," *Industrial Marketing Management,* July 1983, pp. 179–92; F. Doody and W. G. Nickels, "Structuring Organizations for Strategic Selling," *MSU Business Topics,* Autumn 1972, pp. 27–34; Porter Henry, "Manage Your Sales Force as a System," *Harvard Business Review,* March-April 1975, pp. 85–94; Michael S. Herschel, "Effective Sales Territory Development," *Journal of Marketing,* April 1977, pp. 39–43; John Barrett, "Why Major Account Selling Works," *Industrial Marketing Management,* February 1986, pp. 63–74.

4. Kenneth Lawyer, *Training Salesmen to Serve Industrial Markets* (Washington, D.C.: Small Business Management Series No. 36, Small Business Administration, 1975); "Retailers Discover an Old Tool: Sales Training," *Business Week,* December 22, 1980; Wesley J. Johnston and Martha Cooper, "Analyzing the Industrial Salesforce Selection Process," *Industrial Marketing Management,* April 1981, pp. 139–47; J. Michael Munson and W. Austin Spivey, "Salesforce Selection that Meets Federal Regulations and Management Needs," *Industrial Marketing Management,* February 1980, pp. 11–21; A. J. Dubinsky, "Recruiting College Students for the Salesforce," *Industrial Marketing Management,* February 1980, pp. 37–46; George J. Avlonitis, Kevin A. Boyle, and Athanasios G. Kouremenos, "Matching the Salesmen to the Selling Job," *Industrial Marketing Management,* February 1986, pp. 45–54.

5. Stephen X. Doyle and Benson P. Shapiro, "What Counts Most in Motivating Your Sales Force" *Harvard Business Review,* May-June 1980, pp. 133–40; H. O. Pruden, W. H. Cunningham, and W. D. English, "Nonfinancial Incentives for Salesmen," *Journal of Marketing,* October 1972, pp. 55–59; O. C. Walker, Jr., G. A. Churchill, and N. M. Ford, "Motivation and Performance in Industrial Selling: Present Knowledge and Needed Research," *Journal of Marketing Research,* May 1977, pp. 156–68; Douglas N. Behrman and William D. Perreault, Jr., "A Role Stress Model of the Performance and Satisfaction of Industrial Salespersons," *Journal of Marketing,* Fall 1984, pp. 9–21; Thomas N. Ingram and Danny N. Bellenger, "Motivational Segments in the Sales Force," *California Management Review,* Spring 1982, pp. 81–88; "Motivating Willy Loman," *Forbes,* January 30, 1984, p. 91; Z. S. Demirdjian, "A Multidimensional Approach to Motivating Salespeople," *Industrial Marketing Management,* February 1984, pp. 25–32.

6. John P. Steinbrink, "How to Pay Your Sales Force," *Harvard Business Review,* July-August 1978, pp. 111–22; "Managers on Compensation Plans: There Has to Be a Better Way," *Sales & Marketing Management,* November 12, 1979, pp. 41–43; Leon Winer, "A Sales Compensation Plan for Maximum Motivation," *Industrial Marketing Management* 5 (1976), pp. 29–36; Pradeep K. Tyagi and Carl E. Block, "Monetary Incentives and Salesmen Performance," *Industrial Marketing Management,* October 1983, pp. 263–70.

7. Paul Busch and David T. Wilson, "An Experimental Analysis of a Salesman's Expert and Referent Bases of Social Power in the Buyer-Seller Dyad," *Journal of Marketing Research,* February 1976, pp. 3–11; Rosann L. Spiro, William D. Perreault, Jr., and Fred D. Reynolds, "The Personal Selling Process: A Critical Review and Model," *Industrial Marketing Management,* December 1977, pp. 351–64; Rosann L. Spiro and William D. Perreault, Jr., "Influence Use by Industrial Salesmen: Influence Strategy Mixes and Situational Determinants," *Journal of Business,* July 1979, pp. 435–55.

8. Robert H. Collins, "Microcomputer Applications in Selling and Sales Management: Portable Computers—Applications to Increase Salesforce Productivity," *Journal of Personal Selling & Sales Management,* November 1984, p. 75f; Jean Marie Choffray and Gary L. Lilien, "A Decision-Support System for Evaluating Sales Prospects and Launch Strategies for New Products," *Industrial Marketing Management,* February 1986, pp. 75–86; "Rebirth of a Salesman: Willy Loman Goes Electronic," *Business Week,* February 27, 1984, pp. 103–4.

9. John I. Coppett and Roy Dale Voorhees, "Telemarketing: Supplement to Field Sales," *Industrial Marketing Management,* August 1985, pp. 213–16; Roy Voorhees and John Coppett, "Telemarketing in Distribution Channels," *Industrial Marketing Management,* April 1983, pp. 105–12; "Better than a Smile: Salespeople Begin to Use Computers on the Job," *The Wall Street Journal,* September 13, 1985, p. 29.

10. For more on sales presentation approaches, see C. A. Pederson, M. D. Wright, and B. A. Weitz, *Selling: Principles and Methods,* 7th ed. (Homewood, Ill.: Richard D. Irwin, 1981), pp. 224–356. See also Marvin A. Jolson, "The Underestimated Potential of the Canned Sales Presentation," *Journal of Marketing,* January 1975, pp. 75–78; Don Meisel, "Add Sales Power! Ask Questions," *Industrial Distribution,* December 1976, p 64.

Chapter 15

1. "Time out for a 60-Second Epic," *Time,* January 20, 1986, p. 44; "Special Report: Out-of-Home Advertising," *Advertising Age,* May 12, 1986, pp. S1–S10; "Companies Cram Ads in Stores to Sway Shopping Decisions," *The Wall Street Journal,* August 22, 1985, p. 25; "'Ad Space' Now Has a Whole New Meaning," *Business Week,* July 29, 1985, p. 52.

2. "Coen Backs off on '85," *Advertising Age,* July 22, 1985, p. 3.

3. "Ad Spending Fails to Equal Predictions," *Advertising Age,* May 12, 1986, p. 76.

4. Exact data on this industry are elusive. But see "Showing Ad Agencies How to Grow," *Business Week,* June 1, 1974, pp. 50–56; *Statistical Abstract of the United States 1986* (Washington, D.C.: U.S. Bureau of the Census, 1985), p. 400.

5. "A Pained Bayer Cries 'Foul,'" *Business Week,* July 25, 1977, p. 142.

6. William L. Wilkie and Paul W. Farris, "Comparison Advertising: Problems and Potential," *Journal of Marketing,* October

1975, pp. 7–15; Linda L. Golden, "Consumer Reactions to Explicit Brand Comparisons in Advertisements," *Journal of Marketing Research,* November 1979, pp. 517–32; "Should an Ad Identify Brand X?" *Business Week,* September 24, 1979, pp. 156–61; Steven A. Meyerowitz, "The Developing Law of Comparative Advertising," *Business Marketing,* August 1985, pp. 81–86.

7. "Ad Agencies Press Franchisees to Join National Campaigns," *The Wall Street Journal,* January 17, 1985, p. 29; "Co-op: A Coup for Greater Profits," *Marketing Communications,* September 1985, pp. 66–73; "Sears Pulls in Its Advertising Umbrella," *Advertising Age,* May 5, 1986, p. 32.

8. Richard W. Pollay, "The Subsiding Sizzle: A Descriptive History of Print Advertising, 1900–1980," *Journal of Marketing,* Summer 1985, pp. 24–37; Murphy A. Sewall and Dan Sarel, "Characteristics of Radio Commercials and Their Recall Effectiveness," *Journal of Marketing,* January 1986, pp. 52–60; "Breakout in Billboards," *Dun's Business Month,* May 1985, pp. 40–44; "Confused Advertisers Bemoan Proliferation of Yellow Pages," *The Wall Street Journal,* February 27, 1986, p. 23; "Advertisers Bristle as Charges Balloon for Splashy TV Spots," *The Wall Street Journal,* June 20, 1985, p. 31; Michael Heges, "Radio's Lifestyles," *American Demographics,* February 1986, pp. 32–35.

9. "Why Jockey Switched Its Ads from TV to Print," *Business Week,* July 26, 1976, pp. 140–42.

10. "Study of Olympics Ads Casts Doubts on Value of Campaigns," *The Wall Street Journal,* December 6, 1984, p. 33; "Cost of TV Sports Commercials Prompts Cutbacks by Advertisers, *The Wall Street Journal,* January 15, 1985, p. 37.

11. "Mailing for Dollars," *Psychology Today,* October 1984, pp. 38–43; "Apple Now Major Direct-Mail User," *Advertising Age,* April 14, 1986, p. 36.

12. "And Now, a Wittier Word from Our Sponsors," *Business Week,* March 24, 1986, pp. 90–94; "The Competition Looks on," *Time,* December 24, 1984, p. 53; "The Coming Avalanche of 15-Second Ads," *Business Week,* February 11, 1985, p. 80.

13. "The 15% Media Commission Is on the Way toward Becoming a Relic," *Marketing News,* June 10, 1983, p. 9; "How Agencies Should Get Paid: Trend Is to 'Managed' Systems," *Advertising Age,* January 17, 1977, pp. 41–42; "Do Media Buying Services Sell Their Clients Short?" *Marketing and Media Decisions,* August 1985, p. 49f.

14. "Behind the Scenes at an American Express Commercial," *Business Week,* May 20, 1985, pp. 84–88.

15. George M. Zinkhan, "Rating Industrial Advertisements," *Industrial Marketing Management,* February 1984, pp. 43–48; Pradeep K. Korgaonkar, Danny N. Bellenger, and Allen E. Smith, "Successful Industrial Advertising Campaigns," *Industrial Marketing Management,* May 1986, pp. 123–28; Lawrence C. Soley, "Copy Length and Industrial Advertising Readership," *Industrial Marketing Management,* August 1986, pp. 245–52.

16. William L. Wilkie, Dennis L. McNeil, and Michael B. Mazis, "Marketing's Scarlet Letter: The Theory and Practice of Corrective Advertising," *Journal of Marketing,* Spring 1984, pp. 11–31; Jacob Jacoby, Margaret C. Nelson, and Wayne D. Hoyer, "Corrective Advertising and Affirmative Disclosure Statements: Their Potential for Confusing and Misleading the Consumer," *Journal of Marketing,* Winter 1982, pp. 61–72.

17. Dorothy Cohen, "Unfairness in Advertising Revisited," *Journal of Marketing,* Winter 1982, pp. 73–80; "Lysol's Maker Keeps Fighting FTC over Advertising Claims," *The Wall Street Journal,* February 24, 1983, p. 29; J. J. Boddewyn, "Advertising Regulation in the 1980s: The Underlying Global Forces," *Journal of Marketing,* Winter 1982, pp. 27–35; Gary T. Ford and John E. Calfee, "Recent Developments in FTC Policy on Deception," *Journal of Marketing,* July 1986, pp. 82–103; John S. Healey and Harold H. Kassarjian, "Advertising Substantiation and Advertiser Response: A Content Analysis of Magazine Advertisements," *Journal of Marketing,* Winter 1983, pp. 107–17.

18. "Watchdogs Zealously Censor Advertising Targeted to Kids," *The Wall Street Journal,* September 5, 1985, p. 35; Priscilla A. LaBarbera, "The Diffusion of Trade Association Advertising Self-Regulation," *Journal of Marketing,* Winter 1983, pp. 58–67.

Chapter 16

1. "Aluminum Firms Offer Wider Discounts but Price Cuts Stop at Some Distributors," *The Wall Street Journal,* November 16, 1984, p. 50.

2. Alfred Rappaport, "Executive Incentives versus Corporate Growth," *Harvard Business Review,* July-August 1978, pp. 81–88.

3. Pricing "in the public interest" is often an issue in pricing government services; for an interesting example, see "Price Policy on Space Shuttle's Commerical Use Could Launch—or Ground—NASA's Rockets," *The Wall Street Journal,* March 21, 1985, p. 64.

4. "Harvester Sells Many Trucks below Cost, Citing Need to Maintain Dealer Network," *The Wall Street Journal,* April 19, 1983, p. 8. See also "Pricing Strategy in an Inflation Economy," *Business Week,* April 6, 1974, pp. 43–49.

5. "Leave the Herd and Leap off the Old Price Treadmill," *The Chicago Tribune,* November 11, 1985, Sec. 4, p. 21f.

6. Elliot B. Ross, "Making Money with Proactive Pricing," *Harvard Business Review,* November-December 1984, pp. 145–55; Thomas Nagle, "Pricing as Creative Marketing," *Business Horizons,* July/August 1983, pp. 14–19. See also Subhash C. Jain and Michael B. Laric, "A Framework for Strategic Industrial Pricing," *Industrial Marketing Management* 8 (1979), pp. 75–80; Barbara Coe, "Perceptions of the Role of Pricing in the 1980s among Industrial Marketers," in *1983 American Marketing Association Educators' Proceedings,* ed. P. E. Murphy et al. (Chicago: American Marketing Association, 1983), pp. 235–40.

7. For an interesting discussion of the many variations from a one-price system in retailing, see Stanley C. Hollander, "The 'One-Price' System—Fact or Fiction?" *Journal of Marketing Research,* February 1972, pp. 35–40. See also Michael J. Houston, "Minimum Markup Laws: An Empirical Assessment," *Journal of Retailing,* Winter 1981, pp. 98–113; "Flexible Pricing," *Business Week,* December 12, 1977, pp. 78–88.

8. Alan Reynolds, "A Kind Word for 'Cream Skimming,'" *Harvard Business Review,* November-December 1974, pp. 113–20.

9. Stuart U. Rich, "Price Leadership in the Paper Industry," *Industrial Marketing Management,* April 1983, pp. 101–4; "OPEC

Member Offers Discounts to Some Amid Downward Pressure on Oil Prices," *The Wall Street Journal,* November 16, 1984, p. 4.

10. For an excellent discussion of laws related to pricing, see Louis W. Stern and Thomas L. Eovaldi, *Legal Aspects of Marketing Strategy: Antitrust and Consumer Protection Issues* (Englewood Cliffs, N.J.: Prentice-Hall, 1984).

11. John Liefeld and Louise A. Heslop, "Reference Prices and Deception in Newspaper Advertising," *Journal of Consumer Research,* March 1985, pp. 868–76. Individual states often have their own laws; see, for example, "States Crack down on Phony Price-Cutting 'Sales,'" *The Wall Street Journal,* January 30, 1986, p. 1.

12. "The FTC Redefines Price Fixing," *Business Week,* April 18, 1983, p. 37; "FTC Accuses 6 Title Insurers of Price Fixing," *The Wall Street Journal,* January 8, 1985, p. 8; "Price-Fixing Charges Rise in Paper Industry Despite Convictions," *The Wall Street Journal,* May 4, 1978, p. 2; "Plywood Makers Agree to Settle Antitrust Suit," *The Wall Street Journal,* December 5, 1982, p. 3. See also Mary Jane Sheffet and Debra L. Scammon, "Resale Price Maintenance: Is It Safe To Suggest Retail Prices?" *Journal of Marketing,* Fall 1985, pp. 82–91. For discussion concerning European countries, see *Market Power and the Law* (Washington, D.C.: Organization for Economic Cooperation and Development Publication Center, 1970), p. 206.

13. Morris L. Mayer, Joseph B. Mason, and E. A. Orbeck, "The Borden Case—A Legal Basis for Private Brand Price Discrimination," *MSU Business Topics,* Winter 1970, pp. 56–63; T. F. Schutte, V. J. Cook, Jr., and R. Hemsley, "What Management Can Learn from the Borden Case," *Business Horizons,* Winter 1966, pp. 23–30.

14. "Is the Cost Defense Workable?" *Journal of Marketing,* January 1965, pp. 37–42; B. J. Linder and Allan H. Savage, "Price Discrimination and Cost Defense—Change Ahead?" *MSU Business Topics,* Summer 1971, pp. 21–26; "Firms Must Prove Injury from Price Bias to Qualify for Damages, High Court Says," *The Wall Street Journal,* May 19, 1981, p. 8.

15. Lawrence X. Tarpey, Sr., "Who Is a Competing Customer?" *Journal of Retailing,* Spring 1969, pp. 46–58; John R. Davidson, "FTC, Robinson-Patman and Cooperative Promotion Activities," *Journal of Marketing,* January 1968, pp. 14–18; "The FTC Gets Tough on 'Promo' Payments," *Business Week,* November 24, 1973, p. 30; L. X. Tarpey, Sr., "Buyer Liability under the Robinson-Patman Act: A Current Appraisal," *Journal of Marketing,* January 1972, pp. 38–42.

Appendix B

1. Checking the accuracy of forecasts is a difficult subject. See D. M. Georgoff and R. G. Murdick, "Manager's Guide to Forecasting," *Harvard Business Review,* January-February 1986, pp. 110–20; P. L. Bernstein and T. H. Silvert, "Are Economic Forecasters Worth Listening to?" *Harvard Business Review,* September-October 1984, pp. 32–41; P. R. Wotruba and M. L. Thurlow, "Sales Force Participation in Quota Setting and Sales Forecasting," *Journal of Marketing,* April, 1976, pp. 11–16; E. Jerome Scott and Stephen K. Keiser, "Forecasting Acceptance of New Industrial Products with Judgment Modeling," *Journal of Marketing,* Spring 1984, pp. 54–67.

Chapter 17

1. "How to Sell Computers Today—And How Not to," *Business Week,* September 2, 1985, pp. 70–72.

2. Marvin A. Jolson, "A Diagrammatic Model for Merchandising Calculations," *Journal of Retailing,* Summer 1975, pp. 3–9.

3. Mary L. Hatten, "Don't Get Caught with Your Prices Down: Pricing in Inflationary Times," *Business Horizons,* March 1982, pp. 23–28; "Why Detroit Can't Cut Prices," *Business Week,* March 1, 1982, p. 110; Douglas G. Brooks, "Cost Oriented Pricing: A Realistic Solution to a Complicated Problem," *Journal of Marketing,* April 1975, pp. 72–74.

4. Approaches for estimating price-quantity relationships are reviewed in Kent B. Monroe, *Pricing: Making Profitable Decisions* (New York: McGraw-Hill, 1979). For a specific example, see Frank D. Jones, "A Survey Technique to Measure Demand under Various Pricing Strategies," *Journal of Marketing,* July 1975, pp. 75–77; or Gordon A. Wyner, Lois H. Benedetti, and Bart M. Trapp, "Measuring the Quantity and Mix of Product Demand," *Journal of Marketing,* Winter 1984, pp. 101–9.

5. Benson P. Shapiro and Barbara P. Jackson, "Industrial Pricing to Meet Customer Needs," *Harvard Business Review,* November-December 1978, pp. 119–27; "The Race to the $10 Light Bulb," *Business Week,* May 19, 1980, p. 124.

6. For an example applied to a high-price item, see "Sale of Mink Coats Strays a Fur Piece from the Expected," *The Wall Street Journal,* March 21, 1980, p. 30.

7. B. P. Shapiro, "The Psychology of Pricing," *Harvard Business Review,* July-August 1968, pp. 14–24; C. Davis Fogg and Kent H. Kohnken, "Price-Cost Planning," *Journal of Marketing,* April 1978, pp. 97–106.

8. "Strategic Mix of Odd, Even Prices Can Lead to Increased Retail Profits," *Marketing News,* March 7, 1980, p. 24.

9. Peter C. Riesz, "Price versus Quality in the Marketplace," *Journal of Retailing,* Winter 1978, pp. 15–28; John J. Wheatly and John S. Y. Chiu, "The Effects of Price, Store Image, and Product and Respondent Characteristics on Perceptions of Quality," *Journal of Marketing Research,* May 1977, pp. 181–86; Arthur G. Bedeian, "Consumer Perception of Price as an Indicator of Product Quality," *MSU Business Topics,* Summer 1971, pp. 59–65; N. D. French, J. J. Williams, and W. A. Chance, "A Shopping Experiment on Price-Quality Relationships," *Journal of Retailing,* Fall 1972, pp. 3–16; J. Douglas McConnell, "Comment on 'A Major Price-Perceived Quality Study Reexamined,'" *Journal of Marketing Research,* May 1980, pp. 263–64; K. M. Monroe and S. Petroshius, "Buyers' Subjective Perceptions of Price: An Update of the Evidence," in *Perspectives in Consumer Behavior,* ed. T. Robertson and H. Kassarjian (Glenview, Ill.: Scott Foresman 1981), pp. 43–55.

10. Stephen Paranka, "Competitive Bidding Strategy," *Business Horizons,* June 1971, pp. 39–43; Wayne J. Morse, "Probabilistic Bidding Models; A Synthesis," *Business Horizons,* April 1975, pp. 67–74; Kenneth Simmonds and Stuart Slatter, "The Number of Estimators: A Critical Decision for Marketing under Competitive Bidding," *Journal of Marketing Research,* May 1978, pp. 203–13.

11. For references to additional readings in the pricing area, see Kent B. Monroe, D. Lund, and P. Choudhury, *Pricing Policies and Strategies: An Annotated Bibliography* (Chicago: American Marketing Association, 1983). See also "Pricing of

Products Is Still an Art, Often Having Little Link to Costs," *The Wall Street Journal,* November 25, 1981, p. 29f.

Chapter 18

1. "Countertrading Grows as Cash-Short Nations Seek Marketing Help," *The Wall Street Journal,* March 13, 1985, p. 1f; David B. Yoffie, "Profiting from Countertrade," *Harvard Business Review,* May-June 1984, pp. 8–17.

2. "U.S. Increases Its Exports, Despite Problems," *The Wall Street Journal,* June 11, 1985, p. 6; "Strong Dollar or No, There's Money to be Made Abroad," *Business Week,* March 22, 1985, p. 155; Robert T. Green and Arthur W. Allaway, "Identification of Export Opportunities: A Shift-Share Approach," *Journal of Marketing,* Winter 1985, pp. 83–88; Daniel C. Bello and Nicholas C. Williamson, "The American Export Trading Company: Designing a New International Marketing Institution," *Journal of Marketing,* Fall 1985, pp. 60–69; "How Coke Runs a Foreign Empire," *Business Week,* August 25, 1973, pp. 40–43.

3. E. S. Browning, "A Top Japanese Firm in Electronics Finds U.S. Market Difficult," *The Wall Street Journal,* March 25, 1985, p. 1f; see also Robert Guenther, "Forest-Products Concerns Urge Using Wood for Latin Houses," *The Wall Street Journal,* September 19, 1984, p. 35.

4. E. S. Browning, "U.S. Concerns Trying to Do Business in Japan Face Government, Market, Cultural Barriers," *The Wall Street Journal,* July 8, 1985, p. 16.

5. John A. Quelch, "How to Build a Product Licensing Program," *Harvard Business Review,* May-June 1985, p. 186f.

6. F. Kingston Berlew, "The Joint Venture—A Way into Foreign Markets," *Harvard Business Review,* July-August 1984, pp. 48–55; "GM Is Leading Bidder for Joint Venture with Egypt's State-Owned Auto Firm," *The Wall Street Journal,* September 12, 1985, p. 37; "Ford Joint Venture Plans to Expand Taiwan Capacity," *The Wall Street Journal,* November 15, 1984, p. 2.

7. Theodore Levitt, "The Globalization of Markets," *Harvard Business Review,* May-June 1983, pp. 92–102; Gary Hamel and C. K. Prahalad, "Do You Really Have a Global Strategy," *Harvard Business Review,* July-August 1985, pp. 139–48; "Playing the Global Game," *Fortune,* November 16, 1981, p. 111f.

8. Thomas Hout, Michael E. Porter, and Eileen Rudden, "How Global Companies Win Out," *Harvard Business Review,* September-October 1982, pp. 98–108; "Multi-national Firms Now Dominate Much of World's Production," *The Wall Street Journal,* April 18, 1973, p. 1f; "Japanese Multinationals Covering the World with Investment," *Business Week,* June 16, 1980, pp. 92–99; David A. Heenan and Warren J. Keegan, "The Rise of Third World Multinationals," *Harvard Business Review,* January-February 1979, pp. 101–9.

9. "Japanese Firms Set up More Factories in U.S., Alarm Some Americans," *The Wall Street Journal,* March 29, 1985, p. 1f.

10. "McDonald's Brings Hamburger (with Beer) to Hamburg," *Advertising Age,* May 30, 1977, p. 61; "Haute Couture, with Catsup," *Time,* May 12, 1986, p. 69.

11. John A. Quelch and E. J. Hoff, "Customizing Global Marketing," *Harvard Business Review,* May-June 1986, pp. 59–68; Warren J. Keegan, "A Conceptual Framework for Multinational

Marketing," *Columbia Journal of World Business,* November 1972, pp. 67–78; "Playtex Kicks off a One-Ad-Fits-All Campaign," *Business Week,* December 16, 1985, pp. 48–49.

12. "Dole and Del Monte Are Staying Put—No Matter What," *Business Week,* November 18, 1985, pp. 58–59; Thomas W. Shreeve, "Be Prepared for Political Changes Abroad," *Harvard Business Review,* July-August 1984, pp. 111–18; "Ford's Mexico Plant to Heed Export Call," *The Chicago Tribune,* April 7, 1985, Sec. 7, p. F9; Victor H. Frank, Jr., "Living with Price Control Abroad," *Harvard Business Review,* March-April 1984, pp. 137–42; Michael G. Harvey and James T. Rothe, "The Foreign Corrupt Practices Act: The Good, the Bad and the Future," in *1983 American Marketing Association Educators' Proceedings,* ed. P. E. Murphy et al. (Chicago: American Marketing Association, 1983), pp. 374–79.

13. "U.S. to Boost Tariffs on European Pasta in Response to EC Citrus Discrimination," *The Wall Street Journal,* June 21, 1985, p. 31; "Philips Finds Obstacles to Intra-Europe Trade Are Costly, Inefficient," *The Wall Street Journal,* August 7, 1985, p. 1f.

14. William Copulsky, "Forecasting Sales in Underdeveloped Countries," *Journal of Marketing,* July 1959, pp. 36–37; John S. McClenahen, "The Third World Challenge," *Industry Week,* May 28, 1984, pp. 90–95.

15. J. S. Hill and R. R. Still, "Adapting Products to LDC Tastes," *Harvard Business Review,* March-April 1984, pp. 92–101; *The Wall Street Journal,* August 8, 1968, p. 1.

16. Christopher A. Bartlett, "MNCs: Get off the Reorganization Merry-Go-Round," *Harvard Business Review,* March-April 1983, pp. 138–46; James M. Hulbert, William K. Brant, and Raimar Richers, "Marketing Planning in the Multinational Subsidiary: Practices and Problems," *Journal of Marketing,* Summer 1980, pp. 7–16.

Chapter 19

1. "Life in the Express Lane," *Time,* June 16, 1986, p. 64.

2. James U. McNeal, "Consumer Satisfaction: The Measure of Marketing Effectiveness," *MSU Business Topics,* Summer 1969, p. 33; Robert B. Woodruff, Ernest R. Cadotte, and Roger L. Jenkins, "Modeling Consumer Satisfaction Processes Using Experience-Based Norms," *Journal of Marketing Research,* August 1983, pp. 296–304; Hiram C. Barksdale and William D. Perreault, Jr., "Can Consumers Be Satisfied?" *MSU Business Topics,* Spring 1980, pp. 19–30.

3. For classic discussions of the problem and mechanics of measuring the efficiency of marketing, see Stanley C. Hollander, "Measuring the Cost and Value of Marketing," *Business Topics,* Summer 1961, pp. 17–26; Reavis Cox, *Distribution in a High-Level Economy* (Englewood Cliffs, N.J.: Prentice-Hall, 1965).

4. Alan R. Andreasen and Arthur Best, "Consumers Complain—Does Business Respond?" *Harvard Business Review,* July-August 1977, pp. 100–1; see also Claes Fornell and Robert A. Westbrook, "The Vicious Circle of Consumer Complaints," *Journal of Marketing,* Summer 1984, pp. 68–78; Hiram C. Barksdale, Jr., Terry E. Powell, and Earnestine Hargrove, "Complaint Voicing by Industrial Buyers," *Industrial Marketing Management,* May 1984, pp. 93–100; Theodore Levitt, "After the Sale Is Over . . .," *Harvard Business Review,* September-October 1983, pp. 87–93.

5. Alan R. Andreasen, "Judging Marketing in the 1980s," *Journal of Macromarketing* 2, no. 1 (1982), pp. 7–13; Robert Bartels, "Is Marketing Defaulting Its Responsibilities?" *Journal of Marketing,* Fall 1983, pp. 32–35; Gene Laczniak, "Frameworks for Analyzing Marketing Ethics," *Journal of Macromarketing* 3, no. 1 (1983), pp. 7–18.

6. E. H. Chamberlin, "Product Heterogeneity and Public Policy," *American Economic Review,* May 1950, p. 86.

7. Arnold J. Toynbee, *America and World Revolution* (New York: Oxford University Press, 1966), pp. 144–45; see also John Kenneth Galbraith, *Economics and the Public Purpose* (Boston: Houghton-Mifflin, 1973), pp. 144–45.

8. Russell J. Tomsen, "Take It Away," *Newsweek,* October 7, 1974, p. 21.

9. "Intellectuals Should Re-Examine the Marketplace; It Supports Them, Helps Keep Them Free, Prof. Stigler," *Advertising Age,* January 28, 1963; E. T. Grether, "Marketing and Public Policy: A Contemporary View," *Journal of Marketing,* July 1974, pp. 2–7; "Deregulating America," *Business Week,* November 28, 1983, pp. 80–82.

10. Frederick Webster, *Social Aspects of Marketing* (Englewood Cliffs, N.J.: Prentice-Hall, 1974), p. 32.

11. Paul M. Mazur, "Does Distribution Cost Enough?" *Fortune,* November 1947.

12. John H. Antil, "Socially Responsible Consumers: Profile and Implications for Public Policy," *Journal of Macromarketing* 4, no. 2 (1984), pp. 18–39; James T. Roth and Lissa Benson, "Intelligent Consumption: An Attractive Alternative to the Marketing Concept," *MSU Business Topics,* Winter 1974, pp. 30–34; Robert E. Wilkes, "Fraudulent Behavior by Consumers," *Journal of Marketing,* October 1978, pp. 67–75; "How Shoplifting Is Draining the Economy," *Business Week,* October 15, 1979, pp. 119–23; Warren A. French, Melvin R. Crask, and Fred H. Mader, "Retailers' Assessment of the Shoplifting Problem," *Journal of Retailing,* Winter 1984, pp. 108–15.

13. Dan R. Dalton and Richard A. Cosier, "The Four Faces of Social Responsibility," *Business Horizons,* May/June 1982, pp. 19–27; Y. Hugh Furuhashi and E. Jerome McCarthy, *Social Issues of Marketing in the American Economy* (Columbus, Ohio: Grid, 1971); James Owens, "Business Ethics: Age-Old Ideal, Now Real," *Business Horizons,* February 1978, pp. 26–30; Steven F. Goodman, "Quality of Life: The Role of Business," *Business Horizons,* June 1978, pp. 36–37; Stanley J. Shapiro, "Marketing in a Conserver Society," *Business Horizons,* April 1978, pp. 3–13; Johan Arndt, "How Broad Should the Marketing Concept Be?" *Journal of Marketing,* January 1978, pp. 101–3.

Illustration Credits

Chapter 1 3 (left) Minute Maid Country Style Juice, *courtesy The Coca-Cola Company;* (center) Cars, *W. Strode/Four by Five;* (right) Sign, *Roy Morsch/The Stock Market;* 4 Tennis racquet ad, *courtesy Wilson Sporting Goods Company;* 6 Women with posters, *Richard Gross/After-Image, Inc.;* 7 Computer-aided design, *courtesy The Black & Decker Corporation;* 8 Supermarket, *Joseph Sterling: Click/Chicago;* 10 (left) Family in bank, *courtesy Household International;* (right) Buying bananas, *Tom Tracey/After-Image, Inc.;* 11 Going out of business, *Brent Jones;* GTE ad, *courtesy GTE;* 13 Exhibit 1–1, Wroe Alderson, "Factors Governing the Development of Marketing Channels," *in* Marketing Channels for Manufactured Products, *ed. Richard M. Clewett (Homewood, Ill.: Richard D. Irwin, 1954), p. 7;* Pottery making, *Bruce Thomas/The Stock Market;* 14 Exhibit 1–2, *adapted from Wroe Alderson, "Factors Governing the Development of Marketing Channels,"* in Marketing Channels for Manufactured Products, *ed. Richard M. Clewett (Homewood, Ill.: Richard D. Irwin, 1954), p. 7;* 15 Third world, *Luis Villota/The Stock Market;* 16 Volvos, *Phillip Wollick/The Stock Market;* Sorting plastics, *Gabe Palmer/The Stock Market;* 17 Exhibit 1–3, *adapted from William McInnes, "A Conceptual Approach to Marketing,"* in Theory in Marketing, 2nd ser., ed. Reavis Cox, Wroe Alderson, and Stanley J. Shapiro (Homewood, Ill.: Richard D. Irwin, 1964), pp. 51–67; 18 Exhibit 1–4, *model suggested by Professor A. A. Brogowicz, Western Michigan University;* Test kitchen, *Craig Hammell/The Stock Market*

Chapter 2 23 (left) Product development team, *Ronald Seymour: Click/Chicago;* (center) Account rep and customer, *courtesy Du Pont;* (right) Woman with Borden products, *courtesy Borden, Inc.;* 26 Consumer affairs panel, *courtesy Ford Motor Company;* 27 Managers at table, *Jon Feingersh: Click/Chicago;* 28 Cancer billboard, *courtesy American Cancer Society, Inc.;* 29 Exhibit 2–2, *adapted from R. F. Vizza, T. E. Chambers, and E. J. Cook, Adoption of the Market Concept—Fact or Fiction (New York: Sales Executive Club, 1967), pp. 13–15;* 30 Hospital billboard, *courtesy Smyrna Hospital;* 32 L'eggs, *Don Smetzer: Click/Chicago;* 33 Buying stereo, *Gabe Palmer/The Stock Market;* 35 Group with storyboard, *Craig Hammell/The Stock Market;* 38 Paint ad, *courtesy Pittsburgh Paints;* 41 Model T, *Bob Chwedyk/Star Publications;* Airline advantage card, *courtesy American Airlines*

Chapter 3 57 (left) Group with map, *Camera Graphics;* (center) Toothpaste, *Jim Whitmer Photography;* (right) Computer graphics, *Camera Graphics;* 58 Exhibit 3–2, Igor Ansoff, Corporate Strategy *(New York: McGraw-Hill, 1965);* 60 Bic lighter ad, *courtesy Bic Corporation;* 61 Hallmark card shop, *Kirk Schlea/Berg & Associates;* 64 Video ad, *courtesy Kartes Video Communications;* 65 Couple at easel map, *courtesy Bureau of Business Research/University of Nebraska—Lincoln;* 70 Tribune ad, *courtesy The Chicago Tribune;* 72 Videodisc ad, *courtesy McDonnell Douglas Corporation;* 76 Rental sign, *Glennon P. Donahue: Click/Chicago;* 77 Couple at bar, *Michael Philip Manheim/Gartman Agency;* 80 Swimmers, *Rick Meyer/The Stock Market;* Desktop computer, *Jon Feingersh: Click/Chicago;* 81 (left) Crest ad, *courtesy The Procter & Gamble Company;* (right) Colgate ad, *courtesy Colgate-Palmolive Company;* 82 Exhibit 3–15, *Russell I. Haley, "Benefit Segmentation: A Decision-Oriented Research Tool,"* Journal of Marketing, July 1968, p. 33

Chapter 4 87 (left) Made in USA label, *courtesy Burlington Industries;* (center) Meeting, *Alvis Upitis/The Image Bank;* (right) Electronic warning system, *courtesy Motorola;* 92 Sorting potatoes, *Martin Rogers: Click/Chicago;* 96 Woman with portable PC, *courtesy Hewlett-Packard Company;* 97 Made in USA billboard, *Vautier de Nanxe: Click/Chicago;* 100 Cigarette warning label, *Billy E. Barnes: Click/Chicago;* 101 Biker, *J. Blackman/The Stock Market;* 102 Exhibit 4–8, *map developed by the authors based on data from* Statistical Abstract of the United States, 1986, *p. 12;* 103 Exhibit 4–9, Statistical Abstract of the United States, 1986, *p. 25;* 104 Buying stereo, *Gabe Palmer/The Stock Market;* Home-building couple, *Michael Philip Manheim/Gartman Agency;* 106 Exhibit 4–10, Statistical Abstract of the United States, 1986, *p. 450;* 107 Exhibit 4–11, Statistical Abstract of the United States, 1986; Capsule hotel, *Chad Ehlers: Click/Chicago;* 108 Exhibit 4–12, *map developed by the authors based on data from* Statistical Abstract of the United States, 1986, *p. 440;* 111 Exhibit 4–15, *adapted from M. G. Allen, "Strategic Problems Facing Today's Corporate Planner," speech given at the Academy of Management, 36th Annual Meeting, Kansas City, Missouri, 1976*

Chapter 5 115 (left) Two businessmen, *Jon Feingersh/Uniphoto;* (center) Market research, *Richard Gross/Stock Imagery;* (right) Market research pollster, *Ellis Herwig/The Picture Cube;* 117 IRI prompt TV screen, *courtesy Information Resources, Inc.;* 118 Marketing managers, *Comstock, Inc.;* 123 Statistical Abstract, 1986, *Irwin staff photo;* 124 Focus group, *Richard Gross/Stock Imagery;* 125 Questionnaire, *courtesy Mid-America Research, Inc.;* 126 Computer telephone survey, *Craig Hammell/The Stock Market;* Market researcher and customer, *courtesy The Campbell Soup Company;* 127 Scanner montage: Store, *courtesy Dominick's Finer Foods;* Cameramann International Photos; Taste test, *Camera Graphics*

Chapter 6 133 (left) Stereo shopping, *Chuck Keeler: Click/Chicago;* (center) Women shopping, *Steve Leonard: Click/Chicago;* (right) Grocery shopping, *Walter Bibikow/The Image Bank;* 135 Exhibit 6–1, *adapted by the authors from "Consumer Expenditure Survey, Interview Survey, 1982–83," Bulletin No. 2246, U.S. Department of Labor, February 1986;* 136 Exhibit 6–2, *adapted from William D. Wells and George Gubar, "Life Cycle Concept in Marketing Research,"* Journal of Marketing Research, August 1968, p. 267; see also Patrick E. Murphy and William A. Staples, *"A Modernized Family Life Cycle,"* Journal of Consumer Research, June 1979, pp. 12–22; 139 Perrier, *Don Smetzer: Click/Chicago;* 140 Exhibit 6–5, *adapted from C. Glenn Walters, Consumer Behavior, 3rd ed. (Homewood Ill.: Richard D. Irwin, 1979); R. M. Liebert and M. D. Spiegler, Personality, 3rd ed., (Homewood, Ill., Dorsey Press, 1978); and others;* 142 Beauty treatment, *courtesy Revlon, Inc.;* 145 Exhibit 6–8, *Joseph T. Plummer, "The Concept and Application of Life-Style Segmentation,"* Journal of Marketing, January 1974, pp. 33–37; Betty Crocker montage, *courtesy General Mills, Inc.;* 146 Kellogg's Frosted Flakes, *Don Smetzer: Click/Chicago;* Today's Marriage ad, *courtesy Dell Magazine Group;* 147 Exhibit 6–9, *adapted from Steven L. Diamond, Thomas S. Robertson, and F. Kent Mitchell, "Consumer Motivation and Behavior,"* in Marketing Manager's Handbook, ed. S. H. Britt and N. F. Guess (Chicago: Dartnell, 1983), p. 239; 149 Cabbage Patch Kids, *Jeffrey W. Myers/Stock, Boston;* 150 Exhibit 6–11, *adapted and updated by authors from H. Kassarjian and Thomas S. Robertson, eds.,* Perspectives on Consumer Behavior, 3rd ed. (Glenview, Ill.: Scott, Foresman, 1981), p. 318; and the work of the Bureau of Applied Social Research, Columbia University, New York; Buying iron, *Cezus: Click/Chicago;* 153 Coupon, *courtesy Ralston Purina Company*

Chapter 7 157 (left) Diabetes Control Center, *courtesy American Home Products Corporation;* (center) Sportswear buyers, *courtesy Sears;* (right) Brass rod inspection, *courtesy B. P. America: Paul Fusco/Magnum;* 158 Exhibit 7–1, County Business Patterns—United States, 1986, *p. 1;*

Statistical Abstract of the United States, 1986; 1982 Census of Construction Industries; 1982 Census of Service Industries; 1982 Census of Agriculture; 1982 Census of Wholesalers; 1982 Census of Retailers; 1982 Census of Manufactures; 159 Exhibit 7–2, *data adapted from* 1982 Census of Manufactures; 162 (left) Die cutter ad, *courtesy Wm. C. Staley Machinery Corp.;* (right) Bearings ad, *courtesy Bearings, Inc.;* 163 Exhibit 7–5, *Patrick J. Robertson and Charles W. Faris,* Industrial Buying and Creative Marketing *(Boston: Allyn & Bacon, 1967), p. 33, reprinted by permission of the publisher;* 165 Grain sampler, *Cameramann International;* 166 (left) Solutions ad, *courtesy United States Robots;* (right) McMaster-Carr ad, *courtesy McMaster-Carr Supply Company;* 167 Computerized inventory ordering, *courtesy The Southland Corporation;* 169 Supermarket, *Ted Horowitz/The Stock Market*

Chapter 8 175 (left) Orange juice manufacturing, *Ron Sherman/ Uniphoto;* (center) Marketing managers, *courtesy The Gillette Company;* (right) Hertz counter, *Cameramann International;* 178 Procter & Gamble products, *Jim Whitmer Photography;* 179 (left) Pipes, *courtesy United Brands;* (right) Drive-in, *Martin Rogers/After-Image, Inc.;* 183 Holiday Inn sign, Don Smetzer: Click/Chicago; 187 Lumbering, *Cary Wolinski/Stock, Boston;* 188 (left) Aluminum wheels, *courtesy Alcoa;* (right) Computer supplies, *courtesy Unisys Corporation;* 189 Window washers, *David Perla/ After-Image, Inc.;* 193 Cans of peas, *Don Smetzer: Click/Chicago;* 194 (left) Boise Cascade packaging, *courtesy Boise Cascade Corporation;* (right) Kids with lunch drinks, *courtesy The Coca-Cola Company*

Chapter 9 201 (left) Technicians reviewing prototype, *courtesy Alcoa;* (center) Business manager and customer, *courtesy Du Pont;* (right) Pringles lab, *courtesy The Procter & Gamble Company;* 204 Cookies, *Don Smetzer: Click/Chicago;* 207 Tide, *Don Smetzer: Click/Chicago;* 209 Exhibit 9–4, *adapted from Frank R. Bacon, Jr., and Thomas W. Butler,* Planned Innovation *(Ann Arbor: University of Michigan, Institute of Science and Technology, 1980);* 210 Exhibit 9–5, *adapted from Management Research Department, Booz, Allen & Hamilton, Inc.;* 211 Exhibit 9–6, *adapted from Philip Kotler, "What Consumerism Means for Marketers,"* Harvard Business Review, *May–June 1972, pp. 55–56*

Chapter 10 215 (left) Warehouse, *courtesy Toys "R" Us;* (center) Retailer stocking shelves, *courtesy Wetterau, Incorporated;* (right) Ryder auto carrier, *courtesy Ryder System;* 217 Golf shop, *R.I. Pasley/Stock, Boston;* 218 Filling orders, *courtesy The Southland Corporation;* 220 TV dish, *Cameramann International;* 222 Exhibit 10–3, Statistical Abstract of the United States, 1986, *p. 591;* Exhibit 10–4, *adapted from B. J. LaLonde and P. H. Zinzer,* Customer Service: Meaning and Measurement *(Chicago: National Council of Physical Distribution Management, 1976); and D. Phillip Locklin,* Transportation for Management *(Homewood, Ill.: Richard D. Irwin, 1972);* 223 Coal cars, *Cameron Davidson/After Image, Inc.;* 225 (left) Loading ship, *Peter Fronk: Click/Chicago;* (right) Loaded ship, *William H. Clark: Click/Chicago;* Storage silos, *Wayne Bladholm;* Old warehouse, *Mary Ellen Zang;* 226 Distribution center, *courtesy Fleming Companies, Inc.;* 231 7-Eleven suppliers, *courtesy The Southland Corporation;* 235 Exhibit 10–9, *adapted from D. J. Bowersox and E. J. McCarthy, "Strategic Development of Planned Vertical Marketing Systems," in* Vertical Marketing Systems, *ed. Louis Bucklin (Glenview Ill.: Scott, Foresman, 1970)*

Chapter 11 239 (left) Toys "R" Us store, *courtesy Toys "R" Us;* (center) Store interior, *Mark Segal: Click/Chicago;* (right) Shoppers, *Chuck Keeler: Click/Chicago;* 241 Saks Fifth Avenue, *Cathy Melloan: Click/ Chicago;* 242 Exhibit 11–2, *adapted from Louis Bucklin, "Retail Strategy and the Classification of Consumer Goods,"* Journal of Marketing, *January 1963, pp. 50–55;* 243 Selling shoes, *courtesy W. R. Grace & Co.;* 245 Save Mart sign, *courtesy Wetterau Incorporated;* 247 Laneco shopper, *courtesy Wetterau Incorporated;* Quick Mart, *courtesy The Southland Corporation;* 248 Catalogs, *Don Smetzer: Click/Chicago;* 250 Buying video cassettes, *courtesy Fleming Companies, Inc.;* 252 Exhibit 11–6, *based on data from* 1982 Census of Retail Trade; 253 Sears store, *courtesy Mid-America Research, Inc.*

Chapter 12 259 (left) Food delivery, *courtesy IU International;* (center) Warehouse, *Chuck Keeler: Click/Chicago;* (right) Wholesaler, *Glenn Steiner/Joan Kramer and Associates;* 260 Wholesale showroom sign, *Cameramann International;* Computerized warehouse, *courtesy Baxter Travenol Laboratories, Inc.;* 261 Southland ad, *courtesy Southland Distribution Center;* 262 Exhibit 12–1, *based on data from* 1982 Census of Wholesale Trade; 266 Cheese, *Reprinted by permission of Land O'Lakes,*

Inc.; Rack jobbers, *Mary Ellen Zang;* 269 Farmers and broker, *courtesy International Business Machines Corporation;* 270 Automated warehouse, *courtesy Foster Wheeler*

Chapter 13 275 (left) Balloons, *Vince Streano: Click/Chicago;* (center) Promotion managers, *Gabe Palmer/After-Image, Inc.;* (right) Bike race, *Tim Welek/Stock Imagery;* Cap'n Crunch cereal, *Don Smetzer: Click/ Chicago;* 283 Pepsi "Tipping Can" display, *courtesy PepsiCo Incorporated;* 285 Examining camera, *Cameramann International*

Chapter 14 291 (left) Salesman and buyer, *Eric Roth/The Picture Cube;* (center) Beverage salesman, *Gregg Mancuso/Uniphoto;* (right) Sales manager and staff, *Jon Feingersh/Uniphoto;* 293 Rep and managers in factory, *Lee Balterman/Gartman Agency;* 295 Order getter, *Martin Rogers: Click/Chicago;* 296 Technical training, *courtesy Rockwell International Corporation;* 299 Missionary sales rep, *Mary Ellen Zang;* 302 Training group, *courtesy The Goodyear Tire & Rubber Company;* Asking for order, *Jim Pickerell: Click/Chicago;* 304 Exhibit 14–2, *figure suggested by Professor A. A. Brogowicz, Western Michigan University;* 305 Computer-assisted telephone selling, *courtesy Owens-Illinois*

Chapter 15 311 (left) Product management team, *Bob Krist;* (center) Magazines, *Richard Gross/Stock Imagery;* (right) Ad layout, *Jay Freis/The Image Bank;* 313 Exhibit 15–2, Advertising Age, *September 24, 1987, p. 1;* 314 Exhibit 15–3, *adapted from R. J. Lavidge and G. A. Steiner, "A Model for Predictive Measurements of Advertising Effectiveness,"* Journal of Marketing, *October 1961, p. 61;* 316 Diet Sprite ad, *courtesy The Coca-Cola Company;* 318 Exhibit 15–4, *data from Standard Rate and Data Service and estimates from May 12, 1986,* Advertising Age, *p. 76;* 319 MTV logo, *courtesy MTV Networks;* Specialty magazines, *Don Smetzer: Click/Chicago;* Direct-mail ads, *Mary Ellen Zang*

Chapter 16 327 (left) Ralphs Giant Supermarket, *courtesy Federated Department Stores, Inc.;* (center) Clearance sign, *Ron Bowman/Uniphoto;* (right) Business meeting, *Charles Feil/Stock, Boston;* 333 Camera prices, *Cameramann International;* 336 Hertz ad, *courtesy The Hertz Corporation*

Appendix B 359 Exhibit B–4, Sales & Marketing Management, *July 28, 1986, p. C-60ff.*

Chapter 17 363 (left) Buying furniture, *John Coletti/The Picture Cube;* (center) Vegetable stand, *Jeffry W. Myers/Stock, Boston;* (right) Calculating, *Richard Gross/Stock Imagery;* 365 Drill, *Don Smetzer: Click/Chicago;* 366 Toothpaste on shelves, *Chris Jones/The Stock Market;* 373 Milk on shelves, *Peter Menzell: Click/Chicago;* 374 Houston Instrument ad, *courtesy Houston Instrument;* 377 Hanes ad, *courtesy Adams-Miller Corp.*

Chapter 18 381 (left) Penaten Baby Oel, *courtesy Johnson & Johnson;* (center) Marketing meeting, *Alvis Upitis/The Image Bank;* (right) Vicks Cool Drops, *courtesy The Procter & Gamble Company;* 382 Coca-Cola ad, *courtesy The Coca-Cola Company;* 383 Japanese Liquid Paper, *courtesy The Gillette Company;* 385 Japanese plant in USA, *Billy Barnes: Click/Chicago;* 386 Tokyo McDonald's, *Greg Davis/The Stock Market;* 387 Exhibit 18–3, *adapted from Warren Keegan, "Multinational Product Planning: Strategic Alternatives,"* Journal of Marketing, *January 1969, p. 59;* 393 British Lean Cuisine transit ad, *Mary Ellen Zang;* 394 Exhibit 18–6, *map drawn by J. F. McCarthy;* 395 Exhibit 18–7, *adapted from Norton Ginsberg,* Atlas of Economic Development, *by permission of the University of Chicago Press;* 396 Exhibit 18–8, Statistical Abstract of the United States, 1986, *p. 838; and* Yearbook of National Account Statistics, 1981, *Vol. II (New York: United Nations, 1983), pp. 5–10;* Foreign soda signs, *William S. Nawrocki/Nawrocki Stock Photo;* 397 Exhibit 18–9, Yearbook of National Account Statistics, 1981, *Vol. II (New York: United Nations, 1983), pp. 5–10*

Chapter 19 401 (left) Captain Power products © *Landmark Entertainment Group 1987, courtesy Mattel, Inc.;* (center) Quality control, *W. Strode/Four by Five;* (right) Shoppers, *Chuck Keeler: Click/Chicago;* 403 Customer reply cards, *Mary Ellen Zang;* 407 Aerobic weights ad, *courtesy Spenco Medical Corp.;* 408 Using microwave, *Mary Ellen Zang;* 410 Shoplifter warning, *Mary Ellen Zang*

Appendix C 415 Exhibit C–1, Northwestern Endicott Report, 1985 *(Evanston, Ill.: Northwestern University, The Placement Center);* 416 Exhibit C–2, *adapted from Charles G. Burck, "A Group Profile of the Fortune 500 Chief Executive,"* Fortune, *May 1976, p. 172;* 421 Exhibit C–4, *adapted from Lila B. Stair,* Careers in Business: Selecting and Planning Your Career Path *(Homewood, Ill.: Richard D. Irwin, 1980) and other sources*

Author Index

Subject Index

Glossary

Accessories   short-lived capital items—tools and equipment used in production or office activities.

Accumulating   collecting products from many small producers.

Administered channel systems   various channel members informally agree to cooperate with each other.

Administered prices   consciously set prices aimed at reaching the firm's objectives.

Adoption curve   shows when different groups accept ideas.

Adoption process   the steps that individuals go through on the way to accepting or rejecting a new idea.

Advertising   any paid form of non-personal presentation of ideas, goods, or services by an identified sponsor.

Advertising agencies   specialists in planning and handling mass selling details for advertisers.

Advertising allowances   price reductions to firms further along in the channel to encourage them to advertise or otherwise promote the firm's products locally.

Advertising managers   managers of their company's mass selling effort in television, newspapers, magazines, and other media.

Agent middlemen   wholesalers who do not own (take title to) the products they sell.

AIDA model   consists of four promotion jobs: (1) to get Attention, (2) to hold Interest, (3) to arouse Desire, and (4) to obtain Action.

Allowance   (accounting term) occurs when a customer is not satisfied with a purchase for some reason and the seller gives a price reduction on the original invoice (bill) but the customer keeps the goods or services.

Allowances   reductions in price given to final consumers, customers, or channel members for doing "something" or accepting less of "something."

Assorting   putting together a variety of products to give a target market what it wants.

Attitude   a person's point of view toward something.

Auction companies   agent middlemen who provide a place where buyers and sellers can come together and complete a transaction.

Automatic vending   selling and delivering products through vending machines.

Average cost (per unit)   the total cost divided by the related quantity.

Average fixed cost (per unit)   the total fixed cost divided by the related quantity.

Average variable cost (per unit)   the total variable cost divided by the related quantity.

Average-cost pricing   adding a "reasonable" markup to the average cost of a product.

Bait pricing   setting some very low prices to attract customers but trying to sell more expensive models or brands once the customer is in the store.

Balance sheet   an accounting statement that shows a company's assets, liabilities, and net worth.

Basic list prices   the prices that final customers or users are normally asked to pay for products.

Basic sales tasks   order getting, order taking, and supporting.

Battle of the brands   the competition between dealer brands and manufacturer brands.

Belief   a person's opinion about something.

Bid pricing   offering a specific price for each possible job rather than setting a price that applies for all potential customers.

Birth rate   the number of babies per 1,000 people.

Brand familiarity   how well customers recognize and accept a company's brand.

Brand insistence   customers insist on a firm's branded product and are willing to search for it.

Brand managers   manage products—often taking over the jobs formerly handled by an advertising manager.

Brand name   a word, letter, or a group of words or letters.

Brand non-recognition   a brand is not recognized by final customers at all even though middlemen may use the brand name for identification and inventory control.

Brand preference   target customers will usually choose the brand over other brands, perhaps because of habit or past experience.

Brand recognition   customers remember the brand.

Brand rejection   potential customers won't buy a brand unless its image is changed.

Branding   the use of a name, term, symbol, or design—or a combination of these—to identify a product.

Breakthrough opportunities   opportunities that help innovators develop hard-to-copy marketing strategies that will be very profitable for a long time.

Brokers   agent middlemen who specialize in bringing buyers and sellers together.

Bulk-breaking   dividing larger quantities into smaller quantities as products get closer to the final market.

Buying center   all the people who participate in or influence a purchase.

Buying function   looking for and evaluating goods and services.

Capital item   a long-lasting product that can be used and depreciated for many years.

Cash discounts   reductions in the price to encourage buyers to pay their bills quickly. 2/10, net 30, for example, means that a 2 percent discount off the face value of the invoice is allowed if the invoice is paid within 10 days.

Cash-and-carry wholesalers   like service wholesalers, except that the customer must pay cash.

Catalog showroom retailers   stores that sell several lines out of a catalog and display showroom—with backup inventories.

Central market   a convenient place where buyers and sellers can meet face-to-face to exchange goods and services.

Channel captain   a manager who helps direct the activities of a whole channel and tries to avoid—or solve—channel conflicts.

Channel of distribution   any series of firms or individuals who participate in the flow of goods and services from producer to final user or consumer.

Clustering techniques   approaches used to try to find similar patterns within sets of data.

Combination export manager   a blend of manufactur-ers' agent and selling agent—handling the entire export function for several producers of similar but non-competing lines.

Combined target market approach   combining two or more sub-market segments into one larger target market as a basis for one strategy.

Combiners   firms that try to increase the size of their target markets by combining two or more segments.

Commission merchants   agent middlemen who handle products shipped to them by sellers, complete the sale, and send the money (minus their commission) to each seller.

Communication process   a source trying to reach a receiver with a message.

Community shopping centers   planned shopping centers that offer some shopping stores as well as convenience stores.

Comparative advertising   advertising that makes specific brand comparisons—using actual product names.

Competitive advantage   means that a firm has a marketing mix that the target market sees as better than a competitor's mix.

Competitive advertising   advertising that tries to develop demand for a specific brand rather than a product category.

Competitive environment   the number and types of competitors the marketing manager must face, and how they may behave.

Complementary product pricing   setting prices on several related products as a group.

Components   processed expense items that have become part of a finished product.

Consumer Product Safety Act   a 1972 law that set up the Consumer Product Safety Commission to encourage more awareness of safety in product design—and better quality control.

Consumer products   products meant for the final consumer.

Consumerism   a social movement that seeks to increase the rights and powers of consumers.

Containerization   grouping individual items into an economical shipping quantity and sealing them in protective containers for transit to the final destination.

Contract manufacturing   turning over production to others while retaining the marketing process.

Contractual channel systems   various channel members agree by contract to cooperate with each other.

Convenience (food) stores   a convenience-oriented variation of the conventional limited-line food stores.

Convenience products   products a consumer needs but isn't willing to spend much time or effort shopping for.

Convenience store   a convenient place to shop— either centrally located "downtown" or "in the neighborhood."

Cooperative advertising   middlemen and producers sharing in the cost of ads.

Cooperative chains   retailer-sponsored groups, formed by independent retailers, to run their own buying organizations and conduct joint promotion efforts.

Copy thrust   what is to be communicated by an ad's words and illustrations.

(Corporate) chain store   one of several stores owned and managed by the same firm.

Corporate channel system   corporate ownership all along the channel.

Corrective advertising   ads to correct deceptive advertising.

Cost of sales   total value (at cost) of the sales during the period.

Cues   products, signs, ads, and other stimuli in the environment.

Cultural and social environment   affects how and why people live and behave as they do—and has a direct effect on consumer buying behavior.

Culture   the whole set of beliefs, attitudes, and ways of doing things of a reasonably homogeneous set of people.

Cumulative quantity discounts   reductions in price for larger purchases over a given period, such as a year.

Customer service level   how rapidly and dependably a firm can deliver what customers want.

Dealer brands   brands created by middlemen.

Decision support system (DSS)   a computer program that makes it easy for a marketing manager to get and use information as he is making decisions.

Decoding   the receiver in the communication process translating the message.

Demand-backward pricing   setting an acceptable final consumer price and working backward to what a producer can charge.

Department stores   larger stores that are organized into many separate departments and offer many product lines.

Derived demand   demand for industrial products is derived from the demand for final consumer products.

Description (specification) buying   buying from a written (or verbal) description of the product.

Determining dimensions   the dimensions that actually affect the purchase of a specific product or brand in a product-market.

Direct type advertising   competitive advertising that aims for immediate buying action.

Direct-mail advertising   selling to customers via their mailboxes.

Discount houses   stores that sell "hard goods" (cameras, TVs, appliances) at substantial price cuts.

Discounts   reductions from list price that are given by a seller to a buyer who either gives up some marketing function or provides the function himself.

Discrepancy of assortment   the difference between the lines a typical producer makes and the assortment wanted by final consumers or users.

Discrepancy of quantity   the difference between the quantity of products it is economical for a producer to make and the quantity normally wanted by final users or consumers.

Dissonance   tension caused by uncertainty about the rightness of a decision.

Distribution center   a special kind of warehouse designed to speed the flow of goods and avoid unnecessary storing costs.

Diversification   moving into totally different lines of business—which may include entirely unfamiliar products, markets, or even levels in the production-marketing system.

Diversion in transit   redirection of railroad carloads already in transit.

Door-to-door selling   going directly to the consumer's home.

Drive   a strong stimulus that encourages action to reduce a need.

Drop-shippers   wholesalers who take title to the products they sell but do not actually handle, stock, or deliver them.

Dual distribution   when a producer uses several competing channels to reach the same target market.

Early adopters   the second group in the adoption curve to adopt a new product, these people are usually well respected by their peers and often are opinion leaders.

Early majority   a group in the adoption curve that avoids risk and waits to consider a new idea after many early adopters have tried it and liked it.

Economic and technological environment   affects the way firms and the whole economy use resources.

Economic men   people who logically compare choices in terms of cost and value received to get the greatest satisfaction from spending their time, energy, and money.

Economic needs   needs concerned with making the best use of a consumer's limited resources—as the consumer sees it.

Economic system   the way an economy organizes to use scarce resources to produce goods and services and distribute them for consumption by various people and groups in the society.

Economies of scale   as a company produces larger numbers of a particular product, the cost for each of these products goes down.

Emergency products   products that are purchased immediately when the need is great.

Empty nesters   people whose children are grown and who are now able to spend their money in other ways.

Encoding   the source in the communication process deciding what it wants to say and translating it into words or symbols that will have the same meaning to the receiver.

Equilibrium price   the going market price.

Exclusive distribution   selling through only one middleman in a particular geographic area.

Expense item   a product whose total cost is treated as a business expense in the period when it is purchased.

Expenses   all the remaining costs that are subtracted from the gross margin to get the net profit.

Experimental method   a research approach that compares the responses of groups that are similar, except on the characteristic being tested.

Export agents   manufacturers' agents who specialize in export trade.

Export brokers   brokers in international marketing.

Export commission houses   brokers in international trade.

Exporting   selling some of what the firm is producing to foreign markets.

Extensive problem solving   the type of problem solving involved when a need is completely new or important to a consumer—and much effort is taken to decide how to satisfy the need.

Facilitators   firms that provide one or more of the marketing functions other than buying or selling.

Factor   a variable that shows the relation of some variable to the item being forecasted.

Factor method   an approach to forecast sales by finding a relation between the company's sales and some other factor (or factors).

Family brand   a brand name that is used for several products.

Farm products   raw materials grown by farmers, such as oranges, wheat, sugar cane, cattle, poultry, eggs, and milk.

Federal Fair Packaging and Labeling Act   a 1966 law requiring that consumer products be clearly labeled in easy-to-understand terms.

Federal Trade Commission (FTC)   government agency that polices antimonopoly laws.

Financing   provides the necessary cash and credit to produce, transport, store, promote, sell, and buy products.

Flexible-price policy   offering the same product and quantities to different customers at different prices.

Focus group interview   an interview of 6 to 10 people in an informal group setting.

Form utility   provided when someone produces something tangible.

Franchise operation   a franchiser develops a good marketing strategy, and the retail franchise holders carry out the strategy in their own units.

Freight absorption pricing   absorbing freight cost so that a firm's delivered price meets the price of the nearest competitor.

Full-line pricing   setting prices for a whole line of products.

General merchandise wholesalers   service wholesalers who carry a wide variety of non-perishable items such as hardware, electrical supplies, plumbing supplies, furniture, drugs, cosmetics, and automobile equipment.

General stores   early retailers who carried anything they could sell in reasonable volume.

Generic market   a market with broadly similar needs and sellers offering various and often diverse ways of satisfying those needs.

Generic products   have no brand at all other than identification of their contents and the manufacturer or middleman.

Gross margin (gross profit)   the money left to cover the expenses of selling and operating the business.

Gross national product (GNP)   the total market value of goods and services produced in a year.

Gross sales   the total amount charged to all customers during some time period.

Heterogeneous shopping products   shopping products that the customer sees as different—and wants to inspect for quality and suitability.

Homogeneous shopping products   shopping products that the customer sees as basically the same—and wants at the lowest price.

Hypotheses   educated guesses about the relationships between things or what will happen in the future.

Ideal market exposure   when a product is widely enough available to satisfy target customers' needs but not exceed them.

Implementation   putting a marketing plan into operation.

Import agents   manufacturers' agents who specialize in import trade.

Import brokers   brokers in international marketing.

Import commission houses   brokers in international trade.

Impulse products   products that are bought quickly as unplanned purchases because of a strongly felt need.

Indirect type advertising   competitive advertising that points out product advantages—to affect future buying decisions.

Individual brands   different brand names used for each product.

Industrial products   products meant for use in producing other products.

Innovation   the development and spread of new ideas and products.

Innovators   the first group to adopt new products.

Inspection buying   looking at every item.

Installations   industrial products that are important capital items such as buildings, land rights, and major equipment.

Institutional advertising   advertising that tries to develop goodwill for a company or even an industry—instead of a specific product.

Intensive distribution   selling a product through all responsible and suitable wholesalers or retailers who will stock and/or sell the product.

Intermediate customers   any buyers who buy for resale or to produce other goods and services.

Introductory price dealing   temporary price cuts to speed new products into a market.

Inventory   the amount of goods that are being stored.

Job description   a written statement of what an employee (for example, a salesperson) is expected to do.

Joint venturing   in international marketing, a domestic firm entering into a partnership with a foreign firm.

Jury of executive opinion   forecasting by combining the opinions of experienced executives—perhaps from marketing, production, finance, purchasing, and top management.

Just-in-time delivery   reliably getting products to the customer just before the customer needs them.

Laggards   prefer to do things the way they have done in the past and are very suspicious of new ideas—see *adoption curve.*

Late majority   a group of adopters who are cautious about new ideas—see *adoption curve.*

Leader pricing   setting very low prices on some products to get customers into retail stores.

Learning   a change in a person's thought processes caused by prior experience.

Licensed brand   brand that sellers pay a fee to use.

Licensing   selling the right to use some process, trademark, patent, or other right—for a fee or royalty.

Life-style analysis   the analysis of a person's day-to-day pattern of living—as expressed in his Activities, Interests, and Opinions—sometimes referred to as AIOs or psychographics.

Limited problem solving   when a consumer is willing to put some effort into deciding the best way to satisfy a need.

Limited-function wholesalers   merchant wholesalers who perform only some wholesaling functions.

Low-involvement purchases   purchases that do not have high personal importance or relevance for the customer.

Lower-lower class   (13 percent of the population) consists of unskilled laborers and people in non-respectable occupations.

Lower-middle class   (36 percent of the population) consists of small business people, office workers, teachers, and technicians—the "white-collar" workers.

Macro-marketing   a social process that directs an economy's flow of goods and services from producers to consumers in a way that effectively matches supply and demand and accomplishes the objectives of society.

Magnuson-Moss Act   1975 law requiring that producers provide a clearly written warranty if they choose to offer any warranty.

Mail-order wholesalers   sell out of catalogs that may be distributed widely to smaller industrial customers or retailers.

Management contracting   the seller provides only management skills—the production facilities are owned by others.

Manufacturer brands   brands created by manufacturers.

Manufacturers' agents   agent middlemen who sell similar products for several noncompeting producers for a commission on what is actually sold.

Manufacturers' sales branches   separate businesses that producers set up away from their factories.

Markdown   a retail price reduction that is required because customers won't buy some item at the originally marked-up price.

Markdown ratio   a tool used by many retailers to measure the efficiency of various departments and their whole business.

Market   a group of potential customers with similar needs and sellers offering various products—that is, ways of satisfying those needs—or a group of sellers and buyers who are willing to exchange goods and/or services for something of value.

Market development   trying to increase sales by selling present products in new markets.

Market growth   a stage of the product life cycle when

industry sales are growing fast—but industry profits rise and then start falling.

Market information function   the collection, analysis, and distribution of all the information needed to plan, carry out, and control marketing activities.

Market introduction   a stage of the product life cycle when sales are low as a new idea is first introduced to a market.

Market maturity   a stage of the product life cycle when industry sales level off and competition gets tougher.

Market penetration   trying to increase sales of a firm's present products in its present markets—usually through a more aggressive marketing mix.

Market potential   what a whole market segment might buy.

Market segment   a relatively homogeneous group of customers who will respond to a marketing mix in a similar way.

Market segmentation   a two-step process of: (1) naming broad product-markets and (2) segmenting these broad product-markets in order to select target markets and develop suitable marketing mixes.

Market-directed economic system   individual decisions of the many producers and consumers make the macro-level decisions for the whole economy.

Marketing company era   a time when, in addition to short-run marketing planning, marketing people develop long-range plans—sometimes 10 or more years ahead—and the whole company effort is guided by the marketing concept.

Marketing concept   the idea that an organization should aim all its efforts at satisfying its customers—at a profit.

Marketing department era   a time when all marketing activities are brought under the control of one department—to improve short-run policy planning and to try to tie together the firm's activities.

Marketing information system (MIS)   an organized way of continually gathering and analyzing data to provide marketing managers with information they need to make decisions.

Marketing management process   the process of (1) planning marketing activities, (2) directing the implementation of the plans, and (3) controlling these plans.

Marketing mix   the controllable variables that the company puts together to satisfy a target group.

Marketing model   a statement of relationships among marketing variables.

Marketing orientation   trying to carry out the marketing concept.

Marketing plan   a written statement of a marketing strategy and the time-related details for carrying out the strategy.

Marketing program   blends all of the firm's marketing plans into one "big" plan.

Marketing research   procedures to gather and analyze new information to help marketing managers make decisions.

Marketing research process   a five-step application of the scientific method that includes (1) defining the problem, (2) analyzing the situation, (3) getting problem-specific data, (4) interpreting the data, and (5) solving the problem.

Marketing strategy   specifies a target market and a related marketing mix.

Marketing strategy planning   finding attractive marketing opportunities—and developing profitable marketing strategies and plans.

Markup   a dollar amount added to the cost of products to get the selling price.

Markup (percent)   the percentage of selling price that is added to the cost to get the selling price.

Markup chain   the sequence of markups used by firms at different levels in a channel—determining the price structure in the whole channel.

Mass marketing   the typical production-oriented approach that vaguely aims at "everyone" with the same marketing mix.

Mass-merchandisers   large, self-service stores that have departments emphasizing "soft goods" (housewares, clothing, and fabrics) and that sell on lower margins to get faster turnover.

Mass-merchandising concept   the idea that retailers can get faster turnover and greater sales volume by charging lower prices that will appeal to larger markets.

Mass selling   communicating with large numbers of customers at the same time.

Merchant wholesalers   wholesalers who take title to the products they sell.

Message channel   the carrier of the message.

Metropolitan Statistical Area (MSA)   an integrated economic and social unit with a large population nucleus.

Micro-marketing   the performance of activities that seek to accomplish an organization's objectives by anticipating customer or client needs and directing a flow of need-satisfying goods and services from producer to customer or client.

Middleman   someone who specializes in trade rather than production.

Missionary salespeople   supporting salespeople who work for producers—calling on their middlemen and their customers.

Modified rebuy   the in-between process where some review of the buying situation is done—though not as much as in new-task buying or as little as in straight rebuys.

Monopolistic competition   a market situation that develops when a market has (1) different products and (2) sellers who feel they do have some competition in this market.

Multinational corporations   firms that make a direct investment in several countries and run their businesses depending on the choices available anywhere in the world.

Multiple buying influence   the buyer shares the purchasing decision with several people—perhaps even top management.

Multiple target market approach   segmenting the market and choosing two or more segments—each of which will be treated as a separate target market that needs a different marketing mix.

National accounts sales force   salespeople who sell directly to large accounts such as major retail chain stores.

Nationalism   an emphasis on a country's interests before everything else.

Natural products   raw materials that occur in nature such as fish and game, lumber and maple syrup, and copper, zinc, iron ore, oil, and coal.

Need-satisfaction approach   a type of sales presentation in which the salesperson develops a good understanding of the individual customer's needs before trying to close the sale.

Needs   the basic forces that motivate an individual to do something.

Negotiated contract buying   agreeing to a contract that allows for changing the purchase arrangements.

Neighborhood shopping centers   planned shopping centers that consist of several convenience stores.

Net   an invoice term that means that payment for the face value of the invoice is due immediately—also see *cash discounts.*

Net profit   what the company has earned from its operations during a particular period.

Net sales   sales dollars the company will receive.

New product   a product that is new in any way for the company concerned.

New unsought products   products offering really new ideas that potential customers don't know about yet.

New-task buying   when a firm has a new need and the buyer wants a great deal of information.

Non-cumulative quantity discounts   reductions in price when a customer purchases a larger quantity on an individual order.

Non-price competition   aggressive action on one or more of the Ps other than Price.

Odd-even pricing   setting prices that end in certain numbers.

Oligopoly   a market situation that develops when a market has (1) essentially homogeneous products, (2) relatively few sellers, and (3) fairly inelastic industry demand curves.

One-price policy   offering the same price to all customers who purchase products under essentially the same conditions and in the same quantities.

Open to buy   a buyer has budgeted funds that he can spend during the current time period.

Operating ratios   ratios of items on the operating statement to net sales.

Operating statement   a simple summary of the financial results of the operations of a company over a specified period of time.

Opinion leader   a person who influences others.

Order getters   salespeople concerned with getting new business.

Order getting   seeking possible buyers with a well-organized sales presentation designed to sell a product, service, or idea.

Order takers   salespeople who sell to the regular or typical customers.

Order taking   the routine completion of sales made regularly to the target customers.

Packaging   promoting and protecting the product.

Penetration pricing policy   trying to sell the whole market at one low price.

Personal needs   an individual's need for personal satisfaction unrelated to what others think or do.

Personal selling   direct face-to-face communication between a seller and a potential customer.

Phony list prices   misleading prices that customers are shown to suggest that the price they are to pay has been discounted from "list."

Physical distribution (PD)   the transporting and storing of goods to match target customers' needs with a firm's marketing mix—within individual firms and along a channel of distribution.

Physical distribution (PD) concept   all transporting and storing activities of a business and a channel system should be coordinated as one system—which should seek to minimize the cost of distribution for a given customer service level.

Physiological needs   biological needs such as the need for food, drink, rest, and sex.

Pioneering advertising   advertising that tries to develop demand for a product category rather than a specific brand.

Place   making products available in the right quantities and locations—when customers want them.

Place utility having the product available where the customer wants it.

Planned economic system government planners decide what and how much is to be produced and distributed by whom, when, and to whom.

Planned shopping center a set of stores planned as a unit—to satisfy some market needs.

Pool car service allows groups of shippers to pool their shipments of like goods into a full rail car.

Population in marketing research, the total group you're interested in.

Positioning shows where proposed and/or present brands are located in a market—as seen by customers.

Possession utility obtaining a product and having the right to use or consume it.

Prepared sales presentation a memorized presentation that is not adapted to each customer.

Prestige pricing setting a rather high price to suggest high quality or high status.

Price what is charged for "something."

Price discrimination injuring competition by selling the same goods at different prices.

Price fixing sellers illegally getting together to raise, lower, or stabilize prices.

Price lining setting a few price levels for a product line and then marking all items at these prices.

Primary data information specifically collected to solve a current problem.

Private warehouses storing facilities owned or leased by companies for their own use.

Producers' cooperatives work almost as full-service wholesalers with the "profits" going to the producers who are members.

Product the need-satisfying offering of a firm.

Product advertising advertising that tries to sell a specific product.

Product development offering new or improved products for present markets.

Product liability the legal obligation of sellers to pay damages to individuals who are injured by defective or unsafe products.

Product life cycle the stages a new product idea goes through from beginning to end.

Product managers manage products, often taking over the jobs formerly handled by an advertising manager—sometimes called brand managers.

Product-market a market with very similar needs and sellers offering various close substitute ways of satisfying those needs.

Production actually making goods or performing services.

Production era a time when a company focuses on production of a few specific products—perhaps because few of these products are available in the market.

Production orientation making whatever products are easy to produce and then trying to sell them.

Professional services specialized services that support the operations of a firm.

Profit maximization objective an objective to get as much profit as possible.

Promotion communicating information between seller and potential buyer to influence attitudes and behavior.

Prospecting following down all the "leads" in the target market.

Psychographics the analysis of a person's day-to-day pattern of living—as expressed in his Activities, Interests, and Opinions—sometimes referred to as AIOs or life-style analysis.

Psychological pricing setting prices that have special appeal to target customers.

Public warehouses independent storing facilities.

Publicity any unpaid form of non-personal presentation of ideas, goods, or services.

Pulling getting consumers to ask middlemen for the product.

Purchase discount a reduction of the original invoice amount for some business reason.

Purchasing agents buying specialists for their employers.

Pure competition a market situation that develops when a market has (1) homogeneous products, (2) many buyers and sellers who have full knowledge of the market, and (3) ease of entry for buyers and sellers.

Pure subsistence economy each family unit produces all the goods it consumes.

Push money (or prize money) allowances allowances (sometimes called "PMs" or "spiffs") given to retailers by manufacturers or wholesalers to pass on to the retailers' sales clerks for aggressively selling certain items.

Pushing using normal promotion effort—personal selling, advertising, and sales promotion—to help sell the whole marketing mix to possible channel members.

Qualifying dimensions the dimensions that are relevant to a product-market.

Qualitative research seeks in-depth, open-ended responses.

Quantitative research seeks structured responses that can be summarized in numbers—like percentages, averages, or other statistics.

Quantity discounts discounts offered to encourage customers to buy in larger amounts.

Quotas   the specific quantities of products that can move in or out of a country.

Rack jobbers   merchant wholesalers who specialize in non-food products that are sold through grocery stores and supermarkets—they often display such products on their own wire racks.

Raw materials   unprocessed expense items—such as logs, iron ore, wheat, and cotton—that are handled as little as is needed to move them to the next production process.

Rebates   refunds to consumers after a purchase has been made.

Receiver   the target of a message in the communication process, usually a customer.

Reciprocity   trading sales for sales—that is, "if you buy from me, I'll buy from you."

Reference group   the people an individual looks to when forming attitudes about a particular topic.

Regional shopping centers   large planned shopping centers that emphasize shopping stores and shopping products.

Regrouping activities   adjusting the quantities and/or assortments of products handled at each level in a channel of distribution.

Regularly unsought products   products that stay unsought but not unbought forever.

Reinforcement   occurs in the learning process when the consumer's response is followed by satisfaction—that is, reducing the drive.

Reminder advertising   advertising to keep the product's name before the public.

Requisition   a request to buy something.

Research proposal   a plan that specifies what marketing research information will be obtained and how.

Resident buyers   independent buying agents who work in central markets for several retailer or wholesaler customers from outlying areas.

Response   an effort to satisfy a drive.

Response rate   the percent of people contacted in a research sample who complete the questionnaire.

Retailing   all of the activities involved in the sale of products to final consumers.

Return   when a customer sends back purchased products.

Return on assets (ROA)   the ratio of net profit (after taxes) to the assets used to make the net profit—times 100.

Return on investment (ROI)   ratio of net profit (after taxes) to the investment used to make the net profit—multiplied by 100 to get rid of decimals.

Risk taking   bearing the uncertainties that are part of the marketing process.

Robinson-Patman Act   a 1936 law that makes it illegal to sell the same products to different buyers at different prices—if it injures competition.

Routinized response behavior   mechanically selecting a particular way of satisfying a need when it occurs.

Safety needs   needs concerned with protection and physical well-being.

Sales decline   a stage of the product life cycle when new products replace the old.

Sales era   a time when a company emphasizes selling—because of increased competition.

Sales forecast   an estimate of how much an industry or firm hopes to sell to a market segment.

Sales managers   managers concerned with managing personal selling.

Sales presentation   a salesperson's effort to make a sale.

Sales promotion   those promotion activities—other than advertising, publicity, and personal selling—that stimulate interest, trial, or purchase by final customers or others in the channel.

Sales promotion managers   managers of their company's sales promotion effort.

Sales territory   an area that is the responsibility of one salesperson or several working in a coordinated effort.

Sales-oriented objective   an objective to get some level of unit sales, dollar sales, or share of market—without referring to profit.

Sample   a part of the relevant population.

Sampling buying   looking at only part of a potential purchase.

Scientific method   a decision-making approach that focuses on being objective and orderly in testing ideas before accepting them.

Scrambled merchandising   retailers selling any product lines that they think they can sell profitably.

Seasonal discounts   discounts offered to encourage buyers to stock earlier than present demand requires.

Secondary data   information that has already been collected or published.

Segmenters   aim at one or more homogeneous segments and try to develop a different marketing mix for each segment.

Segmenting   an aggregating process that clusters people with similar needs into a market segment.

Selective distribution   selling through only those middlemen who will give the product special attention.

Selective exposure   our eyes and minds seek out and notice only information that interests us.

Selective perception   people screen out or modify

ideas, messages, and information that conflict with previously learned attitudes and beliefs.

Selective retention   people remember only what they want to remember.

Selling agents   agent middlemen who take over the whole marketing job of producers—not just the selling function.

Selling formula approach   a sales presentation that starts with a prepared presentation outline, gets a customer to discuss needs, and then leads the customer through some logical steps to a final close.

Selling function   promoting the product.

Senior citizens   people over 65.

Service wholesalers   merchant wholesalers who perform all the wholesaling functions.

Shopping products   products that a customer feels are worth the time and effort to compare with competing products.

Shopping stores   stores that attract customers from greater distances because of the width and depth of their assortments.

Simple trade era   a time when families traded or sold their "surplus" output to local middlemen, who sold these goods to other consumers or distant middlemen.

Single target market approach   segmenting the market and picking one of the homogeneous segments as the firm's target market.

Single-line (limited-line) stores   stores that specialize in certain lines of related products rather than a wide assortment.

Single-line (or general-line) wholesalers   service wholesalers who carry a narrower line of merchandise than general merchandise wholesalers.

Situation analysis   an informal study of what information is already available in the problem area.

Skimming price policy   trying to sell the top of the demand curve at a high price before aiming at more price-sensitive customers.

Social class   a group of people who have approximately equal social position—as viewed by others in the society.

Social needs   needs concerned with love, friendship, status, and esteem—things that involve a person's interaction with others.

Sorting   separating products into grades and qualities desired by different target markets.

Source   the sender of a message.

Specialty products   consumer products that the customer really wants and is willing to make a special effort to find.

Specialty shop   a type of limited-line store—usually small and with a distinct "personality."

Specialty stores   stores for which customers have developed a strong attraction.

Specialty wholesalers   service wholesalers that carry a very narrow range of products and that offer more information and service than other service wholesalers.

Standard Industrial Classification (SIC) Codes   codes used to identify groups of firms in similar lines of business.

Standardization and grading   sorting products according to size and quality.

Staples   consumer convenience products that are bought often and routinely—without much thought.

Statistical packages   easy-to-use computer programs that analyze data.

Status quo objectives   "don't-rock-the-boat" pricing objectives.

Stimulus-response model   the idea that people respond in some predictable way to a stimulus.

Stockturn rate   the number of times the average inventory is sold in a year.

Storing function   holding goods until customers need them.

Straight rebuy   a routine repurchase that may have been made many times before.

Strategic (management) planning   the managerial process of developing and maintaining a match between the resources of an organization and its market opportunities.

Super-stores   stores that try to carry not only foods, but all goods and services that the consumer purchases routinely.

Supermarket   a large store specializing in groceries—with self-service and wide assortments.

Supplies   expense items that do not become a part of a final product.

Supporting salespeople   salespeople who support the order-oriented salespeople—but don't try to get orders themselves.

Target market   a fairly homogeneous (similar) group of customers to whom a company wishes to appeal.

Target marketing   a marketing mix is tailored to satisfy some specific target customers.

Target return objective   a specific level of profit as an objective.

Tariffs   taxes on imported products.

Team selling   sales reps working together on a specific account.

Technical specialists   supporting salespeople who provide technical assistance to order-oriented salespeople.

Technological base   the technical skills and equipment that affect the way the resources of an economy are converted to output.

Telephone and direct-mail retailing   allows consumers to shop at home—usually placing orders by mail or phone and charging the purchase to a credit card.

Telephone selling   using the phone to find out about a prospect's interest in the company's marketing mix and even to make a sales presentation or take an order.

Time utility   having the product available when the customer wants it.

Total cost   the sum of total fixed and total variable costs.

Total cost approach   evaluating each possible PD system and identifying all of the costs of each alternative.

Total fixed cost   the sum of those costs that are fixed in total no matter how much is produced.

Total variable cost   the sum of those changing expenses that are closely related to output—such as expenses for parts, wages, packaging materials, outgoing freight, and sales commissions.

Trade (functional) discount   a list price reduction given to channel members for the job they're going to do.

Trade-in allowance   a price reduction given for used products when similar new products are bought.

Trademark   those words, symbols, or marks that are legally registered for use by a single company.

Trading stamps   free stamps (such as "Green Stamps") given by some retailers with each purchase.

Traditional channel system   a channel in which channel members make little or no effort to cooperate with each other.

Transporting function   the movement of goods from one place to another.

Trend extension   extends past experience to predict the future.

Truck wholesalers   wholesalers who specialize in delivering products that they stock in their own trucks.

Unfair trade practice acts   set a lower limit on prices, especially at the wholesale and retail levels.

Uniform delivered pricing   making an average freight charge to all buyers.

Unit-pricing   placing the price per ounce (or some other standard measure) on or near the product.

Universal functions of marketing   buying, selling, transporting, storing, standardization and grading, financing, risk taking, and market information.

Universal product code (UPC)   special identifying marks for each product that can be "read" by electronic scanners.

Unsought products   products that potential customers don't yet want or know they can buy.

Upper class   (2 percent of the population) consists of people from old, wealthy families (upper-upper class) as well as the socially prominent new rich (lower-upper class).

Upper-lower class   (38 percent of the population) consists of factory production line workers, skilled workers, and service people—the blue-collar workers.

Upper-middle class   (11 percent of the population) consists of successful professionals, owners of small businesses, or managers for large corporations.

Utility   the power to satisfy human needs.

Validity   the extent to which data measures what it is intended to measure.

Value-in-use pricing   setting prices that will capture some of what customers will save by substituting the firm's product for the one currently being used.

Vendor analysis   formal rating of suppliers on all relevant areas of performance.

Vertical integration   acquiring firms at different levels of channel activity.

Vertical marketing systems   a whole channel focuses on the same target market at the end of the channel.

Voluntary chains   wholesaler-sponsored groups that work with "independent" retailers.

Wants   "needs" that are learned during an individual's life.

Warranty   what the seller promises about its product.

Wheel of retailing theory   new types of retailers enter the market as low-status, low-margin, low-price operators and then—if they are successful—evolve into more conventional retailers offering more services with higher operating costs and higher prices.

Wheeler Lea Amendment   law that controls unfair or deceptive acts in commerce.

Wholesalers   firms whose main function is providing wholesaling activities.

Wholesaling   the activities of those persons or firms that sell to retailers and other merchants, and/or to industrial, institutional, and commercial users, but that do not sell in large amounts to final consumers.

Wholly-owned subsidiary   a separate firm owned by a parent company.

Zone pricing   making an average freight charge to all buyers within specific geographic areas.